PROCEEDINGS OF THE FORTY-FIFTH COLLOQUIUM ON THE LAW OF OUTER SPACE

INTERNATIONAL INSTITUTE OF SPACE LAW
OF THE
INTERNATIONAL ASTRONAUTICAL FEDERATION

10 OCTOBER – 19 OCTOBER 2002
HOUSTON, TEXAS

AIAA

Published and Distributed by
AMERICAN INSTITUTE OF AERONAUTICS AND ASTRONAUTICS

ISBN
1-56347-625-8

Printed in the U.S.A.

IISL BOARD OF DIRECTORS 2002-2003

Dr. Eilene M. Galloway
4612 29th Place, N.W.
Washington, DC 20008-2105 USA
T 1-202 362 1337
F 1-202 362 1337
E (c/o Marcia Smith) E mssmith@crs.loc.gov

Dr. Peter Jankowitsch
Secretary-General
Oesterreichisch-Französisches Zentrum
Salzgries 19/16
A-1010 Vienna AUSTRIA
T 43-1 535 23 35
F 43-1 533 89 27
E jankowitsch@nextra.at

Dr. Gabriel Lafferranderie
Legal Adviser, European Space Agency
8-10 Rue Mario Nikis
75738 Paris Cedex 15 FRANCE
T 33-1 5369 7162
F 33-1 5369 7560

Dr. Martin Menter
4701 Willard Avenue (Apt 1726)
Chevy Chase, Maryland 20815-4632 USA

Prof. Dr. Priyatna Abdurrasyid
Tetana Duta Konsulindo
Pondok Pinang Center, Bloc A24
Jl. Ciputat Raya, Pondok Pinang
Jakarta 12310 INDONESIA
T 62-21 750 7373
F 62-21 751 1068 (preferably use fax)
E priyatna@indosat.net.id/ priyatna@cbn.net.id

H.E. Judge Dr. Vladlen S. Vereshchetin
International Court of Justice, Peace Palace
Carnegieplein 2
2517 KJ Den Haag THE NETHERLANDS
T 31-70 302 24 69
F 31-70 302 2409
E v.s.vereshchetin@icj-cij.org

Amb. Eugeniusz Wyzner
Vice-Chariman
International Civil Service Commission
Two United Nations Plaza, Room DC2-1050
New York, N.Y. 10017 USA
E wyzner@un.org

Prof. Dr. Gennady P. Zhukov
Ap. 84, Komsomolsky Prosp. 33
119 146 Moscow RUSSIA
T 7-095 245 76 85
F 7-095 433 73 85
E (c/o Dr Veschunov) dir@intersputnik.com

INTRODUCTION BY N. JASENTULIYANA PRESIDENT

I consider it to be a great honor to have been reelected as President of the International Institute of Space Law (IISL). In appreciation of the trust and confidence placed on me, I hope to carry forward with enthusiasm the work of the Institute that is regarded as the leading non-governmental organization in the field of space law.

I am happy that during my previous tenure, the Institute was able to advance its work in several important areas:

(i) Following a report submitted by a Task Force, the Board and the General Assembly accepted suggestions for a new vision for the Institute that would also enhance the Institute's work with the United Nations. In adopting the report, the Institute has established guidelines for its research efforts and several members are already undertaking work on topics of interest to them, the results of which will be considered and if appropriate adopted as Institute Policy Papers.

(ii) On the recommendation of another Task Force established by the Board, the Institute considered and adopted a series of changes to its Statutes and bylaws, in order to clarify and strengthen a number of their provisions.

(iii) A series of IISL Regional Meetings has been initiated by the Institute, the first of which was held in Singapore in March 2001 in collaboration with the Society for International Law of Singapore (SILS). The second of the series will be held in Beijing in April 2003 in Collaboration with the Chinese Institute of Space Law (CISL) and other Chinese sponsoring organizations.

(iv) The Institute has also begun to co-sponsor some space law meetings and symposia held both at the national and international level that are considered of benefit to its members and are useful in promoting space law.

(v) With a view to encouraging interdisciplinary discussion of space issues, the Institute organized a Plenary Session in collaboration with IAF at the annual International Astronautical Congress beginning with the Rio Congress in 2000. The IISL organized Plenary Sessions were attended by over one hundred participants and dealt with topics of interest to lawyers, policy specialists and high level managers of space programs from the governmental and commercial sectors. The Panelists were CEOs and other senior level managers from industry and government.

(vi) The annual Manfred Lachs Space Law Moot Court Competition judged by the Judges of the World Court was extended in 2000 to cover the Australasian region that joined teams in the competition from the United States and Europe. This year, the competition will be further extended to cover teams from Canada and China, thus enhancing the international character of this competition that has become one of the premier moot court competitions.

(vii) With the able assistance of an Honorary Director, The Institute was able to issue a new publication on the Institute's history and it was released at the World Space Congress in Houston in 2002.

(viii) With the strong support and commitment of one of the Institute's young members who volunteered his services, the Institute developed a web site for IISL which began operations in the spring of 2002. The site is constantly being expanded to serve the members of the Institute and promote its work. Greater use is also now made of the Internet and e-mail to help the Institute keep in regular contact with its members.

(ix) The Institute continued to promote membership and in particular the active participation of younger members. This is indicated by the large number of papers presented by young authors at the Rio, Toulouse and Houston colloquia and the enthusiastic participation of a greater number of university students in the Manfred Lachs Moot Court Competition. The Institute supported this important trend in establishing in 2001 the new Diederiks-Verschoor award for the best paper presented by a young author at the annual colloquium.

(x) The Institute also continued to work closely and strengthen its cooperation with the United Nations, contributing to the annual report on the Highlights in Space published by the United Nations for the use of COPUOS as well as the wider academic and professional community. The Institute, in collaboration with the ECSL, continued to organize an annual symposium for the benefit of members of the Legal Sub-Committee of COPUOS. At the invitation of the United Nations, the Institute now submits an annual report on the Institute's activities for the consideration of the Legal Sub-Committee. The Institute also continued its links with the ECSL and ILA. In recognition of the important developments in the area of private international law aspects of space activities, the Institute, through the active participation of its members, collaborated in the work of UNIDROIT, which drafted a protocol on the protection of space assets.

(xi) Last but not least, the Institute firmly established a tradition of holding an annual dinner on the occasion of the Manfred Lachs Space Law Moot Court Competition. Courtesy of sponsors, the Institute has been able to invite members to the annual dinner at no charge.

During my new tenure, I expect to continue to build on these and other new initiatives in enhancing the role of the Institute in the formulation and practice of space law and policy. I have no doubt that the Institute, with its rich international membership, should be able to play a critical role in future developments relating to space activities, particularly on emerging issues in the area of private international space law.

Finally, I wish to place on record my appreciation of the support extended by the membership of the Institute that continues to be its strength. Ms. Daria Lopez-Alegria and those who sponsored and helped with the arrangements for IISL activities at the World Space Congress deserves special thanks for the strong organizational and generous financial support, which made the Houston activities an outstanding success. I am grateful to our members Ram Jakhu, Steven Doyle and Stephan Hobe who assisted in preparing the Institute's reports to the United Nations. Andrei Terekhov, Chairman of the committee that prepared the publication on the status of Treaties, and JoAnn Clayton who collaborated in compiling the manuscript for the Institute's annual proceedings deserve the Institute's thanks. Steve Doyle spent a great deal of his time by volunteering to bring out the new History of the Institute and I am grateful for his cooperation. Thanks are also due to Patricia Sterns and other members who helped in numerous ways to ensure that the annual Colloquium, the Moot Court, the dinner and other activities were a success. Above all, it is the indispensable work of our outstanding Secretary Tanja Masson-Zwaan who labored throughout the year in coordinating all aspects of the program that is responsible for the success of the Institute's work, and we are all grateful for her outstanding contribution. I look forward to working with our dynamic Secretary and our ever-supportive Treasurer Dr. Frans von der Dunk in serving the Institute and its members in the coming year.

Annex: General Information

Background

The International Institute of Space Law (IISL) was founded by the International Astronautical Federation (IAF) in 1960. The IISL replaced the Permanent Committee on Space Law which the IAF had created in 1958 under the chairmanship of Andrew G. Haley. Since 1958, the IISL has held annual colloquia on space law in many nations. The IISL presently has elected individual and institutional members from over 40 countries, who are distinguished for their contributions to space law development. While a component of the IAF, the IISL is authorized to function autonomously in accordance with its Statutes.

The purposes and objectives of the Institute include the cooperation with appropriate international organizations and national institutions in the field of space law, the carrying out of tasks for fostering the social science aspects of astronautics, space travel and exploration, the organization of meetings and colloquia on juridical and sociological aspects of the space sciences, and the publication of proceedings, reports and other publications. Each year, the Institute publishes a report of the Standing Committee on the Status of International Agreements Relating to Activities in Outer Space, headed by Dr. A. Terekhov.

The financial resources of the Institute are derived from membership dues, research grants, remuneration received from the sale of its publications, and donations received from individuals, associations, institutions, foundations, and other organizations with interests in the development of law governing space activities. The headquarters of the International Institute of Space Law are located at 3-5 rue Mario Nikis, 75015 Paris, France.

IISL and the United Nations

IISL members have been appointed by the International Astronautical Federation as Official Observers to annual sessions of the United Nations (UN) Committee on the Peaceful Uses of Outer Space and its Legal Subcommittee. In addition, the IISL has, like in past years, prepared a report on legal developments under contract with the UN, to be published in the annual Highlights in Space Report, and provides yearly reports on its activities to the Legal Subcommittee.

In 2003, the IISL will again co-organize a symposium for the delegates and staff of the Legal Subcommittee session; the Coordinator of the program is Ms. Tanja Masson-Zwaan. The symposium will deal with the Registration Convention.

45th IISL Colloquium

The 45th IISL Colloquium was held from 14-18 Oct. 2002 in Houston, Texas, USA, during the Second World Space Congress (WSC), 10-19 October 2002. Nearly 100 persons attended the sessions and most of the 66 papers were presented.

The following sessions were held:

Session 1: Space Assets: Legal Aspects of Financing and Risk Management.
Chairmen: Dr. A. Dula and Ms. F. Schroeder, USA, Rapporteur: Mr. Wayne White, USA
Session 2: ISS and the Law
Chairmen: Dr. A. Farand, ESA and Mr. J. Maclure, USA, Rapporteur: Mr. Kenneth Weidaw, USA
Session 3: International Security and Military Uses of Outer Space: Legal Implications
Chairmen: Prof. J. Galloway, USA and Dr. E. Fasan, Austria; Rapporteur: Mr. Marco Ferrazzani, ESA
Session 4: Other Legal Matters, Including Legal Aspects of Launch Services
Chairmen: Dr. K.U. Schrogl, Germany and Ms. JoAnn Clayton Townsend, USA; Rapporteur; Ms. Yuri Takaya, Japan

The IISL held another successful Plenary Event on "Space Business in the Early 21st Century: More than Telecom?". Speakers were: Antoine Bouvier, CEO of Astrium, Terry Hart, President, Loral Skynet, Jay Honeycutt, President of Lockheed Martin Space Operations, and Pascale Sourisse, President of Alcatel Space. The panel was coordinated by Chris Stott, President and CEO of ManSat LLC and the IISL President.

IISL Publications

The Proceedings of the Houston Colloquium will be published by the AIAA.

Dr Doyle presented his new book: *Origins of International Space Law and the International Istitute of Space Law Of the International Astronautical Federation* (Univelt, 2002). This work introduces the origins of writing on international space law and its early development. Beginning with legal works early in the 20th century, the study traces developing literature, organizational formation, and gradually increasing international cooperation in the development of international space law.

Manfred Lachs Space Law Moot Court Competition

The 11th Manfred Lachs Space Law Moot Court Competition was held during the Houston Colloquium. Semi-finals were held on Tuesday 15 October, and the Finals were held on Thursday 17 October. Three Judges of the ICJ judged the Finals: H.E. Judge Koroma, H.E. Judge Buergenthal and H.E. Judge Elaraby. The Institute is very grateful that they accepted to travel to Houston, thus enabling us to continue our unique tradition of having World Court Judges for the Finals.

In the European Round, 7 teams participated, in the USA 5, and in the Asia-Pacific region there were 11 teams. The winners of the preliminary rounds were, respectively, the University of Warwick, UK, Georgetown University Law Center, Washington DC, USA, and the University of New South Wales, Sydney, Australia. Australia, the team with the highest score for written briefs, moved directly to the Finals, whereas the USA and UK first met in the Semi Final. The USA won this, then met Australia in the Final, was victorious there as well, and brought home the Manfred Lachs Trophy. The Sterns and Tennen Award for Best Oralist was won by Victoria Williams of the US team, and the Eilene M. Galloway Award for Best Brief was won by the Australian team. All students received certificates.

With the invaluable help of Ms. Daria Lopez-Alegria of SpaceBridges, a Houston based consultant, we had managed to secure the support of a large number of law firms, space corporations, universities, government agencies, international organizations and individual IISL Members, to whom IISL is most grateful.

The Colombe d'Or, an elegant restaurant in Houston was the location for the IISL Dinner that followed the Finals. The University of Houston had provided the location for the finals.

A report on the competition, the case and the winning briefs are published in this volume. The competition will be held for the 12th time in Bremen, Germany in October 2003.

Awards

A Distinguished Service Award was presented to Prof. Jonathan Galloway.

The second "Dr. I.H.Ph. Diederiks-Verschoor Award" for best paper presented at the IISL Colloquium by a young author was given to Mr. Ricky Lee from Australia, for his paper "The *ius ad bellum* in outer space: the interrelation between Article 103 of the Charter of the United Nations and Article IV of the Outer Space Treaty." Prof. Fernandez-Brital donated the Medal.

The Board also adopted a Resolution to thank several persons who have made continuing and long-term efforts to promote the IISL. These resolutions were read at the annual dinner and will be given to these persons in the form of a certificate. They are:

- Ms. JoAnn Clayton (USA), for her work on the Proceedings,
- Mr. Ricky Lee (Australia), for his work on the Asia Pacific moot court round and for creating and maintaining a moot court website,
- Ms. Daria Lopez-Alegria (USA/ Switzerland), for arranging all the sponsors of the moot court and arranging all the logistics,
- Mr. Sergei Negoda (Ukraine), for creating and maintaining our new website,
- Ms. Patricia Sterns (USA), for managing the IISL's social and COSPAR cooperative functions at the WSC.

V. Space Law Conference Beijing

The Chinese Institute of Space Law (CISL) will host the next regional conference in Beijing, China, from 6-8 April 2003. This meeting is following up on the first regional conference, held in Singapore in 2001. The **"Space Law Conference 2003: Asia, a Regional Force in Space"** is organized by IISL and the the China Institute of Space Law (CISL). Sessions will be held on the following topics:

- National Space Programmes, Policies and Legislation in Asia
- Trade Issues, including Insurance, Financing, Asset protection, Export controls
- Commercial Use of Space, including Launching
- Protection of Developing Countries' Interests, Including Access to Space
- Space Applications: Remote Sensing & Telecommunications

46th IISL Colloquium

The 46th IISL Colloquium will be held from 29 Sept. – 3 Oct. 2003 in Bremen, Germany. The following sessions will be held:

Session 1: New Issues Relating to Nuclear Power Sources
This session will address legal issues relating to the use of nuclear devices (including radioisotope heating units, radioisotope thermoelectric generators, and nuclear reactors) for space operations (including heat, power or propulsion) in Earth orbit, beyond Earth orbit, or for launching spacecraft from the surface of the Earth.
Chairs: Prof. Stephan Hobe, Germany and Ms. Marcia Smith, USA
Rapporteur: Ms. Gerardine Goh, Singapore

Session 2: Space Traffic Management and Navigation
International and national legal and institutional implications of the management of space traffic and the navigation of space vehicles, e.g. through GNSS. This topic includes the relationship between general principles of space law and the establishment of future 'space standards and recommended practices'.
Chairs: Dr. Lubos Perek, Czech Rep., and Prof. José Monserrat Filho, Brazil
Rapporteur: Dr. Sylvia Ospina, Colombia

Session 3: Space Law and International Security
This session will address questions of missile non-proliferation (new international code proposed for MTCR) and related issues.
Chairs: Prof. Yuri Kolossov, Russia and Mr. John Gantt, USA
Rapporteur: Dr. Liara Covert, Canada

Session 4: Other Legal Matters
Including the 40th anniversary of the 1963 "Declaration of Legal Principles Governing the Activities of States in the Exploration and Use of Outer Space": achievements and the future development of space law
Chairs: Mr. Hermann Ersfeld, Germany and Prof. Maurice Andem, Finland
Rapporteur: Dr. Peter van Fenema, Netherlands

Manfred Lachs Space Law Moot Court Competition

The semi finals and finals of the 12th Manfred Lachs Space Law Moot Court Competition will be held during the 2003 Colloquium in Bremen. The case was written by Michael Davis and Ricky Lee (Australia). Preliminary competitions will be held in Europe, the USA and the Asia Pacific.

Dr. I.H.Ph. Diederiks-Verschoor Award

Authors will again be invited to apply for this Award.

VII. 47th IISL Colloquium

The 47th Colloquium on the law of outer space will be held during the IAF Congress in October 2004 in Vancouver, Canada. The session topics for this colloquium will de decided in the Spring of 2003.

Elections 2002

Board of Directors:

Prof. Böckstiegel was elected Honorary Director in recognition of his singular contributions to the analysis and development of space law. In addition, three new directors were elected (one to replace Prof. Böckstiegel and two in view of the amendments to the statutes that increase the number of board members from 18 to 20):

- Prof. Elisabeth Back Impallomeni (Italy)
- Prof. Stephan Hobe (Germany)
- Prof. Rosa Maria Ramirez de Arrellano (Mexico)

Six other directors were re-elected for a new term.

Lastly, Dr. Jasentuliyana was re-elected as President, in recognition of his outstanding and continuing service to the IISL and its mission in the field of space law and international cooperation and encouraging the free expression and exchange of ideas relevant to space law and policy.

Members:

The following members were elected throughout 2002:

Prof. Philippe Achilleas
Université de Paris XI
2 Place Wagram
75017 Paris, FRANCE
T 33 1 40 53 03 73
E achilleas@jm.u-psud.fr

Ms. Ulrike M. Bohlmann
Legal Department, European Space Agency
8-10 rue Mario Nikis, 75015 Paris, FRANCE
ulrike.bohlmann@esa.int

Dr. Tony Carro
Solar System Program Division
NASA
Code SE-NASA HQ
Washington DC 20546-0001, USA
T 1-202 358 0349
F 1-202 358 0349
E acarro@hq.nasa.gov

Mr. Luis F. Castillo Argañarás
Adj. Professor
University of Buenos Aires
Arenales 2021 poison 3 Dpto 5
Buenos Aires 1124, ARGENTINA
T 11-4821 6673
F 11-4821 6673
E lfcastillo@uade.edu.ar

Dr. Liara M. Covert
20, Horton road
Rothesay, New Brunswick, E2H 1P8, CANADA
1-506 847 0219
liarac@yahoo.com

Mr. Alvaro Fabricio Dos Santos
National Institute for Space Research (INPE)
Av. dos Astronautoas 1758, Jardim de Granja, 12227-010
Sao Jose dos Campos SP, BRAZIL
1-55 12 3945 6022
1-55 12 3945 6015
alvaro@dir.inpe.br

Mr. James E. Dunstan
Garvey, Schubert, Barer
1000 Potomac Street NW, 5th Floor
Washington DC 20007, USA
T 1-202 298 2534
F 1-202 965 1729
E jdunstan@gsblaw.com

Mr. Gary Epstein
Latham & Watkins
555 Eleventh Street, NW, suite 1000
Washington DC 20004-1304, USA
T 1-202 637 2249
F 1-202 637 2201
E gary.epstein@lw.com

Mr. Hermann Ersfeld
Head of Legal Matters,
Space Infrastructure Division, Astrium GmbH
P.O. Box 286156
28361 Bremen, GERMANY
T 49-421 539 4587
F 49-421 539 5849
E Hermann.Ersfeld@astrium-space.com

Mr. John P. Janka
Latham & Watkins
555 Eleventh Street, NW, suite 1000
Washington DC 20004-1304, USA
T 1-202 637 2289
F 1-202 637 2201
E john.janka@lw.com

Mr. Philip S. Makiol
Institute of Air and Space Law
University of Cologne
Albertus Magnus Platz
D 50923 Cologne, GERMANY
1-49 221 470 4017
1-49 221 470 4968
philip.makiol@uni-koeln.de

Mr. Alberto Marchini
Secretary, ECSL, c/o ESA
8-10 rue Mario Nikis
75015 Paris, FRANCE
E Alberto.Marchini@esa.int

Mr. Christopher J. Murphy
Senior Legal Advisor, International Bureau
Federal Communications Commission (FCC)
445, 12th Street, SW
Washington DC 20554, USA
T 1-202 418 2373
F 1-202 418 2818
E cmurphy@fcc.gov

Ms. Franceska O. Schroeder
Milbank, Tweed, Hadley & McCloy
1825 I Street NW, Suite 1100
Washington DC 20006, USA
1-202 835 7519
1-202 835 7586
fschroeder@milbank.com

Mr. Christopher Stott
President and CEO, Mansat LLC
1542 Mija Lane
Seabrook, Texas 77586, USA
T 1-281 228 9155
F 1-281 229 99176
E chris.stott@mansat.com

Ms. Yuri Takaya
Secretary, Institute of Space and Astronautical Science (ISAS)
1-22-712, Nagatsuta, Midori-ku
Yokohama-shi, Kanagawa-ken 226-0027, JAPAN
1-81 45982 4336
1-81 45982 4336
yuritakaya@hotmail.com

Dr. Douglas A. Vakoch
Social Scientist, SETI Institute
2035 Landings Drive, Mountain View , California 94043, USA
1-650 960 4514
1-650 961 7099
vakoch@seti.org

Photos from the 45th Colloquium on the Law of Outer Space

Moot Court Finalists, N. Jasentuliyana, and ICJ Judges Buergenthal, Koroma, and Elarby

L. Perek

J. Gabrynowicz, J. Monserrat, R. Monserrat

J. Rummel (COSPAR), P. Sterns

F. von der Dunk

T. Masson-Tzaan, G. Goh

A. Terekhov, N. Jasentuliyana, K.-U. Schrogl, K. Takaya

N. Jasentuliyana, Marcia Smith, Milton Smith

ICJ Judges and Dean Rapoport (U. of Houston Law School)

Amb. Jankowitsch

E. Fasan

J. Clayton-Townsend, M. Roberts, E. Galloway, M. Smith

C. Cristol, V. Kopal

University of New South Wales Team, winners of the Eilene M. Galloway Award for Best Written Brief, and Dr. Galloway

V. Williams, USA, receiving Sterns and Tennen award for Best Oralist

TABLE OF CONTENTS

LEGAL IMPLICATIONS OF MILITARY USES OF OUTER SPACE

OTHER LEGAL MATTERS, INCLUDING LEGAL ASPECTS OF LAUNCH SERVICES

ADDENDA

Session 1: SPACE ASSETS: LEGAL ASPECTS OF FINANCING AND RISK MANAGEMENT

Chairmen: A. Dula, USA, and F. Schroeder, USA

Rapporteur: W. White, USA

IAC-02-IISL.1.01

CRITICAL ISSUES IN THE UNIDROIT DRAFT SPACE PROTOCOL

Paul B. Larsen, Georgetown University Law Center*

The objective of the Space Protocol is to create a document that will protect financiers thus giving them confidence to loan money for space ventures. It is in their interest that the Protocol be as sweeping as possible without ambiguous exceptions that will cause doubt whether they are adequately protected. A Protocol that has many exceptions and reservations creates uncertainty in the minds of financiers about the risks of financing The Protocol also must be simple, certain and easily understood in order to be workable. For example an open-ended blanket treaty provision that the Protocol is subject to and subservient to existing space law might incorporate public international law extraneous to the private law purposes of the Protocol. If those public law provisions contain ambiguities, they could create uncertainty for private investors about the scope of legal protection for their assets. The space industry working group was conscious that this could undermine the intended uniformity and predictability of the Protocol's legal regime. The working group thought it is essential that the Protocol advance and increase the confidence and feeling of security of financiers. 1/

The Space Protocol, like the Aviation Protocol, is based on private international law governing the relationships among private parties. To understand the Space Protocol provisions, it helps to read the corresponding provisions in the Aviation Protocol. 2/ This will be even more important as practical experience and case law develop under the Aviation Protocol. The establishment of a Supervisory Authority and Registry under the Aviation Protocol will have particular value as a precedent for the Space Protocol's similar arrangement. 3/

A. Coexistence of the Space Protocol with Space Law Treaties

The Outer Space Treaty (hereinafter OST) 4/ obligates States Parties to ensure that national activities in outer space, whether they are governmental or nongovernmental, be performed in compliance with the provisions of the treaty. Furthermore, OST, Art. IX, obligates States to conduct their outer space activities "with due regard to the corresponding interests of all the other States Parties to the Treaty." If States' activities in outer space may cause harmful interference with the activities of other States then they must consult with other States before proceeding. 5/ The States parties must supervise private activities of their nationals in outer space for compliance. 6/ Consequently, in order to respect existing space law, all interested parties agree on a governing principle of having no conflicts between public law space treaties and the private law Space Protocol. 7/ This principle is incorporated in the text of the Protocol. Its preamble recognizes "the established principles of space law, including those contained in the international space treaties under the auspices of the United Nations." 8/ Acceptance of the no-conflicts principle arose out of a study by a special industry working group which examined the existing space law and did not find any conflicts with the current draft of the Space Protocol. 9/ The COPUOS Consultative Group agreed with the no conflicts principle and recommended "that appropriate language should be incorporated within the text of the space protocol to the extent necessary to ensure the integrity and respect for the rights and obligations of States in accordance with those principles." 10/ The chairman of the Legal Subcommittee, Prof. Kopal, in his address to the working group stressed the importance of this principle in saying " the nature of the relationship between the two regimes needed to be clarified expressly in the text of the preliminary draft Protocol, at least in the preamble thereto." 11/

B. Space Assets

The Space Protocol regulates space assets. 12/ Its definition of space assets is very broad in order to afford all assets in a space project protection by the Protocol. It includes property that has been launched into outer space, manufactured in outer space, and property that has been returned from space. The definition includes space assets on Earth intended for launch into outer space; intangible rights to control satellites, contractual rights, proceeds and revenues and other rights yet to be established. The Protocol's scope also includes debtor's rights to payments or performance under agreements secured by or associated with space assets. These associated rights 12/ include permits, licenses, authorizations or equivalent instruments granted or issued by national or intergovernmental bodies including authorities to control, use or operate space assets and include authorizations to use orbital positions, transmission and reception of radio signals from or to space assets, in each case "to the extent permissible and assignable under the laws concerned." 14/ In addition the associated rights include rights to payments or other performance due a debtor by a person relating to space assets, and a debtor's contractual rights secured by or associated with such space assets. 15/

The Protocol's definition of space assets is broader than the definition of space objects in the space law treaties. 16/ "Space object" concerns property that has been launched into outer space whereas "space assets" include property on the surface of the Earth. 17/ Is consistency of the Protocol's definition with the definition under existing international space law necessary? This is an important question because all the space law conventions concern space objects. 18/ For example, the Registration Convention, Art. II, mandates registration of space objects; registration identifies the state which has jurisdiction and control over the object; thus registration has bearing on ownership of the space object. 19/ Consistency of definition of "space object" with "space asset" is probably not necessary because the Protocol's purpose differs from the purpose of existing space law: The Protocol is concerned primarily with private law and with the protection of financiers who enter into private law contracts, whereas the existing space law is primarily public law. However, the broader definition of space assets has the consequence that some space assets are not subject to the international space law treaties because they are not defined as space objects. 20/

C. The Registry

The registry of financial interests is visualized as a computer bank that is accessible by computer. The registry will be open on a 24 hour basis so that it can be electronically accessed and searched at any time from anywhere in the world. 21/ The Space Protocol will not only establish a registry for space assets that is separate from aviation equipment, it will also establish a registry that is separate from the current U.N. registry established under the Registration Convention. 22/ Establishment of a separate registry for space assets would have several advantages: Several space-faring countries, including the United States, support the principle that existing space law treaties should not be changed by the Space Protocol. 23/ Use of the current U.N. Registry to register international interests might require amendment of the Registration Convention, whereas a separate Protocol registry would satisfy the principle of no change to existing space law. Nevertheless, the separate registries could still provide a limited identification link between the two registries. 24/

Persuasive argument for separate registries are that the Space Protocol and Registration Convention registries serve different purposes. The Protocol's registration is by individual companies whereas the Registration Convention's registration is by States. 25/ Secondly, the purpose of the Space Protocol is to regulate the relationship between creditors and debtors, whereas the Registration Convention's purpose is to determine which State has jurisdiction and control over space objects. 26/ Furthermore, as mentioned above, 27/ the scope of the Registration Convention is more narrow that that of the Protocol. Therefore, the space working group, as indicated in the Space Protocol, 28/ favors a Protocol registry that is separate from the Registration Convention's registry, perhaps operated by a private contractor, under the supervision of the Supervisory Authority. Equipment must be identifiable for the purpose of registration. The Space Protocol, influenced by the Aviation Protocol, favors use of the manufacturer's name or serial number and model description and the intended location of the space asset. 29/ Parts of space assets may be registered separately and several different modes of registration are contemplated. The space working group agreed that multiple search criteria would enhance the reliability of searches in the computerized data base. 30/

The Supervisory Authority will appoint and dismiss the Registrar. 31/ All liability of the Registrar shall be covered by liability insurance or by a financial guarantee as directed by the Supervisory Authority. 32/

D. Supervisory Authority.

Art. 17 of the Convention would create a Supervisory Authority to appoint and supervise the Registrar, provide for continuity of the Registry and perform several administrative functions. 33/ The Space Protocol provides that the Authority will be appointed by the diplomatic conference. 34/ Furthermore, the Supervisory Authority shall be immune from legal and administrative process. 35/ A commission of experts, to be nominated by the States, may be appointed by the Authority to assist the Authority with its duties. 36/ The Supervisory Authority may adopt regulations placing in special escrow the command codes for access and control of space assets. 37/

Full reimbursement of all the Supervisory Authority's expenses will be essential to its function. 38/ Thus all the cost of the Supervisory Authority relating to appointing, supervising and regulating the Registrar will be recovered from the fees charged for use of the registry's facilities and services. 39/

The Supervisory Authority under the Space Protocol has not yet been finally identified. UNIDROIT has approached the United Nations, which has indicated interest. 40/ COPUOS asked for guidance from the U.N. Legal Counsel about whether the United Nations can serve as Supervisory Authority. 41/ However, other intergovernmental organizations are also interested in serving as Supervisory Authority. 42/ Service of the United Nations or another intergovernmental organization as Supervisory Authority would not change the basic nature of the Space Protocol as being "a transactional private law treaty;" because, as Loren Clark and Jeffrey Wool point out, the involvement by an intergovernmental organization would be merely incidental to the core purpose of the Protocol. 43/

E. Liability Issues

The COPUOS consultative group is of the view the effect of the Space Protocol on liability for space activities should be studied. 44/ At issue is examination of the interaction between the Space Protocol and Articles II and III of the Liability Convention. 45/ Article II makes the launching State absolutely liable for damage caused by its space objects on the Earth's surface and to aircraft in flight. 46/ Art. III makes the launching state liable for damage to space objects caused by its negligence in outer space. 47/ The question is how can the launching State maintain oversight and control over a space object if the object has been transferred to creditors who are located in another State and subject to its jurisdiction? Such transfer to creditors in another State could take place if the financier, in accordance with his rights and remedies under the Convention, Art. 8 takes physical or constructive possession of space objects which they have financed. Suppose the financier decides to operate the space object and the space object causes surface damage or damage in outer space? The launching State could be liable under the Liability Convention. The launching State would then try to seek recourse from the operator (financier) who might be located in another country and difficult to hold responsible. Such recourse action would not be based on the Liability Convention, nor on the Space Protocol but could be based a separate agreement among States, or on specific local law, or on assumption of liability. 48/

Because the Liability Convention holds the launching State liable, this brings into issue the Convention's definition of launching State as "(i) a State which launches or procures the launching of a space object; a State from whose territory or facility a space object is launched." 49/ The space law treaties, including the Liability Convention, were drafted at the time when Governments conducted most space activities. 50/ The Liability Convention implies government operation. The Convention's drafters did not provide for individual liability of private satellite operators when the space assets have been transferred, whether by sale, lease or secured financing, to private operators in countries that are not launching states. 51/ Nevertheless, the Space Protocol can work in tandem with the Liability Convention. The Protocol requires that the name of the financier having financial interests in space assets be listed in the Space Protocol's registry. 52/ States would benefit from the enhanced transparency resulting from the existence of and access to the registry to be established under the Space Protocol States would better be able to assess their potential liability under the Liability Convention and their supervisory functions under Art VI of the Outer Space Treaty. 53/ Consequently, the liability of the launching state under the Liability Convention does not appear to be undermined by the Space Protocol.

The problem is with the Liability Convention's definition of "launching State." 54/ The COPUOS Legal Subcommittee previously established a special working group on the problem of "launching State." 55/ That working group is particularly concerned with improving the application of the Liability and Registration Conventions. 56/ The COPUOS Legal Subcommittee established a three year work plan on the definition of "launching State." 57/ However, some COPUOS member States noted that the definition of launching State has not caused any current problem and " that governmental and private launches were occurring on a regular basis and were able to proceed with the support of private insurance." 58/

Regarding the liability of the Supervisory Authority and the Registrar for negligent acts or omissions in performance of their duties, the Convention 59/ provides for immunity of the Supervisory Authority, 60/ and provides that the Registrar may buy insurance to cover the Registrar's liability. 61/ The Space Protocol reinforces these protections from liability. 62/

F. Jurisdiction

The Convention permits the parties to a finance contract to choose the exclusive forum to adjudicate disputes arising under the contract. 63/ The chosen forum does not need to have a connection with the transaction or with the parties. The chosen forum has jurisdiction to grant temporary relief in order to preserve the space asset, to repossess or immobilize it. 64/ The Space Protocol Article XX confirms that the waiver of sovereign immunity from the jurisdiction of the court specified in the Convention or regarding enforcement under the Convention is binding and shall confer jurisdiction and allow enforcement. 65/

The contractual freedom to choose a forum may be contrasted with the Outer Space Treaty, Art VIII: 66/

> A State Party to the Treaty on whose registry an object is launched into outer space is carried shall retain jurisdiction and control over such object, and over any personnel thereof, while in outer space or on a celestial body.

Art. VIII governs State responsibility. It does not govern private party rights. Private parties may, under the Convention and the Space Protocol, agree to change the national jurisdictional rules that govern a contract. 67/ The contractual objective will normally be for the debtor to seek to stipulate that disputes be settled in an impartial forum.

Finally the Convention provides that the courts of the place where the registrar is located shall have jurisdiction to issue orders against the Registrar and to award damages. 68/

G. Choice of Law.

The Space Protocol 69/ provides that the parties to a financing agreement or contract of sale may agree on the law which shall govern the contract. The law chosen by the parties would be the domestic law of the designated state.

H. Space Protocol Interaction with ITU International Law and Regulations

The COPUOS Legal Subcommittee focused on the interaction of the Space Protocol with the Constitution, Convention and Radio Regulations of the International Telecommunication Union (ITU), in particular on treaty obligations in the situation when space assets are transferred from one country to another. 70/ Some COPUOS delegates wish to have more active ITU participation in this discussion. 71/ Examples of Space Protocol interaction with the ITU legal instruments are: The general provisions under the ITU Constitution 72/ give the ITU Member States the right to terminate illegal radio transmissions. 73/ ITU Member States may suspend international telecommunication service after due notice to ITU. 74/ The space working group's view is that there is no conflict with the ITU legal instruments because the operators of communication satellites and thus the financiers take possession of those satellites subject to ITU's established priority of telecommunications on safety of life. 75/

Fortunately, ITU participated actively in the space industry working group through its former ITU General Counsel, Alfons A.. E. Noll. 76/ Furthermore, UNIDROIT sent a formal request to the Secretary General of ITU asking ITU to study the relationship between the Space Protocol and the ITU instruments. ITU responded that the Space Protocol does not contradict the ITU instruments, nor does the Protocol overlap with these instruments. 77/

The reasons for ITU's absence of concern with the Space Protocol relate to its view of the Protocol's private law regulation of the contractual rights of financiers and debtors. In ITU's view the Protocol does not regulate or supersede the public law regulatory functions of ITU. Financiers and debtors are very conscious of the importance of satellite operators complying with the ITU legal instruments when they enter into financing or lease contracts. The parties conclude their financing contracts expecting compliance by the satellite operators with applicable governmental authorizations, including existing ITU rules and regulations. They accept that the ITU laws and regulations regulate the legal use of radio frequencies and orbital locations. 78/

FOODNOTES

1. UNIDROIT 2002, Study LXXIIJ - Doc. 11 at 9.

2. Aviation Protocol to Convention on International Interests in Mobile Equipment, U.N.Doc A./AC.105/C.2.2002/CRP.3

3. Preliminary Draft Protocol on Matters Specific to Space Assets, UNIDROIT 2002, Study LXXIIJ – Doc. 10 (Space Protocol), Chapter III.

4. Treaty on Principles Governing the Activities of States in the Exploration and Use of Outer Space, Including the Moon and Other Celestial Bodies, 610 U.N.T.S. 205(OST), Art VI.

5. Id. Art. IX.

6. Id. Art. VI.

7. See U.N. Committee on Peaceful Uses of Outer Space, Report of the Legal Subcommittee on its forty-first session held in Vienna from 22 to 12 April 2002, U.N.Doc A/AC.105/787 (COPUOS Report)

8. Space Protocol, supra n. 3, Preamble.

9. Id. at vi.

10. COPUOS Report supra n. 7, at 24.

11. UNIDROIT Doc. 11, supra n. 1, at 7.

12. Space Protocol, supra n.3, Art. 1.

13. Id.

14. Id.

15. "Associated rights" means(i) any permit, license, authorization or equivalent instrument that is granted or issued by a national or intergovernmental or other international body or authority to control, use or operate a space asset, relating to the use of orbital positions and the transmission, emission or reception of radio signals to and from a space asset, which may be transferred or assigned , to the extent permissible and assignable under the laws concerned; (ii) all rights to payment or other performance due to a debtor by any person with respect to space assets; and (iii) all contractual rights held by a debtor that are secured by or associated with the space assets."

16. Registration Convention, 1023 U.N.T.S. 15, Art. 1.

17. Space Protocol, supra n. 3, Art. I.

18. All the space law treaties refer to space "objects."

19. See OST, supra n. 4, Art. VIII.

20. See definition of space assets in Space Protocol, supra n. 3, Art I.

21. Id. Art. XIX. The act of registration notifies the public of the existence of the security interests in space assets and of the priorities of creditors' interests.

22. Registration Convention, supra n. 16, Art III.

23. COPUOS Report supra n. 7. U.S. Delegation statements during discussion in COPUOS experts group.

24. COPUOS Report, supra n. 7, at 15.

25. Registration Convention, Supra n. 16, Art II states that launching States shall register space objects.

26. Registration Convention, supra n. 16, Art. II.

27. Supra at n. 16.

28. Space Protocol, supra n. 3. Also see UNIDROIT Doc. 11, supra n. 1.

29. Space Protocol, supra n. 3, Art. VII. Note that the Registry is based on registration of assets rather than on registration of debtors.

30. UNIDROIT Doc. 11, supra n. 1, at 9.

31. Convention, supra n. 2, at Art. 17 (2)(b)

32. Convention, supra n. 2, Art. 28 (4), Space Protocol supra n. 3, Art XIX. The Registrar will be liable for negligent record keeping.

33. Convention, supra n. 2, at Art. 17.

34. Space Protocol, supra n. 3, Art . XVII.

35. Convention, supra n. 2, Art. 27

36. Space Protocol, supra n. 3, Art. XVII.

37. Id., Art. 17(4).

38. COPUOS Report, supra n. 7, at 15.

39. Convention, supra n. 2, Art.17(2), Space Protocol, supra n. 3, Art XIX.

40. Id.. UNIDROIT Doc. 11, supra n. 1, at 6.

41. COPUOS Report, supra n. 7, at 18.

42. UNIDROIT Doc. 10, supra n. 3, at xv.

43. Clark and Wool, Entry Into Force of Transactional Private Law Treaties Affecting Aviation, 66 J. Air L. & Com. at 1407.

44. COPUOS Report, supra n. 7, at 14.

45. Space Protocol, supra n. 3; Liability Convention, 961 U.N.T.S. 18.

46. Id. Liability Convention, Art. II: "A launching State shall be absolutely liable to pay compensation for damage caused by its space object on the surface of the Earth or to aircraft flight."

47. Id. Art III: "In the event of damage being caused elsewhere than on the surface of the Earth to a space object of one launching State or to persons or property on board such a space object by a space object of another launching State, the latter shall be liable only if the

damage is due to its fault or the fault of persons for whom it is responsible."

48. Liability could be based on bilateral agreements under which another state assumes all liability of a launching state; liability could be based on the statutory law of a State or on its law of Torts; it could also be based on assumption of liability either through the finance agreement or if the permitting authority required that the financier as receiver of title assumed liability.

49. Liability Convention, supra. n. 45, Art I.

50. The Liability Convention was finalized in 1972. All the space law treaties were negotiated in the 1967 – 1979 time frame.

51. Only launching States are liable under the Liability Convention, supra n. 45. References to States may include international intergovernmental organizations if they accept rights and obligations under the Liability Convention, see Art. XXII.

52. Space Protocol, supra n. 3, Art VII. Identification of space assets in the Registry shall include the name of he debtor and the creditor, their addresses, description of the space assets, date and location of launch, and description of separately identifiable component part.

53. OST, supra n. 4, Art. VI.

54. Liability Convention, supra n. 45, Art. I.

55. COPUOS Report, supra n. 3, at 16.

56. Id., at 26. Chairman of the COPUOS special working group on "launching State" is Mr. Kai-Uwe Schrogl, Germany.

57. Id. at 16.

58. Id. at 16.

59. Convention, supra n. 2, Art. 27.

60. Id., Space Protocol, supra n. 3, Art. XVII. See supra n. 32.

61. Convention, supra, n. 2, Art. 28.

62. Space Protocol, supra n. 3, Art. XIX.

63. Convention, supra n. 2, Art. 42.

64. Id. Art. 43.

65. Id. Arts. 42 and 43.

66. OST, supra n. 4, Art. VIII.

67. Convention, supra n. 2, Arts. 42 and 43; Space Protocol, supra n. 3, Art XVII.

68. Convention, supra n. 2, Art. 44.

69. Space Protocol, supra n. 3, Art. VIII.

70. ITU Constitution, Project 2001, Legal Framework for the commercial use of Outer Space (Satellite Communications), 8/9 June, 2000, Berlin, Germany, at 314 – 316.

71. COPUOS Report, supra n. 7, at 14.

72. ITU Constitution, supra. n. 69, Arts. 33 – 48.

73. Id. Art. 34.

74. Id. Art 35. The ITU requires radio stations to have licenses.

75. See Larsen, UNIDROIT Draft Space Protocol, 44 Colloquium on Law of Outer Space (2001).

76. UNIDROIT Doc.11, supra n. 1, at 3.

77. UNIDROIT Study LXXIIJ, S.W.G. ,4th Sess., W.P. 3 (2001). Also see Larsen, supra n. 775.

78. Id.

THE CONCEPTS OF ASSETS and PROPERTY: Similarities and Differences, and their Applicability to Undertakings in Outer Space

SYLVIA OSPINA, JD, LLM

ABSTRACT
UNIDROIT 's Preliminary Draft Protocol on Matters Specific to Space Assets was revised and modified in 2001. Whereas the first drafts addressed "SPACE PROPERTY", the revised version speaks of "SPACE ASSETS".

This paper will examine these changes and the implications thereof, particularly in view of the trend toward privatization of outer space activities, and the context provided by Article II of the Outer Space Treaty.

Introduction

The concept of "property" is probably older than man-made law itself./[1]/ Land (real property) is an immovable and finite resource, ownership and use of which gained in importance with the expansion of sedentary societies. Humankind's desire to possess things eventually led to the extension of the concept of "property" to include movable and personal goods, as well as intangibles./[2]/

While humans have sought to possess tangible items or objects, we have also sought to imbue intangible ones with certain qualities, valuable characteristics, or "assets"./[3]/ Assets can include property of all kinds, real and personal, tangible and intangible, as well as the perceived value of a characteristic./[4]/ Hence, the term "asset" has broader connotations, comprising far more than merely tangible property. Assets also could include access to and use of nature's elements, "global commons" like the oceans, air, and outer space.

Perhaps a desire to be owner and master of nature's elements has always been in the human spirit. Certainly in our days, wanting to be owners and masters of air and outer space, including orbits and parts of the radio frequency spectrum, would seem to confirm this latent desire.

A question arises, namely whether these intangible assets, the commons of all mankind, can be made the subject of private security interests, as proposed in the UNIDROIT Convention on International Interests Mobile Equipment, and the Preliminary Draft Protocol on Matters Specific to Space Assets./[5]/ Is this kind of convention essential to encourage participation of private parties in space activities, or merely to protect their massive investments in them? A brief look at private sector involvement in this area may be helpful, before examining UNIDROIT's proposals.

The Private Sector and Space Activities

Even before the adoption of the Outer Space Treaty, proponents of space activities foresaw that the private sector would be involved in these. Private entities, such as COMSAT/[6]/,

---

International Telecommunications / Space Law Consultant. Senior Member, AIAA., Full Member IAA, Member IISL Board of Directors. Contact:sospina@bellsouth.net were specifically created to develop and deploy the early communications satellite systems, which have been, and still are the most lucrative use of outer space. These activities, however, were "subject to appropriate governmental regulation,"/[7]/ a caveat that was included in the Outer Space Treaty: the State Party to the Treaty would bear international responsibility for national activities in outer space, whether carried out by governmental or non-governmental entities (including private parties). Further, "[the] activities of non-governmental entities shall require authorization and continuing supervision by the appropriate State Party to the Treaty."/[8]/

State Parties to the Treaty, and by extension, their nationals, "shall retain jurisdiction and control over [a space object]...while in outer space or on a celestial body. Moreover, "[o]wnership of objects launched into space is not affected by their presence in outer space...or by their return to earth."/[9]/ I.e., owners remain responsible for their space object, even at the end of its useful life, whether in orbit or not. In addition, under the terms of the Liability Convention, they are liable for damage caused by their space object./[10]/ Thus, from early on, private parties have been involved in space activities, subject to State authorization, and the States Parties to the treaties assuming responsibility for them.

In the last few years, the State's financial involvement has diminished, while the private sector has taken the lead, but the space treaties remain unchanged. Do the basic concepts of ownership, responsibility, and liability, as found in space law need to be changed, to accommodate private sector initiatives, or are they broad enough to allow for its greater participation in space activities, albeit subject to State authorization?

While States assumed the risks for their decisions (and investments) in earlier times, at present private parties seem eager to engage in space activities, but less willing to assume the concomitant risks and responsibilities. Thus, UNIDROIT's Protocol proposes to make investments in space activities less risky, by providing certain mechanisms for securing at least financial interests in these activities, and in procedures related to them.

UNIDROIT's Definition of "Space Property", now "Space Assets"

UNIDROIT has been engaged for more than a decade with drafting a Convention to secure financial interests in movable property (mobile equipment). It has achieved some measure of success in relation to its Convention on Mobile Equipment, as well as to its Protocol on Aircraft equipment. Since 1997, it has been involved in drafting a Protocol specific to objects that are launched, or used to launch objects to outer space.

Interestingly, the Draft Protocol provides a definition of "associated rights" before, or prior to defining "space asset". The definitions need to be read together, and perhaps in reverse order, as presented in this paper. Thus the far-reaching scope of the current definition of "associated rights" becomes more apparent, as will be elaborated upon, infra.

Earlier versions of the draft Protocol referred to space objects as "space property", but in September 2001, the term "assets" replaced "property". According to one author, certain jurisdictions require that the term "property" refer to rights in land or tangible, quasi-corporeal objects as opposed to personal rights, and thus, intangible assets could be excluded. Thus, the term "assets" is "...useful in order to harmonize the conceptual differences between different legal systems under a uniform international Protocol."/[11]/

Article I (2) (f) of the Protocol provides the following definition of "space asset":

(i) any separately identifiable asset that is in space or that is intended to be launched and placed in space or has been returned from space;

(ii) any separately identifiable component forming part of an asset referred to in the preceding clause or attached to or contained within such asset;

(iii) any separately identifiable asset or component assembled or manufactured in space; and

(iv) any launch vehicle that is expendable or can be reused to transport persons or goods to and from space.

As used in this definition, the term "space" means outer space, including the Moon and other celestial bodies."/[12]/ [Emphasis added.]

The Protocol's definition of "space asset" is broader, yet clearer in some respects, than the Liability Convention's definition of "space object" as provided in Art. I (d): "The term "space object" includes component parts of a space object as well as its launch vehicle and parts thereof."/[13]/

The Protocol's definition of "space", as including the Moon and other celestial bodies, would seem to be a first attempt at defining "outer space", which is not defined in any of the outer space treaties drafted by the United Nations. (The Protocol, however, does not offer a delimitation of outer space from air space.) Could this last clause be interpreted to mean that the Moon and other celestial bodies are also "space assets", since they could be adjudged to be "separately identifiable assets", albeit assets that have not been placed in outer space by humans? While they may be "space assets", or space-based resources, they are not "space property"; i.e., celestial bodies, including the Moon and asteroids, are not subject to appropriation, nor subject to property rights./[14]/

Some authors contend that even though national appropriation of the Moon and other celestial bodies is forbidden, private parties may still have property rights on those bodies./[15]/ Other authors maintain that what is forbidden to a State (the non-appropriation principle found in the Outer Space and Moon Treaties) is not allowed to private parties, either. This would seem to be a more logical tenet. It is acknowledged, however, that the issue of appropriation vs. non-appropriation needs to be resolved, in view of the potential liabilities and responsibilities of States (the Parties to the treaties) whose private entities are engaged in commercial space activities./[16]/

While the space treaties and customary international space law do not allow for the national or individual appropriation of outer space or its resources, this does not mean that endeavours by private parties are not allowed, nor that the *use* of outer space by private entities is prohibited. Quite the contrary, without the involvement of the private sector, many space activities, particularly satellite communications, would not have flourished as they have. Most of the satellites in orbit are currently owned and operated by private entities, and provide services to most of the world's population.

Man-made and launched satellites, clearly fall within UNIDROIT's definition of "space assets", and are the space property or assets of various corporations and consortia. While the Moon and other celestial bodies, orbits and the radio frequency spectrum may be "space assets", none of them may be appropriated, or transformed into private property. The "Associated Rights" proffered by the Protocol, however, could result in converting some of these intangible space assets, particularly orbits, orbital positions, and radio frequencies, into "property". This will be discussed at greater length, infra.

A last observation in regard to space assets: since the Protocol's definition includes objects manufactured or assembled in space, presumably it would include those assets manufactured or assembled on the International Space Station (ISS) as well. Could there be some conflicting claims to ownership of intellectual property rights, or in relation to the manufacture of objects or assets on the ISS, and interests secured under the Protocol? To avoid controversies in future, it is submitted that the International Governmental Agreement (IGA) amongst the partners involved in the construction and assembly of (and future manufacturing on) the ISS should be examined, to ensure that no provisions or clauses in either the IGA or the proposed UNIDROIT Protocol are in conflict with each other. An analysis of international conventions on intellectual property and copyrights would also be helpful, to avoid future disputes. A thorough discussion of these issues is beyond the scope of this paper, however, and will not be addressed here.

"Associated Rights"

Article I of the Protocol provides a definition of several "associated rights", only one of which will be discussed here. For clarity's sake, the term "*license*" will be used hereinafter, in reference to concessions, authorizations, permits, or licenses granted by a governmental authority, and only as they may relate to telecommunication satellite systems. These have required massive investments, but most of the investors in the non-geostationary satellite systems (non-GEOs, or GMPCS) have experienced huge economic losses, and little, if any return on their investment./[17]/ "Associated rights" as they may relate to remote sensing or navigation (GPS) satellite systems, will not be examined.

Currently, Article I (2) (a) states that "associated rights" means:

(i) *any permit, license, authorization or equivalent instrument that is granted or issued by a national or intergovernmental or other international body or authority to control, use or operate a space asset, relating to the use of orbital positions and the transmission, emission or reception of radio signals to and from a space asset, which may be transferred or assigned, to the extent permissible and assignable under the laws concerned;*

(ii) *all rights to payment or other performance due to a debtor by any person with respect to space assets; and*

(iii) *all contractual rights held by the debtor that are secured by or associated with the space assets.*/[18]/ [Emphasis added]

Several issues related to this very broad definition, such as "associated rights" in relation to national law, and their relation to outer space-related law, have been discussed at COPUOS and other venues./[19]/ There seems to have been, or to be little discussion, however, of an issue which this author believes is fundamental: the gradual taking over of key government functions by the private sector. The Protocol seems to view licenses as negotiable property, as commodities in which a financial interest can be secured; thus, licenses begin to acquire characteristics or traits of "property" that can be transferred or assigned, even attached. But licenses are not negotiable property, nor are they a right.

Licenses: Privileges or Property?

One law dictionary defines "license", in pertinent part, as follows: "The *permission* by competent authority to do an act which, without such permission, would be illegal, a trespass or a tort"; "privilege from state or sovereign"... A *permit, granted by an appropriate government body*, generally for a consideration, to a person, firm or corporation ...to carry on some business subject to regulation under the police power. *A license is not a contract between the state and the licensee, but is a mere personal permit. Neither is it property or a property right.*"/[20]/ [Emphasis added.]

Whether called "permits, licenses, authorizations, or equivalent instruments," these are not rights, but are essentially privileges and/or prerogatives, granted by an official governmental entity, to facilitate some activity, whether on earth or in outer space./[21]/ It is an official entity that decides, on the basis of certain criteria, whether a license is granted or not.

Obtaining a license is not an entitlement or a basic right, in the sense that the government has no option but to grant it. Were it otherwise, the official granting of licenses could become a superfluous activity. Human society, however, has not evolved to the point that all activities can be allowed without some government sanction, or be taken over by the private sector. Thus, the granting or withholding of licenses still remains an important governmental function, one unlikely to be delegated to the private sector. To reiterate, "*a license is a mere personal permit; it is not property or a property right.*"

A few examples may begin to illustrate the fact that licensing, launching and operating an international satellite system is very complex, and though it may require large amounts of money, not all aspects can be monetarily quantified or converted into a financial asset, or "commodified"./[22]/

Despite the "globalization" trend, every nation involved in outer space affairs, has a different licensing system, and may have different requirements and milestones that must be met prior to engaging in any facet of space activities, including the use of the radio frequency spectrum (RFS). These requisites are part of a nation's sovereign right to regulate the activities of its nationals, and paradoxically, in this age of "globalization," national regulations are limited in scope, applicable only within the State's territory.

Licensing requirements differ not only from country to country, but also vary, depending on the kind of communication system involved, and even on the kind of antenna(s) involved. A couple of examples are provided. In some jurisdictions, operators of "VSAT" (Very Small Aperture Terminals) systems are granted "blanket licenses"; i.e., they are authorized to install a certain number of these terminals without having to go through the whole licensing procedure for each one. The antennas themselves may be owned by different persons; the satellite system itself may be owned by one entity, operated by another, and services provided by yet other entities. These could all be in different jurisdictions, each with unique licensing requirements.

Another example: in the USA, hand-held sets used to access the GMPCS satellite systems, such as INMARSAT, IRIDIUM or Globalstar, are considered "earth stations" by the FCC, and need to be "commissioned" (licensed) by the FCC. In other countries they are not deemed to be earth stations, but still require an official sanction, at least a certificate of homologation (that the equipment meets certain technical standards or requirements) prior to use./[23]/

Tracking and controlling a satellite and transfer of command codes raise many issues related to national security, and to export control laws and policies. A thorough analysis of these is beyond the expertise of this author and ambit of this paper, but these issues should be closely examined by technical experts as well as by potential signatories of the Protocol./[24]/ It is submitted, however, that licenses issued for these purposes will not be easily transferable to private investors, due to national security / defense implications.

In most jurisdictions, licenses cannot be transferred from the original applicant to a different party without the prior authorization of the entity that granted the license in the first place. If it can be transferred, the original licensee often has to keep the license for a specified time period prior to requesting authorization to cede it, a request that may be approved or rejected by the authorities. If the government were not involved, a new "business" could flourish -trafficking in licenses, without official approval of the transfer- thereby supplanting a major role of the government.

As to licenses to use certain orbits and occupy particular orbital positions, neither the International Telecommunication Union (ITU) nor any other international entity regulates the choice or use of orbits. The proponents of (and investors in) the satellite system usually are the ones who decide in which orbit(s) they want to locate their satellite(s), and the frequency bands they propose to use. One Administration/[25]/ submits this information to the (ITU), so that all existing and planned telecommunication systems that could be subject to harmful interference may co-ordinate with the proposed one. The ITU merely endeavors to ensure that no harmful interference is caused between the many systems that use the radio frequency spectrum. Thus, it would be difficult to secure a financial interest in, or transfer a license for the use of a particular orbit or orbital position, as proposed in UNIDROIT's Protocol, since these choices are not subject to regulation.

Other factors may further complicate the issue of securing financial interests in licenses. While UNIDROIT seeks to secure and protect financial investments, national security issues are predominant, and will supersede financial ones, especially after 9/11/01. Many components of spacecraft and launch vehicles are classified as weapons, subject to stringent export controls. Further, many commercial satellite systems are used for official (and military) communications, which could complicate the attachment of any financial interest or revenues generated by the system or service providers. A question arises: is it likely that governmental agencies involved in national security will approve the transfer of "any" license, or all "associated rights", including revenues that could inure from their operation, to private parties, as proposed by UNIDROIT?

As may be deduced from the above, licensing a satellite system, or any of its component parts, as well as the use that is made of the spacecraft, are complex matters, involving any number of governmental agencies even in just one jurisdiction. Thus, it may take longer than the drafters of the Protocol envisage to transform licenses – a government prerogative – into negotiable private property.

UNIDROIT is not the only entity that advocates greater control and jurisdiction by the private sector, particularly in the use the radio frequency spectrum, which could lead to licenses being converted into property rights. There are other advocates of "propertyizing" the spectrum; i.e., endowing the radio frequencies, an intangible yet physical phenomenon, with the same "status" as granted to physical, tangible, real estate./[26]/

A first step, already taken, is auctioning the use of parts of the radio frequency spectrum. The parties that favor these auctions argue that those who value it most will acquire the spectrum and make more efficient use of these scarce resources. Auctioning the spectrum for *national* telecommunication systems has brought much money to the public coffers, but many of the consortia that have "won" the spectrum are unable to pay the price they bid. If the "winners" are unable to use the spectrum, should they be allowed to "warehouse" it? To whom should this acquired spectrum / "property" revert: to the government that issued the license to use it in the first place, or to the corporation that "acquired" this "property"?

This question highlights an inherent difficulty with spectrum auctions: they create certain expectations. The winning investor is likely to consider that he is entitled to more than just the *use* of the frequencies or orbital position- he may perceive them as his "property", over which he has exclusive control, not subject to government regulation. It seems that those who advocate privatizing the spectrum view this acquisition (which is merely a right to use the RFS,) in the same manner as obtaining any other commodity or property./[27]/

To date, the auctions have involved spectrum for national use by terrestrial wireless systems (microwave or cellular telephony). At the international level, auction of the spectrum is not favored, not even by the US's Federal Communications Commission (FCC). Recent legislation states that the FCC "shall not have the authority to assign by competitive bidding orbital slots or spectrum used for the provision of international or global satellite communication services."/[28]/

Neither the FCC, nor any other Administration can sell the spectrum or orbital locations, since these do not belong to anyone; they are part of the global commons;/[29]/ governments are mere stewards of the radio frequency spectrum./[30]/ And the international steward of these natural resources *par excellence* is the ITU which, though it does not issue any licenses for their use, should remain the international steward or "allocator" of these global commons.

One author notes that transforming the spectrum from public commons to private electronic real estate would fundamentally change the relationship between the people and global commercial enterprises"/[31]/. One result would be that a few media companies could end up controlling the most important facets of human enterprise –communications- that are basic to all human endeavors.

At present no one "owns" the resources in outer space, such as the orbits, orbital positions and radio frequencies, and no one should be able to acquire property rights in them. However, these global commons would be "privatized" if the Protocol's wording were accepted. In turn, this would bring the Protocol in direct conflict with a key provision of the Outer Space Treaty/[32]/, namely Article II, which states:

> "Outer space, including the moon and other celestial bodies, is not subject to appropriation by claim of sovereignty, *by means of use or occupation, or by any other means.*" [Emphasis added.]

If licenses to use the spectrum or an orbital location are considered "rights" (rather than privileges) the result will be the appropriation by private parties of outer space resources, a clear violation of the spirit and the wording of the Outer Space Treaty.

Conclusion and Recommendations

In the last decade the "privatization pendulum" has swung nearly 180 degrees, and the results –some good, some less favorable- are now being seen and felt the world over. More recently, many telecom corporations have bloomed and withered, despite massive investments in both satellite and fiber optic cable systems. Unfortunately, some of these economic downfalls have been accompanied by revelations of fraud and corporate wrong-doing.

In addition to making investors leery, these failures would indicate the need for on-going government supervision, rather than leaving everything in the hands of private parties. Elected officials can be voted in or out of office, and while private sector executives can be hired or fired, the shareholders have little control over corporate officials. Do we want to give the private sector more control over communications, allowing a few financial institutions or corporations to become the owners of licenses, of the radio frequency spectrum and other global resources?

While "privatization" and "globalization" are blurring borders between countries, the various national legal systems still need to be taken into account. The Nation-State and national regulators still have important roles to play, roles that should not be ceded to the private sector. Lack of government leads to insecurity at all levels –personal, financial, and legal uncertainty-, which in turn, leads to greater insecurity at all levels, putting everything into question. Thus, in seeking greater financial security for investors, the Protocol may have the effect of creating greater uncertainty and insecurity in non-financial areas.

While UNIDROIT's attempts to reach some unification in private international law are commendable, it is submitted that several points of the proposed Space Protocol would benefit from further discussions. In particular, greater dialogue with the ITU, and operators of global and international satellite systems, would be helpful in clarifying the interrelationship among the technical, financial and legal aspects of space objects and natural resources.

Undeniably, licenses and permits are valuable assets; without them, few activities can be undertaken. However, whether these government prerogatives can be converted into property rights in which a financial interest may be secured is debatable. Thus, the definition of "associated rights" in relation to space assets will likely remain the subject of debate and clarification. Even UNIDROIT has noted that "the issues of how to define and how to deal with 'associated rights' pose a number of problems which will continue to attract attention and to trigger both technical and doctrinal discussions."/[33]/

In seeking clarification, the following points should be taken into account:

1. Licenses are not rights, nor "associated rights", as presented by UNIDROIT. As discussed, supra, they are privileges granted by an official entity and are not negotiable property.
2. Users of the radio frequency spectrum, orbits and orbital positions need to remain aware that they are mere users, not owners, of these global commons. National governments are the stewards of these resources, which are allocated and allotted to them by the international steward, the ITU.
3. These global commons are part of outer space, and are not subject to national (or private) appropriation, by any means, as stated in Article II of the Outer Space Treaty.
4. "Associated rights" as stated in Art. I (2) (a) (i) of the Protocol should be re-named "Ancillary Privileges". Just as "space property" was changed to "space assets", to take into account the divergent views on "property" that exist in the different legal systems, the term "privilege" better represents the true nature of licenses, authorizations or permits.

Perhaps this slight change in terminology, would add clarity, and help overcome the reticence of some of the potential signatories of the Protocol. The governments would retain control of the licensing process, authorizing their nationals to *use* space resources but not permitting their privatization.

Outer space, the common heritage or province of mankind, should remain a global commons, and not be subject to privatization, "property-zation", by national or private entities, or by any other means.

---

[1] One of the Ten Commandments tells us that we shall not covet our neighbor's goods (or property).

[2] Black's Law Dictionary states that property may be classified as either real or immovable, or personal and movable. St. Paul, Minn., West Publishing Co.

[3] This same dictionary provides the following definition of **intangible property:** "such property [that] has no intrinsic and marketable value, but is ...evidence of value..." "Other **intangibles** include property that is a "right" rather than a physical object. Examples would be patents, stocks, bonds, goodwill, trademarks, franchises and copyrights." [Emphasis added.]

[4] Ibid. "An **intangible asset** is defined as a non-physical, noncurrent asset which exists only in connection with something else, such as the goodwill of a business." [Emphasis added.]

[5] UNIDROIT is the acronym for the International Organization for the Unification of Private Law, headquartered in Rome, Italy. UNIDROIT has drafted a Convention on international interests in mobile equipment, and Protocols specific to the rolling stock of railroads, to aircraft, and to "space assets." The full title is "Convention on International Interests in Mobile Equipment, preliminary draft protocol thereto on matters specific to space assets." Opened to signature in Cape Town, South Africa, November 2001. [Cited hereinafter as the Protocol.]

[6] The Communication Satellite Corporation has its genesis in Section 102 (c) and Sec. 301 of the 1962 Communication Satellite Act. P.L. 87-624; 76 STAT 419. Through this Act President Kennedy sought to bring the benefits of satellite communications to the world, especially to developing countries, and "to provide the widest possible participation by private enterprise" in commercial satellite communications.

[7] Ibid., Sec. 102 (c).

[8] Art. VI, Treaty on Principles Governing the Activities of States in the Exploration and Use of Outer Space, including the Moon and Other Celestial

Bodies. Entered into force October 1967. [Cited as the Outer Space Treaty hereinafter].

[9] Ibid., Art. VIII. Could this article be interpreted to mean that entities engaged in space activities are also responsible for mitigating space debris that may result from their activities?

[10] Convention on International Liability for Damage Caused by Space Objects. Entered into force 1972. [Cited as the Liability Convention hereinafter.]

[11] Neil Hazan, The UNDROIT Preliminary Draft Protocol on Matters Specific to Space Assets.
Term Essay (unpublished). McGill University 2002. Discussions held at COPUOS also reflect the concern of different delegations as to the inclusion of certain intangibles in "property". See UN documents A/AC.105/763; A/56/20, *inter alia*. See also footnotes of the Draft Protocol discussions held at Evry, France, Sept. 2001. At that meeting it was agreed to adopt the term "space assets" in preference to "space property", 'in response to concerns regarding the implications under civil law of the term "property"'. UNIDROIT, www.unidroit.org.

[12] Protocol, *supra*, note 5, Art. I (f).

[13] Art. I (d), Convention on International Liability for Damage Caused by Space Objects. Entered into force 1972. [Cited hereinafter as the Liability Convention.]

[14] Art. II, Outer Space Treaty, supra note 8. Art. 11 (2) of the Moon Treaty reiterates the non-appropriation doctrine, although Art. 6 allows States Parties to this Treaty to "collect on and remove from the Moon samples of its minerals and other substances". Agreement Governing the Activities of States on the Moon and Other Celestial Bodies. Entered into force 1984.

[15] P. Dasch, M.M. Smith, A. Pierce, "Conference on Space Property Rights: Next Steps; IISL Proceedings 1999, pp.174-178. See also W. White, Implications of a Proposal for Real Property Rights in Outer Space. IISL Proceedings 1999, pp.366-373.

[16] P. Sterns, G.H. Stine, L. Tennen, "Preliminary Jurisprudential Observations Concerning Property Rights on the Moon and Other Celestial Bodies in the Commercial Space Age. IISL Proceedings 1996, pp.50-60. (For other discussions on property rights in space, see '96,'97,'98 IISL Proceedings).

[17] Billions of dollars were devoted to the development of the Global Mobile Personal Communication Services/Systems (GMPCS), such as ICO, Iridium, Orbcomm, Globalstar, Teledesic, Skybridge, Ellipsat, inter alia. While some projects have not materialized yet, those that are in service have had to seek protection of the US Bankruptcy courts. Is it coincidence that UNIDROIT's Space Assets Protocol was drafted in 1997, at which time many of the GMPCS consortia had already launched, or were planning to launch their satellites? Being able to secure an interest internationally in satellite systems such as the GMPCS would be very appealing to the financial sector, especially since the GMPCS consortia were incorporated in a variety of jurisdictions, had investors from many different countries, and legal systems. It would make sense, from a legal and financial perspective, to be able to secure these massive loans through an international convention, like the one proposed by UNIDROIT.

[18] Protocol, supra, note 5, Article I (2) (a). Revised in Rome, Italy, February 2002.

[19] See, for example, UNGA, A/AC.105/C.2/L.225, Jan.2001, para. 19,in which it is stated that "Such associated rights are regarded as being inextricably linked to a satellite and integral to its commercial value." Also A/AC.105/763, April 2001; A/57/20, June 2002. Also M. Stanford's presentation at UNISPACE III, July 1999, and UNIDROIT's Secretary-General, H. Kronke assessment, included in "Project 2001- Legal Framework for the Commercial Use of Outer Space", Karl-Heinz Bockstiegel, Ed. Carl Heymanns Verlag, Koeln, Germany, 2002.

[20] Black's Law Dictionary, supra, note 2.

[21] Perhaps the licensing system with which most people are familiar is the driver's license, which is issued by a governmental entity. A driver's license is highly personal, and cannot be assigned, transferred, or re-issued to a third party without prior official authorization. Should licenses pertaining to space activities be more easily transferable than drivers' licenses, in view of the numerous national security (and not only financial security) issues involved?

[22] One author notes that the "new culture of hypercapitalism" tends to "commodify" all experiences. As to telecommunications, he cites some studies that advocate that the entire radio frequency spectrum should be converted into private property to be sold, leased or otherwise developed, thus eliminating the need for a FCC, or any other kind of regulatory body. Jeremy Rifkin, "The Age of Access", Jeremy Tarcher/Putnam, New York (2000) p.226 ff.

[23] The GMPCS were subject of a Memorandum of Understanding, the GMPCS MOU, whose overriding purpose, *inter alia,* was to facilitate the bringing into service of the mostly privately owned GMPCS systems world-wide. The GMPCS MOU was drafted primarily by private parties; its proposed regulations are not legally binding until adopted into national legislation. The lack of harmonized regulations, as would be provided by an international treaty, may have been a contributing factor to the GMPCS systems' lack of success.

[24] P. Larsen & J. Heilbock , "UNIDROIT Project on Security Interests: How the Project Affects Space Objects. 64 J. Air L. & Commerce 703 -770 (Summer 1999). The authors recognize that there are a number of problem areas with the Protocol, one of which is the 'bundling of rights, interest, privileges and properties in the satellite business'. (P.736).

[25] The ITU defines Administration as "any government department or service responsible for discharging the obligations undertaken in the {ITU's] Convention and Radio Regulations." Ch.1, Art. I, Sect. I, 3.1.1. ITU Radio Regulations. The ITU "Administration" is similar to the State of Registry of the space object, as required in Art. VIII of the Outer Space Treaty and in Art. I (c) of the 1976 Convention on Registration of Objects Launched into Outer Space.

[26] Several economists are promoting this notion. A recent article by Prof. Lawrence J. White, attempts to provide a parallel between real estate and the spectrum, and proffers reasons as to why they should be treated in a like manner. ""Propertyzing" the Electromagnetic Spectrum: Why It's important and How to Begin". NYLS J. Media Law & Policy, Vol. IX, No.1, Fall 2000 (22-48). See also, Rifkin, supra, note 22, who makes references to various initiatives in the U.S. Congress to "privatize" the spectrum.

[27] Rifkin, supra, note 22, pp 227 ff..

[28] Section 647, P.L. 106-180, March 2000, the "Open-market Reorganization for the Betterment of International Telecommunications Act., the "ORBIT" Act.

[29] V. Kopal "Outer Space as a Global Common", Proceedings of the IISL, 1997, pp.108-118. See also Rifkin, supra, note 22.

[30] See Fishman, W.L., "Property Rights, Reliance and Retroactivity Under the 1934 Communications Act. Fed. Communications Law Journal, Vol. 50 No. 1 (2-51), 1997.

[31] Rifkin, supra, note 22, p. 227.

[32] Art. II, Outer Space Treaty, supra note 8. But see fn 2, of the Protocol Draft (Evry 2001), to the effect that there are no conflicts between the Protocol and the principles incorporated in the UN's Space treaties.

[33] H. Kronke, "The Draft UNIDROIT Convention..." Included in "Project 2001- Legal Framework for the Commercial Use of Outer Space", Karl-Heinz Bockstiegel, Ed. Carl Heymanns Verlag, Koeln, 2002, at p. 655.

IAC-02-IISL.1.04

DEVELOPING COUNTRIES AND THE UNIDROIT PROTOCOL ON SPACE PROPERTY

Álvaro Fabricio dos Santos
National Institute for Space Research (INPE)
São José dos Campos, SP, Brazil
alvaro@dir.inpe.br

ABSTRACT

Outer space has become a prosperous area for business. The commercialization of space activities would increase if countries or companies received more financial support. Space activities involve a high level of risk, however, which is why financial institutions are reticent to advance credit. The International Institute for the Unification of Private Law[1] (UNIDROIT) is interested in finding legal ways to satisfy commercial and financial needs by improving creditors' guarantees. A draft protocol on matters concerning space assets has been proposed to be considered at the Convention on International Interests in Mobile Equipment. The following paper explains why this UNIDROIT draft protocol has been included as an item on the agenda of the Legal Subcommittee of the United Nations Committee on Peaceful Use of Outer Space (COPUOS), showing why this subject has attracted the attention of both developing and developed countries.

INTRODUCTION

Space activities involve a high level of risk. There are risks when a space object is launched, when damage may occur due to vibration and the extreme launch conditions. There is further risk when a space object is being put into its orbit, and the rocket or the on-board computer may not work. There are additional risks when a space object is in orbit; if it does not work well, there is not much that may be done to fix it. Insurance is required and insurance premiums are prohibitive. The total cost of development and launching is, therefore, usually in the millions of dollars. Most private companies and world governments in developing countries need outside financing.

There is currently little credit available. The standardization of private national laws is desirable in order to provide more stable commercial relationships, thereby reassuring creditors through increased trading confidence and legal guarantees.

Lack of credit obviously affects developing countries the most. Yet, it would be wrong to conclude that developed countries have nothing to gain from improved credit conditions. Companies from developing countries are not able to carry out a whole space project technically or financially. If there were a line of credit, companies from developing countries could contract the specialized services of companies from developed countries. Developed countries would benefit directly through the commercialization of components and satellites, thus increasing jobs, profits, and subsequent tax revenues. Thus, all countries would benefit from improved financing conditions.

Financial institutions, however, are loathe to assume the high risks of space ventures. Besides the technical risks, there is the added risk that governments or companies will default on payments in a loan agreement. Creditors obviously want to be surrounded by guarantees in order to assure the assets are reclaimed and fines are paid in the event of a breach of contract. All of these risks have to be considered in a financial operation. Financial institutions would feel more confident to lend money if there were a solid international legal framework to protect them.

This legal framework has been successfully introduced through the UNIDROIT statute in the area of aeronautics. Article 7 of the 1988 UNIDROIT Convention on International Financial Leasing "*enshrines a rule recognizing the enforceability of the lessor's real rights – which, in most cases, that is other than in cases typically involving sub-leases, will mean the lessor's ownership – in a leased asset against the trustee in bankruptcy and unsecured creditor of his lessee*"[2].

The UNIDROIT Governing Council approved a proposal to elaborate a new draft UNIDROIT Convention on International Interests in Mobile Equipment at its 76th session, held in Rome from 7 to 12 April 1997. To carry out this decision, the UNIDROIT Governing Council also decided to establish work groups in order to prepare three different protocols which would be linked to the Convention, namely: a) a protocol on airframes, aircraft engines and helicopters; b) a protocol on railway rolling stock; and c) a protocol on space assets.

THE CAPE TOWN DIPLOMATIC CONFERENCE

The text of the Convention on International Interests in Mobile Equipment was finalized, adopted, and opened for signature in 2001 at the diplomatic conference that was convened under the co-sponsorship of UNIDROIT and the International Civil Aviation Organization (ICAO) in Cape Town, South Africa, from 29 October to 16 November 2001. Delegations from sixty-eight States and fourteen international organizations attended the conference. This Convention created a legal document of international scope for the three categories of mobile equipment. As of August 2002, twenty-two States had already signed the Convention.

At least three States must adhere to the Convention before it may be considered a binding UNIDROIT document. According to Article 49.1, the Convention goes into effect on the first day of the month following the expiration of three months after the date of the deposit of the third instrument of ratification, acceptance, approval or accession. It is important to remark that a State may initially adhere merely to the Convention, although the Convention will only enter into effect in that State when it also adheres to one protocol. While the Convention helps create a basic international legal framework, it does not provide specific regulations that are set up in the protocols. States frequently wait to sign the Convention when they are in agreement with at least one protocol. This explains the importance of each protocol and the necessity of a careful analysis of their terms.

It was, therefore, a significant advancement in Convention proceedings when the text of the aircraft objects protocol was approved and opened for signature at the Cape Town Conference. Twenty-two States have already signed this protocol[3]. The railway rolling stock and the space assets protocols are still being discussed in their respective forums.

THE SPACE ASSETS PROTOCOL

The President of UNIDROIT invited Mr. Peter D. Nesgos[4] to organize and chair the space assets work group to prepare the preliminary draft Protocol on matters specific to space assets. This work group (hereafter called "Space Work Group") has already had five meetings, the first in Los Angeles on 1 July 1997, the second in Rome on 19 and 20 October 2000, the third in Seal Beach, California, on 23 and 24 April 2001, the fourth in Evry Courcouronnes, near Paris, on 3 and 4 September 2001, and the fifth in Rome, on 30 and 31 January 2002[5].

At the fourth meeting of the Space Work Group, the expression "property", often used in civil law, was considered too broad a term because it included authorization, licenses, and mechanisms to protect intellectual property, as well as non-disclosure information. The UNIDROIT protocol on space assets (hereafter called "Protocol") aimed to protect only the commercial relationship between a creditor who has given financial support and the debtor who wants to have a space asset. Moreover, "space assets" is the expression adopted in space treaties. Thus, the expression "space asset" was considered more suitable than "space property"[6].

According to Article I.2 (f) of the Protocol, "space assets" means: "(i) any separately identifiable asset that is in space or that is intended to be launched and placed in space or has been returned from space; (ii) any separately identifiable component forming a part of an asset referred to in the preceding clause or attached to or contained within such asset; (iii) any separately identifiable asset or component assembled or manufactured in space; and (iv) any launch vehicle that is expendable or can be reused to transport persons or goods to and from space".

The Protocol tries to provide ample guarantees for creditors. In case of breach of contract, the creditor is able to require either the repossession or the control of a space asset from the Contracting State where the debtor is located (see Article XI). In practice, however, the current text of the Protocol provides no legal mechanism for repossession where there are multiple creditors.

The following scenario illustrates the problem. Suppose that the satellite's transponder was financed by one creditor; the payload was financed by another creditor; and the infrared camera by a third. Suppose the debtor did not honor its commitment and the transponder's creditor wants to take possession of the satellite to sell it to a third party.

When this situation occurs with aircraft, the creditor just requires the removal of the financed equipment and the plane is grounded until the problem is solved. This procedure cannot be adopted when the satellite equipment is in outer space. Its retrieval from space would be so expensive that it would probably be cheaper to produce another one.

Although the Protocol foresees the possibility of a creditor taking possession of the space asset, the rights of the other creditors cannot be infringed upon. Article XI, item 6, alternative "B" of the Protocol stipulates that: "The space asset shall not be sold pending a decision by a court regarding the claim and the international interest". "International interest" refers to different international creditors, as specified in Article 2 of the UNIDROIT Convention. So, in the above example, the creditor would not be able to sell the satellite to get its money back.

The cooperation of Contracting States is also an important issue. In case of insolvency, the role of administrative authorities from the Contracting State where the debtor is located is fundamental to assure the creditors' rights. According to Article X (6.b) of the Protocol, the administrative authorities shall cooperate and assist the creditor in the exercise of its rights. The judicial court of the Contracting State where the debtor is located also shall cooperate to obtain a speedy resolution to the problem (Article XII.2 of the Protocol).

The Protocol will only be well accepted when creditors have due protection of their rights. In order to assure the creditors' rights in cases of insolvency, the process must be expedited. Furthermore, the possession of the financed asset should be assured to the creditor *inaudita altera pars*. In this step, UNIDROIT needs to establish censure for those Contracting States which put up obstacles to the exercise of creditors' rights. If there are no harsh measures to avoid insolvency, the Protocol probably will not obtain the desired number of adherences.

It is important to establish a clear difference between "Launching State" and "Contracting State". The first - "Launching State" – according to the definition from space treaties, is the national government responsible for space activities that are carried out either by its governmental or non-governmental entities[7]. In case of any damage caused by space objects, the "Launching State" will be fully responsible for the payment of any indemnity, even when a private company undertakes the launching[8]. The second - "Contracting State" – is the national government of the country where the debtor or creditor(s) reside which has adhered to the UNIDROIT Convention. The Contracting State is not bound to pay any debts to the creditor, when the debtor is a private company. In this case, the Contracting State is only bound to obtain "speedy relief" to solve the problems, as is mentioned in Article XIII of the UNIDROIT Convention.

In 2000, UNIDROIT considered that the draft of the Protocol was ready to be submitted to COPUOS, because the approval of the UN Committee would lend substance to the Protocol and make it more effective.

The discussion of the Protocol was inserted in the agenda of the COPUOS Legal Subcommittee as a decision of said Committee in its 43rd Session, in 2000[9].

In conclusion, the mission of the UNIDROIT Space Work Group is still not finished, because its members are following the discussions in the COPUOS Legal Subcommittee and updating the Protocol's text.

THE DISCUSSION IN THE COPUOS LEGAL SUBCOMMITTEE

Some countries believed that such a subject should not be examined by COPUOS, because it was related to private commercial interests. However, this position was rejected by the majority of COPUOS member States who believed any subject involving space activities should be discussed by COPUOS. It is important to mention that such an understanding is consonant with item 7 of the United Nations Declaration on International Cooperation in the Exploration and Use of Outer Space for the Benefit and in the Interest of All States, Taking into Particular Account the Needs of Developing Countries[10], *in verbis*: "The Committee on Peaceful Use of Outer Space should be strengthened in its role, among others, as a forum for the exchange of information on national and international activities in the field of international cooperation in the exploration and use of outer space".

At its 40th session, from 2 to 12 April 2001, the COPUOS Legal Subcommittee agreed to the establishment of an ad hoc consultative mechanism to review the issues related to the preliminary UNIDROIT draft Protocol, in accordance with a proposal introduced by the delegation of Belgium[11]. The mechanism would make it possible to undertake, if necessary, intersessional work group meetings at the convenience of interested member States. As of the first semester of 2002, two meetings had been held, the first one in Paris, France, from 10 to 11 September 2001, and the second in Rome, Italy, from 28 to 29 January 2002.

In the Paris work group meeting, the main items on the agenda were: (i) the relationship of the proposed new international regime to the existing body of space law; (ii) the nature and framework of the international registration system; (iii) the role of COPUOS and its Legal Subcommittee in the future development of the project; (iv) the form and manner by which the COPUOS Legal Subcommittee would transmit its views, findings, and recommendations to UNIDROIT; and (v) the future status of the item on the agenda of the COPUOS Legal Subcommittee.

By the time of the Rome work group meeting, the UNIDROIT Convention had already been approved and opened for signature. Thus, the main items on the agenda were: (i) the follow-up on the work group meeting in Paris; (ii) further consideration of the compatibility of the preliminary draft Space Assets Protocol and space law; and (iii) consideration of the preparation and content of the recommendations to be submitted to the COPUOS Legal Subcommittee at its 41st session, which was to be held in Vienna, Austria, from 2 to 12 April 2002.

At this 41st session of the COPUOS Legal Subcommittee, item 8 of the agenda, regarding the UNIDROIT Protocol, was, incontestably, the topic that caused the most debate because the question of incompatibilities between the Protocol and the current legal framework in existing space law was raised. In the 42nd session, in 2003, this subject will certainly engender new and intense discussions.

Actually, the Protocol has brought a little bit of vitality to the agenda of the COPUOS Legal Subcommittee, which has been immobilized by the stalemate regarding changes in the texts of the five space treaties currently in effect.

COPUOS, which had a fundamental role in the cold war period, once again has the opportunity to do a great service to mankind, especially to developing countries by suggesting improvements in the wording of the Protocol and supporting reform in the UN space treaties.

POSITIONS FROM SOME DEVELOPING COUNTRIES

Most developing countries have agreed with the discussion of the Protocol by COPUOS; however they have examined the terms of that instrument carefully. The following countries are cited because their statements made during the last two sessions of the COPUOS Legal Subcommittee summarize the basic issues under debate.

Brazil's Position

Brazil sustains that COPUOS is the appropriate forum for the discussion of the Protocol as well as any other subject regarding space activities, including those carried out by private entities. At the 41st session of the COPUOS Legal Subcommittee, in 2002, the representative of Brazil, Mr. Leite da Silva, said, "*It is also important to stress that the discussion of this subject has to aim toward the prevention of any conflicts between the UNIDROIT Protocol and the five United Nations Treaties. In the case of any conflict, the dispositions of the five United Nations Treaties should always prevail*".

Brazil considers that "*the question of transfer of space objects is the central issue to be solved in the relationship between the Registration Convention and the UNIDROIT Protocol on Space Assets*". Brazil believes that "*it would be quite adequate and convenient that to be registered according to UNIDROIT Protocol any space object should first be registered according to the Registration Convention, which must be considered as the general and superior register of all objects launched into outer space*".

The Brazilian Space Agency has issued rules regarding authorization and licensing to carry out space activities in Brazilian territory[12], in accordance with this legal philosophy, although the Protocol does not present any conflict with such rules. If Brazil adheres to the Protocol and if a Brazilian company receives the financing of a space asset, only the Brazilian company, which will be responsible for the space activity, will be held liable under the requirements established by the Brazilian Space Agency. No requirements will be imposed on the foreign entity which will give financial support to the Brazilian company. In other words, only the party carrying out space activities in the Brazilian territory is bound to Brazilian Space Agency regulations.

China's Position

At the 40th session of the COPUOS Legal Subcommittee in 2001, China's representative, Mr. H. Huikang, presented several substantial remarks about the Protocol. The first question brought up by the Chinese representative was a question of definition of terms and how to determine the actual commercial value of an asset.

"*How to define the concepts of space equipment or space property in legal terms for the purpose of financing and providing collateral and security for space activities? In a broader sense, space equipment belongs to the mobile equipment category and, therefore, may become a subject for the readjustment of the legal regime on international interests in mobile equipment. However, space equipment as property in the sense of civil law is different in many respects from ordinary mobile equipment like railroad rolling stock or aircraft. Apart from the unique character of their location in outer space, the commercial value of space equipment often depends on their functions and usage and their orbital positions*".

The second issue dealt with the difficulties of mixing public and private legal regimes. The Chinese representative said, "*How to harmonize a securities regime which is of a private law character with international space law which is public law in nature and avoid inconsistency with the latter's basic legal principles? Here, a basic conceptual issue is involved, namely, is the proposed new regime based on private international law and civil and commercial law or international space law. Specifically, is it based on the proposed aircraft protocol or existing treaties governing outer space? And different lines of thinking will lead to different conclusions*"[13].

At the end of his statement, the Chinese representative concluded that the Protocol was not ready for the examination by COPUOS and recommended that the Secretariat of that Committee, in liaison with UNIDROIT, present a new draft of the Protocol to be examined in the next session of the Legal Subcommittee, in 2002. At the 41st session of the COPUOS Legal Subcommittee, in 2002, China, once more, said that the Protocol should be reviewed because its text was still not ready for a critical analysis.

Mexico's Position

Mexico supports the debate of the Protocol by COPUOS, stressing that the integrity of the five United Nations space treaties should prevail over the Protocol. At the 41st session of the COPUOS Legal Subcommittee, in 2002, the representative of Mexico, Ms. M.T. Rosas Jasso, said her delegation recommended that the United Nations act as the Supervisory Authority through its Office for Outer Space Affairs (OOSA). Her delegation also recommended that the OOSA Secretariat examine the principles of the supervisory and/or registrations authority in order to determine the financing structure as well as operational and registration proceedings. Ms. Jasso stated it would be convenient to have a legal opinion from OOSA Secretariat regarding whether a COPUOS mandate would be legally binding as a Supervisory Authority. At that session, Mexico emphasized the need to consider the legal effects of transferring space assets, according to existing law.

CONFLICT WITH THE EXISTING LEGAL FRAMEWORK

At the end of 2001, OOSA sent a list of questions to the COPUOS member States in which it asked them if there were any conflicts between the Protocol and the five United Nations space treaties[14]. As of the 41st session of the COPUOS Legal Subcommittee, in 2002, four States had answered the questions; namely, Australia, Austria, the Czech Republic, and the Netherlands. Three of these four States understood that the Protocol did not present any apparent contradictions with the five space treaties.

However, in that same session, the representative from Belgium, Mr. J.F. Mayence, identified the point of conflict, namely, differences in the registration systems of the UNIDROIT documents and the UN Registration Convention. In the UNIDROIT registration system, the ownership of a space object may be changed whenever it is required. So, if there is a breach of contract, the creditor may transfer the possession of a space object to a third party, which will be liable for that space object. This transfer is registered in the UNIDROIT system. This kind of transfer is unforeseen in the

UN Registration Convention. There is no mention of a Contracting State because at that time only national governments and private entities within their boundaries were considered. Thus, in the UN Registration Convention the Launching State remains liable for the space object even if it has been sold to a third party, presumably also from an entity within national boundaries[15].

Actually, it is still not clear how the registration system foreseen by UNIDROIT will work. It presupposes any space asset which has been bought through a financing operation must be registered. Thus, it can be said that registry is a *sine qua non* condition for a creditor to exercise its rights in the case of a breach of contract[16]. Nevertheless, different creditors may finance different parts of the space object. So, according to the UNIDROIT registration system, a satellite, for instance, may have many registry parties. Multiple registries do not occur in the UN Registration Convention, where only one State is admitted as the Registry State[17]. To integrate both registration systems, a change of the text in the Protocol could be proposed in which the Contracting State where the company controlling the satellite is located would be the sole register.

A second problem in the two registration systems involves the definition of what should be registered. According to the Protocol, an object qualifies as a space asset whether or not it has actually been placed in orbit. So, it should be registered in the UNIDROIT system, even if it is not launched to outer space. This system differs from that which is used in the UN Registration Convention where only a space object that has been launched to outer space may be registered[18].

There are many obstacles to the integration of both registration systems. The simultaneous registry in the UN Registration Convention and in the Protocol would only be feasible if there were just one creditor. However, it becomes impossible when the ownership of a space object is changed, because one system admits the transfer of ownership and the other does not. In fact, the UN Registration Convention must be changed in order to foresee the possibility of transferring ownership of a space object. Considering the current development of space activities, there are no weighty reasons to maintain this stalemate. The commercialization of satellites now happens frequently, but the UN Registration Convention makes no legal provision for such transactions.

The question has been raised as to whether it would be possible for both registration systems to operate independently. Separate registration systems would mean that space assets registered under the UNIDROIT system would not have to be registered under the UN Registration Convention. If such an understanding prevailed, the UN Registration Convention would be unable to fulfill its primary objective which is to assure the pacific and equitable exploration of outer space. Commercial ventures would fall entirely outside of the UN Registration Convention. And these are arguably the most important space objects to supervise. So, the idea of both systems operating independently of each other is not viable.

SOME CONCLUSIONS

It is undeniable that the Protocol provokes interest from developing countries that want to have improved financing mechanisms in order to pursue their space activities. The Protocol also sparks interests from developed countries, which foresee the opportunity to increase the business of their aerospace industries. Moreover, financial entities are interested in the Protocol's approval as long as guarantees can be provided in case of a breach of contract.

From the statements made in the two last sessions of the COPUOS Legal Subcommittee, it may be concluded that developing countries are, nonetheless, concerned about discrepancies between the Protocol and the existing legal framework. They believe the Protocol should be subordinate to the UN space treaties through some form of integrated registration system which currently is not feasible because the treaties are outmoded.

The existing impasse between the registration system proposed by UNIDROIT and that system which is established in the UN Registration Convention could be solved if the text of the UN Registration Convention were modified.

Some governments have expressed the opinion that any change in the texts of the five space treaties is impossible. Dr. Yuri M. Kolosov, Professor of International Law in Moscow, Russian Federation, explained and countered this position when he said: "*Most probably the restrained attitude towards the initiative to develop a new 'Space Bible' is caused by fears of some States that this process might lead to the revision of the basic principles that have proved their viability. There are, of course, certain safeguards to avoid such situation. First of all, it can be ensured by the principle of consensus, which will remain the cornerstone of the future negotiation process. Secondly, a 'package-based' procedure may be widely applied to the negotiation process.*" [19]

At the 41st session of the COPUOS Legal Subcommittee, in 2002, Mr. S.Leite da Silva, on behalf of Brazil, supported the Russian proposal to establish a single UN space convention that would update the texts of the five existing space treaties. The Brazilian representative said: "*The world has changed and we can't be leashed to the past, proceeding as if nothing new had been happen in these last decades*".

Without any doubt, COPUOS is the appropriate forum to discuss the Protocol. Its Legal Subcommittee needs to work toward international consensus in international law and commerce. Even countries without space assets should participate in the discussion and support necessary reforms to UN space treaties so that the current ad hoc commercialization of space does not persist. Without a sound legal framework, space will remain the domain of the financially privileged.

References

---

[1] See "www.unidroit.org"

[2] Stanford, Martin – "The Creation of a New International Regimen Governing the Taking of Security in Space Assets: A Window of Opportunity for the Financing of Commercial Space Activities" – paper presented in the 10th International Space Insurance Conference (London, 8 July 2002).

[3] Data available in August 2002

[4] Expert consultant on international space finance matters (Milbank, Tweed, Hadley & McCloy, New York).

[5] Data available in August 2002

[6] In the title of this paper the expression "space property" was maintained just to retain the terms which were being used in the agenda at the 41st session of the COPUOS Legal Subcommittee, in 2002. At the end of that session, "space assets" officially replaced the expression "space property".

[7] See Article VI of the Outer Space Treaty.

[8] See Article II of the Liability Convention.

[9] See the United Nations Official Records of the General Assembly, Fifty-fifth Session, Supplement # 20 (A/55/20), and paragraph 167.

[10] Approved by the United Nations General Assembly Resolution # 51/122.

[11] See document prepared by OOSA reference A/AC.105/763, paragraph 94 (www.oosa.unvienna.org).

[12] See "www.agespacial.gov.br"

[13] See document prepared by OOSA reference COPUOS/LEGAL/T.649 pages 4/6.

[14] See document prepared by OOSA reference A/AC.105/C.2/2002/CRP.4.

[15] For more about the Registration Convention read the author's paper "Brazil and the Registration Convention" published by the American Institute of Aeronautics and Astronautics in the Proceedings of the Forty-Fourth Colloquium on The Law of Outer Space, pages 78/86.

[16] For more about the UNIDROIT Space Assets Protocol, read the paper "The Prospective Unidroit Convention on International Interests in Mobile Equipment as Applied to Space Assets" written by Dara A. Panahy.

[17] See Article II.2 of the Registration Convention.

[18] Se Article II.1 of the Registration Convention.

[19] In his paper "Is It Time to Develop a Universal Comprehensive Convention on The Law of Outer Space?"

IAC-02-IISL.1.06

EVOLUTION OF SPACE LAW IN FRANCE
MAIN LINES OF THE 2002 STUDY REPORT FOR THE MINISTER

by Philippe Clerc[1]
Space and Aeronautical Department, Ministry of Research, Paris- France

INTRODUCTION

France bears the international obligation to authorise and supervise space activities under its jurisdiction and can be liable for damage caused by space objects launched from Kourou (French Guiana) and/or by companies registered in France. The current national framework for the activities carried by Arianespace, Starsem, Eutelsat and for the Ariane European launcher operated from the Guiana Space Centre (CSG) is adequately regulated on the basis of relevant programmatic, contractual and administrative legal regime. But in consequence of the liberalisation of the telecommunications market, of the privatisation of international organisations and State owned companies and of the increasing private demands to access CSG facilities, further regulations could be needed.

In this context, the French Ministry of Research's Space Department has convened in 1999, during 2 years, more than 100 technical and legal experts organised in several working groups to propose an upgraded national legal framework for space activities. This constituted working groups dealt with: launching (to implement a licence procedure, considering the responsibility of France and international competition rules), earth observation (for licensing and data policy), telecommunications and navigation, and space objects property and security regime (linked to the registration convention and the Unidroit Space Protocol).

The report of this work named "Space Law Evolution in France Study" was presented to the Minister of Research by March 2002.

The present author has driven the overall study on behalf of the French Research Ministry's Space Department. This paper presents the report's general content

1) Scope of the study

The study is strictly limited to space activities, that is to say mainly the launch services and the life of the satellites in orbit, when these activities are likely to come under national legislation. The services themselves, television broadcasting and telecommunications, as well as the problems of frequency are not dealt with directly, since these questions do not specifically depend on space law. Only the satellite observation and navigation services were tentatively developed since they are not currently covered by specific systems. Manned flight and the status of astronauts are covered by specific international

---

[1] **This paper only binds its author's opinion and shall not commit its employer in any way.**

agreements and were not examined in this study which mainly concerns the French national space activities.

2) Structure of the report

The report is divided into two parts:

1) General measures common to all space activities;
2) Measures specific to each of the three sectors which are the launch services, Earth observation and radiocommunications. This part is in fact based on the reports of the Chairmen of each of the work groups concerned.

The first part describes: In chapter 1 "Public missions for regulation, authorisation, monitoring and control of space actitivities", the activities which are under the responsibility of the public sector in application of international space law, as regulatory (legislative or reglementary), authorising, monitoring and licencing authority when they are directly operated by the government or by concession.

Chapter 2 "Support for the development of the market and of private initiative", deals with : the private and commercial activities and the legal systems specific to them[2]: the chain of responsibility between the different private players, taxation, (the intellectual property system, the status of property and of safety on space objects, and the conditions for market access.

3) Main findings:

In its introduction, the study highlights the importance of the multiplicity of the challenges linked with producing a national legal framework which goes beyond the basic questions of responsibility.

Among these challenges for France, we can note in particular those of sovereignty, safety and defence, foreign policy, cooperation, humanitarian aid and respecting international treaties, construction of "space Europe" around the European Union, the European Space Agency (ESA) and their respective members, industrial competitiveness, the development of the space application market, and the ethical questions.

It therefore appears that the continuity of the space power status, in addition to a maintained effort in the budgetary and technological fields, must also be supported in France and in Europe by a specific legal system which controls and favours space activities.

The inventory of elements forming the current legal framework in France however shows that this framework is acceptable for the current programs, when these are developed or operated under the responsibility of public organisms, particularly CNES, and when a legal link (contractual at least) has been defined between these space activities and the State which ultimately assumes the international responsibility for them. However, the procedure consisting of treating the legal problem on a case by case basis, from a conventional or contractual point of view and by program, sometimes led to a system which is difficult to read, badly consolidated and lacking in clarity for the new entrants.

In addition, the liberalisation of the space sector leads us to rethink the type of legal bond existing between the new private operators and the French State by posing the question of the implementation

2 That is to say, beyond private law, the legal systems of all disciplines which can restrict or facilitate these private or commercial activities.

of a public authorisation and monitoring system for these activities.

3.1 Implementation of a public authorisation and monitoring system for space activities

After giving a reminder of the commitments which result from the 1972 United Nations Convention on responsibilities (in case of damages), the report fully justifies the necessity for a legal framework for space activities (launches and satellite operations) and more specifically to:

- create a licence (or authorisation) obligation for all launches carried out either from France or from abroad by or for a French national;
- take into consideration all the "national space activities", including when France is not the initial launch State (possible cases of satellites bought in orbit by a French national);
- identify all the space objects and debris likely to involve the State's responsibility or that of its nationals;
- ensure that, when its is considered by an international jurisdiction to be the launch State responsible for a liability, France has the legal means to obtain the reimbursement of the sums it may have to pay to the victims;
- have the technical means and an operational and independent administrative organisation allowing the State, in all circumstances, to assume its international responsibilities and to ensure its national law is correctly applied.

Since it concerns the application in national law of the 1975 United Nations Convention on licencing space objects, the report makes several suggestions concerning the operation of the French national register, given the commercial development of space activities:

- the opportunity to produce an informational text (regulatory act, circular or simple guide) describing in detail the licencing procedure between the various authorities concerned (CNES, Foreign Ministry, Ministry responsible for space...). CNES effectively plays the role of controller or coordinator without this prerogative being formalised;
- define the list of additional information to be provided in this national register (in addition to that required by article IV of the 1975 Convention), in particular to process the authorisation and licence demands linked with the operations and service provided by the satellite to be launched;
- the reason for mentioning the ownership status with respect to the satellite and its component is the following: identification of owners and of possible guarantees covering this object given the links to be envisaged with a future international guarantee system as studied by Unidroit;
- provide information for the intellectual property system relating to the satellite, its components and its mission: patents, applicable law, holder(s) of operator's rights, holder(s) of the copyright on the transmitted data;
- indicate in which conditions the register can or must be modified during the satellite's lifetime (change of satellite orbit or of its mission), and more specifically the procedures for notification of possible transfer of ownership of the space object in orbit? This preoccupation results from the consequences that such a transfer

could have on the responsibilities of the States (acceptance of the new licences...) on the licences given to operate the satellite and, with respect to the rules, on the exportation of sensitive technologies and goods;

- detail the procedures for objects launched from foreign countries by companies covered by French law or for French customers, and vice versa for the licencing carried out by foreign operators or international organisations which have their headquarters in France (ESA, Eutelsat company...) ;
- determine the conditions for public access to the register by reconciling transparent access to public data and the confidentiality linked with the contracts;
- mention, where applicable, the fees and taxes to be paid during licencing, the penalties and the excess charges for late or non registration...

At the same time, a doctrine must explain the consequences of national licencing: in terms of jurisdiction and responsibility of the French State (particularly in the case when the launch takes place abroad), in terms of corporeal and incorporeal property, and of the rights to operate or use the space object.

3.2 Perimeter of a national legal framework regulating space activities

The report defines the perimeter of a national legal framework regulating space activities. It uses a functionalistic definition of space activities stating that a space activity is any activity aiming to launch a space object or to have it launched[3], or any operation necessary for the operation of such objects (i.e. telemetry, monitoring and control of space objects, activities placing and maintaining satellites on-station) and including all other activities carried out in outer space or on a celestial body (Moon and other planets). The scope of the national framework also depends on the nationality of the players concerned. The report states that by the combined application of articles VI and VIII[4] of the 1967 Space Treaty, it is the vocation of our national law to extend its influence, and even its application (at least by default), beyond the national sphere, particularly with respect to European, international, public or private entities which have their headquarters in France (ESA in Paris and at the Guiana Space Center (CSG), Arianespace, the new Eutelsat company) or to companies covered by French law carrying out their activities abroad, such as Starsem. The application of such extra-territorial national law must however remain "compatible"

3 A space object can be defined as any spacecraft designed to carry payloads or astronauts into space.

4 Article VI: "The States adhering to the Treaty have international responsibility for national activities in outer space, including the Moon and the other celestial bodies, whether they be undertaken by government organisms or by non-government entities, and for ensuring that the national activities are carried out in accordance with the terms of this Treaty. The activities of the non-government entities in outer space, including the Moon and the other celestial bodies, must be continously monitored by the appropriate State adhering to the Treaty. In the case of activities carried out by an international organisation in outer space, including the Moon and the other celestial bodies, the responsibility for respecting the terms of this Treaty is the responsibility of this international organisation and of the States adhering to the Treaty who are part of the said organisation."
Article VIII: "The State adhering to the Treaty, on whose register an object launched into outer space is listed will retain under its jurisdiction and its control the said object and all the personnel of the said object, when it is in outer space or on a celestial body. The ownership rights for the objects launched into outer space, including the objects brought to or constructed on a celestial body, as well as their components, remain intact when these objects or components are in outer space or on a celestial body, and when they return to Earth. The objects or components of objects found beyond the limits of the State adhering to the Treaty, on whose register they are listed must be returned to the State adhering to the Treaty, who must, on request, provide identification data before the objects or components can be returned."

with that of the other sovereign laws implicated, particularly where services are concerned (telecommunications, audiovisual...).

The study develops different criteria for authorising a "right to use" a space activity and to licence the corresponding space object by making a difference between the qualities specific to the demander (his status, his solvability, his guarantees, his track record, where applicable, particularly in terms of debris...) and the criteria linked with the type of activity envisaged: the technical criteria (certification), the conditions linked to national defence, the level of risk and responsibility for the State, the other authorisations obtained linked with the system, taxation of applications...

The report then examines the authorities which will be responsible for approvals (authorisation, certification, licencing) of space objects and for their surveillance (safety, security, monitoring placing and maintaining the satellite on-station and debris), both of which can be taken together. The approach chosen is a careful one: it does not suggest that a new public establishment be created, due in particular to the low volume of authorisations to be given and of the risks of duplicating (or scattering) means and skills.

3.3 Application of the concept of public service

We must also make a distinction according to the purpose of the public interest or industrial and commercial program. For this special attention has been given with respect to the concept of "public service", on certain public space systems generating new applications whose operation as given from the beginning to the private sector without the legal context being clearly qualified. Among these systems, we can mention civil Earth observation, navigation, positioning by satellite and launch services.

Unlike other applications which are already operational outside the space sector, like telecommunications, television broadcasting, meteorological, or information gathering which may have been attached to the mission of the appropriate organisms (France Telecom, TDF, Météo France, French Ministry of Defence...), these new systems had to create an *ad hoc* operating system for themselves, very often in the context of a concession between the space agency and a commercial company or subsidiary, created for this purpose, operating in the market in the context of an exclusivity. This structure is aimed at a very wide range of customers or to a user community from the point of view of sector and status, who are spread all over the world, badly structured and very often not aware of future potential uses, hence the term "latent user" currently used with respect to observation and navigation systems.

The legal status and the long-term financing system for such systems are still uncertain since the relations established at the start of the program between investors (originally the agencies), the operators, and the users for a preliminary system cannot be broken down indefinitely into recurrent series, in a context which becomes more operational, more international and more competitive.

The question of the application of "public industrial and commercial service" is therefore posed more specifically in the Earth observation sector, by analysing this activity's current organisation and with the legitimate preoccupation of preserving the economic balance and the development of this activity in an ever uncertain market.

As an illustration, the experience of the relations between CNES and the company responsible for broadcasting SPOT observation satellite images seems to indicate that this system could satisfy the usual public service or public interest criteria5.

In any case, it appears quite inappropriate to wish to unreservedly submit such information systems to the ordinary laws of competition[6] as long as the market has not reached full maturity and as long as the private sector cannot substantially assume the necessary investments.

However, the Treaty of Rome[7] can authorize legitimate concessions to the ordinary laws of competition in favour of companies responsible for the management of public economic interest services. In addition, community law allows exceptions to the prohibiting of the "refusal to sell" in favour of activities guaranteeing public order or national security which can give a legal basis to a possible national system of "security control of data distribution" (cf. work of the General Secretariat of National Defence and of GirSpot)[8].

The difficult discussions on the concept of Private Public Partnership applied to the Galileo program in the context of a rapprochement between the European Union and ESA, highlights however the difficulty of converging at European level in favour of a common concept of public service.

The application of public service rules to certain space activities basically remains a political, economic and social question which is outside the scope of this study. At best this study can identify the domains of application which must be explained.

In these conditions, it seemed appropriate to position ourselves more upstream, by asking Bertrand du Marais9 for a detailed study of the rules in force in France and in Europe around the concept of public service, in order to analyse the opportunity and the conditions of their application to space activities. It must also be noted that this legal analysis is then placed in a dynamic and future-orientated perspective by concerning, in a personal manner, some space sector liberalisation scenarios.

---

5 That is to say a major interest for administrations (richness of the space observation information from the military, strategic, political, scientific and socio-economic points of view), the public financing of investments (technical operator's satellite and ground network, including part of the maintenance costs), a control by the government, the shareholding and compensatory mechanisms or "ISIS" type promotions, the implementation of concessionary rules of ordinary law (exclusive concession, security control of data distribution, international status of direct receiving station, low licences), respect for traditional principles like the principle of equality between users, the principles of adaptation and continuity (continuity of an operational sector garanteed by CNES since 1986, from Spot 1 to 5 then continued with adaptations in the context of the Pleiades program)...

6 If we consider remote sensing as a purely commercial and competitive activity, the prohibiting of "anticompetitive agreements" of article 81-1 of the European Union Treaty (ex article 85.1 of the Treaty of Rome), and that of "abuse of dominant position" of article 82 (ex article 86), or the implementation of restrictions to the aid given by the States in article 87 (ex article 92) which threaten to distort competitiveness, could affect the legal security of a public satellite data distribution system which would be based on a total concession to a commercial company, which is almost free of charge, exclusive and world-wide.

7 article 86-2 of ex Article 90-2

8 And in particular, article 122-1 of the Consumer Code which reiterates the terms of article 33 of Order no. 86-1243 of 1st December 1986: "it is prohibited to refuse a consumer the sale of a product or the provision of a service, except for a legitimate reason, and to subordinate the sale of a product to the purchase of an imposed quantity or to the concomittant purchase of another product or a service as well as to subordinate the provision of a service to that of another service or the purchase of a product...».

9 Senior Civil Servant attached to the Council of State who also intervened as first participant in this report.

This study, annexed to the report, is based on a typological analysis of the different activities of the space sector with respect to the traditional criteria of public service. It reveals four main categories:

- purely competitive activities: telecommunications services;
- regulated competitive activities: rewarding contracts in favour of public organisms, commercial Earth observation, availability of test facilities...;
- clearly public service activities: State or inter-agency international cooperation, fundamental research, upstream technological research (R&T), space object qualification and certification, management, organisation and availability of launch facilities, scientific program, military programs;
- administrative police activities: security and safety, "space" frequency allocation function, organisation of space object qualification and certification, space surveillance.

The work group devoted to Earth observation by satellite, presided by Jean-Claude Lummaux[10], makes a clear distinction between private or commercial systems and public systems[11].

The private and commercial systems are those for which investments are financed from private funds (equity capital, debt, public issue...). Such systems, without prejudicing the rules of free competition, must receive prior authorisation delivered by the government, in particular to guarantee that the following are respected:

- French international undertakings and responsibilities (article VI of the 1967 Treaty, 1986 Principles on remote sensing, 1972 Convention on responsibility for space damage, ITU (International Telecommunications Union) rules in terms of frequencies);
- texts relative to defence and national security (upstream control of blocking, of programming and disclosure of data);
- fundamental rights of the citizen (private life, right of image, business secrecy...).

The public systems are financed by the State for public interest purposes. The data from these systems can be distributed by public (case of scientific instruments) or commercial (case of Spot satellites) organisms. In this last case, the convention between the State, a public entity, and the commercial operator is similar to a delegation of public service as it guarantees, in addition to the conditions mentioned above: system continuity, no restriction or discrimination for data access, economic balance of the concession and exclusivity of the distribution activity. This leads to ensuring that there is a clear legal and accounting distinction between the activities of the operator, which depend on the distribution of the licenced data, and those of his own added-value services.

Without prejudging the various typologies above, the requirement was largely expressed during the group meetings, to formalise as transparently as possible and whatever the activity or the chosen status, the legal links between the

---

10 Jean-Claude Lummaux intervened in the reports and studies which concerned related subjects:

- member of the previously mentioned French Planning Office workshop which led to the "Public data dissemination and the digital revolution" report;
- rapporteur and writer of the report "The prospects of the evolution of geographical information and the consequences for the French National Geographic Institute (IGN)", by Guy Lengagne, deputy mayor of Boulogne sur Mer

11 See Part 3, Chapter 2

different public and private players concerned, to reinforce the legal security of their relations.

This study on the concept of public service therefore appears fairly independent of space law and seems to be able to be treated separately from a space legislation context in the strict sense. We suggest that this be gone into in greater detail, in particular in the context of groups and committees already set up to monitor the programs, Pleiades and Galileo for example, by duly taking into consideration the security and defense aspects and the interactions with the European Union and ESA.

3.4 Other measures relative to market developments and private initiatives

The report then in part 2, under the title "Support for market development and private initiatives", deals with other questions not directly linked to the authorisation and control context, and which are more specifically concerned with private law or current legal practices applicable in the industrial world. The report does not propose to produce a private legal system specific to the space sector, but rather to specify or adapt, where necessary, due to the specific nature of space activities, the branches of national law concerned as in private law, particularly property and real security law, intellectual property law, civil and contractual liability law, insurance law, and at public law level, in setting out an authorisation and monitoring system for space activities in France, without forgetting the fiscal aspects.

Of the points which require targeted action, we will mention in particular:

- The confirmation of the systems of responsibility used between private players in the space sector (for over 20 years). According to a legal practice largely recognised and accepted internationally due to the specific nature of the risks from the technical point of view and of the costs, the participants in a launch activity (satellite manufacturers, equipment manufacturers, launch operators, satellite operators, customers...) are all bound by specific contractual agreements where the economy is that "each one individually deals with the damage caused to his own persons and property", and abandons, where applicable, all claims against those responsible who are protected by 'no-claim clauses and guaranteed agreements" or determines responsibility limitations. The manufacturers concerned (Arianespace, EADS Launch Vehicle, Astrium, Alcatel Space Industries, Snecma...), and also the insurers, desire that French law, like that of the United States of America, incorporate these practices in the texts and that in this manner what is implicit becomes explicit for the recognition of the validity of such clauses[12].

- The limit of responsibility for launch operators must be formalised in a legal or reglementary framework. The French State, in conformity with its international and European agreements currently obliges Arianespace to take out responsibility insurance for damage which could be caused to third parties during an Ariane launch to a limit of four hundred million francs (60 Meuros). This limit corresponds to the responsibility limit left to the

---

12 In particular, by reference to the terms of the French civil code and of the jurisprudence relative to the contractual responsibility and to the guarantee against latent defects, particularly since the transposition of the 1985 European directive on the responsibility for defective products.

responsibility of Arianespace by the State which covers the indemnities beyond this limit. However, this insurance obligation does not result from a law. It would be desirable, for transparency and stability, that this insurance obligation be translated into a legal form[13] and generalized to all launch operators liable to launch satellites for which the French State would be the launch State in the sense of the Convention on responsibility of 29 March 1972 (cf. Soyuz at Kourou hypothesis).

- The obligation to insure satellites for risks in orbit with respect to third parties must be envisaged. This obligation, expressly planned for by English law, does not currently exist in France particularly concerned with Eutelsat. The amount of this type of policy is not very high given the probabilities of collision in orbit.

- The overall analysis of the tax context of space activities in France has not indicated any basic problems. The legibility of this system could however be improved. In the hypothesis where the above different systems should be rediscussed, a certain amount of European reciprocity must be preserved and the advantages given to this sector of activity must be maintained, given those allocated by competitor countries.

- Coherence must be sought in terms of intellectual property, between space law and the different aspects of patent law. Some measures require to be specified in national law: the status of inventions and patents in space, the extent of the protection (implementation of infringement action...), possible conflicts with the principle of non appropriation of space (case of patented orbits...) and the temporary presence exception (impossibility to seize space objects "in transit" on the launch site).

Like certain countries (United States), it is proposed to extend the application of French patent law to space objects and to their components which are under French jurisdiction or control, in conformity with article VIII of the 1967 Space Treaty (effects of licencing and conservation of property, jurisdiction and control systems in space).

In addition, the "launch" manufacturers (Arianespace and EADS LV...) desire that, since the temporary presence exception already applies in France to vehicles in transit (ships, aircraft, trains), it be extended to spacecraft and space objects so that their commercial partners are not exposed to possible infringement actions by third parties, in particular on the Guiana Space Center site. European satellite manufacturers are also favourable to this exemption, but more especially to benefit from a reciprocity for their objects in transit on United States territory as the United States has allowed the temporary exception only for nationals of countries which allow the same exception to American nationals.

- The clarification of the laws of ownership and guarantees concerning space objects also seems to be a necessity to favour the development of private space activities, in order to guarantee new methods of financing them. This question alone has justified the creation of a specific work group (group 4). This group suggests that the French "Property law" make reference to the space object, in the same way as ships and aircraft, under a specific system of licenced mobile property, depending on the Civil Code.

---

13 Thus following the practice adopted by all the States which have already implemented specific space legislation, and particularly the United States.

In parallel, it appears necessary to unify the different rules of guarantees at the international level, in particular by supporting the action of Unidroit for the implementation of the Convention and the Space Protocol, while encouraging constructive dialogue with CUPEEA (United Nations Committee for the Pacific Use of Outer space), due to the interdependences with space law and to the necessity to harmonise the respective licencing systems, or even to combine them under a same authority. This action with respect to Unidroit is carried out in France[14] by the Foreign Affairs and Justice Ministries, which have received group 4's contributions, and the contributions of the space aeronautics department in the context of this study.

This group also desires that the system of guarantees recommended by Unidroit be studied, beyond the strict framework of space law, by the international, European (EU) and national (DiGITIP, ANFR, ART, CSA...) authorities which are competent in terms of "services" licences (telecommunications, audiovisual...). It is important that the transfer of ownership of a space object, or of its use, to a creditor benefiting from an international guarantee is accompanied in the most foreseeable, or even automatic, conditions possible, by the transfer of all its associated rights (responsibility, frequencies and orbital positions, operating licences).

- Finally, favouring access to the market and the respect for free competition, for the commercial activities, is one of the priorities mentioned in the report[15]. This question is specifically developed in chapter 2 of the report, in addition it underlies all the conclusions of group 3 concerning radiocommunications (Part Three: Specific measures - Chapter 3). These contradictions inherent to commercial space activities seriously penalise their development.

The adoption of legislation specific to space activities is therefore a privileged solution to resolve this antagonism observed throughout the study between the requirement to have space activities controlled by the States and that of favouring the development of a space application market at the European and

---

14 To favour Unidroit's approach, the national civil law and the French rules on private international law must be adapted in parallel to reduce all sources of conflict between different creditors (national, international, with their respective priviledges ...) in favour of the creditor who benefits from an international guarantee. Public international law, in particular United Nations space law (1967 treaty...), must also provide for the possibility of taking control of a satellite, transfer of property or of its use to a secured creditor or even its retention. In particular, it is important to specify in which conditions a State can allow or refuse the transfer of ownership or retention of the secured property, given its responsibilites in case of damage. Finally, the **national licencing register** items must be defined in consequence, whatever their form (law, ministerial order, circular...) specifying the mandatory or optional, confidential or public endorsements.

15 Following the world and European liberalisation process for the telecommunications and audivisual communication sectors, the space radiocommunications activities have been integrated in a market whose dominnt principle is, and must remain, that of **free access**. In France, this principle results from the "freedom of commerce and industry", laid down during the Revolution and now considered as a fundamental legal principle. In the context of the European Union, this principle refers to the **freedom of establishment,** it also tends to become the common rule in the context of the World Trade Organisation and of the general agreement on trade and services. It therefore opposes all national measures confering exclusive rights without justification. These principles of free access and of fair competition can, as developped above, clash with other restrictions which are just as valid particularly with respect to the application of space law (responsability of States, obligation to authorise and control activities, licencing...), national security restrictions (exports of war materials, technologies or sensitive imagery), of rules linked with the use of rare resources like those of frequencies and orbital positions, or of other public restrictions (particularly audiovisual).

world level in an appropriate competitive environment.

4) Conclusion and outlook:

The question of the construction of a legal framework specific to space applications is posed more specifically with respect to future systems, delegated or operated by the private sector, but more generally the need for coherent regulations, guaranteeing the current practices appears to be more and more necessary, and is the subject of insistent requests by contractors, operators, insurers and financiers and legal professionals.

The high participation, at the best level, in the work groups set up for this prospective approach is evidence of this.

Of the main actions which can result from this study, we must note:

- the interest, as a priority, of creating in France a general framework for the authorization of space object launches, of licencing and surveillance of space activities (launchers and satellites) regulating, in particular, the question linked with the State's responsibilities;
- given the specific nature of the space activities, the need to specify or adapt certain branches of national law, particularly property and real security law, the law of intellectual property, the law of civil and contractual liability, and insurance law;
- the pertinence of clarifying the concept of public service applied to space activities, in particular in the European context of the European Union and the European Space Agency;
- and in this respect, the interest of specifying the context of CNES missions in its interactions with its supervisory authorities, and more generally the interest of better understanding the roles of the States and their regulatory action in the above European context.

SPACE DEBRIS

G. Lafferranderie[1]
Former ESA Legal Adviser, Chairman of ECSL

The Legal Subcommittee of COPUOS appears to be close to starting the very necessary debate on space debris. Some encouraging indications have already been received; however working methods remain to be defined, and a list compiled of specific, detailed issues to be examined in the context of existing space law, taking into account the work that has been done by other bodies and the regulatory mechanisms that have been studied (and adopted) at the national and international level. My impression (for the time being it is no more than that) is that the time is ripe for work to begin, that the necessary consensus is within reach. As we said here above detailed and specific legal questions need to be formulated, questions that arise from an examination of the technical work that has already been done. The broadly exploratory phase is ending, and we now have a better idea of the direction to follow and guidelines to observe. It is time for the lawyers to strike out in that direction; the groundwork has been done, as the documentary record and recent works show. It is not my intention to review those achievements, nor is this necessary. Instead, I wish to present a report that I delivered to the Legal Subcommittee at its April session. The issues addressed in it struck a chord, to judge by the reactions at the meeting.

This paper will also describe some possible procedures to be considered, and the form and contents of legal texts that might be produced.

Section 1: The ECSL report

This report was distributed at the 41st session of the Legal Subcommittee as A/AC.105/C.2/2002/CRP.5, dated 27 March 2002. It was discussed as a CRP (Conference Room Paper) under the agenda item entitled "Information on the activities of international organizations", which recently has become a regular item in Legal Subcommittee meetings. Even though there is no specific item on the Subcommittee's agenda entitled "space debris", at least now the issue (which concerns all countries, whether they are party to the Outer Space Treaty or not) has been discussed and debated in this form.

The report examines the responses to a questionnaire (copy attached) that was designed by the ECSL and widely distributed to ECSL members and some non-members. It considers past analysis and proposals put forward in the Legal Subcommittee, the Scientific and Technical Subcommittee and at international colloquiums (such as those organised by the International Institute of Space Law, the International Academy of Astronautics, the International Bar Association, Committee Z, and the Academy of

[1] Represents only the personal views of the author and does not commit the organisation to he belongs.

International Law, Space Law Committee). The report also examines work of the Inter-Agency Space Debris Coordination Committee (IADC) presented to the Scientific and Technical Subcommittee, the results of national research, and existing national regulations and policies.

Against the background of this documentation, concrete, fundamental legal questions can be formulated, such as: what do the existing instruments (I would certainly include technical regulations, and indeed give them a certain priority) address already, what do they cover incompletely, and what are the important issues not addressed to date?

Elaborating a generally accepted legal definition of the term "space debris" is frequently seen as the place to start, to judge by the amount of ink that has been spilled on the subject. However, none of the instruments in force (1967 Outer Space Treaty and others) so much as use the term, let alone provide a definition. It is worth asking if the search for a generally agreed definition is perhaps the wrong place to start; should it be allowed to impede? Next, what type of legal instrument is required? Should the Outer Space Treaty be amended, along with the other treaties, or should a 'special instrument' be adopted along the lines of the proposal which the Institute of International Law brought forward at Buenos Aires in 1994?

To continue the list of questions: does a piece of space debris (or orbital debris) constitute a space object, or a component of a space object? Is it subject to registration? What happens when space debris causes damage in outer space, in the air, or on the ground (knowing that a large proportion of objects, mostly debris, falls into the South Pacific Ocean)? A related question is, what are the consequences of the transfer of ownership of a space object or component in space (including debris) at a time when commercialisation and privatisation of space activities are becoming widespread, particularly if the owner, operator or commercial user goes bankrupt? These are some of the issues that need to be addressed. In attempting to do so, the legal expert needs a measure of humility to realise that the answers to questions and concerns that are perfectly legitimate (particularly in the light of Article I paragraph 1 of the Outer Space Treaty) will be conditioned by increasingly sophisticated and varied technical responses, so that a definitive, ultimate settlement is likely to remain elusive. Scientists and engineers, on the other hand, need to recognise that this means that obligations and duties need to be solidly anchored in legal instruments that are universally enforceable, under both international treaties and national space law (drafted specifically to accommodate future technical progress). In this connection I am thinking particularly of the process for granting launch licenses, insurance and technical regulations.

It is important to resist the temptation to seek a simple answer to these questions in an inherently fluid situation. The legal complexity of space objects (see the aerospace objects calls for a suitably nuanced response. The starting point should be those concerns that existing law clearly fails to address: abandonment of a space object in orbit (recognition? liability?); transfer of ownership of a space object; recovery of a space object; the basis for liability in case of damage in outer space (collision), in airspace and on the ground. Should the distinction between "active" satellites and others be formalised? What is the appropriate way of handling environmental or health hazards associated with space objects (e.g. nuclear power sources) appropriately taken into account?

The ECSL report concludes that items of space debris constitute space objects, and that existing space law already provides some answers and guidelines. It is reasonable therefore to start by examining the questions of whether and to what extent existing technical and legal provisions address the concerns of the international community.

Section 2: Proposals

First, how can the existing texts and procedures be used more fully?

- Inform the international community: immediate notification of any event giving rise to space debris (including degradation of an existing space object into space debris), providing full information, including a forecast of re-entry time and place and any special procedures for dangerous or harmful objects, with continuous updates.

- Cooperation and technical assistance (cf. Article XI of the Outer Space Treaty), coordinated use of tracking, observation and recovery systems. None of these measures require new legal instruments to be adopted or existing ones to be amended.

- Preventive measures, in particular by means of launch licensing, insurance etc.

- Debris reduction measures (e.g. passivation of launcher stages) have been identified by the IADC and the Scientific and Technical Subcommittee and taken up in certain national space legislations. These evolving technical provisions need the broadest possible legal recognition.

Second, what options are open if, for the reasons discussed above, no basis is found for a new legal category to deal with space debris, nor for formally amending the existing space treaty?

- First of all, gather up in a high-level policy document those technical measures that have been defined by the stake-holders, operators and launching authorities, which are already being followed by and large. One way to do this would be by way of a resolution of the UN General Assembly. This will obviously not make the Scientific and Technical Subcommittee of the COPUOS redundant, any more than the IADC or the International Academy of Astronautics. On the contrary, such a step will provide top-level validation of their work. Such a resolution would call on countries to apply existing instruments more fully, in particular the Convention on Registration of Space Objects, and to use article VI of the Outer Space Treaty to adopt appropriate national legislation (launch licensing). It would also outline the Legal Subcommittee's working objectives and the concrete items requiring legal work.

- Concerning the Legal Subcommittee's plan of work: on the basis of current procedure, the Legal Subcommittee is obliged to wait until the Scientific and Technical Subcommittee has produced enough documents and closed out its deliberations. This is a patently unrealistic requirement; for one thing, there is a perpetual need for some ongoing review and refinement. Certainly, the Legal Subcommittee needs to be briefed on the technical issues before commencing its work, but how should this briefing process be organised, and who should be involved? Compiling required documentation will be a preliminary task but is not the answer. A dialogue is needed between the two subcommittees, with the participation of the IADC. This might take the form of a one or two-day joint session, in the framework of an ordinary Legal Subcommittee meeting. Each delegation would be accompanied by its counterpart from the Scientific and Technical Subcommittee, and the STS Chairman would be in attendance. The Legal Subcommittee could then commence its own work the following year by identifying pressing legal problems dealt with inadequately or not at all at present. In doing so, it would draw on presentations from a range of legal experts from the International Institute of Space Law, the Academy of International Law etc. As for the form of the international 'instrument' (which in no way makes national legislation redundant), various options might be considered. At the present time, the form that appears most appropriate is a declaration of principles; this is a solemn form used by the UN for particularly grave matters, like the Declarations of 1963 and 1996. Representatives of member states at that time affirmed their will to abide by the Declarations even though the latter lacked formal treaty character.

– Several delegations expressed their appreciation of the ECSL's report before the Legal Subcommittee and COPUOS. Some, such as the French delegation, proposed that draft principles be prepared, in the same way as was done, for example, with the Principles Relevant to the Use of Nuclear Power Sources in Outer Space.

This appears to me to be the most reasonable approach. The international community cannot wait any longer for legal deliberations to be started by the body of experts it has set up for the purpose. The technical groundwork has been done, and the time is ripe for a consensus to be sought.

I trust that the ECSL report and the proposals that have come out of it will be useful in putting the finishing touches on a road map that will allow us finally to start to move in the direction we all know we must take.

RECENT BIBLIOGRAPHICAL REFERENCES

Article based on the presentation made at the forty first session of the UNCOPUOS legal subcommitte, Vienna 2-12 April 2002.

Proceedings of the Third European Conference on Space Debris, March 2001:

- Gabriel Lafferranderie, *Spaces Debris and Related Legal Issues*, Third European Conference on space debris, ESOC; Darmstadt (Germany), 19-21 March 2001
- Armel Kerrest, *Space Debris, Remarks on Current Legal Issues,* Idem.
- Franz G. Von der Dunk, *Space Debris and the Law,* Idem
- Marietta Benkis, Kai Uwe Schrogl, *The 1999 UNCOPUOS Technical Report on Space Debris (2002-2005): Perspectives and Legal Consequences,* Idem

Proceedings of the Workshop on Space Law in the Twenty First Century; Session Eight, July 1999, Office for Outer Space Affairs, UN Office in Vienna, 2000.

Report of the Scientific and Technical Subcommittee on its Thirty-Ninth Session, Vienna, February 2002, A/AC-105/

Report of the Legal Subcommittee on its Forty-First session, Vienna, 2-12 April 2002, A/AC-105/787

Report of the COPUOS on its fifty seventh Session, Vienna, June 2002, A/57/20

52nd International Astronautical Congress, Toulouse, France, October 1-5 2001, International Institute for Space Law:

- Cf. E. Jason Steptoe, *Legal Standards for Orbital Debris Mitigation: a Way Forward*

51st IAF Congress, Rio de Janeiro, 2000:

- Cf. Edward A. Frankle, *International Regulation of Orbital Debris,* IISL-00- IISL-4-15 (2000)

Interagency space debris coordination Committee (IADC), IADC space debris Mitigation Guidelines, IADC.02.01, 12 April 2002-07-18

Documents and reports, in particular:

- U.S. Government Orbital Debris Mitigation Standard Practices, December 2000
- Space Debris Mitigation Standard, NASDA-STD-18, March 28 1996
- CNES Standard Collection, Method and Procedure Space Debris, RNC-CNES-Q-40-512, Issue 1 Rev., April 19 1999
- Space Technology Items, General Requirements, Mitigation of Space Debris Population. Russian Aviation and Space Agency Standards, October 134-1023-2000
- ESA Space Debris Mitigation Handbook, Release1.0, April 7 1999
- European Space Debris Safety and Mitigation Standards, Issue 1, rev. , September 27 2000
- International Academy of Astronautics, Position Paper on Orbital Debris, Edition 2001
- Federal Communications Commission, IB Docket N° 02-54, Notice of Proposed Rule Making, Released March 18, 2002

Space Debris Questionnaire
G. Laferranderie

I. Definition/status

1. Do you believe that a legal definition of the notion of "space debris" is needed? If yes, please explain.

2. Do you have an idea what such a definition should look like?

3. Do you believe that the existing space law texts are adequate on this point? (cf. draft instrument adopted by the International Law Association at Buenos Aires in 1994)

4. What legal form should an instrument take?
--amendment to existing instruments
--additional protocol
--separate agreement
--adoption of the principles by a resolution of the General Assembly of the UN
--solemn interpretation by the states party to the treaties in question

II. Contents

1. What should go into the legal instrument (apart from the definition, international assistance, prevention, and technical details on specific categories of object)?

2. What measures, if any, should be taken on recovery, in your view?

3. What role can/should the COPUOS play, in your view? Is an information and consultation mechanism necessary? What would be the implications for the launching state?

4. Should an international register be established? Should this be done by a solemn interpretation by the states parties to the treaties in question? Should such a registry include 'military' space objects?

5. What provisions do you believe are required in cooperation agreements and launch contracts? What recommendations should be made to manufacturers of space objects?

III. What should be the future role of the IADC under the authority of COPUOS?
Should IADC membership be extended to non-space faring nations?

IV. National licensing systems
Should national launch licensing systems include specific obligations on the applicant?

V. Should the measures agreed by the United Nations (via COPUOS) automatically apply to the private sector?

1. If you said "yes," what legal means would you suggest?

2. How far should the competence of the state having jurisdiction (launching state) extend, and what obligations should this entail? (Insurance? How high?)

VI. Other remarks (or comments or proposals) you may wish to make?

IAC-02-IISL.1.09

CHALLENGES TO SPACE LAW IN THE 21st CENTURY – PROJECT 2001 PLUS*

Prof. Dr. Stephan Hobe, LL.M. (McGill)
Director
Institute of Air and Space Law
University of Cologne
stephan.hobe@uni-koeln.de

Jana Kristin Hettling, LL.M. (Leiden)
Research Associate
Institute of Air and Space Law
University of Cologne
jana.hettling@uni-koeln.de

I. Abstract

At the edge of the 21st century the development of society as well as of international law is marked by the phenomenon of globalization and in Europe additionally by a deepening of integration in the framework of the European Union. Traditional schemes of international relations and of international law are ever more altering due to progressive changes in science and technology and equally due to changes in global politics. A fundamental characteristic of the new era of globalization and Europeanization is a certain withdrawal of states from their conventional role in international relations as well as an increase of the importance of new actors in the international society. Recently, privatization and commercialization have also affected space activities. In order to examine in detail in which way space law either mirrors those changes or needs to be reformed itself, the German Aerospace Center DLR and the Institute of Air and Space Law of the University of Cologne have jointly initiated the Project 2001 Plus, building upon the successfully concluded Project 2001.

II. The Impact of Globalization on International Space Law

Usually globalization is regarded as a primarily economic phenomenon relating to the increasing interaction of national economic and financial systems through intensifying relations in international trade, investment and capital flows.[1] Though, it is essential to note that important changes in cross-border social, cultural and technological exchange also form part of the incident of globalization. With instantaneous communications, knowledge and culture can be shared around the world easily and timely and a large variety of problems of geographic distance no longer exists. Sociologists and political scientists tend to define globalization as a vanishing of frontiers, a decoupling of space and time where distance becomes a factor of declining importance and where economic, political and socio-cultural relations are created and maintained on a global level[2]. Within this emerging framework, a retreat of state authority is an essential characteristic[3]. Globalization is shifting authority from the level of the state to different kinds of public and private actors[4], e.g. to transnational enterprises or NGOs. For instance one can observe a decreasing function of the modern state to direct and influence respective business transactions. Commercialization and/or privatization of originally public services -such as in telecommunications, postal services, meteorological organizations- can be found in more and more areas that affect international relations as well as every day life.

However, it is still states who are the original and major subjects of international law. Here the existing controversy between globalization and international public law is becoming obvious. While the former is characterized by a decline of state authority and influence and by a disappearance of national frontiers, the latter is a system based on national sovereignty, created by states and mainly addressing states. Consequently the new range of global interaction in various fields is pressuring and challenging international law to come to terms with the contemporary structural changes in the reality of international relations. It is the unique function of the law to apportion rights and duties to those subjects it considers fit and worthy enough to hold them[5]. Taking this into consideration, it cannot be denied that in the course of time, international law has proved to be a system open for gradual structural changes and able to respond to the demands of modern times. In the Lotus Case of 1927 the Permanent Court of International Justice still stated that: "International Law governs the relations between independent States. The rules of law therefore emanate from their own free will as expressed and established in conventions or by usages generally accepted as expressing principles of law and established in order to regulate the relations between these co-existing independent communities or with a view to the achievement of common aims. Restrictions upon the independence of States cannot therefore be presumed."[6]

By defining international law simply as a law of passive co-existence the 1927 Lotus judgement fits into the historical period of the League of Nations which failed to prevent World War II and thereby evidenced its weakness as an international institution.

The structure and understanding of international law changed, however, in 1945 with the foundation of the United Nations Organization, introducing a prohibition of the right to warfare in article 2, paragraph 4 of its Charter.[7] Having experienced horrific damages and suffering during World War II, the international community was now ready to emphasize the aim of preserving international peace by acts of solidarity and active engagement such as safeguarding human rights, raising social standards and supporting developing countries. The American lawyer of German descent, Wolfgang Friedman, took notice of this change of paradigm as a change from a law of co-existence to a law of cooperation[8].

The emerging template of globalization can now be regarded as a next challenge to international law[9]: the law has to adapt to the growing interdependence of states, to an augmentation of competition in an international free trade system intensified by the diffusion of technology[10], to the increasing importance of the non-governmental sector and to various new actors on the scene.[11] Such an emergence of free trade and intensifying technological competition can also be observed when it comes to space activities. Whereas in the early hours of space endeavour exclusively states were engaged in the use of outer space, in recent years commercial space activities have increased dramatically. The originally scientific and military character of space undertakings began to change progressively as opportunities arose to conduct space activities for commercial purposes. With the rising profitability of activities in certain fields, especially in the area of telecommunications, the increasing curiosity and interest of the private sector lead to a gradually evolving tendency of relocating parts of the activities to the non-state side[12]. In 1996 the global commercial utilization of space hardware had reached 53% and thus went beyond government expenditures[13]. Though, this development is not yet reflected in the present state of space law which provides only very few and sometimes inappropriate provisions for the commercial use of outer space and especially the use by private enterprises.[14] So far, the legal regimes dealing with space activities are mainly public law regimes which cannot bind private entities, at least not directly. Nonetheless, private space activities can involve the same risks and dangers as the same activities conducted by public bodies. Moreover, to the amount that international organizations are subjects of international space law, they are rather regarded as a vehicle of cooperation for states and not as individual and self-determining actors on the international scene. Consequently policy makers as well as legal researchers and practitioners have to face the issue as to which further development and elaboration of space law might be desirable.[15]

III. The Concept of Project 2001 Plus

For the promotion and further development of the commercial use of outer space, the Institute of Air and Space Law of the University of Cologne in cooperation with the German Aerospace Center (DLR) jointly carried out the Project 2001. The project aimed at giving a first overview over the most striking effects and consequences of privatization and commercialization of space activities. It did so by investigating the present state of the law for the main areas of commercial uses of outer space with the purpose to name and classify the gaps in the legal framework as well as to make concrete suggestions for possible future legislation[16]. The project concentrated on 6 specific areas (privatization, launch and associated services, remote sensing, telecommunication, space stations, national space legislation), and for each of these areas a working group of international experts was established. In the course of the year 2001 Project 2001 was successfully terminated with an international space law colloquium in Cologne and the results of the respective working groups have recently been published[17].

Built upon the conclusions and recommendations of Project 2001, the new *Project 2001 Plus* has been initiated to take a closer insight into the legal problems of privatization and commercialization of space activities. This new project intends to consider in particular aspects of the emerging globalization and Europeanization in space activities as well as in the aviation market. The deepening of integration in the framework of the European Communities and the European Union implies new questions also for space related undertakings. For instance, the European Space Agency (ESA) and the European Union jointly work on an intensification of their inter-relationship in order to create a coherent and highly competitive environment for the European strategy for space. This involves a large variety of institutional law questions as well as practical questions for space operations which need to be examined carefully. Contemplating the space industry, Europeanization also affects competition laws within the Union and relations with partners around the world. Furthermore the existence of multinational space corporations (such as Sea Launch) and the respective absence of appropriate national space legislation are causing severe difficulties in the application of the space treaties, most prominently the Liability Convention and the definition of the launching state according to the convention. Finally, globalization and Europeanization considerably affect commercial navigation, remote sensing and telecommunication satellite services.

Hence, the research activities of the Project 2001 Plus will come to pass in six specified subject areas, to be examined in an envisaged timeframe between 2002 and 2005:

1. Institutional relationship between ESA and EU / European space strategy
2. National space legislation
3. Fair competition in the conduct of space activities
4. Commercial space applications (navigation, telecommunication, remote sensing)
5. Current legal issues with regard to the international space station
6. Consequences of globalization for air transport

For the promotion of scientific and intellectual exchange a *working group* of international experts will be established for each of these six areas. Each working group will be coordinated by two experts from the particular field, one from DLR and one from the University of Cologne. Overall scientific project management is in the hands of Prof. Dr. Stephan Hobe, LL.M. (McGill), Director of the Institute of Air and Space Law at the University of Cologne.

Every working group will convene at an *international workshop* where the experts have the opportunity to present and exchange their views on the respective subjects. Discussions are supposed to define concrete possible developments of the law and make practical suggestions to close gaps in present legislation.

Every workshop will issue *proceedings* through an *own publication series* of the project containing the presentations of speakers, extensive legal background material, as well as a list of further references of articles and books published in the fields. In addition, reports on the current status of the overall project and the working groups are planned to be presented at international meetings and colloquia.

The project shall be concluded by an international law conference currently planned for the end of 2005 where all the concluding reports and recommendations from the working groups can be presented and discussed. The final proceedings will contain the ultimate versions and reports from all discussed fields.

The working groups are supposed to start their activities several months before the respective workshop will take place in order to secure an adequate preparation and sufficient background knowledge in the concerned area. The *first workshop* on the future institutional relationship between ESA and EU will take place in Brussels in December 2002[18].

IV. Conclusion

International law is codified international policy and thus a product of its environment. It has emerged in line with the prevailing notions of international relations. In order to safeguard its role in the international system it must be in harmony with the realities of the age[19]. The phenomenon of globalization is reinforcing the trend away from the exclusivity of the state and towards a stronger acceptance and involvement of non-state entities in the international law-making-process. International law needs to continue to move into new fields covering e.g. such issues as the commercial use of outer space. The Project 2001 Plus takes into account the current development in the international system and intends to find solutions for legal problems resulting from the globalization and Europeanization of the space industry.

References:

[1] Good description of the different aspects of globalization by Michael Likosky (ed.), Transnational Legal Process, Butterworth 2002, Jost Delbrück, Structural Changes in the International System and ist legal Order in the Era of Globalization, Schweizerisches Jahrbuch für Internationales und Europäisches Recht 1/2001, 1 et seq.

[2] Simon Reich, What is globalization? Four Possible Answers, Working Paper #261, Kellogg Institute for International Studies, 1998, 18f.

[3] See Stephan Hobe, Völkerrecht im Zeitalter der Globalisierung, Perspektiven der Völkerrechts-entwicklung im 21. Jahrhundert, Archiv des Völkerrechts 37 (1999), 253.

[4] Philip G. Cerny, Paradoxes of the Competition State: The Dynamics of Political Globalization, Government and Opposition 32/2, 1997, 270.

[5] See Malcolm N. Shaw, International Law, 4th Edition, 1997, 137 et seq.

[6] PCIJ Judgements, Series A, No. 9, 18.

[7] For a more general description see e.g. Otto Kimminich/Stephan Hobe, Einführung in das Völkerrecht, 7th ed. 2000, 61 et seq.

[8] Wolfgang Friedman, The Changing Structure of International Law, 1964, 50 et seq.

[9] For a description see Stephan Hobe, Völkerrecht im Zeitalter der Globalisierung, Archiv des Völkerrechts 37 (1999), 253, 261 et seq; id., Globalization: a challenge to the Nation State and to International Law, in: Likosky (ed), note 2, 378 et seq.

[10] Simon Reich, What is globalization? Four Possible Answers, Working Paper #261, Kellogg Institute for International Studies, 1998, 12.

[11] For a description of the development of the European legal order and its repercussion on national legal orders see Stephan Hobe, Europarecht, 2002, passim.

[12] Stephan Hobe, Harmonization of National Laws as an Answer to the Phenomenon of Globalization, Proceedings of Project 2001 –Legal Framework for the Commercial Use of Outer Space, 2002, 638.

[13] See Susanne Reif, Procedural Programme of Project 2001, Proceedings of Project 2001 –Legal Framework for the Commercial Use of Outer Space, 2002, 51.

[14] The only explicit mentioning in the still existing legal order for outer space activities is art. VI of the Outer Space Treaty of 1967.

[15] See for a description of some of the short-comings of the curent legal situiation in the actual globalized international framework Stephan Hobe, The Relevance of Current International Space Treaties in the 21st Century, Paper presented at the Celebration of the 50th anniversary of the McGill Institute of Air and Space Law in April 2002, (publication forthcoming).

[16] Karl-Heinz Böckstiegel, Welcome and Introduction, in: id. (ed.), Proceedings of Project 2001 –Legal Framework for the Commercial Use of Outer Space, 2002, 4.

[17] Karl-Heinz Böckstiegel (ed.), Project 2001 – Legal Framework for the Commercial Use of Outer Space, Studies in Air and Space Law, Volume 16, Carl Heymanns Verlag, Cologne 2002.

[18] Further information can be obtained through the internet site of the Institute of Air and Space Law, http://www.uni-koeln.de/jur-fak/instluft/

[19] See also Malcolm N. Shaw, International Law, 1997, 36 et seq.

IAC-02-IISL.1.10

PRIVATEERING AND PROFITEERING ON THE MOON AND OTHER CELESTIAL BODIES: DEBUNKING THE MYTH OF PROPERTY RIGHTS IN SPACE

P.M. Sterns*
L.I. Tennen**
Law Offices of Sterns and Tennen***
Phoenix, Arizona, U.S.A.

ABSTRACT

The increasing role of the private sector in space creates virtually limitless opportunities. It is axiomatic that activities in space must be conducted in compliance with the applicable requirements of the *corpus juris spatialis*. Unfortunately, in their zeal to manufacture a profit, some proponents give insufficient consideration to the implications and ramifications of their ventures *vis-a-vis* the extant law of outer space, particularly in relation to the non-appropriation principle. Still other purveyors of proposals are more disingenuous, proffering elaborate yet analytically inadequate rationales to justify either abrogating or disregarding the legal framework applicable to activities in space, especially in regard to assertions of so called "property rights" in space, on the Moon, and on other celestial bodies. This article examines the fallacies of these propositions, and demonstrates that such claims of property rights are both unnecessary and counterproductive to the development of commercial space.

* Director IISL, Member IAA, ASIL, ABA, IBA, ILA, Senior Member AIAA

** Former Commissioner, Arizona Space Commission, Member IISL, IAA, IEAS, ASIL, ILA, Senior Member AIAA

*** Member IAF

INTRODUCTION

"Got $16? Buy acre on moon" So proclaimed the headline in a recent newspaper.[1] According to this article, deeds to an acre on the lunar surface are being sold by an outfit calling itself the "Lunar Embassy." The individual behind this questionable enterprise, Dennis Hope, claims to own the moon on the basis of an alleged loophole in the Outer Space Treaty – the absence of a reference to private entities in the non-appropriation principle in article II, which provides that "outer space, including the Moon and other celestial bodies, is not subject to national appropriation by claim of sovereignty, by use or occupation, or by any other means."

The assertion that private individuals and corporations are not subject to article II is like a bad penny. It keeps reappearing in various incarnations. Whether promoted by charlatans like the Lunar Embassy with simple profit making schemes, or touted by more elaborate machinations and constructs, the contention that the private sector needs to and can claim areas of celestial bodies without violating the Outer Space Treaty is a myth. The exploration and use of space holds the promise of significantly advancing the quality of life for all mankind. Nevertheless, the promotion of unfounded and unwarranted fictions and fallacies could prove antithetical and counterproductive to the interests of commercial development of space.

PRIVATE ENTITIES AND THE *CORPUS JURIS SPATIALIS*

The Outer Space Treaty and other international conventions applicable to space were drafted during a period when governments were the major participants in space activities. The private sector initially was limited to the roles of contractors and suppliers to governments. The space treaties did not have as their primary purpose the regulation of commercial activities and the relationships among private entities or between states and private entities. In this regard, the *corpus juris spatialis* is neither expressly "pro" nor "anti" free enterprise.[2] Nevertheless, the law of outer space recognizes that the private sector will be a significant factor in the commercialization of space applications.

The absence of comprehensive and detailed regulation of space commerce does not equate to either a *laissez-faire* philosophy, where the first in time has total and unfettered control over resources on celestial bodies, nor does it equal a complete ban and prohibition of all commercial use of extraterrestrial materials.[3] There can be no serious question but that the private sector is subject to the rule of law, even while operating or conducting activities in outer space.[4] The *corpus juris spatialis*, and the Outer Space Treaty in particular, contain several provisions which recognize and promote the role of private entities in space.[5]

The Outer Space Treaty expressly provides that non-governmental entities, including private individuals, companies and organizations, have the right to conduct activities in space, including on the moon and other celestial bodies, subject to the authorization and continuing supervision of the appropriate state party.[6] Several provisions of the Outer Space Treaty may have special relevance in the context of activities by the private sector. In addition to the non-appropriation provisions of article II, the Outer Space Treaty provides that all states have a right of access to space on the basis of equality (article I); states retain jurisdiction over their personnel and objects, even when in outer space (article VIII); and states are to prevent harmful interference with the activities of other states parties (article IX). The Moon Agreement goes much further that the Outer Space Treaty in the recognition and regulation of the exploitation of lunar resources.[7] In addition, states parties to the Moon Agreement have agreed to undertake to establish an international regime to govern the exploitation of such resources.[8]

Of paramount importance to commercial activities in space is that the *corpus juris spatialis*, and the Outer Space Treaty in particular, has been instrumental in preserving space and celestial bodies for peaceful purposes, and preventing the spread of arms and military fortifications and maneuvers beyond this planet. The maintenance of outer space for peaceful purposes has fostered an environment where activities by both the public and the private sectors can be conducted, without the necessity of defensive armaments.[9] Nevertheless, this peaceful, non-militarized environment could be jeopardized if the non-appropriation principle is disregarded or abrogated.[10]

The opponents of the non-appropriation principle all too often have attempted to characterize the issue as one of "property rights." The focus on "property rights" is misplaced. While the non-appropriation principle prohibits the claim to an area of a celestial body, extraterrestrial resources may be extracted and utilized for scientific as well as commercial purposes.[11] Thus, the focus should be on the regulation of the use of extraterrestrial resources.[12]

No serious proposal has yet been made which is dependent upon the fee simple ownership of lunar or other extraterrestrial property to conduct a profit-making activity *in situ* separate and apart from the claim of property ownership. Numerous examples exist where a private entity is able to profitably extract resources from land it does not own. Grazing leases on public lands, offshore oil platforms, and logging rights are all examples where profit is available to private enterprise despite the absence of property ownership.[13] The fee simple ownership of extraterrestrial property similarly is irrelevant to the profitability of a venture providing products or services derived from celestial resources. Ownership is relevant only where it is intended that the source of the profit is derived from the claim of ownership, and the corresponding alienation thereof for economic consideration.[14]

THE CASE AGAINST THE NON-APPROPRIATION PRINCIPLE

Several assertions have been made by the opponents of the non-appropriation principle to justify the claim that article II of the Outer Space Treaty does not apply to private entities. The Lunar Embassy, for example asserts that the Outer Space Treaty mentions only national appropriation, in other words, appropriation by states. The absence of an express reference to private entities in article II of the Outer Space Treaty is proclaimed to be a loophole.[15] This contention conveniently ignores the provisions of the Moon Agreement, which expressly mention private entities in relation to the non-appropriation of celestial bodies.[16]

To bolster his argument, Hope asserts that he "registered his claim" to the moon and all planets and other moons in the solar system with the United States, Russia, and the United Nations.[17] From the absence of an acknowledgment of receipt of this "registration," Hope wishfully concludes that his claim has received an official seal of approval. Hope's reliance on the absence of a response is misplaced. His procedure of sending notice registration of his "claim" is self-fabricated and lacking in any official countenance. Moreover, neither the U.S., Russia nor the United Nations had any obligation to respond to Hope, even assuming that the "notice," in fact, was received.[18] States do not have any obligation to respond to claims such as Hope's, or to every other crackpot scheme.

The arguments advanced to justify an exemption for private entities from the provisions of article II of the Outer Space Treaty often are similarly lacking in substance, logic and/or credibility. For example, Benson, a vociferous opponent of the non-appropriation principle, addressed the issue, as he framed it, whether the Outer Space Treaty denies private property by the non-appropriation provision, and whether the Moon Agreement forbids private property in space? His response consists of three components: first, both the Outer Space Treaty and the Moon Agreement are just "wrong"; second, the Moon Agreement should be thrown "on the garbage heap of history"; and third, the Outer Space Treaty should be changed or ratification should be rescinded.[19]

This argument is not a line of objective reasoning, but a series of subjective, redundant and conclusory *non sequiturs*. A slightly better effort, at least superficially, was made by Dasch, Smith & Pierce, who concluded that private appropriation was not prohibited by the Outer Space Treaty. They claim this conclusion was based on prior drafts of the treaty, and what they judge to have been the intent of the framers.[20] There are two problems with this argument. First, Dasch, Smith & Pierce wrongly imply that there were prior drafts to the Outer Space Treaty which contained terms that conflicted with article II in a manner which supported an exemption for private entities. Second, the "judgment" of the intent is dependent upon the presence of such non-existent prior inconsistent drafts. As such, the judgment is unsubstantiated and unwarranted.

The Outer Space Treaty was drafted by the U.N. Committee on the Peaceful Uses of Outer Space in 1966. The text of article II can be traced directly to U.N. Resolutions 1721 and 1962. Resolution 1721 was adopted by the General Assembly in 1961, and provided that:

> (a) International law, including the Charter of the United Nations, applies to outer space and celestial bodies;
>
> (b) Outer space and celestial bodies are free for exploration and use by all States in conformity with international law and are not subject to national appropriation.[21]

U.N. Resolution 1962, entitled "Declaration of Principles Governing the Activities of States in the Exploration and Use of Outer Space," was adopted by the General Assembly in December, 1963. Article 3 of the Declaration provided: "Outer space and celestial bodies are not subject to national appropriation by claim of sovereignty, by means of use or occupation, or by any other means." Thus, the *res communis* nature of space was confirmed, and general agreement on the non-appropriation principle was reached by the community of nations at an early stage in the space age.[22]

In June, 1966, both the United States and the Soviet Union submitted to COPUOS drafts of an instrument that would later become the Outer Space Treaty. Article 1 of the U.S. draft reflected both Resolutions 1721 and 1962, and provided:

> Celestial bodies are free for exploration and use by all States on a basis of equality and in accordance with international law. They are not subject to national appropriation by claim of sovereignty, by means of use or occupation, or by any other means.[23]

Article II of the Soviet draft similarly provided:

> Outer space and celestial bodies shall not be subject to national appropriation by claim of sovereignty, by means of use or occupation, or by any other means.[24]

The draft treaties were submitted to the Legal Sub-Committee of COPUOS, which approved the text in August, 1966, with the addition of an express reference to the Moon in the phrase "outer space, including the Moon and other celestial bodies." This entire process transpired in less than two months. There were no prior drafts which referred to "private appropriation" or created an exclusion for appropriation by private parties.

The argument that article II of the Outer Space Treaty does not apply to private entities since they are not expressly mentioned therein has been made many times, but must fail for the simple reason that private entities do not need to be expressly listed in article II to be fully subject to the non-appropriation principle. Private entities have the right to conduct activities in space and on celestial bodies, but that right is not unlimited, and is subject to the rule of law. Significantly, the private entity must be authorized to conduct an activity in space by the appropriate state of nationality.[25] But if the state is prohibited from engaging in certain conduct, then it lacks the authority to license its nationals or other entities subject to its jurisdiction to engage in that prohibited activity.[26]

If a state could license its nationals to "privately appropriate" areas of the moon and other celestial bodies, notwithstanding the prohibition against national appropriation in article II of the Outer Space Treaty, then why could a state not also authorize its nationals to conduct other activities, in their capacity as private entities, in contravention of other articles of the Treaty. What is to prevent a state, under that scenario, from licensing its nationals to place nuclear weapons or other kinds of weapons of mass destruction in Earth orbit or on celestial bodies, notwithstanding the prohibitions contained in article IV of the Outer Space Treaty – after all, private entities are not mentioned in that article. Why stop there? Why could a state not "privatize" its nuclear testing procedures, and license a private entity to conduct nuclear weapons tests above ground, in the atmosphere, or in outer space, contrary to the provisions of the Nuclear Test Ban Treaty,[27] which also does not mention private entities. Carried to its logical conclusion, this argument would negate every bilateral or multilateral agreement ever made, since the states party thereto could engage in every activity they agreed to restrict or limit by the convenient subterfuge of conducting the activity through the guise of the private rather than the public sector.

Another line of argument made by the opponents of the non-appropriation principle is that a state could establish a form of registry for recognizing private property rights in space and on celestial bodies, purportedly consistent with the non-appropriation principle. This "consistency" is provided by the artifice of proclaiming this registration scheme "not to be appropriation." For example, Dasch, Smith & Pierce propose that a state establish a unilateral system of recognizing claims to space resources by its citizens. "In doing so, the nation could make it clear that it was *not claiming* sovereignty over such resources, but *simply recognizing the claims* of its citizens (emphasis added)."[28] This is a clear example of a distinction without a difference.

State recognition of claims to extraterrestrial property by its nationals is national appropriation "by any other means," no matter what euphemistic label is employed to mask the obvious. Recognition of claims, however, is only one side of the coin. The other side is the exclusion or rejection of any competing or conflicting claims. The application of this *de facto* exclusion of other states and their nationals by its very nature would constitute a form of national appropriation.[29] Prof. Christol observes that the *res communis* nature of outer space, including the Moon and other celestial bodies, "denies parties the right to establish exclusive rights, including exclusive property rights, in the space environment."[30]

The final line of argument by the opponents of the non-appropriation principle implicitly concedes that "private appropriation" is prohibited, and instead asserts that the policy of non-appropriation is wrong and should be renounced.[31] This may well be a case where they should be careful of what they wish for, as the abrogation of article II of the Outer Space Treaty would be counterproductive to the interests of space commercialization.[32]

The classic age of exploration was characterized by conquest. No specific, uniformly accepted means of acquiring new territories existed, but claims generally were based on discovery and physical presence. Notwithstanding the means of acquisition, however, claims were recognized and enforced on the basis of military power.[33] This historical process continued into the twentieth century, when the community of nations departed from past practice in Antarctica and in outer space. With regard to Antarctica, states had asserted conflicting and overlapping claims, but agreed to freeze such claims with the adoption of the Antarctic Treaty.[34] In outer space, the nations of the world went further and prohibited all claims of appropriation, whether by means of use, occupation, claim of sovereignty or otherwise. Sound policy considerations supported that decision.

When the Soviet Union successfully launched Sputnik I in 1957, the national and international security implications were formidable. The launch of an object into Earth orbit was a stunning demonstration of technology. Apart from whatever benefit that demonstration may have had for ideological or propaganda purposes, the technical capability of the Soviets provided a means to acquire tremendous economic and military advantage.

The Soviet Union achieved one "first" after another in the exploration of space, including the first impact by a probe on the lunar surface in 1959, and the first man in orbit. The international community could have followed the historical precedents of exploration and conquest, but that would have resulted in conceding vast reaches of outer space, including part or even all of the Moon, to the Soviet Union. Any areas of space and celestial bodies not claimed by the Soviet Union certainly would be claimed by one or more other states. Moreover, the claims which could be asserted by the U.S.S.R. would not necessarily be immune from conflicting and overlapping claims. The enforcement of these claims ultimately would depend on military means, and the risk of exporting armed conflict into space would be significant.

An alternative approach to this inevitable conflict between claims in space was available, that of recognizing the *res communis* nature of space, and prohibiting such claims *ab initio*.[35] None of the historical precedents of claiming new lands would be accepted or apply beyond the confines of this planet. The interests of promoting and maintaining international peace and security clearly would be served by the prevention of conflict over competing and conflicting claims to areas of outer space or celestial bodies. In addition, the prohibition of claims of appropriation would serve the interests of helping to assure the right of all states to access to, and the free exploration of, outer space, and to make possible uniform preservation and conservation of celestial environments.[36] This issue was resolved in 1961, by the adoption of the non-appropriation principle in General Assembly Resolution 1721.[37]

The adoption of the non-appropriation doctrine was based on sound fundamental principles. Yet the opponents of article II of the Outer Space Treaty urge that it be renounced and abrogated. However, abrogation of the prohibition against appropriation can be justified only where the original purposes of the doctrine cease to remain applicable.[38] While neglecting to provide an acceptable rationale or justification, the opponents of the doctrine implicitly infer that the absence of the non-appropriation doctrine would benefit space commercialization. But would it really, or is that yet another myth?

The adoption of the non-appropriation doctrine, whether by G.A. Resolution 1721, or by article II of the Outer Space Treaty, unlike the Antarctic Treaty, did not freeze any claims in space, as none had been seriously asserted to that time. Should there be a "space rush" commencing the moment the non-appropriation principle ceases to be applicable, with a clean slate of celestial treasures open and available to be grabbed by the quickest or the strongest? Alternatively, and as a matter of equity, should not all of the potential claims which could have been asserted prior to the entry into force of the Outer Space Treaty be considered to have been impliedly placed on hold, to be resurrected in the event the non-appropriation doctrine is abrogated?

The Russians, under this scenario, as successors in interest to the Soviet Union, would have the historic justification for claiming vast reaches of near-Earth space based on their undeniable first in time discoveries and/or explorations by robotic or human presence. Other nations will lay claim to additional space "properties." The United States could have claims to part or all of the Moon, especially to the areas in proximity to the Apollo landing sites, but also perhaps to robotic soft or crash landing sites. The claims would not be restricted to the Moon, but would extend to Mars, Venus, asteroids, and the outer planets and their moons, with claims based on thinner and thinner explorations, possibly consisting of nothing more than mathematical or theoretical extrapolation. The Bogota Declaration,[39] expressing claims to the geostationary orbit, could be expected to be re-asserted, but this time possibly accompanied by military enforcement measures.

It is clear that the absence of the non-appropriation doctrine would result in conflicting and overlapping claims. This state of affairs would give rise to international tensions and increase the potential for armed conflict. In addition, there would be nothing to prevent states claiming an area from imposing substantial taxes, royalties, duties, auction fees or other charges for the acquisition of rights by private entities to utilize such areas and the resources contained therein on the surface or subsurface, even where the claims thereto overlap.[40] The opponents of the non-appropriation doctrine have yet to articulate how the development of private enterprise in space would be served by the imposition of an economic tribute by various states and entities. If "private appropriation" were sanctioned, separate and apart from the claims of states, the situation would become even more murky and convoluted, and another layer of involuntary tribute potentially could be exacted from entrepreneurial ventures.

The international legal community must seek to achieve the maximum exploration and use of outer space by both the public and private sectors, while preventing the spread of armed conflict beyond this planet. It does not appear that the abandonment of the non-appropriation doctrine would serve that purpose. Indeed, the non-appropriation principle is a major reason why space has remained an arena of peaceful exploration and use. It is submitted that the maintenance of international peace and security, and the prevention of the spread of armed conflict into outer space, serves the interests of space commercialization more than would the abrogation of the non-appropriation doctrine.

Claim Jumping on Celestial Bodies

Pursuant to the requirements of article VI of the Outer Space Treaty for states to authorize and supervise the activities of their private entities in space, many states have adopted domestic licensing regimes.[41] The creation of domestic licensing and regulatory regimes by states constitutes a significant avenue of protection and predictability for private enterprise in space. A private entity which is granted a license to construct a facility and/or to extract and utilize extraterrestrial resources can operate with assurance that it will not have to fortify or otherwise plan and budget for defensive armaments *in situ* on celestial bodies.

Space activities inherently are difficult, risky and expensive. A facility on a celestial body is remote and not readily accessible by just anyone at just any time. In order to visit an installation on celestial body,[42] a mission would have to be planned consisting of a launch of a crewed vehicle; the crew would need to be selected and trained; and a specific mission objective defined, articulated and funded. While these simple facts seem obvious, they often are overlooked by those who advocate "private appropriation." There is one additional fact which also is overlooked: a private entity would need to obtain the authorization of its state of nationality to launch a mission to a facility on a celestial body.

A basic framework for the protection of the private sector in space is established by the following provisions of the *corpus juris spatialis*: first, the requirement of authorization and continuing supervision of private entities by the appropriate state; second, the obligation to prevent harmful interference with the activities of other states; and third, the duty to participate in consultations where such interference may occur. The claim of private ownership to an area of a celestial body is not necessary to protect against interference by other entities.

If the state which licensed the facility desired to interfere with the operations of the licensed entity, it is very unlikely that the state would seek to achieve that goal by launching a mission to overtake the facility by physical means. It would be much more efficient, productive and cost effective, from the perspective of the state, to revoke or restrict the license, or if necessary and appropriate, to utilize the domestic civil or criminal justice system. Under proper circumstances, a state could cancel assignments of frequencies, revoke authorizations, restrict communications, issue injunctions, attach property, or utilize a number of provisional or other remedies under domestic law

It also is unlikely that a licensee would be subject to interference by another entity granted authority to operate by the same state licensing regime. It is doubtful that a license application would be approved which expressed the clear intention to cause physical interference with the operations of a previously licensed facility. The state itself would object to such a purpose, which otherwise could constitute a violation of the peaceful purposes provisions of space law.[43] Moreover, the operator of the licensed facility, or members of the public, may have an opportunity to voice a formal objection to the second license application pursuant to domestic licensing or judicial procedures. Objections based on the potential for interference which would be caused by the second licensee would be well founded. Objections based on expressly stated intentions to cause such interference would be even more compelling.

It is possible, of course, that a second licensee could be granted a license to operate a facility near the vicinity of the first licensed facility, provided that no interference was caused thereby. If both licensees produced the same product or service utilizing extraterrestrial resources, there could be the potential for claims such as infringement of intellectual property rights, and unfair competition. But those types of claims are raised on a daily basis, and resolved on a daily basis, according to extant law. The validity or defense of these actions is wholly unrelated to a claim of ownership of areas of a celestial body.

A facility on a celestial body thus is protected from interference by both the state which licensed the facility, as well as the private entities subject to that same licensing regime. Accordingly, the only other source of terran interference is from other states or their nationals. The claim of private appropriation would not add a scintilla of credibility or substance to the rights of the licensed operator of the facility if a foreign state sought to interfere with the operations directly or through its private entities. The interference with the facility would exist independently of any claim of ownership, as a state which was intent on committing interference directly or through its private entities with a facility licensed by another state would do so in violation of the Outer Space Treaty,[44] and if applicable, the Moon Agreement.[45] Such a state would not be deterred by the assertion of a claim of private ownership of the location on the celestial body.

Whether or not a claim of private appropriation was permitted, the enforcement of the claim, and more importantly, the protection of the personnel of the facility, would occur primarily on Earth and not *in situ*. That is, short of military maneuvers on site at a facility on a celestial body, it can be expected that diplomatic or other mechanisms would be employed on Earth to seek to diffuse and resolve any dispute. Unless the interfering mission was planned in secrecy, consultations between the states would be sought in advance of the interference pursuant to article IX of the Outer Space Treaty. Moreover, if the interfering state refused to engage in the consultations, or if the interfering mission was planned in secrecy, the claim of private appropriation would be meaningless and not add any protection to the operator of the facility.

The *corpus juris spatialis* is maturing in accordance with the scientific and technical progress of human society.[46] Undoubtedly, the law will need to evolve and develop to accommodate the commercialization of space applications. Nevertheless, existing international space law, supplemented by domestic laws, provides a solid foundation for the growth of space commerce.[47] The concern has been expressed, however, that the "combinations of incongruous and contradictory results [of domestic regulation] may be very large."[48] A comprehensive international juridical regime may be preferable to a patchwork of independent and unreconciled national legislation.[49] Further, there may be certain issues which arise which are better suited to international resolution. Nevertheless, domestic legislation may be able to consider subjects not thoroughly covered by international law, and domestic authorities may be able to draft and implement legislation more rapidly than can their counterparts in international fora.[50]

If claims of private appropriation are ineffective, in contravention of the *corpus juris spatialis*, and contrary to the long term interests of space commercialization, than it must be asked what is the benefit of making such claims? There are two economic aspects which would be positively impacted by private appropriation of celestial bodies: the first is the increase in the net worth of the privateering company, artificially inflated by the optimistic valuation of the claimed space assets; and second is the pursuit of profit by the trade in "subsidiary rights" such as leasehold interests, mining rights, easements, and other traditionally alienable property rights. Neither of these economic considerations is directly related to the use of celestial resources, nor to the providing of a product or service uniquely available in the celestial environment. If the intent of the entrepreneur is to capitalize on these economic considerations, that intent should be clearly stated at the outset. Any other course would be disingenuous and deceptive.

The private ownership of unlimited rights to celestial property would add a significant element to the cost of conducting an entrepreneurial venture. That is, the ability of all states to explore and utilize areas on or below the surface of celestial bodies, as guaranteed by the *corpus juris spatialis*, no longer would be a right, but a commodity available only to the highest bidder. Monopolies and other anti-competitive practices would restrict rather than enhance space commercialization. These anti-competitive effects of private appropriation are exemplified by the activities of the Lunar Embassy itself:

> The cost for a piece of the moon has gone up astronomically. Before 2001, Hope sold 17,700-acre tracts for $16, the price he now charges for one acre.[51]

Thus, even while operating in a vacuum, the price structure of the Lunar Embassy has not been stable, but has been arbitrarily manipulated. One can only imagine the proliferation of anti-competitive practices if private appropriation were officially permitted.

CONCLUSION

The assertion that private entities are not subject to the non-appropriation principle, as expressed in article II of the Outer Space Treaty, is a myth, and lacks a cogent analytical foundation. Not only would so called private appropriation be in violation of the *corpus juris spatialis*, but the arguments which have been presented in opposition to article II lack either a legal justification, a factual predicate, or both. Moreover, the abrogation or renunciation of the non-appropriation principle would be antithetical to the interests of space commercialization. Conflicting, competing and overlapping claims would create international tensions, and potentially lead to armed conflict, both on and off this planet.

The extant law of outer space, both international and domestic, provides a basic framework for the development of regulation of space commerce. Domestic licensing regimes, together with international commitments regarding authorization and supervision of private entities in space, prevention of harmful interference, and participation in consultations concerning potentially harmful interference, grant a significant measure of protection for private ventures in space. Claims of fee simple ownership of space property are unnecessary and ineffective to protect private interests from interference. Those who advocate the renunciation and abandonment of the non-appropriation principle are either seeking to increase their own bottom line by disingenuous and deceptive constructs, or lack an appropriate appreciation and respect for international processes. Perhaps most significant in this regard is the tangible benefit the *corpus juris spatialis* has made in maintaining outer space exclusively for peaceful purposes.

Endnotes

1. *The Arizona Republic*, § D, at 1, January 21, 2002.

2. Sterns, Stine & Tennen, *Preliminary Jurisprudential Observations Concerning Property Rights on the Moon and Other Celestial Bodies in the Commercial Space Age*, in PROCEEDINGS OF THE 39TH COLLOQUIUM ON THE LAW OF OUTER SPACE 50, 51 (1997).

3. Sterns & Tennen, *Institutional Approaches to Managing Space Resources*, in PROCEEDINGS OF THE 41ST COLLOQUIUM ON THE LAW OF OUTER SPACE 33 (1999).

4. Clayton-Townsend, *Property Rights and Future Space Commercialization*, in PROCEEDINGS OF THE 42ND COLLOQUIUM ON THE LAW OF OUTER SPACE 159, 166 (2000); de Seife, *Star Wars or Star Peace: The Impact of International Treaties on the Commercial Uses of Space*, in 1 AMERICAN ENTERPRISE, THE LAW AND THE COMMERCIAL USES OF SPACE 73, 97 (1986); Sterns & Tennen, *supra* note 3, at 36.

5. *But see* Golrunia & Bahrami, *Outer Space Treaty in 21st Century: A Change of Concept*, in PROCEEDINGS OF THE 40TH COLLOQUIUM ON THE LAW OF OUTER SPACE 303, 307 (1998).

6. Treaty on Principles Governing the Activities of States in the Exploration and Use of Outer Space, Including the Moon and Other Celestial Bodies, *opened for signature* January 27, 1967, art. VI, 18 U.S.T. 2410, T.I.A.S. No. 6347, 610 U.N.T.S. 205, *text reproduced in* UNITED NATIONS TREATIES AND PRINCIPLES ON OUTER SPACE 3 (2000) [hereinafter referred to as the "Outer Space Treaty"].

7. Agreement Governing the Activities of States on the Moon and Other Celestial Bodies, *entered into force* July 11, 1984, art. 11, 1363 U.N.T.S. 3, *text reproduced in* UNITED NATIONS TREATIES AND PRINCIPLES ON OUTER SPACE 27 (2000), *and* 18 I.L.M. 1434 (1979) [hereinafter referred to as the "Moon Agreement"].

8. *Id.* at art. 11, ¶ 5.

9. Sterns & Tennen, *supra* note 3, at 35, n. 11 (*citing* statement of Mrs. Galloway).

10. See text & notes 31-40, *infra*.

11. Gal, *Acquisition of Property in the Legal Regime of Celestial Bodies*, in PROCEEDINGS OF THE 39TH COLLOQUIUM ON THE LAW OF OUTER SPACE 45 (1997).

12. *See* Christol, *The Natural Resources of the Moon: The Management Issue* in PROCEEDINGS OF THE 41ST COLLOQUIUM ON THE LAW OF OUTER SPACE 3 (1999).

13. *See, e.g.,* 43 U.S.C.A. §§ 315 (grazing); 1181a (timber); 1331 (oil); *see also* Christol, *supra* note 12, at 5 (observing that parties have sold or leased portions of the International Telecommunications Union allotments to third parties, without claiming ownership thereof in light of article 33 of the ITU Convention, which grants only the right to use an orbital position or frequency allocation for a limited period of time).

14. *See* Summary of Discussion, in PROCEEDINGS OF THE 41ST COLLOQUIUM ON THE LAW OF OUTER SPACE 289, 290 (1999) (statement of Dr. Jasentuliyana); see also text & note 51, *infra*.

15. *The Arizona Republic*, *supra* note 1, § D, at 1.

16. Moon Agreement, *supra* note 7, at art. 11, ¶ 3.

17. In an apparent concession that his "registration of claim" is legally insufficient, Hope has solicited from his purchasers affidavits of ownership, on cigarette papers, with the intention to send the affidavits to the Moon and thereby attempt to establish a physical presence on the lunar surface. *See* Pop, *The Men Who Sold the Moon: Science Fiction or Legal Nonsense*, 17 SPACE POLICY 195, 198 (2001).

18. *Id.* at 200.

19. Benson, *Space Resources: First Come First Served,* in PROCEEDINGS OF THE 41ST COLLOQUIUM ON THE LAW OF OUTER SPACE 46, 48 (1999).

20. Dasch, Smith & Pierce, *Conference on Space Property Rights: Next Steps,* in PROCEEDINGS OF THE 42ND COLLOQUIUM ON THE LAW OF OUTER SPACE 174 (2000).

21. International Co-operation in the Peaceful Uses of Outer Space, G.A. Res. 1721(XVI)A, U.N. Doc. A/4987, at ¶ 1(b) (December 20, 1961).

22. *See generally* A. HALEY, SPACE LAW AND GOVERNMENT 123-24 (1963).

23. Draft Treaty Governing the Exploration of the Moon and Other Celestial Bodies, at 4, U.N. Doc. A/AC.105/32 (June 17, 1966).

24. Draft Treaty on Principles Governing the Activities of States in the Exploration and Use of Outer Space, the Moon and Other Celestial Bodies, *text reprinted in* Report, Committee on the Peaceful Uses of Outer Space, at Annex I, U.N. Doc. A/AC.105/35 (September 16, 1966).

25. Outer Space Treaty, *supra* note 6, at art. IX.

26. *See* C.W. JENKS, SPACE LAW 201 (1965); van Traa-Engelman, *Clearness Regarding Property Rights on the Moon and Other Celestial Bodies,* in PROCEEDINGS OF THE 39TH COLLOQUIUM ON THE LAW OF OUTER SPACE 38, 42 (1997); Sterns, Stine & Tennen, *supra* note 2, at 54.

27. Treaty Banning Nuclear Weapons Tests on the Surface of the Earth, in the Atmosphere, or in Outer Space, *entered into force* October 10, 1963, 14 U.S.T. 1313, T.I.A.S. No. 5433, 480 U.N.T.S. 43.

28. Dasch, Smith & Pierce, *supra* note 20, at 178.

29. Pop, *Appropriation in Outer Space, The Relationship Between Land Ownership and Sovereignty on the Celestial Bodies*, 16 SPACE POLICY 275, 278 (2000); Reif, *Project 2001: Conclusions and Recommendations of the Working Group on Privatization*, in PROCEEDINGS OF THE 44TH COLLOQUIUM ON THE LAW OF OUTER SPACE 3, 8 (2002).

30. Christol, *supra* note 12, at 4.

31. Benson, *supra* note 19.

32. *See* Lee, *Creating an International Regime for Property Rights Under the Moon Agreement,*

in PROCEEDINGS OF THE 42ND COLLOQUIUM ON THE LAW OF OUTER SPACE 409, 415 (2000); Sterns, Stine & Tennen, *supra* note 2, at 54.

33. *See generally* Haley, *supra* note 22, at 118-23.

34. Antarctic Treaty, *opened for signature* December 1, 1959, 12 U.S.T. 794, T.I.A.S. No. 4780, 420 U.N.T.S. 71.

35. See *generally* Gorove, *On the Threshold of Space: Toward a Cosmic Law. Problems of the Upward Extent of Sovereignty*, in PROCEEDINGS OF THE 1ST COLLOQUIUM ON THE LAW OF OUTER SPACE 69 (1959); Haley, *Space Age Presents Immediate Legal Problems*, in PROCEEDINGS OF THE 1ST COLLOQUIUM ON THE LAW OF OUTER SPACE 3 (1959); Hyman, *Sovereignty over Space* in PROCEEDINGS OF THE 3RD COLLOQUIUM ON THE LAW OF OUTER SPACE 26 (1961); Fasan, *Contribution*, in PROCEEDINGS OF THE 3RD COLLOQUIUM ON THE LAW OF OUTER SPACE 18 (1961).

36. Lee, *supra* note 32, at 413.

37. See text & note 21, *supra*.

38. Sterns, Stine & Tennen, *supra* note 2, at 53.

39. Declaration of the First Meeting of Equatorial Countries, Bogota, Columbia, December 3, 1976, *text reproduced in* N. JASENTULIYANA & R.S.K. LEE, II MANUAL ON SPACE LAW 383 (1979).

40. *See* Sterns & Tennen, *supra* note 3, at text & notes 43-46.

41. *See generally* F.G. VON DER DUNK, PRIVATE ENTERPRISE AND PUBLIC INTEREST IN THE EUROPEAN 'SPACESCAPE' (1998).

42. *See* Outer Space Treaty, *supra* note 6, at art. XII; Moon Agreement, *supra* note 7, at art. 15.

43. *See* Outer Space Treaty, *supra* note 6, at art. IV; Moon Agreement, *supra* note 7, at art. 3, ¶ 1.

44. Outer Space Treaty, *supra* note 6, at art. IX.

45. Moon Agreement, *supra* note 7, at arts. 8, ¶ 3; 15.

46. Kopal, *What Kind of Institutional Arrangements for Managing Space Mineral Resource Activities Should be Done in a Foreseeable Future*, in PROCEEDINGS OF THE 41ST COLLOQUIUM ON THE LAW OF OUTER SPACE 12, 15 (1999).

47. *See* Kopal, *Outer Space as a Global Common*, in PROCEEDINGS OF THE 40TH COLLOQUIUM ON THE LAW OF OUTER SPACE 108 (1998); Kolosov, *Commentary Paper, Existing U.N. Treaties: Strengths and Needs*, in PROCEEDINGS OF THE WORKSHOP ON SPACE LAW IN THE 21ST CENTURY (Unispace III) 30, 31 (2000); American Astronautical Society, FINAL REPORT, WORKSHOP ON INTERNATIONAL LEGAL REGIMES GOVERNING SPACE ACTIVITIES 1 (2001).

48. O'Donnell, *Benefit Sharing: The Municipal Model*, in PROCEEDINGS OF THE 39TH COLLOQUIUM ON THE LAW OF OUTER SPACE 151, 153 (1997); *see also* von der Dunk, *The Dark Side of the Moon - The Status of the Moon: Public Concepts and Private Enterprise*, in PROCEEDINGS OF THE 40TH COLLOQUIUM ON THE LAW OF OUTER SPACE 119, 122A (1998) (arguing that national legislation can apply only to space objects).

49. von der Dunk, *supra* note 48, at 120.

50. *Id.*

51. *The Arizona Republic*, *supra* note 1, § D, at 2.

This paper is dedicated in memory of my mother, Elsie Tennen. LIT and PMS

Session 2: THE INTERNATIONAL SPACE STATION AND THE LAW

Chairmen: A. Farand, France, and J. MacClure, USA

Rapporteur: K. Weidaw, USA

IAC-02-IISL.2.02

IMPLEMENTATION OF INTELLECTUAL PROPERTY LAW ON THE INTERNATIONAL SPACE STATION

John G. Mannix
Associate General Counsel
For Intellectual Property Law
National Aeronautics and Space Administration
Washington, DC

Introduction

Historically, NASA has led the United States into many great new frontiers in space and technology. One such venture is underway with the building of the International Space Station (ISS). A few months ago, I had the opportunity to see the IMAX movie entitled "Space Station 3D." It provides a clear, up close view of the incredible beauty, complexity and sophistication of the ISS. It included a number of scenes documenting the astronauts and cosmonauts working inside and outside the ISS, which helped me to appreciate the difficult tasks that they perform on a daily basis. The ISS is truly a marvel of innovation, vision and international collaboration. As NASA's predecessor, the National Advisory Committee for Aeronautics (NACA) provided early leadership in aeronautics and provided the initial investment into what we now know as the commercial airline industry, we envision a similar development of commercial enterprise in space through the establishment of the ISS.

In the Commercial Space Act of 1998, the Congress of the United States declared that a "priority goal of constructing the International Space Station is the economic development of Earth orbital space". NASA's response to congressional declarations promoting free enterprise and U.S. economic development based on the International Space Station (ISS) can be found in NASA's Commercial Development Plan for the International Space Station. In this implementation plan, NASA set forth its short-term goal to "begin the transition to private investment and offset a share of the public cost for operating the Space Shuttle and Space Station...." NASA's long-term goal as set forth in the plan is to "establish the foundation for a marketplace and stimulate a national economy for space products and services in low-Earth orbit...." As Ralph Waldo Emerson said, "The future belongs to those who prepare for it." In the past few years, NASA has proceeded with implementation of the initiatives which were set forth in this plan and received multiple commercial offers from industry. Our primary emphasis during this time has been to establish an efficient, "business-friendly" operation for entering into agreements with industry for ISS economic development opportunities.

Innovation and Economic Development

One of the primary methods by which the ISS will create new economic value is through the creation of intellectual property and capitalization of business enterprises involved in licensing new innovations and inventions and developing new commercial products and services. The space environment provides opportunities for research and development that are unmatched anywhere else. The micro-gravity and ultra-vacuum environments of space provide unique opportunities for advancing our understanding of physical and molecular dynamics. Commercial opportunities exist in using the Space Station for research and development, for operation and servicing of the ISS infrastructure, and for development of new capabilities to augment the ISS. Media services and sponsorships may also be near-term commercial opportunities. Industry's involvement in the economic development of the ISS has been part of NASA's vision since the space station was conceived. Protection and ownership of intellectual property are critical to the success of most businesses, especially for those involved in research and development efforts through collaborative business relationships. In speaking with potential commercial users of the ISS, one area of strong interest was how their existing intellectual property was going to be protected and how new innovations and inventions were going to be treated in the international environment of the ISS. In response to this interest, my office prepared a reference guide entitled, "Intellectual Property and the International Space Station: Creation, Use, Transfer, Ownership and Protection" which synopsizes and analyzes the intellectual property provisions in international agreements and U.S. laws that are applicable to the ISS program. The guide details the intellectual property provisions and explains how proprietary data and goods will be exchanged and protected on the way to, from and on the ISS. It is available on the NASA website at http://www.hq.nasa.gov/ogc/iss/main.html. Today, I will provide an overview of the system of agreements, regulations and provisions that set forth the terms and parameters for the treatment of intellectual property and how proprietary data and goods will be exchanged and protected in the ISS environment. I believe these will be of interest to those preparing to invest themselves and their organizations in the utilization of one of the most innovative and exciting facilities of our time.

Framework for Intellectual Property Rights

The five partners who have joined together for the development, operation and utilization of the International Space Station are Canada, Europe, Japan, Russia and the United States. These partners are joined in agreement through the Inter-Governmental Agreement (IGA). In addition to the extensive provisions and procedures within this agreement, NASA has a separate

Memorandum of Understanding (MOU) with each of the partners. The MOUs contain more specific provisions, but do not conflict with the terms set forth in the IGA. In total, these agreements place a premium on proprietary or commercially sensitive information exchanged during the development, operation and utilization of the ISS and establish strict procedures for protecting it.

An International Space Station in which each partner is isolated in its own module and has total control over its own equipment and experiments would be simple from the perspective of intellectual property rights. But that is not the situation on the International Space Station. For one thing, the International Space Station agreements provide for extensive access by the United States to the European and Japanese research elements. Moreover, the partners have the right to barter or sell any portion of their respective allocations to each other or to third parties. Thus, a U.S. based commercial experiment may be performed in or on a Japanese element. The IGA and MOUs attempt to address all the issues that could arise from such arrangements. Naturally though, it is impossible to write a document that can address every possible contingency that may occur in the future.

Limitations on Use and Disclosure of Data

Through the IGA and MOU, each Partner has agreed that they shall respect the proprietary rights in and the confidentially of properly identified and appropriately marked data and goods. Each Partner agrees to protect the marked proprietary data in accordance with the markings. A corollary principle, however, is that third party proprietary data which may be required in order for Partners to carry out their responsibilities with respect to developing, operating and utilizing the ISS will be kept to a minimum. In order to accomplish this goal, the Partners agreed in the IGA to the following provisions:

- Each partner shall respect the confidentiality of appropriately marked data and goods transported on its space transportation system and passing through its communication systems.

- Each partner shall transfer all technical data and goods considered to be necessary by both parties to fulfill the responsibilities of the other partner under the relevant MOUs and implementing arrangements.

- The transfer of technical data for the purposes of discharging the partners' responsibilities with regard to interface, integration and safety shall normally be made without restrictions. If detailed design, manufacturing, and processing data and associated software is necessary for interface, integration of safety purposes the transfer shall be made, but the data and associated software may be appropriately marked.

- Each partner shall take all necessary steps to ensure that the receiving partner and any other persons and entities including contractors and subcontractors shall treat technical data and goods received by it in accordance with all markings.

Each Partner has the explicit responsibility to ensure that its crewmembers comply with a Code of Conduct that has been developed and approved. The ISS Crew Code of Conduct is an enforceable obligation between the respective Partners and their crew members and provides that information obtained by a crew member in the course of performing his or her duties that is proprietary, confidential, or otherwise not generally available shall only be used for official purposes and shall not be used to further private interests. The IGA further stipulates that the withdrawal by a Partner from the ISS partnership shall not affect rights and obligations regarding the protection of technical data and goods, which were transferred under the Agreement.

In addition to our ISS Partners, U.S. civil service employees and U.S. Government contractors may come into contact with commercial data. As an employee of the Federal Government, a civil servant bears the responsibility for proper protection of proprietary data. Failure to take the proper level of protection may subject the employee to criminal penalty. Often working closely with civil servants, Government contractors are involved to some degree in almost all design, development and operational aspects of the U. S. space program, which specifically includes the ISS and the Shuttle programs.
One of the key factors for achieving proper treatment of proprietary or confidential data is that it be properly marked so those that come into contact with data are aware of its nature and the restrictions applied to the treatment of it. Within U.S. Government contracts, the Federal Acquisition Regulation (FAR) clause, 52.227-14, Rights in Data – General, addresses the rights to and protection of data. In general, all NASA contractors agree that to the extent they receive or are given access to data that contains restrictive markings, the contractor will treat the data in accordance with the markings.

Principles of Inventorship on the ISS

I have addressed the safeguards that the Partners have instituted in order to protect the existing intellectual property of commercial users of the ISS. Now, I would like to address the way in which new innovations and inventions emanating from research on the ISS will be treated in the international environment of the ISS.
With respect to patentable inventions the IGA and MOUs set out a framework for cooperation. For example:

- Article 21 of the IGA states that for purposes of intellectual property law, an activity occurring in or on a Space Station flight element shall be deemed to have occurred only in the territory of the Partner State of that element's registry. Thus, an invention made on a U.S. element will be deemed to have occurred in the United States and the entire U.S. Patent Law would apply.

- This is consistent with Article VIII of the Outer Space Treaty of 1967, which states that a party on whose registry an object is launched shall retain jurisdiction and control over that object and over personnel thereof. It also states that launching an object into space does not affect the objects ownership. Each element of the Space Station is clearly an object over which a particular partner state has retained jurisdiction and control. In addition to jurisdiction for criminal activities or personal damages, a state can also extend its intellectual property laws to territories under its jurisdiction. The U.S. statute, 35 U.S.C. § 105, codifies this understanding by stating that "any invention made, used or sold in outer space on a space object or component thereof under the jurisdiction or control of the United States shall be considered to be made, used or sold within the United States for the purposes of this title." By the way, this also follows the analogy used under maritime law for ships at sea. If the International Space Station is going to become a research laboratory for commercial experiments, private entities will want an established body of law upon which to make business decisions. They will not risk millions of dollars without a clear understanding of their legal rights to technical data and innovations emanating from their investment. We have sought to provide this certainty for both the Space Shuttle as well as the territorial elements of the International Space Station. As a practical matter, what makes the situation on the ISS interesting is the close proximity of each Partners' laboratory. But, with the advent of collaboration by scientists over the Internet this is just a further extension of the issues that intellectual property attorneys deal with every day when they have clients involved in collaborative research with colleagues in different countries around the world. Luckily, there is consistency in one key aspect of the patent laws of all of the Partner countries. Each states that if an invention is made in their territory, a patent application must be filed in their patent office before filing in any other patent office, no matter what the nationality of the inventor.

- There are two concepts ingrained in the Space Station cooperation that may lead to interesting negotiations as we move toward more commercial opportunities. As you probably know, the Space Station crew will operate as one integrated team with one commander. The entire crew will operate under a single time line for performance of all operations and utilization activities. The integrated crew concept means that any crewmember, regardless of his or her nationality, could be assigned to perform any utilization activity. For example, a Canadian astronaut could be assigned to perform a U.S. based commercial experiment. If all of the legal requirements of inventorship are met for the territory in which the invention was made, the Canadian astronaut could become an inventor of an invention while working on the U.S. commercial experiment. The second complicating factor, which was mentioned earlier, is that the partners also have the right to barter or sell any portion of their respective allocations. Thus, a U.S. based commercial experiment may be performed in or on a Japanese element. If an invention were made during the course of the experiment, it would be deemed to have occurred in Japanese territory under Japanese patent laws.

- Therefore, we may have a Canadian inventor making an invention while working on a U.S. commercial experiment while operating in the Japanese module. Japanese patent law would apply and the Canadian astronaut would have certain rights based upon his or her invention. Of course, the ability of an astronaut to invent would depend upon the amount of freedom the astronaut has in performing or modifying the experiment. If the experiment is fully scripted so that every step is set forth by the owner of the experiment, then the astronaut performing the experiment would have no opportunity to conceive an invention. This has been our experience on the Space Shuttle where each step of the experiment is scripted in advance. To date, no U.S. astronaut has obtained a patent for an invention made while flying on the Space Shuttle.

- With respect to patent infringement, the temporary presence doctrine, as reflected in the Paris Convention, provides an exception to patent infringement for the use of various articles or parts of a ship or aircraft temporarily in the territory of another State. Article 21 of the IGA extends the doctrine to articles, including the components of an ISS flight element, which are temporarily present in the territory of a Partner while transiting between Earth and the ISS. Thus, operation of an article in the United States (including the period of operation for pre-flight check-out, awaiting launch, and return to Earth) intended for the ESA-registered element would not form the basis for an action for patent infringement during the article's transit through the United States.

Based on the above legal framework and the generally accepted principles of patent, copyright and trade secret laws in the partner states, we have negotiated a number of related ISS agreements with other space agencies and with commercial entities. The intellectual property provisions of the arrangements are unique to the particular activity, and while consistent with the IGA provisions, they necessarily contain carefully tailored data rights and patent rights clauses to best accomplish the mutual goals of the parties involved. Most of these relate to barter arrangements in which one Partner provides ISS equipment in exchange for research time and resources owned by another Partner or one Partner provides launch capability in exchange for equipment, software or services. Additional agreements have also been negotiated to coordinate the provision of international life science research hardware for the ISS so as to avoid equipment redundancy.

All of the above mentioned agreements are consistent with the intellectual property clauses outlined in the IGA, MOUs and implementing arrangements. But in all cases, there are also issues that arise that are not specifically addressed in these documents, for example the rights to the data and inventions resulting from the activity. In each case, unique intellectual property clauses, tailored to accomplish the mutual goals of the parties involved, have been created. These clauses have been negotiated based upon general principles of Intellectual Property Law, the contributions of the Parties and common sense. I have found that the basic legal framework for the ISS is a robust and effective set of principles that form a strong basis for negotiation. As time passes, there will be many more agreements and new issues which will evolve, but I believe that the basic legal framework that has been put in place will allow reasonable individuals to negotiate workable solutions to these issues.

As I stand here and try to predict how the legal documents related to the ISS will evolve and be handled, I am reminded of some others who have attempted to predict the future.

Thomas Watson, the chairman of IBM stated in 1943, " I think there is a world market for maybe five computers."

A senior engineer at IBM in 1968, commenting on the microchip, " But what is it good for?"

Ken Olson, chairman and founder of Digital Equipment Corp in 1977, " There is no reason anyone would want a computer in their home."

Western Union internal memo in 1876, " This telephone has too many shortcomings to be seriously considered as a means of communication. The device is inherently of no value to us."

Decca Recording Co, rejecting the Beatles in 1962, " We don't like their sound, and guitar music is on the way out."

Charles Duell, Commissioner of the US Patent Office in 1899, " Everything that can be invented has been invented."

It is interesting to note that before Orville Wright died in 1948, the first man to walk on the moon was already born. No one in the era of the Wright Brothers could possibly have conceived that we would not only fly, but also break the speed of sound and go off to the moon. We always have the tendency to overstate the short-term and underestimate the long term. There is no question in my mind that we will continue to underestimate what is in store for us in this new century. The ISS and other great endeavors will lead us into new technologies that we cannot even imagine at this time.

Thank you for your interest in the ISS.

APPLICATION OF THE RULES OF THE CODE OF CONDUCT TO THE FIRST CREWS ON BOARD THE INTERNATIONAL SPACE STATION

By

Prof. Gabriella Catalano Sgrosso*

University of Rome (Italy)

Abstract

More than three years after the launch of the first Russian module Zarya the International Space Station is now operational being made up of various pressurised modules, where the astronauts live and work during their stay on board, and of a space lab. The Station is also continuously served by the Russian and American shuttles for the transportation of the crews rotating on the Station, of multi-purpose logistic modules and for the transportation of goods and experiments and lately also of visiting astronauts.

The paper, without debating on the specific rules of the Code of conduct agreed upon by Partner States for the Station's crew, will focus on the aspects concerning its application and especially on the co-ordination between the Code and the internal systems of the Partner States. The paper will also consider the role of the Station Commander, the extension of his authority and the relationship with the Commander of the transport shuttles and with the Flight Director on Ground.

A special focus is placed on the questions concerning the jurisdiction and control over astronauts, from the Station and from transport shuttles, during the many activities outside the vehicle itself.

The increasing amount of visiting astronauts and especially of the "space tourist" has required the elaboration of specific rules which will be examined in this paper.

In conclusion, it is evident that in this initial application, especially for these new situations, the criterion based on citizenship, for the choice of the subject holding jurisdiction and control, is now losing effectiveness. The formulation of common rules, to which the State Partners must submit, or flight rules created for specific missions is the system mostly used also to solve problems concerning jurisdiction over the crew.

1. The Code of Conduct

On September 15 2000, the Multilateral Co-ordination Board (MCB)[i] representing the highest co-operation organ instituted by the Memoranda, approved the Code of conduct for the International Space Station Crew. It is a specific structure of rules of the Space Station programme agreed upon by all participating States in order to regulate the conduct of crew members.

The Code[ii] will "establish a clear chain of command on-orbit, clear relationship between ground and on-orbit management and management hierarchy, set forth standards for work and activities in space, and as appropriate, on the ground, establish responsibilities with respect to elements and equipment, set forth disciplinary regulations, establish physical and information security guidelines, and provide the Space Station

---

*Professor of International Law, Faculty of Economics, University of Rome, Italy; Director ISSL.

Commander appropriate authority and responsibility, on behalf of all the Partners, to enforce safety procedures and physical and information security procedures and crew rescue procedures for the Space Station"[iii].

The agencies are required not only to regulate the conduct of the astronauts according to their own specific personnel policies, in accordance with the IGA and the MOU, but also according to the rules of the Code which the astronauts are required to understand and accept. Crew members are required to conform to the dispositions indicated in the Code, the application of which is in force the moment they are assigned to a specific mission and until post-flight activities are completed. Since art. 5 of the IGA establishes that each State maintains jurisdiction and control over its personnel, it has been necessary to involve the States in the decision and internal application of the Code rules.

For European astronauts, being all members of the European Astronaut Corps (EAC), the mediation for the determination of the Code rules has been carried out by ESA in accordance with the decisional power forwarded by European States. After verifying the accordance of the Code rules with the local legal systems, each government of the European Partners wrote to the Director General of ESA authorising acceptance, that is to say ratification of the Code itself. Subsequently the Director General addressed a directive to the EAC Partners inviting them to subscribe to the terms and conditions of the Code[iv].

In the United States, Japan, Russia and Canada the rules of the Code have become an integral part of the employment terms and conditions for astronauts, whether employment is carried out directly by national agencies or through governmental appointment[v].

Referring to a further detailed analysis on the status of the crew[vi] and on the contents of the Code of conduct, the paper intends to examine some specific aspects concerning the figure of the Commander and the new jurisdiction problems over staff arising during activities towards, on and outside the Station.

2. The Commander

One of the first questions considered on the appointment of the Commander is if the latter should be of a different nationality than Partner States. A disposition has been added to the Code according to which nothing should forbid the Multilateral Crew Operations Panel (MCOP) to appoint an individual of "any" Partner State for the position of Commander. This operation has a double advantage: on one hand it is the first written acknowledgement of the "rotation" principle for such role and on the other it states that no national of a non-Partner State may aspire to the role of Commander.

Section III of the Code of conduct considers in detail the authority if the Station Commander. This authority covers all orbiting elements and all elements which will be added according to the development programme of the Station, it also covers all the personnel on the Station, all activities carried out in and on board the ISS, payload, crew, technical data and information relevant to the programme.

During the negotiation for the drafting of the Code, the possibility of the Commander's authority covering the payload was discussed. The question was solved positively by connecting the possibility of the Commander's intervention to the duty to protect the elements, payloads and Crew on the Station. In fact, the Commander has the authority to carry out any action considered necessary to respect his orders, including enforcement to be used only when immediate security is at risk and when all other systems have failed.

During flight the Commander is responsible for the success of the mission programme. He is authorised to change the crew's daily routine in order to adapt to any unforeseen events or urgent events associated to the crew's safety and to the protection of the Station's elements, and also to conduct critical flight situations. Among other duties, he directs crew activities in accordance with flight regulations, mission plans and consolidated or programmed procedures and under the direction of the Flight Director on

ground, to whose authority the Commander must submit. The Commander must supply the Flight Director with accurate and immediate information on the operational and structural status of the Station, including emergency situations.
The flight regulations indicate specific roles and responsibilities for the Commander and the Flight Director. Furthermore, they also refer decisions planned before the mission and they are intended to reduce the amount of explanations during missions[vii].

3. Extravehicular activity
During the first assemblage period of the Space Station many extravehicular activities have been carried out[viii] in order to manually operate on the external structure of the Station or for the docking of the transport shuttles or the installation of logistic modules for the loading and unloading of goods to and from the Station or for necessary maintenance[ix].
The Liability Convention on damage occurring in Outer Space only refers to the loss of human life or damage to people on board space objects, no mention is made about incidents that may occur during one of the many extravehicular activities. In the event of an astronaut's collision during an EVA mission with a space object registered by another State or in the event of his space-suit bring torn by space debris, according to the Convention this would be a case of collision between space objects. Even the space-suit, necessary for survival in outer space, could be considered a space object within a wider concept referring to any object capable of "assuring human conditions of life or allowing the transit of persons throughout outer space or celestial bodies"[x].
The new question is that of identifying the subject holding jurisdiction over astronauts outside the Space Station and out of the transport vehicle, who could be considered responsible for his activity.
The Outer Space Treaty (art. VIII) links the registration of the space object to the jurisdiction, therefore the launching State "shall retain jurisdiction and control over such subject and over any personnel thereof". The IGA (art. 5.2) joins the quasi-territorial jurisdiction of each Partner State over its own flight elements with personnel jurisdiction on its nationals ("..each Partner shall retain jurisdiction and control over the elements it registers in accordance with paragraph 1 above and over personnel in or on the Space Station who are its nationals). Therefore, jurisdiction is mentioned "in or on the Space Station" and it does not extend out of the physical limits represented by the structure of the Space Station.
The Russian Federation issued a national legislation disposition[xi] solving the question. According to this law the Russian Federation shall retain jurisdiction and control over any crew of a manned space object registered in it. Jurisdiction and control cover all flight stages, from ground activities to return to earth, including extra-vehicular activities during the stay in outer space.
During this first stage of assemblage of the Station American and Russian transport systems have been used, and as soon as they are available other systems of space transportation shall be used. Art. 12 of the IGA concerning transport states that "access and launch and return transportation services shall be in accordance with the previsions of the relevant MOUs and implementing agreements". Initially this meant that the launching State of the transportation vehicle extended its jurisdiction over all the activities concerning the transportation vehicle and planned missions, therefore also extravehicular activities irrespective of astronauts' nationality. If extravehicular activities are linked to the docking to the Station, the Station Commander must co-operate with the transportation vehicle crew acting as shuttle between Earth and Station, in order to ensure the success of operations. The necessary co-operative spirit for the success of the enterprise required Partner States to draw up agreements for each single mission. The Commander's authority, covering all crew members on the ISS, also extends to activities carried out in and on the Station, but the relationship between the Station Commander and the ETOV Commander and their respective authorities are specified by Partners in the flight rules[xii].

In space law, the term "jurisdiction" is always linked to the term "control" referring to aspects of the jurisdiction carried out by the Command Centre on Earth managing the movements of the space object, the normal development of the mission and crew activities[xiii]. The Flight Director on Ground directs the mission and the Commander of the ISS directs operations in orbit, therefore including extra-vehicular activities, under the authority of the Flight Director and in accordance with the flight rules[xiv].

In conclusion, jurisdiction and control over astronauts in extravehicular activity is mainly exercised by the State of the Space object they come from, but during a co-operational programme such as the International Space Station, specific rules will be dictated by actuation agreements and flight rules between Partners.

4. Space tourism

The first specifically tourist journey into space, to the International Space Station, was made on April 30th 2001 by an American industrialist, Dennis Tito, on board the Russian shuttle Soyuz. Mr Tito stipulated a contract with the Russian Space Agency for the amount of approximately 20 million dollars.

The Russian Space Agency's request to allow Mr Tito's access was initially refused because there didn't seem to be enough time for minimum training and NASA feared that the presence on board of an inadequately trained person might interfere with the crew's activity and routine.

Considering the persistent requests from the Russian Agency, the Multilateral Co-ordination Board (MCB)[xv] after having consulted with the Multilateral Crew Operations Panel (MCOP) agreed to the exception unanimously but with some limitations. Therefore, the Russian Agency and the American industrialist agreed to specific behaviour regulations, already foreseen in the flight rules, in the Code of Conduct and in the liability regulations, requiring an intensive training on safety on board and a limited access for the tourist to non-Russian elements of the Station. NASA required the Russian Agency to be liable for any damage that might have occurred to the elements and crews of other Partner States due to the presence on board of the visitor[xvi]. With a policy stipulated with the Aviakos insurance company for one-hundred thousand dollars, the Russian Agency covered liability for eventual damage caused by Mr Tito's presence.

NASA also believed that the normal work routine of the mission should be modified, keeping only fundamental activities for the health and safety of the crew and for ordinary maintenance, in order to guarantee the operational efficiency of the Station and its payload.

On such occasion, the MCB deliberated that Partner States should commit to not suggesting further flights for non-professional subjects until the criteria for selecting crew members were definite and adopted by all Partners[xvii].

The final decision on the matter was made after months of negotiations, during which the MCB agreed to a common regulation applicable to the commercial branch of space tourism. [xviii]: "The rules of road for travellers to the International Space Station". These new criteria are to be applied to all crew members of the Space Station, to professional astronauts and to other participating members such as scientist, tourists, academics and astronauts of non Partner States. The participating crew will not be obliged to perform the intensive training established for professional astronauts of other Partner States, but their freedom of movement and stay on board shall be limited.

The new policy for the selection of the space tourist stresses the necessity to reassure other Partner States on the trustworthiness of the person on board the Station. The so-called "taxi" flights transporting visitors to the Station shall respect previously planned flight priorities. Co-ordination and management of the visitor is totally up to the requesting Partner.

The visitor shall access the space structure by being transported by the vehicle of the Agency with which commercial agreements have been made. Physical requirements for admittance to a space flight are similar to those made for professional astronauts. Abuse of alcohol and drugs, and also criminal records or belonging to organisations unbecoming to the Station's programme are enough to exclude any possibility of taking part in a space flight.

Appointment of participants must be notified at least six months before the planned flight date. The MCOP shall accept the appointment and appeal may be forwarded to the MCB for any eventual refusal.

Two categories of visitors have been established: short term visitors, appointed by the Space Agencies and destined to activities on board the Station such as the conduction of scientific experiments, and visiting crew members such as journalists, tourists, etc.[xix]. The latter shall be trained with the members of the official hosting crew. Short term visitors shall also attend a further week's training at NASA Johnson Space Centre if they are flying on board the shuttle or at RKA Star City if they are flying with the Russian Agency. Visitors must have a good knowledge of Russian language if they are travelling with the RKA or of English if they are travelling with NASA.

Other questions, such as further studies on the problem of liability for eventual damage during a space tourism flight, or details concerning medical requirements and training are being examined by the competent discussion panels.

Commercial exploitation of the Station is now within the space policies of all Partner States and many consider that space tourism might be one of the most important areas for space development[xx]. Requests for space travel and visits to the Station are increasing and a second paying tourist, Southafrican Mark Shulleworth, was taken to the Station on April 25th 2002 by the Russian Agency on board the Soyuz. The southafrican millionaire paid the same amount as Mr Tito but he took a more active part in the space flight. He accepted the previously agreed rules of road and was therefore allowed to move freely on the Station, whereas Mr Tito was only allowed to stay in the Russian module, and also carried out some experiments on genetic engineering.

At present the only possibility is offered by the Russian Agency, because the United States are still considering whether to sustain the development of this commercial branch. The 1996 National Space Policy includes various provisions for the promotion of commercial space activity. There is a general encouragement to introduce this sector of space tourism in the National Space Policy with special attention to the safety of tourists and to the economic activity of carriers offering the service[xxi]. The organisations managing support and regulation of commercial launch activities in the United States could also be appointed the supervision of space tourism [xxii].

5. Conclusions

The Intergovernmental Agreement and the memoranda of Understanding have been established during a phase of the Station programme when Partner States were concentrating on the various aspects to be included within the development of the programme itself. The dispositions on the various stages of development are detailed and clear, whereas those directly linked to usage operations are more vague and therefore require a greater interpretation effort in the event of application to concrete events.

The will to establish a common legal regime on specific questions, as it also happened for the crew Code of conduct, seems to be the direction suggested by doctrine and practice of Partner States for future developments of the legal framework of co-operation for the Station. The Code, to be known, approved and observed by each astronaut in contact with the Station, determines common behaviour rules, the extension of the Commander's authority, hierarchical relationship in orbit and with those responsible for the mission on ground. In actual fact, as an initial application, such rules have been respected.

However, some questions on jurisdiction and control arose in the event of unusual situations, such as when the Station or vehicle's astronauts were engaged in extravehicular activities or in the case of visiting-astronauts.

The novelty of the introduction of the concept of nationality, concerning jurisdiction over the crew, added to the concept of territoriality, according to the IGA rules, appears to be somewhat outdated and no longer justified in these new situations. The 1967 Outer Space Treaty could only have foreseen the existence of single objects, built and registered by a single country. The subsequent existence of an International Space Station in which many countries co-operate and supply personnel, has required the extension of the jurisdiction of the State over its personnel even when it is within a module belonging to another Partner. Hence the link of jurisdiction over the crew to the nationality of each individual and not only to his presence within a specific space object.
However, when crew members of the transport vehicle or members of the Station carry out extravehicular activities, in the event of maintenance or connections, it seems that application of jurisdiction – in some Partner States practice and legislation – is the same of the country the transport vehicle or Station module from where the EVA astronauts come from. Considering the co-operative nature of the programmes to be carried out, there is a need for rules established by parties taking form of "actuation agreements" or "flight rules", such as established by the Code of Conduct, laying down competencies, sphere of command and relationship with the Ground Directors.
Broadening commercial exploitation of the Station to space tourism has led to the presence of visiting-astronauts. For the latter, who are at times not nationals of any Partner State, the concept of nationality for jurisdiction would not be suitable. In this case, specific "rules of road" to be respected have been established.
Finally, the Intergovernmental Agreement is a structure of rules which can be considered as a framing law, since it considers more or less specific details for general questions, while referring more specific questions, such as crew management, to regulating documents on the matter specifically established for the Station.

NOTES

[i]The *Multilateral Coordination Board (MCB)* is made up of members from the Space Agencies of Partner States. The American Agency presides over the board and decisions are taken by common consent. Should the consent not be reached within the established terms, the President is authorised to make the necessary decisions. The Board is responsible for the coordination of the utilization activities of the Space Station, including support services such as transport and communication (art. 8, commas 1.b and 1.c, MOU 1998)

[ii] Code of Conduct for the International Space Station Crew, Doc. ESA7C(2000)14 ANNEX

[iii] Art. 11.8 MOU 1998

[iv] In accordance with the regulations adopted for creating the staff of European astronauts. LAFFERANDERIE, The European Space Agency and the Astronaut's Policy, *Proc. of the 41st Colloquium on the Law of Outer Space, IISL, Melbourne 1998, p. 356;* FARAND, The Code of Conduct for the International Space Station Crews, *ESA Bulletin 105 (February 2000), p. 64*

[v] FARAND, The Code of Conduct for the International Space Station Crew, cit. p.67

[vi] CATALANO SGROSSO, Legal Status, Rights and Obligations of the Crew in Space, *Journal of Space Law*, 1998, vol. 26, n. 2, p. 163 and IDEM, Legal Status of the Crew in the International Space Station, *Proc. of the 42nd Colloquium on the Law of Outer Space, IISL, Amsterdam 1999, p.35*

[vii] Code of Conduct, III, C

[viii] For further details see NASA Human Space Flight website, *International Space Station EVA*, http://spaceflight.nasa.gov/station/eva/index.html

[ix] In june 2002 the space shuttle Endeavour took the crew "Expedition 5" to the Station, to replace the previous crew after six months stay. During their eight days docked to the Station, the shuttle astronauts took three space walks to install the logistic module Leonardo (MPLM) on the Station, to perform maintenance activities and to operate on a partially blocked robotic arm

[x] ESQUIVEL DE COCCA, International Liability for Damages Caused by Persons or Space Objects in Outer Space or on Celestial Bodies to Persons, Properties or Environment in Outer Space or Celestial Bodies, *Proc. of the 42nd Colloquium on the Law of Outer Space, IISL, Amsterdam 1999, p. 50*

[xi] Russian Federation on Space Activity 1993, art. 2 (cosmonauts and crews of piloted space objects):"The Russian Federation shall retain jurisdiction and control over any crew of a manned space object registered in it, during the ground time of such object, at any stage of a space flight or stay in outer space, on celestial bodies, *including extra-vehicular stay*, and return to Earth, right up to the completion of the flight program, unless otherwise specified in the international treaties of the Russian Federation". The English version may be found in *Project 2001 "Legal Framework for*

privatising Space Activities", 19 July 1999, Vienna, Institute of Air and Space Law of the University of Cologne

[xii] Code of Conduct, III, A, W, © and III, B 2

[xiii] see ZHUKOV, Registration and Jurisdiction Aspects of the International Space Station, in *Proc. of the 42nd Colloquium on the Law of Outer Space, IISL, Amsterdam 1999, p. 75*

[xiv] Code of Conduct, III, C "Relationship of the ISS Commander (On Orbit Management) and the Flight Director (Ground Management)"

[xv] The MCB must ensure the coordination of the Partners' activities concerning operation and use of the Station, Memorandum of Understanding, January 28th 1998, art. 8.1.b

[xvi] Official Document of the United States Subcommittee on Space and Aeronautics, on space tourism. June 26th 2001

[xvii] ESA-HUMAN SPACE FLIGHT, *International Space Station partners grant flight exemption for Dennis Tito,*
Internet:
http://www.es.int/export/esaHS/ESA5DOVRXLC_iss_2.html

[xviii] *"Rules of Road" for travellers to the International Space Station.* Document adopted by the MCB to support the development of the new branch of space tourism. See the article published on the MSNBC website.
http://www.msnbc.com/news/694231.asp?cp1=1#BODY, Jan 31st 2002

[xix] *Short-term visitors* are scientists, researchers and those subjects engaged in research activities. *Visiting crew members*: Simple visitors are paying individuals who wish to travel for journalistic or tourism reasons. In the "Marco Polo" mission which departed from Baikonur of April 25th 2002, there were three astronauts on the Russian "Soyuz" shuttle with different qualifications: the *Commander* of the Shuttle, Russian Iuri Ghidzenko, a *short term visitor*, Italian Roberto Vittori – who after having operated as a flight engineer in cooperation with the Soyuz Commander on the Soyuz itself, also conducted a series of experiments, on board the Station, sponsored by the Italian Space Agency within the agreement between ESA, the Russian Space Agency and RSC Energia-, and finally a *visiting crew member*, Southafrican Mark Shuttleworth, the second paying space tourist on the Station

[xx] DISCOVERY ON LINE, *Space Entrepreneurs, Space Tourist,*
Internet :
http://www.discovery.com/stories/science/entrepreneurs/tourist.html; for the increase of space tourism see TAKAYA-LEE, Space Tourism and Permanent Human Settlement: Legal and Regulatory Issues, *Proc. of the 43rd Colloquium on the Law of Outer Space, Rio de Janeiro 2000, p. 142*

[xxi] SCOTT, Policy/Legal Framework for Space Tourism regulation, *Journal of Space Law, 2000,* vol. 23, p.1

[xxii] Title 49, subtitle IX of the US Code designates the Secretary of Transportation (DOT) and his executive agent the Administrator of the Federal Aviation Administration (FAA) as the authorities controlling launch activities

Status of Multilateral Space Agreements in International and United States Law[1]

John B. Gantt, Mizrack & Gantt, Counsellors at Law, Washington D.C. USA
[jbgantt@attglobal.net]

I. INTRODUCTION:

This paper addresses the status in international law and United States law of the constitutive documents underlying the multi-lateral agreements for an International Space Station project. I do this by first describing the relevant international and domestic laws relating to treaties so that the reader understands the framework that determines the status of the ISS instruments, and then apply them to these instruments to determine their status both in international and U.S. law.

When one considers multilateral space treaties, one naturally starts with the five United Nations space treaties, beginning with the 1967 *Treaty on Principles Governing the Activities of States in the Exploration and Use of Outer Space, including the Moon and Other Celestial Bodies.*[i] These instruments all fit the definition of "treaty" as reflected in customary international law and codified in Article 2.1(a) of the Vienna Convention on the Law of Treaties[ii], the latter of which reads:

> 'treaty' means an international agreement concluded between States in written form and governed by international law, whether embodied in a single instrument or in two or more related instruments and whatever its particular designation.

However, there are numerous other international instruments between governments or agencies of governments, mostly bilateral, which pertain to activities in outer space. These range from bilateral memoranda of understanding for the joint development of spacecraft to bilateral agreements for the establishment and operation of space tracking stations.[iii] However, in light of the specific subject matter of this session, this paper is confined to considering the status in international and U.S. law of the multilateral instruments which serve as the constitutive documents pertaining to the development, establishment, operation and use of the International Space Station ("ISS"), in particular, the Intergovernmental Agreement ("IGA") signed January 29, 1998, among the 15 Partner States, and the bilateral Memoranda of Understanding ("MOUs") between the U.S. "Cooperating Agency" (the National Aeronautics and Space Administration ("NASA")) and the Cooperating Agencies of Canada, Europe and the Russian Federation, and the Government of Japan.

The 1998 IGA entered in force 27 March 2001 for Canada, Japan, the Russian Federation and the United States. Although it has not, as of October 2002, entered into force for the European Partner States[iv], their participation in the ISS program continues pursuant to the 1998 "Interim Arrangement" signed by the Partner

States at the time of signature of the IGA in 1998.[v]

In addition, there was an earlier, 1988, IGA[vi] concluded between all of the 1998 IGA Partner States, except for Russia, and which entered into force in 1992 for the United States and Japan. However, it has been replaced by the 1998 IGA, which provides, in Article 25.4, that upon its entry into force, the 1988 IGA shall cease to be in force.

II. FROM THE PERSPECTIVE OF INTERNATIONAL TREATY LAW:

As noted in the foregoing definition of "treaty" in the Vienna Convention, a treaty must be an agreement in writing and governed by international law. Furthermore, Article 2.2 of the Convention stipulates that the breadth of meaning given to the term "treaty" in the Convention is "without prejudice to the use of [the term] or to the meanings which may be given to [it] in the internal law of any State." This is important when considering the use of the term "treaty" in U.S. treaty law in view of the dichotomy in U.S. law between a "treaty" which under Article II of the U.S. Constitution is submitted to the Senate for its advice and consent prior to ratification ("Article II Treaty") and an "international agreement" which is not submitted to the Senate.

Article 5, extends the Convention to any treaty which is adopted within an international organization without prejudice to the any relevant rules of the organization.

Article 18 of the Convention imposes the obligation on a state that has signed a treaty or otherwise expressed its consent to be bound by the treaty pending its entry into force, "to refrain from acts which would defeat the object and purpose of the treaty", unless and until it communicates its intention not to become a party to the treaty.

Article 26 codifies the principle of *pacta sunt servanda* ("agreements must be kept") that every treaty in force "is binding upon the parties to it and must be performed by them in good faith."

Article 31 expresses the general rule of interpretation of treaties. Namely, they shall be interpreted

> "in good faith in accordance with the ordinary meaning to be given to the terms of the treaty in their context and in light of its object and purpose."

III. FROM THE PERSPECTIVE OF UNITED STATES TREATY LAW.

The status of "treaties" under United States law has its origin in Article VI, Sec. 2 of the Constitution:

> The Constitution, and the Laws of the United States which shall be made in Pursuance thereof; and all Treaties made, or which shall be made, under the Authority of the United States, shall be the supreme Law of the Land; and the Judges in every State shall be bound thereby, anything in the Constitution or Laws of any State to the Contrary notwithstanding.

Thus, "treaties" are of equal status with the Constitution (although they must be consistent therewith) and the laws of the United States. However, there are Article II Treaties and there are "other international agreements". Both may be treaties under international law but are treated differently under U.S. law.

In respect to treaty-based international law, the legal system of the United States is in some respects a "dualist" system[vii] in that treaty-based international law remains separate from U.S. municipal law unless and until it is specifically incorporated ("executed") into municipal law through one of several governmental processes. Thus, to automatically become part of U.S. municipal law, the treaty must be "executed.", whether it is an Article II Treaty or an international agreement not submitted to the Senate pursuant to Article II. To avoid confusion when discussing international treaties and their relationship to U.S. municipal law, it is less confusing to refer to them as "international agreements", whether they are submitted to the Senate for advice and consent pursuant to Article II of the Constitution or brought into force for the United States by the President pursuant either to specific congressional approval or a prior congressional authorization or to his plenary or inherent powers as President under Article II of the Constitution.[viii]

Once the international agreement has come into force for the United States, it may become part of municipal law in one of two ways. "[It] can sometimes be deemed to apply automatically as statute-like law in domestic U.S. courts" as a "self-executing" agreement. Or, if the agreement "cannot be deemed to be domestic law, … [it] may require further governmental acts to be implemented [in domestic law]."[ix] To be a "self-executing" agreement, it must not require further action by the Congress (e.g., not require appropriation of funds or where the international agreement, itself, specifically requires the United States to take further legislative action). Whether it is an Article II Treaty or other international agreement, it "is self-executing when it can be directly applied by courts or executive agencies without the need of further measures."[x] If it is not "self-executing," then further legislative action must be taken by the Congress before the instrument becomes a part of U.S. municipal law, assuming the government wishes it to so become.[xi] The question of whether the treaty is self-executing or not does not, of course, affect the international obligation of the United States, once it has ratified the agreement, to carry it out under international law.

If the decision is made by the President not to submit an international agreement to the Senate for its advice and consent as an Article II Treaty, the agreement will then fall into one of three categories of "executive agreements" requiring (for two of those categories) congressional action.

The first of these categories is a "congressionally-*authorized* executive agreement" where Congress has previously delegated authority generally for the President to enter into international agreements in a certain area or with respect to a certain subject matter. For our purposes, a good example of this delegated authority is Section 205 of the National Aeronautics and Space Act of 1958, as amended (the "NASA Act".[xii] Section 205 reads:

> The Administration, under the foreign policy guidance of the President, may engage in a program of international cooperation in work done pursuant to this Act, and in the peaceful application of the results thereof, pursuant to agreements made by the President with the advice and consent of the Senate.

It is important to note that in the presidential signing statement accompanying the signing of the NASA Act in 1958, President Eisenhower singled out section 205 as raising "substantial constitutional questions":

> I regard this section merely as recognizing that international treaties may be made in this field, and as not precluding, in appropriate cases, less formal arrangements for

cooperation. To construe this section otherwise would raise substantial constitutional questions.

The second type of international agreement is a "congressionally-*approved* executive agreement." Once the agreement is negotiated by the executive, it must be submitted to the Congress for approval in the form of a joint resolution before it can enter into force for the United States. It is important to note that the President has plenary authority under Article II of the Constitution to negotiate agreements with foreign governments and need not, for constitutional reasons, first seek Congressional approval to undertake and conclude negotiations. However, for practical and political reasons, he will often coordinate with the relevant committees of Congress to keep them informed as to the progress of negotiations so as to facilitate later obtaining the necessary congressional approval to bring the agreement into force for the United States. This is especially the case with regard to multilateral trade agreement negotiations such as the the World Trade Organization (WTO) negotiations. The WTO agreement, as important as it was to the U.S. economy, was not submitted to the Senate as an Article II Treaty. Instead, it was treated as a "congressionally-approved executive agreement" for which the President, for political reasons, first obtained congressional authority to undertake the negotiations on the basis that when concluded, the agreement would be submitted to the Congress for approval by an up-or-down (i.e., no amendments) vote in both Houses.

The third type of international agreement is a "*presidential* executive agreement". It does not require congressional authorization or approval as long as the substance of the agreement is within the plenary or inherent powers of the President under the Constitution. An example is the President's authority as Commander-in-Chief of the armed forces. Another is with respect to his implicit authority to conduct diplomatic relations with foreign nations derived from his Article II power to "receive Ambassadors and other public Ministers."

In the case of the 1988 ISS IGA and MOUs, they were treated as congressionally-authorized executive agreements pursuant to the Congressionally-delegated authority under Section 205 of the Space Act and section 112 of the NASA Authorization Act of 1988.[xiii]

Also in the case of the 1988 IGA, it was first necessary to obtain specific Congressional legislation in regard to certain matters concerning intellectual property in order to make U.S. municipal law consistent with the U.S. obligations under Article 21.3 of the IGA concerning protection of the secrecy of patent applications. In as much as Article 21.3 was retained verbatim in the 1998 IGA, it too is consistent with U.S. municipal law, and no further congressional action is necessary in that regard.[xiv]

Whether to choose the Article II Treaty route or to proceed on the basis of an executive agreement is a political decision for the Executive Branch.[xv] If the President seeks to proceed and obtain Congressional approval for an executive agreement by way of a joint resolution of Congress, it requires only a simply majority vote of both Houses. If, instead, the agreement is submitted as an Article II Treaty to the Senate it requires an affirmative vote of 2/3rd of the

Senator present. Thus, except for certain categories of international agreements (e.g., disarmament agreements, tax treaties), the Executive generally chooses the congressional-approval route unless it appears that the Senate would not support a joint resolution. Likewise, in the case of the 1988 IGA, the "congressionally-authorized executive agreement" route was deemed the better approach because there was some doubt in 1988 whether a 2/3rd majority vote could be obtained in a timely fashion by going the Article II Treaty route in the Senate.

Within the Executive Branch of the U.S. Government, determination of whether an instrument concluded with a foreign government or an IGO is an international agreement rests with the Secretary of State pursuant to the Case-Zablocki Act of 1972, as amended.[xvi] The Act requires that significant international commitments of the U.S. Government be reduced to writing, and reported to the foreign relations committees of the Congress within sixty days of the entry into force of such commitments. The Act, its implementing State Department Regulations,[xvii] and Circular 175[xviii] define for the purposes of U.S. law what constitutes an international agreement. In addition, they detail the procedures to be followed with respect to negotiating and concluding such agreements and subsequently reporting them to Congress.

In addition to the Case-Zablocki Act, various other acts of Congress that authorize the President to negotiate international agreements, require the submission of such agreements to the relevant oversight committees of the Senate and the House. One such act in the case of NASA was the 1988 amendment to the NASA Act which required that the IGA and MOUs be submitted to the Senate Committee on Commerce, Science and Transportation, and the House Committee on Science, Space and Technology thirty days prior to their entry into force.[xix]

The State Department Regulation concerning coordination, reporting and publication of international agreements, sets forth five criteria to be applied in determining whether any undertaking of the United States constitutes an "international agreement" within the meaning of the Act and of 1 U.S.C. 112a, requiring the publication of significant international agreements. At the least, the first four criteria must be met in order for the undertaking to constitute an "international agreement." The criteria are:

1. *Identity and intention of the parties.*

The parties must be states, state agencies or IGOs. They must intend their undertaking to be legally binding and not merely of political or personal effect. They must intend the undertaking to to be governed by international law although this intent need not be manifested by any reference to third- party dispute settlement mechanisms or any express reference to international law. It will be presumed to be governed by international law in the absence of a choice of law clause.

2. *Significance of the arrangement.*

The undertaking must be significant, and in determining significance the entire context of the transaction as well as the expectations and intent of the parties must be considered.

Examples given in the regulation of arrangements that may constitute international agreements include those that constitute a substantial commitment of funds that would require new appropriations, and those that will require continuing and/or substantial cooperation in the conduct of a particular program or activity, such as scientific or technical cooperation.

3. *Specificity, including objective criteria for determining enforceability.*

Intent of the parties is the key factor in determining whether an arrangement is an international agreement. However, undertakings expressed in vague or very general terms with no objective criteria for determining enforceability or performance are not normally international agreements as they often reflect the intent not to be bound by the agreement.

4. *Necessity for two or more parties.*

Although unilateral commitments may at times be binding, they do not constitute international agreements. Furthermore, the requirement of "consideration" necessary in domestic contract law is not required in international agreements.

5. *Form.*

Although it deserves consideration, form as such is not an important factor. While failure to use the customary form may constitute evidence of a lack of intent to be legally bound, if the general content and context reveal an intention of the parties to enter into a legally binding arrangement the fact that the arrangement does not reflect customary form will not preclude it from being an international agreement.

The Regulations provide that an agency level arrangement can constitute an international agreement if it meets the above criteria, or at least the first four.[xx] In addition, an implementing arrangement may constitute an international agreement if its underlying agreement is general in nature and the implementing arrangement is detailed and meets at least the first four of the above criteria.[xxi]

IV. THE STATUS OF THE ISS IGA AND MOUs IN INTERNATIONAL LAW.

The rights, obligations and responsibilities of the respective Parties to the IGA are expressed in a hierarchy of three instruments: the IGA, the individual MOUs between NASA and each foreign Cooperating Agency (in the case of Japan, the Government of Japan), and a number of subsequent implementing arrangements (IAs). The MOUs are subject to the IGA, and the IAs must be consistent with and subject to the MOUs.[xxii]

A. THE IGA...

The Preamble to the IGA, concludes by stating the intent of the parties to form an international cooperative effort:

> Convinced that working together on the [ISS] will further expand cooperation through the establishment of a long-term and mutually-beneficial relationship, and further promote cooperation in the exploration and peaceful uses of outer space...[the Parties] have agreed as follows :

Article 1.1 establishes a "long-term international cooperative framework among the Partners, on the basis of a genuine partnership" to build, operate and utilize a permanently inhabited international space station for peaceful purposes "in accordance with international law." The IGA further provides for "mechanisms and arrangements designed to ensure that its object is fulfilled."

The IGA "specifically defines" not only the ISS Program, but also the "nature of this partnership" including the respective rights and obligations of the Partners in this cooperation. Hence the intent is to promote cooperation in outer space by working together in the ISS, in a form of contractual intergovernmental venture as opposed to a separate international entity such as an intergovernmental organization. Furthermore, the intent is to do this on the basis of a "genuine partnership" but without creating a partnership-type entity.

Article 2 of the IGA, provides that the Partners will "join their efforts, under the lead role of the United States for overall management and coordination to create and integrate the [ISS]." Thus, the United States, besides contributing the elements identified in the Annex to the IGA, serves as the project manager and coordinator, a necessary role in such a "partnership" established without the creation of a separate "partnership" entity.

As a result, we have an international joint undertaking expressed as a "genuine partnership" by a group of states pursuant to an agreement to be governed by international law. It is an agreement with a singular, defined purpose in which the Partners various rights and obligations are set forth in considerable detail.

However, unlike agreements for the establishment of commercial joint ventures and partnerships, there are no financing mechanisms such as capitalization requirements and a "capital call" provision in the IGA for the ISS program. Instead, each Partner is to develop and fund its own Space Station elements and activities; i.e., there is to be generally no exchange of funds. However, the fulfillment of each Partner's financial responsibilities is made subject to "its funding procedures and the availability of appropriated funds", with the important proviso that

> recognizing the importance of the Space Station cooperation, each Partner undertakes to make its *best efforts* to obtain approval for funds to meet those obligations consistent with its respective funding procedures.[xxiii] (Emphasis added).

This leads to the question of whether the IGA and MOUs are legally binding instruments.

In the case of the United States, this provision limiting the government's fiscal obligation to no more than a "best efforts" obligation, avoids the strictures of "Anti-Deficiency Act"[xxiv] which requires appropriations to be made in advance of the commitment of funds by the federal government. From the fiscal standpoint, this clause makes the IGA consistent with existing U.S. Government fiscal laws thereby avoiding the need for congressional approval of the IGA as well as the appropriation of funds before the IGA could enter into force for the United States.

However, this "best efforts" clause, while not inconsistent with the Anti-Deficiency Act, nevertheless raises other issues with respect to internal U.S. fiscal procedures. In particular, each

Partner "undertakes to make its best efforts to obtain approval for funds … *consistent with its respective funding procedures.*" (Emphasis added). In the case of the United States, the funding approval procedure starts in the Executive Branch. Each year, generally in February, the President submits his budget to the Congress for the next fiscal year. Hearings are then held by various committees of the House and Senate, budget resolutions are adopted, authorization bills are considered and in many cases adopted and finally, by the beginning of the new fiscal year (October 1st), appropriation acts are enacted (or, more often, continuing resolutions are passed in order to avoid a shutdown of those departments and agencies for whom appropriations have not been made). But for present purposes, the key starting point for the Executive is the submission of its budget. And it is the President who has the responsibility to see that the international obligations of the United States are carried out, including those under the 1988 IGA, which is in force for the U.S. and Japan, and the 1998 Interim Arrangement which is in force for all the signatories to the 1998 IGA pending entry into force of the 1998 IGA. In addition, there is the obligation on States, generally, under international law "to refrain from acts which would defeat the object and purpose of a treaty" prior to its entry into force.[xxv]

Moreover, international law requires states to carry out their international obligations in "good faith". "Every treaty in force is binding upon the parties to it and must be performed by them in good faith."[xxvi] And it has been said that this principle could also extend to non-legally-binding agreements:

> However, because good faith applies generally in the legal relations between states, the principle will often continue to be relevant to situations arising from non-legally binding agreements, if those situations are themselves governed by or reducible to, legal rules. For example, factual reliance, perhaps over a long period, on a non-legal agreement may give rise to a legal claim based upon estoppel. More questionably, even insistence on the legal right to disregard a non-legally binding agreement might be challenged as an abuse of right.[xxvii]

Thus, issue of the fiscal obligations of the Partner under IGA Article 15 is centered on when the "best efforts" must first be made. In the case of the United States this is when the executive authority of the United States (the President) presents the budget for the fiscal year in question to the Congress. If the appropriating or approval body (the Congress, in the case of the United States) later fails to approve the necessary funds, the Article 15 obligation of the Partner is excused under the "subject to appropriations" clause of Article 15 to the extent of the lack of funding. However, without the request in the President's budget the chances of obtaining an appropriation of the necessary funds are considerably reduced.

What is meant by "best efforts" in the context of Article 15? It is clear that the U. S. Government could not, consistent with its internal fiscal restraints, permit the IGA to enter into force for it without the "subject to appropriations" clause, i.e., a "condition precedent" to its performance. And since this was likely the case with the other Parties, it was in their mutual interest to seek some greater commitment to avoid the practical appearance of an illusory arrangement, i.e., one in which a Party was committed only if it later obtained funding. Furthermore, reliance just on the principle of good faith and the rule of *pacta sunt* servanda may have been considered, both diplomatically and programatically, too implicit (or, perhaps, under the circumstances, insufficient) for the purposes of an international undertaking of the magnitude and duration of the ISS program. Therefore, just as in commercial contract law where an absolute commitment or assurance of satisfactory performance is impractical for legal, professional or other reasons, greater assurance that necessary funding would be forthcoming on a timely basis to meet programmatic goals, was found in the undertaking of each party to "make its best efforts" to obtain approval of funds to meet its obligations under the IGA.

The phrase "best efforts" has been defined in a municipal law context as

> a standard that has *diligence* as is essence and is imposed on those contracting parties that have undertaken such performance.[xxviii]

From an international law perspective, the *Harvard Research* commented on the principle of "good faith" in fulfilling a treaty engagement as

> requir[ing] that its stipulations be observed in their spirit as well as according to their letters and that what was promised be performed ... honestly *and to the best of the ability* of the party which made the promise.[xxix]

While these criteria – "diligence" and "to the best of the ability" – may appear to overlap, the former is more of an objective criterion, the later being subjective as to the party's ability. Therefore, the "best efforts" criterion appears to be a stronger admonition than relying only on the principle of "good faith", at least in the context of Article 15 of the IGA.

B. The MOUs...

The four MOUs in the ISS Program constitute the first layer of arrangements implementing the provisions of the IGA. Each one is a more comprehensive description of the programmatic undertakings and obligations set forth in the IGA. Pursuant to the Interim Arrangement of January 29, 1998, each MOU will enter into force after signature by the respective representatives of each Party thereto and notification by each Party of that it has completed all necessary domestic procedures for its entry into force.[xxx] At that time, the 1998 MOU is deemed to replace the respective 1988 MOU in the case of two of the MOUs.[xxxi] Furthermore, in three of the MOUs the respective Parties "agree to abide by the relevant terms of the IGA, to the fullest extent possible consistent with applicable domestic laws and regulations."[xxxii]

Pursuant to Article 4 of the IGA, each MOU has as its purpose the establishment of arrangements between the parties to the bilateral MOU implementing the provisions of the IGA on the basis of genuine partnership for peaceful purposes "*in accordance with international law.*"[xxxiii] The specific objectives of the MOUs are: (a) to provide the basis for cooperation of the parties to each MOU; (b) to detail their roles and responsibilities, taking into account those of the parties to each of the other MOUs; (c) to establish the management structure and necessary interfaces to ensure effective planning and coordination of the work and activities in the ISS program; (d) to provide a basis for cooperation that maximizes the total capability of the ISS, accommodates users needs and ensures that the ISS is operated in a safe, efficient and effective manner for both the users and operators; and (e) to provide a general description of the ISS and its elements.[xxxiv]

The subject matter of the various articles of the MOUs in many cases correspond to those of of articles in the IGA, although often going into much greater detail, e.g., the provisions on Management and Crew. In other corresponding articles the language is more similar and one MOU article (Article 15) merely incorporates by reference the so-called "legal articles" (i.e., articles 16 through 22) of the IGA. Of note however, is MOU Article 16, *Financial Arrangement,* which appears nearly verbatim in each MOU and with certain exceptions, is substantively the same as Article 15 of the IGA. One major exception, however, is sub-Article 16.2 in each MOU which, while retaining the subject-to-availability-of-appropriations requirement as a broad excuse from performance, omits the "best efforts" proviso of Article 15.2 of the IGA. Instead, the MOUs, in their respective sub-Article 16.3 requiring notification and consultation by a Partner in the event it incurs "funding problems", add a final sentence in which the MOU Parties

> undertake to grant *high priority* to their Space Station programs in developing their budgetary plans. (Emphasis added).

In view of the fact that the MOU Parties are, except for Japan, governmental space agencies and not the governments, themselves, this distinction between the IGA and the MOUs appears reasonable, since it is the executive heads of government and not the heads of government agencies which control the submission of budgets to the respective legislative bodies for approval. What the "high priority" language provides is an added mutual assurance at the heads of agency level (and at the executive level in the case of Japan) of the fiscal importance to be given their Space Station programs. As in the case of the "best efforts" clause in Article 15 of the IGA, this "high priority" clause in the MOUs serves to enhance the legally binding nature of the MOUs.

Also, it is noted that in the international arena NASA uses the term "MOU" for "significant agreements binding under international law" and which are procedurally consistent with the Case-Zablocki Act and its implementing regulations. NASA considers cooperative activities to be significant which have "major budget impact, are long-term, or have a high degree of programmatic, policy, or political importance. The examples given by NASA expressly refer to the ISS program, as an example of "[a]ctivities that are complex, involve multiple parties, or have unusual organizational arrangements (e.g., ISS)."[xxxv]

V. CONCLUSION.

1. As to the IGA....

On the international plane, the IGA meets the definition of "treaty" in Article 1 of the *Vienna Convention on the Law of Treaties.* It is a written agreement concluded among states in which they have expressed their collective intent that it be governed by international law.

Under United States law, the IGA is treated as a "congressionally-authorized executive agreement pursuant to Section 205 of the NASA Act of 1958, as amended and Section 112 of the NASA Authorization Act, Pub. L. No. 100-147 (1987). It meets all five of the criteria of for an international agreement under the Case-Zablocki Act and Section 181.2 of its implementing State Department Regulation. (1) The Parties to the IGA are states; they have expressed the intent that the agreement be governed by international law, and from its terms taken in context with and in light of its object and purposes, reveals an implicit intent that it be legally binding under international law; (2) It is a significant agreement for a major scientific and technical undertaking in the field of space science costing many tens of billions of U.S. dollars to develop, operate and utilize over an elapsed period measured in decades; (3) its terms have considerable specificity including as to the intent to which the Parties are bound under the agreement at international law; (4) it is a multi-party agreement; and (5) it follows the customary form of international agreements and is denominated as an "intergovernmental agreement."

As to the matter of the status of the IGA provisions in U.S. municipal law, the writer is not aware of whether the Executive Branch has determined that provisions of the IGA are self-executing or if not should be "executed". No legislation has been enacted to do so with respect to the provisions of the Agreement other than as described below. The "legal provisions" (Articles 16 through 22) were considered to be consistent with existing federal law with one exception concerning patent secrecy, Article 21.3. In that case, and legislation was enacted to make U.S. law consistent on that issue. As for the Article 16 regime on cross-waivers of liability, NASA did in 1991 promulgate a regulation pursuant to its broad statutory authority under the NASA Act, implementing these with regard to the 1988 IGA.[xxxvi] Some changes were made to Article 16 in the 1998 IGA, and presumably NASA will in time address whether any changes to its regulation are needed as a result of such changes.

2. As to the MOUs...

The MOUs are not "treaties" on the international plane as that term in defined in the Vienna Convention since they are not agreement concluded between states. Instead, each is an agreement concluded between governmental agencies (except the NASA-Japan MOU which is concluded between a government agency and a foreign state. Nevertheless, they are agreements implementing the provisions of the IGA "in accordance with international law."

Under U.S. law, the MOUs are "agency-level" agreements and would appear to meet the five criteria of 22 CFR sec. 181.2(a) thereby making them international agreements under the Case-Zablocki Act. They do not appear to have been published pursuant to sec. 112b of the Act in the U.S. Government's annual publication, *Treaties in Force*, which also includes other significant international agreements in force for the United States. Moreover, the NASA Procedures and Guidance (NPG 1051.1) expressly confirms this conclusion as to the status of the MOUs as international agreements binding under international law.

[i] 18 UST 2410, TIAS 6347, 610 UNTS 205 (1967). (Hereinafter, the Outer Space Treaty). The other four treaties are: *Convention on International Liability for Damages Caused By Space Objects*, 24 UST 2389, TIAS 2262, 961 UNTS 187 (1971); *Convention on the Registration of Objects Launched into Outer Space*, 28 UST 695, TIAS 8480, 1023 UNTS 15 (1976); *Agreement on the Rescue of Astronauts, the Return of Astronauts, and the Return of Objects Launched into Outer Space*, 19 UST 7570, TIAS 6599, 672 UNTS 119 (1968); and the *Agreement Governing the Activities of States on the Moon and Other Celestial Bodies* , 1363 UNTS 3, 18 ILM 1434 (1984).

[ii] U.N. Doc. A/CONF. 39/27 (1969), 8 I.L.M. 679 (1969), entered into force 27 January 1980. ("Vienna Convention").

[iii] E.g., *Memorandum of Understanding for joint development of the TOPEX/POSEIDON (oceanographic satellite) project*, 1987, TIAS 12207. *Agreement providing for the establishment and operation of a lunar and planetary spacecraft tracking facility on Ascension Island*, 1965, 16 UST 1183, TIAS 5864, 551 UNTS 221.

[iv] Article 25.3(b) of the IGA provides that the IGA shall not enter into force for a European Partner State before it enters into force for the European Partner, which cannot occur until at least four European signatory or acceding States have deposited their instruments of ratification, acceptance or approval "and, in addition, a formal notification by the Chairman of the ESA Council" has been made to the Depositary Government (United States). http://www.state.gov/s/l/13897.htm . Pursuant to its internal rules, the ESA notification will not be made until the governments of its three largest Member States signatory to the IGA (France, Germany and Italy) have completed their procedures. As of 18 October 2002, only Germany and Italy had completed their procedures.

[v] Agreement Concerning Application of the Space Station Intergovernmental Agreement Pending its Entry into Force, signed and entered into force January 29, 1998. (the "1998 Interim Arrangement"). http://www.state.gov/www/global/legal_affairs/treaty_actions_1998.html Article 3 sets forth the Parties "desire to pursue cooperation as provided for in the [1998 IGA] to the fullest possible extent" pending their completion of necessary domestic approvals. The Parties, in Article 4, "undertake, to the fullest extent possible consistent with their domestic laws and regulations, to abide by the terms of the [1998 IGA] until it enters into force or becomes operative with respect to each of them." Article 5 provides that a Party may withdraw from this arrangement upon 120 days' written notice to the others.

[vi] Agreement on cooperation in the detailed design, development, operation and utilization of the permanently manned civil space station, with annex. Done at Washington September 29, 1988; entered into force January 30, 1992, together with bilateral MOUs) concluded between NASA and the Cooperating Agencies of Canada,and Europe and the Government of Japan.

[vii] Henkin, Pugh, Schachter and Smit, *International Law – Cases and Materials,* 153-154 (3 ed., 1993). ("Dualists (or pluralists) regard international law and municipal law as separate legal systems which operate on different levels. International law can be applied by municipal courts only when it had been "transformed" or "incorporated" into municipal law.")

[viii] Specifically, under Article II, Sec. 2, Clauses 1 and 3. In pertinent part they read:

Clause 1: The President shall be Commander in Chief of the Army and Navy of the United States....

Clause 3: ....he shall receive Ambassadors and other Public Ministers; he shall take Care that the Laws be faithfully executed, and shall Commission all the Officers of the United States.

[ix] J.H. Jackson, *The World Trading System – Law and Policy of International Trade Relations,* 63 (MIT Press, 1989).

[x] Y. Iwasawa, *The Doctrine of Self-Executing Treaties in the United States: A Critical Analysis*, Va. J. Int'l L, 627 (1986).

[xi] See, *Foster v. Neilson,* 27 U.S. (2 Pet.) 253, 314, 7 L.ed. 415 (1828) in which Chief Justice Marshall formulated the distinction between self-executing and non-self-executing treaties. "Our constitution declares a treaty to be the law of the land. It is, consequently, to be regarded in courts of justice as equivalent to an act of the legislature, wherever it operates of itself, without the aid of any legislative provision. But when the terms of the stipulation import a contract, when either of the parties engages to perform a particular act, the treaty addresses itself to the political, not the judicial department: and the

legislature must execute the contract, before it can become a rule for the court." See, also, RESTATEMENT 3rd, *Foreign Relations Law of the United States*, § 111(4), comment h., and Reporter's Note 5.

[xii] 42 U.S.C. § 2475.

[xiii] See, *infra.*, fn 17 and accompanying text.

[xiv] In this connection and as a related matter, U.S. Patent Law prior to the enactment of the Patent of Space Act, 35 U.S.C. § 105 (1990) was confined to the territories of the United States. The Act extended the U.S. Patent Law to include the make, use or sale in outer space of inventions on space objects carried on the registry of the United States. Nevertheless, in recognition of the jurisdiction (Art. 5) and intellectual property provisions of the 1988 IGA, the Act contains a specific exceptions in the case of the ISS and in the case of inventions made use or sold in outer space on space objects carried on the registry of a foreign state.

[xv] RESTATEMENT 3rd, *Foreign Relations Law of the United States*, § 303, comment (e) (1987).

[xvi] 1 USC § 112b

[xvii] 22 CFR Part 181.

[xviii] Vol. XI, *Foreign Affairs Manual*, Chapt. 700 (Department of State).

[xix] Pub. L No. 100-147, § 112, *codified at* 42 U.S.C. § 2451 (note 1994). See, Dalton, "National Treaty Law and Practice: United States" which appears in *National Treaty Law and Practice: Austria, Chile, Columbia, Japan, The Netherlands, United States*, Chapt. 6 (Studies in Transnational Legal Policy No. 30, American Society of International Law (Washington, D.C., 1999). Mr. Dalton served for a number of years as the State Department Assistant Legal Advisor for Treaty Affairs and has written an excellent summary of US Treaty Practice to which is appended a number of very useful annexes setting forth examples of the various types of documents used in U.S. treaty practice.

[xx] 22 CFR § 181.3(c).

[xxi] Id., at 181.3(d).

[xxii] IGA, Art. 4.2.

[xxiii] IGA, Art.15.2. The language of Article 15 is identical in both the 1988 and 1998 versions of the IGA.

[xxiv] 31 U.S.C. § 665.

[xxv] Codified at Article 18 of the *Vienna Convention on the Law of Treaties*, entered into force 27 January 1980

[xxvi] *Vienna Convention on the Law of* Treaties, Art. 26. See, I. Brownlie, *Principles of Public International Law*, 620 (5th ed. 1998). See generally, J.F.O'Connor, *Good Faith in International Law* (Reprint, Dartmouth Publ. Co., 1999). O'Connor concludes by offering the following definition of "good faith":

"The principle of good faith in international law is a fundamental principle from which the rule *pacta sunt servanda* and other legal rules distinctly and directly related to honesty, fairness and reasonableness are derived, and the application of these rules is determined at any particular time by the compelling standards of honesty, fairness and reasonableness prevailing in the international community at that time." O'Connor at 124.

[xxvii] *Id.*, O'Connor at 113.

[xxviii] Farnsworth, *Farnsworth on Contracts*, § 7.17b (1990)(emphasis added) (He contrasts "best efforts" with "good faith", the latter being "a standard that has honesty and fairness at its core and that is imposed on every party to a contract."

[xxix] *Harvard Research: Draft Convention on the Law of Treaties*, comment *ad* Art. 20 (Part III, 1935. See, Bing Cheng, *General Principles of Law as Applied by International Courts and Tribunals*, 114 (1953).

[xxx] See, NASA-ESA MOU, Art. 19.1; NASA-Russian Space Agency MOU, Art. 19.1; NASA-Canadian Space Agency MOU, Art. 19.1; and the NASA- Government of JAPAN MOU Art. 19.1, which, however, imposes the further requirement for entry into force of the MOU that the IGA have also entered into force, which it has not as of the date of the presentation of this paper.

[xxxi] NASA-ESA MOU, Art. 19.1 and NASA Government of Japan MOU, Art. 19.2.

[xxxii] Article 19.2 in the NASA-ESA MOU, NASA-Russian Space Agency MOU, and NASA-Canadian Space Agency MOU. The text of Article 19.2 in each of these MOU is identical to the text in Paragraph 4 of the Interim Arrangement of January 29, 1998, except in each MOU provision the undertaking is to abide by the "relevant" terms of the the IGA.

[xxxiii] (Emphasis added). See, e.g., NASA-ESA MOU, Art. 1.1. The substance of Art. 1.1 of each of the other three MOUs is the same as Art. 1.1 of the cited MOU.

[xxxiv] See, e.g., NASA-Russian Space Agency MOU, Art. 1.2.

[xxxv] NASA Procedures and Guidelines (NPG) 1051 Space Act Agreements, Chapt. 3., Non-reimbursable and Reimbursable Agreement with

Foreign Governments or Governmental Entities, § 3.2, Non-reimbursable Agreement/ Memorandum of Understanding, effective December 30, 1998 – December 30, 2003.

[xxxvi] *Cross-waiver of liability for Space Station Freedom activities,* 56 Fed. Reg. 48430, Sept. 25, 1991, *codified at,* 4 CFR § 1266.102.

IAC-02-IISL.2.08

Commitment and Compliance in the Evolution of the ISS Program

Liara Covert, P.h.D., CEDS, Paris, France [liarac@hotmail.com]

Introduction

This paper considers to what extent and under what conditions ISS Partners re-evaluate or modify their notions of *commitment* and *compliance*. Explanations of these terms are offered based on the understanding that patterns of human reactions to legal instruments vary over time, according to domestic and international priorities. Constitutional frameworks of each sovereign State then determine the degree to which international law is applied as part of State municipal laws. [2]

Definitions

The terms *commitment* and *compliance* reflect that laws determine political interactions as much as these interactions can affect the perception of domestic laws and legal institutions.[3]

For this paper, ISS commitments are defined as collectively agreed statements of intent that can have implicit undertones. ISS commitments are explained in the quantifiable means and efforts defined in legal instruments. The statements of intent are explained in ISS instruments by individuals at different levels of authority: e.g., ISS Partner States, Cooperating Agencies and/or professional teams,[4] who interpret commitment and compliance with regard to three types of agreements.

ISS Intergovernmental Agreement (IGA)

The ISS IGA is the highest-level ISS legal regime, comprised of rules grounded in jurisdictions (areas under power and control) of ISS Partner States. Fifteen ISS Partner States[5] signed a treaty on January 29, 1998 to formalize the ISS IGA:

> *"a long term international co-operative framework on the basis of genuine partnership, for the detailed design, development, operation, and utilization of a permanently inhabited civil Space Station for peaceful purposes, in accordance with international law"* (ISS IGA Article 1).[6]

Respective National laws of ISS Partners can then be applied to issues concerning liability,[7] jurisdiction,[8] the protection of intellectual property rights,[9] the exchange of goods and data, criminal matters[10] and other subjects.

ISS IGA goals even outline processes for how Cooperative ISS Partners should identify and achieve "evolutionary capability" (Id., Article 14.1) while engaging in "cooperation reviews" (Id., Article 24) and "exert best efforts" (Id., Article 23) to resolve matters and meet commitments.

A trend towards non-binding instruments influences the interpretation of binding commitment.[11] Progress has been made in managing international disagreements, but approaches could still be improved.[12] Where problems do arise, rarely is there agreement that international law is being violated.[13]

ISS Memorandum of Understanding (MOU)

A second level of ISS legal instruments involves the Cooperating Agencies of the ISS Partner States. They delegated program responsibilities to their respective space agencies.

More specifically, the National Aeronautics and Space Administration (NASA) signed bilateral MOUs with each Co-operating Agency (European Space Agency for Europe, Canadian Space Agency, Russian Space Agency, and Japanese Space Agency). Those instruments detail the roles and responsibilities of the agencies in the design, development, operation and utilization of ISS. They also define the management structure and professional interfaces. The space agencies also agreed to favor Bartering Arrangements which "seek to minimize the exchange of funds while carrying out their respective responsibilities," (MOU Article 16.4).

ISS Implementing Arrangements (IAs)

The third level of ISS instruments is defined by IAs between the space agencies. They have been created to implement and further clarify the ISS MOUs and as such, to delegate some authority to professional teams. They distribute concrete guidelines and tasks among the national agencies.

Compliance at the ISS Partner Level

At the ISS Partner State level, compliance to ISS instruments is achieved when Partner governments alter their behavior and policies, and impose rules and regulations in their societies for the purpose of meeting their collective commitments. This could include references to the ISS Program in media, policy debates, and when forming scientific and policy task forces, allocating budgets, exploring options for research, commercial and other development discussions on national agendas, and in diplomatic exchanges.[14]

Admittedly, with multiple interests to satisfy in different ISS Partner States, specific issues should be addressed rather than aiming to evaluate the success of commitment and compliance of the entire ISS Program. Issues of compliance to ISS-related commitments are based on the context of specific legal and political relationships among actors.[15]

Hypothetical Views of ISS Compliance

An analysis of compliance[16] in the ISS Program should be approached from several perspectives and on the basis of several causal factors. To learn to recognize the different reasons why and how individuals seek compliance leads to gaining a better grasp of the major differences in the kinds of compliance sought and obtained by ISS Partners.

For instance, compliance is reflected when members of ISS Partner governments, Cooperating Agencies and professional teams have approved, discussed or changed their commitments and have further developed a consensus about how these commitments will be implemented. In such cases, compliance may be higher when bureaucratic structures are organized and facilitate the implementation of activities outlined in legal provisions.

The meaning of compliance is further defined in the case where there is a disagreement among parties concerning the meanings of ISS instruments. Here, actors involved in different levels of legal agreements could clarify 'compliance' as the consequence of alleged non-compliance between signatories. Where alleged non-compliance is the consequence of a disagreement, different views or commitments also arise.

In this regard, compliance with ISS instruments as an objective needs to be clarified in terms of first-order compliance (causing respect for standing rules) and second-order compliance (causing respect for authoritative decisions). Interdisciplinary team reviews may determine what level of compliance is necessary. What compliance is expected of governments, Cooperating Agencies or other parties by different levels of authority and the general public, is often seen as a potential problem. Consensus is needed to determine when a violation or breach of an ISS Instrument has occurred, and also to determine an appropriate course of action to react to induce compliance, re-define the commitment and/or facilitate future continued cooperation.

Specific ISS IA Example

Consider a hypothetical scenario related to the ISS IA Crew Code of Conduct (CCOC)[17] where one Partner accuses another Partner of breaching a part of the agreement. Before one can attempt to define commitment and compliance, one must first recognize that this ISS instrument has different legal status and thus different legal meanings for different ISS Partners.[18] The nature of a disagreement could relate to an alleged violation that has already occurred or it could concern anticipated conduct of a State with regard to a planned timeline or another commitment (i.e., an anticipated breach). Much is based on the interpreted compatibility of ISS Partner and Agency regulations.

Possible Reasons for Seeking Compliance

Consider some of the potential reasons for ISS Partners wanting compliance by the other ISS Partners regarding ISS instruments:

a) To protect political, economic, socio-cultural and other interests (why instruments are designed).
b) To uphold a moral principle, whether or not a violation would cause harm.
c) To impact more interactions than they were designed to protect.
d) To avoid the problem of setting precedents for future breaches.

Compliance can also be defined by objectives of parties external to those parties involved in a disagreement. For instance, a non-ISS Partner State with a contractual agreement to provide technical parts to an ISS Partner disagrees with the way it is compensated due to unforeseen economic difficulties of that ISS Partner. The external party could raise questions of ISS Partner compliance. However, perceived legal rights and duties of each party could make such a situation hard to resolve.

Also, the perception of legal status of an MOU varies.[19] When ISS Partners and/or external parties have different views of MOU obligations and their implications, difficulties are likely to arise in attempting to reach consensus about what conduct constitutes compliance.[20]

Consider that ISS Partners on friendly terms with regard to agricultural trade policy may support claims made by these allies in the ISS Partnership.[21] Yet, this standard is not easily accepted as reasonable compliance without the States involved having reasons to support each other that are more directly related to space arrangements.[22]

A broader suggestion is that United Nations (UN) members could examine disagreements concerning commitment and compliance among ISS Partners and then offer independent judgment of the facts with regard to international law. Yet, this approach would be very time-consuming, could offer options based on political alliances and could generally lead to diverse views that would not realistically be heeded by the ISS State Partners.[23]

As it happens, ISS Partners have developed guidelines in the event of the need for dispute resolution.[24] Suggestions can lead to recommendations and possibly even more binding decisions. Ultimately, a point of reference is needed to determine what constitutes compliance.

One should recall that each ISS Partner State has domestic interests while also being a member of the international community with multinational interests to reconcile. If a specific ISS program timeline changes or technical procedures are changed in the short term, this reality has repercussions on the livelihoods and activities of many people in different countries, companies and entities who are increasingly interdependent.

Also, there is a tendency for government to focus on short-term interest when handling issues of commitment and compliance.[25] Consider that a disagreement amongst some ISS Program actors about what constitutes acceptable and unacceptable conduct or interpretation of terms could be perceived as ISS Program compliance by another Partner.

For instance, timelines for the construction of core infrastructure may be met according to ISS Instrument deadlines, but that restrictions in program management and astronaut flights may make the evolution of the program as previously envisaged unrealistic or inappropriate in the long-term.[26] The final sections leading to the conclusion will present perspectives of commitment and compliance from each of the five ISS Partners.

The ISS European (ESA) Partner[27]

Consider some examples of commitment and compliance concerning the ISS European (ESA) Partner:

The 1998 ISS IGA has not yet entered into force for the European Partner. This reality suggests different levels of political commitment by European ISS Partner States.[28]

For example, the 1998 NASA-ESA MOU Article 3.3 (Space Station Elements) states that "ESA will design, develop and provide on orbit the following flight elements, including subsystems, flight software and spares, as required: one ESA pressurized module [...] logistics carriers which provide systems operations support, user logistics and on-orbit supply and orbital transfer vehicles [...]." Article 5 (Major Program Milestones) of the MOU lays out "major targets" and schedules for the completion of specific infrastructure and operations.

Although the ESA-provided European pressurized Columbus module was originally to have been launched by NASA in October 2002, this event has been postponed to October 2004. As a result, the first ESA operational mission utilizing the module, planned to take place in March 2003, is now projected to take place in September 2005. The "Assembly Complete"[29], once foreseen to be December 2003, is now projected for 2005-2006.[30]

Therefore, ESA's notion of commitment and compliance to the ISS Program evolved, in part, according to the delay in the launch of the Russian Zarya module. This event resulted in schedule delays for other ISS Partners. ESA will still complete the Columbus module on schedule. ESA has also enhanced its commitment by taking advantage of the launch delay to release calls for utilization-related experiments earlier than had been planned. ESA's scientific and commercial potential use of the ISS is thus further developed as the result of the delay.[31]

Another ESA perspective on the issue of commitment and compliance in the ISS Program involves the abrupt cancellation earlier this year (2002) of the NASA X-38 Program.[32] The German Space Agency (DLR) had an agreement (MOU) with NASA to develop and contribute heat resistant technology.[33] This was considered a preliminary phase in the U.S.-ESA cooperation to build the ISS crew return vehicle (CRV) intended for eventual ISS crew cargo delivery and return.[34] For budgetary reasons, NASA has pulled out of the CRV program.[35] NASA also apparently proposed an alternative, smaller vehicle. Yet, no formal mention of budget, detailed infrastructure or construction schedule has followed.[36] At the same time, not only is NASA proceeding with technical tests for the contributed German X-30-related technology, but this technology has not yet been returned to Germany which was part of the agreement.[37] This situation paints a confusing picture of commitment and compliance when one compares what has previously been said.

As such, a flexible understanding of commitment and compliance in the ISS Program has evolved based on a process of negotiations subsequent to those of the initial ISS IGA and MOUs, as opposed to an understanding based on what was initially agreed upon. The result of canceling one part of one element of the Program can have a dangerous trigger effect for other Partners who are also in the process of completing interdependent Program elements on coinciding timelines.

Further, it is imperative to recognize the potential for inconsistent objectives of ISS Program participants. Reference to U.S. Public Law 106-391 Section 201(d) pertaining to the issue of "Equitable Utilization" admonishes NASA that in the event any other ISS Partner "willfully violates any of its commitments or agreements for the provision of agreed-upon Space Station-related hardware or related goods or services, the Administrator should, in a manner consistent with relevant agreements, seek a commensurate reduction in the utilization rights of that Partner until such time as the violated commitments or agreements have been fulfilled."

This precatory language "should" reveals a curious situation. In essence, this law demonstrates an attempt to define good faith[38] in the performance of implementing ISS Program instruments. However, if NASA breaches, there is no comparable sanction in section 201 (d), in the federal laws of ISS Partner States or even internal regulations in Cooperating Agencies, that my research has revealed. The failure of mutuality is demonstrated in part by the U.S. Partner in instituting this law without the other Partners doing something similar.

The failure of mutuality is also demonstrated by the other ISS Partners and Cooperating Agencies that do not have a comparable provision. To apply the good faith principle in International Treaty Law, all ISS Partners should adhere. If NASA is to impose this effect as the result of another ISS Partner's breach, shouldn't there be similar effects where there is a NASA violation? It is not very clear whether this is the case.

One of the major concerns of the European Partner is whether or not the US Partner, in view of its recent ISS budget related problems, has already entered into an exercise falling within the scope of Article 23.3 of the IGA pursuant to which: "any Partner which intends to proceed with significant flight element design changes which may have an impact on the other Partners shall notify the other Partners accordingly at the earliest opportunity". These provisions were added to the IGA in 1998 to allow the Partners to assess whether the intended changes are compatible with the ISS Agreements or if these changes entail modification of a Partner's rights and obligations.[39]

The ISS Japanese Partner[40]

Consider some examples of commitment and compliance concerning the ISS Japanese Partner:

Japan is one of two ISS Partners for which the ISS IGA has entered into force.[41]

Another point for reflection is the 1998 NASA-GOJ MOU. Article 3 (Space Station Elements) states that "the GOJ will design, develop and provide on orbit the following flight elements including subsystems, flight software and spares as required: one Japanese Experiment Module (JEM) [...] and logistics carriers which provide system operations support, user logistics and on-orbit supply."

Although the JEM Module hardware was completed on schedule according to ISS Implementing Arrangements, this hardware now sits in the Japanese Tskuba Center. NASDA requested to postpone the launch of the JEM module because of national economic difficulties.[42] Uncertainty with regard to the eventual launch date affects the lives and enthusiasm of scientists and other space professionals, as well as the general public. Utilization and projected crew numbers and experiments are affected and this impact is difficult to measure quantitatively.[43]

In a separate ISS Program-related bilateral agreement, NASDA committed to provide ESA with racks for its Columbus module in exchange for a special freezer. This transaction occurred as planned and demonstrates a level of commitment and compliance with regard to the "no exchange of funds" clause.[44]

Accordingly, there exist provisions to facilitate new kinds of compliance when circumstances evolve. Compliance thus benefits where different ISS Partners adapt to changing circumstances and make efforts to promote mutual understanding. Frank, relaxed discussion is needed such that the facts are clarified and the interpretation of rules or regulations is not placed in doubt.

In addition, NASDA continues to work on completion of the centrifuge it committed to provide to NASA as part of exchange for the JEM Module launch.[45] Upon encountering a variety of obstacles, a NASDA task force recently requested NASA's help to develop facets of the centrifuge. This illustrates a continuing desire to comply with previously agreed upon ISS commitments, albeit in light of changing national circumstances.[46]

The ISS U.S. Partner[47]

Consider some examples of commitment and compliance concerning the ISS U.S. Partner.

The U.S. Partner deposited its notice of acceptance of the ISS IGA on November 17, 1998.[48] This ISS instrument cannot enter into force until Japan, Russia and the U.S. have followed all necessary internal procedures and deposited their instruments defined by international law and protocol for multilateral treaties.[49]

The NASA-ESA MOU Article 3.2 (Space Station Elements) lists flight elements and subsystems that NASA "will provide."[50] For example, NASA agreed to provide "one permanently attached Habitation Module with complete basic functional outfitting to support habitation for four crew members, including primary storage of crew provisions and the health maintenance system." The Habitation Module has been completed and launched, but there are only three astronauts permanently on-board ISS.

The NASA-ESA MOU Article 11.1 states that "Each Partner has the right to provide personnel to serve as Space Station crew from the time the Partner begins to share common operations responsibilities. During the period of the three-person crew, NASA and RSA will be allocated 50% of the crew flight opportunities [...] Following outfitting of the NASA-provided Habitation Module and initial operational verification of the NASA-provided crew return vehicle, when the Space Station has a crew of seven, RSA will be allocated three crew flight opportunities."

For instance, the *Core Complete* term introduced by NASA in particular and the repercussions on the ISS Partner crew issues will be addressed.[51] In terms of clarifying issues of commitment and compliance of the U.S. Partner, it is difficult at this time to see how the agreed upon ISS crew of seven can be realized in the short term.[52] The domino effect is that where sufficient crew and infrastructure remain unavailable, ISS utilization potential cannot grow. Until such time as ISS utilization can increase, initial international plans for scientific research are in jeopardy.[53]

NASA's reactions to commitments to provide infrastructure and personnel are grounded in the NASA institutional view of the character of international agreements.[54] As such, it is important to recognize that, "a NASA MOU is an executive agreement that is bilateral or multilateral in nature, is for activities which are significant in scope [...] and is intended by the parties to be legally binding in accordance with international law."[55]

Nonetheless, the U.S. and foreign nations have not always agreed on the legal status of an MOU in practice. Consider that representatives of Commonwealth governments have not always favored MOUs as a legally-binding arrangement.

More often, in international arenas, the general MOU document has been considered as a 'gentleman's agreement' because of issues of "confidentiality and technical complexity, although representing political commitments of a significant nature."[56] Binding instruments have been used to encourage commitment and compliance where prudence of individual state and agency representatives dictates the perception of State power, characterizes classified technology, identifies ownership of property and clarifies other controversial issues where competition and ideology are then at stake.[57]

The ISS Canadian Partner[58]

Consider some examples of commitment and compliance concerning the ISS Canadian Partner:

The Canadian Partner deposited the ISS IGA for ratification July 24, 2000.[59] It is one of the ISS Partners that has made this IGA national legislation.[60]

According to the 1998 NASA-CSA MOU Article 3.3.a, "CSA will design, develop, and provide the following flight elements of the Mobile Servicing System, including subsystems, flight software and spares, as required: Space Station Remote Manipulator System (SSRMS), Mobile Remote Service Base System (MBS) and One Special Purpose Dexterous Manipulator (SPDM). SSRMS, MBS and the NASA-provided Mobile Transporter comprise the Mobile Servicing Center (MSC)." Article 5 of the same MOU (Major Program Milestones) outlines the timeframe for the completion of this infrastructure as well as the launches.

To recall, Canada provided the SSRMS in April 2001 and the MBS in April 2002. The SPDM is planned to be ready soon. In order to complete necessary tests and integration, it is currently projected that this element will tentatively be launched in 2005. In essence, Canada will soon have provided the infrastructure that meet its infrastructure commitments outlined in the ISS IGA and MOUs.[61]

It is interesting to note that Canada engages in bilateral cooperation agreements with ESA[62] and other ISS Partners in the context of space science projects related and unrelated to ISS. Hence, the completion of ISS infrastructure by the Canadian Partner does not mean other commitments and compliance will not evolve.

The Russian Federation Partner

Consider some examples of commitment and compliance concerning the ISS Russian Federation Partner:

The Russian Federation Partner deposited its ratification (executed national legal procedures) necessary for entry into force of the 1998 ISS IGA.

According to the 1998 NASA-RSA MOU Article 3, the Russian Partner plans to provide a considerable amount of infrastructure. To date, it has provided the Service Module and has begun to provide other program elements. Article 8.3.c.1. (Allocation of Crew Time) states that "During the period of a three-person crew…50% of the crew time will be allocated to NASA and 50% to RSA. The above allocations will be adjusted through implementing arrangements as allocations to other partners."

Recognize that most recently, the Russian re-supply space vehicle arrived at the ISS but that Russian officials stated that their contributions to ISS might have to be temporarily suspended in 2003. This would impact timelines and programs of all other Partners

A significant obstacle to Russia's ISS IGA and MOU commitments is apparent in a letter from Valery Ryumin, head of international space station program office at Energia to William Gerstenmaier, NASA's Space Station program manager. Essentially, Energia lacks the funds needed to build two more Progress vehicles in 2003. The crux is that Energia needs at least 4.5 billion rubles annually (142$ million U.S.) to fulfill its technical commitments to ISS. Yet, Energia received 1.2 billion rubles from the Russian government. This forced the company to take out loans and go into debt of 1 billion rubles. Nonetheless, NASA has "not received any indication from the Russian Aviation and Space Agency that they are not going to meet their commitments."[63]

Conclusion

The issue of how well each ISS Partner lives up to its IGA commitments, as well as to what degree decision-making authorities at other levels comply, is crucial to the overall perception of success of the international cooperation. To compare and contrast how previous ISS commitments have been respected or re-defined, points to issues that require new action. The credibility of respective decision-making levels of the ISS Program can be assessed, in part, based on the politics of international relations. A systematic analysis of compliance with ISS Program commitments is helpful in identifying national priorities, as well as revealing a variety of understandings of identified binding and soft law commitments. As time and a variety of national and international circumstances evolve, there is opportunity for all ISS Partners to challenge, confirm, modify or supplement their previously outlined commitments.[64]

---

[2] Kindred Hugh M., Mickelson Karin, McDorman Ted L., Provost Rene, de Mestral Armand L.C., Reif Linda C., and Williams Sharon A. (2000), *International Law Chiefly as Interpreted and Applied in Canada,* Sixth Edition, Emond Montgomery Publications Limited, pp. 165.

[3] Slaughter Anne Marie (2000), "What International Relations Can Offer International Law", from *International Law and International Relations,* Academie de Droit International, Recueil des Cours, Volume 285, p. 26-30.

[4] Covert (2002), Doctoral Thesis, *International Space Station (ISS) Negotiations and Manned Space Strategy (MSS): Towards the Consideration of a Multinational Astronaut Corps* (MAC), Introduction; (thesis 650 pgs).

[5] The 1998 ISS IGA treaty was signed by the governments of the United States, Canada, Japan, the Russian Federation, and eleven Member States of the European Space Agency (Belgium, Denmark, France, Germany, Italy, The Netherlands, Norway, Spain, Sweden, Switzerland, and the United Kingdom of Great Britain and Northern Ireland), see 1998 ISS IGA.

[6] See also 18 UST 2410, TIAS 6347, 610 UNTS 205 (1967)-- (The Outer Space Treaty). The other four space treaties are: *Convention on International Liability for Damages Caused By*

Space Objects, 24 UST 2389, TIAS 2262, 961 UNTS 187 (1971); Convention on the Registration of Objects Launched into Outer Space, 28 UST 695, TIAS 8480, 1023 UNTS 15 (1976); Agreement on the Rescue of Astronauts, the Return of Astronauts, and the Return of Objects Launched into Outer Space, 19 UST 7570, TIAS 6599, 672 UNTS 119 (1968); and the Agreement Governing the Activities of States on the Moon and Other Celestial Bodies , 1363 UNTS 3, 18 ILM 1434 (1984).

[7] Especially 1998 ISS IGA Article 16 (Cross Waiver of Liability).

[8] Id., Article 5 (Registration; Jurisdiction and Control); Article 6 (Ownership and Equipment), Article 25 (Entry into Force); and Article 27 (Amendments), note here "Amendments to this Agreement, except for those made exclusively to the Annex, shall be subject to ratification, acceptance, approval, or accession by those States in accordance with their respective constitutional processes."

[9] Id., Article 17 (Liability Convention) and Article 21 (Intellectual Property).

[10] Id., Article 22 Criminal Jurisdiction.

[11] "Given the growing use of soft law, it is important to understand the extent to which states and non-state actors comply with non-binding legal instruments, the factors that affect compliance, and the strategies available to increase compliance," Brown-Weiss Edith (2000), "Conclusions: Understanding Compliance with Soft Law", Chapter 9 in *Commitment and Compliance- The Role of Non-binding Norms in the International Legal System*, Edited by Dinah Shelton, Oxford University Press, pp.535; see also concept as apparent in the execution of the 1988 and 1998 ISS IGA, MOUs and between NASA and each of the other ISS Partners (NASDA, CSA, RSA and ESA); Covert (2002, Introduction), supra. note. 4.

[12] "The term 'international agreement' was intended to embrace unilateral engagements of an international character made by one state in favor of another." (Aust, 2000, ICLQ 276); Since the 1998 ISS IGA has only entered into force for only some and not all ISS Partners, this reinforces that views of commitment and compliance to this space program differ.

[13] Black's Law Dictionary describes law as the regime that orders human activities and foreign relations through systematic application of the force of politically-organized society or social pressure (2nd Edition, p. 400); "a rule will be legally-binding if it meets the requirements of a custom, which is a formal source of international law, and its substance will be indicated by state practice, which is the material source of custom. The term *evidence* is then used in the sense that diplomatic correspondence, for example, is evidence of state practice," Harris, D.J. (1998, 23)—*Cases and Materials on International Law*, Fifth Edition, Sweet & Maxwell, London.

[14] See for example, U.S. Public Law 106-391 (106th Congress) which authorizes NASA appropriations for fiscal years 2000, 2001, and 2002 and for other purposes; see Canadian the Civil International Space Station Agreement Implementation Act, S.C., 1999, c.35 Statute No. 999, Article 13-28 and Annexe; ESA Ministerial Meeting 2001 summary and respective ESA Member State Science and Technology Policies.

[15] Henkin Louis (1968), "How Nations Behave: Law and Foreign Policy 253, pp. 256-257.

[16] The Oxford English Dictionary (1996, 285) offers several definitions, from "obedience to a request" and "yielding" to "unworthy acquiescence"; Benedict Kingsbury suggests that, "there is a shared understanding that compliance is adequately defined as conformity of behavior with legal rules, and agreement that the real problems are about such matters as measuring, monitoring and improving compliance," taken from pp. 49, "The Concept of Compliance as a Function of Competing Conceptions of International Law" in *International Compliance with Non-Binding Accords*, Edited by Edith Brown Weiss, Studies in Transnational Legal Policy, No. 29, American Society of International Law, Washington, D.C. 1997; Alternatively, Peter M. Haas states that compliance is explained by "well-established patterns or expectations for patterns [of behavior]" in international relations and ultimately, "compliance is a matter of state choice," taken from "Choosing to Comply: Theorizing from International Relations and Comparative Politics," Chapter 2, Compliance Theories, pp. 43-64, in Shelton, Id. 11.

[17] See 14 U.S. CFR 1214.403 (January 2002). The ISS CCOC an enforceable U.S. federal law yet other ISS Partners do not have such a law.

[18] See supra. note 17 part IV: "the disciplinary policy does not limit a Cooperating Agency's right to apply relevant laws, regulations, policies and procedures to ISS crewmembers, consistent with the IGA and MOUs" and 1214.404 Violations- "subpart within the meaning of 18 USC 799, and whoever willfully violates,

attempts to violate, or conspires to violate any provision of this subpart or any order or direction issued under this subpart may be cited for violating title 18 of the U.S. Code and could be fined or imprisoned not more than 1 year or both" (misdemeanor). In contrast, the ISS CCOC is not an IGO regulation for the European (ESA) Partner, but rather, is perceived as an internal 'soft law' rule. The legal status of this space agency document remains an internal CSA rule because the Executive Committee (President of the Agency and High-level Directors determined that rules external to this government department were unnecessary. There was however, mention of this debate in the study of whether it should be made a national law).

[19] For instance, all governments do not agree that [MOUs] "use treaty language" and "are necessarily "governed by international law", Aust (1986, ICLQ, 795); The United States implemented the Case Zablocki Act which requires that the negotiation and conclusion of international instruments to be notified to Congress and the consultation by agencies with the Secretary of State with respect to proposed agreements. The Department of State publishes them.-- 22 Code of Federal Regulations, Part 181 ; see 46 Federal Register 35917 of 13 July 1981); Canada, Japan, and Russia have different processes of evaluation of these documents.

[20] See ISS IGA Article 7 (Management)---"Management of the Space Station will be established on a multilateral basis and the Partners, acting through their Cooperating Agencies, will participate and discharge responsibilities in management bodies established in accordance with the MOUs and implementing arrangements [...] In these management bodies, decision-making by consensus shall be the goal."

[21] The jury is still out as to whether international cooperation on ISS Programs is more broadly transferable to non-space issues and vice versa. More examples are needed to establish whether obligations met concerning one treaty has any direct links to commitment and compliance to other treaties with the same/similar signatories..

[22] For instance, where two ISS Partner nations are on friendly terms where they agree to reduce specific agricultural subsidies, this in itself does not mean they will support each other in an ISS-related dispute involving other State Partners.

[23] Note that drafters of ISS Instruments recognized the necessity to respect existing international law such as is demonstrated in ISS IGA Aricle 2.1 (International Rights and Obligations)---"The Space Station shall be developed, operated and utilized in accordance with international law, including the Outer Space Treaty, the Rescue Agreement, the Liability Convention, and the Registration Convention." Recognizing existing International Law in the ISS Program does not imply asking current UN members to offer opinions on ISS Partner issues.

[24] See ISS IGA Article 23 (Consultations)--offers four avenues to discuss and determine issues of commitment and compliance: 1. At the level of Cooperating Agencies, in accordance with procedures provided in the MOUs (and also following respective Agency internal reviews and procedures) ; 2. At the level of government, [and if] appropriate for consideration by all the Partners, the United States shall convene multilateral consultations; 3. At the technical level with regard to the two levels mentioned above; and 4. If an issue not resolved through consultations still needs to be resolved, the concerned Partners may submit the issue to an agreed form of dispute resolution such as conciliation, mediation, or arbitration. ; see also differences in ISS MOU Article 18 Settlement of Disputes between NASA and each of the other respective ISS Partners.

[25] "The more that the legal system decides for, and thus, becomes identified with, one side of a major conflict, the less it becomes able to act as an impartial arbiter whose decisions are readily respected." (Fisher, 1981, 25-26); Fisher Roger (1981). *Improving Compliance with International Law.* Procedural Aspects of International Law Series. Volume 14. University Press of Virginia Charlottesville. 370pgs.

[26] Consider that if specific timelines agreed upon by all ISS Partners for programmatic-related launches are willfully ignored or simply not respected by the launching States for diplomatic reasons, then Partners would be forced to devise alternative ways of meeting their commitments; see also Lucid (2002), Pellis (2002) and Gerstenmaier (2002), as well as ESA research experiment projects for ISS, infra. note 38.

[27] See ISS IGA Article 6 (Ownership of Elements and Equipment)---"The European Partner shall entrust ESA, acting in its name and on its behalf, with ownership over the elements it provides, as well as any other equipment developed and funded under an ESA programme as a contribution to the Space Station, its operation or utilization."

[28] According to Andre Farand of the ESA Legal Department in October 2002, eight of the eleven participating ESA Member States have ratified, but of the three big contributing nations necessary for ESA entry into force (e.g., France, Germany, Italy), France has not yet ratified. Thus, the ESA Council has not yet passed a motion to enter the ISS IGA into force for the European Partner. Among the ESA States that began this process earlier, the Kingdom of Spain deposited the ISS IGA for ratification October 1, 1999, the Kingdom of Norway did so and approved the document on May 13, 1999, the Federal Republic of Germany deposited the ISS IGA for ratification January 19, 2000, the Kingdom of the Netherlands deposited and approved the ISS IGA February 11, 2000; See also *Space News* (September 30, 2002, 6) "European Officials Brace for Negotiations with CNES" by Peter B. deSelding where a 2.6% drop in the space budget (1.28 in 2003 versus 1.307) for France will impact its contributions to ESA programs.

[29] Term "Assembly Complete" mentioned ISS MOU Article 5 in the context of finished infrastructure. Compare this term with the definition of "Core Complete" introduced by NASA.

[30] Based on interview with Frederic Nordlund, ESA Washington, D.C. Office, September 27, 2002.

[31] Supra. note 20.

[32] See NASA website (e.g., www.dfrc.nasa.gov/PAO/PAIS/HTML/FS-038-DFRC.html); also MAN Technologie.

[33] See Dogigli M. et al (2001) "Qualification of CMC Body Flaps for X-38" IAF Toulouse presentation. MAN Technologie. Germany.

[34] See ISS NASA-ESA MOU Art. 12.1b, 12.1d (Transportation, Communications and Other Non-Space Station Facilities) and also set forth in implementing arrangements.

[35] There is question as to whether NASA has used "best" or "reasonable" efforts to meet the commitments related to the X-38 Program which was to be a developmental stage for the ISS CRV. Consider IGA Article 12.2---
"Those Partners providing launch and return transportation services to other Partners and their respective users on a reimbursable or other basis shall provide such services consistent with the conditions specified in the relevant MOUs and implementing arrangements."; Although ISS IGA Article 15.2 states,
"Financial obligations of each Partner pursuant to this Agreement are subject to its funding procedures and the availability of appropriated funds," "best efforts" in this case might only be truly demonstrated where the U.S. President requests the appropriations from Congress. This was not done; also Gaede Heather (1999). "What Does Best Efforts Really Mean?" See FindLaw for Legal Professionals, Subject: Contracts: General 1. Gray Cary Ware & Freidenrich, LLP. pp. 1-3
http:///frof.com/articles/artDetail.asp?id=107 ;

[36] Based on interview with Richard Obermann, U.S. House Science Committee, Washington, D.C., September 13, 2002; also consulted Ralf Huber at DLR Washington, D.C. Office.

[37] Based on Communications with Ralf Huber, DLR Representative, Washington, D.C. (October 2002).

[38] See "Definition of the Principle of Good Faith in International Law", Chapter 8 in JK.F. O'Connor (1991) *Good Faith in International Law*, Ashgate Publishers, pp. 117-125, and especially the principles of "honesty, fairness and reasonableness" which require clarification in the context of a given arrangement.

[39] See diplomatic letter from Dr. Hebert Diehl,Chairman of the European Partner's IGA Coordinating Committee and Spokesman for the ISS European Partner to Ralf Braibanti, Director, Space and Advanced Technology Staff, Bureau of Oceans and International Environmental and Scientific Affairs, November 2, 2001.

[40] See ISS IGA Article 4 (Cooperating Agencies) ---"Where a provision of an MOU sets forth rights or obligations accepted by a Cooperating Agency (or, in the case of Japan, the Government of Japan) [...]."

[41] Date of Deposit of ISS IGA for ratification and acceptance, November 17, 1998; according to Robert Lefebvre detailing dates of signing and entering into force of ISS Agreements; confirmed by Mick Schlabs in the NASA Legal Office, Washington, D.C. and Masato Koyama of the NASDA Washington, D.C. Office (September 2002); NASA-GOJ MOU entered into force 28/02/98.

[42] Projected annual JEM operations budget is ~500 million U.S. dollars per year and the entire annual NASDA budget is 1.6 billion.

[43] Based on an interview September 20, 2002 with Masato Koyama, Director of NASDA Washington, D.C.

[44] See ISS MOU Article 16.4 --- " The Parties will seek to minimize the exchange of funds while carrying out their respective

responsibilities in this cooperative program, including through the performance of specific operations activities as provided for in Article 9 or, if they agree, through the use of barter, that is, the provision of goods or services."

[45] See ISS NASA-ESA MOU Art. 12.1.g and NASA-NASDA MOU as well as implementing arrangement.

[46] See ISS MOU Article 16.3---"In the event that funding problems are arising that may affect a partner's ability to fulfill its responsibilities under this MOU, that partner will promptly notify and consult with the other partners. Further, the Parties undertake to grant high priority to their Space Station programs in developing their budgetary plans."

[47] See ISS IGA Article 7.2 (Management)—"The United States, acting through NASA, and in accordance with the MOUs and implementing arrangements, shall be responsible for the management for: overall program management and coordination of the space station."

[48] Acceptance here means ratification, confirmed by the U.S. Department of State, Washington, D.C., July 24, 2000; Based also on communications with Mick Schlabs, NASA Legal Department, Washington, D.C. (July 2002).

[49] 1998 ISS IGA Article 25 (Entry into Force); note ISS IGA entered into force March 27, 2001.

[50] This document is used as an example among the existing NASA-Partner MOUs since there is no NASA-NASA MOU.

[51] Term "Core Complete is not present in the 1998 ISS IGA or NASA MOUs with the other Partners. This differs from the "Assembly Complete" term that was agreed upon by consensus by all ISS Partners: see Article 5.2 NASA-ESA MOU—"assembly of all permanently attached elements listed in Article 3" (parenthetical interpreted as quotation). The term "core complete" was introduced by the U.S. OMB concerning the FY 2002 Budget submission to U.S. Congress on 28 February 2001. This document indicates that completion of the U.S. Core is the point where the basic infrastructure is ready to accept "major international hardware elements," see http://www.whitehouse.gov/news/usbudget/blueprint/bud33.html ; See also Statement of A. Thomas Young, Chairman ISS Management and Cost Evaluation Task Force, Before Science Committee, House of Representatives, November 7, 2001 where 'Core Complete' is defined on page 1—" the core complete program is the original program with the deletion of the Crew Return Vehicle, Node 3, the Habitation module, and the Propulsion module, as well as a reduction in the research budget," www.hq.nasa.gov/congress/young11-7.html ; also ISS Management Evaluation Task Force (or Young) Report that mentions 'core complete' in preface, www.hq.nasa.gov/pub/pao/reports/2001/imce.pdf ; also NASA Advisory Council Meeting Minutes, June 11-12, 2002, mentions 'core complete' in opening remarks, www.hq.nasa/office/codez/nac/mins/0206mins.html.doc; also GAO Report July 2002, Space Station: 'Actions Underway to Reduce costs but Significant Challenges Remain', mentions 'core complete on page 3 and refers again to the term throughout the document, www.gao.gov .

[52] The Russian Soyuz can rescue 3 people. A temporarily docked Space Shuttle could rescue more people; see also The Young Report (2001) which detailed an internal review of NASA overspending on the ISS Program and recommended a complete review of specific management and operations approaches.

[53] See *NASA's Integrated Requirements*, Presentation by Shannon W. Lucid, September 10, 2002, especially slides 9,10, 11 and 12 (of 14) that stipulate and project individual ISS Partner crew time requirements; Dr. Sigmar Wittig, Chairman of the DLR German Aerospace Center also stated in Washington, D.C. on September 10, 2002 that ESA will require 720 hours of crew time per year as of the time the Columbus Module is launched; see also Pellis Neal R.(2002) "ISS Research, Office of Biological & Physical Research.", Presentation to the NASA Advisory Council, September 10-11, 19pgs; Gerstenmaier William (2002), "Response to Research Requirements." Presentation to NASA Advisory Council, September 10, 19pgs.

[54] Note NASA Space Policy Directive NPD 1050.1F--- "Authority to Enter into Space Act Agreements" and Chapter 3 of Space Act Agreements (NPG 1050.1)--- "Non-reimbursable and reimbursable agreements with foreign governments or governmental entities," Appendix 3: Sample Clauses for non-reimbursable and reimbursable agreements with foreign governments or governmental entities"

[55] "Non-reimbursable Agreement/ Memorandum of Understanding", Chapter 3 NASA Space Act Agreements, "Non-reimbursable and reimbursable agreements with foreign

governments or governmental entities," (NPG 1050.1).

[56] See McNeill John H. "International Agreements: Recent U.S. –U.K. Practice Concerning the Memorandum of *Understanding in American Journal of International Law*, Volume 88, Issue 4 (Oct., 1994), 821-826, especially 822-823; Aust Anthony (2000) *Modern Treaty Law and Practice*, Cambridge University Press, 443pgs; Ibid (1986). "The Theory and Practice of Informal International Legal Instruments. 35 I.C.L.Q. 787.

[57] "The intent of drafters to conclude an agreement in written form governed by international law, whatever its particular designation, is determinative," McNeill, supra. note 41 (823); also 22 USC S 2767 (b)(1)-(2) (1988) and 22USC S 2767a(d)(1)(1988).

[58] Based, in part, on communications with Robert Lefebvre, Legal Counsel, CSA (September, 2002).

[59] The Civil International Space Station Agreement Implementation Act,S.C.,1999, c.35, Article 13-28 and Annexe.

[60] See 1998 ISS IGA Article 25 (Entry into Force).

[61] Based on Communications with Benoit Marcotte, Karl-Heinz Gindl, CSA (October 2002).

[62] See Agreement for Cooperation between the European Space Agency and the Canadian Space Agency.

[63] *Space News*, September 30, "Russian Official Warns Lack of Funding May Temporarily Chose Space Station in 2003," Brian Berger and Simon Saradzhyan authors, p.15.

IAC-02-IISL.2.09

LEGAL ASPECTS OF SPACE TOURISM

By

Ram Jakhu* and Raja Bhattacharya**

ABSTRACT

This paper analyses some important aspects of applicable international space law and some national laws that have direct relevance to space tourism. Legal lacunae are identified and suggestions are made with a view to encourage the development of this newest application of space technology.

INTRODUCTION

It is a unique trait of human beings to be curious, to crave to know the unknown, to see the unseen, to unveil the mystic and to conquer the invincible, which attribute to their endeavor to moving from one geographic location to other, and this trait accounts for the birth of tour and travel, including space tourism.

Space tourism has a unique characteristic, which makes it distinguishable from any other fields of Tourism. A visit to the International Space Station (ISS), or any other space stations leaving the human defined territories and crossing the undefined border between airspace and outer space, does not only give such visit an extra-territoriality character, but also makes its visitors a kind of representatives of the people from the planet Earth in a limitless universe.

Normally, tourists do not undertake trips to see the air or the water; they take advantage of these means to see other places. But a space tour is a tour to see and contemplate what outer space is. The feeling of weightlessness is an alluring feature of space tourism. More importantly, space tourism is a branch of tourism where the travelers' state of heath is of prime importance. Thus, it is essential for a space tourist to undergo special and expensive medical fitness training and tests so that he/she could endure such an excursion or tour.

It can be asserted that because of several recent and significant technological developments, safe, reliable, and affordable transportation systems for space travel will become available within the next ten to fifteen years. The availability of such vehicles, meeting high standards of spaceworthiness, will encourage the initiation of commercial space lines and other space travel service providers for routine visits to outer space.

---

* LL.M., D.C.L., Associate Professor, Institute of Air and Space Law, Faculty of Law, McGill University, Montreal, Canada.

** LL.M. candidate, Institute of Air and Space Law, Faculty of Law, McGill University, Montreal, Canada.

From a market research project sponsored by the National Aerospace Laboratory, Japan, it came to light that "surveys of the world's two largest consumer markets and supporting data from Europe, [show] that the price of a return ticket to low Earth orbit should be reduced to between US$10,000 and US$20,000 per person", and further that "a market of the order of one million passengers per year, paying approximately US$10,000 per person, would generate revenues of US$10 billion per year."[1] Therefore, space travel by 'ordinary' or "average" people could become possible in the near future. A study carried out by the World Tourism Organization Statistics Chief, Enzo Paci, points out that short pleasure voyages to outer space will become a reality by 2004 or 2005.[2]

The motivating factors, which will guide tourism of the 21st century are entertainment, excitement and education. The space tourism would be "neither a fantasy nor just a nickname for conventional manned space flights, but an economic activity based on public demand."[3] Actual examples of birth of such an economic industrial activity are the space trips made by Dennis Tito of the U.S. [4] and Mark Shuttleworth of South Africa.[5]

POLICY AND LEGAL ISSUES

It has now been made clear by different studies that unless a definite regulatory framework exists it is difficult to promote space tourism. Several studies have been conducted by governments and private companies in search of a regulatory framework, which could serve as a platform or jumping board for the space tourism industry.

Aviation regulations as a precedent:

It is generally accepted that the existing aviation regulatory framework, after adequate and appropriate modifications and reforms, is compatible to be extended for to space transportation.[6] A group of authors rightly observed that "In view of the trend under way to commercialize NASA's activities, it seems likely that the evolution of

[1] P. Collins, R. Stockmans, M. Maita, Demand for Space Tourism in America and Japan and its Implication for Future Space Activities, 1995. For text see: http://www.spacefuture.com/archive/demand_for_space_tourism_in_america and_japan.shtml (accessed on 5.10.2002)

[2] Francesco Frangialli, "Crystal Ball Gazing", Dossier, The Courier, May-June 1999, p. 2.

[3] Makoto Nagatomo *et al,* "Study On Airport Services For Space Tourism", Proceedings of 6th IS COPS, AAS, For the text see: http://spacefuture.com/archive/study_on_airport_services_for_space_tourism.shtml

[4] Lift off on April 28, 2001 on Soyuz TM-32; De-orbit burn completed at 12:47 a.m. EDT Sunday; Landing completed at 1:42 EDT Sunday, May 6, 2001. For more details see: http://www.space.com/dennistito/ (accessed on 5.10.2002)

[5] Soyuz-TM34 rocket lifted clear of the launch pad at 0626 GMT from Baikonur, Kazakhstan and reached orbit eight minutes later. Soyuz capsule landed at 03.51 GMT. Also see: http://cooltech.iafrica.com/ spacetourist/ news/935985.htm (accessed on 5.10.2002)

[6] P. Collins and K. Yonemoto, "Legal and Regulatory Issues for Passenger Space Travel", IISL-98-IISL-3.09, Proceedings of International Symposium on Space Law, 49th IAF Congress, p.1.

government space activities will belatedly follow the precedent of aviation, with governments' role being progressively cut back from operations to supporting research - and the majority of activities being passenger transportation."[7]

For the purpose of studying the range of legal and regulatory issues, other than those relating to vehicle certification, which are necessary to be resolved before the commencement of the space tourism industry, a new committee called the "Commercial Space Transportation Legislation Research Committee" was established in 1998 in Japan under the chairmanship of Mr. Y. Funatsu, an aviation consultant. On board this Committee are experts possessing extensive aviation operating expertise in advanced technological passenger carrying vehicle and in working for building a bridge between the rocket community and the civil aviation community. The Committee extensively studied the existing aviation regulations and airworthiness standards. This approach parallels with the work being carried out in the U.S.

Since 1996, the U.S. Federal Aviation Administration (FAA)'s Office of the FAA Associate Administrator for Commercial Space Transportation (FAA-AST),[8] has been considering various forms of regulation of reusable rocket operations.[9] Several proposals concerning regulation of commercial facilities in orbit have been made to the FAA-AST,[10] which in turn felt the need of bringing in new regulations by 2005 to integrate space traffic and air traffic.[11] The FAA-AST is comprised of three divisions (a) Space system development (b) Licensing and safety

---

[7] P. Collins, K. Isozaki and R. Wakamatsu, "Space Tourism in Japan - the Growing Consensus", 2nd International Symposium on Space Tourism, 2nd International Symposium on Space Tourism, Bremen, April 21-23, 1999. For text see: http://www.spacefuture.com/ archive/space_tourism_in_japan_ the_growing_consensus.html (accessed on: 26.9.2002)

[8] On October 1, 1995, the U.S. Department of Transportation (DOT) transferred control over the Office of Commercial Space Transportation (OCST) to the Federal Aviation Administration (FAA). William A. Gaubatz, "Comments on Certification Standards for New Reusable Launch Vehicles ", FAA Office of Commercial Space Transportation Panel on Certification Standards for New Launch Vehicles, April 24, 1996, p. (1) . For text see: http://www. spacefuture.com/archive/ comments_on_ certification_standards_for_new_reusable_laun ch_vehicles.shtml. (accessed on 25.9.2002).

[9] P. Collins and K. Isozaki, "The Japanese Rocket Society's Space Tourism Research", International Symposium on Space Tourism, Bremen , 1997, March 20-22. For text see: http://www.spacefuture.com/archive/ the_japanese_rocket_society's_space_tourism_r esearch.shtml. (accessed on: 25.9.2002).

[10] C. Lauer, "Analysis of Alternative Governance Models for Space Business Parks", Engineering Construction & Operations in Space 5, ASCE, Vol. 1, 1996, pp 177-185; and B. Sherwood *et al*, "Government Actions to Enable Space Business Parks ", Engineering Construction & Operations in Space 5, ASCE , Vol. 1, 1996, pp 186-193.

[11] Patricia G. Smith, "Concept of Operations in the National Airspace System in 2005 ", Version 1.0, FAA Commercial Space Transportation, 1999, un-paginated. For the text see: http://www.spacefuture.com/archive/ concept_ofoperations_in_the_national_airspace _system_in2005.shtl. (accessed on: 25.9.2002)

and (c) Systems engineering and training. Active 'Strategies' have been worked out by FAA-AST to accomplish certain well-defined objectives in these three divisions.[12] This plan also outlines strategic support areas, vehicle system approvals and training, which cut across and support FAA-AST strategic focus areas.[13]

An evaluation of the existing Federal Aviation Regulations (FAR's) was conducted to assess their applicability to the design of reusable space vehicles. It was recognized that the existing FAR's do not cover all areas of reusable space vehicle (RSV) design, production, test and evaluation, and operations, but it suggested that the certification requirements for new RSV's can be developed within the existing FAR's, and that the FAR's and policies for RSV should therefore be similar to that of commercial aircraft. Apart from addressing the requirements for passenger space vehicles for having a type design certificate, production certificate, airworthiness certificate, commercial operators license, spaceport license and other approvals, it was emphasized that "Although individual nations need to put their own policies into place, their implementations need to be carried out in an atmosphere of international cooperation. This international planning should begin now during the most formative stages of the Spaceways."[14]

Though there has been a conscious attempt to apply the regulatory system, which is generally followed in case of aviation, however it would have some inherent problems also. The principal of them is the domain of certification. There may be different types of certifications, including the spaceworthiness certificate. "In order to extend existing aviation regulations to apply to passenger space vehicles, appropriate rules concerning vehicle structural integrity and damage tolerance, fire-suppression systems, passenger evacuation standards, maintenance procedures and other matters must be developed."[15] A major practical problem for such type of certification is that these certifications are issued after lots of test runs and if such test runs are applied as a prerequisite mechanism the cost of operation per space flight will be enormous and that can pose a deterrent to the promotion of this industry.

Another important issue is the use of cryogenic propellants. Unlike aviation, the propellants used by space vehicles

---

[12] See 'AST Strategic Plan 2002', FAA-AST. For text see: http://ast.faa.gov/files/pdf/strategicplan2k2.pdf

[13] See http://ast.faa.gov/aboutast/strat_plan.htm

[14] William Gaubatz, "Reusable Space Transportation - The Key Infrastructure Element in Opening the Space Frontier to the Public", Proceedings of 21st International Symposium of Space Technology and Science, May 24-31, 1998, Sonic City, Omiya, Japan. For the text see: http://www.spacefuture.com/archive/reusable_space_transportation_the_key_infrastructure_element.shtml

[15] P. Collins and K. Isozaki, "Legal and Regulatory Issues for Passenger Space Travel", *supra* note 6.

is different in composition and use. It has a close nexus with the safety of the flight also. In case of emergency landing of an aircraft, its fuel is generally jettisoned but in case of a space flight it has to be maintained in flight for a longer time in order to burn out the propellants on board the spacecraft.

Though a preliminary study in Japan showed that the noise level in case of space transport vehicles is far more than the permissible noise level, it is expected that with the passage of time and with the advent of advance technology this can be taken care of. The supporters who encourage space tourism vehemently forward their views that space tourism flights are so rarely flown that they would not affect anybody except the travelers who would be mentally prepared to bear such noise. This problem can also be tackled by constructing spaceport far away from human localities.

The most serious issue that has troubled various study groups is that of space traffic management. Once space vehicles start flying regularly and aircraft traffic would increase with arithmetic progression by then, undoubtedly there could be severe interference between the two services. There would be a need of establishing a body parallel to the International Civil Aviation Organization (ICAO) for space activities.[16] If a similar organization for space traffic is created, possible conflict of their jurisdictions and overlap of operations of space vehicles and civil aviation activities of the two organizations in view of the lack of demarcation between airspace and outer space, need to be resolved.

Unlike airplanes within the atmosphere, spacecrafts in orbit do not maintain fixed positions relative to the Earth's surface, and so a practical procedure for defining orbits needs to be devised and agreed upon.[17] There is an ongoing discussion regarding 'slot management'. To date, allocation of 'slots' has been carried out primarily for the geostationary orbit. Although that orbit is easy to define, the matter of allocating geostationary orbital 'slots' is nevertheless the subject of substantial legal activity involving both telecommunications law and space law.[18] This activity will have some serious implications in defining and

[16] For more discussion on ICAO's role, see below.

[17] P. Collins and T. Williams, "Towards Traffic Control Systems for Near-Earth Space", Proceedings of 29th Colloquium on the Law of Outer Space, IISL, 1986, pp. 161-170; alsowww.spacefuture.com/archive/towards_traffic_control_systems_for_near_earth_space.shtml; and P. Collins, "Legal Considerations for Traffic Systems in Near-Earth Space", Proceedings of 31st Colloquium on the Law of Outer Space, IISL, 1989, pp. 296-303; www.spacefuture.com/archive/legal_considerations_for_traffic_systems_in_near_earth_space.shtml.

[18] J. Thompson , "Space for Rent: The International Telecommunications Union, Space Law, and Orbit/Spectrum Leasing ", Journal of Air Law and Commerce , Vol. 62, 1997, pp. 279-311.

regulating the use of space "traffic lanes" and low Earth orbits.[19]

Security issues will be a major concern from the beginning of the space travel. Any deficiency in security may bring devastation for future prospects of this industry. Therefore, insurance issues will also have important relevance to space travel as they are currently for the aviation industry. Substantial insurance coverage will be needed to make each venture risk-free and a successful one both from the operator's point of view and that of the travelers.

For the sub-orbital flights the question of training may not be so important but for orbital flights it will play a significant role as some formal training to appraise and regulate the behavior of the space tourists in zero/micro gravity environment will be required. Medical certification may also be necessary which may limit the intake of space travelers for orbital flights. The passengers will not only be exposed to physical stress due to a micro/zero gravity environment but also to the high speed with which the orbital flights would operate and the level of endurance a human body could bear. There is also the risk of damaging space radiation, which needs to be taken care of.

For the sub-orbital flights mainly, and in a few cases of orbital flights also, the question of international political relations between States would inevitably come into play requiring compliance of relevant immigration and customs laws.

Another important issue is that of liability. Some authors[20] feel that some regulatory mechanism may be developed similar to the one under the 1929 Warsaw Convention[21] that deals with the limits of liability not only because of the historic role it played in nourishing an infant aviation industry to its present adulthood but also in considering the interests of aviation passengers. However, the attitude and actions of the insurance industry in the wake of September 11, 2001 tragedy should act as a pre-cautionary lesson for not placing utmost reliance on the war risk insurance type clauses which may be applied to space transportation as well. Thus, not only an international treaty is required establishing a Warsaw Convention type regime but equal emphasis should be placed on the other insurance elements which are closely connected to any particular space flight operation. Another serious issue related with orbital space travel operations is the problem of space debris. Though a rosy picture is painted by all the commercial firms in order to promote their prospective space tourism endeavors, the most serious risk about which they are silent is the hazards

[19] L. David, "Surge in Launchers Spurs FAA to Study Traffic Control Plan", Space News, Vol. 9, No 15, 1998, pp. 4 and 19.

[20] Ricky J. Lee et al, "'Space Tourism and Permanent Human Settlement: The Legal and Regulatory Issues', The legal and Regulatory Issues", Colloquium on the Law of Outer Space, (2000), IISL-00-IISL.2.05, at p. 4; P. Collins and K. Yonemoto, "Legal and Regulatory Issues for Passenger Space Travel", *supra* note 6.

[21] Convention for the Unification of Certain Rules Relating to International Carriage by Air, Warsaw, October 12, 1929.

arising out of possible collisions with rapidly increasing space debris, particularly in the low Earth orbit. The insurance premiums inevitably would be high in view of this risk. Unless some parity is drawn between the operational cost (including insurance payable by the space liners) and the cost of travel per passenger, the space tourism industry may suffer irreparably despite the efforts by governmental or non-governmental entities.

It is interesting to note that during the last few years, several space related tax reform bills have been introduced in the U.S. Congress. This shows that the U.S. government is taking important initiatives in space utilization, and if passed, these bills can be expected to encourage space tourism industry as well. Among the bills, are (a) Invest in Space Now Act of 2001(HR 2177),[22] (b) The Spaceport Equality Act (H.R. 1931, S. 1243),[23] (c) The "Zero Gravity, Zero Tax Act" (H.R. 2504),[24] (d) Space Tourism Promotion Act of 2001 (H.R. 2443),[25] and (e) Commercial Space Partnership Act of 1999 (S. 2316).[26]

Legal status of space tourists

The universally accepted designation of a crewmember of a space object is "astronaut". However, there is no definition of the term "astronaut' in the 1967 Outer Space Treaty; [27] the first cardinal treaty which is accepted universally as the *magna carta* of the international space law. Though, the Russians use the term 'cosmonaut' for the same, the term 'astronaut' undoubtedly can be considered to have been legally and universally a recognized term as the Outer Space Treaty (adhered to by Russia as well) refers to this term.

---

[22] To benefit investors of both small start-up launch companies as well as larger well-established ones, the proposed legislation offers two categories of tax credits: one for small space vehicle manufacturers and the other for large ones. See: http://www.spaceprojects.com/tax/#INVEST. http://thomas.loc.gov/cgi-bin/query/D?c107:1:./temp/~c107TjLtax.

[23] To treat spaceports like airports under the exempt facility bond rules. See: http://www.spaceprojects.com/tax/#INVEST. For the text see: http://thomas.loc.gov/cgi-bin/query/D?c107:2:./temp/~c107TjLtax.

[24] To amend the Internal Revenue Code of 1986 to provide tax incentives for investing in companies involved in space-related activities See: http://www.spaceprojects.com/tax/# INVEST. For the text see: http://thomas.loc.gov/cgi-bin/query

[25] To create guaranteed loans and capital gains exclusions essentially for the development of facilities and services directly involved with space tourism. See: http://www.space projects.com/tax/#INVEST. For the text see: http://thomas.loc.gov/cgi-bin/query

[26] To authorize the lease of real and personal property under the jurisdiction of the National Aeronautics and Space Administration to public or private businesses, as well as to local, state and other federal government entities. See: http://www.spaceprojects.com/tax/#INVEST. For the text see: http://thomas.loc.gov/cgi-bin/query/D?c106:1:./temp/~c106GymWKn.

[27] The Treaty on Principles Governing the Activities of States in the Exploration and Use of Outer Space, including the Moon and Other Celestial Bodies (adopted by the General Assembly in its resolution 2222 (XXI)), opened for signature on 27 January 1967, entered into force on 10 October 1967. (96 ratifications and 27 signatures). (hereafter referred to as the Outer Space Treaty).

Under the Outer Space Treaty, each astronaut is regarded as an 'envoy of mankind' in outer space.[28] Astronauts enjoy the assurance of universal assistance from States in the event of accident, distress or emergency landing be it on a territory of a State or high seas.[29] They enjoy the protection of and assistance for being promptly and safely returned to the State of registry of the space vehicle.[30]

In the texts of the international space treaties, (namely the Outer Space Treaty, the Rescue and Return Agreement, and the Registration Convention[31]) there has been the use of three terms for a space traveler, however without any definition of either of them; i.e. 'envoy of mankind', 'astronaut' and 'personnel'. An interesting matter is the status of an astronaut of a particular State *vis a vis* another astronaut of a different State. These envoys of mankind transform into political identities representing two sovereign States; their interrelations, behavior, actions and movements are controlled and dictated by their respective States. So we can see that the status of a space traveler changes with location or situation; an 'astronaut' bearing a explorative and scientific connotation, a 'personnel' bearing administrative connotation, a 'representative of a State' bearing a political connotation, an 'envoy of mankind' bearing a global diplomatic yet humane connotation.

The legal status of a space tourist will have to fit in any of the above-mentioned three terms in conformity with the contemporary space law. However, their legal status seems to be more akin to an astronaut than the others. They have some traits of astronauts, though not all, and as such they can be called as pseudo astronauts. Whatever may be the case any space traveler, under the present regime of space law will remain under the jurisdiction and control of the State under which the concerned space object (the space tour vehicle) is launched.[32] The 'take-off' of a spacecraft will be treated as a launch. Again each space travel venture will be treated as separate launch and a separate space activity and the appropriate State will be internationally responsible for it.[33]

Dennis Tito, the first officially acclaimed space tourist had the status of a space tourist for the public and the

---

28 Ibid., Article V.

29 Ibid. Also see: The Agreement on the Rescue of Astronauts, the Return of Astronauts and the Return of Objects Launched into Outer Space (the "Rescue Agreement", adopted by the General Assembly in its resolution 2345 (XXII), opened for signature on 22 April 1968, entered into force on 3 December 1968. (87 ratifications and 26 signatures). (hereafter referred to as the Rescue and Return Agreement).

30 Ibid.

31 The Convention on Registration of Objects Launched into Outer Space, adopted by the General Assembly in its resolution 3235 (XXIX)), opened for signature on 14 January 1975, entered into force on 15 September 1976. 43 ratifications and 4 signatures. (hereafter referred to as the Registration Convention).

32 Article VIII of the Outer Space Treaty.

33 Article VII of the Outer Space Treaty.

media, a guest cosmonaut for the Russians and an amateur astronaut for the Americans.[34]

It is quite interesting to note that the second commercial space traveler, Mark Shuttleworth, has not been termed as a 'guest'. He has been designated as a 'non-professional cosmonaut.'[35] His mission was not to just travel for pleasure but something more than that which has changed his status from a mere guest to a pseudo cosmonaut intending to carry out a series of experiments on board the International Space Station. According to his spokesman, Barak Geffen, Shuttleworth was "a fully certified member of the Soyuz crew responsible for some of its systems during the flight [and would] conduct several scientific experiments with South African and Russian researchers…"[36] Unlike Tito, Shuttleworth had to undergo rigorous cosmonaut medical check ups, followed by a thorough cosmonaut training, including intense Russian language tuition. He was, in his own words, "Trying to achieve with this program what most countries set out to achieve when they first start a manned space program."[37] Thus Shuttleworth's motivation was not primarily pleasure (which remained the sole driving force of a tourist) but to achieve scientific zero/micro gravity results. The Russians have asserted that they were selling the third seat on Soyuz space shuttle. As per the spokesman of Russian Space Agency, Sergei Gorbunov, "Taking into account our difficult situation, our partners will understand why we shall be forced to sell one of the three seats on Soyuz spaceships.[However], this is not to say that the third seat will invariably be sold to space tourists."[38] Thus, it appears that the Russian view on the status of a space tourist is of a 'non professional cosmonaut'. This is supported by an official statement according to which Shuttleworth was "accompanied by professional cosmonauts."[39] It has already been decided that Lance Bass will be the third tourist.[40] However, according to a Russian official, Bass will receive "training as a simple space tourist like dozens of other amateurs that pay the Gagarin center for a theoretical course and a few thrills, such as low-gravity parabolic plane flights …. [and] will not train as part of the two-person professional crew".[41] Thus for the Russians, Shuttleworth was a 'non-

[34] http://www.spacedaily.com /news/011206 133411.3i4zwq28.html (accessed on: 27-12-01)

[35] http:// www.spacedaily.com/news/020122143 959.qz3jsqlw.html, (accessed on: 22-01-02)

[36] http://www.spacedaily.com /news/011204120 530.hlj8wds3.html (accessed on: 27-12-01)

[37] http://www.spacedaily.com/news/tourism - 02a.html (accessed on: 06-0102)

[38] http://www.spacedaily.com/news/020122 143959.qz3jsqlw.html (accessed on 22-0102)

[39] http://www.spacedaily.com /news/0112051 55750.qi4myfex.html (accessed 27-12-01)

[40] Simon Saradzhyan, "Lance Bass to Resume Cosmonaut Training, Won't Fly Until April at Earliest", 20 September 2002; on line: http://www.space.com/missionlaunches/bass_re sumes_020920.html (accessed on: 27.9.02).

[41] Ibid.

professional cosmonaut' and Bass will be a 'simple space tourist'.

These first space travelers are expected to lead to a host of similar tours from different nations. The borderline between a space tour and a space travel is fading and so is the status of a space tourist, a space traveler and an astronaut.

In determining the legal status of a space traveler an essential question is: 'for what mission?' There may be a secondary query 'under which flag?' The Russian approach of commercializing space made it more important for the West to carve out the importance of the flag bearer of the space traveler. However the importance of a flag warrants great importance considering the specific provisions of the Outer Space Treaty, the Registration Convention, the Rescue and Return Agreement, and the Liability Convention,[42] particularly from the perspective of liability as well as jurisdiction and control.

Licensing:

An important part in space tourism operations is the regulatory regime, at both the international and national levels. This is due to the fact that a space tour vehicle, in its flight to and from outer space, will travel through and/or by using the airspace of several States. Under the 1944 Chicago Convention, each State enjoys "complete and exclusive sovereignty over the airspace above its territory."[43] On the other hand, the 1967 Outer Space Treaty, in its Article 1(2) recognizes the freedom of outer space. Since there is no clear demarcation between airspace and outer space, national legal regimes may dictate the rules and limitation of flights through their respective airspace. There is also no clear acceptance of a right of 'innocent passage' allowing a particular space flight through the sovereign airspace of foreign States.[44] Therefore, a space tour vehicle for its operation would need licenses from the States whose airspace it could be traversing. As space tourism primarily will be a commercial activity, it is likely that some States may be reluctant to grant such licenses or may grant them with costly conditions. In order to minimize this regulatory burden, States should

[42] The Convention on International Liability for Damage Caused by Space Objects, adopted by the General Assembly in its resolution 2777 (XXVI)), opened for signature on 29 March 1972, entered into force on 1 September 1972. 81 ratifications and 26 signatures. (hereafter referred to as the Liability Convention).

[43] The Convention on International Civil Aviation (signed at Chicago, on 7 December 1944), Article 1.

[44] The opinion of the Council of ICAO, as presented by the ICAO Observer to the Legal Subcommittee of the COPUOS at its 1986 session, is that: "(d) The right of innocent passage of spacecraft through the sovereign airspace is proposal de lege ferenda (i.e. a legislative proposal not reflecting the existing law); such right does not exist under the present international law of the air; an unconditional right of passage through the sovereign airspace does not exit even with respect to the civil aircraft and is specifically subject to a special authorization with respect to State aircraft and pilotless aircraft; (e) The operation of spacecraft in the airspace may require operational co-ordination with air navigation services to ensure the safety of air navigation." See document: C-WP/8158 of 15/1/86.

enter into space transport bilateral or multilateral agreements, as is the case in civil aviation.

The other important dimensions of licensing will emerge when space tourism becomes a significant economic activity. "Licensing covers a variety of non-direct investment production operations, involving arms-length cooperation with an external agency (or agencies). Some elements of market transfer are included in this packaged sale of asset services. A spectrum of relationships is possible, ranging from (the rare) simple sale of embodied knowledge or assets (brand name, patent) through franchising, turn key operations, contract manufacturing, management contracts etc."[45] Therefore, space tourism industry will involve a variety of legal licensing like any other regular commercial operation.

At the national level, the U.S. has been the most active country in devising licensing regime and procedures for privately operated reusable space transportation systems. As noted above, since 1995, the FAA-AST has been actively developing licensing procedure for commercially operated reusable space vehicles.[46] The FAA-AST draws its limited authority and/or responsibility to regulate the commercial space transportation industry, from the law regulating Commercial Space Launch Act.[47] At present the FAA-AST grants a license when it determines that an applicant's launch or reentry proposal or proposal to operate a launch site will not jeopardize public health and safety, safety of property, the U.S. national security or foreign policy interests, or international obligations of the United States. The FAA-AST, however, does not license launches performed by and for the U.S. government agencies.[48] The FAA-AST has been considering applying appropriate aviation procedures to the field of private reusable space transport vehicles. Though, the existing FARs do not cover all areas of RSVs design, production,

---

[45] Stephen F. Witt, Michael Z. Brooke, Peter J. Buckley, The Management of International Tourism, 2nd Edition (New York: Routledge, 1992) at p.65.

[46] P. Collins and K. Yonemoto, "Legal and Regulatory Issues for Passenger Space Travel", *supra* note 6.

[47] 49 USC, Subtitle IX, Chapter 701, gave the FAA-AST the responsibility to: · "regulate the commercial space transportation industry, only to the extent necessary to ensure compliance with international obligations of the United States and to protect the public health and safety, safety of property, and national security and foreign policy interest of the United States, ... encourage, facilitate, and promote commercial space launches by the private sector, · recommend appropriate changes in Federal statutes, treaties, regulations, policies, plans, and procedures, and facilitate the strengthening and expansion of the United States space transportation infrastructure." http://ast.faa.gov/lrra/. For the text see: http://ast.faa.gov/ aboutast/701complete.html (accessed on: 29.9.2002). It is should be noted that the 'finding and purpose' of this Act was *inter alia* to encourage the United States private sector to provide launch vehicles, reentry vehicles, and associated services by simplifying and expediting the issuance and transfer of commercial licenses and facilitating and encouraging the use of Government-developed space technology.

[48] http://ast.faa.gov/lrra/. Also see: http://ast.faa.gov/files/pdf/2000rlv.pdf (both accessed on: 29.9.2002).

test and evaluation and operation, it has been suggested that the certification requirements for new RSVs can be developed within the existing FARs and that the FARs and the policies for RSVs should therefore be similar to that of commercial aircraft.[49] There has been recommendation that the FAA-AST should be given further authority and resources to extend its work to include passenger space travel and to license private aircraft to provide zero-gravity flight services to the general public.[50] In fact, in July 2001, a bill has been introduced in the U.S. Congress. If enacted, it will authorize the Secretary of Transportation to issue regulations governing activities related to space tourism.[51]

ICAO and space tourism:

The involvement of the International Civil Aviation Organization in space tourism should also be seriously considered. The space traffic will have to be appropriately and smoothly accommodated with air traffic, which in itself has become so congested. It will take a serious consideration by all States through ICAO, as the forum, to work out a viable solution to this problem. Space and air traffic management issues will be a major factor in the allotment of air 'slots' to both air and space liners. Air and space traffic congestion will also force the States to reorganize their military or defense air routes and will likely result in more stringent rules. ICAO's role will be very important in the near future as a participant in resolving the space traffic issues. It is an interesting question as to whether the States will also empower ICAO with a mandate to deal with space travel safety and security issues, as it does in the civil aviation sector.

Will there be parallel aviation and space treaties or will the present aviation treaties be amended to incorporate, with harmony and without dichotomy, the space travel issues and aspects? Will ICAO be the international organization to formulate a regulatory framework for passenger space travel needs or is there a necessity of establishing a parallel or identical international body for space travel related activities and issues? The U.S. FAA-AST has already "proposed the formation of an International Space Flight Organization (ISFO) to play the role of the International Civil Aviation Organization (ICAO) in relation to space travel."[52] Collins and Funatsu rightly assert "the ISFO would help to coordinate different countries' activities and ensure that agreement is reached on

[49] P. Collins, "Legal Considerations for Traffic Systems in Near-Earth Space", Proceedings 31st Colloquium on the Law of Outer Space, IISL, 1989, pp. 296-303.

[50] Robert L. Haltermann, Report On The First U.S. Space Tourism Conference, "Going Public": Moving Toward The Development Of A Large Space Tourism Business, September 30, 1999. For the text see: http://www.space transportation.org/99ConReport.htm (accessed on: 29.9.2002)

[51] Space Tourism Act 2001, July 2001, (H.R. 2443).

[52] P. Collins, "Space Activities, Space Tourism and Economic Growth", Proceedings of 2nd International Symposium on Space Tourism, Bremen, April 21-23, 1999. For the text see: www.spacefuture.com/archive/ space_ activities_space_tourism_and_economic_growt h.shtml. (accessed on: 28.9.2002).

international procedures and standards in a timely manner".[53]

An interesting proposal from Smith[54] for establishing "Space Transition Corridors" (STC),[55] and supported by Collins and Funatsu,[56] warrants a serious consideration. According to these scholars the STC will enable efficient and economical use of airspace and outer (orbital) space.

[53] P. Collins and Y. Funatsu, "Collaboration with Aviation - The Key to Commercialization of Space Activities", IAF Congress paper no IAA-99-IAA.1.3.03, 1999. For the text see: http://www.spacefuture.com/archive/collaboration_with_aviation_the_key_to_commercialisation_of_space_activities.shtml. (accessed on: 28.9.2002).

[54] Patricia G. Smith, Concept of Operations in the National Airspace System in 2005, Federal Aviation Administration Office of Commercial Space Transportation, February 8, 1999. For the text see: http://www.spacefuture.com/archive/concept_of_operations_in_the_national_airspace_system_in_2005.shtml. (accessed on: 28.9.2002).

[55] Zones linking an area on the ground to an area in orbit reserved for either a vehicle returning from orbit or a launching vehicle, into which aircraft are not permitted for the duration. it is not a permanent fixed route like an air-lane, but a temporary zone defined in space and time within a computerized air traffic control system.

[56] P. Collins and Y. Funatsu, "Collaboration with Aviation - The Key to Commercialization of Space Activities", IAF Congress paper no IAA-99-IAA.1.3.03, 1999. For the text see: http://www.spacefuture.com/ archive/ collaboration _with_aviation_the_key_to_ commercialisation_of_space_activities.html. (accessed on: 28.9.2002).

Registration of transportation vehicles:

In terms of the existing space legal regime, all launches of space objects to or beyond Earth orbit are to be registered nationally and with the United Nations. According to Funatsu "in case of commercial spaceships which are repeatedly launched (or which can be described more appropriately by saying "flown") and space structures which are not launched but built and operated in orbit, this **requirement** (*of being registered with UN*) seems impractical and should not be applicable to these vehicles"[57] (emphasis supplied). He suggests that "the nature of registration for commercial space vehicles should be the same as that for aircraft, the purpose being the establishment of their ownership and identification. It is administered nationally according to ICAO procedures."[58]

The Outer Space Treaty affirms that States shall bear international responsibility for their national activities in outer space.[59] The Treaty also entrusts 'jurisdiction and control' of a spacecraft to the State on whose registry an object launched into outer space is carried.[60] Thus the Registration

[57] Y. Funatsu, "Some Aspects of Space Navigation Law", Proceedings of 2nd International Symposium on Space Travel, Bremen, April 21-23 1999 for text see: http://www.spacefuture.com/archive/ some_aspects_of_space_navigation_law.shtml (accessed on: 28.9.2002)

[58] Ibid.

[59] Outer Space Treaty, Article VI.

Convention, which draws its formulation or legislative basis from the Outer Space Treaty, not only aims to provide identification of space objects but also aims to fix the responsibility arising out of any space activities pertaining to that space object on a launching State. While providing for a detailed procedure regarding registration, the Registration Convention incorporates the same definition of launching State as in the Outer Space Treaty and the Liability Convention.

The Registration Convention provides two fold benefits; i.e. (i) in case of any damage caused to the spacecraft during its flight, (e.g. due to space debris), the responsibility could be attached to the State of registry or for that matter the launching State(s) by identifying the space object (debris) responsible for the damage; and (ii) for fixing responsibility in case of any damage from which a third State suffers.

Whether the 'flag of convenience' practice, as followed in the maritime field, can be applied to space tour vehicles is a time-tested question. Keeping in view the Outer Space Treaty and the Registration Convention, it is clear that even if the flag of convenience is used by a space travel company the victim State will have legal recourse for remedy against the State (of the tour operator), which comes within the definition of a launching State or the State of registry.

[60] Outer Space Treaty, Article VIII.

Liability for damage:

Liability issues may be broadly categorized under two types: criminal liability and civil liability. The former deals with the more human element in space operations and thus essentially involves punitive consequences whereas the latter includes the legal framework of national and international rules and regulations and compensation issues arising out of space operations.

Criminal liability:

In the case of space tourism, criminal liability may arise on two occasions. First in case of the passengers who are going for pre-orbital and orbital flights and secondly the passengers who will be availing/utilizing or staying on a space station or platform. The legal regime of outer space comprising the five international space treaties[61] do not provide for it specifically.

In the first case, guidance may be sought from the existing aviation conventions on this subject which may be said to be the first uniform, universal and collective approach, initiative and action of all nations to effectively tackle the problem of aviation security. There has been a major contribution to the development of international law in the

[61] They are: the 1967 Outer Space Treaty, the 1968 Rescue and Return Agreement, the 1972 Liability Convention, the 1995 Registration Convention, and the Agreement Governing the Activities of States on the Moon and Other Celestial Bodies, adopted by the General Assembly in its resolution 34/68, opened for signature on 18 December 1979, entered into force on 11 July 1984. (9 ratifications and 5 signatures)

field of civil aviation security by different aviation security instruments with the initiative of ICAO.[62] These international legal instruments while creating special criminal jurisdiction of, and international duty upon, the State of registry in respect of or arising out of offences and other acts which can endanger civil aviation, brought the system of universal jurisdiction in international law and granted particular rights, functions and entitlements to the Pilots-in-command which they did not possess earlier under international law. This issue however unfolds another very important aspect relating to the scope of authority and power to be vested to the Commander of a space tourist vehicle. It is advisable to adopt the same scheme both in cases of the application of criminal jurisdiction, liabilities and vesting of authority to the Commander, as they basically deal with issues similar to the safety and security arising out of aviation passengers' misconduct or criminal behavior.

An answer to the second part of the issue, which deals with criminal liability and/or jurisdiction on space stations or platforms may be searched for in a multilateral space station agreement between five Partners States, commonly known as the Inter Governmental Agreement of 1998.[63]

The 1998 IGA is the first exhaustive legal document dealing with different aspects of space activities. Generally criminal matters are dealt with under the respective national criminal legislations and jurisdictions. However, matters relating to criminal liability and/or jurisdiction over crimes occurring on the space station have been given somewhat uniform treatment under Article 22 of 1998 IGA. It not only provides that Partner States "may exercise criminal jurisdiction over personnel in or on any flight module element who are their respective nationals"[64] but also allows other Partners to prosecute the perpetrator, in certain cases. This means that no perpetrator could escape prosecution taking advantage of his/her national criminal legislation or absence of a extradition treaty. Once this framework is fully implemented,

---

[62] To summarize them: The first international instrument was the 'Convention on offences and certain other acts committed on board aircraft' signed at Tokyo (commonly known as Tokyo Convention,1963), followed by the 'Convention for the suppression of unlawful seizure of aircraft' signed in Hague (commonly known as Hague Convention,1970), 'Convention for the suppression of unlawful acts against the safety of civil aviation' signed in Montreal (commonly known as Montreal Convention,1971), 'Protocol for the suppression of Unlawful Acts of Violence at Airports Serving International Civil Aviation, Supplementary to the Convention for the suppression of unlawful acts against the safety of civil aviation done at Montreal' signed in Montreal (commonly known as Montreal Protocol,1988) and 'Convention on the marking of Plastic Explosives for the purpose of Detection' done in Montreal (commonly known as Montreal Convention, 1991).

[63] Agreement among the Government of Canada, Governments of Member States of the European Space Agency, the Government of Japan, the Government of the Russian Federation, and the Government of the United States of America concerning cooperation on the Civil International Space Station, 20 January 1998. (hereafter referred to as the 1998 IGA)

[64] Article 22(1) of the 1998 IGA.

criminal jurisdiction and liability issues in the operation of space tourism could be easily and properly addressed.

The Parties (Partner States) to this Agreement have taken steps towards reforming their national legislations in order to fulfill their respective obligations (particularly those that relate to criminal matters) under the 1998 IGA. The glaring example on this point is that of Canada as it has enacted the *Civil International Space Station Agreement Implementation Act*[65]. By virtue of Section 11 of this Act, Section 7 of the Canadian Criminal Code[66] has been amended in order to incorporate corresponding changes in the liability arising out of criminal behavior of the crewmember(s) on aboard the ISS.

It would be advisable to follow the guideline as set out in the 1998 IGA while attempting to draft and formulate regulations and internationally enforceable rules governing criminal liability issues in space tourism sector.

Civil liability:

The Outer Space Treaty and the Liability Convention bring under their umbrella the entire gamut of issues arising out of launching (including the attempted launching) of space objects (which include component parts of space objects or launch vehicles) and assign liability to the launching State(s) for damage[67] caused to a third party. They cover liability issues for both pre-orbital and orbital accident/damage.

The Liability Convention assigns absolute liability for damage caused on the surface of the Earth and to any aircraft in flight (i.e. the pre-orbital damage) and fault liability for damage caused elsewhere (meaning orbital damage). However it is controversial whether this Convention covers damage caused in orbit by space debris. Liability in such case may not be clearly and strictly assigned to the launching State(s) because of the difficulty in the identification of the origin of the damaging space debris. Some authors believe that the Convention "appears to be primarily concerned with a possible collision between [active] space objects."[68] However, an attempt may be made to take advantage of the Registration Convention to assign liability to the State of registry (which will also be the launching State) if the space debris causing such damage could be identified on the basis of registration under the Convention.

The important liability questions, directly relevant to space tourism, which need to be addressed are: (a) whether a flight undertaken by a space passenger vehicle can be termed as

[65] Statutes of Canada 1999, Chapter 35, as passed by, The House of Commons, 19th November 1999, 2nd Session, 36th Parliament, 48 Elizabeth II, 1999. Bill C-4, assented to on 16th December 1999.

[66] Revised Statutes of Canada, Chapter C-46.

[67] 'Damage' is defined in Article I, to mean loss of life, personal injury or other impairment of health, loss of or damage to property of States or of persons (natural or juridical) or property of international intergovernmental organization.

[68] Glen H. Reynolds and Robert P Merges, Outer space: problems of law and policy, (Boulder, Colo.: Westview Press, 1997), p. 212.

launching, (b) whether space transport vehicles are space objects, and (c) what will be the treatment and status of the passengers or space tourists under the Liability Convention?:

(a) The term 'launch' has not been defined in any of the five international space treaties.[69] If the 'taking off' of a space transport vehicle with space tourists is deemed to be a launch, it would have two opposite repercussions. This can also be termed as the dichotomy arising out of the legal interpretation of the term 'launch'. On the one hand, if it is a space launch, then the definition of launching State[70] squarely applies and the space tourists are covered under the Liability Convention. On the other hand, this interpretation could debar the same tourists from claiming for any damages under Article VII of the Liability Convention.[71]

(b) The term 'space object' has not been clearly defined in any of the five international space treaties. But the use of the word 'an object' in Article VII of Outer Space Treaty, especially in the context of launching, can be deemed to apply to a space transport vehicle. Thus, this interpretation will give rise to a problem and will have bearing on a particular group of space tourists, leading to the following third question.

(c) If space tourists (passengers) from a launching State (having the nationality of that State) are not covered under the Liability Convention; that is to say, if any damage is caused to them from the space transport vehicle (treating the space transport vehicle as a space object) they will be disqualified from making any claim under Article VII of the Liability Convention. This is inconsistent with the entire fabric of liability regime that the space tourism industry has to rely on and will be a serious deterrent to the industry itself.

Article VII of the Liability Convention poses another impediment to space tourism and could have far reaching consequences. It stipulates that the Liability Convention is not applicable to "foreign nationals during such time as they are participating in the operation of that space object from the time of its launching or at any stage thereafter until its decent." If flying of a space transport vehicle to the outer space is deemed to be a 'launch' and if the space vehicle is a space object, then the foreign nationals who are space tourists (passengers) are not sheltered by the international protections granted by the Liability Convention. Thus any space tourist having a foreign nationality will

[69] *Supra* note 61.

[70] According to Article 1 (c) of the Liability Convention, the term "launching State" means: (i) a state which launches or procures the launching of a space object; (ii) a State from whose territory or facility a space object is launched. Similar definition is included in Article VII of the Outer Space Treaty and in Article I (a) of the Registration Convention.

[71] Article VII of the Liability Convention provides that: "The provisions of this Convention shall not apply to damage caused by a space object of a launching State to: (a) nationals of that launching State; (b) foreign nationals during such time as they are participating in the operation of that space object from the time of its launching or at any stage thereafter until its descent, or during such time as they are in the immediate vicinity of a planned launching or recovery area as the result of an invitation by that launching State."

be debarred from making any claim against damage occurring during the space travel. This would not help the space tourism industry to flourish.

So it is in this context that the definitions included in the international space treaties are to be revisited in order to give space tourists the maximum benefit and sense of security against any apprehended damage, which may be incidental to the space operation/travel. It has rightly been observed that "Risks will in any case have to be objectively small or passenger space travel will not be acceptable" to the general public.[72]

The situation can also be perceived from a different perspective. The location of passengers may be either on the ground (in vicinity of the spacecraft during embarkation or disembarkation) or in outer space during the flight depending on its course. If they are on the ground, they may have recourse to remedies for damage caused to them, under the domestic (national) statues or tort law rules. This is also in consonance with customary international law that requires the exhaustion of local remedies. For the passengers in flight or "in the space vehicle, the question of law may be based on the issue of jurisdiction. As the State of registry under the Registration Convention applies its jurisdiction to the spacecraft, any claims for damages incurred by the [passengers] would be pursued within the State of jurisdiction. The liability for injury or death of employees would be covered by domestic occupation health and safety laws."[73]

Thus it is advisable to set up a liability system, which would resemble the Warsaw Convention. This should not only provide protection to the passengers but also encourage operators, as well as the space tourism industry during its infancy phase.

There has been a conscious attempt on the part of different States to bring about national regulatory frameworks for implementing their international obligations relating to liability arising out of space activities. Some of the most important examples of such regimes are:

a) The Australian Space Activities Act, 1998, was adopted with an objective *inter alia* to provide for the payment of adequate compensation for damage caused to persons and property as a result of space activities regulated by the Act.[74]

b) The Japanese Law Partially Amending the NASDA Law, 1998, obligates NASDA to enter into third party liability insurance contracts and binds NASDA to enter into special arrangements by which NASDA shall assume all liability for damage caused

---

[72] P. Collins and K. Yonemoto, "Legal and Regulatory Issues for Passenger Space Travel", *supra* note 6.

[73] Ricky J. Lee and Yuri Takaya , "Space Tourism and Permanent Human Settlement: The Legal and Regulatory Issues", *supra* note 20.

[74] Act. No. 123, 1998, assented to on December 21, 1998, Section 3(b).

to anyone related to the launch in certain cases.[75]

c) The Russian Law on Space Activity, 1993, *inter alia* provides that Russian Federation shall guarantee full compensation for direct damage inflicted as a result of accidents while carrying out space activities in accordance with the legislation of Russian Federation.[76]

d) The South African Space Affairs Act, 1993, conditionally provides immunity against issues of liability for the Minister, his Council, the State and its employees against anything done under the Act.[77]

e) The Swedish Act on Space Activities, 1982 provides that if, on account of its obligations under international agreements, the State has been held liable for damage caused as a result of space activities carried on by person (who had undertaken the space activity), such person shall reimburse the State accordingly, unless special reason warrants against it.[78]

f) The United Kingdom Outer Space Act, 1986, while providing an immunity to person acting as an employee of another and to anything done on the instruction of the Secretary of State, secures payment of compensation as mandatory indemnification to her Majesty's government by any person to whom the Act applies while engaging in space activity, including space launches.[79]

g) The U.S. Commercial Space Launch Act provides that a launch license will be granted once the applicant satisfies the FAA-AST that he has procured an appropriate insurance policy.[80] The policy should cover (a) upto $100 million against loss to the US government, and (b) upto $500 million against third party claims for death, bodily injury, or property damage or loss resulting from an activity carried out under the license. However, in case the damages exceed these amounts, the U.S. government covers them up to a ceiling of $1.5 billion for a single event or incident. In addition, the risk is allocated through reciprocal waivers of liability (excluding willful misconduct) between the licensee, its customers and their respective contractors and subcontractors.

FINAL REMARKS

It is well known that without full governmental participation and

[75] Promulgated as the law (law no. 87) on June 3, 1998 and became effective as of same day. For a detailed analysis of this law, see Masahiko Sato, "The Japanese Legal Framework: Third Party Liability Resulting From NASDA Launch", IISL-98-IISL-2.05, p. 32.

[76] August 20, 1993, Section VII, Article 30 "liability for damage".

[77] Statutes of Republic of South Africa no. 84 of 1993.Assented to 23 June, 1993, date of Commencement: September 6, 1993; Section 21.

[78] Section 6 of the Act (1982:963).

[79] Section 10 of the Act, 1986 Chapter 38.

[80] The Commercial Space Launch Act, 49 USC, Subtitle IX, Chapter 701, Sections 70112 and 70113.

financial support space activities would have remained a myth. However, it came to light through the studies made by different organizations that there is now a growing discontent and apathy of the taxpayers towards funding space travel and tourism, which is basically a commercial venture and will benefit only a handful of private companies and individuals. Thus governments are not fully and enthusiastically investing taxpayers' money in promoting space tourism. They are encouraging private participation not only to develop space transport vehicles but also to commercially exploit them, while keeping the overall control and supervision of the activities under an emerging regulatory framework. In the words of U.S. Congressman Robert Walker "Most of our laws and regulations governing space activity were written to make it easier for the government to function in space. Now we need to make it easier for the private sector to undertake space development."[81]

The unleashing of vast wealth and economic development through space tourism is no longer a hypothesis but a reality that could be achieved soon. The myths about space which reigned its existence in the minds of a common average man is fading away fast as space travel by 'ordinary' people would become possible in the near future.

In order to encourage the viability and commencement of space tourism industry, numerous legal and regulatory issues must be addressed and resolved both at international and national levels in a timely fashion. Some of them are the formulation and enforcement of strict operational procedures, safety standards, security requirements and licensing rules by the respective governments. The resolution of these issues will ensure the safety of space travel and thus will provide impetus to space tourism for the general public.

The existing international space treaties need to be revised in order to resolve severe conflict with the current and future uses of outer space particularly space tourism. It is submitted that they should be consolidated in a single comprehensive consistent and forward looking international treaty, perhaps similar to the 1944 Chicago Convention.

In view of the lack of demarcation between airspace and outer space possible conflict of jurisdictions and overlap of operations, of space vehicles and civil aviation activities need to be resolved either empowering ICAO or if a similar organization for space traffic is created, between the two organizations.

---

[81] L. Roberts, "Space Business incentives, It's time to act", Ad Astra, Vol. 8, No. 2, pp. 38-39.

Session 3: LEGAL IMPLICATIONS OF MILITARY USES OF OUTER SPACE

Chairmen: E. Fasan, Austria, and J. Galloway, USA

Rapporteur: M. Ferrazzani, ESA/Italy

IAC-02-IISL.3.01

INTERNATIONAL AGREEMENTS OF UNLIMITED DURATION:

THE 1972 ABM TREATY*

Carl Q. Christol
Distinguished Professor Emeritus of International Law and Political Science
University of Southern California
Los Angeles, California 90089-0044
Attorney at Law
Member IISL, IAA, AIAA

Abstract

The 1972 ABM Treaty between the United States and the former Soviet Union is, pursuant to Article XV, of unlimited duration. However, this Article allows a party to withdraw if "extraordinary events related to the subject matter of this Treaty have jeopardized its supreme interests." A withdrawing party must give six months advance notice in which it recites what are the extraordinary events causing the notice of withdrawal.

Notice was given to Russia on December 13, 2001 in the form of a presidential statement relying on the basic fact, as recited in the treaty, of a fundamental change in circumstances, namely "that extraordinary events related to the subject matter of this Treaty have jeopardized its supreme interests." Withdrawal became effective on June 12, 2002.

Cited as meeting this condition was the attack on the United States of September 11, 2001 and the ending of the Cold War. This required the creation of a national "limited missile defense of our territory." With the termination of the agreement the United States would be allowed to cooperate with friends and allies in developing missile defenses against long-range threats.

The termination of the agreement and the change in policy have produced expected criticism. On the one had hand it has been suggested that an effective national missile defense system (NMD) is beyond scientific and technical know-how, that its enormous costs could be applied better to a variety of human wants and needs, that the NMD project is destabilizing and that it might contribute to an arms race on the part of America's enemies. On the other side, it is argued that the dangers presented to the United States, particularly by terrorists and rogue States, are so vast that the United States would be derelict in not moving beyond the ABM Treaty.

All things considered, the change in the status quo produced by the termination of the 1972 Treaty, and the manner in which the change was brought about, have added to the debate concerning unilateralism and multilateralism.

1. The Anti-Ballistic Missile Systems Treaty (ABM) Terminated

On May 26, 1972 the United States and the Soviet Union signed the ABM Treaty.[1] It was accompanied by an Interim Agreement and a Protocol. All entered into force on October 3, 1972. At the time of the signature the United States made several unilateral statements. One was entitled "Withdrawal from the ABM Treaty." It referred to the fact that both sides wished to limit strategic defensive arms within five years. If such an expectation were not achieved the United States stated that this would jeopardize U.S. supreme interests and would "constitute a basis for withdrawal from the agreement."

Article XV of the Treaty provided that it "shall be of unlimited duration." It then stated the conditions under which a party would no longer be bound. Derived from a party's national sovereignty, withdrawal would depend on a party's unilateral decision "that extraordinary events related to the subject matter of this Treaty have jeopardized its supreme interests."

2. Reasons Advanced by the United States for Withdrawal

In providing reasons for withdrawals from international agreements States normally urged that there has been a "fundamental change in circumstances" since the date of the original agreement. This was used by the United States in the instant case by referring to the terrorist attack of September 11, 2001. Reference to the Cold War's ending resulted in the conclusion that "our security environment is profoundly different."[2]

The security theory of mutually assured destruction (MAD) was no longer considered to be valid in light of the new cooperative relations between the two States. This theory was to be replaced by one allowing for a "limited missile defense of our territory." Such an approach, it was asserted, was needed to counteract the military potential of "terrorists and rogue states" equipped with weapons of mass destruction and their delivery."[3]

The United States referred to two specific prohibitions in the 1972 agreement. First, the defense of the homeland against ballistic missile attack; second, from cooperating in developing missile defenses against long-range threats with friends and allies.

On June 13, 2002, six months after the announced withdrawal, President Bush repeated as a reason the need for the United States to "develop and deploy effective defenses against limited missile attacks [resulting from] growing missile threats we face."[4] He reemphasized that the withdrawal would now allow the United States to work with "our allies and friends around the world" without breaching the terms of the 1972 agreement. Such activities, he said, would include participation on the part of Russia.[5]

Russia's initial response to the U.S. policy change was disapproval. However, the Bush administration put forward a new State-Strategic Relationship for Russian acceptance. It was urged that the NMD could benefit Russia from possible harm from terrorists and rogue States, and it would be desirable for the United States and the Soviet Union, over time, to reduce the number of their nuclear warheads. This was coupled with the understanding that the United States would continue to pay Russia at least $4 million annually for the decommissioning and safeguarding of its nuclear warheads. Referred to as the Cooperative Non-Proliferation and Threat Reduction Program, it was initiated in 1991. Further cooperation in this area was to be the purchase by the United States from Russia of "Material blended down from Russian highly enriched uranium from dismantled nuclear warheads, for use in civilian nuclear reactor fuel."[6]

A formal product of these bilateral negotiations was the U.S.-Russian Nuclear Warheads Reduction and Limitation Treaty of May 24, 2002. Article I captured the statements of President Bush on November 13, 2001 and those of President Putin on November 13, 2001 and on December 13, 2001, whereby each party to the agreement promised that it "shall reduce and limit strategic nuclear warheads" so that by December 31, 2012, "the aggregated number of such warheads does not exceed 1,700 to 2 ,200 for each party." Pursuant to Article II: "The parties agreed that the START treaty remains in force in accordance with its terms."

Article III dealt with the implementation of the agreement. The parties agreed that a newly constituted "Bilateral Implementation Commission" would facilitate mutually beneficial cooperative measures.

3. Appraisals of the American NMD Policy

Assessments of NMD are varied. They focus on the security needs of the United States and whether the proposed NMD can meet those needs. From the point of view of continuing to rely on the ABM system, there is agreement that the United States had the legal right to give notice to Russia of termination. With the United States and Russia enjoying amicable relations and with new security challenges arising from terrorism and the capability of lesser States to manufacture and launch nuclear warheads, there is such a change of circumstances.

While it remains to be fully proven that the rogue States do have this technical capacity and the political will to undertake such devastating action, America's response must be based on the policy of caution. With this in mind, and assuming the potential employment of nuclear weapons by a hostile country, one can be sympathetic to the fears reflected by a former U.S. Senator, Jesse Helms.

He stated: "But deterrence alone is no longer an effective strategy when the world is tainted by unpredictable tyrants and terrorists who are difficult to target and have little concern for human life, or when an unauthorized or accidental launch of a missile occurs."[7]

Further, the U.S.-Russian Treaty of May 24, 2002, with its progressive elimination of nuclear warheads, and the substitution of a NMD system for the ABM approach, has not guaranteed that on a worldwide basis there will be "progress in disarmament, and possibly a new arms race."[8]

The wisdom of abandoning the ABM treaty will depend not only on the view that the United States needs a new form of protection against rogue States and terrorists but also on the premise that science and technology, present and future, will be able to fashion equipment needed for an effective new NMD policy.[9]

Missile tests conducted up to the end of December 2001, were far from conclusive. It was considered that it was highly speculative if the tested defense equipment could be more reliable. According to an editorial "A national missile defense system would be enormously expensive, and there are no indications it's feasible. The ABM Treaty shouldn't be junked for a 'maybe' defense."[10]

Mr. G.T. Allison, a former U.S. Assistant Secretary of Defense, has asked a number of questions and provided answers respecting the utility of a NMD system. He offered no assurance that the NMD would be ready at any further date. He acknowledged that from the technical point of view it was very ambitious. He observed that over time there could be a feasible system that "has some degree of effectiveness."[11]

Within the American Congress there have been substantial concerns. For example, Senator Joseph R. Biden, Jr., of Delaware, a democrat has attacked the NMD system. His charges included a waste of governmental resources, an increase in world instability, since China would be drawn into an arms race, and that simpler means were sufficient for the delivery of hostile warheads.[12]

Senator Carl Levin of Michigan, also a democrat, as chairman of the Armed Services Committee, stated that the Bush decision was likely to lead to a cycle of development of costly offensive and defensive weapons, "and that kind of arms race would not make us more secure."[13]

When President Clinton first proposed a NMD system he received in January 1999 an estimate from Secretary of Defense William Cohen, that initial costs over a five year period would be $6.6 billion. Late in June, 2002, the Senate agreed to a $7.6 billion budget for missile defense in 2003.[14] This sum took into account the programs being developed in North Korea, Iraq, and Iran. These defense costs are in addition to the $620 million granted to Russia in February 2002 to assist in defraying costs for destruction of the Russian nuclear stockpile, which included different kinds of gases. This was in addition to the annual subvention of $400 million to Russia for the decommissioning and safeguarding of its nuclear warheads.

The cost for maintaining the United States as the world's policeman is very high and growing higher as a result of the war on terrorism. Without taking such costs into account, the Stockholm International Peace Research Institute, which records annual military budgets, has reported the following figures for 2001, in billions of U.S. dollars: United States, $281.4; Russia, $43.9; France, $40; Japan, $38.5; United Kingdom, $37.0; Germany, $32.4; China, $27.0; Saudi Arabia, $26.6; Italy, $24.7; Brazil, $14.1.[15]

5. Conclusion

The jury still has not rendered its decision whether the termination of the 1972 ABM agreement has resulted in a stabilization or destabilization of the security relationship between the United States and Russia and other countries of the world, and in particular with such so-called rogue States as North Korea, Iran, and Iraq.

The United States and Russia have somewhat ameliorated potential tension through their Nuclear Warheads Reduction and Limitation Treaty of May 24, 2002, which was accompanied, albeit reluctantly, by Russia because of U.S. plans for a NMD system.

The Bush administration has emphasized the need for a NMD system to cope with international terrorism. Interestingly, the Clinton administration which can claim pride of authorship for the NMD system, did not refer to terrorism as a basis for this new security theory.

Whether an NMD system meets the test of wisdom, as well as technical feasibility, its ultimate practicability, its huge and almost excessive costs, whether there are other justifiable needs having a greater societal value, such as replacement of the country's aging infrastructure, outer space activities, support for human resources, medicine, and educational needs, the special needs of Afghanistan following the antiterrorism activities of the United States, and the general needs of the developing countries, remain to be seen.

NOTES

1. 23 UST 3435; TIAS 7503.
2. *ABM Fact Sheet*, The White House, Statement of Press Secretary, 1, December 13, 2001.
3. *Ibid.*
4. *Weekly Compilation of Presidential Documents for the Week Ending June 14, 2002*, 1011 (2002).
5. *Ibid.*
6. *U.S. Government Nonproliferation and Threat Reduction Assistance to the Russian Federation Fact Sheet* The White House, Office of the Press Secretary 1, November 13, 2001.
7. Jesse Helms, Bush Was Right to Abandon Treaty, *Los Angeles Times*, B11, December 17, 2001.
8. I. Ivanov, The Missile-Defense Mistake, 79 *Foreign Affairs*, No. 5, 15, September/October 2000.
9. J. Newhouse, The Missile Defense Debate, 80 *Foreign Affairs*, No. 4, 97, July/August 2001.
10. Trading 'Good' for 'Iffy,' *The Los Angeles Times*, B12, 12 December 2001.
11. ABCs of ABM and Missile Defense, *The Christian Science Monitor*, 21, May 31, 2000.
12. *The Los Angeles Times*, A10-11, September 10, 2001.
13. *The Los Angeles Times*, A28, December 14, 2001.
14. *The Los Angeles Times*, A12, June 27, 2002.
15. *The Christian Science Monitor*, 24, June 18, 2002.

THE JUS AD BELLUM IN OUTER SPACE: THE INTERRELATION BETWEEN ARTICLE 103 OF THE CHARTER OF THE UNITED NATIONS AND ARTICLE IV OF THE OUTER SPACE TREATY

Ricky J. Lee*
Hunt & Hunt (Adelaide)
University of Western Sydney, Australia

INTRODUCTION

The exact content of the *jus ad bellum* in space has been the subject of much academic and legal debate since the adoption of the Treaty on Principles Governing the Activities of States in the Exploration and Use of Outer Space including the Moon and Celestial Bodies (the "**Outer Space Treaty**") in 1967. The main provisions in relation to use of force in space are found in Articles III and IV of the Outer Space Treaty. Contrary to common belief, however, the Outer Space Treaty does not expressly prohibit military uses of outer space. The provisions require space activities to be carried out in the interests of maintaining international peace and security, a complete demilitarisation of celestial bodies and a prohibition on the deployment and use of weapons of mass destruction in space.

The Charter of the United Nations (the "**Charter**") provides a further complication in considering the contents and effects of Articles III and IV. It is necessary, when considering the law concerning the use of force in space, to keep in mind Chapter VII and Article 103 of the Charter. Chapter VII contains the codification of the international law on the use of force, while Article 103 provides that the Charter prevails over other international treaties and conventions. Considered together with the Outer Space Treaty, these provisions have the effect of limiting and modifying the rights and obligations of States in relation to the use of force in space.

PROVISIONS OF THE OUTER SPACE TREATY

The United Nations Committee on the Peaceful Uses of Outer Space (COPUOS) has long affirmed the principle that military uses of outer space are to be limited, more so than is the case on Earth. Consequently, the 1967 Outer Space Treaty and all subsequent treaties and General Assembly resolutions and declarations reiterate the principle that there are limitations imposed by international law on the use of outer space for military purposes.

However, the provisions are far from clear in setting out what these limitations are, as it appears to draw distinctions between outer space *sensu stricto*, or the empty space between celestial bodies, and outer space *sensu lato*, which includes both "outer space" and the celestial bodies.[1] The Outer Space Treaty appears to require different restrictions on military activities in different "parts" of outer space.

Specifically, Article IV(1) prohibits the placement of any nuclear weapons and other weapons of mass destruction in outer space. This presumably refers to outer space *sensu lato*, thus including outer space, the Moon and other celestial bodies. However, this provision, or any other, does not prohibit the stationing of any other type of weapon in outer space for military purposes, such as conventional or even laser weapons. In other words, it appears from this provision that States are entitled to use outer space for military purposes, provided that these do not involve deploying or using nuclear weapons and other weapons of mass destruction.[2]

The second paragraph of Article IV of the Outer Space Treaty, which requires the use of celestial bodies to be exclusively for peaceful purposes only, appears to apply only to the Moon and other celestial bodies and not to outer space *sensu stricto*.[3] Both the United States and the Soviet Union pointed out that, by omitting the mention of "outer space" from the peaceful purposes requirement in Article IV, the States have rejected a broad prohibition of military activities in space and restricted the requirement to celestial bodies only.[4]

Even if a broader application is inferred, the precise meaning of what "peaceful" purposes mean are by no means certain. The United States has long argued that the term "peaceful purposes" means "non-aggressive purposes" rather than "non-military purposes".[5] In other words, the Outer Space Treaty implements only the existing obligations under international law for non aggressive use of space, but not to impose a new obligation involving the full demilitarisation of celestial bodies.[6] States are therefore free to deploy weapons, personnel, fortifications and facilities for defensive purposes.

This interpretation may be considered to be contrary to existing interpretations that are found elsewhere in international law. For example, the similarly worded Antarctic Treaty, to which the United States is also a signatory, defines "peaceful" as "non-military" and specific references to military installations are regarded as exemplificative rather than exhaustive in nature.[7] The Soviet Union, for example, takes a contrary view and argued that the Outer Space Treaty prohibits all military activities regardless of their aggressive nature, on celestial bodies.[8] By inference, the interpretation used in applying the Antarctic Treaty should therefore be equally applicable to Article IV of the Outer Space Treaty as well.

The United States is also a signatory to several nuclear non-proliferation treaties and Washington would undoubtedly consider it absurd for States to assert that their development and manufacture of nuclear weapons is for "non-aggressive" purposes only and therefore permissible under the Nuclear Non-Proliferation Treaty and other instruments. As a result, the interpretation suggested by the United States with respect to "peaceful" use of outer space may therefore be contrary to existing principles of international law.

On the other hand, if Article IV imposed obligations beyond its literal meaning, it is difficult to see why the framers of the Outer Space Treaty had chosen to use such specific and restrictive language in the wording of Article IV. If Article IV is intended to imply a broad demilitarisation of outer space, it is unlikely that it would have made specific references to weapons of mass destruction or to have confined the peaceful purposes requirement to celestial bodies only.

Consequently, it is clear that the most appropriate interpretation of Article IV is in fact the literal one. In other words, States are required to observe the prohibition on the deployment and use of force on celestial bodies and the total prohibition on the deployment and use of nuclear weapons and other weapons of mass destruction anywhere in outer space. However, there are no prohibitions on the deployment and use of conventional arms in outer space *sensu stricto* as imposed by Article IV of the Outer Space Treaty and subsequent international space law instruments. This is, of course, provided they are not used in a way in contravention with existing legal principles or against the interest of maintaining international peace and security, as required by Article III.

In fact, the terms of Article III lend further support to the view that Article IV should be read literally rather than to infer a broad demilitarisation of outer space. Article III provides that space activities are to be carried out "in the interest of maintaining international peace and security". Conducting activities in the interest of maintaining international peace and security often involves the use of force, as illustrated by the jurisprudence over the content of Articles 39 and 42 of the Charter.

The preferred view, therefore, is that Article III requires activities in space to be conducted in accordance with international law, especially the interests of maintaining international peace and security, with caveats on such activities imposed by the effects of Article IV. With this context in mind, the next step is then to explore the effects of Article 103 of the Charter, the content of the rights and obligations under Chapter VII and how they interact with Articles III and IV of the Outer Space Treaty to impose restrictions on the use of force in outer space.

EFFECT OF ARTICLE 103

Article III of the Outer Space Treaty states that space activities must be conducted in accordance with international law and the Charter. As a result, it is clear that space activities are governed not only by the principles of the Outer Space Treaty and subsequent instruments but also the existing principles of public international law that generally govern the activities of and the use of force by States on Earth.

It has commonly been accepted that the Charter now provides the authoritative principles of law in relation to the use of force on Earth. It is pertinent, therefore, to consider the application of Article 103 of the Charter. Article 103 states that:

> In the event of a conflict between the obligations of the Members of the United Nations under the present Charter and their obligations under any other international agreement, their obligations under the present Charter shall prevail.

This is further reinforced by the 1980 Vienna Convention on the Law of Treaties, which provides that later treaties prevail over earlier ones except for the application of Article 103 of the Charter.[9] One issue that may affect the application of Article 103 is whether the provision to be overridden by Article 103 may be a codification of a *jus cogens* principle of custom. If that is the case, it is generally accepted that States cannot contract out of *jus cogens* and corresponding obligations. There is some support for the view that the obligations of Articles III and IV of the Outer Space Treaty, regardless of their exact contents and effects, are *jus cogens*. However, the fact that the Charter prevails over all other treaties and the acceptance by all States of the legal effects of Chapter VII on the use of force by States suggest that Chapter VII may have acquired the status of *jus cogens* as well.

While it is clear from a literal reading of Article 103 that the Charter takes precedence over any other treaty, there are two other important points to take into consideration. Firstly, Article 103 provides only for obligations and not rights under the Charter to prevail over other treaties. Consequently, if a treaty revoked a right provided under the Charter, a State cannot rely on Article 103 to continue asserting that right. Secondly, Article 103 deals only with obligations arising under the Charter and, as a result, it is unclear whether it would apply to an obligation arising from the exercise of a power or the discharge of a function under the Charter, such as a decision of the General Assembly or the Security Council.[10] In other words, Article 103 may not require a State to carry out an act in contravention of an applicable treaty provision if the requirement arose from a resolution rather than the Charter itself.

In considering the effects of Article 103 on United Nations decisions, there are three types of decisions that may be made by the United Nations or its principal organs:

1) decisions that are externally binding on States that did not participate in making the decision;

2) decisions that are internally binding on the United Nations only but have external effects; and

3) external decisions that are not binding but in certain circumstances would have binding effect.[11]

Under the Charter, the only externally binding decisions of the United Nations are decisions of the Security Council that are concerned with the maintenance of international peace and security pursuant to Chapter VII.[12] As the obligation to observe such decisions arise directly from Articles 25 and 48 of the Charter, it is an obligation to which Article 103 would have application, as supported by the requirements of Article III of the Outer Space Treaty.

Even though the General Assembly and the Economic and Social Council may make decisions with dispositive force and effect on the external relations of States, they are not decisions that are externally binding.[13] Similarly, a Security Council resolution not made pursuant to Chapter VII would have the same effects. As there is no obligation directly under the Charter for States to comply with such decisions, Article 103 would arguably have no application on any obligation that may be imposed on States arising from such internal decisions.[14]

The final category of decisions includes General Assembly resolutions or those of other organs that contain declarations of legal principles concerning a particular aspect of international activities. In space law, the legal principles concerning remote sensing is an example of such resolutions.[15] These decisions are not binding but, if accepted by the States concerned, it may be considered to be the codification of existing custom or the creation of new custom by simultaneous state practice or, at the very least, *opinio juris*. In other words, the resolution itself is not binding and creates no obligation except for the customary principles contained therein.

As Article 103 deals only with conflicts between obligations arising from the Charter and treaties and not between custom and treaties, there can be no application of Article 103. This is consistent with the view that States can contract out of customary principles by the adoption of treaties unless the principles are *jus cogens* and therefore the resulting *erga omnes* obligations must be observed regardless of the intention and consent of the States involved.

It can be seen from this that Article 103 requires States to observe their obligations:

- directly arising from the provisions of the Charter; or

- binding decisions of the Security Council in relation to international peace and security,

over and above their obligations in subsequent treaties, such as the Outer Space Treaty. In order to analyse the content of the *jus ad bellum* in space, it is therefore essential to consider not only the content of Articles III and IV of the Outer Space Treaty but also the extent of any obligations that arise under the United Nations Charter to which Article 103 may have application.

PROHIBITING THE USE OF FORCE

Article 2(4) of the Charter provides that States are to refrain "from the threat or use of force against the territorial integrity or political independence of any State, or in any other manner inconsistent with the Purposes of the United Nations". This principle has been found by the International Court of Justice to be *jus cogens* and binding on all states as a customary norm.[16]

This blanket prohibition on the use of force is not without exceptions. Under Chapter VII of the Charter, the Security Council may authorise the use of force "to maintain or restore international peace and security" if there is a "threat to the peace, breach of the peace, or act of aggression" for which economic and trade sanctions would be inadequate. Further, Article 51 provides that there is an inherent right by States to use force for individual or collective self-defence "until the Security Council has taken measures necessary to maintain international peace and security".

There have been some instances since the creation of the United Nations where this principle appeared to have been breached or, in other words, there have been several occasions where the operation of Article 2(4) may have been invoked. For example, the ultimatum issued by France and the United Kingdom to Egypt and Israel in 1956, demanding a cease-fire within twelve hours, would be a "threat of force". In 1960, the Soviet Union issued the warning that any unauthorised flights over Soviet territory will result in the bases where the planes flew from being attacked. When Iraq positioned artillery and tanks near its border within range of Kuwait, the United Kingdom stated that to be a "threat to Kuwait and a breach of the provisions of the Charter".[17] It should be noted that the legality of the Persian Gulf War and the NATO attack on Yugoslavia have remained the subject of intense academic debate. In all these cases, it is arguable that such acts, would be in contravention of the Charter if they were not conducted with the authority or approval of the Security Council.

Then there is the qualification that the use of force is only prohibited where it is conducted "against the territorial integrity or political independence of any State". This may be seen as a limiting factor in the prohibition on the use of force. In this way, a distinction can be drawn between annexations or permanent occupations, which infringe the territorial "integrity" of a State, and trespassing, which infringes the territorial "inviolability" of a State. In the *Corfu Channel* case, the United Kingdom argued that Operation Retail, in which the Corfu Channel, located in Albanian territorial waters, was swept for mines after a British ship was damaged, "threatened neither the territorial integrity nor the political independence of Albania".[18]

Brownlie argued against such a limited approach as, in his view, "it is difficult to accept a 'plain meaning' which permits evasion of obligations by means of a verbal profession that there is no intention to infringe territorial integrity".[19] In his view, this provision must be read with the totality of the sovereign rights of a State in regard to its territories.[20] Harris suggested that the territorial integrity issue is irrelevant as the last clause of Article 2(4) amounts to a total prohibition on the use of armed force.[21] This is because one of the Purposes of the United Nations is to "maintain peace and security" and consequently any form of use of force, regardless of whether it infringes the integrity of a State or otherwise, is contrary to the Purposes and therefore in contravention of Article 2(4) of the Charter.

As a result, the use of force can be legally justified under the Charter only where:

1) it is intended and restricted to individual or collective self-defence;

2) it is mandated by a decision of the Security Council under Article 42 of the Charter; or

3) in humanitarian intervention, which is a somewhat controversial justification for the use of force.[22]

Careful analysis of the events since 1945 involving the use of force may well find that this principle is honoured more in its breach than its observance. It does not, however, alter the balance that use of force on Earth is only permitted in those three situations.

It is clear that humanitarian interventions, as a unilateral act without reference to the Charter, cannot attract the application of Article 103. As a result, the conduct of humanitarian intervention operations must respect the limitations imposed by Article IV of the Outer Space Treaty or, namely, the prohibition on weapons of mass destruction and the demilitarisation of celestial bodies. It is difficult to see, in any event, how humanitarian interventions would be affected, presently or in the future, by the limitations imposed by Article IV.

In the case of use of force for self-defence or Security Council mandated actions under Articles 41 and 42 of the Charter, it is important to consider to the application of Article 103 on those specific provisions in Chapter VII of the Charter.

ARTICLE 51: SELF-DEFENCE

Article 51 recognises the inherent right in law of individual or collective self-defence where an armed attack takes place "until the Security Council has taken measures necessary to maintain international peace and security". This doctrine has arguably justified the use of force against Iraq in the defence of Kuwait, even though at the time the armed attack was already complete.[23]

It is interesting to note that Article 51 of the Charter considers collective self-defence to be a right rather than an obligation, as one would have considered collective security to be the responsibility of all States rather than a "right" to be exercised. It may been seen that the States have completely surrendered their sovereignty in relation to the use of force to the Security Council and, as a result, collective self-defence has become a "right" to use force outside the authority of the Security Council.[24] In other words, the "obligation" of collective security is given effect by the other provisions of Chapter VII and the authority under Article 42 and, as a result, all that remains is a "right" to use force in self-defence outside the realm and authority of the Security Council.

Consequently, it is clear that Article 103 would have no application on Article 51 as it applies only to obligations and not rights. The right of a State to use force in self-defence in outer space, therefore, would have to respect the limitations imposed under Article IV of the Outer Space Treaty. From the discussion above, Article IV would not prevent the use of force by States in space, provided it did not involve the deployment or use of weapons of mass destruction and did not involve the use of celestial bodies. States are nevertheless required to observe the same obligations in relation to the *jus ad bellum* and *jus in bello* in space as it does on Earth, as Article III of the Outer Space Treaty applies existing principles of international law on activities in outer space.

ARTICLE 41

Under Article 41, the Security Council can decide on the "complete or partial interruption of economic relations and of rail, sea, air, postal, *telegraphic, radio and other means of communication*" to restore international peace and security.[25]

The Security Council can make a binding decision that communications links with a particular State are to be interrupted. Such a decision would amount to a binding obligation on all States and one that Article 103 would apply. As a result, the States may be required to take steps to ensure that communications with that State is interrupted. These steps would be limited to internal ones as Article 41 would not authorise a State to take external steps to disrupt another State's link and communications that amounts to use of force. This is analogous to shipping links, where each State would be required to ensure that no shipping under its flag reached the target State but cannot undertake a naval blockade or to arrest or attack ships destined for the target State. Similarly, a State can act to interrupt or interfere with satellite communications pursuant to a resolution made under Article 41 of the Charter, but it cannot destroy the communications satellite itself.

For example, in Resolution 221 of 1966, the Security Council determined that supplies of oil from tankers calling at the port of Beira constituted a threat to the peace and called upon both Portugal and the United Kingdom to take action to prevent oil from reaching Southern Rhodesia.[26] This was considered to be action taken by the Security Council under Article 42 rather than Article 41 as it involved the use of military force to undertake a blockade that is excluded from the authority of Article 41.

Applying Article 41 to outer space would mean that, when required, States would have to take steps to ensure that no transmissions from ground segments within their control are relayed through satellites to the target State. It would also mean that satellites registered to other States would similarly be required to cease transmissions to the target State. Such actions would not contravene Article IV of the Outer Space Treaty and, as a result, it would not be necessary to invoke Article 103 of the Charter for such actions to take place. In the case of satellites registered to the target State, Article 41 would not provide the legal authority for the Security Council to require disruptions or interference with the transmissions of those satellites, as it would amount to a use of force by the interfering States.

It is interesting to note that Article 41 does not allow the Security Council to provide for the interruption of space transport or launch activities by other States. This may be the result of the framers of the Charter not anticipating the advent of space activities or it was never intended for the Security Council to have power to interrupt or prevent space activities under Chapter VII. This is difficult to accept because, if the threat or breach to the peace is the proliferation of weapons in space undertaken by a particular State, the Security Council would be powerless to make any decisions pursuant to Article 41 for the prevention of launch activities from taking place. If Article 41 impliedly permits such interruptions or interference, these acts would be carried out by States in the interest of maintaining international peace and security and, provided they are done without the use of weapons of mass destruction, would not contravene the provisions of the Outer Space Treaty.

ARTICLE 42

Article 42 of the Charter provides that the Security Council may decide on the use of force if actions taken under Article 41 are inadequate to restore international peace and security. Traditionally, it has been observed that Article 42 was the only provision in the Charter that allows the Security Council to "take action by air, sea or land forces" where necessary to maintain or restore international peace and security.[27] However, the International Court of Justice had taken a contrary view in the *Certain Expenses of the United Nations* case.[28]

In any event, it is important to note that Article 42 authorises States only to undertake measures by air, sea and land forces "as may be necessary to maintain or restore international peace and security". As a result, there is clearly no mention of operations in space or measures taken by space forces in Article 42. Of course, there is no reason why a State cannot use the authority provided by the Security Council under Article 42 to use force in space by "land" or "air" forces, though this would appear to be contrary to the literal meaning of "air, sea or land forces" in the provision.

There are clearly two perspectives on the content of this limitation in relation to the authority of Article 42 in space. Firstly, it could be seen as limiting the scope of the authority given to the Security Council only to use of force by terrestrial forces and, consequently, the Security Council has no authority to require military action in space. If applied literally, this would mean that the total ban of military force in space, so eagerly sought after by some framers of the Outer Space Treaty, would be achieved, as the only use of force allowed in outer space would have been for self-defence under Article 51 of the Charter. It would also mean that there would be no conflict between Article 42 of the Charter and Article IV of the Outer Space Treaty that would allow Article 103 to permit the use of force on celestial bodies when required to do so under Article 42 of the Charter.

Secondly, it can be pointed out that the first satellite in space was not launched for another fourteen years after the Charter entered into force. As a result, it can be argued that the drafters of the Charter simply did not anticipate the possibility of military combat in space, even though they had intended for the Security Council to be able to decide on the use of all forms of military force.

There is no reason why the scope of Article 42 cannot be altered by consistent and uniform practice by States on the Security Council and, as a result, the Security Council may find itself having the authority to require military actions in space.[29] In any event, such a decision by the Security Council would clearly fall under the scope of Article 103, effectively overriding the provisions of Article IV of the Outer Space Treaty to the extent that force may be used on celestial bodies and may involve the use of weapons of mass destruction.

On the other hand, it should be observed that Article 42 provides for action by "air, sea or land forces" where, if it had intended to mean all "military forces", it would have specified accordingly. Conversely, it can also be suggested that no other forces existed at the time and that the framers had intended to specify all three armed forces for the sake of completeness.

The only remaining argument that is apparent on this subject is that the prohibition of military use of outer space may be a *jus cogens* principle that would prevail over the United Nations Charter or any other treaty. This would be supported by the consistent language of General Assembly resolutions relating to the exploration and use of outer space to be limited to "peaceful purposes" only. However, as discussed above, the provisions of the Charter may have acquired the status of *jus cogens* as well.

On balance, there does not appear to be any overwhelmingly persuasive argument to tilt the balance between the "legalistic" interpretation of Article 42 on the one hand and the "pragmatic" interpretation on the other. In the field of space law, such a divide has grave consequences as it would dictate the ability of States to use military force in space, when supported by the Chapter VII mandate of a Security Council decision. However, this uncertainly is unlikely to be resolved without some practice of the Security Council in the decades to come.

THE DUST SETTLES: *JUS AD BELLUM IN SPATIALIS?*

It would be difficult to specify the exact content of the *jus ad bellum* in space without clarifying the mandate of Article 42 in relation to use of military force in space. However, it is possible to consider the law as it would be in the context of the two possible interpretations and examine the different resulting implications.

Celestial Bodies

In relation to use of force on celestial bodies, the prohibition of non-peaceful use contained in Article IV would apply unless there is a conflicting obligation under the Charter. It is clear that the right of self-defence provided under Article 51 would not extend to celestial bodies. States would be allowed to take action permitted under Article 41 on celestial bodies provided they did not amount to use of force that would have nevertheless contravened existing principles of international law.

With the legalistic interpretation of Article 42, the Security Council would not have authority to require the use of force by States in space, including celestial bodies. As a result, there would be no conflict between the Charter and Article IV (2) of the Outer Space Treaty that would have permitted Security Council-authorised use of force on celestial bodies.

With the pragmatic interpretation of Article 42, it would be open to the Security Council to authorise the use the force in space and on celestial bodies. As States are required under Articles 25 and 48 of the Charter to implement decisions of the Security Council, Article 103 would operate to allow States to use military force on celestial bodies, despite the prohibition contained in Article IV(2) of the Outer Space Treaty. Presumably such authority would permit the use of weapons of mass destruction as well, unless there is a *jus cogens* principle to the contrary that would prevail over the United Nations Charter.

Outer Space

In relation to use of force in outer space, either in Earth orbit or in other parts of the Solar System, Article IV(1) requires only that weapons of mass destruction are not deployed or used in space. In other words, there is no prohibition under the Outer Space Treaty of the deployment or use of military force in outer space. Article 51 of the Charter would allow States to use force for self-defence in outer space provided that such use of military force is necessary and proportionate to the armed attack.[30] In other words, there is no reason why force cannot be used in space if it is necessary and proportionate to respond to an armed attack that took place on Earth.

In relation to the authority to use force under Article 42, the legalistic approach would mean that the Security Council has no legal authority to permit or require the use of military force in space. As a result, the use of force in space would be limited to the context of self-defence. Under the pragmatic approach, the Security Council would again be able to permit or require the use of military force in space under Article 42 of the United Nations Charter.

CONCLUSIONS

It is clear from the above analysis that the limiting provision of international law on the use of military force in outer space is not Article IV of the Outer Space Treaty but Chapter VII of the United Nations Charter as it is the case on Earth. The use of force in space is limited by the permissive provisions of Chapter VII, namely Article 42 in relation to actions mandated or authorised by the Security Council and Article 51 in relation to acts of self-defence.

In order to provide for a definitive *jus ad bellum* in space, it would be necessary to clarify the appropriate interpretation to be placed on the authority of the Security Council under Article 42 in regard to outer space. Such a clarification can be achieved only by the creation of a *jus cogens* principle on the prohibition of military force, or an amendment to the Charter to either expressly include or exclude the use of space forces under Articles 42 and 51. Until either development takes place, however, one would have to be content with the thought that the intended prohibition of military use in space is far from being realised by the provisions of the Charter and the Outer Space Treaty.

Notes

* Member IISL, ILA and IBA. This paper is written in the personal capacity of the author and does not necessarily represent the views of any organisations with which the author is associated.

[1] Outer Space Treaty, Art. IV.

[2] Cheng, *The Legal Status of Outer Space and Relevant Issues: Delimitation of Outer Space and Definition of Peaceful Use* (1983) 11 J. SPACE L. 89 at 102.

[3] Markov, among others, holds the opposite view: see Markov, *The Juridical Meaning of the Term "Peaceful" in the 1967 Space Treaty* (1969) 11 PROC. COLL. L. OUTER SPACE 30.

[4] See the testimony of Ambassador Goldberg in TREATY ON OUTER SPACE: HEARINGS BEFORE THE SENATE COMMITTEE ON FOREIGN RELATIONS (1967) 90th Cong., 1st Sess. 22 at 59; and the statement by the Permanent Representative of the Soviet Union in SUMMARY RECORD OF THE U.N. COMMITTEE ON THE PEACEFUL USES OF OUTER SPACE (1966) U.N.Doc.A/AC.105/C.2/SR.66 at p. 6. See also Lay and Taubenfeld, THE LAW RELATING TO ACTIVITIES OF MAN IN SPACE (1970), at p. 97; and Christol, THE MODERN INTERNATIONAL LAW OF OUTER SPACE (1982), at pp. 29-30.

[5] TREATY ON OUTER SPACE: HEARINGS BEFORE THE SENATE COMMITTEE ON FOREIGN RELATIONS, *supra* note 4, at p. 59; and Christol, *supra* note 4, at pp. 29-30.

[6] Charter of the United Nations, Art. 2(4).

[7] Antarctic Treaty (1959) 402 U.N.T.S. 71, Art. I.

[8] Russell, *Military Activities in Outer Space: Soviet Legal Views* (1984) 25 HARV. INT'L. L. J. 153 at 161; Piradov (ed.), INTERNATIONAL SPACE LAW (1976); and Christol, *supra* note 4, at pp. 28-29.

[9] Vienna Convention on the Law of Treaties (1980) 1155 U.N.T.S. 331, Art. 30.

[10] Lauwaars, *International Law: The Interrelationship between United Nations Law and the Law of Other International Organisations* (1984) 82 MICH. L. REV. 1604 at 1606.

[11] Lee, *The United Nations: From Peacekeeping Success to Peace Enforcement Failures* [2000] AUST. INT'L. L. J. 180.

[12] Charter of the United Nations, Arts. 25 and 48.

[13] *Certain Expenses of the United Nations (Article 17 Paragraph 2 of the Charter)* [1962] I.C.J. Rep. 151 at 163.

[14] Lauwaars, *supra* note 10, at 1607.

[15] Principles Relating to Remote Sensing of the Earth from Outer Space (1986) 41 U.N. G.A.O.R. Supp. 20 (U.N.Doc. A/41/20).

[16] *Case Concerning Military and Paramilitary Activities in and against Nicaragua (Merits)* [1986] I.C.J. Rep. 14.

[17] Sir David Hannay, U.N. Doc S/PV.3431 (16 October 1994), pp. 11-12.

[18] *Corfu Channel Case (United Kingdom v Albania) (Merits)* (1949) Pleadings, Vol. III, p. 296. The Court did not refer to this particular submission.

[19] Brownlie, INTERNATIONAL LAW AND THE USE OF FORCE BY STATES (1963), pp. 267-268.

[20] This view is supported by the 1970 Declaration on Principles of International Law concerning Friendly Relations and Cooperation among States.

[21] Harris, CASES AND MATERIALS ON INTERNATIONAL LAW (5th ed., 1998), p. 866.

[22] *Ibid.* See also Simma, *NATO, the UN and the Use of Force: Legal Aspects* (1999) 10 EUR. J. INT'L. L. 1; Cassese, *Ex iniuria ius oritur: Are We Moving towards International Legitimisation of Forcible Humanitarian Countermeasures in the World Community* (1999) 10 EUR. J. INT'L. L. 23; and Reisman, *Unilateral Action and the Transformations of the World Constitutive Process: The Special Problem of Humanitarian Intervention* (2000) 11 EUR. J. INT'L. L. 3.

[23] Kelsen, THE LAW OF THE UNITED NATIONS: A CRITICAL ANALYSIS OF ITS FUNDAMENTAL PROBLEMS (1951), at p. 792; and Bowett, SELF-DEFENCE IN INTERNATIONAL LAW (1958), pp. 216-218.

[24] Halberstam, *The Right to Self-Defence Once the Security Council Takes Action* (1996) 17 MICH. J. INT'L. L. 229 at 248. After all, as Halberstam stated at 248, "it is difficult to believe that some 180 states would have agreed to give up the most fundamental attribute of sovereignty, the right to use force in self-defence, to an international body and particularly one like the Security Council."

[25] Emphasis added.

[26] Security Council Resolution 218 (1966), S.C.O.R., 21st year, RES. & DEC., p. 5.

[27] See Kelsen, supra note 23, at pp. 744-745.

[28] It can also be based on the consent of the Congolese Government or Art. 51 of the Charter: *Certain Expenses of the United Nations*, *supra* note 13, at 167.

[29] See, for example, Art. 27 of the Charter; and Kelsen, *supra* note 23, at pp. 239-244 and Wolfrum and Philipp, UNITED NATIONS: LAW, POLICIES AND PRACTICE (1995) at pp 1404-1405.

[30] Bowett, UNITED NATIONS FORCES (1964), p. 54.

Missile Defense and International Law

HASHIMOTO, Yasuaki*
Associate Professor
National Institute for Defense Studies
2-2-1, Nakameguro, Meguro-ku
Tokyo 153-8648, JAPAN

Abstract

Some countries such as U.S.A., Russia, Israel, European countries, Japan now study and/or develop missile defense systems against ballistic missiles from other countries including so called rogue countries. Though there is legitimacy for such missile defense by the right of self-defense as well as the doctrine of military objectives, there will happen an unhopeful result, hazardous outer space with debris. This is a kind of dilemma. We have to understand this reality and establish appropriate legal and technical measures to avoid this unacceptable situation.

1. Development of Missile Defense Systems

1) Proliferation of Ballistic Missiles

The number of states holding ballistic missiles is increasing rapidly after the end of Cold War structure. Only the superpowers had ballistic missile technology at the earlier stage of the Cold War era. For example, according to "Military Balance" etc., those countries that deployed ballistic missiles in 1969 were only U.S.A. and U.S.S.R., but they increased in number to 15 nations in 1989 when the Cold War ended. At that time, those new countries were West European countries, such as France, the United Kingdom, West Germany, Italy, etc., East European countries, such as Bulgaria, East Germany, Hungary, Poland, and China in Asia, etc. Now 46 nations possess ballistic missiles in 2002 after one decade passed. Many countries of Africa, Middle East, South America and Asia came to have their ballistic missiles[1]. In those countries, when the political situation is unstable, ballistic missiles might be actually used. In such cases, this situation becomes an unstable factor in that region. Furthermore, the danger that missiles will be transferred to terrorist groups from such states is also concerned.

2) Missile Defense Systems

Based on such a situation, some advanced nations are developing the defense system against ballistic missiles. Some of those are Arrow system developed by Israel, S300/S400 of Russia, MEADS (Medium Extended Air Defense System) developed by West European countries with U.S.A. Actually the systems of Israel and Russia are already in service. Moreover, U.S.A. also develops and builds their missile defense systems now. If those defense systems are completed, the threat of missiles from the so-called rogue states will be minimized.

However, these defense systems will not be available by all nations. The missile defense systems are combined to various technical elements, such as detection of missiles, identification of targets, interception, its evaluation, and further detection of the following missiles. Huge finance as well as high technological skills is required for development and introduction. Systems can be equipped only in advanced countries' areas, such as U.S.A., Russia, Europe and Japan. Consequently, there will emerge two country groups in the world, the countries with missile defense capability, and countries without missile defense capability. That means that the world will be divided into two areas, the area protected from ballistic missiles, and the area not protected.

2. Applicability of International Law to Missile Defense Systems

1) Area of Interception

Because the targets (ballistic missiles) pass through outer space, the interception is done there. Therefore, the problem of the relationship between the international space law and missile interception is raised.

2) Principles applied to Missile Defense in Outer Space

a) Self-Defense

Generally the international space law including Outer Space Treaty regulates the activities of states in outer space. These space related treaties have declared that international law is applied to outer space activities. For example, Article 3 of Outer Space Treaty provides that international law is applied for activities there[2]. In that drafting process, it was interpreted that international law included use of the right of self-defense[3]. Of course, international law does not accept the act of aggression on the Earth, and also is the same in the outer space. Moreover, general international law forbids use of weapons of mass destruction, and also is the same in outer space. Outer Space Treaty forbids strictly carrying weapons of mass destruction on the earth orbit by Article 4. However, as mentioned above, use of the right of self-defense is not forbidden.

How is international law applied to the missile defense systems? First, when missile defense systems are functioned as execution of the right of self-defense, there is clearly a legal basis. By Article 51 of the U.N. Charter[4], when one country is attacked from other countries, she can counterattack the aggressor countries using the right of self-defense. It is natural that this principle is applied also to the activities in outer space.

However, in fact, can the right of self-defense allow all activities? This question should be considered based upon the following reason. In the Cold War era, the use of the right of self-defense to the ICBMs in outer space was a prologue to the full-scale nuclear war between the East and the West. In this case, the right of self-defense directly linked to destruction of the whole Earth, and human beings, though the interception marked a good score. But in that era, the countries with the missile defense capability were only U.S.A. and U.S.S.R. As long as both two countries took a restraint attitude on missile attacks, the conditions could be managed effectively.

On the other hand, while the country with missile defense capability is still limited, the countries holding ballistic missiles are increasing in number. Furthermore, because so-called rogue states are included among those, the possibilities of missile attacks from them are not a nominal situation, but a certain imaginable situation. We have to consider such worst cases of the real war between the advanced countries with missile defense capability and the rogue states.

In those circumstances, sufficient examination is required about what role international law plays about the missile defense as a real imaginable situation.

b) Doctrine of Military Objectives

The missile defense systems, which are interception systems actually used, are ultimate defense systems in a sense. In the modern law of conflict, the targets are restricted to the military objectives in order to avoid unnecessary damage to the non-combatants, ordinary people. Missile defense destroys pinpoint the missile, which flies in outer space. This defense technology just suits the doctrine of military objectives most in that only the military targets are destroyed correctly. Therefore, the influence of the interception will not be supposed to damage others other than belligerents.

However, because of the physical characteristic of outer space, there will happen the different result. The destroyed missile warheads and the interceptor missiles themselves will turn many pieces of debris, and fly like a shower in outer space. Probably, most of such debris fall down toward the earth atmosphere, as shooting stars, and are burned out. On the other hand, some debris might stay on the earth orbit. For the satellites passing through such a debris shower, without any armour on them, space debris on the orbit and/or in outer space are fatal weapon fundamentally. The result by which many warheads were destroyed by the ultimate missile defense system might be such orbital space with debris.

3. After Missile Defense

1) Number of Space Debris Caused by Missile Defense

In the present technology of missile defense, the attainment altitude of interceptor missiles is about 100 to 200km. This altitude now does not have so many debris and at this altitude, target (ballistic missile) is passing through in the boost phase (upward) and the terminal phase (downward). Even if debris occur, it is thought that they may not stay at outer space for a long time. However, a certain amount of debris might stay on the low earth orbit. Moreover, when missile defense technologies, such as space-based missiles as well as land-based interceptors, which go up to higher altitude, are developed in the future, the altitude of interception will rise higher. In such cases, mid-course interception against the warheads will be emerged. The mid-course altitude of ballistic missile warheads reaches almost 1,000km. If we examine some ASAT experiments, one space object will be ruined into hundreds of debris. In the experiment in 1968 by U.S.S.R., a suicide explosive satellite broke up into 100 or more debris[5]. In another experiment in 1985 by U.S.A., a targeted satellite was destroyed into near 300 debris by the collision with an air-launched missile[6]. What missile defense aims as a target is not an artificial satellite but a missile, which passes outer space with a hard nose cone. And the speed is less than the first astronautics velocity (7.9km/s), because this is not a satellite but a ballistic trajectory object. Therefore, it is unknown what number of debris on the orbit will be made from a missile warhead. To be debris on the orbit, such objects need to increase their own speed to the first astronautics velocity or more by the explosion. However, on the other hand, because the number of targeted warheads does not seem single but more, we can imagine the danger of flying some hundred of debris on the orbit. And of course, we can imagine the same danger as on the low earth orbit mentioned above. In this case, the debris shower will fall down not from 100 or 200 km high but from 1,000 km high.

2) Kessler Syndrome on the Low Earth Orbit

Such a situation reminds us of Kessler syndrome. In the present analysis, the outer space around the altitude of 1,000km is already in saturation. It is concerned that the space objects there might collide with existing debris, turn new debris, and hit new space objects again. If missile interception is done on such an orbit, the saturated condition will be severer. This is Kessler Syndrome[7].

The problem in this case is that the outbreak of those debris and the risk of Kessler syndrome are the results of legitimate activities under international space law, which was done against an illegal act like aggression. After doing the right action, the result might become a disincentive factor to all space actors in future.

We here face the special conditions from the characteristic of outer space. In outer space, there is not the same kind of natural resilience as on the Earth like weathering or diffusion.

How should we evaluate such a result by missile defense? The legitimate activities cannot be suspended even if they cause the obstacle for future space utilization. This problem reminds us of the advisory opinion of the International Court of Justice (ICJ) about the use of nuclear weapons in 1996, judges could not decide the legitimacy of such use when the existence of states is at stake [8]. Although ENMOD (Prohibition of Environmental Modification) treaty[9] forbids environmental change of the outer space, it cannot be interpreted forbidding the right of self-defense. ICJ judged in the advisory opinion in 1986 that environmental treaty's obligation could not limit the right of self-defense under international law[10]. Making nothing to the ballistic missiles passing through outer space means only waiting the damage by missiles on the Earth. That is an unacceptable situation for such countries with adequate missile defense capability. On the other hand, polluted low earth orbit in outer space is also not unacceptable for all the space users of the world.

Of course, for the attacked state, it is theoretically possible to ask for war indemnity from the aggressor state, which performed the illegal activities (attacks by ballistic missiles). And also, the third party states being outside the dispute may claim the international liability for the damage, which they have by such illegal activities according to the international law of war. However, it seems difficult for rogue countries to compensate all damage in outer space. And if we have good finance for cleaning outer space, there still be another problem. We have no concrete measure for orbit cleaning at present. Therefore, we are now far from ideal solution on this problem. In missile interception in outer space, this factor might be one of the surrounding problems, but not so small.

4. Future Consideration

1) Opportunism and Reality

We can see a certain situation of international society from the viewpoint of proliferation of ballistic missiles and development of missile defense technologies as its countermeasure. In this situation, we can see a kind of optimism and pessimistic facts, which deny such optimism. There seems optimism in legal sense as well as in technological sense, where the necessity and legitimacy of missile defense are accepted, and further we want to believe that the result from legitimate missile interception must not be any obstruction for our future utilization of outer space. However, we will face a thorny result, outer space with debris shower falls and debris on the low earth orbit. Probably, international law including space law, as well as the law of armed conflict have to be interpreted appropriately in future in consideration of technology and reality.

2) Temporary Conclusion

A specific conclusion cannot be drawn at the time of this analysis. What should be considered at present will be summarized to the following several points.

a) Fully understand the physical characteristic of space anew with scientists as well as engineers.

b) Develop immediately the debris cleaning technology on the international level.

c) Build new appropriate logic for defense of the international society as a whole, not only for defense of one country. Upon this new logic, it may be justified that the whole international society shares the burden for the space cleaning after missile interception.

d) Advance further effort towards the peace and security on the Earth. It might be the best solution for continuing our space utilization. If nobody wants to launch the ballistic missiles, we can keep the outer space quiet and calm.

After all, the temporary conclusion is likely to become a very simple thesis. That is, no peace of outer space without peace on the Earth.

*Any opinion here is the personal opinion of the author, not the opinion of any organization, which the author belongs.

---

[1] *Military Balance 1970-1971, Military Balance 1988-1989, Military Balance 2001-2002*, etc.

[2] Treaty on Principles Governing the Activities of States in the Exploration and Use of Outer Space, Including the Moon and Other Celestial Bodies, 1967.

[3] M.S.McDougal, H.D.Laswell & I.A.Vlasic, *Law and Public Order in Outer Space*, Yale University Press, 1963, p.441.

[4] Charter of The United Nations, 1945.

[5] In this test, ASAT (Kosmos249) and the target (Kosmos248) were broken down into 110 debris. And after 10 days, new ASAT (Kosmos252) made 139 debris.

[6] In this test, the United States used an air-launched missile from F-15. The target, Solwind of P-78 on the 500 km high orbit, was hit and destroyed into 287 debris.

[7] YASAKA, Tetsuo, *UCHU NO GOMI MONDAI -Space Debris* (in Japanese), Shokabou, 1997, pp.88-90.

[8] Legality of the Use by a State of Nuclear Weapon in Armed Conflict, Advisory Opinion, No.96/22, 1996, para.97.

[9] Convention on the Prohibition of Military of Any Other Hostile Use of Environmental Modification Techniques, 1978.

[10] Advisory Opinion (note 8), para.30.

IAC-02-IISL.3.06

THE DOCTRINE "REBUS SIC STANTIBUS" AND THE 1972 ABM TREATY: A BRIEF REFLECTION

"...Therefore all things whatsoever ye would that men should do to you, do ye even so to them: for this is the law and the prophets."[1]

Maurice N. Andem*
Faculty of Law, University of Lapland, Rovaniemi, Finland

ABSTRACT

The 1972 ABM Treaty was concluded between the former Soviet Union and the United States during the Cold War Era. Its purpose was to prevent an arms race in outer space between the two super powers. It laid down the fundamentals for the further development of broad and mutually beneficial co-operation in various fields of mutual interest to the peoples of both countries and in the interest of mankind. In fact, it has been the nucleus of other strategic arms limitation agreements concluded between them.[2]

Towards the end of the year 2001, President George W. Bush, annouced that the United States will no more comply with the provisions of the 1972 ABM Treaty, because of the changing circumstances. What are these circumstances? Will the collapse of the former Soviet Union, for example, be considered as one of the legal grounds for the denunciation of the Treaty vis a vis the doctrine "Rebus Sic Stantibus? Thus, the purpose of this paper is to reflect on the provisions of the Treaty and the Doctrine of "Rebus Sic Stantibus".

Introduction

As a law teacher, I have been pondering on what would have happened in our contemporary world, if human beings (individuals) in all societies had failed to keep the promises made in their intercourse with one another, expressed in the form of agreements or contracts; and between sovereign states, as expressed in various international legal instruments, agreements, conventions, treaties, etc.

In traditional societies, individuals, in their mutual relationships and intercourse, were obligated to perform the promises made to one another. These promises were not in written form, but verbal. The principles of trust, honesty, integrity and good faith were very important in the development of their contractual relations among themselves. This can be seen in the history of the origin and development of various legal cultures and systems of the world - both in developed and developing societies. Furthermore, the development, progress and stability in families, as the primary foundation and unit in all human societies would have not been what they are today if our ancestors had failed to honour and respect their marital contractual obligations. This analogy is also applicable in international intercourse between states.

Roscoe Pound, for example, reflecting on the development of contract in the civil law and Anglo-American common law legal systems, correctly pointed out that:

"Wealth, in a commercial age, is made up largely of promises. An important part of everyone's substance consists of advantages which others have promised to provide for or to render to him; of demands to have the advantages promised, which he may assert not against the world at large but against particular individuals. Thus the individual claims to have performance of advantageous promises secured to him. He claims the satisfaction of expectations created by promises and agreements. If this claim is not secured friction and waste obviously result, and unless some countervailing interest must come into account which would be sacrificed in the process, it would seem that the individual interest in the promised advantages should be secured to the full extent of what has been assured to him by the deliberate promise of another. .....In an earlier chapter I suggested, as a jural postulate of civilized society, that in such a society men must be able to assume that those with whom they deal in general intercourse of the society will act in good faith, and as a corollary must be able to assume that those with whom they so deal will carry out their undertakings according to the expectations which the moral sentiment of the community attaches thereto. Hence in a commercial and industrial society, a claim or want or demand of society that promises be kept and that undertakings be carried out in good faith, a social interest in the stability of promises as a social and economic institution, becomes of the first importance. This social interest in the security of transactions, as one might call it, requires that we secure the individual interest of the promise, that is, his claim or demand to be assured in the expectation created, which has become part of his substance."[3]

We know that our contemporary civil societies would have been in absolute confusion, under-development and chaos, if all subjects of both national laws and international law had no binding legal duty to fulfil all their contractual obligations. This is due to the existence of universal moral values and ethical rules of behaviour which have been developed and perfected in various forms in all human societies over the past two thousand years. These rules have been codified into the corpus of domestic laws of all legal traditions and also in contemporary international law of nations - international law. Furthermore, we know that international treaties (conventions), as the primary source of international law, were concluded for the common good of the state parties and their nationals.

Like national or domestic laws, international treaties are governed by principles which have been codified in the 1969 Vienna Convention on the Law of Treaties.[4] They have played and shall continue to play a major role in the consolidation and strengthening of the existing international relations between states and peoples of the world.

The 1972 ABM Treaty between the former Soviet Union and the United States was concluded thirty years ago in accordance with the provisions of the 1969 Vienna Convention on the Law of Treaties. Moreover, it should be borne in mind that the 1969 Vienna Convention contains provisions relating to the fundamental change of circumstances, which is expressed in the **Doctrine Rebus Sic Stantibus**.

It is interesting to note that I was a fourth-year law student when the late US President Richard Nixon visited Moscow in 1972. I am not convinced of the reasons given by President George W. Bush for denouncing the 1972 ABM Treaty.

Thus, the purpose of this paper is to reflect on the provisions of the 1972 ABM Treaty vis-a-vis the **Doctrine Rebus Sic Stantibus**. Considering that the relevance of the 1969 Vienna Convention on the Law of Treaties to the topic of my paper, it would be useful to examine some of its provisions.[5]

The 1969 Vienna Convention on the Law of Treaties

The Convention was signed in Vienna, on 23 May 1969 and entered into force on 27 January 1980. It consists of a Preamble, 85 articles, which are further divided into eight parts and an annex.

In the Preamble, the States Parties to the Convention, recognized the ever-increasing importance of treaties as a source of international law and as a means of developing peaceful co-operation among nations, whatever their constitutional and social systems. They further expressed their belief that the codification and the progressive development of the law of treaties achieved in the Convention will promote the purposes of the United Nations set forth in the Charter, namely, the maintenance of international peace and security, the development of friendly relations and the achievement of co-operation among nations.

Article 1 stipulates that the Convention applies to treaties between States. The definition of the terms is given in the provisions of Article 2. Article 2 para. 1(a) stipulates that "treaty" means an international agreement concluded between States in written form and governed by international law, whether embodied in a single instrument or more related instruments and whatever its particular designation. According to Article 6, every State possesses capacity to conclude treaties.

Article 11 provides that consent of a State to be bound by a treaty may be expressed by signature, exchange of instruments constituting a treaty, ratification, acceptance, approval or accession, or by any other means so agreed. Articles 12 to 17 elaborate on these means of expressing the consent of a State to be bound by a treaty.

PART III, Section 1 of the Treaty contains two important articles which deal with the observance of treaties (Art. 26 and 27). Article 26 embodies the principle of **pacta sunt servanda**. According to the Black's Law Dictionary, Fifth Edition (1979), **pacta sunt servanda** means that agreements (and stipulations) of the parties (to a contract) must be observed. It stipulates: "Every treaty in force is binding upon the parties to it and must be performed by them in good faith." Pursuant to the provision of Article 27, a party may not invoke the provisions of its internal law as a justification for its failure to perform a treaty. It further provides that this rule is without prejudice to Article 46.[6]

This is an important principle in both private law and international law. Parties to any contracts are supposed to be sincere, trustworthy, honest and to act in good faith. The principle of good faith is one of the most important principles of international law and international relations between States and peoples of the world. It is quite evident that individuals cannot be engaged in any type of contractual relationship or intercourse without the application of the principle of good faith.

Professor Bing Cheng, in this respect, correctly pointed out that: "The law of treaties is closely bound to the principle of good faith, if indeed not based on it; for this principle governs treaties from the time of their formation to the time of their extinction."[7]

This principle is embodied in the provisions of Article 2(2) of the UN Charter. It has been elaborated further in the UN General Assembly resolution 2625 (XXV) of 24 October 1970, **DECLARATION on Principles of International Law concerning Friendly Relations and Co-operation among States in accordance with the Charter of the United Nations**. It stipulates: "Every State has the duty to fulfil in good faith the obligations assumed by it in accordance with the Charter of the United Nations. Every State has the duty1to fulfil in good faith its obligations under the generally recognized principles and rules of international law. Every State has a duty to fulfil in good faith its obligations under international agreements valid under the generally recognized principles and rules of international law. Where obligations arising under international agreements are in conflict with the obligations of the Members of the United Nations under the Charter of the United Nations, the obligations under the Charter shall prevail."

Furthermore, it is interesting to note that the foregoing provisions are also embodied in the provisions of the **FINAL ACT OF THE 1975 HELSINKI CONFERENCE ON SECURITY AND CO-OPERATION IN EUROPE** - thus consolidating the mandatory character of this principle. It stipulates that "The participating states will fulfil in good faith their obligations under international law, both those obligations arising from the generally recognized principles and rules of international law and those obligations arising from treaties or other agreements, in conformity with international law, to which they are parties. In exercising their sovereign rights, including the right to determine their laws and regulations, they will conform with their legal obligations under international law; they will furthermore pay due regard to and implement the provisions in the Final Act of the Conference on Security and Co-operation in Europe. The participating States confirm that in the event of a conflict between the obligations of the members of the United Nations under the Charter of the United Nations and their obligations under any treaty or other international agreement, their obligations under the Charter will prevail, in accordance with Article 103 of the Charter of the United Nations."

As could be seen from the foregoing provisions, the principle of good faith **(pacta sunt servanda)** has been and will continue to be the life line or driving force in the progressive development and codification of international law, including the civil laws of nations. Furthermore, Professor Bing Cheng, in this respect correctly pointed out that, "**Pacta sunt servanda,** now an indisputable rule of international law, is but an expression of the principle of good faith which above all signifies the keeping of faith, the pledged faith of nations as well as that of individuals. Without this rule, "international law as well as civil law would be a mere mockery.""[8]

Article 62 of the 1969 Vienna Convention on the Law of Treaties contains provisions on **"Fundamental change of circumstances"** or the **Doctrine Rebus Sic Stantibus**. Before continuing with my reflection, it would be useful to define the meaning of **"Rebus Sic Stantibus"** According to Black's Law Dictionary, it is "A name given to a tacit condition,said to attach to all treaties, that they shall cease to be obligatory so soon as the state of facts and conditions upon which they were founded has substantially changed."

Bearing in mind the above definition, let us see how this change is elaborated in the provisions of the said Article 62 of the 1969 Vienna Convention. It stipulates as follows:

"1. A fundamental change of circumstances which has occurred with regard to those existing at the time of the conclusion of a treaty, and which was not foreseen by the parties, may not be invoked as a ground for the termination or withdrawal from the treaty unless:
(a) the existence of those circumstamnces constitute an essential basis of the consent of the parties to be bound by the treaty; and (b) the effect of the change is radically to transform the extent of the obligations still to be performed under the treaty.

2. A fundamental change of circumstances may not be invoked as a ground for terminating or withdrawing from a treaty:
(a) if the treaty establishes a boundary; or if the fundamental change is the result of a breach by the party invoking it either of an obligation under the treaty or of any other international obligation owed to any other party to the treaty.
3. If, under the foregoing paragraph, a party may invoke a fundamental change of circumstances as a ground for terminating or withdrawing from a treaty it may also invoke the change as a ground for suspending the operation of the treaty."

The Doctrine Rebus Sic Stantibus and the 1972 ABM Treaty

It can be seen that the foregoing provisions of Article 62 provide basic rules on fundamental change of circumstances. Thus, taking into consideration what has been discussed above, I will now continue with my brief reflection on the topic of my paper.

It will be recalled that the 1972 ABM Treaty between the former Soviet Union and the United States was concluded during the Cold War Era under Brezhnev's foreign policy of **détente**. It was an important and major rapprochement between the two super powers after the World War II. In the Preamble, for example, both State Parties declared their intention to achieve at the earliest possible date the cessation of the nuclear arms race and to take effective measures toward reductions of strategic arms, nuclear disarmament, and general and complete disarmament. They further expressed their desire to contribute to the relaxation of international tension and the strengthening of trust between States.

At this juncture, it should be reiterated that the 1972 ABM Treaty has contributed a lot to strengthening the provisions of the 1967 Outer Space Treaty (OST), particularly in respect of the implementation of Articles I, II, III and IV. Due to lack of space, it is not my intention to examine again the provisions of OST and the ABM Treaty in this paper. This has already been done in my previous papers.[9]

Bearing in mind the above definition on the **Doctrine Rebus Sic Stantibus** and the provisions of Article 62, the question is: what are these fundamental changes of circumstances that have contributed to the denunciation by US President George W. Bush of the 1972 ABM Treaty? Should the peace-loving states and peoples of the world consider the collapse of the former Soviet Union (now succeeded by Russia) as one of the legal grounds for this denunciation? Let us look at the position of the two Presidents during some of their joint press conferences.

In an answer to a question on the ABM Treaty posed by a reporter during a Press Conference by President Bush and President Vladimir Putin, the US President replied as follows:

"Well, I'm convinced that the treaty is outdated and we need to move beyond it. And we're having discussions along these lines. We had good discussions today; we had good discussions in Shanghi; we had good discussions in Slovenia; and we'll have good discussions in Crawford. This is obviously a subject that's got a lot of ramifications to it. I clearly heard what the President has had to say and his view of the ABM Treaty; he's heard what I've had to say. And we'll continue working it. But my position is, is that it is a piece of paper that's codified a relationship that no longer exists -- codified a hateful relationship. And now we've got a friendly relationship. And I think we need to have a new strategic frame work that reflects the new relationship, based upon trust and co-operation. But we we'll continue to work it."[10]

The reasons given above are not legally and logically sound as far as the provisions of the 1969 Vienna Convention on the Law of Treaties mentioned above are concerned. Why should such an important international legal document which has a major role to play in the disarmament process be called "a piece of paper"? It should be pointed out that the 1972 ABM Treaty had contributed a lot to the normalisation of relations between East and West and to the maintenance of international security and peace. It was a great contribution by the two super powers to the efforts of the United Nations in the prevention of an arms race in outer space, the moon and other celestial bodies.

Furthermore, in an earlier Press Conference by the two Presidents in Slovenia on 16 June 2001, President Putin correctly emphasised the importance of the 1972 ABM Treaty in the following words:

"Now, as far as the issue of the antimissile defense, the official position of the Russian government in known. I don't think we need to spend time to yet again declare it. We proceed from the idea that the 1972 ABM Treaty is the cornerstone of the modern architecture of international security. We proceed from the premise that there are elements which unite us with our partners in the United States....Now, as far as the issues proliferation and nonproliferation, I have to say that in our opinion, this is a topic that's very, very closely tied to the ABM Treaty, because many other things are hooked onto this same string, and many threshold states, when it comes to the destruction of a previous accord, can only be happy and say, look, fantastic. Yesterday, we were the threshold, nobody agreed -- nobody took any account of us; now, today, recognize us. This is a problem we're going to have really think very hard about."[11]

We do agree with the position of the Russian President Putin. He is very sincere and honest in reiterating the position of the former Soviet President Mikhail Gorbachev with respect to the 1972 ABM Treaty.[12] It should be noted the political changes in leadership have not affected the official position of the Soviet/Russian government with regards to the performance of the 1972 ABM Treaty.

It is very sad to observe that since the beginning of the 21st Century a lot of events have taken place that have threatened the rule of law in international relations between states and peoples. The respect and sanctity of international agreements are being ignored and undermined by some states for one reason or the other. Proliferation of weapons of mass destruction is increasing daily, more than during the Cold War Era. Hatred, bitterness, fear, wars and lack of respect for human life and the environment could be seen in many parts of the world. The sad event of 11 September 2001 further illustrates the need for states to comply with their obligations arising from international treaties, particularly those arising under the provisions of the UN Charter.

No states or individuals responsible for the implementation of international agreements have the right to annul or denounce unilaterally their obligations without the consent of the other parties. Performance in good faith of all obligations arising from international treaties has been and will continue to be the core in the codification and progressive deveploment of international law and in the consolidation and strengthening of international relations and co-operation between states and peoples of the world. Therefore, the **doctrine rebus sic stantibus** cannot be applied to international law because of its negative impact on international law and relations. Professor Wolfgang Friedmann, in this respect, correctly pointed out that this form negative law-making is, of course, highly unsatisfactory. It creates uncertainty, and leaves a vacuum where there was at least something before.[13] The missile defence system contravenes the provisions of the UN Charter, arms control and disarmament treaties, the 1967 Outer Space Treaty and the 1972 ABM Treaty.

Concluding Remarks and Observations

In the foregoing pages I have tried to reflect on the nature of international treaties, with special reference to the 1972 ABM Treaty between the former Soviet Union/Russia **vis a vis** the Doctrine of Rebus Sice Stantibus. In doing so, I have briefly examined some of the provisions of the 1969 Vienna Convention on the Law of Treaties. The nature of the principle of **pacta sunt servanda** was elaborated and discussed.

In this concluding part of my paper, may I seize this opportunity to point out that the disappearance of the former Soviet Union or the USSR from the political map of the world was a spiritual death, because the regime relied solely on its military might and power. In fact, the Russian government and people are beginning to recognize the importance and the truth in what the Divine WORD says: **"It is the spirit that quickeneth; the flesh profiteth nothing: the words that I speak unto you, they are spirit, and they are life"**;[14] and **"Not by might, nor by power, but my spirit, saith**

the LORD of host".[15] I believe that the Almighty Creator will help them to regain that part of human existence which was neglected by the old regime. Consequently, He will give them a new dynamic role to play in international affairs and politics in the 21st century.

The Russian Federation is the successor State. The strategic and military infractures are still the same, irrespective of the socio-economic problems currently facing the Russian people. The post Cold War Russian government has not withdrawn from or denounced the ABM Treaty or any of the SALT and START Agreements, irrespective of some shortcomings in their interpretation and implementation by both parties.

It should be emphasized that the majority of states and peoples of the world want to live in peace and co-operate with one another in the 21st. century. The human race is already fed up with the hatred, bitterness, lack of neighbourly love and war which had caused a lot of sufferings and sorrows in the world throughout the 20th century. Therefore, it is now time for all the policy-makers and political leaders in the position of authority to listen and comply with the wishes and expectations of the peoples of the world. This is what I consider to be democracy.

The former UN Secretary-General Boutros Boutros-Ghali, in this respect, correctly emphasized that: " Democracy within the family of nations means the application of its principles within the world Organization itself. This requires the fullest consultation, participation and engagement of all States, large and small, in the work of the Organization. All organs of the United nations must be accorded, and play, their full and proper role so that trust of all nations and peoples will be retained and deserved. The principles of the Charter must be applied consistently, not selectively, for if the perception should be the latter, trust will wane and with it the moral authority which is the greatest and most unique quality of that instrument. Democracy at all levels is essential to attain peace for a new era of prosperity and justice."[16] This is very true!

Furthermore, it should be borne in mind that no amount of military build-up on our blue planet - earth or in outer space, moon and other celestial bodies cannot and will not bring peace to human race in the new millennium; but the virtue of loving our neighbours as ourselves in our daily intercourse with one another. Space science and technology in particular have brought states and peoples of all races, traditions and cultures much more closer. Outer space, as the province of mankind, must be zone of peace, harmony and co-operation. It was created perfect and good by the Almighty Creator of the universe. All states and peoples have the divine obligation to respect its sanctity and purity. We have to leave it in a good condition for the unborn generations to come.

Thus, the militarization of outer space, including the moon and other celestial bodies, should be considered as a serious terrorist act and crime against the human race and the Divine Law, because "The earth is the LORD's, and the fullness thereof; the world and they that dwell therein **(Ps. 24:1, 50:12)."**

Finally, I would like to conclude with this quotation from one the world's leading Statesmen, President Abraham Lincoln: **"With malice toward none; with charity for all; with firmness in the right, as God gives us to see the right, let us strive on to finish the work we are in: to bind up the nation's wounds; to care for him who shall have borne battle, and for his widow and his orphan, to do all which may achieve and cherish a just and lasting peace among ourselves, and with all."**[17]

May the golden rule cited on the first page of this paper, be the guiding principle in the actions, words and deeds of all states and peoples of the world throughout the new millennium.

---

1 Gospel of St. Mt. 7:12. This same principle is expressed in Lk 6:31 as follows: "And as ye would that men should do to you, do ye also to them likewise." See also Lv. 19:18; Mt. 22:37-40; Mk. 12:29-31.

2 See, for example, DOCUMENTS OF THE USSR-USA SUMMIT TALKS, June 1973, Novosti Press Agency Publishing House, Moscow (1973); Warfare and Welfare. Integrating Security Policy Into Socio-Economic Policy, Tinbergen, Jan and Fischer, Dietrich, Wheatsheaf Books, Sussex (1987), pp. 116-138.

3 See, An Introduction to the Philosophy of Law, Yale University Press, Yale (1982), pp. 133-134.

4 For details, see, The Work of the International Law Commission, Fourth Edition, United Nations, New York (1988), pp. 260-286.

5 For more details on the Convention, see, for example, Brownlie, Ian, Principles of Public International Law, Third Edition, Clarendon Press, Oxford (1979), pp. 600-632; Harris, D. J., CASES AND MATERIALS ON INTERNATIONAL LAW, Fifth Edition, Sweet & Maxwell, London (1998), pp. 765-858.

6 Art. 46 stipulates: "1. A State may not invoke that its consent to be bound by atreaty has been expressed in violation of a provision of its internal law regarding competence to conclude treaties as invalidating its consent unless that violation was manifest and concerned a rule of its internal law of fundamental importance. 2. A violation is manifest if it would be objectively evident to any State conducting itself in the matter in accordance with normal practice and in good faith."

7 Cheng, Bing, GENERAL PRINCIPLES OF LAW as applied by INTERNATIONAL COURTS AND TRIBUNALS, Grotius Publications Limited, Cambridge (1987), p. 106.

8 Ibid., p. 113. For further comments on the principle, see, Ibid., pp. 106-119.

9 See, e.g., Andem, Maurice N., IISL-97-IISL.4.11 "Implemantation of Article IV of the Outer Space Treaty of 1967 During the 21st. Century", in Proceedings, IISL 40th Coll. on the Law of Outer Space, Turin, Italy (1997); by same author, IISL-00-IISL.4.01 "Implementation of the 1967 Outer Space Treaty in the New Millennium: A Brief Reflection on the Implication of the Proposed Missile Defence Sysytems", in Proceedings, IISL 43rd Coll. on the Law of Outer Space, Rio de Janeiro, Brazil (2000).

10 For more detail, see http://www.whitehouse.gov/news/releases/2001/11/print/20011113-3.html

11 For more detail, see, http://www.whitehouse.gov/news/releases/2001/06/print/20010618.html

12 For more detail, see, REYKJAVIK Documents and Materials, Novosti Press Agency Publishing House, Moscow (1987).

13 For more details, Friedmann, Wolfgang, The Changing Structure of International Law, Stevens & Sons, London (1964), 133-134.

14 John 6:63. See also, Ps. 119:97-112; II Tim. 3:16-17.

15 Zech. 4:6.

16 Boutros Boutros-Ghali, An Agenda for Peace: Preventive diplomacy, Peacemaking and Peace-keeping. Report of the Secretary-General pursuant to the statement adopted by the Summit Meeting of the Security Council on 31 Jan. 1992, p. 47.

17 Second Inaugural Address, 4 March 1865, in THE OXFORD DICTIONARY OF QUOTATIONS, FOURTH EDITION, Edited by Partington, Angela, Oxford University Press, Oxford (1992), p. 422.

Military Space Activity in the Light of General International Law

by Gyula Gál

Péter Pázmány Catholic University
Budapest

The history of human civilization indicates that all technical achievements suitable for military use sooner or later contribute to the means of warfare.

Aviation made the first steps toward the conquest of the airspace when *H. G. Wells* published his utopian work "War in the Air" in 1908. He wrote of air raids by dirigibles against targets of the rear in future wars. In less than 40 years air fleets laid towns in ruins and the first atomic bombs were dropped.

The launching of the first artificial satellites raised the well-founded hope and wish to save this new achievement, the space exploration from this fateful development: space activity should be reserved for peaceful purposes. This principle has been voiced in various private drafts and declarations before UN Resolutions. E.g. the ILA Declaration of Hamburg (1960): „Outer Space and celestial bodies should be utilized only for peaceful purposes to the greatest common profit of all mankind in accordance with the principles of the UN Charter." (1)

Preceding the Space Treaty of 1967 "peaceful use" connected with "common interest" appears again in UN GA Resolutions 1721/XVI and 1962/XVIII. At present, space technology plays an indispensable role in military planning and armed conflicts. The US Air Force Chief of Staff Merriel Mc Peak defined the "Desert Storm" as the first "space war", because in this conflict the full range of military space assets was applied. (2) The well-meant hopes failed – military space activity opened new dimensions of strategy. Whether this development is lawful or violates international law, depends on the interpretation of space law rules (jus speciale) and general international law (jus generale) applying to military space activity.

I

The conviction that space exploration can not be "legibus soluta", it does not take place in a legal vacuum, goes back to the time before the Space Treaty. This led to the recognition that international law should govern international relations relating to space activities. GA Res. 1721/XVI recommended the states to observe the principle that "international law including the Charter of the United Nations applies to outer space and celestial bodies." In Article III of the Space Treaty the principle became treaty law. The validity of general international law in respect of activities on the Moon and other celestial bodies within the solar system other than Earth was confirmed by Article II of the Moon Agreement.

Needless to underline the declaratory character of this treaty stipulations. Space exploration is a geocentric activity constituting legal relations on Earth between states governed by general international law in all respects not covered by special rules of space law.

Artificial satellites launched with military destination appeared in 1958-59 in orbit around the Earth. The first USA military satellite was the SCORE launched at the end of 1958. The Soviet Union started the COSMOS-series in 1962. (3) Only certain orbital elements indicated that the satellites of this system were carrying out a military program. (4) The Soviet Minister of Defense the first time referred to the Soviet military space program in 1985. (5) The real destination of the COSMOS program was disclosed only in 1993.

Before 1967 the Moon-landing seemed to be a problem of the distant future. On the other hand military activity around the Earth was an obvious reality. No wonder that the leading space powers made it clean any attempt within the context of the Space Treaty to demilitarize outer space would make the treaty as a whole inacceptable. (6) Apparently, this motivated the different treaty regulations of military activity in orbit an on celestial bodies usually characterized as partial and complete demilitarization.

Concerning military use of outer space the Space Treaty is rather laconic. It stipulates restrictions for the orbital movements around the Earth and for activities on the Moon and other celestial bodies. In Article IV.1 States Parties to the Treaty undertake not to place in orbit any objects carrying nuclear weapons or any other kinds of weapons of mass destruction, install such weapons on celestial bodies or station such weapons in any other manner. For celestial bodies Article IV.2 prohibits installing nuclear weapons or weapons of mass destruction, testing any type of weapons, establishing military bases and fortifications, conducting military maneuvers with the general obligation to use celestial bodies exclusively for peaceful purposes. Article III of the Moon Agreement reaffirms this prohibitions for the Moon and orbits around the Moon or other trajectory to or around the Moon.

II

The notion „peaceful" occurs in the Space Treaty in four aspects:

1. Common interest in exploration and use of outer space for peaceful purposes (Preamble)

2. *Exclusively peaceful* purposes for celestial bodies (IV.2)

3. Use of military personnel and equipment for peaceful exploration (IV.2)

4. Cooperation in the peaceful exploration (XI)

The Treaty otherwise does not give an authentic **definition of "peaceful"**. Other Space treaties do not help the theory to find an incontestable interpretation of the term.

In my commentary on the Space Treaty I joined the conception that peaceful use of outer space excludes its use for military purposes, i.e. peaceful = non-military. (7) My arguments were footed on general principles laid down in the Treaty: exploration and use of outer space shall be carried out for the benefit and the interests of all countries, it shall be province of all mankind (Article I. 1.) Consequently exploration and use of outer space should be carried on for the benefit of all peoples (Preamble) therefore "peaceful" is more than peace merely as antithesis of war or armistice. (8) An activity will not be peaceful from the absence of aggression, but by the intent of promoting international cooperation and coexistence. I admitted at the same time that above principles in this context constitute additional, restrictive conditions to general international law applicable to space activities. It means therefore, that the equation: peaceful = non-military would be an element of space law as *jus speciale.*

The theory of peaceful = non-aggressive maintains: if a military activity is in conformity with the international law including the Charter of the United Nations, it is lawful. In the system of the U.N. Charter the opposite of "peaceful" is "aggressive". The term non-aggressiveness includes the possibility to apply military activities in outer space lawfully as long as those activities do not aim at direct attack in the sense of the U.N. definition of aggression. (9)

This interpretation has been accepted mainly by American authors, but also authors outside the United States (e.g. *A. Meyer* (10), *E. Fasan* (11), *A. Bueckling* (12)). On the other hand the interpretation "peaceful=non-military" was gaining adherents also in the western literature (e.g. *M. Seara Vázquez* (13), *D. Goedhuis* (14), *M. G. Markov* (15)). The opinion that this view was uniformly accepted by socialist space lawyers is hardly tenable. (16) *G. Zhukov – Y. Kolosov* e.g. acknowledge that in the absence of agreement on the total demilitarization international documents refer to the exploration and use of outer space exclusively for peaceful purposes merely as a goal to be pursued. (17) *E. Kamenetskaya* maintained that military activities may have an aggressive or a non-aggressive character. It cannot be asserted, that international law prohibits any military space activity. (18)

The discussion up to now did not come to a rest. To quote two opinions: Professor *Bin Cheng* thinks that "in order to fit the square peg of the already extensive use of outer space for military purposes into the round and hitherto rather hollow concept of 'peaceful uses' there has unfortunately developed in some quarters the habit of interpreting the term 'peaceful' as applied to outer space as meaning 'non-aggressive' instead of 'non-military'." (19) *R. J. Lee* in a noteworthy paper on the subject states that the use of space has been well established in international law to be exclusively for peaceful purposes only. (20) Whether this statement in the light of interstate practice and development of general international law after the Treaty is justifiable? Non-aggressive military space activity should be accepted as being lawful?

III

One of the arguments for a positive answer is derived from the **dual utilization** of satellites. It is estimated that about 75% of all satellites are functioning for military purposes. (21) Satellites intended for civilian purposes can be used to perform military functions. Under special conditions of global warfare all types of orbital devices can have military aspects. Navigation satellites promote the safety of peaceful navigation, they can be used, however, for the detecting of current position of submarines. Geodetic satellites have the peaceful task of performing exact measurements for science and economy, but they provide data useful for programming the guidance system of ballistic missiles. The same Janus-face have other satellites launched by civil authorities for communication, meteorology and reconnaissance.

This later application has a special importance in respect of permissibility of military space activities. The dual use of remote sensing satellites, especially space reconnaissance for military purposes has been subject of vivid discussions for a long time. Remote sensing itself started as military reconnaissance. Samos-2 launched in 1961 was the first satellite of an officially recognized military program. (22)

Reconnaissance was the first military use of the aeroplane before the first world war. From the possibility of aerial control pacific dreamers concluded that wars will be in the future impossible. There is nothing new under the sun. To military reconnaissance satellites very early peace-keeping role was attributed. (23)

The Space Treaty does not contain general stipulations concerning remote sensing, still less any special rules of remote sensing for military purposes. The Remote Sensing Principles (G.S. Res. 41/65) are of recommendatory character, the Resolution is no binding source of international law. Before and after the Space Treaty under the conditions of cold war authors in East and West inclined to qualify this activity as illegal space espionage. The early socialist literature at first has taken a unanimous stand against the legality of "intelligence satellites". Beside arguments based on general principles of the Space Treaty (Article I) general international law was referred to. In the western literature opinions on the practice of space reconnaissance ranged from theoretical opposition (*D. Goedhuis* (24), *W. Jenks* (25)) to legalization deducted in the same way from general international law. ("Observation from outer space like observation from the high seas is consistent with international law") (26)

The SALT Treaties between the United States and the Soviet Union recognized the legality of military space observation. Remote sensing satellites , though without definition of the term, were accepted as "national means" of monitoring: " For the purpose of providing assurance of compliance with the provisions of the Treaty... each party shall use national technical means of verification at its disposal in a manner consistent with generally recognized principles of international law." The treaties also provide that the parties will not interfere with each others "national technical means". (27)

The acceptance of mutual monitoring by observation satellites and the protection of this activity is contained in agreements between two major space powers. International treaties are not effective "erga omnes". For states not being parties to the treaty it is an "acta inter alios". On the other hand up to now, no formal protests are known to have been made concerning this kind of surveillance by satellites.

In the theory of space law this silence is understood as silent consent and interpreted in different ways. Some authors conclude the institution of a customary law rule. "Having offered the evidence of a long practice and an opinion accepting the military space observation's legality, one could consider that the demonstration of this activity's *customary legality* is complete". (*I. Kuskevelis* (28)) Others are of the opinion that the legality of space reconnaissance follows directly from general international law: "The application of international law to outer space would not inhibit military remote sensing activities, as remote sensing does not involve a threat of use of force." (*R. L. Lee* (29))

I am inclined to think, that the opinio juris manifested by silent consent did not create a *sui generis* customary law rule. It confirms rather the later opinion concerning correspondence of military space reconnaissance with general international law.

IV

Before the Space Treaty the first source of **domestic space law**, the 1958 National Aeronautical and Space Act declared: the policy of the United States is that activities in space should be devoted to peaceful purposes for the benefit of all mankind. One of the promoters of the Act *C. J. Feldman* stated to this wording that peaceful means non-aggressive rather than non-military. (30) NASA as a civilian agency was created to control such activities, except that activities associated with the development of weapon systems, military operations or defense of the United States shall be the responsibility of the Department of Defense (CFR. § 1201.101). The term "peaceful" in the context of the Act in this way applies to both civilian and military activities.

Space law Acts after 1967 referring to principles of the Space Treaty obviously likewise govern both kinds of activities. Prohibitions of Article IV are converted into domestic space law. E.g. in the Law of the Russian Federation (1993) it is prohibited to put into orbit around the Earth or deploy in outer space otherwise nuclear weapons and any kinds of weapons of mass destruction, to use the Moon and other celestial bodies for military purposes, or to carry out activities which are prohibited by international treaties of the Russian Federation. The Russian Space Agency shall be responsible for carrying out space activities for scientific and national-economy purposes. Activities for the purpose of defense and security of the Russian Federation shall be pursued by the Ministry of Defense. In this system, similarly to the domestic law of the United States, military space programs, military space technics and non-aggressive military space activities are treated as being consistent with space law and general international law. (31) The Law of the Ukraine on Space Activities (1996) follows the same model. (32) Other space acts referring to international commitments and responsibilities in respect of the "peaceful utilization of outer space" can not be interpreted in such a way that peaceful utilizations would exclude non-aggressive military space activities.

V

Under the impression of the first achievements of space exploration some military theoreticians considered that the surface of the Earth in the future can be excluded from military operations. Theatre of war would be the outer space where robot weapons of the "belligerents" would wage a fully mechanized "human" warfare. (33) It is quite certain that "in a global space war" blows against launching bases and the whole space infrastructure of the enemy would become inevitable. (34)

As mentioned above, the Golf War demonstrated the importance of military space technology in **armed conflicts** not only for strategic planning but also for tactical actions. Satellite support in the future will grant the superiority against an opponent that does not have such technology.

In the sparkling formulation of *P. Jankowitsch*: in a conflict between two space powers having equal space capability the destruction of an opponent's eyes and ears in space could have an important effect on the outcome. The importance of satellite support increases the potential impact of anti-satellite weapons. (35) We have to add: not only in respect of military remote sensing and communications. All satellites constituting an integral part of nuclear and conventional weapon systems in future conflicts may become targets for military actions.

Article II.4 of the UN Charter contains the basic principle of general international law: threat or use of force in international relations against the territorial integrity or political independence of any state or in any other manner is inconsistent with the purposes of the UN. The Moon Agreement only reaffirms this principle. Any threat or use of force or any other hostile act on the Moon is prohibited. It is likewise prohibited to use the Moon in order to commit any such act in relation to the Earth, the Moon, spacecraft, the personnel of spacecrafts or man-made space objects. International space law in this respect is no veritable *jus speciale*. It is not else than an adaptation of general international law rules to activities connected with the Moon and other celestial bodies within the solar system other than the Earth. (Article I.1)

The existence of any threat to the peace, breach of the peace or act of aggression shall be determined by the Security Council (UN Charter Article 39). In a given case the Security Council should act without having a legally binding definition of the concept "Aggression". The definition of GA Resolution 3314 (XXIX) is merely a guidance in determining the existence of an act of aggression for the purpose of Article 39. Obviously this apply also to military space activities involving threat or use of force, hostile act or act of aggression. The UN Res. contains a list of prima facie act of aggressions. Applying some elements of the enumerated acts to military space activity, an act of "space aggression" against the territory, land forces or air fleets of another state would be technically possible. Thought provoking view of *Y. Kolossov* is that since the list of the UN Res. is not exhaustive, aggressive space activities might comprise cases of support of combat operations of an aggressor state in the course of a military conflict. (36)

Destruction of a space object of another state by own space object or ASAT weapon could be qualified as an "act of space aggression". Otherwise the Security Council in the light of the gravity or the consequences of such conduct would decide what measures shall be taken in accordance with Articles 41 and 42 of the Charter.

VI

In Article IV.1 of the Space Treaty Parties to the Treaty undertake not to place in orbit around the Earth any objects carrying nuclear or other mass destruction weapons and not to station such weapons on celestial bodies and in outer space in any other manner.

Since any **stationing of weapons** in outer space postulates an orbital movement, in the sense of the Space Treaty suborbital military activities are not covered by this provision. The action of an ASAT missile carrying an explosive warhead launched from the ground or from air may be the subject of general international law. On the other hand the wording of the Article demonstrates that this ban is not attached to any delimitation of outer space. (37) It concerns also the so called FOB weapons which are, though partially, placed in orbit.

The meaning of "weapons of mass destruction" is disputed in space law literature.

Biological and chemical weapons are usually considered as such means. Professor *S. Gorove* referred to the relativeness of "mass" as an element of this notion. (38) I am inclined to think that the decisive feature may be derived from general international law (*jus in bello*). Weapon of mass destruction is any technical device. the effects of which make any differentiation between combatants and non-combatants impossible.

Other types of weapons not comprised by Article IV.1 are outside the ban. Orbital objects carrying conventional bombs would be – as compared to ICBM-s – a very costly, disadvantageous weapon. Placing in orbit of revolutionary new weapons: charged particle beam weapons (PBW), directed energy weapon (DEW) or high energy laser (HEL) is not prohibited by the Space Treaty. Beyond the ban of Article IV.1 of the Treaty general international law prohibits neither the placing in orbit such systems. (39) nor equipments increasing the capability of ballistic missiles to hit targets. This is a far more effective space armament than weapons in orbit around the Earth.

VII

"International law including the Charter of the United Nations" raises the question of **self-defense** under the special conditions of "space warfare" Article 51 of the Charter acknowledges this right in case of an armed attack until the Security Council has taken the measures to maintain international peace and security. The possibility of defense in the modern "strategy of seconds" depends on speed. The responsible military commands certainly would have no time to legal considerations faced with an imminent identified attack from space.

In the early literature of space law *J. C. Cooper* stated that neither Article 2 nor 51 of the Charter had limited the fundamental right of a state to oppose force against an imminent attack, or danger threatening its existence. (40) *G. P. Zhukov* rejected this view with the argument that Article 51 does not allow preventive action by way of self-defense. He added, however, that this does not deprive a state of the right to take the necessary and corresponding measures for safeguarding its security. (41) The intention of the authors was not to legalize some kind of preventive war. Practically both opinions on the right of self-defense take into account the special need of extraordinary fast reactions in "space warfare". In this sense I agree with them. The right of self-defense does not commence when e.g. a nuclear weapon hits its target i.e. the armed attack has already taken place. The interception of the attacking object or any other measure for preventing the attack in case of emergency even beyond the state territory would be an act of self-defense.

VIII

The formula: belligerent states A and B, neutral state C is for a number of armed conflicts nowadays hardly applicable. In the light of recent developments the classic notion of **neutrality** raises questions worthy to be considered. The rules of general international law, however, are legally binding for space activities of states being out of the armed conflict. The obligation of the neutral state is a customary law rule to stand out of the war and maintain impartiality toward both parties to the conflict. (42) From this general obligation follows the duty of a neutral nation to abstain from helping or assisting one belligerent to the detriment of another belligerent. (43) The neutral state must give no assistance direct or indirect to either belligerent side. (44)

The Hague Convention V of 1907 sets out the obligations of a neutral state in land warfare corresponding to above principles of international customary law. Concerning transmission of informations the Convention provides among others that the belligerents may not erect wireless stations in neutral territory for the purpose of communicating with their armed forces. They may also not use such installations which prior to the war they have established there for purely military purposes. (45) The U.S. Communications Act (1934) in order to preserve the neutrality of the U.S.

authorized the President to suspend rules and regulations applicable to any or all stations and may cause the closing of any station which is suitable as a navigational aid beyond five miles. (46)

Similar norms corresponding to the technical conditions of "good old times" could be hardly applicable to space neutrality of the age of space communications and remote sensing. Informations from dual capability systems (geodetic, navigation, weather satellites) are utilizable for both sides. On the other hand handing over primary or processed data of tactical importance obtained by reconnaissance satellites of a neutral state to one of the belligerents would be a nonfulfillment of an obligation expressed in the U.N. Res. 41/65 on remote sensing. We quote here Principle IV: this activity shall be conducted with due regard to the rights and interests of other states *not being detrimental to the legitimate rights and interests of the sensed State.*

Subjects of international law of neutrality are states not private entities. A reasonable question is, how could be qualified the sale of data of tactical importance by a nongovernmental, commercial organization to one of the belligerents, State responsibility for the non-state violation of law follows from Article VI of the Space Treaty demanding authorization and continuing supervision by the appropriate state. This concerns remote sensing activity processing and dissemination of data included.

+++

„Ensuring that outer space is devoted exclusively to peaceful purposes has remained a most important goal, but until now that goal has been achievable only to a limited degree. It has not been politically possible to bar arms from the new dimension. It is now, with the cessation of the cold war and with new relations developing between all powers, that *it may be possible to give full effect to the principle of the use of outer space for exclusively peaceful purposes."* The words of *M. Lachs* voiced a vain hope ten years ago. (47) In positive treaty space law the principle of exclusively peaceful purposes has been restricted to the legal status of celestial bodies. Military space activities otherwise are mainly ruled by general international law facing serious new challenges of this last decade.

Footnotes

1.) ILA Report 1960, p. 268. *O. Schachter* a long time before the space exploration was realized believed that potential danger of military satellites would lead to the prohibition of their military use. Legal Aspects of Space Travel. Journal of British Interplanetary Society. 1952, p. 16
2.) *J. M. Filho*: Total Militarization of Space and Space Law: The future of the Article IV of the 67' Outer Space Treaty. IISL Coll. 1967, Proceedings p. 359. (US Armed Forces were supported by 15-20 signals intelligence satellites, 3 weather satellites and up to 16 Navstar Global Positioning Systems)
3.) Soviet experts at the same time pointed out that the Soviet Union has to prepare means and methods for space defense. *V. D. Sokolovsky*: Voyennaya strategiya 2nd ed. Moscow 1963, p. 504
4.) *Almár–Both–Horváth*: Űrtan (Space Science) Budapest 1996, p. 251
5.) *E. Kamenetskaya*: Outer Space and the Term "Militarization". IISL Coll. 1990, Proceedings p. 225
6.) *Bin Cheng*: Studies in International Space Law. Oxford 1997, p. 246
7.) *G. Gál*: Space Law. Budapest–Leyden–Dobbs Ferry 1969, p. 171
8.) "Peaceful, in a sense, is more peaceful than peace itself" *A. Bueckling*: Friedliche Benutzung des Weltraums. Zeitschrift für Luft- und Weltraumrecht 1966, p. 241
9.) *G. C. M. Reijnen*: The Term "Peaceful" in Outer Space. IISL Coll. 1982, Proceedings p. 146
10.) *A. Meyer*: Legal Problems of Outer Space. Journal of Air Law and Commerce 1961/62, p. 253
11.) *E. Fasan*: Weltraumrecht. Mainz 1965, p. 78
12.) *A. Bueckling*: Der Weltraumvertrag. Köln etc. 1980, p. 39
13.) *M. Seara Vázquez*: Cosmic International Law. Detroit 1965, p. 151
14.) *D. Goedhuis*: General Questions on the Legal Regime of Space. ILA Report 1962, p. 83
15.) *M. G. Markov*: La notion de l'utilisation pacifique en droit international cosmique. Revue Générale de l'air 1966, Extrait p. 4
16.) *M. M. Mateesco–Matte*: Outer Space Treaty. In: Encyclopedia of Public International Law – 11. Amsterdam etc. 1989, p. 252
17.) *G. Y. Zhukov – Y. Kolossov*: International Space Law. New York etc., p. 57
18.) *E. Kamenetskaya*: op. cit. Note 5, p. 225. Similarly *G. Reintanz*: Weltraumrecht. Berlin 1978, pp. 80–81. *G. Gál*: Activities on Orbit and on Celestial Bodies. Two notions of peaceful Uses? IISL Coll. 1982, Proceedings p. 86
19.) *Bin Cheng*: op. cit. Note 6, p. 247
20.) *R. L. Lee*: Military Use of Commercial Remote Sensing Data. IISL Coll. 2001, Proceedings p. 246
21.) *S. R. Chowdhury*: The Permissibility or Non-Permissibility of Military Uses of Outer Space. IISL Coll. 1988, Proceedings p. 13
22.) Op. cit. Note 4, p. 255
23.) *I. Münch*: Grundfragen des Weltraumrechts. Archiv des Völkerrechts 1959, vol. 8. p. 171 ("friedenserhaltende Funktion")
24.) *D. Goedhuis* op. cit. Note 14, p. 81
25.) *G. W. Jenks*: Space Law. London 1965, p. 305
26.) *L. C. Meeker*: Observation in Space. Proceedings of the first McGill Conference on the Law of Outer Space. Montreal 1964, p. 82
27.) E.g. 1972 ABM Treaty Art. II, 1972 SALT–I Art. V, 1979 SALT–II Art. XV, 1987 INF Treaty Art. XII. See: *J. Ondřej*: IISL Coll. 1990, Proceedings p. 338-339. *P. Jankowitsch*: Legal Aspects of Military Space Activities. In: Space Law ed. by N. Jasentuliyana. Westport etc. 1992, p. 151-152

28.) *L. Kuskevelis*: The Customary Legality of Military Space Observation and Proposals towards ITS Codification. IISL Coll. 1990, Proceedings p. 310. U.N. Secretary General's Report in International Satellite Monitory Agency. – A/AC.206/14. ("there are no provisions in general international law including space law that would entail a prohibition to carry out monitoring activities by satellites").

29.) *R. L. Lee*: op. cit. Note 20, p. 250

30.) Quoted by *S. M. Beresford*: Surveillance Aircraft and Satellite. Journal of Air Law and Commerce 1961, p. 109

31.) Art. 26–28.

32.) Art. 9.

33.) E.g. *M. N. Golovine*: Conflict in Space. A Pattern of War in a New Dimension. London 1962, p. 119. ("An eventual full-scale orbital war might be the only human solution of the apparently insoluble East-West ideological and political opposition.")

34.) *I. H. Ph. Diederiks – Verschoor*: An introduction to Space Law. Deventer–Boston 1993, p. 128

35.) *P. Jankowitsch*: op. cit. Note 27, p. 154

36.) *Y. Kolossov*: Notions of "Peaceful" and "Military" Space Activities. IISL Coll. 1982, Proceedings p. 118

37.) Military space activity is an *orbital activity*. The spatial approach – recently formulated by *F. G. von der Donk* in an outstanding monography: "space activities stricto sensu should in principle be equated to activities at least partly taking place *in outer space*" – would be hardly applicable to the ban of Article IV. See: Private Enterprise and Public Interest in the European 'Spacecope'. Leiden 1998, p. 13

38.) *S. Gorove*: Article IV of the 1967 October Space Treaty and Some Alternatives for Further Arms Control. In: Maintaining Outer Space for Peaceful Purposes. Proceedings of a Symposium Held in The Hague, March 1984, p. 81

39.) *P. Jankowitsch* rightly states: The exclusion of such systems from the scope of the prohibitions was clearly intentional. It has become of practical military importance. Op. cit. Note 27, p. 147

40.) *J. C. Cooper*: Self-Defense in Outer Space and the United Nations. Zeitschrift für Luft- und Weltraumrecht 1962, p. 198. *O. Schachter*'s reasonable comment: "In almost every case where a state has used force since 1945 it has claimed that it did so on legitimate self-defence." International Law in Theory and Practice. Dordrecht etc. 1991, p. 401

41.) *G. P. Zhukov*: Weltraumrecht. Berlin 1968, p. 36

42.) *P. Guggenheim*: Lehrbuch des Völkerrechts. Basel 1951, p. 997

43.) *R. C. Hingorani*: Modern International Law. Dobbs Ferry–New York 1978, p. 372

44.) *J. G. Starke*: An Introduction to International Law – VIII. ed. London 1977, p.128

45.) *G. Schwarzenberger*: A Manual of International Law. V. ed. London 1967, p. 222

46.) 47 USC Chapter 5. Wire or Radio Communication. Section 606. War Powers of the President.

47.) *M. Lachs*: Foreword to Space Law, ed. by N. Jasentuliyana, Westport etc. 1992, p. X.

IAC-02-IISL.3.08

ELENDILMIR: SATELLITES – THREATS OR THE THREATENED?

Gérardine Meishan Goh, LL.B. (Hons.)*
LL.M. Student, University of London
Singapore
vysionary@hotmail.com

ABSTRACT

Military satellite technology has rapidly evolved beyond the existing framework of international space law. A blitz of anti-satellite weapons has sprung up in response to the myriad military applications of satellites. The various space law documents did not envision the volatile détente between the military applications of, and threats to, artificial satellites.

In this context, this article discusses the inadequacy of the existing legal framework relating to satellites. It deals with the blurring of the distinction between civilian and military satellite technology. It also discusses the impact of commercialisation. Suggestions are made on how to update and build upon the existing legal regime relating to satellites in the military context.

CONTEXT

27 January 1967 saw the birth of new horizons of peace and achievement. The Outer Space Treaty[1] heralded a fresh era of international co-operation and affirmed the peaceful use of outer space.[2] The foundation and heart of space law is the law of peace.[3]

This evolution was diametrically opposite to the evolution of space technology. The phoenix of space technology rose from the ashes of wartime missile technology.[4] The earliest military satellite programme focused on reconnaissance. In 1959, the Corona series was launched amid great secrecy.[5] Beyond reconnaissance, early satellites also carried missile warning systems[6], military communications equipment,[7] and military navigation systems[8]. It is ironic that the law of peace should govern the sciences of war.

This historical paradox must be seen in the prevailing climate of global instability and political tension after the tragic events of 11 September 2001 in the United States. The horrific attacks made the international community realise that peace cannot be taken for granted. Against this backdrop of the war against terrorism and the global struggle for peace, a legal framework is desperately needed to maintain outer space for exclusively peaceful uses. In particular, this paper argues for a legal framework to regulate and protect satellites from being threatened, and from being threats themselves.

---

* LL.B. (Hons.) (NUS), LL.M. Student at the University of London. The views expressed and any errors contained herein are entirely mine. Email: <vysionary@hotmail.com>

This paper moots that the existing framework of international space law is inadequate to regulate and protect satellites from increasing military activity in space. It argues that the international laws of war are applicable equally to the space arena, in accordance with the Outer Space Treaty. It then focuses on the principles of discrimination and proportionality in the international law of war. This paper will propose that, absent a utopia of complete peace in space, a legal framework should be set up to protect and regulate military activities against and pertaining to satellites. To set a background for the proposal, it will first review the significance of satellite applications in space activities as well as the existing framework of international space law.

WHY THE FOCUS ON SATELLITES

Significance of Satellites

It is important to establish a legal régime for military threats to and by satellites. There are several reasons for this. Firstly, satellites have emerged as the foremost use of space-based technology. Myriad applications have sprung out of satellite systems. Remote sensing, direct broadcasting, navigation and telecommunications satellites pepper the Earth's orbits. It is thus important to have a proper legal framework that protects and regulates these systems.

Secondly, satellite applications affect the lives of many people around the world. Remote sensing satellites provide disaster-monitoring constellations that help in natural disaster management. Navigation satellites such as the Global Positioning System (GPS) and Galileo are used by millions everyday. A total breakdown in satellite telecommunications would bring the entire world to a standstill. Threats against satellites can potentially impact the world in many ways.

Thirdly, the use of space technology in warfare has already occurred. Satellites have provided the U.S. military with data and imagery since the Vietnam War. Satellite communications were used in the 1983 Grenada invasion and in Operation Eldorado Canyon in Libya in 1986. In 1988, the Global Position System (GPS) provided navigational support for mine sweeping operations in the Persian Gulf. Operation Desert Storm in 1991 involved the full might of military space systems. Some sixty military and civilian satellites provided support, data, communications and imagery to the Allied war effort against Iraq.[9] This shows a growing reliance on space-based technology. The space environment will eventually become a distinct area of military operations.[10]

With so much at stake, it is clear that the existing legal framework relating to threats to and by satellites is grossly inadequate. A new legal régime is needed. This new framework must account for threats caused by satellites. It should however acknowledge that not all military usage of satellites constitutes a threat. It must also consider the threats to satellites and protect against those threats.

Threats Caused by Satellites

Not all military usage of satellites is bad. Satellites are used to keep the peace via disarmament verification and missile attack detection systems. Military satellite systems such as the GPS also serve many useful civilian purposes. However, some military usage of satellites may cause concern. These include[11]:

(1) Anti-Satellite (ASAT) Satellites: Satellites placed in orbit for the purposes of military manoeuvres against other satellites.
(2) Espionage & Reconnaissance: Satellites that passively collect data (through photography or radio and electronic emission monitoring) and computer-"hacking" satellites.
(3) Missile Tracking / Disabling
(4) Direct Broadcasting for Propaganda

Due to these threats, perceived or real, caused by satellites, information operations can have a devastating effect on a State's infrastructure.

Threats to Satellites

In response to the threats caused by satellites, many countermeasures have been initiated against satellites. These include:

(1) ASAT Weapons: Weapons that blind or destroy the satellite's capabilities. These include electromagnetic, radiation, kinetic energy, hypervelocity, particle beam, explosive proximity and "soft-kill" weapons.
(2) ASAT Satellites: Satellites that act as ASAT weapons.
(3) Software-based / Information based Weaponry: These weapons aim to shutdown satellite operations via access to the satellite's control programming.

Problems with the Development of a Legal Framework for Satellites

The development of a legal framework for satellite raises several difficult issues. These include:

(1) Dual-Use Technology: Many satellites employ dual-use technology for both civilian and military purposes.[12] Military reconnaissance satellites can be used for remote sensing.[13] Weather and telecommunications satellites may be used simultaneously to support both military and civilian purposes.[14] This raises the issue as to whether such satellites can be considered military threats and lawfully targeted.[15] This question is compounded in light of the commercialisation of civilian satellite systems that can be used for military purposes.[16]

(2) ASAT Satellites: Satellites occupy a unique position. They can easily become the very perpetrators of the offences the law intends to protect them from. Any legal framework that aims to protect satellites must also recognise and deal with this issue.

(3) Pace of Technology Advancement: Satellite application technology is among the fastest growing field of science. A legal framework for satellites must ensure that it is not inward looking and narrow. This prevents it from becoming obsolete in the face of new technology.

(4) Information Warfare: A legal framework for satellites must take into account the fact that military threats to and by satellites cover the entire spectrum from hardware-based to software-based threats.

(5) Legal Vacuum: There is no existing legal framework that specifically deals with the military threats to and by satellites. There are only two United Nations (UN) General Assembly resolutions that deal specifically with satellite use: remote sensing[17] and direct broadcasting[18]. However, these two resolutions are not binding, and also do not specifically deal with military satellite activities.

EXISTING LEGAL REGIME FOR THREATS BY AND AGAINST SATELLITES

Existing Space Law Framework

There is no United Nations (UN) treaty or declaration that specifically addresses military satellite applications in space. However, there are several provisions in the existing framework of space treaty law that apply.

The Outer Space Treaty

Article IV of the OST directly addresses the militarisation of outer space:

> States Parties to the Treaty undertake not to place in orbit around the earth any objects carrying *nuclear weapons or any other kinds of weapons of mass destruction*, install such weapons on celestial bodies, or station such weapons in outer space in any other manner.
>
> The moon and other celestial bodies shall be used by all States Parties to the Treaty *exclusively* for *peaceful purposes*.
>
> The establishment of military bases, installations and fortifications, the testing of *any type of weapons* and the conduct of military manoeuvres on celestial bodies shall be *forbidden*.
>
> The use of military personnel for scientific research or for any other peaceful purposes shall not be prohibited. The use of any equipment or facility necessary for peaceful exploration of the moon and other celestial bodies shall also not be prohibited.[19]

Much has been written about what constitutes "peaceful purposes", one of restrictions on State uses of outer space. The former Soviet Union and some other States have maintained the view that "peaceful" means "non-military". However, the rest of the international community has disagreed. Thus, the present view seems to be that "peaceful" means "non-aggressive". Space activity that is in the beneficial interest of all countries is considered "peaceful".[20]

Article IV(2) restricts the use of the moon and other "celestial bodies" to peaceful purposes. The issue here is whether the "peaceful purposes" restriction applies in outer space away from celestial bodies. Christol points out that several States within COPUOS objected to the omission of "outer space" from Article IV(2). This is particularly given the inference that this would allow outer space to be used for non-peaceful purposes. However, the American and Soviet view that "peaceful purposes" apply only to the moon and celestial bodies won out.[21] Thus, "peaceful purposes" does not apply to activities conducted away from celestial bodies.[22] Nonetheless, Article 2(4) of the UN Charter, applicable to space law via Article III of the OST prohibit "non-peaceful" uses of space where this means the aggressive use of force.[23] This points to a limited demilitarisation of outer space and a total demilitarisation of celestial bodies.[24]

Article IV also relates to the legality of ASAT satellites. ASATs deviate from the non-aggressive quality of other satellites. They seem to breach the non-aggressive mandate that is required of all space activities under the "peaceful purposes" restriction.[25] However, the OST does not prohibit conventional weaponry in space, including ASATs. The specific prohibition on weapons of mass destruction and nuclear weapons suggests a differentiation between those weapons and conventional weapons.[26]

Article VI of the OST establishes that States bear "international responsibility for national activities in outer space . . . whether such activities are carried on by governmental agencies or by non-governmental entities."[27] This extends State responsibility, making the State responsible for the space activities of its private citizens or organisations.

Article IX of the OST also provides:

> If a State party to the Treaty has reason to believe that an activity or experiment planned by it or its nationals in outer space, including the moon and other celestial bodies, would cause potentially harmful interference with activities of other States Parties in the peaceful exploration and use of outer space, including the moon and other celestial bodies, it shall undertake appropriate *international consultations before proceeding* with any such activity or experiment.[28] (emphasis added)

Article IX does not differentiate between military and civilian space activities. Thus, it applies to military space operations.[29] If a hostile act could harmfully interfere with a third party State's assets, Article IX requires that the State be consulted. Further, Article IX specifies a timeframe: consultations must occur "before proceeding with any such activity or experiment." Such consultations could notify the belligerent State of the expected offensive. Thus Article IX could create a disincentive to an act of armed conflict. Equally, this could be a disincentive for States to abide by Article IX, so to preserve the element of surprise. Nonetheless, Article IX acts as an obstacle to such hostile acts once "consultations" have occurred, even if the third-party State objects.

The Liability Convention[30]

The Liability Convention unveils a tacit admittance that intentional destruction of space objects might occur under certain circumstances. Article II of the Liability Convention subjects States Parties to absolute liability for damage caused by its space objects on the earth's surface, or to aircraft in flight.[31] Article III imposes fault liability on States for damage by its space object to the space object of another State "caused elsewhere than on the surface of the earth."[32] However, Article VI provides exemption from absolute liability in cases where either the claimant State, or the natural or juridical persons it represents, caused the damage wholly or partially by gross negligence, or an act or omission done with *intent to cause damage*.[33] The exemption for intentional damage caused by a claimant State presumes the possibility that such intentional damage will happen. Despite the prescription of the OST for the "peaceful" use and exploration of space, the Liability Convention clearly recognises the possibility that States intentionally harm space objects. This does not mean that the Convention endorses such actions.[34] However, it suggests that the international community expected that a claimant State might take action for the intentional damage of a space object.

The Registration Convention[35]

Article IV of the Registration Convention specifies that launching States must provide the following information: (a) name of launching State or States; (b) an appropriate designator of the space object or its registration number; (c) date and territory or location of launch; (d) basic orbital parameters (e) general function of the space object. The Convention allows registration to be amply vague. This allows a State to hide the true nature of a military mission. Two provisions of Article IV allow for this: firstly, that the information be provided "as soon as practicable". This allows launching States leeway to delay the registration of the object following the launch.[36] Secondly, it requires the disclosure only of the space object's "general function". This allows States to protect the identity of their military space objects.

The Moon Agreement

The Moon Agreement prohibits the placement of weapons of mass destruction, including nuclear weapons, on the moon itself, in orbit around the moon, or on trajectories to and around the moon, and on other celestial bodies.[37] However, the Agreement's provisions limit its restriction only to weapons of mass destruction. The Agreement's language reflects Article IV of the OST. It requires that the use of the moon be "exclusively for peaceful purposes", and prohibits "any threat or use of force or any other hostile act or threat of hostile act on the moon".[38]

Other Applicable International Treaties

Treaty Banning Nuclear Weapons in the Atmosphere, In Outer Space and Under Water (Limited Test Ban Treaty)[39]

The Limited Test Ban Treaty was adopted before any of the space treaties. It provided the first treaty provision governing the use of outer space. The Treaty forbids

> nuclear weapon test explosion[s], or any other nuclear explosion[s]...(a) in the atmosphere; beyond its limits, *including outer space*; or under water, including territorial waters or high seas; or (b) in any other environment if such explosion causes radioactive debris to be present outside the territorial limits of the State under whose jurisdiction or control such explosion is conducted.[40]

It however does not prohibit non-nuclear weapons such as conventional, biological, chemical, or high energy laser weapons. The Treaty prohibits nuclear explosions for both testing and non-testing purposes. Thus, the Treaty prohibits an electromagnetic pulse in space via a nuclear detonation, particularly as an ASAT weapon.[41]

Anti-Ballistic Missile (ABM) Treaty

The ABM Treaty limits the deployment, testing, and use of missile systems designed to intercept incoming strategic ballistic missiles.[42] Article V(1) provides that "each party undertakes not to develop, test, or deploy ABM systems or components which are sea-based, air-based, *space-based*, or mobile land-based."[43]

Article XII is significant to the long-term military use of space. Article XII(1) codifies the "open skies" principle and formally sanctions the legality of space-based military surveillance as an "essential component of the international arms-control regime."[44]

Need to Expand Upon Existing Principles

Satellites as Space Weapons

Despite the rapid militarisation of space, the term "space weapon" is undefined in international law. One proposed definition of "space weapon" is:

> A space weapon is a device stationed in outer space (including the moon and other celestial bodies) or in the earth environment *designed to destroy, damage, or otherwise interfere with* the normal functioning of an object or being in outer space, or a device stationed in outer space designed to destroy, damage, or otherwise interfere with the normal functioning of an object or being in the earth environment. Any other device with the *inherent capability* to be used as defined above will be considered as a space weapon.[45] (emphasis added)

The second sentence especially acknowledges that space objects not designed as weapons may become weapons if they can "be used" as such. This leaves the definition broad enough to include any object at all. Orbiting objects travel at speeds approximating 17,000 miles per hour. This gives them the "inherent capability" to destroy or interfere with an "object or being in space" or in the "earth environment".[46]

An interesting question arises with respect to the question of dual-use satellite technology. Would a satellite with both civilian and military capabilities be considered a "space weapon"? The situation is complicated if the satellite were owned by civilian entities, or were used by both friendly and belligerent States. Under the law of war, an otherwise inviolable object or person may become a legitimate target for attack if used for military purposes. Similarly, an otherwise inviolable object owned by a neutral becomes legitimately subject to attack if used by a co-owner for belligerent purposes. This would apply to the space assets co-owned by intergovernmental and commercial organisations.

Inadequacy of the Existing Framework of International Space Law

The existing framework of international space law is inadequate to deal with the military use of satellite systems. A complete enunciation of the legal standards applicable to space warfare is needed beyond the existing framework of space law. These standards should state the *jus ad bellum* restrictions on the use of force in space. Matte has observed that space law, including the Limited Test Ban Treaty and the ABM Treaty, seems to "permit, indeed to endorse, the arms race, including the militarisation of space."[47]

There is insufficient specific mention to the laws relating to space warfare, and to the military applications and threats to satellites. Absent such legal standards, the permissive character of international law allows threats to and by satellites with no mechanism for international State responsibility.

Threats to and by satellites are related to the law regulating the use of force. Under the OST a State Party "on whose registry an object launched into outer space is carried shall retain jurisdiction and control over such object."[48] *Prima facie*, this means that a State will retain jurisdiction and control over a satellite registered by itself. A complicated situation arises if that State uses the satellite intentionally and wrongfully to disable another State's satellite. Assuming that doing so amounts to an "armed attack" under the UN Charter, the latter State may disable the former's satellite in self-defence.[49] The law of war allows belligerents to destroy their adversary's weaponry. This means that the latter State can lawfully capture or destroy the former State's satellite, Article VIII of the OST notwithstanding. Hence, the only way that a State can assuredly protect its space assets is to ensure compliance with international law, including space law and the *jus ad bellum*.[50]

It can thus clearly be seen that the law applicable to military threats to and by satellites is governed by a mishmash of international law principles. It is submitted that the existing framework of international space law should be developed to provide a more specifically applicable legal framework for satellite systems.

APPLYING THE LAW OF WAR TO OUTER SPACE

Justification for Applying the Law of War to Outer Space

Two arguments sustain the conclusion that the existing law of war does apply to space warfare: Article III of the OST and the UN Charter, and Martens' clause.

The OST & The UN Charter

Article III of the OST clearly provides that international law applies to space warfare:

> States Parties to the Treaty shall carry on activities in the exploration and use of outer space, including the moon and other celestial bodies, in accordance with *international law*, including the *Charter of the United Nations*, in the interest of maintaining *international peace and security* and promoting international co-operation and understanding.[51] (emphasis added)

Article III applies the restrictions of all international law to outer space activities. This includes the *jus ad bellum*, due to the specific reference to the UN Charter. This provides the strongest evidence that the law of war has been incorporated into military space operations by virtue of the OST.

The UN Charter clearly prohibits the "threat or use of force against the territorial integrity or political independence of any state, or in any other manner inconsistent with the Purposes of the United Nations".[52] However, the actual scope of this prohibition remains unclear. The popular view is it absolutely prohibits the use of force. The sole exceptions are self-defence and authorisation by the Security Council. The alternative argument is supported by the NATO air strikes in Kosovo. It argues that the prohibition relates only to the use of force for purposes inconsistent with the Charter.[53] A State's interpretation of this prohibition on the use of force will have great influence on its use of force in space.

The requirement that a State's use of outer space be "in the interest of maintaining international peace and security" echoes the same wording in the UN Charter.[54] This assumes that military force is lawfully permissible to ensure international order.

Under Article 2(4) of the UN Charter, States may neither use force in international relations, nor threaten it. The Charter's significant focus on force rather than war reflects a considered effort to outlaw all types of armed conflict. Included in the prohibition are cases of both direct military force and indirect military force.

Martens' Clause

The second justification of the application of the laws of war to military space operations relates to the "Martens' Clause". This clause appears in several law of war documents, including the 1907 Hague Convention:

> Until a more complete code of the laws of war has been issued, the high contracting parties deem it expedient to declare that, in cases not included in the Regulations adopted by them, the inhabitants and the belligerents remain under the protection and the rule of the *principles of the law of nations*, as they result from the usages established among *civilised peoples*, from the *laws of humanity*, and the dictates of the *public conscience*.[55] (emphasis added)

The clause reminds States Parties that Treaty prohibitions do not supersede general prohibitions operating by way of principles of the law of nations. The clause covers customary international law and also all rules and principles of the general law of nations.[56]

The continuing applicability of the Martens' Clause is especially significant for space warfare. This is because it is the most technologically innovative form of warfare. The doctrine impliedly envisions the need to regulate means of warfare developed through technological advances. Thus, it is extremely important in the legal framework of space warfare.[57]

The Applicable Law of War

Through history, warring States have developed customary practices seeking to lessen the devastating effects of war. This was summarised by Article 22 of the Second Convention adopted by the 1899 Hague Peace Conference: "The right of belligerents to adopt means of injuring the enemy is not unlimited."[58] The principles distilled from the large corpus of customary international law amount to very few: military necessity, discrimination, proportionality, and humanity.[59] These principles are recognised in subsequent treaty law. They limit the means available for conducting armed conflicts. Of these, two principles in particular concern the scope of this article: Discrimination and Proportionality.

Discrimination

Discrimination requires diligence in the selection of methods, weaponry and targets. This embodies several concepts. The most significant is the distinction between combatants and non-combatants. The law of war prohibits attack of any person deemed a "non-combatant". This means that the lawfulness of the use of force under international law presumes attack only of those qualifying as combatants. The requirement to differentiate rests on the more fundamental principle of military objective.[60] This requires that armed attacks be limited to targets that are military in nature. The destruction of these targets must be to advance the attacker's tactical, operational, or strategic position. Such targets would certainly include inanimate objects.

Thus, Article 48 of the 1977 Protocol I to the 1949 Geneva Conventions states:

> In order to ensure respect for and protection of the civilian population and civilian objects, the Parties to the conflict shall at all times *distinguish* between the civilian population and combatants and *between civilian objects and military objectives* and accordingly shall direct their operations *only against military objectives*.[61] (emphasis added)

Subsequently, Protocol I defines "military objective" relating to objects as being

> limited to those objects which by their nature, location, purpose or use make an *effective contribution* to military action and whose total or partial destruction, capture or neutralisation, in the circumstances ruling at the time, offers a *definite military advantage*.[62] (emphasis added)

Proportionality

The rule of proportionality requires that the use of military force be proportional to the legitimate military objective. This requires a balancing of anticipated military advantage against anticipated damage caused. It prohibits collateral damage to civilians and property that is disproportionate to the military value of the objective.[63] Proportionality applies to a response to a grievance, in relation to the adversary's military actions and to the anticipated military value or the State's own actions, including reprisals.[64]

Articles 48 to 58 of Protocol I to the Geneva Conventions regulate military activity. Those articles define, *inter alia*, the rule of distinction, "attack", "civilians", the rule protecting civilian objects, the rule establishing necessary precautions to be taken in the event of attack and the rule establishing precautions to be taken against the effects of attack.[65]

The general rule allows destruction of targets if it is proportionate to the military objective sought by the destruction. For example, infrastructure targets were lawfully destroyed during the 1991 Persian Gulf War that provided electricity both to the civilian populations and to the Iraqi military.[66] The same rationale applies to dual-use satellites. To the extent a satellite is used for the support of a military purpose, it becomes a military objective and is lawfully subject to attack. This however assumes that the space asset is actually used for such military purpose. It is insufficient that it merely has the potential to be so used.

PROPOSAL: THE DISCRIMINATION / PROPORTIONALITY PRINCIPLE

In a perfect world, space would be used for exclusively peaceful purposes. In the world we live in today, space is already a battlefield. It is crucial for international law to recognise and deal with the military threats to and by space activities, especially in the context of satellite applications.

It is with this necessary pragmatism in mind that this paper proposes the following treaty régime for the regulation and protection of satellite activity in space. This paper does not in any way condone the use of space for non-peaceful uses. The proposed régime is based upon the basic premise that outer space is to be used for exclusively peaceful purposes.

However, in limited exceptional circumstances, States may be forced to threaten the disabling of or actually disable satellites. These exceptions should be limited to the following:

(1) Times of declared war
(2) Self-defence as defined under Article 51 and Chapter VII of the UN Charter, and
(3) Necessity.

Additionally, these exceptions should apply only after all reasonable international consultation and diplomatic efforts have been employed, and have failed.

Before the exceptions can be exercised however, the State intending to disable a satellite should take all reasonable precautions to investigate if such actions would potentially be harmful to a third party State's space assets. If such action can possibly cause harmful interference with the third party State's assets, international consultation in accordance with Article IX of the OST must be initiated. The third party State's concerns and views must be taken into account before any action by the State is taken. The State intending to disable the satellite must state its rationale for doing so, and provide the third party State with any and all reasonable assistance to minimise the damage that could potentially arise as a result of its actions.

Military action against the satellite should take place only upon the strict fulfilment of a two-fold test:

(1) Discrimination
This part consists of three stages:
(a) There must be no other alternative action reasonably feasible but the attack on the satellite.
(b) The disabling of the satellite must be of urgent necessity.
(c) The attack on the satellite in question must be for the

furtherance of the military objective of the State.

Military action should only be *prima facie* legally permissible if these three conditions are strictly met. However, the military action against the satellite will only be considered legal under international law if the second part of the test is fulfilled:

(2) Proportionality

(a) The attack on the satellite must only disable it to the minimum amount required to achieve the military objective of the State.

(b) The satellite must be restored to its normal functioning capabilities once the need for its disability is no longer necessary and urgent.

The State intending to take such action against the satellite must provide compensation and assistance to any third party State whose space assets were harmfully interfered with during the operations. It must also provide compensation and assistance to any party who was adversely affected by the disabling of the adversary State's satellite. Further, it must ensure that the disabled satellite is restored to normal functioning capability.

The important thing to note is that the adversary State's satellite cannot be permanently disabled or destroyed. This is because the State intending to disable the satellite must be internationally responsible for returning the satellite to its original functioning capacity once the need for its disabling is no longer necessary and urgent.

Diagram A illustrates the two-fold test in pictorial form.

Diagram A. Two-Fold Test for Military Action Against Satellites

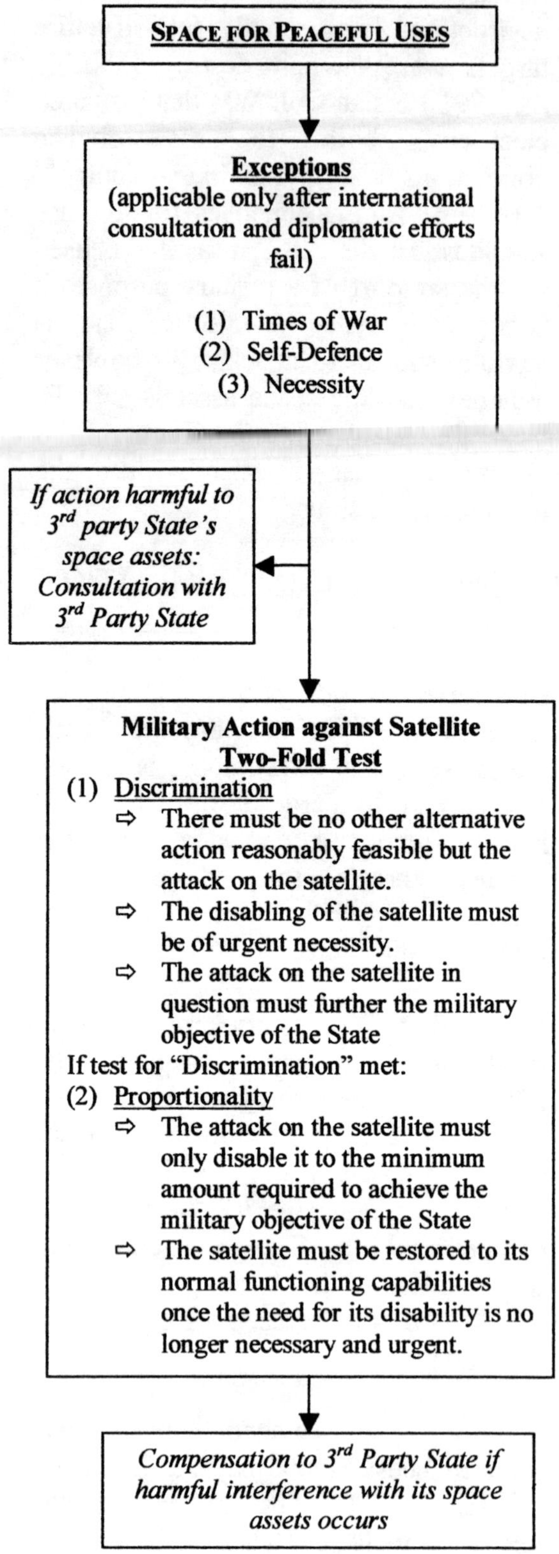

A legal framework that protects and regulates satellites is urgently needed. Attacks by and against satellites can potentially cause an unprecedented degree of harm. Although general principles of international law already exist to regulate the use of force, the need for a specific framework for satellites cannot be overstated.

It is also important to note that the legal framework for space disarmament need not be all-encompassing at once. Small steps are likely to be more palatable to States and the international community. This ensures that a legal framework set up will be more likely to be acceptable to States. This prevents the complete lack of support from space-faring nations that turned the Moon Agreement into little more than a dead-letter.[67]

However, this framework relates to an important area of space activity – satellite applications. This initiative could be the first in a series of declarations or treaties that elaborate upon the exclusively peaceful uses of outer space. It relates to an extremely important area of space activities, both in the sense of military security as well as economic well being. Hence the protection and regulation of satellites is a first step in the correct direction for space law.

More importantly, this area of space law is extremely time-sensitive. It is submitted that this is the best time to push forward an international legal régime for the protection and regulation of military satellite activity. Given the uneasy political climate and the rapidly evolving technology of today, there is more political urgency and practical need for such a régime. This may provide a strong impetus for States to accept such a framework via a declaration in the UN General Assembly. This would provide the groundwork necessary to consolidate the framework into a treaty-based régime. This would then provide the foundation for further initiatives to protect the peaceful nature of outer space.

CONCLUSION

The appalling events of 11th September 2001 in the United States is a grim reminder that we live in a deeply divided world. As a law of peace, space law represents the idealistic ambition for a peaceful world. The ascendant security standard of the space-faring nations is to maintain the "violent peace" on earth and in space. The next two decades will be a time of critical challenge and change for international space law in creating an enduring, peaceful world order.

Seen from the Earth, satellites sparkle on the velvet dark of the night sky like stars. For the star-lovers on earth, satellites should always remain what they were when they were first dreamt up – starlight in the sky that shines our way to greater achievement and peace.

"A light when all other lights go out!
Aiya Eärendil Elenion Ancalima!"[68]

---

[1] Treaty on the Principles Governing the Activities of States in the Exploration and the Use of Outer Space, Including the Moon and Other Celestial Bodies (1967) 610 U.N.T.S 205 [hereinafter "OST"]

[2] para. 4, Preamble to the OST, *ibid.*

[3] de Cocca, M.M.E., "Peace: The Only Way to Return Lawfulness to Space Activities" (1989) 32 Proc. Coll. L. Outer Sp. 317 at 317, Busâk,

"Les Aspects Juridiques des Satellites D'Application" (1978) 20 Proc. Coll. L. Outer Sp. 186

[4] Ramey, R.A., "Armed Conflict on the Final Frontier: The Law of War in Space" (2000) 48 A.F.L. Rev. 1 at 3, see generally, Keegan, J., *A History of Warfare* (1993) at 5

[5] see generally Peebles, C., *The Corona Project: America's First Spy Satellites* (1997)

[6] Peebles, C., *High Frontier: The U.S. Air Force and the Military Space Program* (1997) at 41, Shukman, D., *Tomorrow's War: The Threat of High-Technology Weapons* (1996)

[7] Kutyna, D.J., "Indispensable: Space Systems in the Persian Gulf War" in Hall, R.C. & Neufeld, J. (eds.), *The U.S. Air Force in Space: 1945 to the Twenty-First Century* (1995) 103 at 117

[8] *ibid*

[9] Spires, D.N., *Beyond Horizons: A Half Century of Air Force Space Leadership* (1998) at 244 – 245

[10] Gray, C.S., *American Military Space Policy: Information Systems, Weapon Systems and Arms Control* (1982) at 49

[11] Wingfield, T.C., "Legal Aspects of Offensive Information Operations in Space", (1998), online at <http://www.usafa.af.mil/dfl/documents/wingfield.doc> (Last updated: 2 September, 1998)

[12] Mintz, J., "U.S. Suspends Boeing-Ukraine Rocket Launch", (August 8 1998) Wash. Post. At A14

[13] supra note 5 at 266

[14] Christol, C.Q., *The Modern International Law of Outer Space* (1986) at 28

[15] Cleminson, F.R., "Banning the Stationing of Weapons in Space Through Arms Control: A Major Step in the Promotion of Strategic Stability in the 21st Century", in Beier, J.M., and Mataija, S., (eds.), *Arms Control and the Rule of Law* (1998) at 39

[16] Haeck, "Aspects Juridiques de Certaines Utilisations Militaires de L'espace", (1996) 21:1 An. Air & Space L. 65, Morgan, "Military Use of Commercial Satellites" (1994) 60 J. Air Law & Com. 237 at 317

[17] 1986 Principles Relating to Remote Sensing of the Earth from Outer Space, G.A.Res. 41/65, U.N. GAOR. 95th Plenary Meeting, (3 Dec. 1986)

[18] 1982 Principles Governing the Use by States of Artificial Earth Satellites for International Direct Television Broadcasting, G.A. Res.27/92, U.N. GA OR, (10 Dec 1982)

[19] Article IV, OST, *supra* note 1

[20] Christol, *supra* note 14 at 22

[21] *supra* note 9

[22] Christol, C.Q., "Discussion", in Cohen, M. & Gouin, M.E., *Lawyers and the Nuclear Debate* (1988) at 233

[23] Article III, OST, *supra* note 1

[24] see generally Sgrosso, G.C., "Demilitarisation of Outer Space" (1992) 35 Proc. Coll. L. Outer Sp. 325

[25] Jankowitsch, P., "Legal Aspects of Military Space Activities", in Jasentuliyana, N., *Space Law: Development and Scope* (1992) at 143 and 150

[26] Hurwitz, B.M., *The Legality of Space Militarization* (1986) at 111

[27] Article VI, OST, *supra* note 1

[28] Article IX, OST, *supra* note 1

[29] Vlasic, I.A., "Space Law and the Military Applications of Space Technology", in Jasentuliyana, N., (ed.) *Perspectives on International Law* (1995) 386 at 397

[30] Convention on International Liability for Damage Caused by Space Objects, (Mar. 29, 1972) 24 U.S.T. 2389, 961 U.N.T.S. 187 [hereinafter Liability Convention]

[31] Article II, Liability Convention, *supra* note 30

[32] Article III, Liability Convention, *supra* note 30

[33] Article IV, Liability Convention, *supra* note 30

[34] Article VI(2), Liability Convention, *supra* note 30

[35] Convention on the Registration of Objects Launched into Outer Space, (Jan. 14, 1975), 28 U.S.T. 695, 1023 U.N.T.S. 15 [hereinafter Registration Convention].

[36] Article III, Registration Convention, *ibid.*

[37] Article III(3), Agreement on the Activities of States on the Moon and Other Celestial Bodies, (Dec. 5, 1979), U.N.Doc. A/34/664 (1979) [hereinafter Moon Agreement].

[38] Article III(2), Moon Agreement, *ibid.*

[39] Treaty Banning Nuclear Weapon Tests in the Atmosphere, in Outer Space and Underwater, (Aug. 5, 1963), 14 U.S.T. 1313, 480 U.N.T.S. 43 [hereinafter Limited Test Ban Treaty]

[40] Article I(1), Limited Test Ban Treaty, *ibid.*

[41] see generally, Reynolds, G.H. & Merges, R.P., Outer Space: Problems of Law and Policy (1997) (2nd ed.)

[42] Treaty on the Limitation of Anti-Ballistic Missile Systems, (May 26,1972), U.S.-U.S.S.R., 23 U.S.T. 3435 [hereinafter ABM Treaty].

[43] Article V(2), ABM Treaty, *ibid.*

[44] Article XII, ABM Treaty, *ibid.*

[45] Jasani, B., "Introduction", in Jasani, B. (ed.) *Peaceful and Non-Peaceful Uses of Space: Problems of Definition for the Prevention of an Arms Race* (1991) at 13
[46] see *supra* note 4
[47] Matte M.M., "A Treaty for 'Star Peace'" in Matte, M.M., *Arms Control and Disarmament in Outer Space* (1987) at 190
[48] Article 8, UN Charter, *supra* note 52
[49] Article 51, UN Charter, *supra* note 52
[50] *supra* note 4
[51] Article III, OST, *supra* note 1
[52] Article 2(4), Charter of the United Nations, Art. 10, 1. U.N T.S (1945)
[53] Vlasic I.A., Negotiating and Drafting Agreements Relating to Outer Space, in Matte, M.M. (ed.), *Arms Control and Disarmament in Outer Space: Towards a New Order of Survival* (1991) 203 at 211
[54] Article 1(1), UN Charter, *supra* note 52
[55] Convention (IV) Respecting the Laws and Customs of War on Land, (Oct. 18,1907), (1908 Supp.) 2 Am. J. Int'l L. 90 [hereinafter Hague Convention (IV)].
[56] Article 38, Statute of the International Court of Justice, June 26, 1945, 59 Stat. 1031
[57] Article 1(2), Protocol I, Protocol Additional to the Geneva Conventions of Aug. 12, 1949, and Relating to the Protection of Victims of International Armed Conflicts (Protocol I), Dec. 12, 1977, art. 48, 1125 U.N.T.S. 3.
[58] Convention (II) with Respect to the Laws and Customs of War on Land, (July 29, 1899), (1907 Supp.) 1 Am. J. Int'l L. 129.
[59] Ramey R.A., *supra* note 4
[60] Robertson, H.B., "The Principle of the Military Objective in the Law of Armed Conflict" (1997) 8 A.F. Acad. J. Legal Stud 35
[61] Protocol Additional to the Geneva Conventions of Aug. 12, 1949, and Relating to the Protection of Victims of International Armed Conflicts (Protocol I) *supra* note 57
[62] Article 52(2), *ibid.*
[63] Military and Paramilitary Activities (Nicar. v. U.S.), 1986 I.C.J. 4 at 94
[64]Agora, A.S., "The U.S. Decision Not to Ratify Protocol I to the Geneva Conventions on the Protection of War Victims" (1988) 82 Am. J. Int'l L. 784 at 785
[65] Articles 48, 49, 50 57 and 58, Protocol I, *supra* note 57
[66] Department of Defense Report to Congress on the Conduct of the Persian Gulf War: Appendix O on the Role of the Law of War, 31 I.L.M. 612, 623 (1992).
[67] Gorove, S., "Limiting the Use of Arms in Outer Space: Legal and Policy Issues" (1991), in Gorove, S. (ed.) *Developments in Space Law: Issues and Policies* 255
[68] Frodo: in Tolkien, J.R.R., "Shelob's Lair", *The Lord of the Rings: The Two Towers* (Book Four) (1966, reprinted 1995) at 704

COOPERATION V. CONTROL
MILITARY STRATEGY CHALLENGING LAW

Colleen M. Driscoll, Ph.D.
Director
The Kurtz Institute of Peacemaking
Doylestown PA 18901 USA
cmdriscoll@prodigy.net

ABSTRACT

It has been the contention of the United States government that the present legal structure is sufficient to protect outer space. Thus the U.S. has refused to discuss strengthening the present space law system, either by reaffirming the basic principles which establish positive uses of space, updated definitions of such terms as "weapons of mass destruction", or through negotiations on additional treaty law. However, this contention does not hold up when documented military plans for future warfare are studied. In fact, future plans utilize outer space as part of a war making strategy, one that requires both ground-to-space and space-based weapons. The proposed National Missile Defense system is, in fact, only a first step toward the utilization of space for war making as envisioned by military strategists. There are, however, better ways of assuring the national security and global security, one of which is the development of a law-based management system for outer space and improved treaty law.

INTRODUCTION

"From a military point of view, space is the ultimate high ground." – Air Force General Ralph E. Eberhart, Commander-in-Chief, U.S. Space Command (SPACECOM)

The present United States (U.S.) administration has contended that the present legal structure is sufficient to protect outer space. In numerous statements and documents they have said that the Outer Space Treaty of 1967 (OST)* is sufficient to maintain the peaceful, positive uses of outer space. Recent statements by Ambassador Javits, U.S. representative to the Conference on Disarmament (CD) in Geneva have confirmed this contention:

> ....the United States sees no need for new outer space arms control agreements and opposes the negotiation of a treaty on outer space arms control.
>
> We fully understand that maintaining international peace and security is an overarching purpose that guides activities on earth as well as in outer space, but in the final analysis preserving national security is likewise necessary and essential. For these reasons, the United States sees no need for new outer space arms

* Treaty on Principles Governing the Activities of States in the Exploration and Use of Outer Space, Including the Moon and Other Celestial Bodies, Entered into Force October 10, 1976.

control agreements and opposes negotiation of a treaty on outer space arms control.

And concluding, "There simply is no problem in outer space for arms control to solve."†

There are many flaws in this argument. This paper will discuss those flaws and the definition of national security which, while extolling international cooperation does, in fact, undermine it. It will also discuss the international law to which this argument gives lip service while policy and strategy challenge the law and refuse to participate in strengthening it, no matter what the other States of the world want.

PRECEDENT

During the 1984 presidential campaign NASA sponsored a symposium in which potential cooperative ventures between the United States and the Soviet Union were discussed. They were called the last and best hope for achieving peace.‡ At bilateral and multilateral meetings and within the United Nations (UN), the value, and indeed necessity, for countries to work together has been reiterated, as they recognize their growing dependence on space for communications, information, and basic data.

There are three very pertinent facts about the beginnings of the space age:

1. **It began as a cooperative effort.**
2. **From the beginnings of space exploration a system of international law was developed through the United Nations to maintain the peaceful and positive nature of space use carried out in the interest of all humanity.**
3. **There has always been an overlap between civil and military uses of space.**

As with multilateral activities on earth, so in space the Charter of the United Nations§ applies. Thus the enigma of Article 2.4 versus Article 51 of the UN Charter is evidenced in space law as well as in terrestrial law. When considering allowable military use of space one then has to ask the question: What constitutes use of threat of use of force (2.4) if earth-to-space or space-to-space weapons are deployed? As with the fallout from nuclear weapons, space-based weapons threaten all national borders and the rights of all humans. It would seem that the International Court of Justice (ICJ) decision on nuclear weapons has implications for the issue of space weapons. Now, before weaponization takes place, the General Assembly (G.A.) might well request an opinion of the ICJ on the legality of one or a few countries turning outer space into an arena for war fighting, interpreting how far the protection of the OST goes.**

If States have the right to act in self-defense (51) does that mean that they have the right to introduce weapons into a previously positive-use area, threatening the space systems

---

† Outer Space Remarks by Amb. Eric M. Javits in the Conference on Future Security in Space. New Place, England, May 2809, 2002.

‡ "Panelists Say Joint Adventures in Space Are Crucial to Peace," Philip M. Boffey. *The New York Times*, October 30, 1984.

§ Charter of the United Nations, 1 UNTS. Entered into Force January 1, 1946.

** Legality of the Threat of Use of Nuclear Weapons", ICJ Advisory Opinion of July 8, 1996. UN Doc. A/51/218, 35 I.L.M. 809 & 1343, 1996.

and terrestrial defenses of all other States? If they do so, do not other States have a similar right to defend themselves, thus placing their weapons in space and starting a new arms race? Since space weapons would be deployed, ready-to-use weapons, does this action violate Article 51? In addition, when any State declares a policy of preemptive action, whether defensive or offensive, the caveat in Article 51 that self-defense is allowed when a State and its sovereignty have been attacked is challenged. The temptation to self-interpret Article 51 is endemic among policy makers and military strategists.

U.S. STRATEGY AND POLICY

While the attention of the world is turned to the response to terrorist actions, the U.S. administration's policy and the U.S. military's long-range strategy moves rapidly toward the future. Strategy and plans already declared in U.S. Space Command's Vision for 2020 and U.S. Department of Defense (DoD) Directive 3100.10[1] for the full inclusion of the outer space arena in war making and war fighting strategy have intensified. Vision for 2020 begins: "US Space Command—dominating the space dimension of military operations to protect US interests and investment. Integrating Space Forces into war fighting capabilities across the full spectrum of conflict." The rush toward a National Missile Defense (NMD) and a Theater Missile Defense (TMD), or regional, system also utilize space. Yet the threat that NMD is theoretically supposed to defend against—"rogue states" or terrorists is a threat that is poorly dealt with by a defense against strategic missiles, even if such a defense were proven to be feasible, which is still in doubt.

The Department of Defense became acutely aware of the value of space to their military operations during the Persian Gulf War. This was confirmed in the Balkans where the Global Positioning System (GPS) was used effectively to coordinate the collection of NATO activities. Thus the policies and strategies of the U.S. administration and DoD now include space systems as an essential part of their war planning.

Department of Defense Space Policy of July 9, 1999,[2] which replaced the policy announced in 1987, makes freedom of movement in space vital to U.S. national security. It states that

> Purposeful interference with U.S. space systems will be viewed as an infringement on our sovereign rights. The U.S. may take all appropriate self-defense measures, including if directed by the National Command Authorities, the use of force to respond to such an infringement on U.S. rights.

It also calls for an "operational U.S. space force" to patrol space and guard U.S. interests.

The Commission to Assess U.S. National Security, Space Management and Organization stated that "The U.S. needs to remain at the forefront in space, technologically and operationally....The U.S. must have the capability to use space as an integral part of its ability to manage crises, deter conflicts and, if deterrence fails, to prevail in conflict." On January 11, 2001 the Commission to Assess the Ballistic Missile Threat to the United States,[10] known as the Rumsfeld Commission, was estab-

lished by members of Congress, headed by the nominee for Secretary of Defense, and composed of members who were dedicated to assuring that missile defenses would move rapidly forward. The Commission included former military officers, including some from U.S. Space Command. So while the Commission's findings were presented as if they resulted from a neutral assessment, they were just reaffirming what had been already decided.

As a candidate for President, George Bush had criticized the outgoing Clinton administration for trying to negotiate arms control agreements with Russian President Putin. Bush said "No decision would be better than a flawed agreement that ties the hands of the next president and prevents America from defending itself." [††] Politics, once again, prevails over continuity in U.S. policy. It is no wonder that the Anti-Ballistic Missile (ABM) treaty was considered expendable: one wonders whether other treaties will also be considered an impediment to political and military plans.

In August 2001 General Michael Ryan, retiring Air Force Chief of Staff, said to reporters that "I would think that eventually we're going to have to have capabilities to take things out in orbit. And we had better not be second." He noted that the U.S. is "too dependent" on satellites and although he said that the administration had not made a decision as to whether the U.S. would be the first to place weapons in space, "I would suggest that sometime in the future here we are going to have to come to a policy decision on whether we're going to use space for both defensive and offensive capabilities."[‡‡]

On December 8, 2000 the Air Force, Lockheed Martin Corp., TRW Inc., and Boeing Co. announced a successful test of the optical systems that would be used by a space-based laser (SBL) to shoot out ballistic missiles. [§§] The program is geared to putting an experimental laser in space by 2012 and to testing it against a dummy missile the next year. As of the time of the Fiscal Year 2001 budget, the SBL's expense over its development lifetime was estimated at $30 billion.

The new National Security Strategy to be released in Fall 2002 will describe the administration's new doctrine of preemptive strikes and defensive intervention.[***] Clearly preemptive, or anticipatory military acts are not with the self-defense description of Article 51 of the UN Charter. It is a dangerous policy at best and if one country adopts it, why not the others? Carried into outer space, this policy has the potential to seriously destabilize the world political situation.

On June 25th DoD announced the merger of U.S. Space Command and U.S. Strategic Command, which is in charge of U.S. nuclear missiles. An unidentified DoD official was quoted by Reuters as saying that "I know it sounds like an esoteric corporate

†† "Bush Outlines Post-Cold War U.S. Military Vision," Ann Compton, ABC News, May23, 2000.

‡‡ "U.S. Likely to Put Arms in Space – Air Force Chief," Reuters, August 1, 2001.

§§ A ten-year lead is barely sufficient time to negotiate legal protection against such an act.

***"Bush to Formalize a Defense Policy of Hitting First", David F. Sanger, The New York Times, June 17, 2002.

merger, but it's important in the post-September world to marry warning and response."[†††] This gives technological ability to the preemptive strike policy. On the same day, Lt. Gen. Ronald Kadish, Director of the Missile Defense Agency, announced that a veil of secrecy will be going up around information concerning the development of NMD, presumably to keep adversaries from being able to counter the defense system.[‡‡‡]

This brings up the constitutional issue of how much secrecy by non-elected government officials is allowable in a democratic system of government. At what point in this movement into a whole new realm of exotic weapons and space war fighting does the public have a right to be consulted? A number of public policy issues are involved here. One is the budget, the huge expenditure of public monies now being spent and to be spent on exotic weaponry, some of which will never work, and others which will, in fact, destabilize U.S. national security and global security in the long run. Another has to do with the long-range relationship of the United States with the other countries of the world. Does the American public really want to see our relationship with other counties damaged to fulfill the ambitions of the powerful?

There has been some discussion of the possible creation of a U.S. Space Force because of the growing importance of space for war fighting and planning. The idea of a Space Force came out when Gen. Ronald Fogleman, Air Force Chief of Staff from 1994-97, had a number of studies undertaken on how to best use space resources.[§§§] Then, in its report, the Rumsfeld Commission called for the establishment of "an under-secretary of defense for space, intelligence and information."

At the 18th National Space Symposium in April 2002 Gen. Ed Eberhart, head of U.S. Space Command, Air Force Space Command, and NORAD in Colorado Springs discussed the military's need for a space plane, or sub-orbital bomber. He said that "A reusable launch vehicle will be the key to operating and conquering the space frontier." He also said that it has "....a lot of applications in every one of our missions."[****] Another Space Command spokesman said that planning for a space plane does not mean that the U.S. has made a decision to place weapons in space. Army Maj. Barry Venable said that "peaceful purposes" as established in the OST means "nonaggressive acts", thus defensive weapons can be placed in outer space.[††††] Maj. Venable's comments are another proof of the need to better define what is required in order to maintain the peaceful nature of space use and to protect the legal system for space. Those comments also show the need for clear definitions of defensive v. offensive weapons, among other terms.

There is another future war fighting method which makes use of outer space. How will international

[†††] Reuters, June 25, 2002.
[‡‡‡] AP, June 25, 2002.

[§§§] "Space is essential to our national security," *Florida Today*, March 14, 2000.
[****] "Military High Ground Key To America's Security," Leonard David, Senior Space Writer, Space.com, April 9, 2002.
[††††] "Military explores space planes: Vehicle could drop bombs, fix satellites, general says," John Diedrich, The Gazette, Colorado Springs CO, April 10, 2002. www.gazette.com/stories.

law deal with information systems war fighting, including computer network attacks? SPACECOM is now working on this method which Gen. Richard Myers, then its head, said "will focus on denying, disrupting and degrading systems...."[‡‡‡‡]

The reorganization of its command systems now underway is evidence as to what DoD is thinking as far as future military strategy and what systems are to be important in that strategy. Among the changes, Gen. Richard Myers, former commander of U.S. Space Command, is now Chairman of the Joint Chiefs of Staff. Aerospace officials have been nominated for top positions in the political and military establishments. A Defense Directive issued by the Joint Chiefs of Staff in January 2002 under the direction of Defense Secretary Donald Rumsfeld declares that only the President and the Secretary of Defense have command authority to use nuclear weapons, replacing the former National Command Authority. This gives tremendous power to the Secretary of Defense. [§§§§] One wonders to what extent this power extends to decisions regarding ballistic missile defenses and space weapons.

Using *Global Engagement: A Vision of the 21st Century Air Force*,[4] the Air Force has been restructuring itself in anticipation of future needs. This document uses a term also used in DoD's *Joint Vision 2020:* Full Spectrum Dominance, or "the ability of US forces, operating unilaterally or in combination with multinational and interagency partners, to defeat any adversary and control any situation across the full range of military operations." *Global Engagement* states: "We are now transitioning from an *air* force into an air and *space* force on the way to an evolutionary path to a *space and air* force....The Air Force must plan to prevail in the use of space."

The Memorandum accompanying the issuance of DoD Directive 3100 ' gives the U.S. broad-based self-declared authority to operate in space: "Positions and policies regarding arms control and related activities shall preserve the rights of the United States to conduct research, development, testing, and operations in space for military, intelligence, civil, and commercial purposes...."[*****]

In August 2000 the U.S. ambassador to the CD presented the U.S. administration's version of "peaceful uses." He said

> ....The United States strongly endorses articles I and II of the Outer Space Treaty of 1967, which expressly allow for the free exploration and use of outer space and celestial bodies by all nations. The United States sees no justification for limitations on the right of sovereign States to acquire data from space, and we consider purposeful interference with space systems an infringement on sovereign rights.
>
> ....For us, as for others, the

‡‡‡‡ "Space Command Plans for Computer Network Attack Mission," Paul Stone, American Forces Press Service, March 4, 2000.

§§§§ "Whose finger on the button?," William M. Arkin, The Last Word, Bulletin of the Atomic Scientists, March/April 2002 at 73.

***** *Memorandum for Secretaries of the Military Departments et* al. Department of Defense Space Policy, The Secretary of Defense, July 9, 1999 at 15.

notion "peaceful purpose: does of course allow for activities that support defensive purposes and serve national security goals. [italics added]††††††

If "peaceful purposes is only a "notion" then the decades or work by the General Assembly, Committee on the Peaceful Uses of Outer Space (COPUOS), Office of Outer Space Affairs (OOSA), and the CD as well as the three UNISPACE conferences, will have been for naught. Thus, if the States want to prevent an arms race in outer space they must first clearly define and agree to both "peaceful uses" and "prevention of an arms race" in space as principles of international law. In addition, if the U.S. believes that there is no limitation on the right of States to acquire data, the Remote Sensing Principles also need reaffirming.

THE PATH FROM NMD TO SPACE WEAPONS

Why is there such a rush by the present administration to implement a National Missile Defense system? The Bush administration's Fiscal Year 2003 budget proposes what Bush called "the largest increase in military spending in the last 20 years," which includes a sustained five-year increase. ‡‡‡‡‡ By 2007 the military budget would rise to $451 billion. Much of that money would go to new weapons systems and missile defense research and testing. In the past year development has been stepped up, testing planned, funding authorized, and other countries are being approached in a planned, concerted campaign to secure their compliance with U.S. military plans. First stage deployment is announced for the very near future. Yet there has been no national debate in the United States on whether such a system should be built and whether we want to expend extraordinary amounts of capital on a system whose technical feasibility is questionable at best. Even Sen. Robert Byrd has said that "I believe that it would be both wise and prudent to back off just a little bit on the accelerator that is driving us in a headlong and fiscally spendthrift rush to deploy a national missile defense and to invest billions into putting weapons in space and building weapons designed to act in space....The threat does not justify the pace."§§§§§

It is not even clear that there is a need for such a system. In February 2000 a Central Intelligence Agency analyst told the Senate that "....we project that in the coming years, American territory is probably more likely to be attacked with WMD from non-missile delivery means (most likely from non-state entities) than by missiles primarily because non-missile delivery means are less costly and more reliable and accurate. They can also be used without attribution. Their appeal over missiles makes long-range ballistic missile attack on the United States even less likely."****** The

††††† Conference on Disarmament, CD/PV.858, August 31, 2000. Mr. Grey of the United States speaking, at 5.

‡‡‡‡‡ "Bush Seeks Major Defense Boost", Mike Allen & Thomas E. Ricks, *Washington Post*, January 24, 2002.

§§§§§ "Space Wars," Sen. Robert C. Byrd, *Congressional Record*, September 26, 2001 at S9826-8.

****** Robert Walpole quoted in "National Missile Defences and arms control after Clinton's NMD decision," Daryl G. Kimball and Stephen W. Young. *Disarmament Forum*,

National Intelligence Council Report of 1999 states: "Several other means to deliver weapons of mass destruction to the United States have probably been devised, some more reliable than ICBMs...." There needs to be a slowng down the pace of NMD while the true potential dangers and the alternative methods of dealing with them are considered more fully.[††††††]

NMD has implication far beyond "defense" or "national security." It is, in fact, the first step toward increased militarization, leading to weaponization, of the space environment. Even the first stage weapons of NMD and regional missile defenses, and the testing of those weapons, enter the space environment, as do ballistic missiles. Unlike ballistic missiles they hit a target in space. The legal issues opened up by this one fact are extensive. They include: the debris added to that already crowding space; liability for damage on earth or to the space systems of other countries or commercial enterprises; environmenttal issues that can only be imagined; and denial of free access to parts of space by other countries because of areas closed off due to "national security considerations.'

Even the early version of NMD involves space activities: satellites which use infared detection of the exhaust of a missile,radars, sensors, and the weapon which destroys the missile are all in space. Of course, when the Strategic defense Initiative (SDI) was being developed in the 1980s, it was realized that other countries or groups would respond to SDI by developing a decoy system, hardening their missiles, changing direction, and other ploys to avoid being destroyed en route to their destination. This would have required other responses by the missile defense country, including placing components in outer space with protective zones around them. These "keep out zones" brought up the issue of a violation of the OST Article II prohibition against "national appropriation" of outer space and celestial bodies "by claim of sovereignty, by means of use or occupation, or by any other means."

Future systems also would include Brilliant Pebbles, small satellites in low orbit, each containing small kill vehicles, and space-based lasers mounted on remote-controlled satellites. The first test of the latter is tentatively scheduled for 2012. With no delimitation of airspace and outer space together with freedom of space use, killer low earth satellites (LEOs) and space planes have the potential to challenge the sovereignty of every country on earth.

The Rumsfeld Commission, its members carefully chosen for their pre-conceived support for National Missile Defense, made an obvious determination that NMD was a necessary part of U.S. security. At the CD, Amb. Grey said that "The proposed United Stats national missile defense system would use land-based interceptors, launchers and radars. It would use satellites only to provide early warning and data on threat missiles. This is a far cry from the weaponization of outer space."[‡‡‡‡‡‡]

---

journal of the United Nations Institute for Disarmament Research, January 2001 at 15.

†††††† "Foreign Missile Developments and the Ballistic Missile Threat to the United States Through 2015," National Intelligence Council Report, September 1999.

‡‡‡‡‡‡ Conference on Disarmament, CD/PV

This contrasts with the Rumsfeld Commission statement that "....in the coming period the U.S. will conduct operations to, from, in, and through space in support of its national interests both on he earth and in space."

SOME LONG-TERM IMPLICATIONS OF PRESENT POLICY

The current administration has become so focused on space dominance and NMD that those issues are skewing the political policy process. From the relationship of the U.S. with its NATO allies to the negotiating process in CD, military strategy overrides political cooperation. "This administration, even more than its predecessors, suffers from militarization its policy thought, a significant development in a Washington where the Pentagon has become by far the weightiest an best-financed player in the policy debate."[§§§§§§]

It is obvious that the military needed to be involved in space from the beginning of space use and that military personnel had the training and knowledge to develop the technology and travel into space. However, it is also a fact that NASA was created to engage in civil space activities only. Yet, since 1982 funding has been moving more and more into military space activities and away from civil activities. A Congressional Research Service study of 1985 expressed concern as to what was referred to as the 'militarization of NASA.' In the past year the same concerns have been expressed by Congress as the DoD becomes more involved in the work of NASA.

Although it has been responsible for negotiating significant treaty law, the CD, the negotiating body for arms control, has been at a standstill since 1994. The U.S. blames this on other countries' preoccupation with NMD, while other countries blame it on the U.S. preoccupation with pursuing NMD to the detriment of cooperation and law. A Press Release at the conclusion of the Year 2000 Session of the CD reported that "The United States agreed that it was appropriate for the Conference on Disarmament to keep the agenda item on prevention of an arms race in outer space under review. *But it had also pointed out that there was no arms race in outer space."* [italics added][*******] Perhaps the U.S. administration needs to open Webster's to look up the meaning of "prevention."

China and Russia have both proposed draft treaties on the non-weaponization of outer space at the CD. In June 2002, China, Russia and other countries presented a new draft of ways to prevent weapons in space and the arms race which will ensue. [†††††††]However, China has made it clear that it will not sit back and watch the U.S. build a missile defense system: it will response. One of those responses will be to build more intercontinental ballistic missiles. Another will doubtless be to build its own space weapons in anticipation of a space arms race.

[§§§§§§]"Bush Team's Military Focus Is Skewing U.S. Foreign Policy," William Pfaff, *International Herald Tribune*, June 20, 2001.

[*******] Press Release, CD, 2000.

[†††††††]Possible Elements for a Future International Legal Agreement on the Prevention of the Deployment of Weapons in Out3r Space, Joint Working Paper, CD, June 2002.

What will happen to the commercial space industries if weapons are placed in space? Will they then have to expend the resources to try to harden their systems? Would they find it too expensive or too dangerous for their valuable space systems to place them in an area of questionable safety? Without the ability of the companies to operate their satellites, much of the progress of the past decades would be seriously undermined. In retaliation against U.S. military operations in space, others could target the U.S. comercial space industry. The military and intelligence communities approach is to fear, as they said on March 19, 2002, that "The U.S. faces growing threats to its space dominance...." Included among those involved in what George Tenet, Director of the Central Intelligence Agency (CIA) called "erosion" of the advantage that the U.S. has had in space for decades is the private sector.[‡‡‡‡‡‡‡]

POSSIBLE LEGAL INSTRUMENTS

For over twenty years treaties to assure that weapons would never be placed in outer space have been proposed and presented to different United Nations forums. In the fall of 1981 the Soviet Union introduced prevention of an arms race in outer space onto the agenda of the General Assembly in the form of a Treaty on the Prohibition of the Stationing of Weapons of Any Kind in Outer Space.

In the CD, U.S. Amb. Grey said of the OST and the Limited Test-Ban Treaty of 1963 that "This regime provides the basis for keeping outer space free from the most threatening weapons,"[§§§§§§§] **meaning WMD, especially nuclear weapons. An important effect of the OST was to stop the development and deployment of fractional orbiting bombardment systems (FOBS – space bombs). No one denies that WMD are the immediate, already-deployed weapons. However, the other weapons – space bombs, lasers, kinetic energy, particle beam, explosive proximity – have been in development for decades and are being lab tested.**

Do we once again wait until it is too late to direct the course of history? Had the U.S. and the Soviet Union been willing to place their atomic weapons under international control, as President Eisenhower urged, perhaps the world would not need to fear that terrorists or aggressive States would get access to nuclear weapons. If weapons are to be banned from space, the law is needed now. A few years from now will be too late.

There are a number of ways to go about developing the law. Clear definitions and agreement on basic principles is the first step. A comprehensive treaty would need to ban the testing of weapons in space, anti-satellite weapons, the use of weapons earth-to-space and in outer space itself, and the placement of weapons in outer space. The United Nations would be the forum through which negotiation on a treaty would take place, either in the CD or in a conference called for this specific purpose. Another possible approach

---

‡‡‡‡‡‡‡ "U.S. Space Dominance Faces Growing Threats, Officials Say," Marc Selinger, *Aerospace Daily*, March 20, 2002. www.aviationnow.com/avnow/newschannel.

§§§§§§§ *Request for the Inclusion of a Supplementary Item in the Agenda of the Thirty-Sixth Session, United Nations General Assembly,* U.N.G.A. Doc. A/36/192, 1981.

would be a series of bilateral agreements to protect specific space assets. For example, the Global Positioning System is important enough to all usrs encourage support for rules protecting space assets. There was discussion at the CD of beginning with "rules of the road". However, events are overtaking the feasibility of using this approach, events which are potential threats to U.S. space assets along with those of other countries and commercial industries.

MELDING LAW AND POLICY

The claim that the present legal system for outer space is sufficient for the preservation of that area for peaceful, beneficial uses is ludicrous. There are a number of things which need to be done to preserve the space environment while protecting civil, commercial, and non-weapons military uses of that area.

1. Principles need to be clearly defined and accepted by all the States:

. the OST principles of peaceful uses for the benefit of all humanity and freedom of space from appropriation by any means

. peaceful uses of outer space

. prevention of an arms race

2. Definitions which need to be established and agreed to by all States. Over fourteen years ago in the CD Canada******** made the point that "Prevention of an arms race in outer space clearly involves a significant effort both in defining space weapons and in defining legitimate space activities. " What definitions?

. delimitation of the separation between airspace and outer space

. militarization as differentiated from weaponization

. expanding the definition of WMD to include developing or future weapons

. offensive v. defensive technology

. legitimate military activities in space v. intrusive, aggressive ones

. the rights of the States, the commercial enterprises operating in space, and earth's people

4. The negotiation of a comprehensive treaty/management system

In outer space, as in all other areas of potential conflict, the best, most effective and long-lasting way to protect and create assured security is to create a system which combines global cooperation, national policies, military preparedness, and legal systems so they complement each other and work together. It is the only answer for permanent national and global security.

U.S. Government Documents -
1. DoD Directives 3100, .09, .10.
2. DoD Space Policy
3. H.R.4, National Missile Defense Act
4. *Global Engagement: A Vision of the 21st Century Air Force*, June 26, 1999.
5. DoD *Joint Vision 2010*
6. DoD *Joint Vision 2020*.
7. *National Space Policy*. The White House, Sept. 19, 1996
8. *Nuclear Posture Review*, Jan. 2002
9. *Report of the Commission to Assess US National Security, Space Management and Organization*. PL 106-65, NDAA, FY 2000 S1622.
10.. *Report of the Commission to Assess the Ballistic Missile Threat to the US*. PL104-201, NDAA,FY 1997 S1321(g).
12. SPACECOM, *Vision for 2020*

******** Conference on Disarmament, CD/PV.468, July 26, 1988. Mr. Marchand of Canada speaking at 5.

LEGAL AND POLITICAL IMPLICATIONS OF OFFENSIVES ACTIONS FROM AND AGAINST THE SPACE SEGMENT

Author Iole M. De Angelis

Centre for Defence Analysis, Acquisition Agency French MoD

Arcueil, France

deangelis@cad.etca.fr

ABSTRACT

The Outer Space Treaty had been adopted to avoid the possible denial of peaceful uses of outer space, and because, technically speaking, using effectively a satellite as a weapon was also a difficult task to perform. The problem remains for non-state international actors which are not bound by international treaties.

It is important to remember that the military use of outer space has both stabilizing and destabilizing potential. Military and civilian satellites perform functions that contribute to treaties verification, transparency, confidence building and nuclear deterrence. Putting weapons in space – that is a military use of outer-space – would threaten the instruments and sensors deployed into orbit to monitor potential enemies, control the compliance to disarmament treaties, detect ballistic missile launches, and maintain reliable communications. A sudden attack against such systems would lead to a main international crisis.

In conclusion, the issues related to offensive actions towards and from space shall be taken into consideration not only from a military perspective, but also from a political viewpoint – terrorist actions against the space segment – and from an economical point of view.

TEXT

Hundreds of satellites benefit the people of the world economically, scientifically and by their contribution to international security. So far, activities in space have proceeded without much conflict. Means have been found for regulation and agreement to minimize interference in the radio spectrum, while making more efficient use of limited spectrum resources.

Today, maintaining the peaceful use of space is becoming more complicated due to the privatisation of the notion of security by commercial actors and the emerging of high technology non-state threats, which are not bound by international treaties.

The key questions that this paper addresses can be summarised as follow:

- Is space warfare inevitable?
- What will happen if one country decides to develop and deploy space warfare systems?
- According to some technical scenarios, the use of nuclear, kinetic energy, directed energy weapons and information warfare, what would be the political and legal implications of offensive actions from and against the space segment?

WARFARE IN SPACE

To deter war and to protect the security of the country are the key missions of the Ministry of Defense of all countries of the world. Defense space programs support such missions but, if the prevention and the deterrence fail, it is vital to be able to have the capabilities to defend the nation and its interests.

The access and the use of outer space could be one of the main national interests of a country from a defense and from an economic point of view. In this sense, the question of the inevitability of a space-based conflict seems of primary importance. Especially because there are good arguments in support and against the inevitability of such possibility. In the following paragraphs, we will analyse how and why this situation is not such a paradox as it may seem at a first glance.

Space warfare cannot be avoided

Space leaders understand how the space capabilities might be used as one of the primary instrument of power in pursuit of national and international objectives. In other words, militarily speaking, space is a force multiplier: it allows to gain an advantage in time, maneuver and logistics against an adversary via a more efficient Observation Orientation Decision and Action (OODA) loop. At the same time, space is also a market with growing possibilities not only in the field of services, but also for the exploitation of natural resources.

If we define warfare as a situation of conflict amongst two or more actors that have the purpose to acquire and maintain the control over a resource or a set of resources, then we must conclude that warfare for and in space is highly probable.

Militarily speaking, the developed countries feel the need to be able to project power anywhere on Earth, and, for this purpose to make a large use of space (navigation, observation, communication...). In addition, new capabilities will be developed that can deter attack on and defend national interests and many of these capabilities would be based in space. For this reason, an eventual attack against the space segment could give a strong advantage to the actor that carries out such an action because the current strategic, operative and tactical situation awareness, the superiority in mobility, in logistics, in positioning and the precise guidance of weapons greatly relies upon space technology. For this reason, an actor who would decide to affect the space segment knows the advantage it may gain in term of disorganizing and disturbing its adversary's forces. At the same time, the impact over the public opinion would be very strong and capable to create and maintain a feeling of insecurity that reduces the will to fight or to support the conflict by the population.

In terms of commercial space activities, the possibility to affect the space segment could be used not only as integrated into a military action but also as a commercial action against a competitor in the same field, in particular by reducing the lifetime of the competitor's satellite or by disturbing its missions. This leads to the possibility of conquering the market and ruining the competitor. Of course, such actions are not legal and it is very unlikely that they will take place, but, for the purposes of this paper it is important to take into consideration also non military scenarios.

Politically speaking, affecting or taking down a satellite could have a great effect upon the public opinion. For this reason, a non-state actor may think about such kind of offensive action to attract attention. In particular, the chinese spiritual organization Falung Gong recently hacked the satellite Sinosat in order to send some messages to the population to talk about the repression that the chinese government was operating against them. These kind of actions, are likely to grow in importance and intensity, for this reason there is a strong need to protect the space segment. In any case, the political will is a start, but policy is meaningless if the nation lacks the tools to implement it.

In conclusion, today, space is becoming an area of military operations in its own right—much the same as land, air and sea—not simply a place from which information is acquired and transmitted or through which objects pass.

Space warfare can be avoided

To wring the greatest capability out of the medium of space it is necessary to master highly complex technology; develop new doctrine and concepts of operations for space launch, defensive space operations, power projection in, from and through space and other military uses of space; and operate some of the most complex systems ever built and deployed.

It is complicate to wage war in space, and for this reason, space can be considered as a sanctuary. Even if affecting the space segment can give an important advantage from a military point of view, the technical systems required to do so are very costly, difficult to conceive and to operate in an efficient way. In addition, similar results to an attack against the space segment can be achieved throughout offensive actions against the ground segment.

In terms of commercial space activities, since space warfare is not a loyal concurrence and it is very bad for the image of the company who would be discovered carrying out such actions, the trade off among risks and gains make very unlikely the possibility to use such techniques to gain a market.

In conclusion, space warfare is not a fatality and will not be carried out unless a strong political will of one or more international actors. The term "states" is intentionally avoided, because, nowadays, States are not anymore the only actors on the international arena, and some non-states actors are the most important warring factors to the international security, that includes avoiding the weaponisation of the outer-space.

HOW TO WAGE SPACE WARFARE

It is possible to summarise the political issues related with space warfare as follow:

- The identification of the aggressor, especially if it uses information warfare techniques. It is essential, especially in this field where the use of weapons of mass destruction is possible, to clearly identify the aggressor and the reasons of the attack in order to size the counteraction.
- The management of the public opinion facing such kind of offensive action against its nation satellites. An international actor able to conduct space warfare can also attain the national territory with great damages.
- The feeling, at political level, to have failed a policy of conflict prevention and deterrence of strategic attacks.

Space weapons

Putting weapons in space would threaten the instruments and sensors deployed into orbit to monitor potential enemies, control the compliance to disarmament treaties, detect ballistic missile launches, and maintain reliable communications. At the same time, space weapons can be directed against targets that are still in the atmosphere and in the national territory of a country or in the international sea and air. According to the international law, a boat or an aeroplane is considered as part of the national territory of the country which owns it.

The Outer Space Treaty had been adopted to avoid the possible denial of peaceful uses of outer space. In addition, technically speaking, using effectively a satellite as a weapon was and still is a difficult task to perform. For example, an orbiting laser might take hours or days to be on the target. Weapons of mass destruction are voluntarily omitted because they are the objects of the only specific prohibition to weapons in space, according to the art. 4 of the Outer Space Treaty. In addition, the ABM Treaty prohibits the deployment of space systems with ballistic missiles defence missions (art. 5).

It is currently very difficult to oppose space weapons. For this reason, they could be significantly effective against an adversary. However, there are several ways to counter nation controlled space-based weapons: anti-satellite systems, economic and technological blockade and an international legal system that forbids/restricts such weapons. The problem remains for non-state international actors which are not bound by international treaties. For this reason, the principle established by the United States to tie a common responsibility among the non state-actor Al-Quaida and the State of Afghanistan – that supported and hosted such organisation – is an example that deserves special consideration.

Antisatellite weapons

According to the international customs, the satellites are part of the national territory of the nation's owner. As a result, any attack on the space–based systems is considered as a threat to which armed force, including nuclear force, might be the reply: an attack to the space segment is an attack against the vital interest of a country. In addition, according to the ABM Treaty (art. 12) and the SALT I Treaty (art. 4) the interference in the means used for treaty verification is forbidden.

In a world in which Russia and the United States are no longer enemies, no individual nation has a strong motivation to develop and deploy space weapons for solely military purposes. Such weapons could be seen as inextricably tied to the purpose of achieving space dominance not only for military reasons – achieving full spectrum dominance thanks to a superior information management – but also for economical and political reasons.

It is important to remember that the military use of outer space has both stabilizing and destabilizing potential. Military and civilian satellites perform functions that contribute to treaties verification, transparency, confidence building and nuclear deterrence. A sudden attack against such systems would lead to a main international crisis. For this reason, in February 2000 the Chinese delegation to the United Nations Conference on Disarmament circulated a paper identifying a present and pressing necessity to prevent an arms race in outer space. A treaty forestalling the use of any kind of weapons in space, argued the delegation, would greatly support global peace and security. Moscow agreed with Beijing on this subject.

LEGAL AND POLITICAL IMPLICATION ACCORDING TO DIFFERENT SCENARIOS

Nuclear attack from and against the space segment

Nuclear weapons are a variety of weapons of mass destruction; as we stated before, the art. 4 of the Outer Space Treaty bars the stationing of such kind of weapons in space. In addition, it is also stated that nations are responsible for damages that their space activities may cause to others, perhaps including destruction of the space assets of another nation.

This chapter will focus upon nuclear weapons, because the effects of biological and chemical weapons against a satellite are very limited. Of course, it is still possible to attack ground targets from space with biological and chemical weapons, but it is more cost-effective to carry out such kind of attack with more traditional means.

Nuclear explosions have three main effects: rays effects, mechanical effects and radiological effects.

These effects had been studied by the different countries to understand the advantages and drawbacks of possible uses of nuclear weapons for space warfare. Of course such results are classified and will not be analyzed in this paper.

What it is possible to say is that nuclear weapons used against the space segment will affect not only the satellites targeted, but also all the spacecrafts in a wide surrounding area and will produce space debris. This situation will increase the dimensions and the intensity of the on-going conflict. For this reason, there is not a strong motivation to use nuclear weapons for antisatellite missions, and there is very few chances that the obligations of the different treaties would be compelled.

At the same time, because of technical constraints – lifetime, attitude and control, etc. – the option of placing nuclear weapons into space could not be seen as the most efficient option.

Nuclear weapons raise important political and legal issues. For this reason their development and use had been deeply studied and analysed. At the moment it does not seem that non-state actors may acquire such technology and conduct space warfare at this level.

In conclusion, although the issues related to nuclear weapons are one of the priority of the spacefaring nations, it seems that they are the best studied and those who raises the less uncertainties with respect to the other form of space warfare.

<u>Kinetic energy weapon attack from and against the space segment</u>

None of the Treaties bans the stationing of conventional weapons in space, and such weapons can be used to damage other satellites.

Kinetic energy weapons destroy things by using the energy generated by a moving mass impacting a target mass. Such kind of weapons for space application in the form of antisatellite systems date back to the mid to late 1960s. They can be employed from the ground, air, or space against targets in any medium. Knowing that, the space environment of the future will be one of multiple users of military, civil, and commercial satellites. In many cases, political considerations will prevent or severely constrain military options which involve actually destroying satellites. Having a solid capability in this area, however, will serve to deter similar aggression against satellites and will give the option to counteract if necessary.

The option of placing kinetic energy weapons into orbit to counter air/ground target is very complicate to realise and not efficient. It is much better to conduct such kind of operations in a more conventional way, such as using aeroplanes, missiles, soldiers, etc...

In conclusion, even if there is not a specific legal constraint against the stationing of such kind of weapons into space, the experience shows that they could be used only against other satellites, but the targeting and the guidance process are very complicated.

In addition, there are only few countries in the world able to build and guide missiles – launched by ground or air platforms – able to achieve the orbit and thus attain the satellites. It means, that it is quite easy to discover the author of the action and then organise the proper reaction.

Another effect of the explosion is the production of orbital debris, that jeopardizes the space activities of other actors that are not involved in the conflict. This situation will give them a good reason to be involved in the fight and thus increase the dimensions and the intensity of the conflict.

In conclusion, politically and technically speaking, the use of kinetic energy weapons for space warfare does not seem the most efficient solution to conduct counter-space operations.

Directed energy weapon attack from and against the space segment

A directed energy weapon must be able to generate energy, direct it on the target, propagate it through air or space, to the target, and induce some lethal effect in the target.

Charged particle beams are probably the best at generating, directing, and killing but are clearly the worst at propagating. Neutral particle beams can propagate and kill but cannot yet be generated with sufficient intensities.

In addition, none of the Treaties bans the stationing of directed energy weapons in space, and such weapons can be used mainly to damage other satellites or ballistic missiles, although the ABM and START I treaty prohibits such kinds of actions.

At the moment, the problems related to the development of directed energy weapons systems are mainly technical and related to the following issues: the cost, the need of good weather, the need of no high pollution, the presence of an ecological threat, and the need of big installation to produce the energy needed. Finally, at the moment there is not a strong political interest on such field of research.

In conclusion, although the use of directed energy weapons is very efficient, since it is possible to grade the effects from soft kill to hard kill, the constraints listed above must be taken into serious consideration and they could slow down the development and use of such systems.

Information Warfare attack to the space segment

Space superiority will be one of the key pillars in the future military doctrine because it is the key for an efficient information management. In fact, space superiority means to be able to access to space and to gain a strategic advantage with a more efficient use of space technology than the other international actors.

The purpose of the information warfare actions against the space segment can be identified as following: identify the satellites and their missions, monitor the satellites transmissions, deny the use of its satellites to an adversary, and find the end users of the information with the purpose to gain a position of information dominance against the adversary.

Soft kill systems such as jamming, cyberwar and electromagnetic pulse energy will selectively jam or interrupt a satellite's signals without destroying it. This capability greatly increases the flexibility of space warfare operations. In addition, for achieving the same effects, the technical requirements are lighter than for the other scenarios.

Legally speaking, although some steps had been made to clarify what is legal and what is not in the field of electronic warfare (e.g. it is legal for a country to jam a foreign signal of a foreign satellite inside its national territory), there is a long way forward in the field of the cyberwarfare.

The legal context related to the cyberspace is particularly difficult to define. The first difficulty is related to the absence of a defined territory where laws are enforced, in addition there is no harmonization in the ways of perceiving frauds and the applicable sanctions among the countries. The second difficulty is related to the necessity of a compromise between the data and infrastructure protection and the private life of the people. The third difficulty is related to lack of specific laws and juridical documents related to the cyberspace. Finally, anyone with a computer connected to the Internet could be a potential victim or a potential danger, and it is very difficult to discover the author of a cyberattack.

For these reasons, state and non-state actors may have an interest in carrying out such form of offensive actions to gain a strategic or an economical advantage against its adversary. And, this kind of space warfare operations had already been conducted by non-state actors: not only Sinosat seems to have been hacked, but also Skynet 4, the british military communication satellite.

The use of electronic warfare and cyberwarfare tactics is very efficient: it is possible to grade the effects from soft kill to hard kill. At the same time, the lack of co-ordination among the spacefaring nation in this field jeopardise the freedom of use of outer-space: e.g. a dangerous organisation might stop or hack some broadcasts, and this action will have a great impact on the public opinion and its sense of security.

In conclusion, even if, for most people, the first thought about space dominance goes to the weaponisation of space or the destruction of satellites and spacecrafts, the information warfare threat is the most likely action to be conducted in the near future.

CONCLUSIONS

From an international legal perspective, the development and the deployment of strategic weapons, kinetic energy weapons and directed energy weapons are contained within existing rules, more or less strong, and such issues are being addressed by the international community. The main problem in this area is the same for the international law in general: how to enforce the legislation to prevent an eventual weaponisation of the outer-space?

At the same time, politically speaking, the weaponisation of the outer-space may lead to a "proliferation-like" phenomena, since more and more countries have space capabilities, and will try to protect their interests also in this way. Therefore, it is important to prevent an eventual deployment of weapons in outer-space, and it will be only possible if everybody understand that there is not a political interest in doing that and the need to defend the space segment can be answered with other tools and means.

Although the use of cyberwar and electronic warfare to counter space technology are easily available to many kind of organisations and even to individuals, this issue not only encounters a void of international rules, but it is a question that is very rarely taken into consideration while addressing talking about space warfare.

Summarising, space superiority is not only a matter of military actions, but they shall be addressed also from a political viewpoint – terrorists actions against the space segment – and from an cost/benefit point of view. Unfortunately, the international law binds only the countries, but nowadays there are non-state international actors that shall be taken into serious consideration.

In conclusion, there are three key points related to the achievement of space superiority with military actions: the first one is related to the political will, the second one concerns the non-state actors that are not bind by the treaties and the decisions of the international organisation and, finally, there is a legal blur in the regulation of the cyberspace.

BIBLIOGRAPHY

1. *Air Force 2025*, Air University Press, Maxwell AFB, USA, 1996. All the papers are available at the following Internet site : Internet : http ://www.au.af.mil/au/2025/.

2. ARQUILLA, John J., RONFELDT, David F., *Cyberwar and Netwar: New Modes, Old Concepts, of Conflict*, RAND, RAND Research Review, Santa Monica, USA, Vol. XIX, Numero 2, Fall 1995.

3. BADIE Bertrand, SMOUTS Marie-Claude, *Le retournement du monde. Sociologie de la scène internationale*, Presses de Sciences Po et Dalloz, Paris, 1999.

4. BALENCIE Jean-Marc, *La défense face aux défis et menaces non militaires de caractère stratégique*, Les Cahiers du CHEAr N° 36, DGA, Paris, 1997.

5. BROWN, Michael T., *Terrorist Use of Weapons of Mass Destruction Within the United States : Asymmetric Warfare Paradigm in the 21st Century*, U.S Army War College, USA, 1997.

6. BURROWS William E., *Deep Black. The Startling Truth Behing America's Top-Secret Spy Satellites*, Berkley Books, New York, USA, 1988.

7. CANADAY, Jessie W., *Space Technology : Force Multiplier or False Sense of Security*, Naval War College, Newport, USA, 1994.

8. CHALIAND Gérard, *Anthologie mondiale de la stratégie. Des Origines au nucléaire*, Robert Laffont, Paris, 1990.

9. CHARNAY Jean-Paul, *Terrorisme et culture*, Centre d'Etudes et de Recherches sur les Stratégies et les Conflits, Paris, 1981.

10. CORDESMAN Anthony H., *Defending America, Redefining the Conceptual Borders of Homeland Defense : The Risks and Effects of Indirect, Covert, Terrorist, and Extremists Attacks With Weapons of Mass Destruction - Challenges for Defense and Response* Center for Strategic and International Studies, Washington DC, USA, 2001.

11. CURTIS Schleher D., *Introduction to Electronic Warfare*, Artech House, Norwood, USA, 1986.

12. ESTES Howell Mr., *Space: Fourth Medium of Military Operations,* Defense Resulting no.98, the USA, 1996, pp.1-3.

13. État Major des Armées, Division Emplois, *Instruction 1000. Doctrine interarmées d'emploi des forces en opération*, EMA, Paris, 1999, 2000 et 2001.

14. GARWIN Richard L., *Toward International Security: The Role of Space Weapons, Antisatellite Weapon Tests, and National Missile Defense*, Presentation at the United Nations, New York, USA, 21 October 1999.

15. GROUARD Serge, *La Guerre en Orbite. Essai de politique et de stratégie spatiales*, Economica, Paris, 1994.

16. GUYONNEAU Patrick, SICSIK-PARE Emmanuel, *Surveillance du champ de bataille. Evolution des Besoins et des techniques*, *L'Armament*, n. 52, pp. 79-83.

17. *Joint Doctrine Encyclopedia*, Joint Chiefs of Staff Office, Washington DC, USA, 1997.

18. LIBICKI Martin C, Johnson, Stuart E, *Dominating Battlespace Knowledge,* National Defense University Press, Washington Cd., The USA, 1996.

19. MOLANDER Roger C., RIDDLE Andrew S., WILSON Peter A., *Strategic Information Warfare. A New Face of War*, RAND, Santa Monica, USA, 1996.

20. MUNRO Neil, *The Pentagon's New Nightmare : An Electronic Pearl Harbor*, *Washington Post*, Washington DC, USA, 16 juillet 1995.

21. SELLERS, Jerry J., *Understanding Space. An Introduction to Astronautics*, McGraw-Hill Inc., San Francisco, USA, 1994.

22. STROOMER Michael, *Satellite Communications - Past Present and Future*, *Military Technology*, mai 1996, pp. 60-62.

23. SWENBERG Eric C., *The Effect on Operational and Tactical Surprise by US Military Forces Due to the Proliferation of Unclassified Satellite Imaging System*, US Army Command and General Staff College, Fort Leavenworth, USA, 1995.

24. TIMASHEV Serguei V., KULANDIN Alexander A., *Soviet Space Power Technology*, Wright Laboratory, Wright-Patterson AFB, USA, 1995.

25. United Nations, *United Nations Treaties and Principles on Outer Space*, United Nations, Office for Outer Space Affairs, Vienna, 1994.

26. VOLKOFF Vladimir, *Petite histoire de la désinformation, du cheval de Troie à Internet*, Ed. du Rocher, Monaco, 1999.

27. WAUTELET Michel, *Les Cyberconflits*, Editions GRIP, Bruxelles, 1998.

28. WILSON Thomas R. (Vice Admiral, Director of the DIA), *Global Threats and Challenge Thought 2015*, Statement for the Record, Senate select Committee on Intelligence, 7 Febrary 2001, Washington, USA.

IAC-02-IISL.3.12

"The Vanishing Horizon: Will The Asymmetric Battlefield Make Space-Based Weapons a Reality?"

John W. Heath, Jr.[1]

"How strange. . . that this secret sanctuary should be forsaken by one who had found in it such happiness! For indeed less than an hour later, they halted breathlessly at a curve of the track and saw the last of Shangri-La."[2]

I. Introduction

Space has been our modern, threatened "Shangri-La." While eager to compete in a race to the moon, both the United States and the Soviet Union were hesitant to escalate the Cold War arms race to the heavens. Both sides recognized that seeking military advantage by placing weapons into outer space would be costly and could upset the delicate system of mutual nuclear deterrence in place below. Even with the organized exploration and use of space in its infancy, the superpowers joined with other nations to fashion a system of treaties to limit the future military use of space. While tottering, that treaty system largely succeeded in keeping weapons out of orbit and fostered peaceful, state-sponsored exploration and later private commercial activity.

With the demise of the Soviet Union and the easing of nuclear tensions, the old underpinnings of the treaty system governing space has disappeared. And the sole surviving superpower has increasingly found itself faced with new pressures and new enemies in the following decade. In places such as Somalia, Kosovo and Afghanistan, the United States and its allies have faced loosely organized warlords, terrorist organizations and other non-state actors, who employ unconventional or "asymmetric" tactics to negate the inherent advantages of well-equipped conventional armies. At the same time, the brutality of recent conflicts and outcry for a permanent war crimes tribunal has increased the attention paid to the enforcement of the law of armed conflict. To counter these asymmetric threats while complying with the demands of the law of war, the United States must rely increasingly on technology-specifically space-based technology. Although it has no publicly announced intention to do so, the United States may be enticed to finally field weapons in space to counter the new threats while remaining in the bounds of the law of armed conflict. If this were to happen, the old treaty system governing outer space would not likely prove to be much of a legal obstacle.

Part I of this paper introduces "asymmetric" warfare and explores the problems of fighting modern wars by looking at the American experience in recent conflicts. Part II recounts the demands placed on modern combatants by the international law of armed conflict. Part III examines the potential of space-based weapons to offer advantages on the asymmetric battlefield while satisfying the obligations of the law of war. Finally, Part IV examines how these weapons would fare under the old space law treaty regime.

II. Part I: The Challenge of Modern War

A) What is "Asymmetric Warfare"?

While an increasingly popular concept with defense officials, journalists and other military experts, the term "asymmetry" lacks a definite, widely accepted meaning. In 1999, the Office of the Joint Chiefs of Staff in the Pentagon published the *Joint Strategy Review*. This document defined asymmetric warfare as "attempts to circumvent or undermine US strengths while exploiting US weaknesses using methods that differ significantly from the United States' expected method of operations . . . Asymmetric approaches often employ innovative, nontraditional tactics, weapons or technologies and can be applied at all levels of warfare- strategic, operational, and tactical- and across the spectrum of military operations."[3] However, some observers have commented that the official perception of asymmetry is precisely backwards. They argue that Americans wrongly label foreign threats as "asymmetric" when in fact the United States military is perhaps "the most asymmetric force on earth"; the American military has been wildly successful in exploiting the weaknesses of its enemies through non traditional means of warfare- usually based on superior and innovative technology.[4]

To avoid delving further into this debate and outside the scope of this paper, I will assume that the American way of waging war- exemplified by massed formations of infantry and armor supported by artillery and air power (e.g. Desert Storm)- constitutes the norm (or "conventional" warfare). By contrast, asymmetric warfare encompasses the range of tactics used by an opponent that falls outside of this narrow norm. Recent conflicts such as Somalia, Kosovo, and Afghanistan provide ample illustration of asymmetric warfare in these terms.

B) Characteristics of the Asymmetric Threat

Operation Desert Storm in 1991 demonstrated the futility of trying to match the United States military in kind with conventional forces. The Iraqi Army, the fourth largest in the world at the time, fielded more men and equipment than the German Army fighting in Normandy during the Second World War did.[5] Despite being outnumbered, the Americans with their coalition partners fought a nearly flawless campaign, liberating Kuwait in less than 100 hours of ground combat fighting. Although outnumbered, the Americans made up for lack of numbers through superior intelligence gathering, communication, and firepower. Allied forces could quickly identify targets, disseminate that information to their units and bring tremendous fire upon the enemy- all with minimal exposure of their own forces. America's new asymmetric opponents absorbed these lessons of the Persian Gulf War; in subsequent conflicts, these foes have attempted to minimize their exposure to American firepower and instead draw these conventional forces into combat on their own terms.

New enemies have presented as small a target as possible. Small groups have the advantage of being extremely hard to identify and harder still to pinpoint or track for targeting. On the other hand, dispersed units are more difficult to command and control. Nevertheless, small units acting with minimal guidance from a central authority have been the recurring pattern for recent asymmetric enemies. In Somalia, UN forces failed to subdue the roving bands of clan militia who disrupted relief efforts and eventually killed 25 UN peacekeepers.[6] Hence the Americans targeted the Somali warlords, the driving force behind the clans, in hopes of stopping the attacks. During Operation Allied Force (1999), the Yugoslav Army quickly had to adjust their tactics after the NATO air campaign began. Fixed targets such as roads, bridges, and headquarters buildings were quickly destroyed by NATO aircraft. As such, the Yugoslav Army had to widely disperse their remaining units in the field and force them to operate in smaller and smaller groups.[7] While these units became more difficult to detect and destroy from the air, the effectiveness of their operations was greatly diminished. On the ground, the surviving Yugoslav units proved more susceptible to ambush by the Kosovo Liberation Army (KLA) and less able to carry out their ethnic cleansing mission.[8]

The recent war in Afghanistan presents a mixed picture. With support from American air power and special forces, the opposition Northern Alliance quickly overpowered the Taliban government and military forces on the ground. While the Taliban armed forces were sequestered into strongholds and forced to either surrender or be killed, al Qaeda fighters operating in small cells quietly slipped away into the mountains of East Afghanistan to continue their fight.[9]

Unconventional warriors make the most of the local environment. The Somali gangs operated in the densely packed urban areas of Mogadishu; this maze of narrow winding streets, run down buildings and back alleys made coordinating the efforts of and transporting mechanized forces very difficult. However, these same passages gave the local militiamen an infinite number of places to hide and shielded their movements from view. The Somalis also used crowds of civilians for concealment.[10] Without uniforms, the Somali gunmen had only to hide their weapons to blend into the crowds of sympathetic locals; western forces would have a hard time distinguishing friend from foe.[11] Outside of the cities, the al Qaeda in Afghanistan resorted to the mountains. The al Qaeda cells quickly moved into an elaborate system of caves and tunnels to survive American bombardment, hide from surveillance, and cover up their movements.

Beyond escaping detection and surviving American firepower, an asymmetric opponent will seek to draw conventional forces into close combat. On October 3, 1993, Somali gangs shot down two American UH-60 Blackhawk helicopters.[12] By isolating the surviving crews, they drew an American relief column into their neighborhood and attacked it from the streets and buildings.[13] Although the American task force eventually rescued some of the aircrews, the Somalis killed 18 US servicemen. With the deaths of those soldiers, the Clinton administration subsequently withdrew all American forces from Somalia. In the Shahikot Valley, al Qaeda fighting from the mountain caves attempted (less successfully) to isolate and destroy American ground combat troops sent to root them out.[14] By contrast, the Yugoslav Army was never able to draw NATO ground forces into Kosovo and withdraw after a devastating 78-day air campaign.

III. Part II: The Demands of the Law of War

While the tactics of potential enemies have changed, so have the demands placed on the United States by her allies and the international community at large. The devastating regional conflicts of the 1990's prompted a renewed interest in the enforcement of international humanitarian law and the law of armed conflict. Special ad hoc tribunals were convened to root out and punish war criminals and human rights abusers in the former Yugoslavia and Rwanda. After these tribunals began to enjoy relative success, the international community pushed for the creation of a permanent International Criminal Court (ICC) under the Rome Accord of 1998. While cooperating with the Yugoslavia and Rwanda tribunals, the United States balked at participating with the ICC. Nevertheless, in prosecuting the war in Afghanistan, American practices on the battlefield have, of late, come under more pressure and scrutiny from the international community, as evidenced by the outcry over treatment of al Qaeda detainees at Guantanamo Bay, Cuba.

At the same time that renewed international interest in the enforcement of the law of war has created pressure on future combatants, the United States government has created its own internal pressure. A Department of Defense Directive mandates, "[t]he Heads of DoD Components shall . . . [e]nsure that the members of their respective Components comply with the law of war during all armed conflicts, however such conflicts are characterized, and with the principles and spirit of the law of war during all other operations."[15] Thus the Defense Department has circumscribed the range of potential American military activities more tightly than what the body of treaties and international legal custom require by extending those norms to all operations. Let us examine generally what the law of war requires of a combatant.[16]

The customary international law governing the behavior of combatants once involved in combat can be distilled to four principles: military necessity, humanity, proportionality and discrimination.[17] "Military necessity" limits attacks by belligerents to targets which are not otherwise prohibited and which will confer a military advantage if the attack is successful. For example, a belligerent may not burn out a building for no good reason- there must be some military advantage gained by destroying that building (e.g. an enemy observer was in the top floor of that building). Moreover, if the building has some protected status (e.g. a civilian hospital which contains no enemy troops), that building may not be destroyed whatever the military advantage to be gained. The principle of humanity seeks to limit the kind of weapons that can be used to kill or wound an enemy. Certainly, in legitimate combat, seeking to kill or wound an enemy is not against norms of international law. What the "humanity" principle seeks to limit are the methods which would exacerbate an enemy's wounds or suffering beyond the force required to place that enemy out of combat. In various treaties, certain types of weapons which cause unnecessary harm or suffering have been proscribed including expanding bullets, glass and other non-detectable fragments and blinding lasers. The principle of proportionality requires a belligerent to conduct a balancing test relative to the amount of anticipated collateral damage. Specifically, an attack is "proportional" in the legal sense if the loss of life/destruction to property, incidental to goal of the attack, is not excessive in relation to the concrete and direct military advantages gained by the attack.[18] Finally, the principle of discrimination requires belligerents on both the offensive and defensive to carefully differentiate between combatants and non-combatants as well as between military objectives and protected people/places in launching attack

IV. Part III: The Potential Advantages of Space Based Weapons

Faced with the new pressures of asymmetric threat along with the continuing demands of the law of war, the United States must adapt its strategy to meet the new security demands placed on it. But how? What are the new requirements? Will space based weapons provide the necessary answers?

A) The New Requirements

To defeat an enemy that is tied to no geographic location or particular country but can strike from anywhere, against any target, the United States will need the ability to project force worldwide. In future fights against a stateless enemy, the United States and its allies will not enjoy the luxury of a six-month, Desert Shield-like period in which it can mass conventional forces in relative safety for a strike. While adept at projecting force with land-based and carrier-based aircraft, the American military has had difficulty in getting sufficient conventional forces to far-flung battlefields as evidenced by the Kosovo campaign.[19] In response, the American Army has struggled to reconfigure its force structure to allow for the fielding of lighter, more readily deployable units. If the United States chooses to pursue unilateral, preemptive strikes as mentioned by the Bush administration, the US might not even have the luxury of operating from forward-deployed bases in friendly nations because of increase political tensions. To carry out the wishes of the White House, the US military will need weapons platforms that are capable of global reach without having to operate from the territory or airspace of a third party nation. Once on the battlefield, the American military needs the ability to linger over the area for much greater periods of time. An enemy that operates in small units/cells and waits passively in hiding also leaves few clues as to its whereabouts and intentions. As such, American intelligence gatherers must be able to focus intently on a suspected target for increased periods of time to detect enemy movement or activity. In Afghanistan, the fielding of unmanned aerial vehicles (UAVs) and use of special forces units to conduct reconnaissance patrols with minimal support underscores the need for a sustained intelligence gathering presence in dealing with the asymmetric enemies. When an enemy position is revealed, the American military needs an extremely responsive weapons platform that can successfully mount an attack during the narrow window of opportunity when these kind of opponents are exposed. During the fighting in Afghanistan, armed UAVs discovered senior al Qaeda and Taliban leaders on the move from one hideout to the next; however, the command and control element of these weapons were not responsive enough to successfully engage these targets before they got away.[20] In addition to hunting down the enemy fighters in the open, the American military must have the capability to engage these asymmetric fighters in the places where they hide. The Americans must deny their enemies sanctuary, even if it means being able to shoot into the slum buildings of Mogadishu or penetrate the caves of Eastern Afghanistan. To these ends, the US Air Force continues to refine its precision guided munitions (PGMs) and to experiment with new weapons such as the thermobaric bomb. If enemy cells cannot be identified and engaged, those units must be further isolated. As demonstrated in the Kosovo campaign, small, dispersed units are very difficult to communicate with and control. If the US military can sever communications and coordination between these cells, the units may become ineffective. Finally, all of these tasks need to be accomplished with minimum exposure of US forces and assets. The American military must avoid being drawn into combat if possible on conditions favorable to an enemy as in Somalia. Not only will American casualties be lower but also, as the al Qaeda terrorists have demonstrated, there is a tremendous psychological value to being able to attack with impunity, to strike without presenting a target for the enemy to strike back at. Perhaps regaining the ability to "shoot without getting shot at" will be so psychologically devastating to an enemy as to deter further asymmetric attacks.

At the same time, any new technology must adhere to established legal standards. New American forces must be able to discriminate between non-combatants and combatants, between military objectives and protected places. New weapons systems must be used in a way so as to minimize collateral damage. Any new weapon must not cause unnecessary harm or suffering to any enemy in its employment.

B) A Tempting Alternative

Despite the daunting nature of added operational requirements for American military forces to successfully counter future asymmetric opponents, space based weapons may offer some solutions. What form would these weapons take? What advantages would these weapons offer? What would be their practical limitations?

1) Star Wars Revisited

Most of the proposed space based weapons systems are not new but instead byproducts of the Cold War era thinking. Typically, these weapons fell into two types of categories: anti-satellite weapons (ASAT) and ground attack weapons (i.e. weapons that could deploy from space to hit a target on the earth's surface or flying through the earth's atmosphere).[21] The latter type of weapons, originally designed to attack Soviet ICBMs in flight or in their reinforced silos in the ground, would probably have the most direct relationship to the demands of the modern battlefield. Development of lasers as weapons began in the early 1960's and spurred tremendous interest in the

1980's as part of the Strategic Defense Initiative; the basic idea involved trying to destroy a satellite or missile in space with a laser beam fired from the ground. However, the US Air Force has been experimenting with an Airborne Laser System (ABL) as an interim measure in the development of a comprehensive Ballistic Missile Defense System in the 1990's. The ABL program called for a laser to be mounted in a Boeing 747 aircraft and for this laser to track and engage targets (in this case, ballistic missiles) while the 747 was in flight. Conceivably then, a Space Based Laser (SBL) could be placed on a platform in orbit and be able to strike targets on the earth's surface. Another proposed "directed energy weapon" would be a space based particle beam. Rather than using light as a vehicle to transfer energy to a target, a particle beam weapon would transfer energy by giving off a focused flow of accelerated electrons, much like a bolt of lightning. Related to the laser and particle beam, a Radio Frequency weapon (RF) would rely on a power source and large antenna to broadcast tremendous energy within certain bands of the electromagnetic spectrum in order to disrupt radio communications or destroy sensitive communications equipment over a given targeted area. A second general type of space-based weapons consists of kinetic energy weapons (KE). Originally conceived of as a potential ASAT, KE weapons consist of accelerating a projectile to hypervelocity speeds and destroying a target through the kinetic energy released upon collision. In theory, rods made of extremely resistant materials such as depleted uranium could be accelerated to great speeds in space and directed to strike targets on earth. These rods would be gradually worn away by friction upon reentry into the earth's atmosphere; however, enough of the projectile would strike the target with extreme force (and pressure on the lead end of the rod) so as to penetrate deep into the earth or into a hardened bunker. A final general type of space based weapon involves a vehicle stationed in space, but capable of reentering earth's atmosphere and flying as a conventional aircraft. Such a vehicle could be kept in orbit until needed; when deployed, the vehicle might function in similar fashion to the Predator UAVs operating in Afghanistan- conduct reconnaissance missions, keeping suspected enemy positions under constant surveillance and then engaging enemy target rapidly with conventional missiles when the opportunity arises.

2) The operational advantages of Space Based Weapons

The most readily apparent advantage of placing these systems in orbit is their global reach. With any of these types of weapons in orbit, the United States would have the ability to strike an enemy at any point on the globe without having to buildup a large conventional force or maneuver aircraft into range. Not only could these weapons quickly be in a position ready to fire, but also these weapons, launched from directly above a target, would not have to fly in the airspace of or operate from a third party nation, which might intervene politically to prevent such a strike. The "directed energy" weapons (lasers and particle beam weapons) have the further advantage of being able to strike targets almost instantaneously. Provided that American intelligence could quickly relay targeting information, commanders would be better able to strike an agile enemy moving to and from concealed locations. As with surveillance satellites, individual weapons platforms in geosynchronous orbit could only stay over a given target area for a limited amount of time before moving out of range. A constellation of these types of weapons though could provide some continuous coverage of a particular theater of operations. Considering the reliance of recent opponents on hardened bunkers and caves to provide protection and conceal, the kinetic energy type weapon would be ideal to penetrate these sanctuaries. Furthermore, RF type weapons would be ideal to isolate asymmetric opponents operating in small cells/groups. A RF weapon which could disrupt or destroy a cells' communications equipment would further exacerbate the problem of communicating with or coordinating the action of these units. Imagine isolated al Qaeda cells or small units of the Yugoslav Army completely cut off from each other and their higher echelons of control; these units would be rendered practically ineffective. Finally, given the current technological and financial disparity between the United States and its potential foes, the United States would regain or increase its ability to strike its foes without warning and with minimal exposure of its own forces. The US would be able to strike from even greater distances with virtual impunity and with no signs of a buildup of conventional forces. Once again, the psychological advantage would revert back to the Americans rather than to their opponents.

These space-based weapons could be operated within the limits of the law of war. To field such weapons requires that they have very precise guidance and fire control systems to ensure extremely accurate firing. In theory such weapons would be more precise than the "smart" bombs used in the Persian Gulf, Kosovo and Afghanistan; the highly accurate nature of these space weapons would make it even easier to destroy only the designated target and thereby further reduce the amount of unintended collateral damage. Unlike more "clumsy" conventional bombs that rely on a high explosive charge and/or metal fragments to destroy a target, most of these space weapons deliver massive amounts of energy directly to a target. Especially with directed energy type weapons, the amount of energy delivered could be altered to merely disable targets (in other words, to achieve a "soft" rather than "hard kill"). For example, a RF weapon could be used to damage communications or navigation equipment. As such, the proponent of these types of weapons can vary and control their level destructive force and potentially prevent unnecessary suffering. For example, space weapons could be used only to penetrate and expose a bunker; once the target has been "softened" up, the actual attack could be carried out by more conventional weapons such as aircraft or ground troops. Finally, with better surveillance and increased ability to gather intelligence, space weapons may make it easier to discriminate between legitimate targets and protected persons/places. A UAV deployed from space may be able to linger over a suspect area of a city or cave complex, observe the level of activity in that area and make it possible to determine if that activity is the benign or the work of terrorists preparing to launch an attack.

V. Part IV: The Weak Restraint of Space Law

Space based weapons appear to offer some promising solutions to the types of difficulties experienced in recent campaigns. In addition, these weapons arguably fall inside the limits of use prescribed by the law of war. The remaining question to be examined is whether the weapons are proscribed by the system of treaties and customary international law governing outer space.

A) The Limited Test Ban Treaty

Entering into force on October 10, 1963, the Limited Test Ban Treaty [22] was the first arms control treaty of the Cold War. In relevant part, Article I of the treaty bound each of the parties, " not to carry out any nuclear weapon test explosion, or any other nuclear explosion, at any place under its jurisdiction or control: (a)in the atmosphere, beyond its limits, including outer space . . ."[23] Article I goes even further to ban a nuclear explosion in any environment if the explosion causes radioactive debris to be outside the territorial limit of a state party. In light of the types of space based weapons described earlier, the terms of the Limited Test Ban Treaty would not have much of an impact; however, the treaty would prohibit a category of directed energy weapons that relied on a nuclear explosion for energy. For example, a weapon that could generate an electromagnetic pulse (via a nuclear explosion) and direct that pulse towards a target on earth would be banned under the terms of the treaty. Similarly, a laser that harnessed the energy from a nuclear explosion to direct a beam toward a target on earth would similarly be banned.

B) The Outer Space Treaty

The Outer Space Treaty[24], entering into force on October 10, 1967, is the seminal document of space law. Most relevant to this discussion, Article IV of the Outer Space Treaty prohibits state parties from placing nuclear weapons and "any other kind of weapons of mass destruction" in orbit. Article IV also states that the moon and other celestial bodies be used only for "peaceful purposes" and specifically bans all military bases, weapons testing and maneuvers from all celestial bodies. As mentioned previously, space based weapons functioning on a nuclear explosion principle would be banned. But would all types of these weapons be banned as "weapons of mass destruction?" The term "weapons of mass destruction" is never defined in the Outer Space Treaty. However, in 1948, the UN Commission for Conventional Armaments defined weapons of mass destruction as "atomic explosive weapons, radio active material weapons, lethal chemical and biological weapons, and any weapons developed in the future which have characteristics comparable in destructive effect . . ."[25] Under this definition, the aforementioned space based weapons would not qualify as weapons of mass destruction. These new weapons would engage in pinpoint, precision attacks against limited numbers of personnel, equipment or facilities; these weapons would not have the potential for unlimited, indiscriminate attacks producing the large scale of casualties and destruction cause by a nuclear weapon. What about the limitation of activities in space to those of "peaceful purposes?" Strictly speaking, the treaty only requires that the moon and other celestial bodies be used for peaceful purposes- saying nothing at all about activities on orbit. Even if this requirement were taken to encompass all activities in outer space, the ambiguous nature of the "peaceful purposes" language would defeat any attempt at a meaningful restriction. Looking to subsequent state practice as a guide for determining "peaceful purpose," the signatories of the International Space Station Agreement allowed each member supplying an element of the station "[to] determine whether a contemplated use of that element if for peaceful purposes."[26] As such, the state of the law is that the affected nations have simply agreed to let everyone abide by their own definition of peaceful purposes.

C) Other Treaties and Customary International Law

The Anti-Ballistic Missile Treaty[27], which entered into force on October 3, 1972, might have severely restricted the types of space based weapons the United States could decide to deploy. Article V of the ABM Treaty committed the US and the successor states to the old Soviet Union not to "develop, test or deploy ABM systems or components which are sea-based, land-based or space-based, or mobile land-based."[28] An ABM system under the treaty was a "system to counter strategic ballistic missiles or their elements in flight trajectory..."[29] Directed energy or kinetic energy weapons capable of striking a target on earth could in theory also be used to intercept ballistic missiles in flight. This prohibited dual use might have caused a significant legal barrier to the deployment of such weapons. However, on December 14, 2001, the United States announced its intentions to withdraw from the ABM treaty under the provisions of Article XV effective June 2002.[30]

Lastly, the self defense provisions found in the United Nations Charter and in customary international law would allow for the fielding of space based weapons. Article III of the Outer Space treaty binds state parties to follow international law, including the United Nations Charter, in all activities in space. While the Charter binds all member states to peacefully settle disputes (Article 2(3)) and to refrain from the threat or use of force (Article 2(4)), the Charter allows for broad exercise of the right of self-defense under Article 51.[31] Principles of customary international law go even further recognizing a right of anticipatory self-defense under which force could be used under threat of imminent attack.[32] Within this umbrella of self-defense measures, the United States could find plenty of latitude to field and operate space-based weapons.

VI. Conclusion: The Vanishing Preserve?

"*It came to him that a dream had dissolved, like all too lovely things, at the first touch of reality . . .*"[33] As the conflicts of the past decade demonstrate, the United States and its allies face a far different reality than that of the Cold War, a reality fraught with uncertain enemies and vastly different pressures, politically and militarily. If the technological sophistication were achievable, space-based weapons systems would offer an effective means of countering new types of enemies, employing unconventional, asymmetric tactics. Moreover, these weapons could be successfully deployed and utilized within the bounds of the law of war and the law of outer space. Will these types of space-based weapons be deployed? The answer is unclear. While these weapons may offer one solution, the United States may be able to achieve the same results through conventional land and air forces at a much lower price, politically and economically. The cost of developing the technology for such weapons and then placing them in orbit could be high. Should such a weapons program pass domestic political scrutiny, the United States would still have to wrangle with the disapproval of international allies and neighbors alike. Lastly, should these types of weapons be deployed and thus bring to an end the four decades of sanctuary in space? That question lies beyond the scope of this paper and must be taken up in a different venue.

---

[1] Georgetown University Law Center, JD (2000); Harvard University, AB (1997). The views and opinions expressed in this paper are solely those of the author and do not represent the official policy of the United States Government, any of its agencies, or the United States Army. No classified material was used or referenced in researching or writing this paper.

[2] James Hilton, LOST HORIZON 246 (1933).

[3] Steven Metz, *Strategic Asymmetry*, US Army Command and General Staff College (2001) <http://www-cgsc.army.mil/milrev/English/JulAug01/met.htm>.

[4] *See* Timothy L. Thomas, *Deciphering Asymmetry's Word Game*, US Army Command and General Staff College (2001) <http://www-cgsc.army.mil/milrev/English/JulAug01/thomas.htm> ("The United States may be the most asymmetric force on Earth, but Americans do not see themselves that way. They view others as an asymmetric force or threat when, in fact, they are not. US citizens should be proud to be on the right side of the asymmetric ledger.").

[5] Robert H. Scales, *et. al.*, CERTAIN VICTORY: THE US ARMY IN THE GULF WAR 116 (1994).

[6] Federation of American Scientists, *Operation Restore Hope*, <http://www.fas.org/man/dod-101/ops/restore_hope.htm>; Mark Bowden, BLACKHAWK DOWN 71 (2000).

[7] Federation of American Scientists, *Operation Allied Force*, <http://www.fas.org/man/dod-101/ops/allied_force.htm>.

[8] *Id.*

[9] *See generally* Barton Gellman and Thomas E. Ricks, *US Concludes Bin Laden Escaped at Tora Bora Fight,* WASHINGTON POST, April 17, 2002 at A01.

[10] *See e.g.* Mark Bowden, BLACKHAWK DOWN 111 (2000).

[11] *Id.*

[12] Federation of American Scientists, *Operation Continue Hope*, <http://www.fas.org/man/dod-101/ops/continue_hope.htm>.

[13] Mark Bowden, BLACKHAWK DOWN 125 (2000).

[14] *See generally* Bradley Graham, *Bravery and Breakdowns in a Ridgetop Battle,* WASHINGTON POST, May 24, 2002 at A01.

[15] DODD 5100.77, paragraph 5.3.1 (9 December 1998) <http://www.dtic.mil/whs/directives>.

[16] The Hague Conventions collectively regulate acceptable methods of conducting war while the Geneva Conventions spell out appropriate treatment for persons with special status. Both the Hague and the Geneva Conventions elaborate in greater detail

these general principles of the law of war. I did not go into treaty specifics because of limited space and the fact that such a discussion would carry me beyond the scope of this paper.

[17] For a good discussion of this, *see* Robert A. Ramsey, *Armed Conflict On The Final Frontier: The Law Of War In Space*, 48 AIR FORCE L. REV. 1, 34-44 (2000).

[18] Imagine a bombing strike that destroys a bridge but damages some nearby homes as well. That strike is arguably "proportional" if the loss of the bridge prevents a large enemy force from escaping across the river (i.e. advantage outweighs incidental damage). If the enemy escaped across the bridge hours earlier and the bombing achieves nothing, then the strike is likely not proportional.

[1919] *See* Interview of LTC Ralph Peters *in* Frontline *The Future of War* <http://www.pbs.org/wgbh/pages/frontline /shows/future/experts/taskforce.html>.

[20] *See* Paul A. Rahe, *Bureaucrats vs. Warriors*, National Review Online (October 29, 2001) < http://www. nationalreview.com /comment/ comment-rahe102901.shtml>.

[21] *See generally* Ramsey *supra* note 17, at 18-27. *See also* William L. Spacy II, *Does The United States Need Space-Based Weapons?* Ch. 2 CADRE Paper Air University (1999) <http://research.au.af.mil>.

[22] Treaty Banning Nuclear Weapon Tests in The Atmosphere, in Outer Space, and Underwater, Aug. 5, 1963, 14 U.S.T. 1313, 480 U.N.T.S. 43 (entered into force Oct. 10, 1963)[hereinafter Limited Test Ban Treaty].

[23] *Id.*

[24] Treaty on Principles Governing the Activities of States in the Exploration and Use of Outer Space Including the Moon and Other Celestial Bodies, Jan. 27, 1967, 18 U.S.T. 2410, 610 U.N.T.S. 205 (entered into force Oct. 10, 1967)[hereinafter Outer Space Treaty].

[25] Resolution of the Commission for Conventional Armaments, August 12, 1948 <http://www.yale.edu/lawweb/ avalon/decade/decad253.htm>.

[26] Agreement Among the Government of Canada, Governments of the Member States of the European Space Agency, the Government of Japan, the Government of the Russian Federation, and the Government of the United States of America Concerning Cooperation on the Civil International Space Station, Jan. 29, 1998, art. 9(3)(b) < http://www.nasda.go.jp/lib/space-law/chapter_4/4-2-2-16/4-2-2-169_e.html>.

[27] Treaty on the Limitation of Anti-Ballistic Missile Systems, May 26, 1972, U.S.- U.S.S.R., 23 U.S.T. 3435 (entered into force Oct. 3, 1972) [hereinafter ABM Treaty].

[28] *Id* at art.V(1).

[29] *Id* at art II(1).

[30] US Dept. of State, Diplomatic Note Sent to Russia, Belarus, Kazakhstan, and the Ukraine, December 13, 2001 < http://www.defenselink.mil/acq/acic/treaties/abm/ABMdipnotes1.htm>.

[31] U.N. CHARTER (entered into force Oct. 24, 1945).

[32] *See* discussion of the *Caroline* case. < http://www.yale.edu/lawweb/avalon/diplomacy/britian/br-1842d.htm >(In a series of letters to Lord Ashburton, Secretary of State Daniel Webster lays out the requirements for anticipatory self defense. "It will be for that Government to show a necessity of self-defense, instant, overwhelming, leaving no choice of means, and no moment for deliberation.").

[33] James Hilton, LOST HORIZON 244 (1933).

IAC-02-IISL.3.13

Militarization of Space

María de las Mercedes Esquivel de Cocca*
University of Buenos Aires (Argentina)
mesquivel@2vias.com.ar
mesquivelmerciel@hotmail.com

Abstract

We can see, with pain and sorrow, how there are war, hostilities and violence, in all continents. Space has become an active factor in these events by offering best quality information to our TV sets and showing critical targets to the nations in a dispute. I shall analyze if this last application and any other hostile function of space technology, trespasses what is established in art. IV of the Outer Space Treaty and other similar legal provisions.

Space technology has showed itself as an efficient and hardly comparable means for war, it has also performed as a perfect instrument for education, information, communication, environment protection, and art, as well.

I shall develop the meaning of utilizing space with exclusive peaceful purposes, and which is the real sense of peace. Information provided by satellite applied to war, may also infringe other express space legal provisions, i.e., harm to Earth environment via massive attacks, nuclear contamination or biological effects of an attack to a space predefined target. I shall also compare what some national laws establish on this matter, as well as the attitude of space nations towards the *corpus juris spatialis* provisions.

The development of the principle of international cooperation in the last years, in order to give support to international peace and security, shall be also studied.

Finally, there is a need of establishing namely what can and what cannot be done in the field of space applications in case they can be deviated in order to achieve hostile aims. This regulation must be made by expressing clearly the principle and avoiding any enumeration of activities that could be unfaithfully understood, as it happened with art. IV of the Outer Space Treaty.

Peace

It has been said that *there is no way to peace, peace is the way.* I believe that peace is not a state of things but a feeling born from peoples heart, when order and justice offer an adequate frame to develop men life. It cannot be imposed, for it rises spontaneously when all conditions are given and when man feels that there is no risk in opening arms for embracing instead of closing wrists to fight against others or defend themselves. For this, truthfulness and confidence are necessary.

To achieve peace, it is also necessary to have it as an aim in an immovable propose. Therefore, in accordance to the principle of coherence, one must put all required means in order to reach the goal in mind, or, in better words, in heart.

Moral conditions for Peace: justice, order, thorough will and con-

---

* IAA Correspondent Member and IISL Member,

vincement, constancy, patience, and courage.

There cannot be peace without order and justice. Chaos and injustice bring discomfort and violent feelings in the people. In many countries we can see people claiming or even fighting for a new order of peace and justice, unable to propose alternative ways, they just stay trying to put away what they feel like undeserved. Many reasons could explain this worldwide phenomenon, but is clear that it would be impossible in a climate of justice and order.

To achieve a world in peace, in our times, is a hard task upon each of us as a society. There is a social responsibility in order to put all means towards peace. A special role has been assigned to scientists and technicians, who's knowledge, efforts and experience may change the present state of things.

I have said that peace is a feeling and a goal. As a feeling, is born spontaneously in men's heart, but as a goal, it is a matter of will. The strength of the convincement in the need of peace, will measure the possibilities to achieve it. Peace as a moral, value must be accompanied by other as constancy, patience and courage.

Constancy is an indispensable requisite for it is difficult to change a culture of hostility and domination. It may rise from the conviction in the need to pursue peace as an aim. If not, the most developed part of society: educators, thinkers, artists, scientists, technicians, must preserve it and make possible, from their own role, this cultural evolution. Modern politicians are not able to collaborate in this function because they only search the closest convenience, losing the further scope of the path of peace.

In disarmament documents we often see references to tolerance, and I think this is wrong. Peace does not need tolerance, it requires patience. Tolerance means temporary acceptance of what is believed as wrong, in the idea that no change is possible. We tolerate a bad singer, a smoker, a dirty person, someone ugly, because we know that this disagreeable situation will pass, and we shall be rid of it. By other hand, patience means that we assume that what we do not like may be changed, and that time, the right words, or both, are needed to make the difference, and we are in the position to wait until such a change happens.[1]

Other word easily founded in international instruments is *deterrence*. Another name for cold war, directed to prevent any hostile initiative under the pressure of retaliation. It is far from the path of peace, and near to submission and fear. Moreover, the risk of an error puts the whole world in hazard.

Peace is a worthy goal, it deserves all sacrifices, it requires courage, moral fiber and the decision to face any risk to defend it. Mahatma Gandhi was a true example of what I am saying, he was a man, only a man, but nothing less than a man. He would never rise his hand against a fellow whom he considered essentially equal, in spite of differences. He practiced along his life the basic principle of respectfulness to everything and everybody. Unfortunately our so called civilization could not learn the lesson that took his life. There were other testimonies of fidelity to this principle along history, but I prefer to recall Gandhi because he was an example free of other connotations.

Peaceful purposes

To utilize space for peaceful purposes means to put all means to lead nations to peace. Therefore any action or plan including war or hostile utilization of space, celestial bodies and/or their resources, infringes this principle and must be banned. Article IV of the 1967 Outer Space Treaty (OST), has been interpreted as if the enumeration of banned activities and weapons, is a provision that may be infringed. State parties to the Treaty make public their programs to use satellites for targeting and surveillance of military positions in order to attack or retaliate or defense by revenge. Is this coherent to the principle of utilizing space exclusively for peaceful purposes and in the benefit of all nations? I think it is a sophist way of reading the law and a rough manner to feel it. International relations in these late years is ruled by a legal framework that everybody supports, and simultaneously think, how it could be violated. And we, lawyers and jurists observe them without any question, keeping a coward silence. The role of jurist is to guide society not to lose its values, and, except a few testimonies, we are not accomplishing our duty.

The deployment of weapons in space, will not be regarded as peaceful use of space, irrespective of the public announcements and rationalizations to the contrary, affirmed Sterns and Tennen. They added that the principle that space should be utilized for peaceful purposes has not diminished its utility in the present global climate. The militarization of space would not solve the problem of the balance of terror, and they conclude expressing that the deployment of space weapons systems must occur prior to a complete identification of the ramifications that would result from such activities. [2]

Thus space is "militarized" though not yet "weaponized." In both war and peace, satellites vitally aid our military in inflicting and avoiding damage without being under threat themselves. But no person could say that this militarization observes the simple and clear principle of peaceful purposes. No one with a gun in hands may affirm is moved by a peaceful feeling, if a person has a weapon, whatever the proclaimed purposes are, he/she is decided to use it against another for the reason he/she thinks is useful. Therefore, violence an aggression are previewed and accepted.

Principle of International co-operation

This is an essential principle of Space Law closely linked with the principle of peaceful utilization and to the common heritage of mankind. If space activities are performed in a common space, using common resources, in the benefit of all nations, and with peaceful purposes, it is a logical consequence that they must be developed under the principle of international cooperation. That is why Manuel Augusto Ferrer says that this is a *sine qua non* requisite for a legal space activity.

The thorough meaning of international cooperation, implies two or more active agents. It is co-operating, rather than an agent and a passive subject that allows or consent the action of the first one.

It is hard to put this principle in practice when the parties involved belong to very different stages of development, for this it is necessary to implement a very detailed program and instrument it gradually. When the case is of countries in not too different stages of development, we have to take into account the diagonal cooperation, easier to assume but also needing careful programming.

What happens if this principle is not observed? If a space faring State wants to accomplish the other space principles, as well, it faces the unjust situation of sharing its benefits with those who nothing afforded to the space activity. This is illegitimate and means an illicit enrichment of the passive part in the matter. Other possibility is protecting those who can do less, infringing their condition of equals and submitting them to accept what the "producer" feels as an obligation of generosity, and in the amount considered as enough by the giver.

Those who share efforts, can legal, and ethically, share profits with no danger to spoil their relationship.

In order to evaluate long range results of competence lacking cooperation, Prof. Christol analyzed: "There is a manifest need for the superpowers to modify their policies of competing against each other in outer space arms race in the hope of obtaining what could only be a transitory and fleeting advantage. Such competitive policies do not produce lasting security. They actually harm projects of strategic stability." [3]

We must consider that at the present, mankind shares common problems, a world that, in fact, has no borders, a common outer space with common celestial bodies and resources. It should be a logical consequence easily accepted that peace and international cooperation are not only legal principles to be observed, but also a means for surviving. Since mankind is a subject of international Law, there is a common bond among its members, they belong to the same gender, they should be moved by their human condition, and spontaneously feel links of solidarity among each other, in other words, what we call *affectio humanitatis* should ground space activities.

Present state of violence in space

Today, U.S. intelligence agencies and the military count on some 100 satellites as part of the country's national security. These space-based assets snap detailed images day and night, keeping an eye on global hotspots, even pinpointing missile launchings around the globe for early warning purposes. A satellite that in peacetime uses the global positioning system (GPS) constellation of spacecraft for navigation purposes, may in wartime utilize that same capability to target bombs or remotely piloted vehicles.[4]

Unless appropriate constraints are put on testing of ASATs, there could be a problem. High-speed run-ins with space debris resulting from any ASAT testing could cripple or destroy numbers of satellites in Earth orbit. Sally Reide recalled an encounter with space debris in her first voyage on the space shuttle: "A small but visible gouge in one of the space plane's window appeared about halfway through the flight. Later analysis showed that an orbiting fleck of paint caused the pit", she said. "A fleck of paint is not the same as a small piece of metal traveling at that same speed. So, as soon as you start increasing the amount of junk in low-Earth orbit, you have an unintended byproduct that starts putting some of your own quite valuable satellites at possible risk". [5]

There are many studies reporting the present and near future advancement of weaponization of space, these are two, technical and extended, to be recalled here, but the mere allusion of LEO and MEO satellites that could be used for war purposes deserves a mention. It is this LEO region, closest to Earth, which will be most vulnerable in the near future to earth-based ASATs, "Anti-Satellite" weapons (missiles, lasers, particle beams, etc.), currently under development by several states. For example, the American MIRACL laser has damaged orbiting satellites, as have Russian lasers. The mid-course missile interceptor currently being developed for the U.S. NMD program will be able to target satellites up to altitudes of at least 1200 kilometers. There are many countries possessing IRBMs, missiles having ranges of 3500 km or more; they will be able to reach up to all satellites in LEO. Iraq's al Hussein, a modified Scud-B, could climb to 300 km, enabling it to reach Russia's Cosmos 2370, a military satellite imaging Chehnya. The technical prowess required for great accuracy would not be necessary to harm the targeted satellite: a simple nuclear explosion, or the dispersal of a cloud of pebbles, would suffice to damage all satellites in a large region of LEO for an extended period of time. There is also research underway in the U.S on space-based ASATs – both missiles (e.g., "Brilliant Pebbles" – orbiting, self-guided, self-propelled) and lasers (SBL). There are some 40 to 50 satellites in MEO, "Middle Earth Orbits", orbiting at altitudes between 1000 and 35786 kilometers above the surface of the earth. Presently in this region are science satellites (e.g., the U.S. Chandra and GGS Polar, Japan's Halca and Nozomi, Europe's XMM), and navigation satellites (used for personal, commercial, and military transportation as well as for military targeting). The U.S. military/civilian NAVSTAR Global Positioning System embodies 29 of these satellites whereas the Russian Cosmos, Glonass, and Parus series totals 19 navigation satellites; some of these are non-operating spares. Also in this region are some Russian early warning satellites (Cosmos 2361 and the Oko sat). Most of these MEO satellites are in highly elliptical orbits, dipping into the LEO region during part of their travels. During these close approaches to earth, they would have the same vulnerability as do the LEO satellites. Finally, there are about 300 satellites in GEO, "Geostationary Earth Orbits". These circulate easterly, precisely 35786 kilometers above the Equator with a period of 24 hours; hence they remain stationary with respect to any given position on the surface of the earth. At least 29 of these belong to the U.S. military. Other militaries owning satellites in this region are Australia, Russia, and Britain. These stationary satellites serve for communications, relay, earth observation, search and rescue, weather, and research. There are also constantly staring "early-warning-satellites" (such as the U.S. DSP, and the planned SBIRS High, and the Russian Prognos), designed to detect (and initially track) ballistic missile launchings via the intense infrared emitted by their rocket engines. Some examples of U.S. commercial systems in this region are: DIRECTV, Inc. selling direct-to-home TV broadcasting; Echostar, offering business services; GE American Communications, providing broadcasting, telecommunications, cable programming, business services, direct-to-home TV broadcasting, internet access. Intelsat, Lockheed Martin Global Telecommunications, Loral Skynet, Motient Corp., PanAmSat Corp., and WorldSpace Corp sell similar services. Non-American firms selling such services are based in Japan, Germany, Brazil, France, Spain, UK, Korea, Philippines, Argentina, Netherlands, Indonesia, China, Luxembourg, Israel, Norway, Canada, and Turkey. For the foreseeable future, the only threats to such "far-out" satellites would come either from other such satellites (firing lasers or missiles such as "Brilliant Pebbles") or from the rockets capable of launching such satellites from ground to GEO (releasing conventional or nuclear space mines or gravel clouds). At present only China, France, India, Japan, Russia, Ukraine, and the U.S. possess such rocketry. The author adds that with the possibility of an active use of space weapons, we would be returned to the terror of the

Cold War – without its stabilizing contribution of certain knowledge of the opponent's pre-attack actions. The alternative is *passive* defense of space assets together with a treaty guaranteeing a space sanctuary (equal to no weaponization of space). Though an overwhelming majority of nations in the UN (including all of the technologically adept ones, except the U.S.) have expressed support for a treaty Preventing an Arms Race in Outer Space (PAROS), such a treaty by itself would not be sufficient. There would always be fear of surreptitious weaponization of space by the opponent. (Verification would be difficult; it's hard to determine whether what's inside another's satellite is a forbidden weapon.) Passive defense of satellites would include miniaturization, redundancy, quick re-launch capability, shielding, coding and localization of communications links, and the development of alternative means to achieve current space tasks (e.g., high-altitude drone aircraft for communication and observation). Such an approach would also be expensive – but it would further, not hinder, the development of space industry. It would also further, not hinder, international stability.[6]

Effects of violence in space

The policy question going forward, Sally Ride states, might be simplistically stated as: Does it make sense for the U.S. to place weapons into space? One issue in this regard, she said, is developing and placing in space anti-satellite weapons, or ASATs for short. Unless appropriate constraints are put on testing of ASATs, there could be a problem. High-speed run-ins with space debris resulting from any ASAT testing could cripple or destroy numbers of satellites in Earth orbit. She recalled an encounter with space debris on her first space shuttle voyage. A small but visible gouge in one of the space plane's window appeared about halfway through the flight. Later analysis showed that an orbiting fleck of paint caused the pit, she said: "A fleck of paint is not the same as a small piece of metal traveling at that same speed. So, as soon as you start increasing the amount of junk in low-Earth orbit, you have an unintended byproduct that starts putting some of your own quite valuable satellites at possible risk"[7]

The issue in local legislations

One American lawmaker is already drafting legislation before the U.S. Congress that bans the weaponization of space. Congressman Dennis Kucinich, introduced early this year The Space Preservation Act of 2002. The bill is crafted "to preserve the cooperative, peaceful uses of space for the benefit of all humankind by prohibiting the basing of weapons in space and the use of weapons to destroy or damage objects in space that are in orbit, and for other purposes." The terms "space-based weapon" and "space-based system" mean a device capable of damaging or destroying an object or person — whether in outer space, in atmosphere, or on Earth — by (A) firing one or more projectiles to collide with that object or person; (B) detonating one or more explosive devices in close proximity to that object or person; (C) directing a source of energy against that object or person; or (D) any other undeveloped means.[8]

This draft legislation also calls for an international treaty to preserve space and prevent an arms race in outer space.[9]

The Outer Space Law of the Russian Federation states, in its art. 4, parag. 2, as follows:

"In order to ensure strategic and ecological security it is **<u>prohibited</u>** in Russian Federation:

- to put into the orbit around the Earth or to deploy in outer space otherwise nuclear weapons and any other kinds of weapons of mass destruction;
- to test nuclear weapons and any other kinds of weapons of mass destruction in outer space;
- to use space objects and other space technology as a tool to influence the environment for military and **other hostile purposes**;
- to use the Moon and other celestial bodies for military purposes;
- to create deliberate immediate **threat** to safety of space activity, including safety of space objects;
- to create harmful contamination of outer space which leads to unfavorable changes of the environment, including deliberate elimination of space objects in outer space.

Other space activity under the jurisdiction of Russian Federation, which is prohibited by international treaties of Russian Federation, is not allowed as well."

As we can see it encompasses art. IV of the 1967 Outer Space Treaty and adds some specifications in order to ban activities that might be understood as hostile or potentially hostile.

By other side, we find art 7, in which it opens the door for militarization of space upon de Defense Ministry's decision:

"1. Space activity for purposes of defense and security of Russian Federation shall be pursued by the Ministry of Defense of Russian Federation which shall be responsible for the implementation of the long-term program and annual plans of works **to create and use military space technology** in conjunction with other ministries and departments of Russian Federation.

2. The Ministry of Defense of Russian Federation shall within its competence:

- elaborate draft program and annual plans of works to **create and use military space technology** and, in conjunction with the Russian Space Agency of space technology applied for both scientific and national-economy purposes and for the purposes of defense and security of Russian Federation;
- form and place the state order for works to **create and use military space technology** and, in conjunction with the Russian Space Agency space technology applied both for scientific and national-economy purposes and for **purposes of defense and security** of Russian Federation;
- use space technology for purposes of defense and security of Russian Federation; ...

4. The Ministry of Defense of Russian Federation shall have the right to **temporarily** transfer idle objects of space infrastructure under its jurisdiction to the Russian Space Agency on a contractual basis to be used for space activity for scientific and national-economy purposes."

Art. 13 of this law refers to resources to support the space program, it is interesting to quote the following part:

"...3. The resources of the Russian Space Fund shall be directed towards financing the Federal Space Program of Russia ... for works to create and use space technology, towards supporting space projects **involving innovation and military conversion**, as well as towards projects to use of the results of space activity, among others, for promoting science, education and culture.

A technical initiative towards peace in space

There is a paper that tries to evaluate present state of space militarization and suggests some measures to prevent and eliminate it in the following way:

- ✓ an immediate test ban on ballistic missiles and missiles intended for use in antiballistic missile systems, and a commitment to the complete elimination of these weapons;
- ✓ a formal negotiating machinery for realizing commitments on missile control and disarmament through a series of phased, inter-linked, overlapping stages, each involving ballistic missile reductions and limits on ranges;
- ✓ a pledge not to test and deploy space weapons as a first step to an internationally agreed space weapons ban and the demilitarization of space;
- ✓ the creation of an international monitoring and inspection system to prevent the development, testing and deployment of ballistic missiles and space weapons;
- ✓ a regular public review, reporting, and implementation assessment procedure involving all the parties to the agreement. The essential precondition at this stage would be agreement on the goals and agreement on a negotiating process to move towards them.[10]

As a means to achieve a final banning of space arms race, the authors recommend, as a first step, an agreement freezing space weapons and afterwards the global convention. The agreement would result in a series of phased stages, each being a step towards the ultimate goal. As a reflection of the seriousness of the issue, agreement would be needed at the outset on a moratorium on the further development, testing and deployment of ballistic missiles and antimissile systems. Such a "missile threat freeze" would be like earlier nuclear test ban moratoria that created time and a climate conductive for negotiations. Although not a substitute for a more comprehensive Outer Space Treaty, which would unambiguously prohibit the emplacement of weapons and weapons delivery platforms in space, a launch control regime that included inspections would help reveal efforts by any nation to place weapons in space. A ban on test flights of ballistic missiles could also have an immediate positive impact on the most volatile areas of emerging international arms competition, especially in South Asia, the Middle East and Northeast Asia. Given current political circumstances, an international monitoring and inspection system will be necessary to build trust in the missile control and disarmament regime. Various technical and non-technical means of verification exist to focus on observable rocket characteristics that provide indications of rocket type and performance. The efficiency of verification depends on the stage in the missile life-cycle that is to be controlled.[11]

Argentine doctrine of peace, cooperation, solidarity and mankind

Old Romans thought that if peace is wanted, it is necessary to be ready for war –*si vis pacem, para bellum*– so did our present leaders when they created first cold war, and afterwards followed an arms race that has put humankind in a position of an assured mutual destruction upon governments' decision. Who can have any doubt about the immorality of this scheme, there is no peace born from such a situation, there is fear to begin hostilities because destruction, and suffer for both in the dispute, is assured. The problem with the present state of armamentism is that same pain is sure for those alien to the conflict. It is a mad dance of threat and risk. The possibility of human error adds more hazard to this fact. Cocca always answers to the Latin proposition: ***si vis pacem, para pacem***, if you want peace, prepare for peace. Since peace is difficult to be foreseen at the present, we must prepare for it. This preparation must encompass a cultural evolution towards the conviction of the need of peace based on the necessity of surviving of our common gender.

The last three tables of the Declaration on the Rights of Mankind refer to the principle we are talking about today: peace, solidarity and conscience of race unity:

Table X: Peace

1. Peace is a primordial principle to preserve civilization and its progress, in thus, a vital interest to mankind.
2. Since peace is grounded on a moral order the peoples will begin replacing the force of arms by the value of peace. War will lose its sense when moral and legal order prevail over any other fictitious order. It is an order based on the consensus of men and peoples for the achievements of the ends common to mankind.
3. Peace is the harmonious coexistence of men grounded on concord and founded upon legal and moral order. It presupposes respect for differences, cultural and social integration resulting from cooperation and a fluent communication. It is only possible when spontaneously desired and its necessity acknowledge by the common feeling of men and peoples.
4. Mankind favors anything that brings its peoples together, rejecting what draws them apart and setting aside the persistence in error in the route paved by the legal concept of mankind, which was adopted by acclamation by the United Nations Assembly in 1966 and incorporated as fundamental principle in the 1967 Space Treaty, of universal force today.

Table XI: Solidarity and Integrity

1. Solidarity is today a universal social duty as well as a need arising from interdependence of peoples and the factual elimination of frontiers originated by the new communications technology. Facts bearing isolated consequences exist no longer. This imposes the duty of international cooperation in all activities, particularly in the field of science and technology, for the better achievement of the common welfare in the framework of integration consolidating, in practice, the legal concept of mankind. Solidarity bonds among the peoples assure the equal dignity and they strengthen in reciprocal cooperation.
2. Violence in any of its forms, has a universal impact and social consequences which always imply a damage to human dignity. Relation based on ethics, law and respect for the human condition must be assured by means of a constant education at all levels.
3. The use of any kind of weapons of mass destruction, of a chemical or bacteriological nature, asphyxiating, toxin or similar gases is a crime of lese humanity, irrespective of the scenario where it is used or the number of victims it produces.

4. Mankind has a right to its own integration, and thus, to itself protection from any kind of crime of lese humanity including genocide and gynacide.

Table XII: Conscience of race unity

The human race is one and only. Men constitute a totum which is different from each of their individualities. Unity is strengthen through the common feeling of being necessary elements, in the conscience of the unity of the human race evidenced in the *affectio humanitatis.* [12]

Peace is possible and needs a firm will to achieve it. War, hostilities and all the forms of violence mean to take justice by own hands. If we have to accept war as a legitimate instrument for States, why do we not accept homicide among individuals for revenge or honor reasons? If States take another's goods because they want or need them, why do we not accept a thief? If States do not give good example of what they want to be observed by their citizens, we are faced to a legal paradox .

Conclusions

A. Militarization of space infringes art. IV of the 1967 Outer Space Treaty.

B. Cultural and scientific living forces should undertake the task of seeking peace from their individual position in society, without waiting nor asking support from governments or other political institutions.

C. Peace is a universal need , as well as a social and individual duty. The social responsibility of individuals must be recognized in order to achieve peace.

D. No interest, fear, risk, convenience or otherwise, must allow any person, government, international organizations or else, to infringe legal principles approved and in force.

E. International relations must be based in good faith and any misbehavior in this sense, must be universally condemned.

F. A treaty stopping militarization of space must be agreed.

G. There is no time for doubts, we are very near and capable for self destruction. An attitude of violence denies our condition of good and loyal beings, and our intellectual nature.

Footnotes

[1] M. de las V. Cocca y Esquivel, personal conversation, 14 September 2002.

[2] P..M. Sterns and L.I. Tennen, ***The militarization of outer space: serving peace or provoking crisis***, Proceedings of the 27th International Colloquium on the Law of Outer Space, Lausanne, pub. AIAA,1984, p. 134-145.

[3] C.Q. Christol, Competition to militariza space should be transferred to cooperation to improve the quality of life, Proceedings of the 29th International Colloquium on the Law of Outer Space, Innsbruck, pub. AIAA, 1986, p 11-16.

[4] L. David, ***Space weapons for Earth wars***, Space.com. 15 May 2002, quoting the words of Sally Reide.

[5] L. David. Op cit. loc. Cit.

[6] A. M. Saperstein, ***"Weaponization" Vs. "Militarization" Of Space***.

[7] L. David. Op cit. loc. Cit

[8] L. David. Op cit. loc. Cit

[9] L. David. Op cit. loc. Cit

[10] A. Lichterman, Z. Mian, M. V. Ramana, J. Scheffran, Western States Legal Foundation, ***Beyond Missile Defense,*** Briefing Paper, Prepared for the Non-Proliferation Treaty, Preparatory Committee, Meeting 2002, New York. Sponsored by Nuclear Age Peace Foundation and Abolition 2000,

[11] A. Lichterman, Z. Mian, M. V. Ramana, J. Scheffran, op. cit. loc. Cit.

[12] ***The Buenos Aires Declaration on the XII of the Rights of mankind***, X Congress of the Argentine Association of International Law, Desarrollo Progresivo del Derecho Internacional, aportaciones de organizaciones, tribunales y parlamentos Internacionales, Consejo de Estudios Internacionales Avanzados, Buenos Aires 1991, p. 299.

OPERATIONAL CAPABILITIES AND LEGAL IMPLICATIONS OF A MILITARY SPACE PLANE

A.C. Charania*
SpaceWorks Engineering, Inc. (SEI)
Atlanta, GA U.S.A.
www.sei.aero

ABSTRACT

The potential challenges for the United States military in this upcoming century may require new types of capabilities only achievable through the application of new technologies. One of these potential capabilities includes a Military Space Plane (MSP). An MSP is a concept to use reusable launch vehicle (RLV) technologies in a system to provide the military global access and reach in a timely fashion that could be operational within a decade. New awareness is evident from both recent federal commission reports and activities in Afghanistan of the military's possible need of such capabilities to provide asymmetric advantages. The MSP may eventually become part of a new spaceforce that coordinates the broad range of defensive and offensive space assets. In addition, a new emphasis is being placed upon NASA and the U.S. Air Force to coordinate activity on such a space plane/RLV development. The interaction of civilian and defense agencies for such a program has ramifications, not just in terms of the requirements on a final operational vehicle, but also on the legal charters of both entities. This examination presents operational scenarios for a military space plane in order to derive various legal implications.

NOMENCLATURE

ABM	Anti Ballistic Missile
ASAT	Anti-Satellite
CAV	Common Aero Vehicle
CONOPS	Concept of Operations
CONUS	Continental United States
DoD	Department of Defense
GATT	General Agreement on Trade and Tariffs
GEO	Geostationary Orbit
ISR	Information, Sensors, and Reconnaissance
ISS	International Space Station
KKV	Kinetic Kill Vehicle
LEO	Low Earth Orbit
MSP	Military Space Plane
NASA	National Aeronautics and Space Administration
NMD	National Mission Defense
OTV	Orbital Transfer Vehicle
RBCC	Rocket Based Combined Cycle
RLV	Reusable Launch Vehicle
SLI	Space Launch Initiative
SOV	Space Operations Vehicle
SMV	Space Maneuver Vehicle
TAT	Turnaround Time
TSTO	Two Stage To Orbit
UAV	Unmanned Aerial Vehicle
UCAV	Uninhabited Combat Aerial Vehicle
USAF	United States Air Force
WMD	Weapons of Mass Destruction
WTO	World Trade Organization

*- *Senior Futurist, Member AIAA.*

INTRODUCTION

Over the last decades outer space has gained an amplified importance given the increased interconnectivity of societies through telecommunications. The ever increasing ratio of commercial space launches to government-sponsored space launches is an indication of the importance of outer space as both a corridor of transport and location of resources.

ratio of civilian to military outer space launches was nominally at 5:4 relationship[12]. However, offensive and defensive capacities have not yet emerged. The weaponization of space does not yet exist. However, societies are at a nexus where the motive for such weaponization can be satisfied by the capabilities enabled by new technologies.

Any such MSP will have dual-use capability to service civil and commercial space launch markets. A new MSP will assist in general RLV technology development and operational experience. Technological investment for such a system will be synergistic with those required for commercial RLV development. Investment from the government on a MSP offsets some portion of the commercial risk associated with new RLV ventures. These complicate matters of limiting government offsets to private industry in light of international agreements such as the World Trade Organization (WTO).

This examination attempts to provide some clarity as to what is meant by the most recent incarnation of the U.S. Air Force's military space plane. A review of both concepts and missions is given. From these operational capabilities more insight can be obtained as to any legal implications of the system.

MSP CONCEPT OVERVIEW

A Military Space Plane (MSP) is in essence an atmospheric/space delivery architecture that can consist of multiple stages to deliver payloads into space and onto the surface of earth. The MSP is a delivery mechanism to enable space transportation. A MSP is a version of a reusable launch vehicle (RLV) that has specific abilities required for military users.

Heritage

The United States military, and specifically the United States Air Force (USAF), has a history of programs to investigate technologies and concepts for MSPs. Some of the earliest research involved the Aerospaceplane program and X-planes, which gave the military experience into supersonic flight conditions. Such vehicles included the X-1, Douglas D-558-I, X-15, X-23, and X-24. Subsequent Air Force design efforts included the mid 1950s Bomber Missile (BoMi), the Hypersonic Weapons and Research Development Supporting Program (HYWARDS), the early 1960s Boeing X-20 Dyna-Soar, and the Ballistic Missile Defense Organization's DC-X[13]. The U.S. Air Force was also involved in planning, requirements formulation, and obtaining congressional support for the development of NASA's Space Shuttle.

Recent activity by the United States includes the NASA's X-33, X-34, X-37, and X-40A/B programs. The Air Force Research Laboratory's Military Spaceplane System Technology Office at Kirtland Air Force Base, New Mexico, directs the Space Maneuver Vehicle (SMV) program. Current development programs focus on both short term and long term MSP architectures. The shorter-term programs entail using conventional rocket engines. Long-term technology programs such as the X-43 series of Rocket-Based-Combined Cycle (RBCC) propulsion test beds are designed for operational use at least two decades from today.

MSP Architecture Elements

Current perceptions of the first MSP entail development and Initial Operating Capability (IOC) sometime in the 2010-2015 timeframe. This imagined MSP consists of multiple elements coupled together to provide the war fighter with a flexibility of response. The core component of the architecture is a reusable first stage vehicle known as the Space Operations Vehicle (SOV). The SOV will have the capability of carrying multiple payloads with turnaround times (TATs) measured in hours instead of the current months for the U.S. Space Shuttle. U.S. military scenarios entail building up both a useful demonstrator and full-scale version of the MSP. Concepts within a 5-15 year time horizon most likely will entail some type of Two-Stage-To-Orbit (TSTO) system[10].

Figure 1. Notional Military Space Plane (MSP)

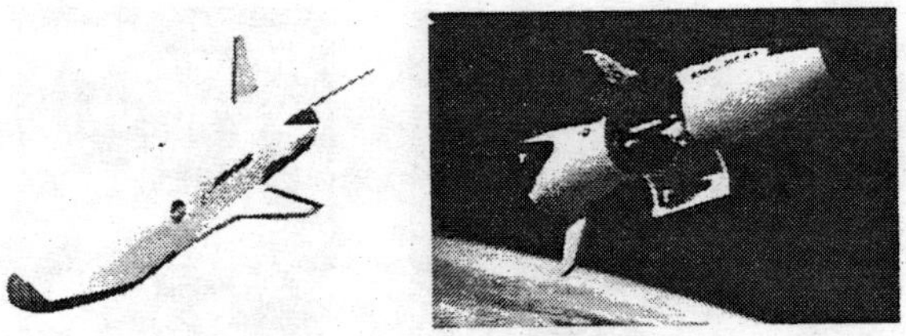

Figure 2. Space Maneuver Vehicle (SMV)

The second stage would consist either of reusable or expendable stages. Reusable stages are referred to as Space Maneuver Vehicles (SMVs). The SMV could itself hold a third/upper stage to carry payloads to higher orbits. Expendable stages are referred to as a Modular Insertion Stage (MIS) that can transport payloads to different orbits. Additional add-on components to the architecture include the Common Aero Vehicle (CAV) that consists of a maneuvering reentry vehicle and an Orbital Transfer Vehicle (OTV) that can move payloads from one orbit to another.

Nominally, the MSP shall be capable of the following[14]:

a. The SOV shall be capable of supporting space control, force application, force enhancement, and force support missions by providing low cost, high ops tempo launches of SMV, CAV, and MIS payloads to mission orbits or trajectories.
b. Orbit-capable and sub-orbital SOVs shall be capable of executing sub-orbital, pop-up profiles that allow safe launch and recovery from U.S. bases.
c. The MSP System shall be capable of autonomous, virtually commanded, or crewed operations depending on future requirements evolution.
d. The MSP System shall provide aircraft-like levels of operability and maintainability to allow high sortie rates.
e. Orbit-capable SOVs shall be capable of supporting once around missions while returning to their launch site.

Table 1 lists sample requirements for a sub-orbital type SOV MSP that can carry a SMV. The sorties requirements are some of the most critical since current turn times for the Space Shuttle are on the order of months.

Table 1. Sample Requirements Matrix for Space Operations Vehicles (Sub-Orbital)[4]

Requirement	Range
Sortie Utilization Rates	
Emergency surge	3-4 sorties/24 hrs.
Turn Times	
Emergency surge	2-8 hours
System Availability	
Mission Capable Rate	75-95 percent
Cross Range	
CONUS pop-up cross range @1200nm	250-400 nm
Mission Duration	
On-orbit time	24–72 hours
Alert Hold	
Hold Mission Capable	15 days
Design Life	
Primary Structure	250-500 sorties
Engine life	100-250 sorties
External Payload Weight	
Carriage Capacity	15,000-20,000 lb
Payload Capability	
Pop-up MIS payload east	2,000 –4,000 lb
Pop-up MIS payload polar	1,000 – 4,000 lb
Maintenance and Support	
Maintenance man hours/sorties	50-100 hours

Notional concepts of the MSP include a phased development cycle wherein a sub-orbital capable MSP could lead to development of an initial capability[11] (see Figures 4 and 5). The sub-orbital architecture assists in technology risk reduction and would be used in an operational mode, not relegated solely to testing. The larger orbital MSP to be built later would enable the use of an OTV. The follow-on orbital vehicle would have a higher cross range capability, pop-up range, and payload capability (15,000-20,000 lbs due east) than the sub-orbital version (2,000 lb due east).

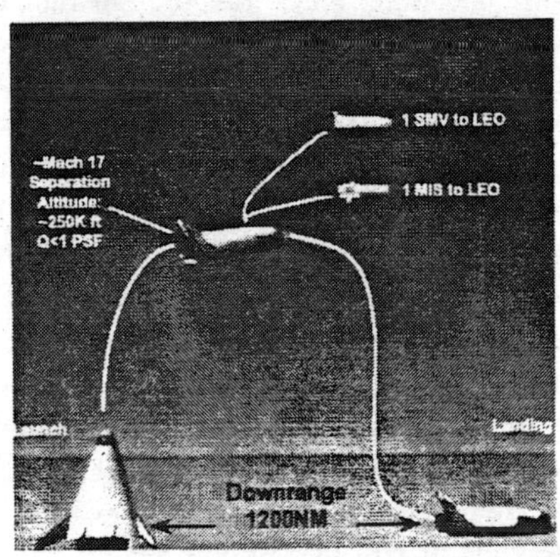

Figure 4. Pop-Up Flight Profile of Notional Sub-Orbital Military Space Plane (MSP)[11]

stages and orbital transfer stages that can be used to carry additional payloads to other destinations. These type of capabilities are just being developed. The weapons area includes offensive and defensive military capabilities such as ASAT, nuclear, and ground capabilities. Thus some payloads represent the current paradigm of space use whereas others represent a fundamental shift in the conception of space into an actual offensive battleground.

Table 3. Sample Payloads for MSP SOV

Type	Detail
Sensors and Telecommunications	Hyper-spectral
	Imaging
	Radar
	SIGNIT
	Meteorological Systems
	GPS
	MILSATCOM
Vehicles (Can also carry payloads)	SMV
	MIS
	CAV
	Micro-satellites
	OTV
Weapons	Precision Munitions (Ground)
	Anti-Satellite (ASAT)
	Electronic Warfare
	Nuclear
	National Missile Defense

Concept of Operations (CONOPS)

There are many components to the operation of a MSP. Figure 7 illustrates a typical timeline of various mission segments of a MSP, from launch to deployment to landing and refurbishment. Launch and landing do not necessarily have to occur at the same location. Keys for the operation of such a system include rapid payload integration, rapid checkout, standard interfaces, and operations flexibility. A sample future scenario for operations for such a vehicle would include an operational fleet of six TSTO systems, with a flight rate of 25 sorties per year, and operational life of 20 years[16]. The baseline mission could consist of the SOV carrying a 15,000 lb payload from Eglin Air Force Base (AFB) in Florida (32 degrees latitude) to an orbit of 140 nmi by 35 nmi. Previous analyses have shown that using conventional rocket engines based upon NASA's SLI program, the configuration sized to 1.5 Mlb gross weight/150 Klb dry weight vehicle (versus 4.5 Mlb gross weight/510 Klb dry weight for the Space Shuttle)[16].

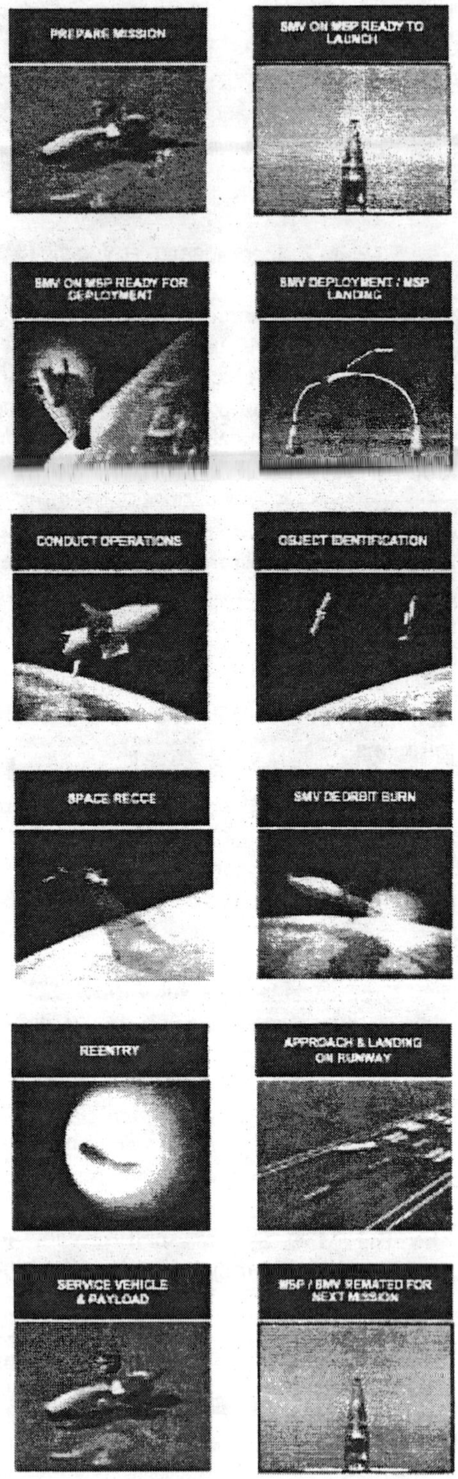

Figure 7. MSP Mission Breakout[11]

LEGAL IMPLICATIONS

There are no specific treaties or regulations that address a MSP in particular. Multiple sets of treaties do discuss various locations of space weaponry and associated military delivery systems. Both customary law and conventions are the two main sources used to obtain clarity as to the relation of space law to the MSP. Conventions, treaties or acts relevant in one degree or another to the legal issues surrounding a MSP include:

- National Aeronautics and Space Act of 1958[17]
- United Nations Charter, Article 51 (1945)[18]
- Nuclear Test Ban Treaty of 1968[19]
- The Treaty on Principles Governing the Activities of States in the Exploration and Use of Outer Space, including the Moon and Other Celestial Bodies (the "Outer Space Treaty", 1967)[20]
- The Agreement on the Rescue of Astronauts, the Return of Astronauts and the Return of Objects Launched into Outer Space (the "Rescue Agreement", 1968)[21]
- The Convention on International Liability for Damage Caused by Space Objects (the "Liability Convention", 1972)[22]
- The Convention on Registration of Objects Launched into Outer Space (the "Registration Convention", 1976)[23]
- The Agreement Governing the Activities of States on the Moon and Other Celestial Bodies (the "Moon Agreement", 1984)[24]
- Treaty between the United States of America and the Union of Soviet Socialist Republics on the Limitation of Anti-Ballistic Missile Systems (the "ABM Treaty", 1972)[25]
- Treaty Between the United States of America and the Union of Soviet Socialist Republics on the Elimination of Their Intermediate-Range and Shorter-Range Missiles (the "INF Treaty", 1988)[26]
- Convention on the Prohibition of Military or Any Other Hostile Use of Environmental Modification Techniques (1976)[17]

Since the current Bush administration in the United States is negotiating with Russia to remove applicability of the ABM Treaty, that treaty will not be extensively covered in this examination. Subsequent issues of whether payloads on the SMV constitute development or deployment of National Missile Defense (NMD) infrastructure will not be covered. In addition, only some of the five United Nations treaties and agreements on space law will be covered.

Military Self Defense

International agreements give justification for military use in self-defense. Article 51 of the United Nations charter states:

> Nothing in the present Charter shall impair the inherent right of individual or collective self-defence if an armed attack occurs against a Member of the United Nations, until the Security Council has taken measures necessary to maintain international peace and security. Measures taken by Members in the exercise of this right of self-defence shall be immediately reported to the Security Council and shall not in any way affect the authority and responsibility of the Security Council under the present Charter to take at any time such action as it deems necessary in order to maintain or restore international peace and security[18].

Thus each nation has this freedom for self-defense if the necessary conditions are met. This would not apply in the case of offensive space assets to be used for a first strike capability. This would also seem to generally preclude preemptive military action. However, an issue to be considered for a MSP, given the role of recent terrorist actions on the American homeland, is the role of preemptive first strike against terrorist targets. The administration of George W. Bush has have promulgated such justification in response to potential Weapons of Mass Destruction (WMD) threats. An operational MSP would become one of the tops assets considered for use in a first strike.

The National Aeronautics and Space Act of 1958 (as amended) explicitly states the civilian agency in charge of aeronautics and space shall have authority except for "activities peculiar to or primarily associated with the development of weapons systems, military operations, or the defense of the United States (including the research and development necessary to make effective provision for the defense of the United States) shall be the responsibility of, and shall be directed by. the Department of Defense."[17] Thus the military is given freedom to conduct research and deployment of system related to aeronautics and space. This international law allows self-defense while U.S. custom allows the military to investigate and develop space technologies.

Legality of Payloads

The MSP concept essentiality consists of combinations of components to deliver payloads for various missions. A MSP without a payload would most likely not be construed as an illegal military application. Only when a payload is applied to the architecture do tactical and legal issues arise. The payload determines the ultimate nature of this transportation system. Application of a payload can change the nature of the destination orbit as well as the duration of the SMV in orbit. The SMV itself is more important when it comes to the issue of legality. The SMV, carried by the booster SOV (which delivers the SMV in nominal Air Force scenarios) can become co-orbit capable, rebuild a constellation, or even perform orbital fly-bys of LEO satellites.

The type of payload is critical to whether such architectures could be in violation of international agreements or conventions. For instance, Article IV of the Outer Space Treaty indicates that state parties cannot place in orbit or station nuclear weapons or WMD. Unlike an intercontinental ballistic missile, a SMV can either directly send its arsenal to a territorial destination or stay in orbit with a weapon. Thus if the arsenal includes WMD material then there may be an issue with the SMV operating for extended periods of time during peacetime "on-station" in orbit.

The issue of payload legality becomes less obvious when it relates to the nature of non-WMD offensive assets. Examples include in-space based kinetic kill vehicles (KKVs) that do damage only to targeted orbiting enemy satellites. The definition of the payload itself is also important. A defensive payload in space could conceivably be reconfigured for offensive purposes. These offensive weapons may have unintended collateral damage in space. Such manipulations of the space environment may violate terms of the 1976 Convention on the Prohibition of Military or Any Other Hostile Use of Environmental Modification Techniques[27]. Generally non-WMD offensive space assets (not restricted by the ABM Treaty) should follow the paradigm of terrestrial weapons and place an emphasis on precision strike.

Uncrewed Nature of the MSP

Notional concepts of the MSP have them being both autonomous and piloted. Uninhabited combat aerial vehicles (UCAVs) and such uncrewed RLVs share similar legal issues. One particular legal issue arises of the classification of cruise missiles in the 1988 INF Treaty. The treaty prohibited the United States and Soviet Union from deploying ground launched cruise missiles with ranges between 500 km and 5.500 km[28]. Some have speculated that UCAVs could be considered such cruises missiles since they are similar to definition in the treaty. In the treaty cruise missiles are defined as unmanned atmospheric vehicles. UCAVs and some variations of the MSP architecture have similar properties: ground launched, uncrewed launch vehicles that have expendable arsenals on board. Future generations of MSPs that have Rocket Based Combined Cycle (RBCC) propulsion systems would more likely fall under these definitions since those systems do use the atmosphere for part of the flight (in place of on-board oxidizer as on conventional rockets systems for near term MSPs). However, the arming of predator UAVs with Hellfire missiles in early 2002 during the U.S. engagements in Afghanistan have shown the military's willingness to rethink the limitations of the INF treaty.

Over-flight Issues

The U.S. military's recent retrenchment when it relates to forward basing of military assets makes the MSP a more viable option for global strike missions. Continental U.S. (CONUS) operations of B-2 bombers in the Kosovo and Afghanistan campaigns demonstrate the attractiveness of such options. MSPs enable CONUS operations that allow for global strike missions. Thus a MSP enables avoidance of international territorial disputes in regards to flying rights over countries on the path towards the terrestrial target.

Coordinated Civil and Military RLV Development

In the United States there has been some recent coordinated movement by both civil and military space leaders to jointly determine if there are potential synergies in development of a RLV. The recent OneTeam/120 Day Study is an example of such coordination between NASA and USAF[29]. Specific architecture requirements of each organization differ. NASA would prefer large payloads that can go to the International Space Station (ISS) orbit whereas the military would prefer a smaller payload class vehicle that can be turned around after landing within a few hours. The military's use of such RLVs would not be as the primary launch service for its satellites (expendable rockets would services these missions).

Given the enormous costs, government assistance is projected to be extensive for any RLV development. Specifically associated with these government efforts may be military subsidies to launch vehicle providers. American, European, Russian, Chinese, Indian, and Japanese launch services receive some type of government support (guaranteed launches, anchor tenancy, facilities development, research and development). World Trade Organization (WTO) conventions discourage governmental subsidies to commercial sectors but exclude military offsets. Specifically this refers to the General Agreement on Trades and Tariffs (GATT) Article XXI, referred to as the "security exception" wherein it allows:

> Governments free reign for trade-related actions taken in the name of national security. The rule states that a country cannot be stopped from taking any such action it deems necessary to protect its essential security interests, or any action "relating to the traffic in arms, ammunition and implements of war."...Article XXI is often called the most powerful exception for WTO member-nations, because governments are allowed to define their "essential security interests" for themselves, and protect their industries while couching their actions in terms of national security[30].

Such items, referred to as non-tariff barriers to trade, are exemplified by Canadian Technology Partnerships that a 1999 WTO dispute panel ruled against. These arrangements assisted Canadian airplane manufacturer Bombardier Aerospace to export regional jet aircraft. These rulings may have an effect of biasing governmental assistance towards military rather than civilian offsets.

Future global launch market forecasts project more commercial than government launches on an annual basis. Any future RLV endeavor (whether civilian or military) will most certainly have a role to play in the commercial launch industry. Possibly unlike previous military funded programs to enhance technologies, these RLV programs seek development of vehicles that could immediately be used to service the commercial marketplace. Given current launch forecasts, commercial utilization may outweigh military. Foreign governments could charge a military RLV-enabled country as being anti-competitive, as some European governments have charged with respect to American expendable launch vehicles. The level of involvement of civilian space agencies with military counterparts in development of such new capabilities may have to be monitored.

CONCLUSION

Since the beginning of exploration of outer space, a myriad of concepts have been explored for civil, commercial, and military purpose. As one of those concepts, the MSP should more appropriately be thought of as a delivery mechanism than an actual weapon. Subsequently, the legality of a MSP is inherent upon the payload it carries.

Various MSP configurations exist, both defensive and offensive with easy interchangeability between either. The SOV portion of the architecture may not be capable by itself of positioning weapons in space. However, additional add-on components like the SMV and CAV could be used for offensive space purposes. On-orbit, sustained operations available through use of such upper stages attached to the SOV entail more legal issues than the SOV by itself. The employment of such a system and associated on-board payloads determines the applicability of international legal conventions and treaties.

MSPs should not be dismissed based upon legal grounds since they similar to existing launch vehicles. MSPs enable much faster response times and global access. MSPs have the capability to provide asymmetric capabilities to upset the reaction times of adversaries. However, the capabilities of the SOV/SMV may not enable revolutionary classes of payloads but can deliver existing or evolutionary payloads in differing manners.

REFERENCES

1. McFaddin, David W., Lt. Col., USAF, "Can the U.S. Air Force Weaponize Space?" Degree Research Report, Advisor: Dr. Joan Johnson-Freese, Air War College, Air University, Maxwell Air Force Base, Alabama, April 1998.

2. Callahan, William H., Jr., "Space Weaponization", National Defense University, National War College, April 20, 2000, submitted in fulfillment of course 5605.

3. Parker, Dewey, Major, USAF, "Access to Space: Routine, Responsive and Flexible Implications for an Expeditionary Air Force", Air Command and Staff College, Air University, Maxwell Air Force Base, Alabama, April 1999.

4. Thompson, David, D., Major, USAF, "The Need for a Dedicated Space Vehicle for Defensive Counterspace Operations", Air Command and Staff College, Air University, Maxwell Air Force Base, Alabama, April 1998.

5. Report of the Commission to Assess United States National Security Space Management and Organization, on-line, Internet, 11 January 2001, available from http://www.defenselink.mil/pubs/space20010111.html.

6. Space Commission member speaks of findings, Capt. Brad Swezy, AFSPC Public Affairs, on-line, Internet, 11 January 2001, available from https://www.patrick.af.mil/45SW/PA/INTERNAL/MISSILER/2001/Mar01/16Mar/space_commission.htm.

7. Hamel, Michael, Maj. Gen. (Sel), "Space Commission Implementation: An Air Force Perspective", HQ US Air Force, Directorate of Space Operations and Integration.

8. General Accounting Office, "Military Space Operations: Planning, Funding, and Acquisition Challenges Facing Efforts to Strength Space Control". GAO-02-738, September 2002.

9. NASA-USAF OneTeam, "The Military Space Plane: Providing Transformational and Responsive Global Precision Striking Power." Peterson AFB, Colorado, January 2002.

10. Anttonen, John, Capt., "U.S. Air Force Space Operations Vehicle", AIAA98-1568, 8th International Space Planes and Hypersonic Systems and Technology Conference, Norfolk, VA, April 27-30, 1998.

11. Anarde, Russ, Brid. Gen., "Military Spaceplane (MSP) and Reusable Launch Vehicle Study".

12. Gen Michael P. C. Carns, USAF, Retired, A COMMENTARY, Airpower Journal - Summer 1995.http://www.airpower.maxwell.af.mil/airchronicles/apj/carnes.html.

13. Jenkins, Dennis R., "Space Shuttle: The History of the National Space Transportation System", Dennis R. Jenkins: Cape Canaveral, Florida, 2001.

14. Verderame, Kenneth, Mjr., USAF, "System Requirements Documents for a Military Spaceplane System.", Military Spaceplane System Technology Program Office, Air Force Research Laboratory, Kirtland AFB, New Mexico, version 4.2, February 12, 2001.

15. Verderame, Ken, Lt. Col., "MS1-A: Military Spaceplane System and Space Maneuver Vehicle", Presentation, Air Force Research Laboratory, 27 October 1999.

16. Hatakeyama, S. Jason, McIver, Keith L., Embler, Jon D., Gillard, William G., Jackson, Lee, "Operability Sensitivities of Airbreathing and Rocket Propulsion for a Two-Stage-To-Orbit Space Operations Vehicle (SOV)", AIAA-2002-3903, 38th Joint Propulsion Conference, July 7-10, 2002, Indianapolis, IN.

17. National Aeronautics and Space Act of 1958, 26 May 1972, on-line, Internet, 15 September 2002, available from http://www.hq.nasa.gov/ogc/spaceact.html

18. United Nations Charter, Article 51, 26 June 1945, on-line, Internet, 15 September 2002, http://www.un.org/Overview/Charter/chapter7.html.

19. Treaty on the Non-Proliferation Of Nuclear Weapons (NPT), Signed July 1, 1968, Entered into force March 5, 1970, on-line, Internet, 15 September 2002, available from http:// www.un.org/Depts/dda/WMD/npttext.html

20. The Treaty on Principles Governing the Activities of States in the Exploration and Use of Outer Space, including the Moon and Other Celestial Bodies (the "Outer Space Treaty", adopted by the General Assembly in its resolution 2222 (XXI)), opened for signature on 27 January 1967, entered into force on 10 October 1967, 96 ratifications and 27 signatures (as of 1 February 2001).

21. The Agreement on the Rescue of Astronauts, the Return of Astronauts and the Return of Objects Launched into Outer Space (the "Rescue Agreement", adopted by the General Assembly in its resolution 2345 (XXII)), opened for signature on 22 April 1968, entered into force on 3 December 1968, 87 ratifications and 26 signatures (as of 1 February 2001).

22. The Convention on International Liability for Damage Caused by Space Objects (the "Liability Convention", adopted by the General Assembly in its resolution 2777 (XXVI)), opened for signature on 29 March 1972, entered into force on 1 September 1972, 81 ratifications and 26 signatures (as of 1 February 2001).

23. The Convention on Registration of Objects Launched into Outer Space (the "Registration Convention", adopted by the General Assembly in its resolution 3235 (XXIX)), opened for signature on 14 January 1975, entered into force on 15 September 1976, 43 ratifications and 4 signatures (as of 1 February 2001).

24. The Agreement Governing the Activities of States on the Moon and Other Celestial Bodies (the "Moon Agreement", adopted by the General Assembly in its resolution 34/68), opened for signature on 18 December 1979, entered into force on 11 July 1984, 9 ratifications and 5 signatures (as of 1 February 2001).

25. Treaty between the United States of America and the Union of Soviet Socialist Republics on the limitation of Anti-Ballistic Missile Systems, 26 May 1972, on-line, Internet, 15 September 2002, available from http://www.state.gov/www/global/arms/treaties/abm/abm2.html.

26. Treaty Between the United States of America and the Union of Soviet Socialist Republics on the Elimination of Their Intermediate-Range and Shorter-Range Missiles (the "INF Treaty", 1988)

27. Convention on the Prohibition of Military or Any Other Hostile Use of Environmental Modification Techniques (December 10, 1976).

28. Lazarski, Anothony J., Lt. Col., "Legal Implications of the Uninhabited Combat Aerial Vehicle", Aerospace Power Journal, Summer 2002, June 3, 2002.

29. Industry Day Briefing, "NASA-USAF Reusable Launch Vehicle Development", NASA-USAF OneTeam, January 17, 2002.

30. "Taiwan may invoke GATT Articles XXXV, XXI in WTO bid, Fang Wen-hung, Staff Reporter, Central News Agency, http://www.taiwan.com.au/Polieco/Policies/WTO/200007/28a.html, 2002.

PREVENTION OF THE OUTER SPACE WEAPONIZATION

Gennady P.Zhukov
The People s Friendship University
Moscow, Russia. E-mail: ***intlaw@mail.rudn.rssi.ru***

Abstract.
The main task of this paper is to analyze and to discuss the present binding regime of the outer space deweaponization and particular measures on consolidation and strengthening of this regime. In particular the following problems are discussed in this paper:

1. The international terrorism as a main present-day obstacle on the way to the universal ban of the space-based ABM systems.
2. The urgent need to strength the regime of inviolability or immunity of satellites due to the international terrorism threat. This may be obtained by turning of the appropriate bilateral agreements between the Russian Federation and the USA into multilateral Treaties. Such ˙immunity¨ would cover all operating space objects, irrespective of their military or civil designation.

This approach is quitejustified taking into consideration that military sattelites enhanced international peace and security and had broad advantages as a counter-terrorism means.

3. Strengthening of confidence among the states of antiterrorist coalition when carrying out peaceful space activity by raising of the degree of transparency on the pre-launch stage of space activity, including satellite inspection before ignition.

4 Other measures of using space objects for international security of the antiterrorist coalition.

1.The Outer Space Deweaponization Regime in Force

The binding rules of international space law ban to place only some kinds of weapons in orbit around the earth, what from the point of view of international law may be qualified as establishing a partial deweaponization regime in outer space. After the universal prohibition of the deploying space based Anti-Ballistic Missile (ABM) Systems or their components development, and of anti-satellite (ASAT) weapons it will be possible to speak about establishing of an international legal regime of complete deweaponization in outer space eliminating any kinds of weapon in a peaceful time from outer space. The process of outer space partial deweaponizasion originated from the date of signing on August 5, 1963 the Moscow Treaty banning nuclear weapons tests in atmosphere, in outer space and under water (Partial Test Ban Treaty-PTBT)[1] The significance of the 1963 Partial Test BanTreaty is, that it has forbidden any nuclear weapons test explosions in outer space. Such prohibition encouraged the non-proliferation of nuclear arms race in outer space and eliminated the hazard for normal operation of satellites that are very sensitive to an electromagnetic impulse resulting from nuclear explosions in space. The 1963 Moscow Treaty has prevented the problem of contamination of outer space with radiation, and also the use of space for conducting experimental tests of X-ray lasers with nuclear pumping. Unfortunately, this treaty does not establish international monitoring system.The States Parties to the Moscow Partial Test-Ban Treaty have the right to carry out control of its observance only with the help of their national technical means (N M). The 1963 PTB Treaty, by protecting outer space from any nuclear explosions, did not contain any prohibition of placing of nuclear weapon in outer space. This gap was filled in by the conclusion of the Treaty on Principles Governing the Activities of States in the Exploration and Use of Outer Space, including the Moon and Other Celestial Bodies (Outer Space Treaty-OST) in 1967.[2]

Particular importance has the article 4 of the Outer Space Treaty which prohibits "to place in orbit around of the Earth any objects carrying nuclear weapons or any other kinds of weapons of mass destruction, install such weapon on celestial bodies, or station such weapons in outer space in any other manner" The term "weapons of mass destruction" includes such kinds of weapons, as nuclear, chemical and biological payloads, and other payloads, comparable with them in terms of destructive striking power, including those, which can be created afterwards.The prohibition of placing in space of the indicated kinds of weapon concerns also the objects with nuclear weapons on board carrying out fractional orbital flight.

Thus, the 1963 PTB Treaty clearly and unambigiously prohibiting nuclear explosions in outer space, along with the 1967 Outer Space Treaty banning to place nuclear and other kinds of a weapons of mass destruction into outer space, may be regarded as efficient contribution to the prevention of an arms race in outer space.The Convention on the Prohibition of Military or any other Hostile Use of Environmental Modification Technique (Environmental Modification (ENMOD) Convention) of 1977[3] plays an important role in the establishment of rules to curb the use of new means of warfare.The Convention defines both the term environmental modification technique and the boundaries within which the Convention is applicable,including the outer space environment.The ENMOD Convention prevents the threat of the so called "geophysical war" and considered some of possible modifications of the environment through the use of special satellite The Convention would, to a certain extent, protect satellites against interference resulting from disturbance of the environment through which they travel. Convention provides for consultations between States Parties to the Convention, or through the machinery of the United Nations. In particular, the consultation through the convening of a Consultative Committee of Experts is provided as appropriate means of verifying States obligations.Unfortunately, this Convention does not become universal one.A number of limitations of military use of outer space (as in quantitative, and in a qualitative sense) is contained in bilateral agreements between Russia, as a legal successor of the former USSR, and the USA.

Till now, the idea was to ban separate kinds of weapon in outer space. However, in the space agreements in force referring to moon and other celestial bodies the most far-reaching weapons prohibitions are established. Pursuant to the 1967 Outer Space Treaty the Moon and other celestial bodies should be used "exclusively for peaceful purposes". The approximate list of kinds of activity forbidden on the Moon and on other celestial bodies, includes the ban to install any objects carrying nuclear weapons or any other kinds of weapons of mass destruction.

The list of possible forbidden kinds of weapons on the moon and other celestial bodies was supplemented and extended by the article 3 of the 1979 Agreement Governing the Activities on the Moon and Other Celestial Bodies[4] where, along with already listed kinds of forbidden activity, there are mentioned: not placing in orbit or other trajectory to or around the moon objects carrying nuclear weapons or any other kinds of weapons of mass destruction, or placing or using such weapons on or in the moon.

It is necessary to mention, that the provisions of the Moon Agreement are applied also to other celestial bodies of the solar System, besides the Earth. In the legal terms the regime established for the moon and other celestial bodies, may be qualified as a complete deweaponization. As to the near space only the regime of partial deweaponisation is established. The Law of the Russian Federation on Space Activity not admits "the space activity, forbidden by the international treaties to which the Russian Federation is a party."

2.The Problem of Prevention of an Arms Race in Outer Space.

The problem of prevention of an arms race in outer space has been debated on the United Nations sessions of the General Assembly for decades. Since 1981 a number of the United Nations General Assembly resolutions made a recommendation to the Committee on Disarmament (1979-1983) and since 1984 to the Conference on Disarmament (CD) to negotiate the conclusion of the multilateral agreement or agreements on the prevention of an arms race in outer space as a matter of priority. In 1982 a new subject, Prevention of an Arms Race in Outer Space (PAROS), became an item of the Committee of Disarmament agenda. From the moment of conclusion of the 1967 Outer Space Treaty the international community did not manage to reach the uniform understanding on the further measures to be undertaken on the ways of Prevention of an Arms Race in Outer Space. The support for these General Assembly resolutions has led to the conclusion of agreement on establishment of the Ad Hoc PAROS Committee in 1985 within the framework of the Conference on Disarmament. The Ad Hoc Committee has never become a permanent subsidiary body of the

CD. Therefore, since 1984 the General Assembly resolutions request the CD to establish or reestablish the Ad Hoc Committee "...with a view to undertaking negotiations for the conclusion of an agreement, as appropriate, to prevent an arms race in all its aspects in outer space".Over the past period the complex of ideas and proposals of the States on this problem was put forward. First of all it is necessary to mention the proposals on prevention of an arms race in outer space. This problem has been debated on the sessions of United Nations General Assembly and CD by decades.In 1979 Italy has submitted "Additional Protocol to the 1967 Outer Space Treaty " to the Committee on Disarmament with the view to preventing an Arms Race in Outer Space[5] .Two proposals were put forward by the former Soviet Union to the United Nations General Assembly in 1981 and 1983.The first proposal was the Draft Treaty on the Prohibition of the Stationing of Weapons of Any Kind in Outer Space.[6] The second proposal was the Text of the Draft Treaty on the Prohibition of the Use of Force in Outer Space and from Space Against the Earth.[7] Among concrete aspects of the prevention of an arms race, the proposals on complete prohibition of the Anti-Satellite weapons (ASAT) were put forward on the UN General Assembly Sessions and the CD Meetings.It is necessary to take into account, that the express prohibition on carrying out of the ASAT tests is not provided by the agreements in force. The unilateral moratorium of the former Soviet Union on the development of the ASAT weapons has been declared in 1983. The Russia Federation as a successor of the former USSR continues to observe this moratorium. Statement submitted by the delegation of India to the CD in 1987 has proposed the conclusion of a multilateral agreement which would transform the de facto moratorium observed by the USSR and the US on the development of ASAT weapons into a universally binding commitment covering both the dismantling of existing systems and the production of new ones. [8] The idea was supported by a number of developing countries and China. In 1989 Sweden made a proposal on the prohibition of the ASAT systems. The delegations of the Netherlands, Sri-Lanka, Great Britain and Pakistan also expressed the opinion in favor of an inhibitory action or limitation of the ASAT systems.

Attempting to put the problem out of deadlock, many States acted with idea of adoption of partial measures by ensuring "immunity" of artificial satellites of the Earth. Among them were the Netherlands, Canada, Australia, Argentina, Poland, Hungary, Bulgaria, Germany, France, Great Britain, Japan, Indonesia, Pakistan, Sri-Lanka etc. The problem of inviolability of satellites, or their "immunity" has remained at the level of discussion, and nobody addressed it in the 90s.Practically speaking, the SALT-1 and SALT-2 Treaties are belived to provide for the immunity of satellites performing verification functions on an arms limitation and desarmament. Other satelites that enjoy immunity are those that perform communication functions directly sanctioned by the Nuclear Accident Agreement of 1971 and the subsequent Agreement on the Prevention of Nuclear War of 1973, as well as the "Hot Line" Treaties. All mentioned Agreements are of bilateral character (between the Russia and the USA), and in this connection the problem on the right of other countries to similar "inviolability" repeatedly arose.Hot discussions took place on the CD sessions concerning the right of the States to self-defense in outer space and on legal protection of satellites. All this has not allowed to achieve a common consensus on such a complex issue as the satellite "immunity". The discussions in the CD sessions demonstrate that with reference to space activity and taking into account the need to consolidate the efforts against international terrorism, more positive result can be achieved in the field of the confidence-building measures (CBMs). The CBMs may be subdivided into three main sets of measures whose aim is to establish confidence among States concerning their space activities:

1) Measures intended to obtain greater transparency and predictability in prior notification of a space object launch, including prelaunch inspection procedures of satellites.

2 Measures within the framework of the "traffic rules", sometimes referred to as the Rules of Behavior would be used for the establishment of measures to increase the safety of space objects and predictability of space activity, including notification on change of a satellite orbit, rules concerning space debris and space maneuvers.

3) The Space Code of Conduct regarded as a mechanism to reduce misinterpretation of space activity and inadvertent collision with other functioning space object. The elaboration of this Space Code of Conduct would constitute a concrete step towards the development of space order, and is an important "institutional" measure at the same time.

Lately, a number of countries attempted to attract attention of the CD sessions participants to the necessity of taking measures on raising transparency and predictability in space activity and, in particular, on the problems of verification and control [9] In 1989 the French Government came back to its 1978 proposal for the establishment of an International Space Monitoring Agency (ISMA) by offering, in addition, the creation of an International Trajectography Center (UNITRACE)[10] and Satellite Image Processing Agency (SIPA)[11] In 1993 a similar proposal was made with regard to the Center of Notification about Start of Space Objects and Ballistic Missiles (CNSSOBM). In 1987 the USSR put forward the proposal on creation of an International Space Inspectorate (ISI)[12] to verify the non-deployment of weapons of any kind in outer space followed by the proposal of creation the International Space Monitoring Agency (ISMA)[13]

In 1987 Canada proposed "the PAXSAT Concept"[14] as a verification measure which provided for the use of space-based remote technology for verification of non-deployment of the ASAT weapons and compliance with Treaty. It also provided for the space-to-ground observation and first of all in Europe, regional verification of conventional forces and weaponry. It is necessary to emphasize that the proposals of France, USSR and Canada mutually supplemented one another, however, within the framework of the CD nothing was made on elaboration of the unified draft. During last ears China and Russia have taken the lead in calling for the negotiation of a new multilateral treaty prohibiting the deployment of weapons in space and restricting its use for peaceful purposes. China, France and Russia have called for the negotiation of a new multilateral treaty prohibiting the deployment of weapons in space and restricting its use for peaceful purposes. These calls have been supported by other states, including Canada and Sri Lanka.In the Conference on Disarmament, China proposed in 1999 the re-establishment of an ad hoc negotiating committee under item three of the CD agenda, Prevention of an arms race in outer space (PAROS). This proposal has been backed in principle by Russia. In 2001 China intensified its diplomatic efforts to open substantive negotiations on space weapons In June 2001 the Chinese delegation introduced a proposed draft agreement. Under this proposal, states would agree not to test, deploy or use in outer space any weapons, weapon systems or their components. Not to test, deploy or use on land, in sea or atmosphere any weapons, weapon systems or their components that can be used for war-fighting in outer space. Not to use any objects launched into orbit to directly participate in combatant activities

It necessary to menshen the russian proposals made in 2000 and 2001 to create an European ABM non strategic system. On the opinion of the american expert J.Pike the USA, for its part, has shown little interest in agreements that would constrain its military activities in space, where it enjoys unrivalled superiority.[15] The author of this paper believes that the CD sessions participants have a real possibility of successful advancing of elaboration of the multilateral agreement or agreements on the prevention of an arms race in outer space.

3. The Problem of Outer Space Neutralization

With the complete and partial dewaeponization of outer space there is tightly connected the problem of neutralization.

The outer space neutralization means the establishment of an international legal regime in outer space which would eliminate carrying out of military operations, defeating of enemy objects situated in outer space, on the ground, in the air and in water by means of a space-based weapon, as well as defeating of space objects by means of ground, sea and air-based weapons.The outer space neutralization would eliminate the transformation of outer space into the theater of warfare and platform for an armed attack against enemy states. From the point of view of international law it would mean establishment of the regime of complete neutralization in outer space. The measures of partial neutralization are possible also. It is useful to remember that the 1979 Moon Agreement contains provisions prohibiting any threat or use of force or any other hostile act or threat of hostile act on the moon. It s likewise prohibited to use the moon in order to commit any such act or to engage in any such threat in relation to the earth, the moon, spacecraft, personnel of spacecraft or man-made space objects. In the absence of the complete outer space neutralization regime the flight of the ballistic missiles designed for military application in space are not be considered forbidden.The advancement of the neutralization regime into outer space would be based on the jus cogens principle of contemporary international law proclaiming non-use of force or threats of force. In space as well as in any other province of mankind activity, the States should be guided by the fundamental principles of international law fixed in the Charter of the United Nations, including the principle which obliges all UN Members to refrain from the threat or use of force in their international relations (p.4 art.2 of the UN Charter).

Thus, according to the general norms of the international law, the States are obliged to abstain from any hostile operations when carrying out space activity, to settle their international conflicts and disputes by peaceful means. In particular, it means non-acceptance of any violent interference with the rightful activity of an automatic or manned space object of another country by demolishing or damaging such object, its capturing or displacing from orbit.It is necessary to take into account that the 1967 Outer Space Treaty reconfirmed the applicability of the United Nations General Assembly resolution 110(II)) to outer space passed in November 3 1947, which condemned propaganda designed or is likely to provoke or encourage any threat to the peace, breach of the peace or an act of aggression. The former USSR was inspired by idea of implementing the above mentioned provisions in the separate legally binding document and put forward in the 1983 Draft Treaty on the Prohibition of the Use of Force in Outer Space and from Space Against the Earth. In this Draft the principle of non-use of force in outer space and from outer space received the complete expression both from the point of view of legal obligations of the States, as well as from the point of view of its reinforcement by the measures of material character prohibiting creation, test and deployment of the space facilities used for agressive purposes. Thus, the important proposal that was meant to implement by means of treaty a fundamental principle of international law with reference to activity in outer space, from outer space to the Earth, and from the Earth to outer space was put forward. Unfortunately, this draft was not translated into life.

In the time of confrontation between the USSR and the USA a positive step was made by conclusion of the Agreement on Measures to Reduce the Risk of Outbreak of Nuclear War Between the US and the USSR (Nuclear Accident Agreement) of 1971, the subsequent Agreement on the Prevention of Nuclear War of 1973,as well as the Agreement on Measures to Improve the US-USSR Direct Communications Link ("Hot Line"Modernization Agreement) of 1971.Russia as a successor of the former Soviet Union strictly fulfills the obligation of these agreements. The first of these agreements requires Parties to notify each other immediately about the signs of interference with their early warning systems or related communication facilities, including those in outer space, if such interference could create a risk of nuclear war; to notify in cases of unauthorized or unpredictable incident connected with a possible detonation of nuclear weapon; about detection of unidentified objects by their early warning systems; about missiles launched from the territory of one state in the direction of another. After a series of consultations held between the the Russia and the USA on May 30 1994 the Agreement on the end of targeting of strategic missiles against each other was signed that practically was realized during 1995. The American and Russian onboard missile computers with divided war heads, were switched to the "zero" flight programs (tasks) put into memory of computers together with other real flight programs.In 1995 Great Britain and China also declared about the cease of targeting of the misilles at the territory of Russia and other nuclear powers. The shortcoming of such measure is that it is not subject to the control and can be quickly put on the reverse. Nevertheless, this Agreement has a great political value and is based on mutual confidence.According to the article 51 of the United Nations Charter, each state has the inherent right of individual or collective self-defense if an armed attack takes place against a Member of the

United Nations until the Security Council has taken measures necessary to maintain international peace and security. Since the near-Earth outer space is not declared to be eliminated from an act of warfare in case of armed conflict between the States, according to the binding norms of international law including the United Nations Charter, it is necessary to recognize lawfulness of the use of outer space for a retaliatory strike against the State supporting international terrorism in case of an armed attack as a valid self-defense measure.

In the agenda of each session of the United Nations General Assembly we may find included two items: ˙Prevention of an arms race in outer space¨ and ˙International cooperation in peaceful use of outer space¨. One may regard these items as two sides of the coin. The problems covered by these items are debated in details annually: the first one in the It is necessary to remark, that the success in international cooperation on the peaceful use of outer space is out of harmony with the problem of prevention of placement of any kinds of weapons in outer space.

At the same time the annual resolutions of the UN General Assembly on this problem find broad support of the international community. Nobody dares to vote against such resolution.

4.The Military Satellite Systems Against International Terrorism.

From the beginning of a space age the military considerations were key factors of space activity of the States. At present-day situation the satellites of various functions (early warning, communication, data acquisition, reconnaissance and navigation) were actively used and continue to be used with the purposes of raising efficiency of ground armed forces, especially in the fight against international terrorism. At the same time such satellites are not a weapon in the sense of that word since they do not create by themselves the threats of armed attack in outer space or from outer space.

Moreover, this satellite system promotes maintaining of stability in the international relations. For this reasons the reconnaissance and data acquisition satellites are effective means used for the verification of the observance by some States of non proliferation of nuclear and other weapons of mass destruction and non violation by them of the appropriate agreements. Such satellite systems are under international protection as the national technical means of the verification and control. Similar protection is enjoyed by the early warning satellites. With the help of space communication facilities the more reliable operative connection of the statesmen is organized in the strained situations. By this way the probability of making the incorrect retaliatory decisions in critical political situations is reduced. At the same time it s necessary to take into consideration that the activities of such satellite systems are tightly connected with ground armed forces of the States.

NOTES

[1] United Nations Treaty Series,vol.480, .6964.
[2] United Nations Treaties and Principles on Outer Space.United Nations,New York,1999, p.3-7.
[3] Official Records of the General Assembly, A/RES/3172, 1977,Annex
[4] United Nations Treaties and Principles on Outer Space.United Nations,New York,1999, p.22-29
[5] Commity Disarmament. CD/9-1979,March 26
[6] Official Records of the General Assembly,A/36/192, 20 August 1981
[7] Official Records of the General Assembly,A/38/194, 23 August 1983
[8] Conference on Disarmmament CD/PV 428 1987 August 6
[9] Prevetion of an Arms Race in Outer Space:A Guide to the discussions in the Conference on Desarmament.UNIDIR.NY 1991, p.117-128.
[10] Conference on Disarmmament CD/937, 1989 July 21
[11] Conference on Disarmmament CD/OS/OW.59 1993 March 12
[12] Conference on Disarmmament CD/PV 428 1987 August 6
[13] Conference on Disarmmament CD/PV.410 1987 April.30
[14] Conference on Disarmmament CD/PV 410, 1987 April 30.
[15] John PIKE The military uses of outer space.SIPRI YEARBOOK 2001.Armamants, disarmamants and international security.Stockholm International Peace Research Institute. Oxford University Press 2001.Chapter 11

IAC-02-IISL.3.18

GNSS FOR MILITARY USES OR PEACEFUL USES?

Yuri Takaya
Graduated from LL.M. International Institute of Air and Space Law
Leiden University, Kanagawa, JAPAN

ABSTRUCT

Global Navigation Satellite System is originally developed for military purposes, though; its applications are recognized as globally multipurpose for peaceful uses.
Since the early 1990s, it has been used for military purposes in outer space. The last case was that, after US Terrorists Attacks on 11 Sept. 2001, the U.S. used its own GNSS namely GPS for the testing of National Missile Defense on 18 Jan. 2002.
In this paper, the author would verify the illegality of GNSS uses for military purposes, with stress on 'space benefit' under Space Benefit Declaration, and 'international cooperation' under Principle of International cooperation and Mutual Assistance, which are international customary law to oblige States Parties to use outer space for peaceful purposes, in order to avoid destabilization of outer space.

1. What is GNSS?

Global Navigation Satellite System (GNSS) is a space-based radio positioning system for communication and navigation. It uses either or both Global Positioning System (GPS), developed by the U.S., and Global Orbiting Navigation Satellite System (GLONASS) developed by the USSR, to provide accurate positioning and the real time navigation information for safety. Besides two 'public' GNSS, EU has worked on building Galileo, which would be operational on commercial basis.
The basic system of GPS, which is operated and financed by the U.S. Air Force, uses the Navigation Satellite Providing Time and Range (NAVSTAR) satellites [1], and its constellation consists of 21 operational satellites and 3 active spares. The orbital constellation consists of 6 orbital planes, each inclined with respect to the equatorial plane by about 55 degrees. The arrangement of 24 satellites and associated ground monitor stations ensure that there are 4-12 satellites above the horizon available for simultaneous measurements for 24 hours.

2. GNSS Applications for Space Benefits

The main benefit of GNSS is to make a single navigation system that offers continuous 'public' services, resulting in reduction of accidents by enhancing accuracy of position and velocity measurements. It has been applied to diversifying current applications[2], recognized through UNISPACEIII [3] and a series of the UN/USA GNSS Workshop[4]. It was concluded that GNSS needs regional and global cooperation for seamless worldwide uses to create international community between civil authorities, governments and industry representatives[5].

3. GNSS for Military Uses

Since the early 1990s, the U.S. has used GPS for military purposes in outer space.

3.1. National Missile Defense (NMD)

Originally GPS was designed and developed in the late 1960s and the early 1970s as joint program of Navy and Air Force as the space-based sensors for communications and navigation for military uses. Its scope was extended early in its development for complementary civil uses as well.

The functions of GPS is not easily divided into civilian or military program as both sectors use communications, navigation, weather, and remote sensing/reconnaissance satellites namely dual-use technology.

Since the 104th Congress, satellites to attack ballistic missiles have been considered in President Reagan's 1983 announcement that initiated a Strategic Defense Initiative (SDI) to study the viability of building a ballistic missile defense system to protect the U.S. and the allies. The Clinton Administration renamed that SDI as the Ballistic Missile Defense Organization (BMDO) to created Theater Missile Defense (TMD) during the Persian Gulf War, rather than NMD. The Bush Administration has changed the name to the Missile Defense Agency (MDA)[6].

Despite space defense program, NMD is still controversial in the U.S. For example, H.R. 2977 would ban U.S. space-based weapons and require the U.S. President to take action to adhere international treaties to assure that the missile defense system uses satellites for early warning, communication, and other support functions.

On 18 January 2002, the Department of Defense (DoD) demonstrated the operational and live-fire testing of 161 military systems by using GPS, which failed to prove the confident capability of the NMD[7].

In fact, NMD either in space or on the ground requires GPS for early warning, communications and other support functions. The above testing relies on data from a GPS beacon for targeting ICBM to help plan the intercept and assist mid-range tracking. To make use of GPS data is suitable for early testing, to verify if the missile defense system is tracking the warhead correctly even though it is not enough acquisition support.

3.2. NMD and the ABM Treaty

The ABM Treaty has played a significant role to stabilize outer space since the 1970s. In May 1972, the U.S. and the USSR concluded the Treaty on the limitation of Anti-Ballistic Missile Systems (the ABM Treaty) that prohibits the deployment of ABM systems for the defense of a nations' territory, or an individual region, or defenses that has capability to provide the base for such a defense.

The ABM Treaty bans, in detail, the development, testing, and deployment of sea-based, air-based, space-based, or mobile land-based ABM systems and its system components including interceptor missiles, launchers, and radar sensors. It allows each party to withdraw after giving 6 months notice on the condition that extraordinary events related to the subject matter of this Treaty have jeopardized its supreme interests[8]

The Clinton Administration had outlined for NMD in 1999 that needed to deploy 100 interceptor missiles at a single site in Alaska[9]. It might have included space-based sensors, namely GPS and other components that the ABM Treaty would have banned. The Administration was in effort to modify the ABM Treaty to allow a limited deployment.

After the USSR, the Clinton Administration determined that Russia would be the successor to the Soviet Union for the Treaty and signed a Memorandum of Understanding (MoU) on

Succession (targeting Russia, Ukraine, Belarus, and Kazakhstan) in September 1997, however, it did not enter into force.

The Bush Administration announced its intention of withdrawal from the ABM Treaty on 13 Dec. 2001 to enable the U.S. move beyond the limits in the treaty to deploy missile defenses, and that took effect on 13 June 2002. It has sought to develop and deploy an integrated, layered system to defend the U.S., its forces, and allies from missile of all ranges. It preferred 'Missile Defense', rather than 'National Missile Defense', with its concept that could combine defenses against shorter, medium, and longer-range missiles in an integrated defense systems.

3.3. After the U.S. Withdrawal from the ABM Treaty

Russia has regarded the ABM Treaty as the cornerstone of strategic stability, which control the entire network of agreements that reduce offensive nuclear weapons. Therefore, it criticized the U.S. withdrawal from the Treaty, which would upset not only strategic stability between the U.S. and Russia, but also international communities, and would provoke a new, threatening international arms race.

After the U.S. Terrorist Attacks on 11 Sept. 2001, Russia immediately took action to offer its support to the U.S. war on terrorism, by allowing the U.S. forces to use bases in former Soviet republics and by sharing intelligence and Russian knowledge about Afghanistan. Therefore, when the U.S. announced to give Russia the six-month notice of withdrawal from the Treaty on 13 Dec. 2001, a new framework for mutual strategic relations came necessary for stability, and they made efforts for a new treaty limiting strategic offensive weapon until when the U.S. withdrawal took effect. Both Presidents signed a Joint Declaration outlining a new framework for cooperation between the two nations.

In regard to arms control, Russia had abided the 1993 START-II Treaty (Strategic Arms Reduction Treaty), which has not entered into force, would have banned Russia from the deployment of land-based strategic ballistic missiles with multiple warheads. After the U.S. withdrew from the ABM Treaty, Russia indicated its neglect of START II as a counter to the U.S. decision.

4. 'Peaceful' Controversy

The definition of 'peaceful' in Article IV of the 1967 Outer Space Treaty (the 1967 OST), regarding disarmament of outer space, has been debated for many years. Although the 1959 Antarctic Treaty, which influenced on Article IV, uses 'peaceful' as 'non-military', the U.S. interpreted it into 'non-aggressive' that can read rather subjective in the following cases[10];

- During the 1990-1991 Persian Gulf War, GPS was used as space-based sensors in near real-time for communications.
- During the 2001-2002 Afghan War, GPS supported the U.S. by pointing out the locations where they were as well as enemy target.
- On 18 January 2002, DoD used GPS for the operational and live-fire testing of 161 military systems that demonstrated.

It is classical but important to review Article 2 (4) of the Charter of the United Nations (the UN Charter) to trace back the definition of 'peaceful';

'All members shall refrain in their international relations from the threat or use of force against the territorial integrity

or political independence of any State, or in any other manner inconsistent with the Purposes of the United Nations.'

Taking into consideration that many developing countries depend on the applications of GPS, it is threatening to use it for military purposes in outer space. Therefore military uses of GPS including the testing NMD are inconsistent with *the Purposes of the UN*.

4.1. Disarmament Articles

As long as space technologies are dual-use which exist in outer space already, the space defense strategies would require the more complicated formation of space technologies for war on Earth or in outer space or places between them. Therefore it is necessary to review the existing disarmament articles to avoid destabilization in outer space.

First it needs to be noted that the deployment of GNSS itself is not illegal as long as they do not carry nuclear weapons or weapons of mass destruction [11]. However, even GNSS seems non-aggressive, it could be categorized as some kind of weapons [12] that support weapons of mass destruction by offering communications and navigation for military purposes.

Article IV of the 1967 Space Treaty bases on the proposal that was made by the U.S. President Eisenhower who submitted it in the United Nation in 1960 [13]. He suggested 'to promote the peaceful use of space and utilize the new knowledge obtainable from space science and technology for the benefit of mankind[14]', quoting from the Antarctic Treaty which was concluded in 1959[15]. In addition, the USSR President Khrushchev also stated that it 'prepared to conclude an agreement which provide for the prohibition of the use of outer space for military purposes [16]'. Interpreting from those statements, they intended to avoid the next arm race in outer space.

4.1.1. Article IV (1) of the 1967 OST

Despite their first intention, the interpretation of Article IV of the 1967 OST has been open to States Parties for leaving places to install weapons in outer space. In the broad sense, compared with Article IV (2), which uses the term 'prohibit', nothing in Article IV (1) itself prohibits placing of any other type of weapons in outer space, including the moon and other celestial bodies[17]. Therefore, it is possible to interpret that, under international law and Article IV (1) of the 1967 OST, States Parties enable to use the whole of outer space for military purpose except placing nuclear weapons and weapons of mass destruction, by ignoring the first intention of two Presidents. Also, it could be interpreted that States Parties enable to use force in outer space for self-defense under the rules of international law and Article 51 of the United Nations Charter[18].

4.1.2. Article IV (2) of the 1967 OST

On the other hand, the original intention of disarmament was taken clearly in Article IV (2) of the 1967 OST that stipulates 'States Parties should use the Moon and other celestial bodies exclusively for peaceful purposes'. No activity of a military nature is allowed on the moon and the other celestial bodies. However, as long as it lacks the term 'in orbit', placing Early Warning Satellites[19] in orbit, under the U.S. space defense programs, is not illegal, even though it would provoke strong arguments over the legality of such military uses of outer space.

According to Article IV (2) '...the testing of any type of weapons and the conduct of military namoeuvres on celestial bodies shall be forbidden...', and in fact GPS was used for the testing of National Missile Defense on 18 January 2002. That conduct seems to have infringed on Article IV (2), however, the testing was conducted in orbit, not 'celestial bodies', which does not break any law directly.

The illegality of GPS uses for military purposes depends on the definition of 'peaceful' in Article IV consistent with general international law, especially under Article 2 (4) of the UN Charter[20].

4.1.3. Non-aggressive' or 'Non-military'?

In 1960, the U.S. President Eisenhower before the General Assembly of the UN presented a proposal [21], and the following statement influenced on Article IV of the 1967 OST.

> *'3. We agree, subject to appropriate verification, that no nation will put into orbit or station in outer space weapons of mass destruction. All launchings of space craft should be verified in advance by the United Nations.'*

At that time, the U.S. seemed in the position of 'non-military' for uses of outer space. However, in 1962, he presented the interpretation of 'peaceful' as follows;

> *'Outer space should be used for peaceful, that is, non-aggressive and beneficial - purposes. ...Until this (adequate safeguards) is achieved, the test of any space activities must not be whether it is military or non-military, but whether or not it is consistent with the United Nations Charter and other obligations of law.[22]'*

In addition, the U.S. National Space Policy of 1989 and 1996 expressed that 'outer space should be used for peaceful purposes and for the benefit of all countries, *including activities for national security and defense.*'

That military-oriented tendency arose with support of following assertion;

(a) 'Non-military' interpretation is not appropriate since space technologies are dual use and also using military personnel and facilities.
(b) There was nothing in general international law or even the UN Charter that obliged States not to use outer space for military purposes[23].
(c) The right of self-defense is kept under Article 51 of the UN Charter by Article III of the 1967 OST.
(d) The term 'peaceful' cannot be defined by Article I (1) of the 1967 OST, because the benefit and the interest of each country is different[24].

Contrary to 'non-aggressive' theory, the definition of 'non-military' has been claimed by the USSR since 1966 at the Legal Subcommittee of the COPUOS [25]. The representative stated that any program for military purposes must not be justified even for the interest of national or regional security, because it was manifest that such activities would lead to war.[26]

The definition of 'non-military' is based on the following assertion;

(a) The 1959 Antarctic Treaty, which influenced on the draft of the 1967 OST, has the definition of 'non-military' in Article I (1) as follows;

> *1. Antarctica shall be used for peaceful purposes only. There shall be prohibited, inter alia, any measures of a military nature, such as the establishment of military bases and fortifications, the carrying out of*

military maneuvers, as well as the testing of any type of weapons.

(b) Military aggressive activities are not consistent with international law and violate Article 2 (4) of the UN Charter[27]. According to Article III of the 1967 OST, it is not appropriate to define 'peaceful' as 'non-aggressive' because it is exceptional interpretation in other international law.

In regard to GPS for military uses, it does not infringe on Article IV (1) or (2) of the 1967 OST, due to the location and the limited terminology of that Treaty. However, such activities threat international peace and security, which is illegal under Principle of International Cooperation and Mutual Assistance.

4.2. GNSS under Article III of the Moon Agreement

It has been pointed out that the number of ratification for the Moon Agreement [28] weakens its persuasiveness. The main obstacle for States Parties to ratify is that the Moon Agreement might prevent them from commercializing their space activities in outer space, as well as from militarizing outer space. Although, its legal significance should be reviewed seriously since unanimous approval was given to the form of the UN General Assembly Resolution of the Moon Agreement.

Article III (3) of the Moon Agreement, which prohibits military uses 'in orbit or other trajectory to or around the moon', does not include 'in Earth Orbit' where GNSS is deployed (20200-km altitude). Then GPS uses for military purposes does not infringe, however, such terminology should not be restrictive to the place where military acts may take place in consideration for that space technology has been developed faster than space law has.

5. Legality of GNSS for Military Uses

As applications of GPS have been diversified globally, the concern of developing countries focuses on the balance of space benefit and threat of aggressive act in outer space. In order to take precautions, legality of space activities needs to be verified under Principle of Mutual Assistance and International Cooperation[29].

5.1. Under Principle of Mutual Assistance

Legality of GNSS for military uses depends on the definition of 'benefit' and 'interests' of Article I (1) of the 1967 OST, which provides 'the exploration and use of outer space, ...shall be carried out for the benefit and in the interests of all countries, ...'. In principle, Principle of Mutual Assistance prohibits space activities for the benefit and in the interests of specific countries or region. Since the current military uses of GNSS were for the Gulf War, Afghanistan War and the testing of NMD, such uses are benefit for specific countries, the U.S. and its allies. Therefore such acts are infringing on Article I (1) of the 1967 OST which is binding.

5.2. Under Principle of International Cooperation

Principle of International Cooperation is international customary law that bases on the UN Charter and the 1970 Declaration of Principle of Friendship and Cooperation[30]. In Article III of the 1967 OST, the Principle reflects in Article I, IX and X of the 1967 OST.

That Declaration has the same purpose and principles of Article I and II of the UN Charter that obliges States Parties to cooperate each other to maintain international peace and security. In addition, such cooperation needs to be consistent with the UN Charter, even in outer space, to contribute to develop the mutual understanding, strengthen the friendly relations between States and peoples recalling the preamble of the 1967 OST.

Therefore, GNSS uses for the interest of specific States, including military purposes, which might destabilize international peace and security, are illegal under Principle of International Cooperation.

5.3. Under Space Benefit Declaration

GNSS has potential application to create, maintain and share 'space benefit[31]' that might solve the global problems under Principle of International Cooperation. In 1988, Legal Subcommittee of the COPUOS decided to add the 'space benefit' issue on the agenda of its 1989 session[32] and to establish a working group on that agenda item[33] in the same year. Such an attempt was realized during the 1991 session[34] resulting in 'Space Benefit Declaration'[35], adopted by the General Assembly of the United Nations in 1996. Afterward, in 1999, this Declaration[36] contributed to the UNISPACEIII[37] resulting in the Vienna Declaration[38].

The impact of the "Space Benefit Declaration" on Principle of International Cooperation was analyzed as follows[39];

- It provides an authoritative interpretation of the cooperation principle of Article I of the 1967 OST and finalized a North-South debate on the introduction of forced cooperation and transfer of resources. It prevents further confrontation on a general political level.
- It confirmed that the freedom of the exploration and utilization of outer space as well as reminds the space powers - in a productive and mutually fruitful manner - to fulfill their obligation to conduct their activities for the benefit of all countries, which means that the space powers should foster international cooperation - on an equitable and mutually acceptable basis. It leads to that developing countries interested in space activities have now higher incentives to put their energies in a "demand-pull" instead of waiting for a politically induced "technology push" by their own efforts well-prepared.

Those interpretations of 'space benefit' would give a hint to the definition of 'peaceful' in line with Principle of International Cooperation. For example, Principle I stipulates;

1. International cooperation [...] shall be conducted in accordance with the provisions of international law, including the Charter of the United Nations and the Treaty on Principles Governing the Activities of States in the Exploration and Use of Outer Space, including the Moon and Other Celestial Bodies [...]"

It repeats the contents of Preamble and Article I of the 1967 OST. And Principle III states;

3. All States, [...] should contribute to promoting and fostering international cooperation on an equitable and mutually acceptable basis. In this context, particular attention should be given to the benefit and the interests of developing countries and countries with incipient space programmes stemming from such international cooperation conducted with countries with more advanced space capabilities.

It clarifies that space powers must involve developing countries into space activities. The Space Benefit Declaration does not intend to force cooperation since it stipulates that such cooperation needs 'on an equitable and mutually acceptable bases'. However, it shall enhance international or intergovernmental space cooperation through implementation of recommendations of UNISPACEIII. In regard to GNSS, that is the aim of holding the UN/USA GNSS Workshop[40] in 5 developing countries.

6. Conclusion

The application of GNSS has been expanding for peaceful uses even though GPS has been developed for military uses.

After the U.S. Terrorists Attacks on 11 Sept. 2001, the U.S. Space Defense Policy has been developing NMD fully, which provokes destabilization of outer space. Before the withdrawal of the ABM treaty took effect on 13 June 2002, GPS was used for the testing of targeting ICBM to help plan the intercept and assist mid-range tracking for NMD.

Before complete placing weapon in outer space, it is indispensable to review the definition of 'peaceful' in Article IV of the 1967 OST, regarding disarmament of outer space, which has been debated over decades. Even it is clear that the 1959 Antarctic Treaty, which influenced on the 1967 OST, uses 'peaceful' as 'non-military', however, 'non-aggressive' is general opinion inconsistent with Article 2 (4) of the UN Charter.

Although Article IV of the 1967 OST bases on President Eisenhower's proposal, submitted in the UN in 1960, his original intention was not took over to the existing Article IV (1). Even States Parties may use outer space for military purposes, in self-defense in accordance with the rules of international law and Article 51 of the United Nations Charter[41].

Under Article IV (2) of the 1967 OST, no activity of a military nature is allowed on the moon and the other celestial bodies. However, as long as it lacks the term 'in orbit', placing Early Warning Satellites in outer space, under the U.S. space defense programs, does not infringe on this Article, even though it would provoke strong arguments over the legality of such military uses of outer space.

Military activities in outer space should be considered under Principle of International Cooperation and Mutual Assistance, which are international customary law consistent with the UN Charter.

Under Article III (3) of the Moon Agreement, GPS uses for military purposes do not infringe. Although it lacks the term of 'in Earth orbit' to apply the case of GPS, such terminology should not be restrictive to the place where military acts may take place in consideration for that space technology has been developed faster than space law has.

Space Benefit Declaration supplements the definition of 'peaceful' by Principle I, which repeats the contents of Preamble and Article I of the 1967 OST. According to Principle III, it clarifies that space powers must involve developing countries into space activities.

In conclusion, due to the location of GPS and the limited terminology of Article IV of the 1967 OST, there is no specific article, which prohibits States Parties from using GPS for war or NMD. However, such military uses in outer space are destabilizing outer space, threatening international peace and security, and illegal under Principle of International Cooperation and Mutual Assistance.

---

[1] Introduction to GPS Applications, <http://ares.redsword.com/GPS/apps/introduction/toGPS.htm> (Last accessed: 2 Oct. 2002)

[2] The current GNSS applications are as follows;

- Forest management and mapping to assess the forest resources, accurate and updated information on forest.
- Precision agriculture to improve production efficiency by adjusting crop treatments to conditions existing at specific areas within fields with GPS, GIS and remote sensing system.
- Disaster management to interconnect the safety management operations vertically and horizontally.
- Environment and Geographic Information System to identify water sector features in different parts of the country.

Besides above, GNSS is used for aviation, maritime, land transportation, mapping, geodesy and land surveying, Earth science, meteorological and climate applications, atmospheric sensing and sounding, agriculture, timing and telecommunications, spacecraft, mineral prospecting, and public safety.

[3] The Third United Nations Conference on the Exploration and Peaceful Uses of Outer Space (UNISPACE III), based on General Assembly Resolution 52/56: International Cooperation in the Peaceful Uses of Outer Space, UN Doc. A/Res/52/56 (1997).

[4] A/AC. 107.771, 'United Nations/United States of America Workshop on the Uses of Global Navigation Satellite Systems', aiming (a) to bring the benefits of the availability and use of GNSS signals to the awareness of decision makers and technical personnel from potential user in particular in developing countries; and (b) to identify actions that could be taken and partnerships to be established by potential users.

[5] See, A/CONF.184/BP/4, 27 May 1998

[6] In regard to the budget for space defense program, the 107th Congress of the U.S. has showed the figure that the FY 2002 budget of $15.761 billion, a FY2003 request of $18.481 billion, which includes the management of a Space-Based InfraRed System (SBIRS) in order to develop new early warning satellites, space control capabilities, and management of military and intelligence space activities in general.

[7] Arms Control Association: Arms Control Today, Boese, W., "December Missile Defense Tests Yield One Success, One Failure", online at <http://www.armscontrol.org/act/2002_01-02/misdeftestjanfeb02.asp> (Last accessed: 02 Sept. 2002)

[8] United States Arms Control and Disarmament Agency, Arms Control and Disarmament Agreements, Text and Histories of the Negotiations, Washington, D.C. (1990)

[9] Congressional Research Service: The Library of Congress, CRS Issue Brief, Order Code IB10034, Steven Hildreth, A., and Woolf, Amy F., "National Missile Defense: Issues for Congress", online at <http://www.fas.org/spp/starwars/congress/1996_r/crs96441.htm> (Last accessed: 5 Sept. 2002)

[10] Congressional Research Service: The Library of Congress, CRS Issue Brief for Congress, Order Code IB92011, Marcia S. Smith, "U.S. Space Programs: Civilian, Military, and Commercial", online at <http://www.cnie.org/nle/crsreports/science/st-57.pdf> (Last accessed: 4 Sept. 2002) at 6

[11] In the United Nations Commission for Conventional Armaments, it was resolved that 'weapon of mass destruction should be defined to include atomic explosive weapons, radioactive material weapons, lethal chemical and biological weapons, and any weapons developed in the future which have characteristics comparable in destructive effect to those of the atomic bomb or other weapons mentioned above', UN S/C.3/32/Rev.1 (18.8.48).

[12] 'What weapon is in outer space already? It's GPS.' the lecture was given by Prof. John M. Logston, Space Policy Institute, George Washington University, at Department of Space Policy and Law, Summer Session Program 2002 of International Space University.

[13] Cf. A/AC.105/C.2/SR.65 (22.7.66), at 9-10 (USA); ibid. /SR.66 (25.7.66), at6-7 (USSR).

[14] 'Introduction to Outer Space', An Explanatory Statement prepared by the President's Science Advisory Committee 1 (1958)
[15] 1 Dec. 1959, Comnd. 913 (1959), 402 UNTS 71.
[16] "President Khrushchev to the President", 38 Department State Bull. 814 (1958).
[17] Cheng, B., "Studies in International Space Law", Clarendon Press Oxford (London: 1997) at 518
[18] Cheng, B., "Military Use of Outer Space", *The Utilization of the World's Air Space and Free Outer Space in the 21st* Century, (Kluwer Law International: 2000) at 330.
[19] The present Early Warning Satellites are as follows;
- Space Based InfraRed System (SBIRS): DoD of US has attempted to develop more capable satellites to provide early warning of foreign missile launches for support missile defense objectives.
- Space-Based Lasers: SBL have been funded since President Reagan announced the 'Star Wars' program in 1983 in the context of missile defense.
[20] The Charter of the United Nations, Article 2 (4): 'All Members shall refrain in their international relations from the threat or use of force against the territorial integrity or political independence of any States, or in any other manner inconsistent with the Purposes of the United Nations.'
[21] GAOR. GA(XV) A/PV.868 (22.9.60), at 45, para. 48
[22] A/AC.1/PV.1289(3.12.62), at 13.
[23] See, Cheng, B., "The Military Use of Outer Space in International Law", in E.G. Bello and Prince Bola A. Ajibola, San (eds), 1 Essays in Honour of Judge Taslim Olawale Elias 81992), at 63.
[24] *Supra note* 1, at 109
[25] The Committee on the Peaceful Uses of Outer Space, established on 12 December 1959 under UNGA Resolution 1472 (XIV)
[26] A/AC. 105/C. 2/SR. 58, p3-14
[27] 'All Members shall refrain in their international relations from the threat or use of force against the territorial integrity or political independence of any state, or in any other manner inconsistent with the Purposes of the United Nations'.
[28] Agreement Governing the Activities of States on the Moon and Other celestial Bodies, 18 Dec. 1979, 18 *ILM* 1434; 1363 UNTS 3.
[29] *Supra note* 1, at 109
[30] Declaration on Principles of International Law Concerning Friendly Relations and Co-operation Among states in Accordance with the Charter of the United Nations, UNResolution2625 (XXV), 24 Oct. 1970
[31] On the early handling the subject, see, Jasentuliyana, N,. "Article I of the Outer Space treaty Revisited", Journal of Space Law 1989, (17,2), at 129-144, here at. 130-136
[32] See, the Report of the Legal Subcommittee on the Work of Its twenty-seventh session, UN Doc. A/AC. 105/411 of April 8, 1988, paras. 37-72.
[33] See, the Report of the Legal Subcommittee on the Work of Its Twenty-Eighth Session, UN Doc. A/AC. 105/430 of April 26, 1989, paras. 53 and 60.
[34] See, the Main Committee the Report of UNCOPUOS 1990, UN Doc. A/45/20, para. 120
[35] Declaration on International Cooperation in the Exploration and Use of Outer Space for the Benefit and in the Interest of All States, Taking into Particular Account the Needs of Developing Countries, UNGA Resolution 51/122, 13 Dec. 1996
[36] See, UN Doc. A/AC.105/385, 411 and 430
[37] Based on UNGA Resolution 52/56: International Cooperation in the Peaceful Uses of Outer Space, UN Doc. A/Res/52/56 (1997).
[38] See, The Space Millennium: Vienna Declaration on Space and Human Development, which was the final resolution to be adopted by UNISPACE III.
[39] See, Marietta Benko and Kai-uwe Schrogl, "The UN Committee on the Peaceful Uses of Outer Space Adoption of a Declaration on 'Space Benefits' and Other Recent Developments", in ZLW, Jg 2/1997 at 233.
[40] See, Chapter 2
[41] *Supra note* 18, at 330.

PROPAGANDA VIA SATELLITE[1]

Philippe Achilleas
Director of the Institute of Space and Telecommunications Law
University Paris Sud – 11[2]
France
Philippe.achilleas@idest-paris.org

Abstract

This paper deals with international regulation of propaganda via satellite. The author gives the international definition of propaganda and explains the applicable law by analyzing space law, human rights law, communications law, the law of peace and security and international penal law.

Introduction

In the context of the cold war, the debate over television broadcasting via satellite was, in the beginning, strongly linked to the question of propaganda. The socialist countries, lead by the USSR, hammered out the same idea at every international conference related to the issue: the satellite was nothing more than a vehicle for further distribution of bourgeois propaganda[1]. The question of propaganda via satellite was thus placed at the center of the debate by the States who had, at the time, the most recourse to its use[2]. At the time, the socialist countries were concerned that their internal communication systems would become porous to occidental propaganda. The legitimacy of these States had been founded, in great part, on the control of information and the closing of borders to all communications coming from abroad. The concerns over propaganda via satellite are still present today as evidenced by the concerns surrounding television broadcasting by satellite. In 1999, the Turkish government attempted to prohibit the retransmission of the Kurdish channel MedTV broadcasted by Intelsat and Eutelsat, accusing the channel of acting as a vehicle for separatist propaganda. More recently, following the events of 11 September 2001, the US government strongly criticized the information channel Al Jazeera, presenting it as a vector of anti-American propaganda and an organ for inciting terrorism. Finally, the inauguration by Israel in July 2002 of a satellite channel broadcasting in Arabic to the Middle East was intended to combat war propaganda which, according to the Hebrew State, was being broadcast by 140 Arabic channels inciting hatred for Israel across the rec eiving populations[3]. This paper deals with the international regulation of propaganda via satellite and will first define propaganda according to international law (1) before going on to study the applicable law (2).

---

[2] P. Achilleas is also Part-time resident faculty in Policy and Law at the International Space University central campus.

1. The notion of propaganda in international law

According to a study conducted by UNESCO, "the notion of propaganda implies efforts deliberately organized with a view to influence the attitudes and behavior of others, even if this influence is more often hoped for rather than anticipated, desired rather than foreseen"[4]. Propaganda is, by its nature, a planned and voluntary action. Continuity and duration are indispensable to its efficacy. The action of one sole channel cannot qualify as propaganda unless it is demonstrated that the channel represents the unique source of information for the targeted population. The USA was therefore incorrect in claiming that Al Jazeera's broadcasting of video footage of Osama Ben Laden during the bombings over Afghanistan in the autumn of 2001 amounted to terrorist propaganda. In another respect, propaganda can be distinguished from information by its goal – the former is intended to influence, the latter is intended to enlighten. Al Jazeera had not, at any time, employed conscious efforts to influence the populations of the receiving countries.

International law condemns, above all, war propaganda, which is defined as any organized utilization of the media with the intention of provoking international armed conflict. However, the mobilization of its population by a State victim of an armed aggression does not constitute an act of propaganda. International law equally prohibits subversive propaganda which is intended to alter the internal order of another State and which could therefore be comparable to interference in domestic affairs. That said, a State party to an international armed conflict could legally carry out propaganda activities intended to discourage the population and demoralize the troops of the enemy camp. International law also prohibits other specific forms of propaganda, for example, genocide propaganda, apartheid propaganda and racist propaganda. However, the defamatory propaganda proposed by J. B. Whitton[5], was never, for its part, recognized by international law even though certain States currently consider themselves to be victims. Beijing, for example, considers that "the American media defamed China in a systematic, organized and planned manner"[6]. Although international law does attach sanctions to defamation, this is more general and independent of the notion of propaganda.

2. The applicable law

Although space law is vague regarding the prohibition of propaganda (a), human rights law (b), communications law (c) the law of peace and international security (d) as well as international penal law (e) condemn propaganda initiatives.

a. Space law

Space law contains no direct provisions on the prohibition of propaganda. However, several initiatives have attempted to incorporate regulation of propaganda into the texts relating to space. In the Soviet proposal for the declaration of principles on space, proposed to COPUOS in 1962, the final version of which was adopted in 1963, paragraph 5 condemned the use of space for the purposes of war propaganda, or propaganda considered to be nationalist, racist or which provoked hate amongst nations[7]. According to Moscow, without a prohibition on propaganda, all satellite communication systems would be naturally compromised. In parallel, Brazil considered that television via satellite would contribute to the dissemination of a false and degrading image of Third-world countries. Its delegation proposed to include in the declaration a prohibition on propaganda favoring war, the class struggle, racial or religious propaganda and propaganda which is offensive to a third party country[8]. The United States however rejected any reference to propaganda and favored the adoption of a very general text without mention of specific space activities[9]. A similar debate saw the USSR and the USA in opposition in regard to the drafting of the 1967 Treaty on Principles Governing the Activities of States in the Exploration and Use of Outer Space, Including the Moon and Other Celestial Bodies. In the end, the definitive versions of both texts, the 1963 Declaration[10] and the 1967 Treaty[11], contain no direct clauses prohibiting propaganda. However, their preambles do refer to the United Nations General Assembly Resolution 110(II) of 3 November 1947 which condemns propaganda. Even the resolution adopted by the General Assembly in 1982 relating to direct broadcasting by satellite makes no reference in its articles to the question of propaganda[12].

It therefore comes down to looking to general international law, in conformity with article III of the Outer Space Treaty, to identify the relevant rules for regulating propaganda via satellite.

b. <u>Human rights law</u>

The Universal Declaration of Human Rights of 10 December 1948[13] and the International Covenant on Civil and Political Rights of 16 December 1966[14] recognize, in their respective articles 19, the right to freedom of information without consideration of borders which applies to all mediums of distribution, including satellite, and to all content including that which may shock or disturb. In this light alone, the use of satellites for broadcasting propaganda would be legal. However, the 1966 Covenant imposes two series of restrictions on this freedom. Firstly, article 19 § 3 states that freedom of information can be subject to certain restrictions which must be expressly set down by law and which are necessary for the safeguarding of national security or public order. Secondly, article 20 § 1 provides that propaganda in favor of war is prohibited by law. The same provision is made in article 20 § 2 for propaganda aimed at inciting national, racial or religious hate which constitutes incitement toward discrimination, hostility or violence. Several reservations were made, however, in relation to this article[15]. On the question of incitement to racism, the 1966 Covenant must be read in the light of the International Convention on the Elimination of All Forms of Racial Discrimination, concluded on 21 December 1965[16], which condemns, in its article 4, "all propaganda ... based on ideas or theories of superiority of one race or group of persons of one color or ethnic origin, or which attempt to justify or promote racial hatred and discrimination in any form...".

c. <u>Communications law</u>

The Convention of 23 September 1936 on the Use of Broadcasting in the Cause of Peace is the only international treaty exclusively devoted to propaganda and disinformation[17]. The first article of the Convention prohibits subversive propaganda, whereas article 2 prohibits war propaganda. By virtue of article 6, it is up to the States to ensure and verify that the provisions of the Convention are applied through appropriate instructions and regulations addressed to broadcasting services placed under their direct control, either by including these in the clauses of the constitutive charters of autonomous national broadcasting institutions, or in the conditions imposed upon concessionary companies or the rules applicable to other private enterprises. At the international level, article 7 of the Convention provides for a progressive mechanism for the peaceful settlement of disputes: diplomatic negotiations, appeal to the good offices of the International Committee on Intellectual Co-operation, arbitration and judicial settlement[18].

d. The law of peace and international security

Given that the principal aim of the United Nations is to maintain international peace and security, it was normal for the Organization to take a stance on the question of propaganda. The UN has maintained a firm and clear position on this point in prohibiting propaganda in so far as it threatens international peace. First, propaganda, regardless of whether it relates to war or subversion, is considered to be a violation of article 2 § 4 of the United Nations Charter[19]. Secondly, the General Assembly rapidly condemned propaganda content through the adoption of specific resolutions. On 3 November 1947, the General Assembly adopted, in conformity with the Charter, Resolution 110 (II). This text was written in continuation of the UN Charter and, aiming to preserve future generations from the scourge of war[20], condemned all forms of propaganda which are either designed or likely to produce or encourage any threat to peace, breach of the peace or act of aggression. A second text, Resolution 381(V) on the condemnation of propaganda against peace was adopted on 17 November 1950[21].

e. International penal law

International penal law condemns propaganda in two respects. Firstly, it sanctions against genocide propaganda. On 9 December 1948, in reaction to the genocide perpetrated by the German nazi regime which had blatantly used the media for genocide propaganda, the Convention on the Prevention and Punishment of the Crime of Genocide was signed[22]. Recent history has shown us that this technique is far from being abandoned. Most notably in Rwanda, the media was used as a means to incite genocide through the broadcasts of *Radio et Télévision libre des Mille Collines*[23]. Article III of the Genocide Convention prohibits "direct and public incitement to commit genocide". Similarly, apartheid propaganda or direct incitement to its commission are prohibited by article III of the International Convention on the Suppression and Punishment of the Crime of Apartheid, adopted by the General Assembly in its Resolution 3068 (XXVIII) of 30 November 1973.

---

[1] See notably: B. G. DUDAKOV, "Some International Legal Issues on the Direct Television Broadcast Satellites", *Proceedings of the 14th Colloquium on the Law of Outer Space*, IISL, Brussels, Belgium (1971), 1972, p. 165.

[2] In effect, at the start of the 1960's, the expenditure of the USSR and the States of the Warsaw Pact for propaganda purposes amounted to 1.5 billion dollars per year - 2 % of their GNP and 20 times more than the expenditure of the United States for the same cause - F. BENHALLA, *La guerre radiophonique*, Paris, PUF, 1983, p. 28.

[3] *Satellite Week*, 1 July 2002, p. 6.

[4] T. MARTELANC, S. SPLICHAL, B. PACLIC, A. FERLIGOJ, V. BATAGELJ, M. D. MURKO, *Les émissions radiodiffusées vers l'étranger et la compréhension internationale - émissions étrangères destinées à la Yougoslavie*, Etudes et documents d'information n° 81, Paris, UNESCO 1978, p.7.

[5] J. B. WHITTON, "Propaganda and International Law", *RCADI*, 1948-I, volume 72, pp. 543 - 658.

[6] D. XIAOHUA, "Pourquoi et comment les médias américains œuvrent à diffamer la Chine", *Bejin Information*, n° 31, 4 August 1997, pp. 9-13.

[7] For the initial Soviet proposal see: UN Doc. A/AC.105/C.2/L.1; for the modified Soviet proposal see: UN Doc. A/AC.105/C.2/L.6.

[8] *Report of the COPUOS*, 5th Session, UN Doc. A/5549/add.1 (1963), p. 21.

[9] UN Doc. A/AC.105/C2/SR.1, p. 8.

[10] Declaration of Legal Principles Governing the Activities of States in the Exploration and Uses of Outer Space (General Assembly resolution 1962 (XVIII) of 13 December 1963).

[11] *UNTS*, volume 610, p. 205.

[12] UN Principles Governing the Use by States of Artificial Earth Satellites for International Direct Television Broadcasting (resolution 37/92 of 10 December 1982).

[13] The Declaration is annexed to UNGA Resolution 217 A (III).

[14] *UNTS*, volume 78, p. 277.

[15] Denmark, Finland and Sweden declared they did not want to apply this provision, judging that to vote against war propaganda risked limiting freedom of expression. Luxembourg stated, for its part, that article 20 must be applied taking into account freedom of expression. Other States like Malta, the United Kingdom and Switzerland considered that they were not obliged to legislate in the domain covered by article 20 § 1. The United States noted that article 20 could not oblige them to adopt measures which restrain the freedom of expression and association protected by the Constitution and the laws of the United States.

[16] *UNTS*, volume 1500, p. 161 – The text was adopted by the General Assembly in its Resolution 2106 A (XX).

[17] This Convention was the work of the League of Nations. The League of Nations examined the question of broadcasting propaganda in 1926 resulting in a Resolution adopted by the consultative and technical committee for communication and transport (SDN, JOSDN, 1926, p. 1141). In September 1933, its Assembly authorized the Committee on Intellectual Cooperation (the equivalent of UNESCO) to prepare a proposal. The Treaty, adopted in 1936, was not signed by Germany, Italy and Japan who operated at the time propagandist policies and refused to become parties.

[18] On 17 December 1954, the UN General Assembly adopted Resolution 841 (IX) relating to the International Convention on the Use of Broadcasting in the Cause of Peace. In its first paragraph, the text asks States Parties to the Convention if they will accept that the functions originally conferred by the Convention on the League of Nations be transferred to the United Nations.

[19] This article provides that "All Members shall refrain in their international relations from the threat or use of force against the territorial integrity or political independence of any state, or in any other manner inconsistent with the purposes of the United Nations".

[20] Preamble, para. 1

[21] The text clarifies, in paragraph 2, the notion of propaganda against peace, by including two situations : incitement to conflict or acts of aggression and measures which tend to isolate people from all external contact.

[22] *UNTS*, volume 78, p. 277.

[23] This station, known as "Hate Radio", was used between 1 January and 31 July 1994 to broadcast programs conceived to provoke inter-ethnic hate and to incite the population to kill or commit acts of violence against the Tutsi minority as well as against others for reasons of political alliance.

ACQUISITION OF SPACE WEAPONS, THE LEGAL, POLITICAL AND MILITARY IMPACT FOR INTERNATIONAL PEACE AND SECURITY

Johanna Catena LLB
Law Graduate student,
University of Hertfordshire
Kent, England
xgx86@dial.pipex.com

Abstract

At the dawn of a new century an immediate danger is upon us: The weaponization of outer space, including potential cost implications of ushering an era of peace and prosperity. Can such statements be explained as pure sentimentality for hopes of a new era? Or is the danger misplaced that the threat to peace and security is an ever more ominous? The Outer Space Treaty prohibits placing in orbit nuclear and other weapons of mass destruction, but this does not include other military systems. These other systems may involve anti-satellite weapons, (ASATS), directed and Kinetic Energy Weapons that may emit laser beams or use their mass from space to intercept ballistic missiles, hostile satellites and eventually ground targets. The Outer Space Treaty states that space should be for peaceful purposes, but what does that mean in the context of acquiring space weapons? Reaching consensus upon delimitation question would be useful to determine when a space weapon is a space weapon. The fabric of these legal implications is being held together with a single thread through political mistrust and self-interest motivated by national security measures. Adopting a more progressive use of outer space this will immediately enhance political relations and global stability.

Militarization of outer space has been a source of debate since Russia launched their first satellite, Sputnik-I as the potential of space was realised, the space race begun. This would not, however, have been possible if it was not for the development of Rocket, which culminating from centuries of technological development into establishing modern astronautics and aviation.

The origin of rocket warfare can be traced as early as thirteen century AD where the Chinese used black powder to create an explosive force. The propellant did not reach Europe until mid thirteen century which was through an English scientist called Roger Bacon. During the beginning of the 1800's the rocket went through a number of improvements the first being in India where they adopted the use of metal cylinders, secondly Sir William Congreve made it possible to choose between a ball charge or incendiary warhead. He also greatly improved the accuracy of the rocket. Thirdly, William

Hale successfully designed the rocket to spin. However the gun became an extremely effective weapon for the military thus the use of rockets declined up until the beginning of the Second World War 1939.

The vision for rockets, however, had changed in between the end of nineteen century to the start of W.W.II. Russian engineer Konstantin Tsiolkovsky was stimulated by the ideas of space travel and was also greatly influenced by Jules Vernes, a fiction writer. Born death; and at the age ten caught scarlet fever and also with the death of his mother a few years later required him to study at home. Books became a great interest, particularly in the area of mathematics and physics. Tsiolkovsky worked as a teacher and also a researcher in to aeronautics and astronautics. His ideas and experiments were highly developed and ingenious. Tsiolkovsky was the first in Russian to build a wind tunnel using a modest grant from the Academy of Sciences. He went on to develop innovative aircraft designs. He published his first book regarding the possibilities of using rockets as means to travel into space, in 1895 and was called 'Dreams of Earth and Sky'. However it was his thesis that dealt with the possibility of using multi stage, liquid-fuelled rockets that marked his most serious work on astronautics. Tsiokovsky's paper was called 'Exploration of space Using reaction Devices' and dealt with the theoretical problems may arise through space travel, describing in detail a full mission into space, as well as laying down fundamental mathematical principles in order to gain an understanding to these problems. Tsiokovsky only theorized and chose never to build a rocket, he envisaged his ideas would not come about until 21st century.

Robert Goddard, an American scientist and founding father to modern rocket science continued Tsiokovsky's work, although he was unaware that a schoolteacher in Russian shared an almost identical vision for outer space. Goddard was greatly influenced by H G Wells novel, 'War of the Worlds'. His ultimate goal was to create a workable machine that could propel into space and eventually mars. He was the first to design high altitude rockets, establishing the nozzle and combustion chamber he went on to constructing and launching them. He also explored the use of liquid oxygen and hydrogen as propulsion and also being the first to build a rocket motor using liquid fuels that was used later by the Germans for the design of the V-2 rocket. After initial experiments with liquid fuelled rockets in Roswell, he published his findings in 1936 called 'Liquid Propellant Rocket Development'. Goddard's experiments in Roswell closed upon the decline in interest in rocket science. He died of throat cancer just before rocket propulsion took another leap forward.

Although the idea of space travel was yet to be fully accepted amongst, the public and it took the work of Hermann Oberth of Germany, founder to German Rocket Society, to engage the publics' imagination as well as fellow scientists. His famous paper in 1923 'The Rocket Into Interplanetary Space' and in 1929 'Ways to Space flight' advanced previous theories of the problems that may be encountered by manning a space flight e.g. space walks, interplanetary travel and using liquid propellant rocket motors. He worked for Wernher Von Braun in Peenemünde where the first ballistic missile was tested the V-2, which was subsequently used for space travel.

However from 1936, it was the renewed military interest in the rocket that led to the development of the V-2 in Germany, subsequently the visions of space travel were put on hold. This was exactly as military interests declined during end of the nineteenth century to 1930, when space travel then took precedence.

Von Braun read Hermann Oberth's paper 'The Rocket Into Interplanetary Space' which encouraged him to apply himself at school, in particular to mathematics because it was a source of frustration for him in his inability to understand Oberth's mathematical principles. The capabilities of Von Braun and liquid fuelled rockets attracted attention from Capt. Walter R Dornberger who provided Von Braun with financial support through arranging a research grant from the Ordnance Department of Germany. Von Braun's early interest in space was replaced during the Second World War. Rocket science was suffering from financial difficulties as military interest intercepted through renewed rigor thus firmly grounding the rocket as an effect weapon capable of causing huge devastation. Von Braun and his team of scientists designed the long range V-2 ballistic missile and Wernher Von Braun remarked upon Goddard's work by saying how Goddard had taken years off their work enabling them to complete the V-2 much earlier than expected and this was due to Goddard's experiments.

The V-2, meaning Vengeance Weapon 2 was successfully tested in Peenemünde, north-eastern Germany, proclaiming Germany as the forefront of technology. This was the site where they launched many V-2 missiles against England, France and Belgium inevitably causing immense destruction and causalities.

After the Second World War Braun and his team of scientists surrendered to the U.S. troops and they transferred to the US Ordnance Corps at White Sands where advanced studies were made into captured V-2 missiles. However, space, was not a high priority until the launch of the Sputnik-1 in October 1957 from the Soviet Union. The space race had begun. Braun and his team of scientists subsequently launched the first USA Satellite just 3 months later (January 1958), called the Explorer 1. Also, the US government in 1958 established National Aeronautics and Space Administration (NASA).

The Soviet Union were the first to launch a manned space flight Vostok 1, where Yury A Gargarin was the first cosmonaut in 1961, one trip was made around the earth, lasting for just over hour and a half. The first woman cosmonaut was Valentina V. Tereshkova in June 1963. Voskhod was the next step in Soviet technologies, which enable the soviets to launch a flight that had the capability of taking more than one cosmonaut. Voskhod 2 was launched on March 18th 1965 and Alexei Leonov conducted the first space walk making it (approx) sixty-two years later from Tsiokovsky's paper prophesizing that such events would not occur until 21st century. Soviet Union did not launch a manned flight to the moon choosing to send lunar probes to collect data. Neil A Armstrong and Edwin E. Aldrin were the first USA astronauts to walk on the lunar surface from the Apollo 11 mission in 1969 conducting scientific experiments and collecting samples. The potential of space was being acknowledged with great importance, particularly as a means to extend military operations through satellite and strategic defense initiatives.

Thus, military presence in space is not founded just on weapons but also through military surveillance systems. These include image satellites, which are high-resolution cameras to identify images /objects on the ground and radar satellites. Electronic Intelligence systems are spy satellites that intercept data, international voice traffic and faxes, etc. Nuclear test detectors: Infrared satellites, which can detect thermal radiation and act as a missile warning system and Geodetic satellites for self guided cruise missiles. Other such satellites, known as support systems, such as communication/relay satellites ensure command and control in exchanging information between other relay satellites; weather satellites and navigation satellites that are part of the Global Positioning System. It is interesting to note that there is both a civilian and military purpose to satellites as well as to launch vehicles and ground stations. For example through Disarmament Treaties ballistic missiles that are to be retired can be used as civilian satellite launchers. Also, high-resolution imagery for remote sensing used for civilian purposes such as monitoring climate change and natural hazards can be used as a support to planning military operations. This highlights the problem of how the distinction between military and space systems has become blurred with dual- purpose technology.

Militarization of outer space has been a source of ongoing debate since the launch of Sputnik but what exactly is meant by it?

In the Oxford Dictionary, the general meaning of militarization appears to be dependant upon interpretation, for example, to utilize and equip [space] with military forces and defenses. Infact this interpretation is quite convenient as missile defense could easily be read into the meaning. Also, by adding 'weapons' alongside forces a definition is arising but it remains inadequate as defenses is too general and is silent upon the uses of military satellites. On the other hand, militarization could simply be used as a 'means to give space a military usage' or perhaps 'to adapt space for military use' and again highlights the same problems found in the first interpretation. Thus establishing a definition upon the 'militarization of outer space' presents immediate difficulties. I have highlighted two aspects that perhaps require clarification. The first, that militarization is through acquisition of 'space strike weapons' which has the capabilities of destroying ballistic missiles as well as destroying any ground, sea and air based weapons systems which pose a threat to space satellites and/or space defense systems.

The second aspect is that militarization occurred upon launching satellites solely for military purposes. This view, however, is not shared, in particular by Russian if one recalls the debates and proposal submitted by Russia to the UN in 1958 and again in 1981; the draft treaty entitled 'Treaty on the Prohibition of the Stationing of Weapons of Any Kind'. However, other countries such as Italy in their draft proposals to the UN believe surveillance systems should also be included in the total prohibition and condemnation of all military activities in outer space. Although these technologies do provide verification on arms control, which some countries have argued in support of such systems, which are needed to adhere to various international agreements, verifying Chemical Weapons Conventions and reducing the number of nuclear weapons and generally maintaining strategic stability. Also, military surveillance systems should not be included as militarizing outer space and subsequently in the debate for prohibition, particularly as they would prevent an adversary from launching a surprise attack. On the other hand, this could provoke an outbreak of hostilities, as it is possible to miscalculate the other countries capabilities thus intensifying an arms race in outer space by intensifying the debate on space defense systems. Difficulty can be highlighted upon analyzing the peaceful and non-peaceful uses of outer space, which is synonymous to establishing a definition.

Thus, not only had the technology which opened space for scientific exploration became dual purpose as they were cultivated through weapons, space itself was being contemplated as a means to conduct and control warfare through the use of space based laser and X ray weapons through strategic defense initiatives. The technology, behind the idea was not available, however, the United Nations recognized that space in the future might become the new battlefield to direct wars on the terrestrial surface, subsequently recognizing the need to establish new rules governing the conduct of human activities in space. Thus in 1967 the Outer Space Treaty was signed focusing on the peaceful uses of outer space and to explore space 'in the interest of maintaining international peace and security and promoting international cooperation and understanding,' Article 3 Outer Space Treaty.

In the preamble of the Treaty it states, 'recognizing the common interest of all mankind in the progress of the exploration and the use of outer space for peaceful purposes', also in Article IV paragraph 2, "the moon and other celestial bodies shall be used exclusively for peaceful purposes…'. Peaceful has remained undefined in the Treaty and has caused considerable difficulty resulting in, as highlighted above, two schools of thought as to what constitutes the military uses of outer space. Article 31(1) of the Vienna Convention on the Law of Treaties states that the ordinary meaning must be interpreted to words in a treaty. However before a meaning to the peaceful uses of outer space can be ascertained it would be prudent to define the boundaries of outer space so one can further define when a 'space weapon' is a space weapon.

Satellites also require detailed analysis arriving at criteria to its components, functions and users, thus, making it easier to highlight any aggressive nature that may interfere with the 'peaceful uses of outer space'. The attempt is to arrive at a compromise and resolve the different schools of thought within space law so international space law can forge ahead with the development of new technologies.

The starting point is the delimitation of the boundaries of outer space. The Outer Space Treaty 1967 is silent upon the definition of outer space. Thus how has the Treaty worked without such a definition? Space capabilities have considerably advanced since the signing of the Treaty as space is in danger of evolving predominately into a base to utilize space based military operations.

In 1959, the ad hoc Committee of UN concluded upon the question of delimitation of boundaries that it was not something that required immediate priority. However in 1966 COPOUS as requested by General Assembly (UNGA Res 2222 (XXI Dec 19 1966) to initiate the study upon the delimitation of boundaries. The question was henceforth on the agenda of the Legal Sub Committee (see Report of the Legal Subcommittee on the work of the sixth session 19-may –14 July 1967 to the COPUOS UN Doc A/AC .105 /37of Jul 14 1967) and has continued to do so going through various transitions before settling in the 24th Session of LSC, for a current version.

There are two different approaches to delimitating the boundaries. The first is known as the spatial definition. This area is dependant upon the properties of the earth's atmosphere. Layers of the atmosphere are divided into trosphere, stratosphere, mesosphere and thermosphere establishing the altitude to each layer with the aim of delimitating where a spacecraft can, without any further application of force, complete a full orbit around the earth.

There are two different approaches to delimiting the boundaries. The first is known as the spatial definition. A detailed explanation can be found in the paper called Boundaries in Space by Caesar Voute in the book 'Peaceful and Non Peaceful Uses of Outer Space... edited by Bhupendra Jasani (14). In a brief explanation of Caesar Voute paper the spatial approach is where layers of the atmosphere are divided to determine the altitude to each layer with the aim of delimiting where a spacecraft can, without any further application of force, complete a full orbit around the earth. By delimiting the boundaries 'air' i.e nitrogen and oxygen is found in the heterosphere, which consists of troposphere, stratosphere and the mesophere at an altitude of 90-100 km. The temperature reversals between these layers are also relevant to delimitation of air from outer space. Beyond this altitude the concentration of nitrogen and oxygen change and this can be considered as outer space. This region is known as homosphere. The lowest perigee of an orbiting satellite, which without using any further propulsive force to complete a full orbit around the earth would be impossible, as it would burn up or re-enter in the earth's atmosphere, is at an altitude below 100/110km. However tethered satellites can move below an altitude 100-110km in a full orbit, but in order to sustain its orbit it must be maintained by an upper satellite, which is moving beyond this altitude.

Some space weapons orbiting in a transition zone between the altitude of 70km and 110km, where the air would be sufficiently thin, could still be effective. Here is the difficulty in defining a space weapon. The delimitation according to the lowest perigee of a satellite has been favored by those states preferring the spatial approach, at an altitude of 100km above sea level. However, this approach does not consider tethered satellites, as they are an important exception to the 100km proposed altitude delimitation. Although as it is dependant upon the upper satellite to maintain its orbit it would make further sense to consider the tethered satellite as an extension of the upper satellite, which is moving above an altitude of 100-110km. In this instance, the tethered satellite would reside under space law. Whether the space powers would agree to such rigid interpretation is doubtful, as it may work too disadvantageous to the space power. Although if one followed a strict spatial approach, by defining the layers, temperature and air density the extension argument would have no foundation as it is moving in 'airspace'. A way round this would be to apply a functional approach to tethered and its connected upper satellite by establishing its nature and type of space activity. If a non-peaceful activity was discovered and its purpose is to function as a space weapon the tethered satellite would automatically fall under the extension principle and be governed by space law. It would be useful to list permitted military activity for example for verifying arms control, which should fall under the guidance of an International Arms Verification Agency.

Thus a possible definition could be:

Outer Space (according to the lowest perigee

of an orbiting satellite; [except in the case of a tethered satellite where sec 1 (b) applies]) is;

1 (a) where an object which is orbiting at an altitude of 100km and upwards and/or travelling in the 'homosphere' region can;

i) Complete a full orbit without any artificial propulsion system
and/ or prevented from the atmospheric density causing the object to burn up or re-enter the earth's atmosphere;

ii) Where the eccentricity of the space object is dependent on the density profile of the atmosphere, which varies greatly with temperature and pressure and changes with time, outer space shall fall beyond the final temperature reversal between mesosphere and thermosphere boundaries.

i) 'Temperature reversal' in this instance is the difference between lowest perigee of an orbiting satellite [tethered satellites being the exception] and the altitude at which the final temperature reversal occurs between the mesosphere and thermosphere boundaries.

Exceptions;
1 (b) i)Space Weapons see below for definitions and 1(c).

ii)Tethered Satellites are two satellites connected by a rope or chain;

Where one satellite moves in outer space as defined in 1 (a) maintains the orbit of the second satellite that is moving below 100km.

In this instance the satellite moving below 100km shall be considered a space object irrespective of the altitude it is moving in if;

i) the nature of the mission is astronautical and/or objectives is military the rules of space law shall apply...

The second approach is as stated above the functional approach to the question of delimitating outer space. The location of the boundaries between air and outer space would no longer be necessary by adopting this approach; rather it would require a definition of the nature of the space activity. However further problems arise as a distinction would need to be made between spacecraft and aircraft and this would further involve a definition of spaceflight and air flight. A catalogue of all useable orbits for civilian and military satellites would need to be established perhaps by an International Satellite/Launch Agency. Although such an Agency would be extremely beneficial anyway as most useable orbits have limited places e.g. geostationary orbit and through this proposed agency they can monitor and keep track of all civilian satellites. There could be a sub-committee for commercial satellites and those that are not would fall under the main head of the agency. Military satellites would fall under as proposed above an International Arms Verification Agency. A current map of all satellites currently in orbit would also be useful.

This approach does not define outer space at all but analyses how space is used and seems quite favorable in that respect. It is very possible to have the best of both worlds and adopt a spatial to delimitating space and functional approach to catalogue civilian and military satellites.

The next question is how the spatial and the functional approach compare with the characteristics of the space weapon. It might be useful to define the different kinds of space weapons before proceeding any further.
There are four kinds of space weapons

summarized from a very good book by Bob Preston called Space Weapons and Earth Wars 2002 Rand see chapter 3 and associated appendixes for more detailed definitions, (13).

Directed Energy Weapons (DEW), which travel at long distances at the speed of light.

The next three weapon systems use either their own velocity and mass or conventional explosives, by using the chemical energy that is stored in these explosives to destroy their targets.

Kinetic-Energy Weapons against missile targets (KEWAMT)
Kinetic Energy Weapons against Surface Targets (KEWAST)
Space-Based Conventional Weapons against Surface Targets (SBCWAST)

More weapons systems that are specific are Anti-Satellite Weapons (ASAT) their sole purpose is to either impair or destroy command and control satellites. The emerging issue is the destabilizing effect to international peace and security if such weapons were used particularly if there is heightened tension between those states that may use ASAT capabilities.

DEW consists of laser torches, where enough power must be given to the beam to reach a destructive level. Thus enough energy must accumulate whilst the beam holds it target in order to destroy it. To destroy ballistic missiles it would require millions of watts of power and huge logistics costs for developing and deploying such weapons. Electronic Jammers are also DEW, which are tuned into the frequency ranges around target areas by using a radio transmitter. They generate enough power by focusing on those target receivers to compete with their intended signals.

Some of the problems associated with developing and deploying DEW's include:

1. The distance between the laser and missile launch points fluctuates in such a predictable way giving the opponent the opportunity to launch as many missiles as possible to saturate the defense. In this situation, the laser torch must be able to quickly retarget, after destroying the first initial target, with sufficient fuel to destroy the next target:

2. Vulnerable in boost phase as well as being restricted to the amount of targets the laser can destroy during this phase.

3. The altitude of the DEW is of importance as the further away the weapon is from the target the fewer missiles it can destroy during boost phase.

Thus, the effectiveness of DEW is compromised the higher the altitude the intensity of the beam decreases and in turn the kill rate decreases. Even if the weapon traveled at a low altitude, there is still the possibility of saturating the defense. To remedy that problem a constellation of weapons would need to be deployed. For purposes of a Missile Defense program, other weapon systems would need to be augmented to prevent saturating the defense.

Listed above are three different kinds of mass to target weapons; KEWAMT is confined to targets that are either leaving the atmosphere or are above the atmosphere; the other two, KEWAST & SBCWAST need to penetrate the atmosphere in order to reach their targets.

KEWAMT would be effective in providing an additional layer of defense to DEW's by intercepting the target using a high velocity impact. The weapon is then very small but as in DEW, their response time is very short so a constellation of weapons would be required to prevent defense saturation. The propulsion costs would be kept to a minimal as each weapon leaves its orbital base. The base would have to be at a low altitude; otherwise, the interceptor may burn out before the target is destroyed. Otherwise, additional propulsion and costs would be needed, as low mass objects would not retain their velocity at higher altitudes.

The problems associated with DEW's are essentially those of KEWAMT as well as the interceptor needs to stay in the atmosphere and this means that it will unable to engage in targets below 60kim. However more importantly the target missile may carry chemical or biological material and upon its interception hazardous debris might survive re-entry, disperse, and fall within the vicinity of a state's homeland.

KEWAST use their own mass to destroy targets at extremely high velocities. Thus they must be large enough to survive re-entry, as they do not destroy their targets outside the atmosphere, but must penetrate the atmosphere at a speed that will generate a destructive effect. The orbit of these weapons, to maintain their accuracy in a vertical trajectory, could either be low, where a great number of weapons near the target area would be needed; or at a higher altitude where a smaller number of weapons could be deployed. The most suitable orbit could either circular for more global coverage or an elliptical orbit, which is less costly and reduces the coverage.

KEWAST are effective against slow-moving targets such as ships and fuel tanks. However to achieve the high velocity impact needed to cause a destructive effect the velocity would need to match that of an intercontinental ballistic missile.

The advantages of acquiring KEWAST and basing them at a high altitude would be the distance between ground sensors thus saturation would be less likely and this would increase the coverage of space. The downside would be the logistical cost and the effort involved deploying such weapons as well as the length of time it would take to reach the target.

Conventional Weapons against terrestrial targets are more responsive and easier to maneuver compared to the high velocity KEWs need to re-enter the atmospheres. To respond promptly to targets on earth multiple weapons would need to be in orbit.

Space weapons can then be divided into categories; ground to space; air to space, space to ground, space to air. These could be further divided into the lowest perigee of a space weapon and a provision could be included that such weapons shall be governed by space law and a subsequent provision could also be included in space law, for example.

1) (c) Military satellites shall be permitted if in this proviso;

i. the nature of the mission and the objectives is to comply with existing treaties on verifying arms control, which shall be monitored by an International Arms Verification Agency.

Using the above descriptions of the different kinds of space weapons one could attempt to arrive at definition. However, it would be very difficult to arrive at a neat definition, as the simplest way would be generate a list, which would constantly be generated of all space weapons and future weapons with description of all their capabilities. The next stage could be either to ban them or allow states to acquire and deploy such weapons. There can be no provisions for limited use of space weapons as once acquisition occurs other counties (as with nuclear weapons) will eventually acquire and deploy such weapons and if those countries have an existing dispute international peace will be adversely affected if such weapons were used threateningly. Further problems will arise in arms controls for such weapons and by not allowing acquisition these problems can be avoided.

The next issue is whether the acquisition of Space Weapons would be fully compatible with Article 2 under the UN Charter, which prohibits the use of force or the threat of use of force, and Article 51 when faced against an armed attack the right to self defense. Satellites and the space activities of another State would be protected as Article 2.4 would prohibit any aggressive interference. Thus implying any introduction to weapon systems in outer space could constitute a threat of force including weapon systems such as KEWAST and DEW designed to destroy ground targets on Earth by directing their mass or energy beam from outer space would be prohibited. The open question is whether interference with space weapon systems would be justified under Article 51 as a right of defense? However there is continued debate as to whether 'armed attack' described in the Treaty means for example justifying a preemptive action or opposing views stress Article 51 can only be uterlised within the 'context of an armed attack' as opposed to responding to a threat with an preemptive action.

'Peaceful' in the Outer Space Treaty 1967 remains very contradictory particularly after the above analysis as two possible interpretations could be attributed to it, either 'peaceful' means non-military or apart from those that are prohibited by international law. Since the sSputnik launch, space powers have used space technology to effect military planning. As previously highlighted it can be quite problematic in distinguishing between civilian or military satellites. Perhaps an approach would be to follow the suggested list approach to define space weapons, although would it be possible to cover all eventualities? The easiest approach is to exclude such weapons then have to go through eliminating or controlling them.

However in attempting to define 'peaceful' other tTreaties have adopted the term therefore this would be a useful starting point to analyze how these treaties have interpreted peaceful. Article 1 Antarctic Treaty 1959 states:

"Antarctic shall be used for peaceful purposes only...' and prohibits ' any measures of a military nature...as well as any weapons. ' Although it is a very good guide it may prove extremely difficult to apply to the Outer Space Treaty, as it clearly does not ban all military uses of space. This can be seen as an example of the continuing military interest on space by not defining clearly what is or not permitted.

The UN convention on the Law of the Sea 1982 adopts the term peaceful purposes. Article 88 suggests that peaceful does not mean non-military as naval vessels are on the high seas and explosive tests have been conducted on the high seas. So where does the Outer Space Treaty stand? The difficulty surrounding the Treaty regarding the military uses of space is its inability to define in clear terms 'weapons of mass destruction'.

Article IV (1) does not permit states to place 'in orbit around the earth any objects carrying nuclear weapons of mass destruction, install such weapons on celestial bodies, or station such weapons in outer space in any other manner.' The general meaning of weapons of mass destruction is understood to include nuclear, biological and chemical weapons. Thus if the destructive capability is equivalent to the above weapons then future weapon systems may fall under the treaty.

Article IV (2) explicitly bans the establishment of military bases and testing of weapons on the moon and celestial bodies as they are exclusively for peaceful purposes Also Article XII of the Outer Space Treaty gives other States party to the Treaty the right of inspection of all installations, equipment, stations and space vehicles, subject to notice and minimal interference with operations, on the moon and celestial bodies only. Outer space is not provided for in this provision.

However Article IX gives States party to the treaty the right to request a consultation if they have reason to believe an activity or experiment planned by another State Party in outer space, including the moon and other celestial bodies would cause harmful interference with activities in the peaceful exploration of outer space, the moon and celestial bodies, and interfere with activities of other State Parties. There are safeguards in the Outer Space Treaty to ensure space is used peacefully, although it does not go far enough.

The place to start is to find the ordinary meaning to peaceful, as stated in the Vienna Convention on the Law of Treaties 1969 Article 31 (1). To determine whether some or no military uses is permitted. However 'some military uses' may prove problematic as does this mean just surveillance / arms verification or can weapons which are not covered in the space treaty be included. Thus, it would be useful to analyze the practice of the states upon application and interpretation of the treaty Article 31(3). Thus, 'peaceful' cannot mean non-military, as using a satellite to aid ground control and targeting could be argued as a non-peaceful use of outer space. The ordinary meaning of peaceful according to The Concise Oxford English Dictionary (1989 pg 753) Peaceful is 'characterized by 'peace' one belongs to a state of peace and not violating or infringing peace.' Thus, 'peace' in the Oxford English Dictionary means freedom from war and harmony between people.

Perhaps the approach to define peaceful is to attempt to categorize all military including future uses and assess them on the merits as to whether these military/weapon systems would have serious consequences to international peace and security. By finding, the non- peaceful activities this may help to some degree in characterizing 'peaceful'. There is, however, an emerging issue that is unfolding in this analysis, it is not defining peaceful but defining what is the acceptable extent to the military uses of outer space and is consistent with the UN Charter and other obligations under international law. Thus to determine the acceptable extent to the military uses of space it is unfortunately dependant upon the national security interests of the concerned state. Thus if those interests are served through that particular activity then it will be deemed peaceful. For example the analogy of equating the law of the sea with outer space. the naval ships merely observing the high seas as are military satellites in space and therefore not contrary to international law. In addition, states see their observance satellites as maintaining international peace and security. Thus to split the definition of peaceful and non-peaceful is only hindering the problem and how to move forward to present clear policies on the peaceful uses of outer space.

Other Multilateral treaties in the effort to use space for peaceful purposes are the Limited Test Ban Treaty of 1963, Convention on Environmental Modification of 1977 and the Moon Agreement of 1979 as model for the future use of outer space. Bilateral agreements such as SALT I and II and the Anti Ballistic Missile Treaty have prevented escalation of an arms race in space and what the future holds for these Agreements.

Article one of the Limited Test Ban Treaty states:

1. Each of the Parties to this Treaty undertakes to prohibit, to prevent, and not to carry out any nuclear weapon test explosion, or any other nuclear explosion, at any place under its jurisdiction or control:

(a) In the atmosphere; beyond its limits, including outer space; or under water, including territorial waters or high seas;

This was the first international Treaty, which addressed outer space and received over 100 ratifications. The concern for nuclear testing was radioactive debris that could contaminate the environment, which could have devastating effects. In paragraph 2 of Article 1 States must refrain from causing or participating in any nuclear test explosion in any of the prohibited environments listed in paragraph (a). The effect of a nuclear explosion in space would effectively destroy all satellites in orbit with possible radioactive debris re-entering the atmosphere. If any states should want to withdraw from the Treaty, it would be a devastating blow to nuclear reduction and international peace.

Although it does not initially ban the development of nuclear weapons, it certainly hinders the process if it cannot be tested,

The Convention on the Prohibition of Military or Any Other Hostile Use of Environmental Modification of 1977 (ENMOD) refers to the degradation to the environment through environmental modifications for military purposes. Thus by harnessing environmental modification and techniques for peaceful purposes could, 'contribute to the preservation and improvement of the environment for the benefit of present and future generations,' whereas 'military or any hostile use of such techniques could have effects extremely harmful to human welfare.' Article 1, States agree not to engage that would have severe long-term effects, in military or harmful use of environmental techniques. Article 2 defines techniques as' through the deliberate manipulation of natural processes.. The dynamics, composition or structure of the earth, including its biota, lithosphere, hydrosphere and atmosphere, or outer space.'

The Moon Agreement 1979 reiterates and enlarges upon the provisions in the Outer Space Treaty. Articles 3, paragraphs 3 extended the prohibition of placing nuclear weapons in orbit on or around the moons trajectory and other celestial bodies. Paragraph 4 in Article 3 forbids the establishment of military bases and testing of any type of weapons but allows military personnel for scientific research or for other peaceful purposes. Although a great deal of debate has arisen to the meaning of peaceful purposes in the Outer Space Treaty and this Treaty does not offer any resolution as to its meaning. Pargraph 2 is an interesting inclusion as it prohibits any threat or use of force or any other hostile act or threat of hostile act on the moon is prohibited...'

including committing or engaging in any such threat in relation to the earth , the moon, spacecraft, personnel of spacecraft or man-made space objects.' Although does this take away the right to self defense under Article 51 of the UN Charter?
Bilateral efforts to prevent an arms race in space resulted in SALT, Strategic Arms Limitation Talks, 1 Agreement of 1972. The Treaty Between the US and USSR on the Limitation Of Anti-Ballistic Missile Systems, ABM Treaty for short was the most important Treaty during the arms limitation talks to be concluded. Also the Interim Agreement on Strategic Offensive Arms was completed and adopted, where launchers to inter-continental ballistic missiles (ICBM) including submarine launchers have been frozen. Also each party must not interfere with national technical means of verification, but it does not mean ASAT weapons are prohibited, as protection is only given to systems that are used to verify the SALT 1 Agreement. SALT II Treaty on the Limitation of Strategic Offensive Arms was not ratified in 1979 but it has been accepted as an informal agreement amongst the parties.

The most significant provision in the ABM Treaty is Article V where 'each Party undertakes not to develop, test, or deploy ABM systems or components which are sea-based, air based, space based, or mobile land based.Article 2 defines ABM systems as, 'a system to counter strategic ballistic missiles or their elements in flight trajectory, currently consisting of ABM interceptor missiles, launchers and radars. However a single fixed land base system may be deployed within 150 mile radius centered on each countries capital.
Article IX provides that states do not deploy ABM systems outside its national territory assuring the viability and effectiveness of the Treaty. Also to assure 'compliance with the provisions of this treaty, each Party shall use national technical means of verification through for example surveillance measures employing satellites and radars. The Treaty is unclear as to whether conducting research on ABM systems would violate the Treaty. Each side has a different perspective to the interpretation of the Treaty. Plans for research in ABM systems that is specifically prohibited in Article V have intensified since the passing of the Treaty. Through this debate and the desire to deploy weapons with laser, particle or even x-ray capabilities, as part of a missile defense program appears to have rendered the ABM Treaty redundant, hence a rather abrupt analysis.

In the Text of the Joint Declaration by President George Bush and President Vladimir Putin on the New Strategic Relationship Between the United States of America and the Russian Federation dated Friday May 24, 2002....

'...the United States and Russia have agreed to implement a number of steps aimed at strengthening confidence and increasing transparency in the area of missile defense, including the exchange of information on missile defense programs and tests in this area, reciprocal visits to observe missile defence tests, and observation aimed at familiarisation with missile defense systems. They also intend to take the steps necessary to bring a joint centre for the exchange of data from early warning systems into operation.

The United States and Russia have also agreed to study possible areas for missile defense cooperation, including the expansion of joint exercises related to missile defense, and the exploration of potential programs for the joint research and development of missile defense technologies, bearing in mind the importance of the mutual protection of classified information and the safeguarding of intellectual property rights. The United States and Russia will, within the framework of the NATO-Russia Council, explore opportunities for intensified practical cooperation on missile defense for Europe....'

This is a complete u-turn from the ABM Treaty and for the purposes of arms control it could be interpreted as huge blow particularly with the possibility of mass acquisition through NATO cooperation. Also the effect to the developing world through mass expenditure in deploying such systems where mutual distrust already exists could further alienate them where resources for humanitarian aid is urgently needed.

Conclusion

The inter-relationship between weapons and space systems have made the distinction between civilian and military satellites increasingly hard. This dual purpose technology has long followed space since the launch of Spuntnik and consequently where space has been seen as an attractive forum to further military capabilities. In 1967 a blueprint was set for the future conduct of space powers that space should be for the heritage of mankind but the vagueness of certain terms has lead to difficulty in defining 'peaceful' and 'weapons of mass destruction' (WMD) as there is much debate as to whether x-ray lasers are WMD. These vague terms can be seen as continuing the political military interests in developing and deploying space weapons. But in order to define space weapons a consensus to the delimitation question regarding outer space needs to be reached. This is a very problematic area as is defining space weapons and as I have demonstrated cannot easily be solved. This highlights the choicesthat need to made either all space weapons are banned, some selectively prohibited or all are allowed . If all weapons are banned then immediately this diffuses the definitions and arms control problems. The other two choices will create problems within verification procedures, particularly as mass acquisition occurs which can be seen as an inevitable consequence to weapons development.

Other Multilateral treaties, particularly Limited Test Ban Treaty work alongside the Outer Space Treaty very effectively, however the bBilateral treaties have suffered. With the withdrawal of ABM Treaty the deployment of space weapons is real possibility. This Treaty served as a very difficult legal implication to bypass same for the Limited Test Ban Treaty for hindering weapons development. The fabric of these legal implications is being held together with a single thread through political mistrust and self-interest motivated by national security measures. It appears each implication whether it is legal, political or military interlinks with each other. Therefore it follows one implication is a consequence from the other. Thus to avoid all the consequential implications of deploying weapons is to channel the resources for positive and more far reaching purposes; to the developing world. The immediate effect to international relations by creating a closer and efficient cooperation with developing countries would enhance international peace. By using the UN as a forum to enable and fund the participation and inclusion for space programs. This could be a foundation to adopting a more progressive use of outer space.

The acquisition of space weapons and the affect to the developing world will have serious implications in dividing the gap further regarding the economic disparities for less powerful and rich countries. The expenditure involved in deploying space weapon systems could be strongly argued as taking away valuable resources in funding a more global civilian activity, whereby the developing world has increased opportunities to influence policy and participate in civilian activity. For example if the developed world placed factories for space components in the developing countries this will help to support their economy, as well as job and educational opportunities. Developing Countries could have the opportunity to bid for contracts in designing space technology through global tendering and in turn will help to circulate money around the world, giving the developing countries the opportunity to become self sufficient. Also extending science education and creating a program for astronauts in developing countries will have a positive psychological effect to relations and to global peace.

Bibilography

1.Understanding conflict resolution: war, peace and global system – *P Wallensteen* Sage Publications ISBN – 0761966676

2.Terrorism, Assymmetric warfare and weapons of mass destruction *Anthony Cordesman* ISBN – 0275974278

3. Strategic Thinking: an introduction and farewell – *Philip Windsor(ed)* ISBN 1588260240

4. Democracy and war: the end of an illusion, *Errol A Henderson* ISBN – 1588870763

5. Sanctions and the search for security challenges to UN action *David Cortight, George A Lopex* ISBN – 158826078X

6.Way out there in the blue Published 2000 ISBN 0684844168 & 0743200233 (*Frances Fitzgerald*)

7.Tellers War, the top secret story behind the star wars deception - *William J Broad* ISBN 0671701061 Simon & Schuster 1992

8.Technical Problems in the verification of a ban on space weapons - UN 1993 *Rodionov Stovislav* ISBN – 9290450800 research paper 1014-4013 no.17

9.Seeking New World Vistas: The Militarization of Space, *Roger Handberg* May 2000 Praeger, ISBN – 0275962954

8.Ballistic Missile Defence and the future of American Security : Agendas, Perceptions, Technology and Policy – *Roger Handberg* Praeger December 2001 ISBN - 0275970094

9.Defense Policy choices for Bush Admin 2001 – 2005 Published March 2001 *Michael E. O'Hanlon* ISBN – 0815700792

10.Rockets Red Glare *James Wirt* Westview Press 2001 ISBN 0813364507

11.Prevention of an Arms Race in Outer Space… *Pericles Gasparimi Alves* UNA 287A/162 ISBN- 9290450568

12.Outer space, a source of conflict or co-operation *Bupendra Jasari* United Nations Univ 1991 ISBN 9280807595

13.Space Weapons Earth Wars *Bob Preseton* RAND 2002 ISBN 0833029371

14.Peaceful and Non-Peaceful Uses Of Space UNIDIR ed *Bhupendra Jasani Taylor*

15.International Space Law and the United Nations- *Nandasiri Jasentuliyana* -Kluwer

Session 4: OTHER LEGAL MATTERS, INCLUDING LEGAL ASPECTS OF LAUNCH SERVICES

Chairmen: K.U. Schrogl, Germany, and J. Clayton-Townsend, USA

Rapporteur: Y. Takaya, Japan

IAC-02-IISL.4.03

PERCEPTIONS ON THE DEFINITION OF A "LAUNCHING STATE" AND *SPACE DEBRIS RISKS*

By Professor Dr. Maureen Williams
University of Buenos Aires / Conicet
Chair - Space Law Committee – International Law Association

1. Introduction

The purpose of this paper is to pursue work on the elucidation of the launching state issue in light of the space treaties in force and recent developments concerning commercial space activities. A number of contradictions may be traced on this matter today whose consequences are undesirable in the present state-of-the-art. The lack of consensus on the term "launching state" -let alone "launching authority", as worded in the Astronauts Agreement- has been pointed out by the doctrine with increased frequency and becomes a matter of concern in the present world scenario.

A second matter of concern is based on the obscurity of the concept of reference vis-à-vis the emerging risks of damage caused by space debris, especially having in mind the growing participation of private entities in space activities and the existing doubts on the ability of these private enterprises to prevent damage resulting therefrom. The difficulties involved in the lack of agreement on the concept of "launching state" become particularly dangerous in this context. For these reasons the paper will also be addressing some of those difficulties with a view to paving the way for realistic solutions on this question.

2. Outlining the problem

The issues of responsibility and liability for space activities are strongly related to launch services. These, in turn, call for more precise national laws on the matter given the unprecedented growth of private activities in space.

Part of the doctrine, among who most of the members of the ILA Space Law Committee may be counted, consider that Article VI of the 1967 Outer Space Treaty entails an obligation of States to enact national laws on the authorisation and supervision of activities of non-governmental bodies in outer space[1]. Therefore, at first sight, commercial space activities in general - and launch services, in particular - appear conveniently covered in the present state-of-the-art by Article VI of the 1967 Treaty provided States Parties observe in good faith their obligations to authorise, supervise and, as the case may be, to implement an efficient licensing system[2].

Be that as it may, some clarifications would be helpful at this stage without falling into too detailed regulations. To this end, the general idea is to think in terms of an agile, short protocol or any other kind of separate instrument designed for supplementing and giving a more precise legal framework to Article VI of the 1967 Treaty.

Professor Hobe -one of the four Special Rapporteurs of the ILA Space Committee- studied this question in depth to determine whether any adjustments were needed for the 1967 Space Treaty to be more consistent with the participation of private enterprises in space. The result was a Draft Protocol which stands out for its simplicity and which, together with the Final Report of the Committee on "Review of the Space Treaties in View of Commercial Space Activities – Concrete Proposals" *was thoroughly discussed in April 2002 at the New Delhi Working Session of the ILA Space Law Committee. The Report -containing the Protocol- was subsequently adopted by consensus at the Plenary Session of the 70th Conference of the International Law Association[3]. Hereunder the text of the proposed Protocol.*

Suggested Protocol to the 1967 Outer Space Treaty

Article 1: (amendment to Article I, 3, of the OST)

1. States Parties hereby agree that the use of outer space and celestial bodies is inclusive of all commercial uses.

2. States Parties are free to define the way in which they shall implement the principle of international co-operation. All commercial uses of outer space and celestial bodies shall be carried out for the benefit and in the interest of all states, irrespective of their degree of economic or scientific development, and shall be the province of all mankind. Particular account shall be taken of the needs of developing countries.

Article 2: (amendment to Article VI of the OST)

States Parties undertake to enact national legislation concerning authorisation and continuing supervision of space activities carried out by non-governmental entities.

Article 3: (amendment to Article VIII of the OST)

States Parties are under the obligation to register any object launched into outer space both on their national register and on the international register maintained by the Secretary-General of the United Nations in accordance with the Convention on the Registration of Objects launched into Outer Space.

Article 4: States Parties undertake to adopt an international legal instrument on the peaceful settlement of disputes which should include provisions for binding mechanisms. In this sense, the 1998 ILA Convention on the Settlement of Disputes related to Space Activities is referred to as a model[4].

In the process of elaboration of the above-mentioned Final Report of the International Law Association, among the terms of reference of the Space Law Committee the need to clarify the meaning of the term "launching state" was listed. Professor Kopal -Special Rapporteur for the Registration Convention- paid considerable attention to Article I of this text, recommending improvements on that Article in connection with definitions and, particularly, improvements on the definition of a "launching state".

The problem is indeed not new. It existed already within the context of the 1968 Astronauts Agreement which refers to a "launching authority" and no longer to a "launching State", The problem continued when the 1972 Liability Convention and the 1975 Registration Convention were adopted and went back to the term "launching State", originally used by the 1967 Space Treaty.

Naturally, in those days, problems were mainly of an academic nature. It was not easy to imagine the pace at which, a few years on, commercial activities in the new areas would be progressing. This phenomenon, however, had the virtue of simplifying certain traditional institutions and making them more agile. An illustrative example is provided by comparing dispute settlement procedures involving sovereign States –subjects par excellence *of public international law-, as would have been the case in the initial stages of space exploration, and the nowadays prompt and simple means available to parties to a dispute in the field of private international law and, particularly, international commercial arbitration.*

Thus, the long-standing controversy over state sovereignty and compulsory jurisdiction, and its sometimes very thorny implications, is nowadays losing momentum as a result of the participation of private companies in the use of outer space. In the present scenario many more actors are participating and an increasing number of private enterprises are investing heavily in space activity.

Professor Kopal –whose views were widely supported by the ILA Space Law Committee-believed that the best way to update the definitions embodied in Article I of the Registration Convention was by means of a separate agreement - possibly a protocol - to supplement the Convention.

Another course of action which was seen with favour was the adoption of a UNGA Resolution to shed light on the definitions issue. Having in mind the fact that the political will of the international community and, especially, of the space-faring nations, is not prepared for changes, such as drastic amendments to the Space Treaties in force, Professor Kopal's realistic recommendation was to take a cautious approach concerning any such course of action[5].

Even though the Registration Convention is not so closely related to the activities of private entities in space as are the 1967 Space Treaty and the Liability Convention, it is, undoubtedly, very closely linked to the latter and an indispensable complement thereof. Hence, the restricted scope of the definitions contained in Article I of the Registration Convention is clearly insufficient in the world of today.

3. Towards descriptions and clarifications

In the present international context the concept of "launching State" stemming from the Space Treaties in force appears outdated. A glaring example is provided by the formula "procure the launching" which is common to the Outer Space Treaty and the Liability and Registration Conventions and which raises, as will later be seen, not a few doubts.

On the occasion of Unispace III, in a discussion paper entitled "Existing United

Nations Treaties: Strengths and Needs"[6] *submitted by Professor Kopal, the need for review is clearly evident. This conclusion, in fact, was a common denominator in most sessions of the meeting. In this sense, Session 8 of the UN Workshop, entitled* "Maintaining the Space Environment", *refers in its* Summary Report *to the need to define the term "space object" and some other terms*[7] *amongst which, no doubt, "launching state" takes pride of place.*

As observed at the outset it is perhaps wise at this point in time to attempt descriptions rather than definitions. As is known, "to define" implies "to limit" and the idea is precisely the opposite. A description, for its very essence, can never be exhaustive.

It should be borne in mind as well that within the Working Group set up by the Legal Subcommittee of Copuos in 2001 as agenda item 9, under the chairmanship of Dr. Kai-Uwe Schrogl, the underlying idea was that no authoritative interpretation of the concept of launching state could emerge therefrom. An international intergovernmental conference would be essential when the time came to agree on any new formula. In the meantime it is for the doctrine to provide down-to-earth ideas leading to viable solutions.

4. Recent advancements on the launching state issue and the meaning of "procurement"

When dealing with commercial space activities, and particularly with launch services, the outstanding issue nowadays is the identification of the launching state. As pointed out earlier the Space Treaties are not too precise on this question. The fact that the Astronauts Agreement introduces the term "launching authority" -even though the Liability and Registration Convention went back to the "launching state" formula- is clearly indicating that not only States who launched or procured a launching, or from whose facilities a launching occured should be considered as such. This idea existed, no doubt, in the mind of the drafters of the 1968 Agreement.

Another source of doubt and controversy surrounds the meaning of the term "procurement", especially when private entities are involved in space activities. A first hurdle to overcome is, therefore, to agree on what should be understood by "procurement". An elucidation of this term is essential before any progress on the "launching state issue"[8] is attempted.

In this quest, Edward Frankle and E. Jason Steptoe (General Counsel and Associate General Counsel, respectively, of NASA) provide food for thought with their pointed observations based on experience. I shall focus on some of the issues raised in their presentation to a Workshop on "Commercial Launch Activities" *held in Bremen on 19 January 2000 as part of the activities included in Project 2001 on the Legal Framework for the Commercial Uses of Outer Space*[9], *headed by Professor Karl-Heinz Böckstiegel and his team from Cologne University.*

As may be expected when streamlining this paper, a very realistic approach is reflected. The authors put an accent on the need for states to examine the treaties currently in force and all available mechanisms before embarking in the creation of new law. It is important, they underline, to centre attention on state responsibility for licensing, continuing supervision of non-governmental entities and to make sure that a just compensation is always readily available [10]. Commercial mechanisms are favoured for solving controversies which are essentially commercial. To this end the authors suggest encouraging States to maintain active licensing programmes and adequate compensation arrangements. Such approach, in their view[11], is a good alternative to lengthy procedures aimed at establishing the precise scope of state responsibility. No doubt this idea would go a long way in avoiding conflicting interpretations of the existing treaties within the complex structure of public international law.

Let us now move on to the analysis of the term "procure the launching", common to the 1967, 1972 and 1975 Space Treaties. Also in this field the above-cited experts follow a very pragmatic approach. On the basis of Article I of the Liability Convention and the possibilities established thereby (participation in a launching activity, procurement of a launching and use of launch facilities as requirements to be a launching state) the authors point out that liability exposure exists when a launch takes place from national or international territory. Yet, the space treaties do not define any of these terms.

However , when following the authors' reasoning further one cannot but agree with them that the least clear of the bases to attribute liability to a state is when it "procures a launching"[12]. This expression lends itself to misinterpretations which are even more serious where private enterprises are involved. The drafting of the space treaties, on this point, does not appear consistent with the present era of commercialisation of space activities. These shortcomings, however, are not enough to justify the introduction of changes thereto.

Interesting, for its implications, is the research carried out by Frankle and Steptoe in connection with the drafting history of the space treaties. One of their conclusions, stemming from the Liability Convention, is that "to procure" was intended to mean active and substantial participation in launching activities[13]. This interpretation is in line with Article 31 of the Vienna Convention on the Law of Treaties laying down rules on interpretation which should be carried out in accordance with the ordinary meaning to be given to the terms in the context and in the light of the object and purpose of the treaty.

In short, the NASA experts identify a few examples of what the drafters intended to be the meaning of "procures a launching", as follows:

- Exceptional arrangements in which a state might induce another state to conduct a launch from the first state's territory, presumably with its active participation in launching decisions[14], or
- Cases in which the state arranging the launch plays a substantial role in the project.

However so, it remains to be established what the situation would be when all actors involved in launching services are private parties. It can be argued, in accordance with Article VI of the 1967 Space Treaty, that the State cannot say it knew "nothing about it" if we have in mind the obligations of authorisation and supervision resulting from that Article.

As indicated by Dr. Schrogl, the responsibility and liability of states also occurs for commercial activities of non-governmental entities. Consequently, national laws should also include rules on indemnification and compensation[15].

Therefore, the most practical solution is for States Parties to the 1967 Treaty to enact national laws establishing effective licensing systems for private enterprises operating launch services. Indeed, as underlined earlier, this is an obligation arising from the Treaty whereby states should act in good faith to make the licensing mechanisms fully reliable. In this context Article 27 of the Vienna Convention establishing that provisions of internal law may not be invoked to justify a failure to perform a treaty is fully applicable.

An overall conclusion is, therefore, that is not necessary to change international treaties in connection with the launching state issue and that lacunae *should be covered by national legislation laying down effective procedures for authorising, supervising and licensing private enterprises operating launch services and, in general, conducting activities in outer space*[16].

On the occasion of the International Colloquium held in Cologne to mark the end of Project 2001, the Working Group on Launch and Associated Services expressed similar views. A consensus is therefore growing to the effect that the terms "launching state" and "launching authority" should not be changed in the space treaties as this would entail a very complex procedure of amendments at a time when the political scenario is not really prepared for it. Consequently, the role to be played by national space legislation in the present time is of major importance.

5. The Copuos Working Group on the concept of "launching state"

At the outset of the fortieth session of the Legal Subcommittee of Copuos a Working Group was set up with the mandate of reviewing the concept of "launching state". This task was to be carried out without amending or interpreting the existing treaties, as the terms of reference for the Group proclaimed. On this occasion the importance of national legislation and licensing régimes were highlighted once again. The Working Group also invited states and international organisations to send information on state practice, including states that did not currently have national space laws[17]. Presentations were made on these points by Australia, China, France, Sweden, the United Kingdom, the European Space Agency, the International Law Association, the International Astronautical Federation and the International Mobile Satellite Organisation[18].

A wide range of opinions were voiced on the occasion. Some delegations remarked that, even though Article V of the Liability Convention provided for the joint and several liability of all launching states for damage caused by a space object, it was still possible for States to conclude arrangements modifying and apportioning liability between them. This stand would set aside to some extent the "launching state issue". It seems, in fact, a reasonable mid-way response to that issue without falling into unwanted interpretation efforts.

A practical example of national space legislation bridging the gaps left by international law without the need to amend the existing treaties is provided by the United Kingdom. This country has enacted specific national law on space activities. The presentation made by the British delegate to the Working Group on the occasion in question focused on the 1986 Outer Space Act applicable to UK nationals, including individuals and corporations, and to activities carried out in the UK or elsewhere. This meant establishing jurisdiction over space activities, requirements to obtain a licence (after ensuring that the activity should not jeopardise public health or national security), penalties, registration requisites and the obligation to indemnify the government for liability [19].

One of the remaining problems, as pointed out to the Working Group by the delegation of France[20], might result from new launching techniques and increasing commercialisation of space activities. Furthermore, some concern was shown in cases of launching from an international territory which could lead to "forum shopping" or flags of convenience on the part of private entities. This assumption, however, could be adequately solved through appropriate arrangements between the entities concerned.

It is expected that the newly-established Working Group within the Legal Subcommittee of Copuos, with the mandate of dealing with the very wide topic of the status and application of the five United Nations Treaties on Outer Space, will continue work on the review of the launching state issue in light of the most recent experiences, state practice and doctrine on the basis of the general idea that the existing space treaties ought not to be amended.

6. Space Debris Risks in a Changing Scenario

Indeed the risk of damage resulting from space debris is infinitely higher now than at the time of drafting the Space Treaties the last of which -the Moon Agreement- was adopted in 1979. As a consequence of the growth of the commercial aspects of space activities the issue is no longer one for academic discussion alone. The possibility of damage has grown considerably in the present world scenario.

The problem was addressed -following the interdisciplinary approach that identified the Unispace III Workshop referred to previously- by a number of participants who expressed their preoccupation for a question likely to become unmanageable unless some specific international regulation is agreed upon. Among them, let us pause briefly on Professor Kerrest's very precise remarks on prevention and mitigation of space debris, made at the last Session of the Workshop entitled "Maintaining the Space Environment"[21].

In the view of this author, speaking of prevention, at this stage, did not seem realistic. If we are to get involved in the mitigation of space debris one cannot escape the fact that costs involved in any such procedure are astronomic. Moreover, it is fair to say, as pointed out by Professor Kerrest[22], that no private entity would be prepared to accept those costs unless its competitors followed suit. This is a natural rule of the market underlying commercial space activities.

In this respect a short reference will be made to a recent South American experience[23]. When the Argentine Republic decided to embark in the construction of its first domestic satellite –which was launched into GEO in 1997- an international bid was opened to establish who would be in charge of this construction. When discussing the various conditions and modalities of the agreements the possibility of having a clause whereby the operator of the satellite should be made responsible for its removal from GEO at the end of its active life was envisaged. In practice, however, this idea did not materialise as it implied a disadvantage for that operator *vis-à-vis* others who were not obliged to any such removal procedures. In fact, the operator in question, in order to comply with that obligation, would have to use the last available power of the satellite for the removal operation, with the consequent reduction of the active life of the satellite.

In light of these facts and realities it is not difficult to conclude that the commitment originating in Article VI of the 1967 Space Treaty should be seen as an obligation imposed on States to adopt national laws on this topic. Furthermore, as private enterprises may tend to switch nationalities, it is reasonable to suggest that States and international organisations be encouraged to accept and duly observe the outer space treaties in force. In the pursuance of these objectives the principle of international co-operation appears of significant value.

7. Outlining conclusions

Finally, a couple of conclusions have been designed for each of the topics addressed in this paper.

(a) the launching State issue

From the foregoing paragraphs it follows that references to a "launching State" and "launching authority" in the existing space treaties should remain as they stand. The general view appears to be totally against introducing amendments to these texts.

This leaves us with the possibility of drafting a separate international instrument dealing with an updated concept of launching consistent with the contemporary reality. The idea is good in spite of the political will of space-faring nations not being the best at the moment.

For these reasons the accent should be on national space legislation. This course of action, to be seen as mandatory in accordance with Article VI of the 1967 Space Treaty is, by and large, simpler, more agile and possibly more effective.

Naturally, States should act in good faith when passing national laws on the issues of authorisation, supervision and licensing of private enterprises to operate launch services and ensure the availability of a just compensation to avoid the international obligations becoming a dead letter.

(b) space debris risks

In the present international context, where the space activities of private entities are growing in a scale without precedent, space debris risks become an aggravated problem. It is doubtful whether these commercial enterprises, in the event of damage caused by launching operations, will be able to meet the ensuing liability issues. Here again a sound insurance system, coupled with effective domestic legislation, seem at the moment the most realistic answer.

References

1 See REPORT OF THE 70TH CONFERENCE OF THE INTERNATIONAL LAW ASSOCIATION, New Delhi, 2-7 April 2002, Space Law Committee. Most of the members of this Committee see this obligation as implicit in Article VI of the 1967.

2 It should be noted that some authors, like Professor Kolosov, firmly hold the view that problems arising in connection with the activities of private enterprises in space should be left entirely to national space legislations. See Proceedings of the Workshop on Space Law in the Twenty-First Century", p.31, Unispace III, Technical Forum, July 1999.

3 This Report and ensuing ILA Resolution were introduced by the ILA representative to the Forty-Fifth Session of the UN Committee on the Peaceful Uses of Outer Space, in Vienna, on 6 June 2002.

4 See op.cit. in note 1, chapter on the Review of the 1967 Outer Space Treaty in View of Commercial Space Activities – Concrete proposals.

5 See op.cit. in note 1 supra, chapter on the Registration Convention.

6 See "Proceedings of the Workshop on Space Law in the Twenty-First Century", at p. 19, Unispace III, Technical Forum, July 1999, Vienna, where the author makes reference to a Working Paper submitted by Germany to the LSC of Copuos (Doc. A/AC.105/C.2/L.211/Rev.1 of 30-o3-1998). Cf. Eilene Galloway, in her Commentary Paper, at p. 27.

7 See op.cit. in note 6 supra, p.217.

8 Project 2001 very clearly underlined the "launching state issue" from its initial steps, particularly in the context of one of its Working Groups addressing the issue of "Launch and Associated Services". See "Project 2001: Legal Framework for the Commercial Use of Outer Space", Carl Heymanns Verlag 2002, p.73 et seq.

9 Project 2001 was conducted by Professor Karl-Heinz Böckstiegel, Cologne University, between 1998-2001. The Project, of undoubted international scope and implications, came to a close in May 2001, and was marked by a Colloquium entitled "Project 2001: Legal Framework for the Commercial Use of Outer Space – Recommendations and conclusions to develop the present state of the law". The book, edited by Karl-Heinz Böckstiegel, was published in 2002 by Carl Heymanns Verlag KG (Köln, Berlin, Bonn, München).

10 See Frankle and Steptoe, "Legal Considerations affecting Commercial Space Launches from International Territory", Proceedings of the Workshop on "Legal Framework for Commercial Launch and Associated Activities", Bremen, January 2000" (Project 2001), p.68.

11 Ibid., p.65.

12 Ibid., p.66.

13 Ibid., p. 67.

14 For example, as indicated by the authors, the San Marcos project which brought together the US and Italy and where NASA was conducting launches with Italy both from US territory and the Indian ocean. Italy, as pointed out by Frankle and Steptoe, took active part in these launchings and this was sufficient to constitute "procurement" from the US.

15 See Karl-Uwe Schrogl, "Responsibility and Liability – Need for national regulation (including harmonisation)", in Proceedings of the Workshop on Commercial Launch Activities, Project 2001, Bremen, January 2000, pp.155-157.

16 This conclusion is in line with Professor Kopal's thinking on the cautious approach to be taken when considering amendments to the space treaties and stressing the need to "ease identification through national and international space regulation". It coincides as well with the stand of the ILA reflected in the Report of the Space Law Committee to the London 2000 and New Delhi 2002 Conferences (op. cit. in note 4) where Prof. Kopal was the Special Rapporteur for this topic.

17 UN Doc. A/AC.105)763, Annex II, p. 22.

18 See Conference Room Paper A/AC.105/C.2/2001/CRP.10.

19 Ibid., p. 23.

20 See Doc. A/AC.105/738 (20 April 2000), p.18 and Doc.A/AC.105/763 (24 April 2001), p.24.

21 This was Session 8 of the Workshop chaired by Ambassador Qizhi He (China) and where the present writer acted as rapporteur and coordinator. See op.cit. in note 1, pp. 195-217.

22 See Commentary Paper to Session 8, op.cit. in note 2, p. 216.

23 See, by the present writer, EL RIESGO AMBIENTAL Y SU REGULACIÓN, Abeledo-Perrot, Buenos Aires 1998, p.50. This question was examined deeply in the framework of the "Ubacyt Projects" conducted by the University of Buenos Aires from 1992 to date, under the direction of the present writer.

IAC-02-IISL.4.04

A new look at the „launching State"

The results of the UNCOPUOS Legal Subcommittee Working Group „Review of the concept of the ‚launching State'" 2000-2002[1]

Dr. Kai-Uwe Schrogl
German Aerospace Center (DLR), Cologne, Germany
kai-uwe.schrogl@dlr.de

Charles Davies
U. N. Office for Outer Space Affairs (UNOOSA), Vienna, Austria
charles.davies@oosa.un.or.at

Abstract

The legal concept of the „launching State" is a crucial element of two of the United Nations treaties on outer space: the Liability and Registration Conventions. It identifies, inter alia, those states that may be liable for damage caused by a space object and would have to pay compensation in such a case. Furthermore, „launching States" may also be responsible for registering a space object.

The concept was the subject of a working group of the Legal Subcommittee of the United Nations Committee on the Peaceful Uses of Outer Space (UNCOPUOS). This working group conducted its deliberations from 2000 to 2002 and presented its conclusions during the 2002 session of the Legal Subcommittee. These conclusions, accepted by the Member States of UNCOPUOS, will be put forward to the UN General Assembly in autumn 2002. They are the first result of intergovernmental discussions on the question of whether the legal concept of the „launching State" is still adequate, and how it is applied, in view of the changing environment of space activities.

This paper analyses the issues that have arisen in the application of the legal concept of the „launching State" that led to the establishment of the working group on this subject in the Legal Subcommittee of UNCOPUOS.

It also presents in detail the results of the deliberations of the working group and discusses the consequences of these results for the further development of space law on the international as well as the national level.

1. Making the concept of the „launching State" an issue

The term "launching State" is based on Art. VII of the Outer Space Treaty and formulated identically in Art. I(c) of the Liability Convention and Art. I(a) of the Registration Convention the following way:

> „The term ‚launching State' means:
> (i) A State which launches or procures the launching of a space object;
> (ii) A State from whose territory or facility a space object is launched;"

[1] *Kai-Uwe Schrogl* was Chairman of the UNCOPUOS Legal Subcommittee's Working Group on the review of the concept of the „launching State", and *Charles Davies* was Secretary of the Working Group. The authors present their personal views; this paper does not reflect the views of the United Nations or DLR. They would like to thank *Petr Lála*, *Robert Wickramatunga* and *Philip McDougall* for their support and contributions during the conduct of the Working Group. An updated version of this paper will be published in the German Journal of Air and Space Law (ZLW).

This concept has recently been challenged by a specific space activity: the SeaLaunch venture.[2] Established in 1995, it launched its first test vehicle in 1999 and started full operations in 2000. It comprises a number of features, each making it difficult to fully apply the concept of the „launching State" at first glance:

- it is a private venture comprising companies from numerous States (in particular U.S.A., Russia, Ukraine, and Norway),
- the headquarters of the company were located in the Cayman Islands, a U.K. overseas territory, but recently moved to Long Beach, California, U.S.A.,
- the rockets are launched from a converted oil drilling platform on the high Seas.

The potential problems in identifying one or more „launching States" in this setting were first brought up in academic circles. In particular, Prof. Armel Kerrest from the University of Brest, beginning in 1997, examined these questions.[3] Following this signal, numerous institutions and fora, in particular the International Institute of Space Law (IISL) and the European Centre for Space Law (ECSL), continued the discussion of this issue in the academic field.[4]

The issue is particular in a second respect, since it was immediately taken up by policy- and law-makers. Agreement on a number of older proposals for new agenda items for the Legal Subcommittee has not been reached, a good example being legal aspects of space debris, which was first proposed almost one decade ago. Another example of an issue that was taken up rapidly by the Subcommittee, however, was nuclear power sources, which was put on the agenda following a major accident. Since no accident and particular legal conflict had happened with the „launching State", its acceptance as an agenda item in the Subcommittee had to coincide with other developments. The prime coincidence was that in 1998 a new agenda item had been established in the Legal Subcommittee dealing with the „Review of the Status of the Five Legal Instruments Governing Outer Space". Europe, at that time, wanted to contribute to this new item and singled out the Registration Convention, which – in its view – could be improved through various measures. It therefore prepared a working paper containing five proposals how to improve the Registration Convention comprising for example the introduction of time limits for furnishing information and extending information requested on space objects.[5] One of the five proposals concerned the concept of the „launching State" and contained the following proposal: para „11(c) (...)it should be investigated whether the definition of the term „launching State" still adequately covers all launching activities;(...)". The „launching State" had thus immediately become „an issue".

---

[2] www.sea-launch.com

[3] *Armel Kerrest*, Launching spacecraft from the sea and the Outer Space Treaty: The SeaLaunch project, IISL-97-IISL.3.15 and *Armel Kerrest*, The Launch of Spacecraft from the Sea, in: *Gabriel Lafferranderie/Daphne Crowther* (eds.): An Outlook on Space Law over the Next 30 Years, The Hague/London/Boston (Kluwer) 1997, 217-233.

[4] See e.g. *Edward Frankle/E. Jason Steptoe*, Legal Considerations Affecting Commercial Space Launches From International Territory, IISL-99-IISL.4.02; *Armel Kerrest*, Remarks on the Notion of Launching State, IISL-99-IISL.4.03; *Marialetizia Longo*, Legal Aspects of Launching Space Objects From Non-Terrestrial Sites, IISL-99-IISL.4.08; *Edward Frankle*, Once a Launching State, Always *The* Launching State?, IISL-01-IISL.1.04; *Alvaro Fabricio dos Santos*, Brazil and the Registration Convention, IISL-01-IISL.1.11; *Kai-Uwe Schrogl*, Is the legal concept of the „launching State" still adequate?, 3rd ECSL Colloquium on International Organizations and Space Law (Perugia), 1999, 327-329; *Christian Kohlhase/Philip S. Makiol*, Report of the „Project 2001" Working Group on Launch and Associated Services, in: *Karl-Heinz Böckstiegel* (ed.): „Project 2001" – Legal Framework for the Commercial Use of Outer Space, Cologne (Carl Heymanns) 2001, 55-102; *Roger Close*, UK Outer Space Act 1986: Scope and Implementation, in: *ibid.*, 579-590. The concept of the „launching State" was already highlighted in connection with the drafting of the Principles on the Use of Nuclear Power Sources in Outer Space in 1992 (Principle 2), see *Marietta Benkö/Gerhard Gruber/Kai-Uwe Schrogl*, The UN Committee on the Peaceful Uses of Outer Space: Adoption of Principles Relevant to the Use of Nuclear Power Sources in Outer Space and Other Recent Developments, in: ZLW(42,1) 1993, 35-64, here 38-39.

[5] Working paper submitted by Germany on behalf of 19 other European States (Member States of the European Space Agency (ESA) and States having signed cooperation agreements with ESA), UN Doc. A/AC.105/C.2/L.211/Rev.1 of 30 March 1998.

2. Establishing the work plan 2000-2002 on the agenda of the UNCOUPOS Legal Subcommittee

The issue of the legal concept of the „launching State" entered the agenda of the UNCOPUOS Legal Subcommittee with a comparably short preparatory period. This is particularly remarkable since the agenda setting process in the Legal Subcommittee used to be extremely slow and complex. In 1999, however, the working methods of the two Subcommittees were reformed and a more dynamic agenda setting procedure was established.[6] This coincided with the holding of the Third United Nations Conference on the Exploration and Peaceful Uses of Outer Space (UNISPACE III), which gave additional support to the establishment of such new mechanisms.

It was a productive coincidence that the European proposal of 1998 to improve the Registration Convention[7] met with this trend. The proposal was generally well received at that time. Not only the sheer number of co-sponsors – 20 States out of the then 61 Member States of COPUOS – but also the precisely and clearly drafted text led to a positive presentation. Basic disagreement, however, was voiced by the Russian Federation, which countered with a „holistic approach". In other words, single treaties should not be discussed individually, because of close links between the five United Nations treaties on outer space. Instead, all these treaties should be discussed, either in parallel or consecutively, and only then could changes or supplements be adopted. The European working paper in para. 10 had already acknowledged that, among other things, a clarification of the definition of the „launching State" in the Registration Convention would have an impact on the same definition in the Liability Convention and that a supplement to the Registration Convention in this respect should also expressly cover the definition of „launching State" wherever it appeared in other United Nations treaties on outer space. It is important to note that the Russian Federation did not voice any objections to the objectives of the European proposal, but differed only on matters of methodology. Since it was not possible to reach an agreement in the Legal Subcommittee (in addition to the Russian resistance, the United States had at that time not yet concluded their internal evaluation of the proposal), the discussion on the European proposal was taken up again in the session of the main Committee in June 1998, „with a view to possibly reaching consensus" as had been recommended by the Legal Subcommittee.[8]

Building on this mandate, Germany led the negotiations at the main Committee meeting in June 1998. It became clear very quickly, however, that neither Russia nor the United States would accept the European proposal as it stood. In addition to the Russian concern with considering any single treaty in isolation, the United States was unable to agree on a new agenda item which would or could lead to an official interpretation or amendment of an international treaty. In order to achieve a compromise, and in place of the entire European package of proposals on measures to improve the Registration Convention, the question of the adequacy of the concept of „launching State" was singled out as an issue on which agreement might be reached. Further discussion on the other points (new elements of information for notification and incorporation of relevant parts of the Principles on the Use of Nuclear Power Sources in outer Space) was postponed.

Having received the support of Russia, the European States had to go through intensive negotiations with the United States before a final agreement could be reached. While Europe proposed an immediate decision on a new agenda item

---

[6] See *Volker Liebig/Kai-Uwe Schrogl*, Space Applications and Policies for the New Century, Frankfurt/Main (Peter Lang) 2000, 168-175.

[7] See *Marietta Benkö/Kai-Uwe Schrogl*, The UN Committee on the Peaceful Uses of Outer Space: Introducing the Agenda Item „Review of the Status of the Five Legal Instruments Governing Outer Space" and Other Recent Developments, in: ZLW (47,4) 1998, 525-530, the text of the proposal is reprinted at 534-538.

[8] See the Report of the Legal Subcommittee on the work of its thirty-seventh session (23-31 March 1998), UN Doc. A/AC.105/698 of 6 April 1998, para.72.

with a three-year work plan (containing Analysis of the present situation, Consequences for existing space law and Recommendations), the United States was only ready to accept that UNCOPUOS would invite presentations on new launch systems and ventures, to be given in both its Scientific and Technical Subcommittee and its Legal Subcommittee in 2000. In addition to committing itself to participate in inter-sessional consultations before the 1999 session of the Legal Subcommittee, with a view to possibly reaching consensus at the Legal Subcommittee session on the introduction of a new agenda item in the Subcommittee starting in 2000/2001. The German government was asked to host these inter-sessional consultations.

The Report of UNCOPUOS at its 1998 session reflected this compromise with the following wording:

> „150. Some delegations noted that there was a need to consider the adequacy of the concept of the „launching State" as contained in the Registration Convention and the Liability Convention. They proposed that the Legal Subcommittee should consider this topic beginning in 2000 under a three-year workplan in a working group.
>
> 151. The view was expressed that more analysis in this area was required before agreement could be reached on a new item for the Legal Subcommittee dealing with this matter.
>
> 152. The Committee noted that inter-sessional consultations among interested delegations before the Legal Subcommittee session in 1999 would be welcome in order to seek a consensus on this matter.
>
> 153. The Committee agreed that the Scientific and Technical Subcommittee and the Legal Subcommittee would invite special presentations on new launch systems and ventures at their sessions in 2000 with a view to attaining a better understanding of these launch activities."[9]

It is not often that UNCOPUOS agrees to hold inter-sessional consultations on new agenda items, and this case demonstrated the sincere determination of the interested States to find a positive conclusion for that question. Following the request by UNCOPUOS, Germany hosted the inter-sessional consultations, which took place on 9 December 1998 in Bonn. The outcome of these consultations perfectly matched the expectations, since an agreement was reached on the scope and content of a three-year work plan[10], which was informally discussed at the Legal Subcommittee and formally adopted at the session of UNCOPUOS in 1999. The respective part of the UNCOPUOS Report reads:

> „114. The Committee agreed that a new item entitled „Review of the concept of the ‚launching State'" should be included in the agenda of the Legal Subcommittee. The item would be considered by a working group during a three-year period beginning in the year 2000 in accordance with the following schedule of work:
>
> 2000 Special presentations on new launch systems and ventures
>
> 2001 Review of the concept of the "launching State" as contained in the Convention on International Liability for Damage Caused by Space Objects (Liability Convention) and the Convention on Registration of Objects Launched into Outer Space (Registration Convention) as applied by States and international organizations
>
> 2002 Review of measures to increase adherence to and promote the full application of the Convention on International Liability for Damage Caused by Space Objects and the Convention on Registration of Objects Launched into Outer Space."[11]

With this agreement, the Legal Subcommittee was ready to take up a new legal problem for the first time since the 1980s. The working group accepted that

---

[9] Report of the Committee on the Peaceful Uses of Outer Space, UN Doc. A/53/20 (1998), part II.D.4 (a).

[10] Report on the inter-sessional consultations on the concept of the „launching State", UN Doc. A/AC.105/C.2/L.217 of 1 March 1999.

[11] Report of the Committee on the Peaceful Uses of Outer Space, UN Doc. A/54/20 (1999), part II.C.4(b).

challenge and aimed from the beginning at working in a concentrated manner on the legal concept of the „launching State".

3. Questions regarding the application of the legal concept of the „launching State"

Since the Liability Convention entered into force in 1972, a number of trends in space activities have created new issues of interpretation under the Convention. One such trend is a continuing increase in the number of countries that carry out launch activities. In 1972, the vast majority of launches were carried out by the two major space powers: the United States and the Soviet Union. This is no longer the case. International cooperation in space activities is also increasing, with examples like the International Space Station, involving resource-sharing and technological cooperation between 16 countries and manned by international teams of space explorers. Involvement of the private sector in launch activities is also continually increasing, and some launches are now carried out by multinational private enterprises, like the French-Russian „Starsem" marketing partnership, the German-Russian „Eurockot" commercial launch service provider, and SeaLaunch. A final trend, of course, is a continuous development of new and improved space technologies.

This section outlines some questions that have been raised by various governments and commentators[12] regarding application of the concept of the „launching State". In addition, it includes examples of state practice that demonstrate how some of these issues are being addressed by national authorities.

3.1 Issues relating to territories and facilities

To what extent is a country liable when that country participates in the launch „only" by making its territory available?

Under the Liability Convention, all the „launching States" for a particular space object are jointly and severally liable. There is no explicit distinction between States procuring the launch of a space object and States from whose territories and facilities a space object is launched.

In other words, the Convention offers a high degree of protection to victims of damage. The classification as „launching States" of States from whose territories and facilities a space object is launched – which may have limited control over the space object and may not be at fault for damage in any way – is clearly designed to offer an additional level of protection to the victim.

In practice, countries that participate in launches only by making their territories or facilities available normally conclude agreements under Article V(2) of the Liability Convention, which states: „The participants in a joint launching may conclude agreements regarding the apportioning among themselves of the financial obligation in respect of which they are jointly and severally liable." However, „Such agreements shall be without prejudice to the right of a State sustaining damage to seek the entire compensation due under this Convention from any or all of the „launching States" which are jointly and severally liable." For example, China's practice with respect to launches from Chinese territory is to conclude agreements limiting its liability, as between the various „launching States", to the point at which the payload is placed correctly into the proper orbit. Thereafter, the State with jurisdiction and control over the space object must pay any damage that the „launching States" are liable for under the Liability Convention.

This is an important issue and possible pitfall for developing countries making their territories available for launches. But it is also a safeguard for technologically appropriate, careful and responsible conduct of launching activities. Under the Liability Convention, countries making their territory available for a launch are jointly and severally liable under the Liability Convention for the entire value of any

[12] See supra footnotes 3 and 4.

damage caused by the space object for which they are a „launching State". It is therefore important for these countries to ensure they are protected – as between the „launching States" – through the negotiation of agreements under article V(2) of the Liability Convention.

Launches from international territory

How does the Liability Convention address launches from international territory? It has been reasoned that launches from international territory (like launches by SeaLaunch from the high seas) create a lacuna in application of the Liability Convention. The State from whose territory a space object is launched may often be the „launching State" that can be identified most easily and objectively, and the only one that cannot be freely chosen by a private entity carrying out a launch. In the case of launches from international territory, like the high seas, the launch is not taking place from the territory of any State, which may result in the victim's State being unable to identify any „launching State" from which to claim damages under the Liability Convention.

A similar problem might be the adoption of flags of convenience. The Liability Convention provides for the liability of „launching States". One way for „launching States" to limit their liability is to establish a system to review the safety of launches before they are licensed by the national authorities. In fact, ensuring the safety of space activities is an important policy behind most national space laws.[13] If private entities carrying out a launch can choose their „launching States", this would result not only in difficulties with claiming liability for any damage, but might also result in less stringent safety rules being applied to the launch in the first place, making accidents more likely.

On the other hand, it is worth noting that many space launch licensing regimes require authorization for certain launches outside national territory in which the country's nationals are involved. For instance, the United States requires a license for launches and related activities by (a) individuals who are citizens of the United States and (b) entities organized or existing under the laws of the United States or a [U.S.] state, and (c) entities organized or existing under the laws of a foreign country if the controlling interest (as defined by the Secretary of Transportation) is held by an individual falling under categories (a) or (b). For activities outside the territory of any country, a license is required for entities in category (c) unless the United States Government and the Government of a foreign country agree that the foreign country has jurisdiction over the launch.[14] Under this provision, the United States requires a launch license for launches by SeaLaunch, in which Boeing, a U.S. company, participates.

It should also be noted that the United States law and similar launch licensing regimes that are in place in other countries like Australia, Japan, Russia, South Africa, Ukraine and the United Kingdom, require licensees to obtain third-party insurance and/or demonstrate their ability to pay potential claims by third parties („financial responsibility"). Under some laws, this insurance or financial responsibility may be required to cover „maximum forseeable loss", or should be appropriate from the viewpoint of potential victims.[15]

Launches from international territory mean there is no State from whose territory the space object is launched. In addition, entities launching from vessels on the high seas may choose the flag state for their launch platform. However, in practice and at present, potential victims are given some protection by authorities applying national insurance and safety requirements to launches by their nationals from international territory.

What type or level of property interest should a State have in a „facility" before it

[13] Review of the concept of the „launching State" - Report of the Secretariat, UN Doc. A/AC.105/768 of 21 January 2002, Section E, paras. 21-23.

[14] 49 United States Code, section 70104.

[15] Review of the concept of the „launching State" - Report of the Secretariat, UN Doc.A/AC.105/768 of 21 January 2002, Section F, paras. 24-26.

can become a „launching State" under the Liability Convention?

Unlike the State from whose territory a space object is launched, the State or States from whose facility a space object is launched may not be so easy to identify. For instance, what about a State that has (or whose national has) financed the building of a space launch facility, or that might even have taken possession of the facility after default by the original owner?

The authors are not aware of any simple answer to this question – it seems like a judgement call. The issues are similar to those concerning which States qualify as States that have procured the launch of a space object. Limiting the number of „launching States" will mean there are fewer States for the victim's State to turn to for compensation. Increasing the number of „launching States" increases the number of States that must protect themselves from possible liability by enacting insurance and safety review regulations, which may be duplicative and costly both for Governments and owners of launch facilities. Again, a State that is at risk of being liable as a launching State because of an interest in a space launch facility, may wish to protect itself from liability – as between the launching States – by concluding agreements under article V(2) of the Liability Convention.

Launches by aircraft

Launches by aircraft – like the U.S. Pegasus launcher, which has been operational since 1990 – may create some questions of interpretation. The main question is at what point the launch takes place.

Under Article 1 of the Chicago Convention on International Civil Aviation, a State has complete and exclusive sovereignty over the airspace above its territory. The question remains whether this complete sovereignty would qualify airspace above a States territory as „territory" under the Registration and Liability Conventions. A further complication would be introduced by the fact that separation between the aircraft and the Pegasus launcher normally takes place over the ocean, in most cases probably outside the territorial sea of the country concerned. If „launch" is defined as separation between the aircraft and the satellite, then it may be impossible to identify a State from whose territory a space object is launched.

If one determines the launch to take place when the launch vehicle takes off, then it will be possible for a potential victim to identify a national territory from which the space object is launched.

Where is the point that a „launch" by an aircraft takes place is also a question under the Registration Convention. The few countries that have included the location of a Pegasus launch in the information provided to the Secretary General under the Registration Convention have indicated that the launch occurred from a point on dry land, rather than in the air.[16] In other words, these registrations would consider the airplane carrier to be just another part of the launch vehicle.

It might also be appropriate to consider an analagous situation: the launch of satellites by another reusable launch vehicle, the United States Space Shuttle. The satellites are deployed at some point while the Space Shuttle is in orbit, and remain in orbit after the Shuttle returns to Earth. The date of launches by the Space Shuttle is normally registered with the United Nations as the take-off date of the Space Shuttle, although practice is not completely uniform. In the case of the launch by the Argentinian satellite SAC-A by Space Shuttle Endeavour, the date of launch was listed by Argentina as the date of separation between the space object and the Space Shuttle.[17]

3.2 States procuring the launch of a space object

Under the Liability and Registration Conventions, a State „procuring the launch of a space object" is a „launching State". Perhaps one of the most difficult issues

[16] UN Doc. A/AC.105/INF/397 of 8 March 1993, UN Doc. ST/SG/SER.E/317 of 15 January 1997, UN Doc. ST/SG/SER.E/326 of 20 October 1997.
[17] UN Doc. ST/SG/SER.E/351 of 1 February 1999.

concerning the „launching State" is determining which countries fall in to the category of States procuring a launch.

One difficulty that has been raised is a difference between the English and Russian translations of the word to „procure". In English, the word „procure" indicates that the State paid for or obtained some benefit from the launch. On the other hand, the official translation for „procures" in the Russian version of the Registration and Liability Conventions, *organizyet*, indicates that the State has organized the launch.[18]

One major concern is the sheer number of countries that may now be involved with a launch and could potentially fall within the category of procurers of a launch. This means that a lot of countries have to analyse whether they may be held liable as a „launching State" and, if they may, take steps to limit their liability or ensure that it can be paid.

For instance, discussions in the Legal Subcommittee considered the typical „delivery in orbit" arrangement, in which the satellite builder, the launch service provider and the satellite operator may each come from different countries. In fact, each may themselves involve various different countries.[19]

One approach would be the inclusive approach. In order to give fullest possible protection to potential victims, one could interpret procurers of a launch broadly and include a large number of countries as „launching States". However, there are costs to this approach. First, business may be faced with a burden of regulation, or „red-tape-costs", in several States for the launch of a single space object. Second, in order to cover potential international liability, each State procuring the launch might set insurance requirements for the entity carrying out the launch. This may be problematic in the case of a procuring State, since this country may have limited access to information on the launch technology (e.g. because of technology transfer regulations) and may therefore find it difficult to quantify reasonable risks. It may also see little benefit from encouraging launch activities and may have limited ability to supervise the launch. In order to protect themselves in light of the limited information available to them, these States may set insurance requirements that are unreasonably high and burdensome on the launch service provider.[20]

Which States are procurers of a launch is again probably a matter of judgement. As mentioned, an inclusive approach favours potential victims but may result in real costs to Government and launch service providers. One potential approach is to consider ways to streamline licensing procedures for launches that may involve a number of procuring States. The broader possibility of harmonizing voluntary practices under the Conventions is addressed in Section 5 of this paper.

3.3 Fault

For damage caused elsewhere than on the surface of the Earth, the „launching State" – following Article III of the Liability Convention - is liable only if the damage is due to its fault or the fault of persons for whom it is responsible. However, the Convention does not elaborate further on the requirements for „fault". A fault determination in space is certainly more complicated than that on the roadways, where vehicles are controlled by human beings and are required to follow a set of predetermined traffic rules.

With a rising amount of space activities, the elaboration of space traffic management rules in a time perspective of ten to twenty years has therefore been identified as a necessity to answer this question, and address a number of related issues. It was more than a coincidence that the annual International Institute of Space Law/European Centre for Space Law Symposium during the Legal Subcommittee

[18] This point was made by the Russian delegation during deliberations in the working group.

[19] Review of the Concept of the „launching State" - Report of the Secretariat, UN Doc. A/AC.105/768 of 21 January 2002, para. 48.

[20] Review of the Concept of the „launching State" - Report of the Secretariat, UN Doc. A/AC.105/768 of 21 January 2002, para. 49.

session in the year 2002 (when the Working Group on the „launching State" finalized its work) dealt with „Prospects for Space Traffic Management".[21] In addition, the International Academy of Astronautics established a study group on this issue in the year 2001.

3.4 Reusable launch vehicles

Are multiple launches of a reusable launch vehicle considered as separate launches under the Liability and Registration Conventions? Some state practice exists on this issue under the Registration Convention. Separate missions of the United States Space Shuttle are registered separately with the United Nations.

3.5 Jurisdiction and control

Under Principle 2(1) of the Principles Relevant to the Use of Nuclear Power Sources in Outer Space[22], the „launching State" is defined as a State which exercises jurisdiction and control over a space object with nuclear power sources on board at a given point in time relevant to the principle concerned. While an integral part of the „launching State" definition in the Principles on the Use of Nuclear Power Sources in Outer Space, „jurisdiction and control" is not mentioned explicitly in the Liability and Registration Conventions' definition of a „launching State". To what extent is it relevant?

Lack of jurisdiction and control over a space object obviously makes it difficult to prevent the space object causing damage. This may be especially relevant to liability for damage elsewhere than on the surface of the Earth, which is fault-based and not absolute. Of course, it is still possible for a State without jurisdiction or control over a space object at the time that the space object causes damage to be partially at fault for the damage, for instance if damage is caused by a preexisting design or orbit failure.

The fact that jurisdiction and control is not an explicit requirement for „launching States" under the Liability Convention raises the possibility of States that procured a launch being absolutely liable for damage that they could not prevent. This is perhaps similar to the situation of States from whose territory a space object is launched. These „launching States" may seek to negotiate agreements limiting their liability – as between the „launching States" – under Article V(2) of the Liability Convention.

One of the most commonly discussed issues is what happens when ownership or control over satellites is transferred from one State to another. In particular, must a State „procuring the launch of a space object" have been an original „launching State", or can it become a „launching State" at later point?

On this issue, it is worth noting an example of practice under the Registration Convention. Satellite BSB-1A was originally registered with the United Nations by the United Kingdom following its launch from the United States in 1989.[23] Subsequently, the satellite was listed as „Sirius 1" on the Swedish register of objects launched into outer space, which was conveyed to the United Nations in UN Doc. ST/SG/SER.E/352 of 19 February 1999, following purchase of the satellite in orbit in 1996. This seems to indicate that Sweden considered itself to be a „launching State" for this satellite under the Registration Convention, since the „State of registry", which registers the satellite with the United Nations, must be a „launching State" under the Convention. The authors are not aware of any Swedish involvement with this satellite at the time it was launched.

Another, perhaps better known, case of a change in the State of registry for satellites is that of the transfer of satellites AsiaSat-1, AsiaSat-2, APSTAR-I and APSTAR-IA from

[21] The Proceedings of this Symposium, which took place on 2 April 2002 are contained in UN Doc. A/AC.105/C.2/2002/CRP.7 of 4 April 2002. For early ideas on this issue see *Lubos Perek*, Traffic Rules for Outer Space, IISL-82-IISL-09; for recent discussions see *American Institute of Aeronautics and Astronautics*, International Space Cooperation: Addressing Challenges of the New Millennium, March 2001, 7-14; and for specific aspects related to air traffic see *U.S. Federal Aviation Administration*, Concept of Operations for Commercial Space Transportation in the National Airspace System, 14 January 2000.

[22] UNGA Res. 47/68, adopted on 14 December 1992.

[23] UN Doc. ST/SG/SER.E/219 of 24 April 1990.

the United Kingdom to the Hong Kong Special Administrative Region of China on 1 July, 1997.[24] This was the date of the transfer of power in Hong Kong from the U.K. to China, and the transfer of the State of registry must have been a result of this transfer of power. This is another example of a transfer in the State of registry of a satellite. On the other hand, China clearly *was* an original launching State in this case, since the satellites in question were launched from Xichang launch center in south-west China.

It is quite possible that none of the original „launching States" for a space object may have jurisdiction and control over the space object. If a „launching State" under the Liability Convention is required to be an original „launching State", this could mean that none of the States subject to international liability under the Liability Convention have the ability to prevent damage being caused by the space object in question. This situation could be avoided, however, if a „launching State" is not required to be an original „launching State". A possible argument for this approach would be that the State in question has obtained some benefit from the launch, even though it was not involved when the launch took place.

3.6 International organizations

The Registration and Liability Conventions provide for the possibility of international organizations to declare their acceptance of the rights and obligations provided for in the Conventions. For this to be effective, a majority of the States Members of the organization in question must be States Parties to the Convention in question as well as the Outer Space Treaty.

If the international organization has not declared its acceptance of the rights and obligations in the Convention, or if a majority of its members are not Parties to the Outer Space Treaty and the Convention in question, how are the „launching States" determined? Would all the Member States of that organization be „launching States"?

[24] UN Doc. ST/SG/SER.E/333 of 3 April 1988 and UN Doc. ST/SG/SER.E/334 of 3 April 1998.

On a side note, some international organizations have recently privatized. For instance, Eutelsat (which declared its acceptance of the rights and obligations in the Liability Convention) is now a private company, which would presumably mean its declaration of acceptance is no longer effective.

4. The deliberations in the Legal Subcommittee

„Review of the concept of the ‚launching State' was considered by the Legal Subcommittee under the three-year work plan referred to in section 2 above. In the Legal Subcommittee, a Working Group, open to all 64 Member States of UNCOPUOS, was set up during each year that considered the agenda item on „Review of the concept of the ‚launching State'".[25]

In the year 2000, presentations on new launch systems and ventures took place not only in the Legal Subcommittee, but were also included as an item on the agenda of the Scientific and Technical Subcommittee. These presentations helped delegations to obtain practical, up-to-date information from a number of perpectives.[26] Governments gave presentations on national launch service programmes, launch vehicles that are currently in use, as well as those that are under development. Representatives of international commercial ventures like Starsem and Eurockot also gave presentations to the Scientific and Technical Subcommittee and the Legal

[25] The Reports of this Working Group are contained in the respective Reports of the Legal Subcommittee on the work of its thirty-ninth (2000), fortieth (2001) and forty-first sessions (2002), UN Docs. A/AC.105/738 of 20 April 2000, Annex II, A/AC.105/763 of 24 April 2001, Annex II and A/AC.105/787 of 19 April 2002, Annex IV.

[26] They are contained in UN Doc. A/AC.105/C.2/2000/CRP.8 of 30 March 2000 for the Scientific and Technical Subcommittee (with presentations by representatives from France, Germany, India, the Russian Federation and the United States) and in UN Doc. A/AC.105/C.2/2000/CRP.12 of 5 April 2000 for the Legal Subcommittee (with presentations by representatives from France, Germany, Japan, the Russian Federation and the United States).

Subcommittee. A few presentations outlined national laws and procedures for licensing launches into outer space, as well as questions that were being faced by national authorities in applying the „launching State" concept. Finally, the Working Group started to consider the scope of work during its three-year work plan. It was agreed that the Working Group should not aim at an authoritative interpretation of the concept of the „launching State" concept, in part because of views by some countries that such an interpretation was not necessary since both Conventions were functioning well, and in part because of procedural concerns that the Legal Subcommittee was not the appropriate body to amend or provide an official interpretation of the Liability and Registration Conventions.

During the second year of the work plan, in 2001, the Working Group reviewed how the concept of the „launching State" was being applied by States and international organizations. That year, various States and international organizations made presentations on their national space laws, or procedures for licensing launches into outer space.[27] The Working Group also considered – in more depth than in 2000 – some of the issues facing national authorities when applying the concept of the „launching State" in practice. The Working Group also had the benefit of a study by the Secretariat summarizing various national space laws,[28] as well as a compilation of national space laws and international agreements relevant to the concept of the „launching State".[29]

Finally, in 2002, the third year of the work plan, the Subcommittee reviewed measures to increase adherence to and promote the full application of the Registration and Liability Conventions. It had before it a report by the Secretariat, which had been prepared at the Subcommittee's request. The report contained a synthesis of state practice in applying the concept of the „launching State", which addressed subjects like state jurisdiction over space activities, ensuring the safety of space activities, third-party insurance and financial responsibility requirements, and cross-waivers of liability.[30] The document also summarized some of the issues that had been raised by States during the first two years of the work plan (see Section 3 above). Based on provisions of existing national space law, the final section of the document listed elements that could be included in national space legislation and licensing regimes.

5. The Conclusions of the Working Group and further perspectives on the future of the legal concept of the „launching State"

The final year of the work plan had the task of reviewing measures to increase adherence to the Liability and Registration Conventions and promote their full application. During this session, the Chairman presented the Working Group with draft conclusions.[31] The idea was to present the Working Group with some possible concrete actions that could be taken based on its review of the concept. The draft conclusions were developed by analysing the positions, goals and concerns that countries had expressed during the first two years of the work plan, in 2000 and 2001.

After considering the Chairman's proposal, the Working Group adopted an amended version as the Conclusions of the Working

[27] They are contained in UN Doc. A/AC.105/C.2/2001/CRP.10 of 11 April 2001 (with presentations by Australia, China, France, Sweden, the U.K., ESA and the International Law Association).

[28] Review of existing national space legislation illustrating how States are implementing, as appropriate, their responsibilities to authorize and provide continuing supervision of non-governmental entities in outer space – Note by the Secretariat, UN Doc. A/AC.105/C.2/L.224 of 22 January 2001.

[29] UN Doc. A/AC.105/C.2/2001/CRP.5 of 27 March 2001. Most of these texts can also be found on the web site of the UN Office for Outer Space Affairs at (http://www.oosa.unvienna.org/SpaceLaw/spacelaw.htm).

[30] Review of the Concept of the „launching State" - Report of the Secretariat, UN Doc. A/AC.105/768 of 21 January 2002.

[31] Draft Conclusions of the Working Group on agenda item 9, „Review of the concept of the ‚launching State'" – Proposal submitted by the Chairman, UN Doc. A/AC.105/C.2/C.2/L.234 of 26 March 2002.

Group. These Conclusions were then endorsed by the Legal Subcommittee.[32] They are reprinted in the Annex to this article.

The Conclusions – in addition to summarizing discussions during the three-year work plan – contain the following three main recommendations.

> First Recommendation (para. 10): *„The Working Group recommended that States conducting space activities consider steps to implement national laws to authorize and provide continuing supervision to activities of their nationals in outer space and implement their international obligations under the Liability Convention, the Registration Convention and other international agreements.(...)"*

As of April 2002, there were 82 States Party to the Liability Convention and 45 States Party to the Registration Convention. For the many States that are not party to either or both of these Conventions, the first step to increase adherence to and promote the full implementation of these Conventions would be to accede to them. These treaties do not only provide benefits to space powers. Liability of the „launching State" under the Liability Convention, or identification of space objects under the Registration Convention benefit spacefaring and non-spacefaring countries equally.

States that are Party to the United Nations treaties on outer space must, of course, comply with their international obligations under these treaties. In some countries, it might be necessary to enact some kind of implementing law. Among other things, „launching States" that are parties to the Registration Convention would have to set up a national registry under the Registration Convention and make provision for providing the required information to the United Nations.

The recommendation of the Working Group, more broadly, refers to national laws „to authorize and provide continuing supervision to activities of their nationals in outer space". Under article VI of the Outer Space Treaty, authorization and continuing supervision of the activities of non-governmental entities in outer space is the responsibility of the „appropriate State Party to the [Outer Space] Treaty". The recommendation of the Working Group is therefore close to the language in the Outer Space Treaty. However, the Working Group refers to authorization and continuing supervision by States of activities of their „nationals". This reflects current State practice, in that many national space laws cover both activities on national territory and activities by the State's nationals outside national territory.

The Working Group also listed four benefits that national space laws could provide to countries enacting them. First, the law can effect a country's jurisdiction and control over a space object. If a „launching State" lacks control over a space object, then it may be impossible for the State to prevent damage being caused by the object. The State may therefore be liable for damage caused by the space object yet unable to prevent the damage from occurring. There is therefore a benefit to States establishing jurisdiction and control over space objects launched by their nationals, as consistent with international law.

Second, national space laws may reduce the risk of launch accidents and other damage. Many national laws require launches to be reviewed for safety before they can be licensed by the government. By reducing the risk of launch accidents, safety reviews serve the public interest, and by helping to prevent damage from space objects, also help the „launching States" concerned avoid liability.

Thirdly, national space laws can establish insurance and financial responsibility requirements for launches, which help ensure the prompt payment of a full and

---

[32]Conclusions of the Working Group on agenda item 9, entitled „Review of the concept of the ‚launching State'" as contained in the Report of the Legal Subcommittee on its Forty-first session, held in Vienna from 2 to 12 April 2002, UN Doc. A/AC.105/787 of 19 April 2002, Annex IV, Appendix.

equitable measure of compensation to victims, a need expressed in the preamble to the Liability Convention.

Fourth, national space laws can provide mechanisms for governments that are internationally liable under the Liability Convention to receive indemnification from any non-governmental entities that caused the damage. The Liability Convention applies to States Parties; it is governments that are directly liable under the Convention. For this reason, it may benefit governments to ensure that they can receive this money back from any non-governmental entities that caused the damage.

Finally, the Working Group identified some practical sources of assistance to States seeking to develop national space laws. First, it made extensive reference to a proposal for "building blocks" of national space legislation, which was presented by the International Law Association during the course of the work plan.[33] Second, it made reference to the two documents prepared by the Secretariat, which had summarized provisions of existing national space legislation.[34] Third, the Working Group noted that the UN Office for Outer Space Affairs could serve as a resource for legal information and assistance.

> Second Recommendation (para. 14): *„The Working Group recommended, following common practice, that States consider the conclusion of agreements according to Article V, paragraph 2, of the Liability Convention for each stage of a mission with respect to joint launches or cooperation programmes."*

As mentioned earlier (see section 3.1 above), „launching States" – which may have varying degrees of participation in a launch – are jointly and severally liable for damage caused by the space object in question. In other words, States with limited participation in a space activity may be liable for the full amount of damage caused by that activity. The common solution adopted by these countries is to conclude agreements that specifically limit their liability, as between the „launching States".

> Third Recommendation (para. 18): *„The Working Group recommended the consideration of harmonizing voluntary practices that would provide useful guidance in a practical context to national bodies implementing the United Nations treaties on outer space."*

This recommendation addresses two issues. First, it addresses the concern that – because of an increase in international cooperation in space activities – there could be a large number of potential „launching States" for any particular space activity. This might mean that the countries involved protect themselves from liability by imposing confusing or duplicative safety, liability and/or financial responsibility requirements on the launch service provider.

Second, harmonized practices may provide some guidance in a practical context to national bodies that are responsible for implementing the United Nations treaties on outer space. Of course, individual national authorities or even groups of national authorities cannot determine authoritatively whether or not they are „launching States"; this is a question of international law. Adopting the practices of other States does have the effect, however, of consistency, avoiding countries arriving at different interpretations that may be confusing for the launch service provider. It should also be noted that while harmonized practices cannot authoritatively interpret the Liability and Registration Conventions, it may be possible for certain practices to *be used* to interpret these Conventions, for instance under article 38 of the Statute of the International Court of Justice or even article

---

[33] These „building blocks" have been worked out in the framework of „Project 2001"; see *Michael Gerhard/Kai-Uwe Schrogl*, Report of the „Project 2001" Working Group on National Space Legislation, in: *Karl-Heinz Böckstiegel* (ed.), „Project 2001" – Legal Framework for the Commercial Use of Outer Space, Cologne (Carl Heymanns) 2001, 529-564, here 556-557.

[34] UN Docs. A/AC.105/768 of 21 January 2002 and A/AC.105/C.2/L.224 of 22 January 2001.

31(3)(b) of the Vienna Convention on the Law of Treaties.[35]

At the end of its Conclusions, the Working Group encouraged States Parties to the Registration Convention to implement the Convention in a manner that will best assist the identification of space objects, ensure the United Nations Register of Objects Launched into Outer Space is as complete as possible, and avoid duplicate registrations.

The Working Group encouraged States Parties to the Liability Convention to implement the Convention in a manner that will best ensure the prompt payment under the terms of the Convention of a full and equitable measure of compensation to victims of damage caused by space objects.

These two paragraphs closely follow the wording in the Preambles to the respective Conventions (with the addition of the rather logical call for Parties to avoid duplicate registrations under the Registration Convention).

National authorities implementing the Conventions are not interpreting them under international law. Nevertheless, the approach taken by the Conclusions of the Working Group is consistent with the general rule for interpretation of a treaty on the international level: „in good faith in accordance with the ordinary meaning to be given to the terms of the treaty in the light of its object and purpose".[36]

While the nature of space activities has changed greatly since the 1970s, when the Liability and Registration Conventions entered into force, the purpose of the Conventions has not. Even though it may be difficult for carefully negotiated treaties like the Liability and Registration Conventions to keep up – at least explicitly – with rapid developments in a field like space, States Parties can keep the original purpose of these Conventions in mind when developing national laws and practices.

Annex

Conclusions of the Working Group on agenda item 9, entitled „Review of the concept of the ‚launching State'" as contained in the Report of the Legal Subcommittee on its Forty-first session, held in Vienna from 2 to 12 April 2002, UN Doc. A/AC.105/787 of 19 April 2002, Annex IV, Appendix

1. The term "launching State" is an important concept in space law. It is based on article VII of the Treaty on Principles Governing the Activities of States in the Exploration and Use of Outer Space, including the Moon and Other Celestial Bodies (the "Outer Space Treaty", General Assembly resolution 2222 (XXI), annex and formulated identically in article I (c) of the Convention on International Liability for Damage Caused by Space Objects (the "Liability Convention", resolution 2777 (XXVI), annex) and article I (a) of the Convention on Registration of Objects Launched into Outer Space (the "Registration Convention", resolution 3235 (XXIX), annex) as follows:

> "(c) The term 'launching State' means:
>
> "(i) A State which launches or procures the launching of a space object;
>
> "(ii) A State from whose territory or facility a space object is launched;"

It identifies inter alia those States which may be liable for damage caused by a space object and which would have to pay compensation in such a case. Furthermore, a launching State is responsible for registering a space object consistent with the Outer Space Treaty and the Registration Convention.

2. The Liability Convention entered into force in 1972, and the Registration Convention entered into force in 1976. Changes in space activity since that time include the continuous development of new technologies, an increase in the number of States carrying out space activities, an increase in international cooperation in the peaceful uses of outer space and an increase in space activities carried out by non-governmental entities.

3. Based on a proposal by certain European countries (A/AC.105/C.2/L.211/ Rev.1) and following intersessional consultations in Bonn on 9 December 1998 (A/AC.105/L.217), the Legal Subcommittee conducted a review of the concept of the launching State under a three-year work plan, during its sessions from 2000 to 2002. The Subcommittee established a Working Group to consider the issue, under the Chairmanship of Kai-Uwe Schrogl (Germany).

4. Under the three-year work plan, the Working Group considered the following issues, from the Legal

[35] Following the adoption of the Conclusions, the proposal was made to take the three Recommendations and make them the centerpiece of a UN General Assembly Resolution providing them the same status as e.g. the Remote Sensing Principles or the Space Benefits Declaration. This proposal did not find consensus and was transferred for further consideration to the session in 2003 but without recreating the Working Group nor with the mandate of re-drafting the Recommendations or the Conclusions as a whole. These Conclusions have found their final form in 2002.

[36] Article 31 („General rule of interpretation") of the Vienna Convention on the Law of Treaties of 1969.

Subcommittee's thirty-ninth session, in 2000, to its forty-first session, in 2002:

2000	Special presentations on new launch systems and ventures
2001	Review of the concept of the "launching State" as contained in the Liability Convention and the Registration Convention as applied by States and international organizations
2002	Review of measures to increase adherence to and promote the full application of the Liability Convention and the Registration Convention

5. The Working Group noted that its conclusions did not constitute an authoritative interpretation of or proposed amendments to the Registration Convention or the Liability Convention.

6. The Working Group considered, following technical presentations at the thirty-seventh session of the Scientific and Technical Subcommittee, in 2000, new launch systems and ventures and other aspects of space activity that might raise questions of interpretation under the Liability Convention and the Registration Convention. The Working Group also examined existing State practice regarding the concept of the launching State, including the provisions of national space laws and international agreements. That illustrated how States were implementing their obligations under the Liability Convention, the Registration Convention and other international agreements and how States were addressing some issues of interpretation under those agreements in a practical context. Special presentations at the Scientific and Technical Subcommittee were compiled and distributed as conference room paper A/AC.105/C.2/2000/CRP.8. Presentations at the Legal Subcommittee were compiled and distributed as conference room papers A/AC.105/C.2/2000/CRP.12, A/AC.105/C.2/ 2001/CRP.5 and A/AC.105/C.2/2001/ CRP.10.

7. In 2002, the final year of the work plan, the Working Group reviewed measures to increase adherence to and promote the full application of the Liability Convention and the Registration Convention. The findings and recommendations of the Working Group are set out below.

8. The Working Group noted that, as of April 2002, the Liability Convention had become binding for 82 States and the Registration Convention had become binding for only 44 States; in addition, 97 States were parties to the Outer Space Treaty. The Working Group noted with concern the relatively low level of participation in those treaties, although almost all spacefaring nations had ratified or implemented the instruments and some international intergovernmental organizations had declared their acceptance of the rights and obligations provided for in the conventions. The Working Group expressed the hope that Member States that had not yet done so would consider binding themselves to those conventions. The Working Group stressed that the conventions offered important benefits to all countries, not only to spacefaring countries, in particular by establishing that a launching State was absolutely liable to pay compensation for damage caused by its space object on the surface of the Earth or to aircraft in flight and by assisting in the identification of space objects. However, those provisions were only applicable to States that adhered to the relevant instruments.

9. The Working Group noted that some questions of interpretation under the Liability Convention and the Registration Convention were being addressed on a regular basis by national space regulatory bodies and intergovernmental organizations that had declared their acceptance of the rights and obligations provided for in the Liability Convention and the Registration Convention. Arrangements such as launch marketing ventures and international financing of space objects, for instance, required the participating States to analyse whether they were States "procuring the launch" of the space object in question. National authorities were interpreting "activities in outer space" to determine which activities of non-governmental entities they would authorize and supervise under article VI of the Outer Space Treaty.

10. The Working Group recommended that States conducting space activities consider steps to implement national laws to authorize and provide continuing supervision of the activities of their nationals in outer space and to implement their international obligations under the Liability Convention, the Registration Convention and other international agreements. The Working Group noted that the implementation of national legal provisions on space could benefit the country concerned in ways such as: (a) affecting the country's jurisdiction and control over the space object; (b) reducing the risk of launch accidents and other damage in connection with space activities; (c) providing fast and effective compensation for such damage; and (d) providing mechanisms for a government that is internationally liable under the Liability Convention to receive indemnification from any non-governmental entities that caused the damage. The Working Group noted that the Office for Outer Space Affairs could serve as a resource for legal information and assistance for countries seeking to develop national space laws, in particular developing countries.

11. The Working Group took note of a proposal from the representative of the International Law Association for elements, or "building blocks", for national space legislation, including: (a) authorization of space activities (interpretation of the term "space activities"; application to activities with regard to territory and legal or natural persons; observation of principles in the United Nations treaties on outer space, such as preventing harmful contamination; sharing the financial risk of liability between governmental and non-governmental actors; and observation of the obligation concerning cooperation and mutual assistance); (b) supervision of space activities (through periodical information either provided by the owner of an authorization or collected by a public authority concerning the terms of the authorization; through sanctions in case of non-observance of the terms of the authorization; and through revocation or suspension of the authorization in the case of non-observance of its terms); (c) registration of space objects (interpretation of the concept of space object; setting up a national registry; determination of the supervisory authority; content of entries in the registry (the five items of information to be provided under article IV, paragraph 1, of the Registration Convention); additional information such as the mass of the space object; a safety assessment when a nuclear power source is involved; registration of non-functional objects and objects that have re-entered the Earth's atmosphere; possibility of changes to the registered information; and access to the registry); (d) indemnification regulation (implementation of a right of recourse if the (launching) State has paid indemnification to another State under article VII of the Outer Space Treaty and under the Liability Convention, even if the damage has been caused solely by a non-governmental entity; and indemnification limited to a certain fixed sum or to the

insured sum, beyond which the State can guarantee payment (problem of fair competition)); and (e) additional regulations, with all points mentioned linked to the problem of "fair competition" (regulation of insurance, patent law and international property issues); and export control regulation (because of the ongoing discussions of the International Institute for the Unification of Private Law (Unidroit) on international interests in space property, special regulations on this issue should not be implemented on a national basis at the moment). The Working Group viewed the proposal as identifying useful elements for States to consider in developing national space legislation.

12. The Working Group noted that provisions of existing national space laws could also serve as a useful resource for countries seeking to develop national space laws and that the following documents, which had been considered by the Working Group during the course of its work, had provided a review of national space law provisions:

(a) Review of existing national space legislation illustrating how States are implementing, as appropriate, their responsibilities to authorize and provide continuing supervision of non-governmental entities in outer space (A/AC.105/C.2/L.224);

(b) Report by the Secretariat on the review of the concept of the "launching State" (A/AC.105/768).

13. The Working Group noted that several States could be jointly and severally liable for damage resulting from an overall space activity, notwithstanding their respective limited participation in that space activity.

14. The Working Group recommended, following common practice, that States consider the conclusion of agreements in accordance with article V, paragraph 2, of the Liability Convention for each stage of a mission with respect to joint launches or cooperation programmes.

15. The Working Group noted proposals for entering into such agreements in cases, among others, in which one State participated in the launch only by making its territory or facility available. In those cases, the Working Group noted that States providing launch services sometimes concluded agreements limiting their liability for damage caused by a space object, as between the launching States, to the point at which the payload was placed successfully into the proper orbit.

16. The Working Group noted that national space laws had elements in common and that, in some cases, governments and non-governmental entities were adopting similar practices under the Liability Convention and the Registration Convention.

17. The Working Group noted that it was common for several States to be involved in a single launch. Those States might consider themselves at risk of being liable as "launching States", including "States procuring the launch". Therefore, the third-party liability insurance requirements of several States might be imposed on any particular stage of the launch, with the highest requirements prevailing.

18. The Working Group recommended the consideration of harmonizing voluntary practices that would provide useful guidance in a practical context to national bodies implementing the United Nations treaties on outer space. Agreements or informal practices to streamline the separate space licensing procedures of various States involved in a launch might reduce insurance costs and regulatory burdens for private industry and regulatory costs for governments. For instance, it might be valuable to consider ways of reducing the number of countries that set duplicate third-party insurance requirements for a particular launch or launch stage. States could also consider voluntary harmonized practices regarding on-orbit transfer of ownership of spacecraft. In general, such practices would increase the consistency and predictability of national space laws and help avoid lacunae in the implementation of the treaties. The Working Group noted that voluntary harmonized practices could be considered on a bilateral or multilateral basis, or on a global basis through the United Nations.

19. The Working Group noted that not all space objects launched into outer space had been registered in the United Nations Register of Objects Launched into Outer Space.

20. The Working Group encouraged States parties to the Registration Convention and intergovernmental organizations that had declared their acceptance of the rights and obligations provided for in that Convention to implement the Convention in a manner that would best assist the identification of space objects, ensure the United Nations Register of Objects Launched into Outer Space was as complete as possible, and avoid duplicate registrations.

21. The Working Group encouraged States parties to the Liability Convention and intergovernmental organizations that had declared their acceptance of the rights and obligations provided for in that Convention to implement the Convention in a manner that would best ensure the prompt payment under the terms of the Convention of a full and equitable measure of compensation to victims of damage caused by space objects.

IAC-02-IISL.4.06

BRAZIL-UKRAINE PARTNERSHIP FOR THE USE OF THE ALCANTARA LAUNCH CENTER

Valnora Leister *
LLM, DCL[1]
José Monserrat Filho **
Brazilian Society of Aerospace Law (SBDA)
Brazilian Society for the Advancement of Science (SBPC)

"To prohibit a great people from making all that they can of every part of their own produce, or from employing their stock and their industry in the way they judge most advantageous to themselves, is a manifest violation of the sacred rights of mankind." Adam Smith[2].

Introduction

The paper analyzes the motivations, the goals and the legal aspects of the Brazil-Ukraine Technological Safeguard Agreement and the Memorandum of Understanding relating to the commercial use of the Brazilian Alcantara Launch Center (CLA) by Ukrainian rockets Cyclon-4. Both documents have been signed during the Brazilian Presidential delegation visit to Kiev, January 16-17, 2002.
The paper also examines the relationship between the Brazil-Ukraine Agreement and the 2000 Brazil-US Technological Safeguard on the use of Alcantara Center by US private enterprises.

The Brazilian-Ukrainian Agreement depends on the success of the Brazil-US Agreement in view of the predominant position of US clients in the world the use of Alcantara Center by US private enterprises.

The Brazilian-Ukrainian Agreement depends on the success of the Brazil-US Agreement in view of the predominant position of US clients in the world commercial launch market.

However, the Brazil-Ukraine arrangements (Agreement plus Memorandum) are wider, more ambitious and go far beyond the technological safeguard concerns: they envisage some co-operative projects that can improve the space position of both countries.

While the Brazil-US Agreement prevents any possibility of space technological transfer, the Brazil-Ukraine arrangements foresee joint work in launch vehicle technology, which is a very difficult enterprise to implement. But if the Brazil-Ukraine Agreement succeeds, maybe we will see a new star in the sky of the space activities of our days.

This paper begins with a discussion of the logistics of the creation of the Alcantara Space Center, examines the restrictions imposed by the US on the export of launching technologies from the CLA and the hopeful agreement with Ukraine, and draws some conclusions on

---

* Address: 1911 Worth Van Buren Street, Arlington, VA, 22205, USA. Phone: 70017035343733. E-mail: <valnoral@iadb.org>. The views expressed in this paper are personal opinions of the authors and do not reflect the views and opinions of their employers.

** Address: Av. Oswaldo Cruz, 73/701, Flamengo, Rio de Janeiro, RJ, CEP 22250-060, Brazil. Phones: 55 21 2552-9036 and 2552-6073. E-mail: <monserrat@ax.apc.org>

the obstacles that the safeguards on transfer of technology impose on the growth of space activities for the "benefit of mankind."[3]

The Brazilian Launching Center In Alcantara (CLA)

The Alcantara Spaceport is located in the State of Maranhão, in the north of Brazil, only 2.18 south of the Equator, offering advantageous position for launchings into the Geostationary Transfer Orbit. This location permits: a) launches to the East with great fuel savings thanks to the Earth's rotation in relation to the tangential velocity of the vehicle, and b) excellent condition for equatorial and polar launch.

Construction of the Alcantara Spaceport began in 1983, with the first satellite launching six years later, after nearly US$ 300 million had been spent on roads, electricity, a command center, an airport and other infrastructure. Since then, 276 satellites and rockets have been launched from Alcantara Spaceport, including 36 by NASA, though the great majority of these were suborbital rockets.[4]

The Alcantara Spaceport occupies an area of 620 sq. km. and an infrastructure able to hold many launch pads and area available to install new commercial launch sites for space vehicles. Now it has around 580 employees.

Since undertaking the commercialization of Alcantara Spaceport, Infraero has seventeen enterprises interested in using it. Among them the most important are:

- FiatAvio/Yuznoye , a consortium interested in launching the rocket Cyclone-4;
- Lockheed Martin (USA), interested in negotiating the temporary installation of a platform for the launching of its rocket Athena;
- Orbital Sciences Corporation (USA) interested in launching its rocket Pegasus and in installing a platform for the launching of its rocket Taurus;
- Mart Macron Space (France/Israel), interested in launching the French-Israeli rocket Leolink;
- Boeing (USA), interested in installing a complex for launching its rocket Delta IV;
- Beal Aerospace (USA), requesting conditions and costs for the implementation of a launching site for its rocket BA-2;
- International Launching System (USA/Russia) interested in installing a launching site for its rocket Angara/Atlas V;
- Mitsubishi (Japan), interested in the installation of a launching site for its vehicle J-II.

The Commercialization of Alcantara

In December 1997, the Brazilian State Company Infraero, then in charge of the commercialization of the Alcantara Spaceport, was negotiating with the Italian Corporation Fiat Avio an agreement for a program of launchings. On April 7th, 1998, Infraero had signed a Memorandum of Understanding with Fiat Avio and the Ukranian Enterprises Yuzhnoye and Yuzhny, for the launching of the Ukrainian rocket Tsyklon-4 (a liquid-fuel, three-stage rocket based on the Soviet SS-9 ballistic missile). Before this event, Fiat Avio and Yuzhnoye, on behalf of the two Ukrainian enterprises, signed a strategic Agreement, creating a joint venture for the commercialization of the Tsyklon-4 rocket launchings. They estimated that this rocket would be an efficient vehicle for launching satellites, being reliable, economic and therefore, competitive. Fiat Avia saw an excellent opportunity for a global cellular telephone company. Thus, the interest in having an Agreement with Infraero.

The American enterprise Motorola, asked by Fiat Avio to participate in the business with its own satellites, consulted the US Government on the subject, in accordance with the US legislation. Then, the US Government sent a "non paper" — an officially unpublished document — to the Italian Government recommending that an agreement on Brazilian spaceport should not be concluded.

This non-paper stopped completely the negotiations between Fiat Avio and Infraero. Both the Italian and Ukrainian companies lost interest, because they sensed that the deal was not welcome by the US State Department.

At this stage, the Brazilian diplomacy had been mobilized to try to overcome the obstacle placed in the first opportunity for an international business using the Alcantara Spaceport.

The first attempts of Brazilian authorities o approach the US Government were unsuccessful. The first positive results of the Brazilian efforts were on June 11, 1999, during an official visit of the Brazilian President Fernando Henrique Cardoso to US President Bill Clinton, who decided to open discussion on CLA. Then a Brazilian delegation was received in the State Department, and the US non-paper was included in the official conversations. On June 12, 1999, the National Security Council received the Brazilian delegation. On April 18, 2000 the Agreement was signed, and is now pending ratification by both Houses of the Brazilian Congress to enter into force.

The Agreement between USA and Brazil[5]

In the first paragraph of the Agreement's Preamble, the Government of US and Brazil stress their desire "to expand the successful cooperation carried out under the Framework Agreement on the Cooperation in the Peaceful Uses of Outer Space of March 1, 1996", signed by them. In fact, as we will see, the Agreement is not exactly an instrument of cooperation, but of technological safeguards. It would be a true instrument of cooperation if it would provide some technological transfer, training human resources or contribution to the development of the Brazilian national space program. That is not the case.

The main purpose of the Agreement is to prevent all unauthorized US vehicle and satellite technology transfer to Brazilian institutions and enterprises at the Alcantara Spaceport. In return, Brazil is to benefit from this agreement to the extent that US enterprises launch in the future from Alcantara Spaceport, taking advantage of its positioning and security.

But for the US the safeguards aim at the VLS Brazilian program, since the US never accepted the VLS program. To the US, the VLS could be used for military purposes. In 1988, the US led the Missile Technology Control Regime, known as MTCR [6]— to block the construction of VLS. Since 1994, Brazil took steps to approach the MTCR, creating the needed dual technology export control legislation. In October 1995, Brazil's membership in the MTCR was approved unanimously at the regime's 10th plenary meeting in Bonn, Germany. Acceptance in the MTCR was the outcome of a series of policy changes initiated by Brazil in early 1994 to address international missile proliferation concerns. that Brazil joined, without reservation, the Missile Technology Control Regime (MTCR), in 27 October 1995, after long negotiations with the USA Government, which led Brazil to adopt the Law 9.112/95, establishing internal controls on dual use technologies, particularly missiles and parts of missiles.

The measures adopted by the Brazilian Government in this matter were considered a firm compromise not to produce and not to export any means of delivery (missiles) of mass destruction armaments. In February 1994 Brazil created the Brazilian Space Agency of civil character and in 1995 the Brazilian National Congress approved of control of export of dual technology. Moreover, Brazil reiterated the purpose of using outer space exclusively for peaceful purposes. But, apparently, Brazil's decision to join the MTCR does not guarantee to Brazil a more trustworthy and flexible treatment by the US.[7]

A very important aspect of the USA-Brazil Agreement is that it also rules on agreements with other governments having jurisdiction and control over entities substantially involved in Launch Activities with the participation of American enterprises. The substantive scope and provisions of such agreements are to be equivalent to those of the USA-Brazil Agreement, and as otherwise agreed between the Parties. In particular, such agreements shall obligate such other governments to require their Licensees to abide by arrangements substantively equivalent to the Technology Control Plans that the USA Government shall ensure that US Participants abide by pursuant to paragraph 4 of Article IV to this Agreement.[8]

Thus the Brazilian Government has to sign with other countries safeguard agreements with the same scope and the same contents as this one. Moreover, the USA-Brazil Agreement obliges other governments to require from their licensees — industries that have developed their own space technology – that they avoid technology transfers, in the same way that the US treats its own licensees.

The Agreement signed between Ukraine and Brazil

In the 60s and 70's Ukraine came to host factories and research institutes from the USSR directed to military space activities. When the USSR was dissolved, Ukraine, as an independent country was left with a well-endowed space sector, including the factories for the rocket Zenit, Ciclone and Dniepr. In order to keep its space industries alive, Ukraine start looking for partners, and signed 30 cooperative agreements, three being with Brazil.[9]

The first agreement with Brazil, for Friendly Relations and Cooperation, dates from October 25, 1995.

On November 18, 1999, the two countries signed a Framework Agreement for Cooperation in the peaceful Uses of Outer Space. Its article 3 listed the areas of cooperation as including space launching systems; research and development, and operation of space launching vehicles, satellites and other space systems – all being areas which directly relate to the Alcantara Space center.

Furthermore, Article 5 opened the doors to the participation of other entities of third countries in the Cooperation programs. Article 7 favored the participation of public and private sectors of both countries.

Later on, the Safeguard Agreement was signed together with a Memorandum of Understanding (MOU). This MOU has 8 paragraphs defining the commercial use of Alcantara by means of Ukrainian rockets. By means of the MOU the Brazilian Space Agency (AEB) and the National Ukraine Space Agency(NSAU) would start to launch Cyclone rockets.

It clarifies that:

- the Launching at CLA would be for peaceful and commercial purposes exclusively,
- both countries would try their best to finance the project.
- Issues relating to the property of equipment and new construction, distribution of work and the launching program would be defined by

complementary mutual agreements to the Framework Agreement.

Regarding international legislation, the parties agreed to move towards a joint policy to define "the Launching state", to meet a key requirement of the Convention on Responsibility for Damage caused by Space Objects", as well as to regulate questions regarding licenses and insurance.

The MOU also addresses environmental issues. A key aspect of the MOU also was its affirmation of the non-exclusive nature of the bilateral cooperation, clearly stating that the Agreement would not pose any obstacle to cooperation with other countries.

In 2002, Brazil and Ukraine were obliged to reach a further agreement to comply with the provisions of the US Technological Safeguards that any country should sign a similar safeguard agreement with Brazil, if it were participating in Alcantara launch-related activities that included US enterprises and industries. To observe this requirement, Brazil and Ukraine signed a Safeguard Agreement in Kiev on January 17, 2002.

The Brazil-Ukraine agreement, along with the safeguard agreement earlier signed with the US, are now under review by the Brazilian Congress before a final decision is made on their implementation. Some observers expect the Ukrainian agreement to be approved before action is taken on the US agreement, whose provisions are considered too restrictive by many in the Brazilian Congress. The outcome of this decision could be crucial, given that US companies are considered potential customers of the Brazil- Ukrainian efforts as well as potential providers of launch services.

While the approval of the Safeguard agreements are pending, NSAU representatives, including its President, visited AEB last April and signed a New MOU for a detailed plan of action. A Working group has been established to examine the technical conditions and the infrastructure needed to establish a join-venture to manage the enterprise, including the construction of a new platform for the launching of the Cyclone 4 in Alcantara. The tasks of the Working group include preparing:

- costs of the project
- definition and responsibilities of each country
- evaluation of the world launching market
- the return on investments to be made, and
- analysis of legal questions and the documentation required for the formal creation of the joint venture, including participation of state enterprises of both countries.

Studies already performed indicate that the joint venture could launch annually from 5 to 10 satellites, which could generate an income of up to US$500 million. It is expected that from 2006 CLA would be able to launch from Cyclone 4 up to 6 satellites per year, at a cost of Us$40 million per launching.[10] As the negotiations within this Working Group are now well advanced, Brazil faces an urgent need reach a final decision on ratifying the technological Safeguards Agreement with the USA to fully commercialize Alcantara.

Major differences between the Agreements

The basic difference between the US and the Ukrainian agreements is that the Brazil-USA agreement seeks to close any opportunity for transfer of technology and cooperation. It further reinforces obstacles, in Article 3 of the Agreement, to the development of the VLS program. This is to prevent Brazil from using resources from launching activities from Alcantara to further the development of the VLS program in Brazil or other countries. This Article conforms to US policy regarding the Non-proliferation of Missile technology (MCTR).

The Technology Safeguard Agreement between Ukraine-Ukraine does not have any similar provision. Ukraine and Brazil welcome each other's development, including an option for further development of joint programs. Both countries aim to solve their financial problems by joining efforts in finding innovative solutions to satisfy global market demand. The Ukrainian Government appears to sense more possibilities for cooperation and mutual benefit if Alcantara enters the world market.

Conclusions

The success of the Brazil- Ukraine Agreement depends on the approval by the Brazilian Congress of the US- Brazil Agreement. But the ratification of the US agreement by the Brazilian Congress, does not assure the success of the program. The success depends on the US Government also authorizing the American private companies to launch from Alcantara.

Brazil and Ukraine are hopeful that the US Government will apply the proposed safeguards in a positive and constructive way. Otherwise, it will raise uncertainties about the launching market and the participation of the American enterprises. US firms as well as others in the global market will clearly have their "free enterprise" activities curtailed and profits cut because of these restrictions. Even key conservative politicians in the US have recognized that its US Export Administration Act "represents a compromise between two conflicting goals, protecting national security and promoting US business interests abroad", as remarked Senator Phil Gramm, Texas Republican during the review of the US Export Administration Act. [11]

At a time of growing polarization in international relations, the importance is rising of international cooperation in the area of space activities, especially launching activities. Neutral systems are needed to avoid technological dominance and likely ensuing market concentration. Steps to build trust among foreign partners in opening space could strengthen relationships between established and emerging spacefaring powers.

Laws and policies which qualify almost all satellites as 'arms' (subject to strict export controls) and mix the concepts of security and trade, discourage cooperation between launch companies, will certainly slow down the development of safe, depolilticized, and affordable access to space – and raise opportunities for collusion and concentration of power on the part of favored launching organizations. [12]

The US Government considers that potential threats from emerging economies pose a challenge to the country's security interests and defense capabilities. Yet national security controls and restrictions can be misused for trade-related reasons (that is, prevention of the entrance of other countries in the controlled market) and not exclusively for the prevention of transfers of arms of mass destruction (national security concerns).

Thus, if the uses of outer space are truly to "benefit all mankind," a new approach to promote the international use of the technology applied in outer space should be in place. Bilateral restrictions imposed by governments on the export of technologies applied in commercial space ventures, such as the ones contained in the Brazil-US Technological Safeguards agreement, pose a bottleneck for the growth of activities that could bring economic and social development to the less developed countries. In their place, international mechanisms should emerge that release constraints upon peaceful cooperation and commercial development in space. Such frameworks could accelerate technological and scientific developments, lead to reductions in launch costs, and engage the aspirations of people around the planet. All of these steps can help ease international tensions.

If the US-Brazil Alcantara Agreement enters into force, and Brazil does gain ground in the international launching market, this will be the result of a particular bilateral understanding.

However, it would be even better if the use of launching facilities around the world would be the result of a global agreement, which when put into place could benefit several countries and private enterprises, following accepted international principles of fair competition and global democracy to develop space for the benefit of mankind.

Taken with national licensing systems on commercial space launching, it is clear that bilateral technological safeguard Agreements limit opportunities for commercial launch organizations to operate in a truly international and depoliticized manner. From the standpoint of free access to space by all countries and its enterprises, the restrictions imposed reflect further insights from Adam Smith:

"*People of the same trade seldom meet together, even for merriment and diversion, but the conversion ends in a conspiracy against the public, or in some contrivance to raise prices*"

"*A monopoly granted either to an individual or to a trading company has the same effect as a secret in trade or manufactures. The monopolists, by keeping the market constantly under stocked, by never fully supplying the effectual demand, sell their commodities much above the natural price, and raise their emoluments... greatly above their natural rate.*"[13]

References:

1) Valnora Leister is a Brazilian Attorney, working in Washington DC. The views expressed are personal opinions from the author and do not reflect the views of her employer.

2) Adam Smith, in the year of the Declaration of Independence passing a judgment upon the system of control which for more than a century England had exercised over the economic activity of her colonies.

3) See the Treaty on Principles Governing the Activities of States in the Exploration and Use of Outer Space, including the Moon and other Celestial Bodies- UN Resolution of 13/12/63, adopted by the UN General Assembly in December 19, 1966, opened for signature in January 27, 1967 and in force since October 10, 1967.

4) Commercial Use of the Alcantara Space Center- Report of the Brazilian Space Agency, April 18, 2000- Http://www.agespacial.gov.br

5) For further details see the paper on "Brazil-USA Agreement on Alcantara Launch Center, Proceedings of the Forty-Third Colloquium on the Law of Outer Space, 2-6 October 2000, Rio de Janeiro, Brazil, by Monserrat Filho, José and Leister, Valnora.

6) The Missile Technology Control Regime (MTCR) is an informal political arrangement to control the proliferation of rocket and unmanned air vehicle systems capable of delivering weapons of mass destruction and their associated equipment and technology. The MCTR was formed in 1987 by Canada, France, Germany, Italy, Japan, the United Kingdom and the United States. Membership has expanded to 29 countries as of June 1998. The MCTR is not a treaty but a voluntary agreement among member countries sharing a common interest in controlling missile proliferation. MCTR members meet at least once a year in a plenary session to exchange information, discuss policy issues, and examine ways to improve the Regime in *the MTCR Annex Handbook, a on line publication designed to assist in implementing export controls on MCTR Items.*

7) Brazil has demonstrated in the national as in the international level, its firm compromise with the disarmament cause and the non-proliferation of dual use technologies. Brazil has stopped its incipient nuclear program, and the following measures were taken: i. the Federal Constitution (Article XXIII, Article 21) prohibits nuclear activities not for peaceful purposes; ii. Brazil has moved its space program from the military arena to civilian jurisdiction under the Brazilian Space Agency (APB) reporting to the

Ministry of Science and Technology and, iii. Brazil has ratified agreements and treaties for disarmament (such as the Agreement signed with Argentina, and the International Agency of Atomic Energy, the Tlateloco Treaty, the Treaty on the Non-Proliferation of Nuclear Weapons *[NPT]*, the Convention on the Prohibition of Chemical Weapons and the Ottawa Convention on Territorial Mines). The Report also points out that Brazil joined, without reservation, the Missile Technology Control Regime (MTCR), in 27 October 1995, after long negotiations with the USA Government, which led Brazil to adopt the Law 9.112/95, establishing internal controls on dual use technologies, particularly missiles and parts of missiles.

8) This paragraph states that "Each party shall ensure that all persons under the jurisdiction and/or control of that Party's state who participate in or otherwise have access to Launch Activities shall adhere to the procedures specified in this Agreement.The Government of the US shall require US Licensees involved in Launch Activities at the Alcantara Spaceport to conclude a Technology Control Plan reflecting and containing the relevant elements of this Agreement. The Government of the Federative Republic of Brazil shall ensure that Brazilian Representatives comply with their obligations as set forth in Technology Control Plans. The Government of the US shall ensure that US Participants comply with their obligations as set forth in the Technology Control Plans."

9) See Monserrat Filho, José, "A Parceria Brazil e Ucrania para o Uso Comercial do Centro de Lançamento de Alcantara" Paper presented at the 5th Annual reunion of SBPC, University of Goias, July, 2002.

10) News Release from the Brazilian Space Agency, dated September 18, 2002.

11) The Commercial Space Launch Act 1988 applies to any launching activity conducted in the territories of the US and also to overseas launching activities of any foreign corporation in which a US national holds a controlling interest – the office of the Assistant Administrator for Commercial Transportation (AST) provides a licensing system for commercial operations and requires the operators to take out liability insurance up to the amount of maximum probable loss.

12) In the US, exports of technologies used for launching spacecraft are considered of dual use and therefore subject to the control of the government The Arms Export Control Act (22USC 2778(a) and 2794(7) revised in 1993 provides that the President shall designate the articles and services deemed to be defense articles and defense purposes. The items so designated constitute the United States Munitions List, whose designations are made by the Department of State with the concurrence of the Department of Defense. This list includes among others: Missile technology, launch vehicles, rockets (including but not limited to meteorological and other sounding rockets), missile and space launch vehicle power plants and all specifically designed or modified components, parts, accessories, attachments and associated equipment for the articles in this category. Also, technical data directly related to the manufacture or production of any defense articles are designated as significant military equipment. The regulations require that "any person who engages in the US in the business or either manufacturing or exporting defense articles is required to register with the Office of Defense Trade Controls."

13) The Wealth of Nations, vol. 1,bk. 1, ch.10 and ch.7

LAUNCHING ALCANTARA INTO THE GLOBAL SPACE ECONOMY - THE 2001 BRAZILIAN NATIONAL SPACE LAW

The Continuing Story Of National Implementation Of International Responsibility And Liability, Part II

Frans G. von der Dunk*
International Institute of Air and Space Law, Leiden - The Netherlands
F.G.vonderDunk@law.leidenuniv.nl

Abstract

In the summer of 2001, with the Administrative Edict No. 27, Brazil became the ninth nation world-wide to establish a national space law in the narrow sense of the word – an act focusing exclusively on space activities and prominently including a system for encapsulating private participation in such activities within the state's jurisdiction, international responsibilities and international liabilities. After five Western states, two former communist nations and the special case of South Africa, Brazil may pride itself on being the first proper developing state taking such a fundamental step.

No doubt, the prospect of opening up the Alcantara launch base to international or even foreign launch operations in a manner beneficial to Brazil constituted a major reason behind the enunciation of the Brazilian Edict. Recently, Brazil has concluded the first international agreement – with the Ukraine – to this end, whilst discussions with the United States and the Russian Federation are ongoing.

The paper will address the international (legal) background to the enunciation of the Edict, in particular taking into consideration the fact that Brazil is the first proper developing state creating a national space law. It will also describe and analyse its contents, and evaluate the possibilities offered by it, as well as the obstacles still present. Finally, it will briefly touch upon the relationship between the Edict and the international negotiations referred to above.

1. Introduction

It is by now beyond doubt, that a major consequence of the Outer Space Treaty's[1] Articles VI, VII and VIII, of the Liability Convention[2] and of the Registration Convention[3] is the requirement for an increasing number of states to regulate private space activities by means of national legislation largely or exclusively dedicated to space and space activities.

This is not the place to go into the details of these provisions, or even into the major uncertainties and the absence of clarity still surrounding some of the key concepts concerned. Much attention has been devoted to these issues by experts, but for the present purpose the following summary should suffice.[4]

Firstly, Article VI of the Outer Space Treaty calls upon states to authorise and continuously supervise "national activities in outer space", if conducted by private entities, as they would anyhow be

* The author is particularly grateful to Prof. José Monserrat Filho of Rio de Janeiro, Brazil, for providing an English translation of the Brazilian Edict and explaining much of the background to the text.

held responsible for them at the international level. Secondly, Article VII of the Outer Space Treaty provides for liability for damage caused by space objects in such a fashion that states are made liable also if the damage should actually be attributed to a private space activity. This fundamental liability-clause is, of course, considerably elaborated and expanded by the Liability Convention. Thirdly, Article VIII of the Outer Space Treaty, reinforced by the Registration Convention, offers states an additional means of actually exercising authorisation and supervision over private space activities, at least to the extent these involve nationally registered space objects.

As has also been reflected in many expert opinions, as a result of the gradually increasing involvement of private entities in space activities over the last decades a growing number of states have enacted national space-dedicated legislation to deal with such involvement.[5] At present, still more states seriously consider the need or desirability to follow those examples.[6]

2. The Brazilian Edict and Regulation

The most recent addition to the list is Brazil, where in 2001 an Administrative Edict was issued dealing with the most prominent aspects of private participation in outer space activities.[7] In doing so, Brazil became the first developing nation with proper national space legislation. Thus, it is of special interest from the perspective of globalisation and 'normalisation' of space activities to analyse this Edict, and to evaluate how it fits into international space law as briefly sketched above, in comparison with the few non-developing states with national space legislation.

In doing so, the paper will focus on four elements which are of major importance. The first element is that of the licensing obligation as such, and the general aspects as to scope and extent. The second concerns the subject of liability, in particular with a view to obligations to compensate damage occurring in view of the potentially enormous financial consequences. The third focuses on a problem of special importance for developing states: the need to find a balance between the desirability to attract foreign capital (especially from developed nations) whilst maintaining the (economic) sovereignty required to ensure that Brazil would also benefit sufficiently from any space activities under the Edict. Finally, another topic of special importance for developing nations concerns international co-operation, at this point mainly at the intergovernmental level. This concerns the various co-operation schemes of Brazil with the Ukraine, the United States and Russia.

The Administrative Edict of 20 June 2001, which was issued by the Brazilian Space Agency (AEB) under the authority of the Ministry of Science and Technology, actually consists of two parts. Even if the name 'Edict' may perhaps suggest otherwise to some readers, it is a binding piece of law under the Brazilian legal system, and may for example be directly invoked before a court.

The Edict proper contains four operative Articles, of which the first one is the most important. It provides for approval of the Regulation which is enclosed and which in turn deals with the substance of private involvement in space activities.[8]

Further to the Edict, the Office for Standards and Licensing may enact implementing regulation on technical and administrative actions related to the licensing procedures.[9] The Edict itself revokes a previous Administrative Edict which dealt with the Brazilian Space Agency's role *vis-à-vis* possible private participation in space activities[10], whilst the enclosed Regulation enters into force upon publication in the Brazilian Union's Official Gazette.[11]

It is thus the Regulation which provides for the substantive issues related to the licensing of private space activities, arguably the most important element of any national space law in the narrow sense of the word.[12]

3. General Aspects: the Licensing Obligation

The first aspect which draws attention when scrutinising the Regulation is that it focuses exclusively on *launching* activities.[13] In this respect it follows the same road as Norway[14] and Australia[15], and to some extent also the United States where originally separate Acts were established for launch activities.[16] In addition, it may be noted that as far as satellite communications as a space activity is concerned, in general terms it would fall within the scope of authority of the Brazilian Ministry of Communications, and within the scope of applicable Brazilian legislation on telecommunications.[17]

The intention of Edict and Regulation, in short, clearly is to focus on the possibilities offered by Brazil's operating launch site Alcantara[18] in Maranhão (and possibly also the launch site at Barreira do Inferno in Natal) to attract and generate interesting economic activities and the related economic development.

More to the point, the Regulation focuses on private participation in such activities explicitly: it does *not* apply "to space launching activities that could be carried out by Brazilian governmental organisations or bodies".[19] Whilst of course this means that *foreign* governmental launch activities from Alcantara would in principle also fall under the regime provided for by the Regulation, it is rather hypothetical such a case would arise without a specific state-to-state agreement superseding the Regulation's provisions on relevant points.

The obligation for any private entity interested in carrying out launching activities in Brazil to obtain a license provides the basis for governmental control over the ensuing activities. The Brazilian Space Agency AEB, an autonomous but federal organisation with a civil nature, is entrusted with the competence to issue such licenses, as well as controlling and supervising them, and if necessary, taking enforcement action with respect to them.[20] Such actions are further specified already to a considerable extent in the Regulation[21], whilst other aspects of the licensing process are also spelled out in quite some detail. This concerns the documentation to be produced,[22] enabling procedures for licensing,[23] and administrative sanctions and appeals.[24]

In short, the AEB avails of competencies and mechanisms to assert supervision and control which seem quite sufficient at this stage to fulfil the requirements of Article VI of the Outer Space Treaty.

As has already arisen from the previous reflections, the scope of Edict plus Regulation and the ensuing licensing obligations is confined to launching activities from Brazilian territory[25]. One might perhaps read from this that Brazil interprets the phrase "national activities" as relevant for Article VI of the Outer Space Treaty as referring to "activities conducted from national territory", although it is more likely that for merely practical reasons – the focus on Alcantara – the possibility of Brazilian (private) companies becoming decisively involved in launch activities *outside* Brazil has simply not been taken into consideration. Legally speaking, however, arguably under Article VI of the Outer Space Treaty international responsibility of Brazil may arise for such activities as well.

The license itself is defined as "the administrative deed (...) granted to a juridical person, single, an association or consortium, for the purpose of carrying out space launching activities on Brazilian territory".[26]

It may be noted further, that licenses shall "only be granted to juridical persons, single as well as associations or consortia, having headquarters or a representation in Brazil".[27] The first category – having headquarters in Brazil – actually reflects the traditional general international law-criterion for the nationality of a private juridical entity.[28] In other words: the Regulation refers here to Brazilian private entities recognised as such under international law.

The second category – having a representation in Brazil – refers consequently and by contrast to non-Brazilian private companies, and will therefore be dealt with further below.

4. Licensing and Liability

One of the major issues of importance to deal with in the context of the license concerns the consequence of state liability as determined at the international level. Under the Liability Convention Brazil qualifies as a "launching state" – and hence as a liable state – in respect of every space object launched from Brazilian territory.[29] This, irrespective of whether Brazil itself has also procured the launch, i.e. of whether a Brazilian space object is being launched into outer space, and more importantly, also irrespective of whether private entities are involved in, or even conducting the launch.

The consequences of such international liability of Brazil in respect of every launch, including private ones, from Alcantara is obvious.

For damage caused to another space object thus launched Brazil would be held liable to the extent the claimant could prove fault on the part of Brazil (or the entity actually in charge).[30] When the damage caused by such space object would be inflicted upon the earth's surface (or to aircraft in flight) Brazil would not even be allowed to plead absence of fault, since absolute liability applies to such cases.[31] It may be noted that the Regulation defines relevant cases of damage closely following the terms of the Liability Convention.[32]

Once liability has been established, moreover, the compensation which Brazil would have to provide to the claimant, would be in principle without limit, since it has to result effectively in *restitutio in integrum*.[33]

It is obvious – as is clear also from the other existing national space laws to the extent dealing with launches – that in any given case the license offers an excellent option to deal with these issues.

Firstly, in the license a derogation clause may be inserted, essentially obliging the licensee in applicable cases to reimburse any international third-party liability claim which the government concerned would be obliged to honour under the Liability Convention. So far, two general approaches to the derogation issue can be distilled from the existing examples of states which have established some form of national space legislation.

Either reimbursement is statutorily comprehensive, allowing at best for the option on the part of the government to *ad hoc* desist from claiming full reimbursement, or a statutory limit to compensation is provided for.[34] In the latter case, the clear intention of the governments is to stimulate private launch activities by offering launch service providers a realistic possibility to either self-insure or obtain commercial insurance, and consequently accepting that in catastrophic cases quite likely the national treasury will have to be called upon to bear the part of the claim over and above the maximum.

Secondly, the license may provide for obligatory insurance – usually up to a maximum amount – in order to ensure that in any real-life case financial resources are there to actually reimburse the government – at least to the extent of the maximum insurance. This approach is followed by some if not all of the national space laws so far enacted.[35]

In the case of Brazil, where the reimbursement and insurance obligations are dealt with together, there seems to be room for granting a cap to the reimbursement obligation in a given case. The AEB, the authority granting the licenses, may "assess liabilities" in case of an application for a license.[36] Also, the "economic and financial qualification" of a particular license applicant will be considered in the licensing process.[37] In this context finally the "purchase of insurance to cover possible damages to third parties, according to the degree of risk of the activities to be carried out by the applicant, where appropriate, in the value previously established by the AEB" has to be proven.[38]

Whilst nowhere a direct provision may be found in the Regulation that such insurance coverage includes the reimbursement of possible claims which the Brazilian government may face under the Liability Convention as a consequence of the licensee's activities, a later Regulation ensured that in the license proper such reference will be included.[39]

Following from this, then, the phrasing of "in the value previously established by the AEB" indicates that somehow such liability, respectively reimbursement obligation, will, or at least in individual cases may, be subjected to an – as of yet unspecified – maximum. For proper juridical certainty, however, one would have to wait for a new and broader law currently under discussion, where the tendency seems to be towards adopting the 'maximum probable loss' approach known from United States and Australian national space legislation.

5. Foreign Participation in Brazilian Launches

In particular for a developing country like Brazil, in order to develop the economy in such a highly technological and expensive sector as the space industry, notwithstanding the impressive home-grown capabilities in this area substantial participation in one way or another of foreign capital – in particular of a private nature – and know-how is evidently desirable, if not plainly necessary.

Developing countries are in such a situation always confronted with a dilemma, however: the best way to attract foreign capital and foreign participants is to allow them a large measure of freedom and discretion in handling their business affairs, yet the larger such freedom and discretion is, the more the country concerned runs the risk of loosing not only control over, but also major benefits from the economic activities thus generated.[40] Moreover, also wider issues of sovereignty, e.g. as to national security, may be at stake.

How this balance is going to be realised in the case of Brazil is not yet fully elaborated. The Regulation provides the first general parameters: for a start, in principle it allows – as mentioned – foreign juridical entities to be granted a license in case of representation of such an entity in Brazil.[41] 'Representation' in this context refers to physical presence through a local office; by contrast, e.g. the presence of a person empowered to represent a company in contractual negotiations, or of a bank account of the company with a Brazilian bank is not sufficient.

This provision is further elaborated in that alongside other relevant documentation a decree of authorisation has to be shown in order for a license application to be successful,[42] and even more concretely, "documentary evidence that the applicant has legal representation in Brazil with express powers to be subpoenaed and to answer both at administrative and court levels".[43]

More particular controls in regard of foreign applicants to protect Brazilian sovereign interests are also to be found. The applicant has to confirm being informed about "local conditions, including the Security Regulations and Procedures established by the AEB or by the Launch Center".[44] He has to commit himself to safeguarding applicable technology transfer regulations, "as determined by the pertinent authority of the Brazilian Government".[45] The AEB reserves its right to consult in the course of the licensing process *inter alia* with Brazilian governmental bodies on security and foreign policy interests of Brazil, and how these should be reflected in a particular license.[46]

Article 14 of the Regulation furthermore is exclusively dedicated to foreign licensing applicants. It obliges such entities to present proper documents from their respective home states "as to their being licensed to perform the launching activities intended."[47] An interesting issue would arise wherever such home state does *not* itself have a relevant licensing system in place, but apparently such cases are for the time being left to be dealt with in a pragmatic *ad hoc* manner.

Also, the AEB is expressly authorised to make grant of a license dependent upon the existence of safeguard agreements relating to technology transfer between the home state of the foreign enterprise and the Brazilian government,[48] which amongst others fulfils Brazilian obligations under international law to ensure non-proliferation of particular military or dual-use goods for example under the Missile Technology Control Regime (MTCR).[49]

Thus, the Regulation seems to provide in particular the AEB with sufficient competencies and instruments to ensure that Brazil's interests – not just of an economic nature, but certainly including those as well – can be duly protected in the course of licensing foreign launch service providers interested in Alcantara. Whilst these provisions seem fair and reasonable – for example, no specific economic or financial restraints in terms of capital transfers are provided for by the regulation – the proof of the pudding is in the eating: whether foreign entities involved in launch service provision will come to a similar conclusion will probably depend on the way the first few licenses will turn out to deal in detail with these issues.

6. International Co-operation

From an abstract perspective, the development of international co-operation schemes has been mentioned as another important approach for a developing country to develop a sector of the economy of such knowledge- and capital-intensive nature as the space business.

And indeed, Brazil has entered into bilateral co-operation agreements with the United States as a participating entity to the International Space Station[50] and on participation of US launch companies in launches from Alcantara, and with the Ukraine equally on launches from Alcantara, whereas discussions with the United States, Russia, Germany, France and India on further co-operative agreements are taking place.[51] The bottom line of all these international co-operation efforts, however, is that they concern *intergovernmental* agreements, with the accompanying political overtones.

In January 2002 Brazil and the Ukraine signed a Technological Safeguard Agreement and a related Memorandum of Understanding relating to the commercial use of the Zyklon-4 launch vehicle from Alcantara. Consequently, the Ukrainian government announced its willingness to invest the money needed to construct a special launch pad at Alcantara suitable for the Zyklon-4.

Both agreements together also are generally envisaged to help convincing the Brazilian National Congress to approve a similar Safeguard Agreement between the United States and Brazil of April 2000 relating to participation of US launch companies in launch operations at Alcantara.[52]

As mentioned, in view of the rather exclusive focus of the Regulation on private launch activities and the licensing thereof,[53] the Regulation does not refer to such international co-operative efforts at all. And indeed, it is quite unlikely that any foreign government, interested in launching from Alcantara under a multilateral or bilateral co-operation agreement, will accept to enter itself the licensing process as provided for by the Regulation. In the event of such an interest, it will rather be dealt with directly in the agreement, or in elaboration of it, which agreement will then replace the licensing process proper. Private launches under such bilateral agreements however would be another matter, nothing in principle precluding application of the licensing process under Edict and Regulation.

Of course, this is largely a matter of conjecture, and it remains to be seen how the Edict and the Regulation either directly or indirectly might relate to the intergovernmental arrangements alluded to.

7. Concluding Remark

With a view to the international legal background to the Brazilian national space legislation as discussed, one final remark is due here. Whilst registration of space objects as such, in line with the requirements of Article VIII of the Outer Space Treaty and the Registration Convention, is not provided for by the current Edict and Regulation, a later Regulation did provide therefore.[54] Brazil clearly qualifies as a launching state in respect of any space object launched from Alcantara, and hence qualifies as potential state of registration.[55]

However, Edict and Regulation do provide for the registration by AEB "of licenses for carrying out space launching activities on Brazilian territory".[56] In view of the close link between the licenses and the launch phases of space objects, and the many details to be collected by the AEB for the purpose of granting a license, in effect this provision comes quite close to materially fulfilling the obligations under the Registration Convention – provided at least that the relevant elements of the registration will be openly accessible.

In sum, the Brazilian Edict and ensuing Regulation form a first coherent effort to establish a transparent, fair and balanced legal framework for private space launches from Alcantara. The waiting is for private license applicants, whether Brazilian or foreign, whether under the umbrella of a bilateral agreement such as the Brazil-Ukraine one or on their own account, but the basis is there: from a legal perspective Alcantara is ready to be launched into the global space economy.

---

[1]. Treaty on Principles Governing the Activities of States in the Exploration and Use of Outer Space, including the Moon and Other Celestial Bodies (hereafter Outer Space Treaty), London/Moscow/ Washington, adopted 19 December 1966, opened for signature 27 January 1967, entered into force 10 October 1967; 6 ILM 386 (1967); 18 UST 2410; TIAS 6347; 610 UNTS 205.

[2]. Convention on International Liability for Damage Caused by Space Objects (hereafter Liability Convention), London/ Moscow/Washington, adopted 29 November 1971, opened for signature 29 March 1972, entered into force 1 September 1972; 10 ILM 965 (1971); 24 UST 2389; TIAS 7762; 961 UNTS 187.

[3]. Convention on Registration of Objects Launched into Outer Space (hereafter Registration Convention), New York, adopted 12 November 1974, opened for signature 14 January 1975, entered into force 15 September 1976; 14 ILM 43 (1975); 28 UST 695; TIAS 8480; 1023 UNTS 15.

[4]. For those interested in the author's personal views, reference may be had to Private Enterprise and Public Interest in the European 'Spacescape' (1998), pp. 17-38, which also contains references to a considerable body of expert opinion. See further e.g. M. Uchitomi, *State Responsibility/Liability for "National" Space Activities*, in Proceedings of the Forty-Fourth Colloquium on the Law of Outer Space (2002), pp. 51-60; G. Gal, *State responsibility, jurisdiction and private space activities*, in Proceedings of the Forty-Fourth Colloquium on the Law of Outer Space (2002), pp. 61-4; L.F. Castillo Argañarás, *Some Thoughts on State Responsibility and Commercial Space Activities*, in Proceedings of the Forty-Fourth Colloquium on the Law of Outer Space (2002), pp. 65-70.

[5]. Arguably, in 1969 Norway was the first state to enunciate a proper national space law dedicated primarily to dealing with private involvement in space activities, closely followed by the United States when in 1970 it declared its licensing system under the 1934 Communications Act to be applicable to private operators undertaking space communications activities. Apart from Brazil, to date the following further states have chosen to develop such national space laws: Sweden (1982), the United Kingdom (1986), Russia (1993), South Africa (1993), the Ukraine (1996), and Australia (1998). In addition, the People's Republic of China's Special Administrative Region of Hongkong has its own Space Ordinance since 1999.

[6]. Cf. e.g. on the case of Germany: K.F. Nagel, *Current Plans for National Space Laws – Germany*, in 'Project 2001' – Legal Framework for the Commercial Use of Outer Space (2002), pp. 565-9; on the case of France: P. Clerc, *French Current Plans for a National Space Legal Framework*, in 'Project 2001' – Legal Framework for the Commercial Use of Outer Space (2002), pp. 591-9.

[7]. Administrative Edict No. 27 (hereafter Edict), of 20 June 2001, entered into force 21 June 2001, Ministry of Science and Technology.

[8]. Regulation on Procedures and on Definition of Necessary Requirements for the Request, Evaluation, Issuance, Follow-up and Supervision of License for Carrying out Space Launching Activities on Brazilian Territory (hereafter Regulation). See Art. 1, Edict.

[9]. See Art. 2, Edict.

[10]. Administrative Edict No. 8/AEB, of 14 February 2001; see Art. 3, Edict.

[11]. Art. 4, Edict. As mentioned, the Edict entered into force 21 June 2001.

[12]. See on this discussion also e.g. F.G. von der Dunk & S.A. Negoda, *Ukrainian national space law from an international perspective*, 18 Space Policy (2002), p. 15; F.G. von der Dunk & A. Nikolaisen, *Vikings First in National Space Law; Other Europeans to Follow*, in Proceedings of the Forty-Fourth Colloquium on the Law of Outer Space (2002), pp. 111-2.

[13]. Cf. already the full title of the Regulation. Art. 1(1), Regulation, defines "space launching activities" for the purpose of the Regulation.

[14]. Act on launching objects from Norwegian territory into outer space, No. 38, 13 June 1969.

[15]. An act about space activities, and for related purposes (hereafter Australian Act), No. 123 of 1998, assented to 21 December 1998; despite the fact that the title suggests otherwise, the Act exclusively deals with launching and re-entry of spacecraft, as

opposed to e.g. satellite communications or remote sensing.

[16]. Commercial Space Launch Act, Public Law 98-575, 98th Congress, H.R. 3942, 30 October 1984; 98 Stat. 3055; as amended by the Commercial Space Launch Act Amendments, Public Law 100-657, 100th Congress, H.R. 4399, 15 November 1988; 49 U.S.C. App. 2615; 102 Stat. 3900; and by Commercial Space Transportation – Commercial Space Launch Activities, 49 U.S.C. Subtitle IX – Commercial Space Transportation, Ch. 701, Commercial Space Launch Activities, 49 U.S.C. 70101-70119 (1994). The Commercial Space Act of 1998 *inter alia* amended these acts, whilst effectively incorporating them.

[17]. E.g. General Law on Telecommunications No. 9.472, of 16 July 1997, in particular Chapter III on the organisation of telecommunications services, including those provided by satellite.

[18]. See on the history of the Alcantara launch base e.g. J. Monserrat Filho & V. Leister, *Brazil-USA Agreement on Alcanatar Launching Center*, in Proceedings of the Forty-Third Colloquium on the Law of Outer Space (2001), p. 329.

[19]. Art. 1(2), Regulation.

[20]. Art. 1, Regulation. The AEB itself had been established by Law No. 8854 of 10 February 1994. See further Art. 3, mandating the AEB to enter into agreements with or hire public and private bodies in order to carry out the necessary supervision and controlling activities.
Further details of the licensing process were provided later by means of Administrative Edict, No. 5, of 21 February 2002.

[21]. See Art. 4, Regulation.

[22]. See Artt. 6-14, Regulation.

[23]. See Artt. 15-19, Regulation.

[24]. See Artt. 20-24, Regulation.

[25]. Cf. title of the Regulation itself, as well as Art. 1.

[26]. Art. 2, Regulation.

[27]. Art. 6, Regulation.

[28]. To be exact, traditionally public international law has used the double criterion of state of incorporation and state of location of headquarters. In practice of course normally both criteria will point to the same state, and even if not, one might well argue that the actual location of headquarters, more akin to such concepts as 'effective link' than mere legal incorporation, should weigh more in determining a company's nationality under international law. Cf. the famous Barcelona Traction case: Case Concerning the Barcelona Traction Light and Power Company, Limited (Second Phase)(Belgium v. Spain), International Court of Justice, 5 February 1970, I.C.J. Rep. 1970, 4.

[29]. Cf. Art. I(c)(ii), Liability Convention. In respect of Alcantara furthermore, at least also under the criterion of the ownership of the launch facility Brazil qualifies as launching, hence liable state.

[30]. See Art. III, Liability Convention.

[31]. See Art. II, Liability Convention.

[32]. Cf. resp. Art. 5, Regulation, further referring to a Resolution of the AEB, CSP/AEB/No. 51 of 26 January 2001, on liability and the international conventions to which Brazil is a party, and (in particular) Art. I(a), Liability Convention.

[33]. Cf. Art. XII, Liability Convention.

[34]. The latter is the case only in the United States, where a maximum limit to reimbursement of US$ 500 million is provided for; cf. Sec. 16(a)(1) & (2), Commercial Space Launch Act as amended; and Australia, where no amounts however have been provided statutorily, only the concept of calculating 'maximum probable loss' is invoked to cap the reimbursement liability in a given case; cf. Sec. 48(3), Australian Act. Though not a case of national space legislation proper, capped reimbursement applies also to Arianespace, where the part of any international third-party liability claim over FF 400 million will be born by France without an obligation resting upon Arianespace to reimburse that part; Artt. 3(9), 4(1), Declaration by Certain Governments Relating to the Ariane Launcher Production Phase, original version of 14 January 1980, repeatedly updated later. See e.g. V. Kayser, Launching Space Objects: Issues of Liability and Future Prospects (2001), p. 142.

[35]. See e.g. for the United Kingdom Sec. 5(2)(f), Outer Space Act, 18 July 1986, 1986 Chapter 38; also R. Close, *UK Outer Space Act 1986: Scope and Implementation*, in 'Project 2001' – Legal Framework for the Commercial Use of Outer Space (2002), pp. 587-9; for the Russian Federation Art. 25(1), Law of the Russian Federation on Space Activities, 20 August 1993, effective 6 October 1993 (and amended 1996).

[36]. Art. 4(V), Regulation.

[37]. Cf. Art. 6(III), Regulation; further Art. 9.

[38]. Art. 9(III), Regulation.

[39]. See Art. 4, also Art. 9(2) sub VI, of the Regulation under Administrative Edict No. 5 (*supra*, note 20).

[40]. Cf. e.g. in detail J. Monserrat Filho & V. Leister, *The Discussion in the Brazilian National Congress of the Brazil-USA Agreement on Technology Safeguards Relating to the Use of Alcantara Spaceport*, in Proceedings of the Forty-Fourth Colloquium on the Law of Outer Space (2002), pp. 377-9.

[41]. Art. 6, Regulation.

[42]. See Art. 7(IV), Regulation.

[43]. Art. 7(V), Regulation.

[44]. Art. 8(IV), Regulation.

[45]. Art. 8(V), Regulation.

[46]. Cf. Art. 12, Regulation.

[47]. Art. 14(1), Regulation.

[48]. Cf. Art. 14(3), Regulation.

[49]. Brazil became a member of the MTCR in 1995; cf. H.P. van Fenema, The International Trade in Launch Services (1999), pp. 153-4; Monserrat Filho & Leister, *The Discussion in the Brazilian National Congress*, 378, 381-2.

[50]. See e.g. M.H. Fonseca de Souza Rolim, *The USA-Brazil Implementing Arrangement on the International Space Station: Interpretation and Application*, in Proceedings of the Forty-Fourth Colloquium on the Law of Outer Space (2002), pp. 87-96.

[51]. With Germany, actually an interesting project on micro-gravity experiments on sounding rockets launched from Alcantara is being executed.

[52]. Agreement between the Government of the Federative Republic of Brazil and the Government of the United States of America on Technology Safeguards

associated with the US participation in launches from the Alcantara Spaceport, of 18 April 2000; see further Monserrat Filho & Leister, *The Discussion in the Brazilian National Congress*, pp. 377 ff.; Monserrat Filho & Leister, *Brazil-USA Agreement*, pp. 328-34.

[53]. Cf. Art. 1(2), Regulation; further Artt. 2 & 6.

[54]. See Art. 19 of the Regulation under Administrative Edict No. 5 (*supra*, note 20).

[55]. It may be noted that so far Brazil is not a party to the Registration Convention, though currently in the process of becoming one; cf. A. Fabricio dos Santos, *Brazil and the Registration Convention*, in Proceedings of the Forty-Fourth Colloquium on the Law of Outer Space (2002), pp. 78-85.

[56]. Art. 27, Regulation.

THE IMPACT OF ARMS LIMITATION AGREEMENTS AND EXPORT CONTROL REGULATIONS ON LAUNCH ACTIVITIES

Steven R. Freeland*
University of Western Sydney, Australia

Ricky J. Lee†
Hunt & Hunt (Adelaide)
University of Western Sydney, Australia

INTRODUCTION

It has been commonly observed that the commercial launch industry is a global one. For example, a commercial launch operator located in Australia may use a Russian launch vehicle, along with its associated technical data, equipment and software, while utilising European or Australian technology in relation to launch safety analysis or control mechanisms and engaging United States consultants to assist in the venture.

The involvement of a number of States will also, invariably, give rise to legal and political constraints relating to the (un)willingness of the various participants to "share" their space-related technology, either for reasons of national security or commercial primacy. For example, the recently released United States Administration document "The National Security Strategy of the United States" evidences all too clearly the deep concerns that State has in relation to maintaining its military technology supremacy.

This paper looks at some of the significant implications and regulatory impact of arms limitation treaties, notably START, and export control regulations of Australia, Russia and the United States on the operations of a commercial launch operator.

THE START RÉGIME

Negotiated between the United States and the Soviet Union (as it then was), the START régime was intended to limit the number of "strategic offensive arms" deployed in both States. The types of missiles affected by the START régime are intercontinental ballistic missiles ("**ICBM**") and submarine launched ballistic missiles ("**SLBM**"). The régime comprises two main treaties: the 1991 START I agreement, which provided for the basic framework of reductions in ballistic missiles; and the 1993 START II framework, which provided for a further reduction of missiles in Russia and the United States and has not as yet been implemented by the parties.[1]

Article IV(1) of START I limits the number of non-deployed ICBMs that either State can keep in storage. Paragraph 1(a) of Article IV limits the number of non-deployed ICBMs to 250, except for "retired" ICBMs with only single warheads that are exempt pursuant to the Thirty-

Seventh Agreed Statement of the Agreed Statements Annex to START.[2]

Article IV(4) limits the number of ICBMs and SLBMs for space launch purposes in several ways. Firstly, the parties are allowed no more than five space launch facilities, which cannot overlap as ICBM bases. Article IV(11)(c) further requires that each space launch facility to be located no less than 100km from any ICBM base for silo or rail launchers or ICBM deployment areas. Space launch facilities are not subject to inspection under the START régime. In the Memorandum of Understanding of 1 January 2002, the most recent of the regular reporting instruments required under START, the United States indicated that the Vandenberg Space Launch Complex was its only space launch facility, containing converted ballistic missiles with two launchers. In the case of Russia, Nenoksa, Svobodny and Plesetsk are space launch facilities containing a total of eight launchers, with four ICBMs also located at Svobodny.

As for the launch vehicles themselves, Article IV(4) provides that the total number of launchers must be limited to twenty, with mobile and silo launchers limited to twelve.[3] The number of ICBMs or SLBMs allowed at each space launch site is limited by the number of launchers permitted at the site. The reason for limiting the number of civilian launches of converted ballistic missiles is to prevent either State from testing their missiles under the guise of civilian space launches.

Russia and the United States did not agree as to the implications of the START régime on the conversion of Soviet SS-25 missiles into launch vehicles. The issue was resolved in the Joint Statement No. 21 of 23 September 1995 of the Joint Compliance and Inspection Commission (**"JCIC"**). In that Joint Statement, the "Start" launch vehicle, which comprises one SS-25 first stage, one SS-25 third stage and one or two SS-25 second stages, would not be considered to be an ICBM being stored in stages or to be a variant of an ICBM that is prohibited under START. The number of converted Start vehicles would nonetheless be limited by Article IV(4) of START I. While it is not necessary under START for space launch facilities to be inspected, the Joint Statement requires the provision of technical data, development plans, schematic drawings or photographs and telemetric changes.

One significant provision in the Joint Statement is the allowance for Russia to export its converted launch vehicles, particularly the Start, to other countries. The Joint Statement affirmed that START did not prohibit the movement of space launch vehicles to facilities outside Russia or the United States but that the country concerned must retain ownership and control of the space launch vehicles, their launchers and support equipment during its transportation. As a result, it would be necessary for Russia to maintain ownership and control of any exported Start vehicles.

In the case of Australian launch operators, Australia and Russia concluded the 2001 Agreement on Cooperation in the Field of Exploration and Use of Outer Space for Peaceful Purposes (referred to as the **"Intergovernmental Agreement"** or the **"IGA"**), partly with the view of allowing Russian Start vehicles to be launched from Australian facilities. As Russia must maintain ownership and control of Start launch vehicles under the START régime, it poses additional difficulties for its compliance with launch licensing and regulatory frameworks of other countries, as well as the applicability and export and import controls.

EXPORT CONTROLS

The globalised nature of the space launch industry means that it is inevitable that launch operators will have to import launch vehicles, payloads, components, software, technology and know-how. As space technology is generally sensitive in the context of the geopolitical military and strategic balance, States such as Australia, Russia and the United States have all implemented regulations in compliance with their international obligations on export controls relating to space technology.[4] The two main international treaty regimes on export controls that impact on launch services are those implemented under the Wassenaar Agreement on Export Controls for Conventional Arms and Dual Use Goods and Technologies (the "**Wassenaar Agreement**") and the Missile Technology Control Regime ("**MTCR**"), to which all three countries are parties

The Wassenaar Agreement

The Wassenaar Agreement entered into force in 1996 as the successor regime to the Coordinating Committee on Multilateral Strategic Export Controls ("**COCOM**") of the North Atlantic Treaty Organisation ("**NATO**") that was established during the Cold War. It has 33 founding members, which include Australia, Russia and the United States.[5]

The Wassenaar Agreement imposes two major obligations on its members:

- the notification of arms transfers and the reporting of transfers or denials of transfers of items contained in the agreed lists;[6] and
- the maintenance of export controls through domestic legislation to ensure that the transfer of items in the agreed lists do not contribute to the development of military capabilities that undermine international and regional security.[7]

Article III of the Wassenaar Agreement sets out the Control Lists, which comprise the Dual-Use Goods and Technologies List and the Munitions List. The Dual-Use List is further divided into a general list (Tier 1) as well as two annexes of sensitive items (Tier 2) and very sensitive items (Subset Tier 2). The responsibility for implementing export controls on the two Control Lists rests with the governments of the member States.[8]

The items relating to space launches that are contained in the Munitions List include:

- rockets, missiles and related equipment or accessories (ML4);
- various propellants capable of being used in rockets, except for liquid oxygen (ML8); and
- technology and equipment used for the production of controlled items in Part 1 of the Munitions List (ML18).

The items relating to space launches that are contained in Part 3 of the List include:

- telemetry and telecontrol equipment in launch vehicles (5A101);
- space launch vehicles (9A004);
- liquid propulsion systems (9A005);
- solid propulsion systems (9A007);
- hybrid propulsion systems (9A009);
- any components or sub-systems of the above vehicles or systems;
- software designed or modified for the development, design, modelling and simulation of systems, vehicles and related equipment or technology (9D001 and 9D103); and
- technology for the production of any of the above (9E001).[9]

The transparency framework for notifications of arms transfers under the Wassenaar Agreement requires disclosure by governments of items exported, as well as denied applications and reasons for such denials. The arms transfers notification requirements are:

1) licences for the export of dual-use goods and technologies denied to

non-member States and the reasons for their denial, to be notified to member States on an aggregate basis;

2) all licences issued or denied to non-member States for the export of sensitive items on the Dual Use List and the reasons for any denials, to be notified to member States on an individual basis; and

3) all transfers of items on the Munitions List to non-member States to be notified to member States on an aggregate basis.[10]

The MTCR Guidelines

The MTCR was concluded in 1987 between Canada, France, Germany, Italy, Japan, the United Kingdom and the United States to limit the proliferation of nuclear weapons technology. This was achieved by requiring member States to impose export controls on technology related to missile systems. The MTCR applies to systems capable of delivering a 500kg warhead to a distance of 300km. Since 1987, a further 25 States, including Australia and Russia, have become members of the MTCR.[11] As a result of the Persian Gulf War, the MTCR was extended in 1992 to cover smaller missiles capable of deploying chemical or biological weapons over short or intermediate ranges.

The MTCR Guidelines for Sensitive Missile Related Transfers require member States to exercise restraint in transferring items on the MTCR Annex to "any destination beyond the Government's jurisdiction or control" and to consider such transfers on a case-by-case, rather than a general categorical basis.[12]

In considering the transfer of any items on the MTCR Annex, the Member State is required to take into account:

- concerns relating to the proliferation of weapons of mass destruction;
- the missile and space capabilities of the recipient State;
- the significance of the transfer in the context of the development of delivery systems for weapons of mass destruction by the recipient State; and
- any assurances given by the recipient State in relation to their use and restraint from re-exporting.[13]

The member States are required under the MTCR Guidelines to obtain assurances from the recipient State that, without the consent of the original Member State:

- the items received will not be used for proliferation purposes;
- no changes will be made to the use of the items;
- no modifications or replications of the items will be undertaken; and
- the items will not be transferred to a third State.[14]

The MTCR Annex comprises two categories of items, which include both the hardware and equipment and the relevant technology, including software and technical data. Category I items, comprising Items 1 and 2, are items of the greatest sensitivity in the framework of MTCR export controls. All other Items in the MTCR Annex constitute Category II and are less sensitive in the context of technology transfers.

The items relating to space launches that are contained in Category I of the MTCR Annex include:

- complete rocket systems and space launch vehicles (Item 1); and
- complete sub-systems used in rockets and launch vehicles as well as equipment used in the production of individual rocket stages, engines and re-entry systems (Item 2).

The items relating to space launches that are contained in Category II of the MTCR Annex include:

- rocket motor cases and liquid propellant control systems (Item 3);
- propellants and constituent chemicals for propellants (Item 4);
- structural materials and structures usable in Item 1 systems;
- flight control systems and related technology for Item 1 systems;
- launch support equipment, facilities and software for Item 1 systems; and
- specifically designed software and modified computers for modelling, simulation or design integration of Items 1 and 2 systems.

Domestic Implementation

Each member State of the Wassenaar Agreement and the MTCR has legislated to implement a system of export controls on space and missile related technologies. Some States have opted to implement controls on the Control Lists of the Wassenaar Agreement and the items of the MTCR Annex only, while others have supplemented them with additional items also considered to be of a sensitive nature.

Australia

In Australia, those export controls required under the Wassenaar Agreement and the MTCR are implemented through the *Customs (Prohibited Exports) Regulations 1958* (Cth) and s 112 of the *Customs Act 1901* (Cth). Part 1 of the Defence and Strategic Goods List directly implements the Munitions List contained in the Wassenaar Agreement. Part 3 of the Defence and Strategic Goods List implements the Dual Use Goods and Technologies List contained in the Wassenaar Agreement.[15] The items in the MTCR Annex are also incorporated into the Australian List.

In the case of launch operators, it may be necessary from time to time to export, temporarily or permanently, software or hardware items on the Defence and Strategic Goods List that were created in Australia or, perhaps more likely, previously imported into Australia from a third State. The Department of Defence has responsibility for administering export controls on relevant items on the List under the Regulations.[16] The Regulations require a licence to be obtained from the Australian Government for the export of items contained on the List.

Table 1. Australian Export Permits

	Permit / Licence	Coverage
PART 1	Military Export Approval (MEA)	Export of a specified quantity of goods to a single specified recipient.
	Military Export Licence (MEL)	Export of unspecified quantities of goods to one or multiple recipients.
	Military In-Principle Approval (MIP)	Marketing of goods to potential customers (does not permit export).
	Military Temporary Export (MTT)	Goods that will be returning to Australia (eg. trials or demonstrations).
	Military Return to Manufacturer (MRM)	Returning goods to overseas manufacturers (eg. for warranty repairs).
	Military Return to Owner (MRO)	Returning goods to overseas owners.
PART2/ 3	Individual Export Permit (IEP)	Export of a specified quantity of dual-use goods to a single recipient.
	Export Distribution Licence (EDL)	Multiple shipment of an unspecified quantity of dual-use goods overseas.
	General Export Licence (GEL)	Export of a range of dual-use goods to recipients in specified States.
	Maintenance Return and Repair (MRR)	Returning or sending dual-use goods for repair or repaired goods overseas.
	Service Supply Licence (ESS)	Goods shipped in support of a maintenance or service program.

In order to obtain an export permit or licence under the Australian export control régime, it is necessary to provide the required supporting documentation. For goods contained in the Munitions List (or Part 1 of the List), the exporter would be required to supply an "End-User and Non-Transfer Certificate" that satisfies the requirements of Paragraph 5 of the MTCR Guidelines relating to assurances from recipient States. Alternatively, the recipient State may supply an International Import Certificate to indicate that it intends to control any intended or unintended re-export of the goods. For dual use goods contained in Part 3 of the Defence and Strategic Goods List, a "Statement by the Ultimate Consignee or Purchaser" is required, setting out the intended use of the item by the recipient State.

Russia

In Russia, the *Law on Military-Technical Cooperation of the Russian Federation with Foreign States 1998* requires governmental approval before exports of "military products" can be made.[17] "Military products" are defined as "arms, military equipments, operations, services and the results of intellectual activity, including the exclusive rights to them (intellectual property), and information in the military-technical sphere".[18]

"Arms and military equipment" is defined to include:

- delivery and launch systems;
- relevant facilities, equipment and technologies for the development of delivery and launch systems; and
- telemetry and telecontrol devices.[19]

The law effectively provides for a monopoly on the export of controlled items from Russia for the Russian Government and organisations with a government majority ownership.[20] As a result, only the Russian Government and agencies or entities established by the Government can engage in the export of launchers and launch related technologies.

In the case of foreign launch operators seeking the export of technology, the regulatory procedure is implemented by the (rather grandly named) 1998 Government Decree on Authorisation of the Procedure for the Consideration of Official Applications from Foreign Customers and Interdepartmental Coordination of Decisions for the Conduct of Foreign Economic Transactions with Products for Military Applications. This Decree provides for the mechanism by which foreign entities may apply for the export of Russian technology.

The United States

The International Traffic in Arms Regulations ("**ITAR**")[21] were enacted under s 38 of the *Arms Export Control Act 1976*, which gave authority to the Department of State for the regulation of the export of articles, services and technology related to defence. The export controls under ITAR operate by prohibiting exports to certain countries or requiring the licensing of certain activities in relation to items on the U.S. Munitions List.

On the launch vehicle side of the equation, Category IV of the U.S. Munitions List includes launch vehicles and any apparatus, device, material or technical data for handling, control, activation, monitoring, detection, protection, discharge or detonation of launch vehicles. As for the payload side, Category XV includes spacecraft and their ground control stations, as well as associated equipment, accessories, attachments and technical data.

The definitions provided under ITAR include software within the term "technical data". As we have already seen, the list of articles on the MTCR Annex also includes launch support equipment, facilities and software, including those specially designed for modelling, simulation or design integration. The MTCR Annex is incorporated as s 121.16 of the United States Munitions List.

The main requirements of the ITAR are:

1) any United States manufacturer or exporter of Munitions List articles is to be registered;[22]

2) any temporary import, temporary or permanent export of an article on the Munitions List, including technical data, is to be licensed,[23] unless it is imported for the purpose of exhibition or marketing;[24]

3) the export of technical data relating to articles on the Munitions List is to be licensed;[25]

4) the provision of technical assistance by U.S.-based specialists or consultants to foreign parties requires approval; and

5) exports to a defined list of countries are prohibited as being contrary to the security and foreign policy of the United States or its efforts against terrorism.[26]

In the case of United States launch operators, these provisions would require a licence for the temporary import of any non-U.S. payload for the purpose of launch, along with any non-U.S. launch vehicle, component, software or technology. If the launch operator is utilising technology from foreign sources, a temporary import licence under ITAR or a licence for the permanent import regulated by the Department of the Treasury may be required.[27]

In the case of foreign launch operators, there are several implications arising from ITAR:

1) the use of any U.S.-based defence article or equipment in relation to the launch must be exported;

2) if the payload is of U.S. origin, the export of the satellite is governed by the Department of State under ITAR;

3) the import of any equipment, software or technical data for a U.S.-based consultant to provide technical assistance requires a temporary import licence;

4) the use of any U.S.-based software or technical data would similarly have to be exported; and

5) the engagement of any U.S.-based specialists or consultants would constitute technical assistance and require State Department approval.

With the exception of temporary import, most of the regulatory requirements relating to export and technical assistance from the United States can be covered by an approved technical assistance agreement deposited with the State Department.

Implications for Commercial Launch Operators

The START Régime

One unique feature of the commercial launch industry is that, regardless of the location and nature of ownership or control of a particular launch operator, it is nevertheless part of a global and interdependent industry. As a result, there is often a heavy reliance on the flow of launch systems, equipment and technology across national boundaries.

There are three important implications of the START régime on a non-Russian commercial launch operator. Firstly, Russia is required to maintain ownership and control of the Start launch vehicle even if it is exported to another country. This makes compliance with local licensing and regulatory laws somewhat difficult for launch operators. The launch operator can choose to ask the domestic government to defer to the competence of the Russian officials operating the launch vehicle, or it would have to "export" and "import" any relevant documentation and technical data to satisfy the local regulatory agencies.

Secondly, if Russia maintains ownership and control of the launch vehicle, it is unclear whether the launch vehicle and the relevant control equipment would have left the "territory or control" of Russia. If the applicability of export controls depend on territorial boundaries, then Russia would nevertheless have exported the items and require compliance with export controls, even though the exporter and the importer would have remained the same Russian entity. This would also have the effect of limiting the number of countries that can operate Start launch vehicles to those that can satisfy Russia of their peaceful intentions in utilising the technology. Conversely, if they depend on the jurisdictional control of the items, then a persuasive argument can be made that export controls would not be applicable. This may well be contrary to the spirit of the export control régime, as missile technology would have left Russian territory and no controls would have been imposed on their possible proliferation.

It should also be noted that the export control régimes of some countries, for example ITAR, require the importer of controlled items to be a domestic entity rather than a foreign one. This would prevent a Russian entity undertaking the import of Russian technology into the United States without a United States entity as partner.

Thirdly, JCIC Statement No. 21 requires the disclosure of technical data, development plans, schematic drawings or photographs and telemetric changes in relation to converted ICBMs used as launch vehicles. Where a payload has been integrated into a launch vehicle, this may require trade secrets or other confidential information to be disclosed by the launch operator or its customer. Without further clarification, this may inhibit the willingness of commercial payload operators to utilise Start launch vehicles for their launch requirements.

Export Controls

In the global launch industry, the flow of technology between countries has become an important feature for the survival and development of the industry. A launch operator in Australia, for example, that relies on Russian technology would be required to import:

- the launch vehicle, either as a complete system or as a combination of complete sub-systems;
- all related equipment, software and technology relating to the development, control, modelling, simulation and operation of the launch vehicle;
- telemetry and telecontrol systems on board the vehicle and the ground segment of such systems;
- all technical data in relation to the items above; and
- the payload.

As mentioned previously, the launch vehicle and its sub-systems constitute Items 1 and 2 of the MTCR Annex, while the other items are controlled in Category II of the MTCR Annex. All of these items are provided for in the Dual-Use Goods and Technologies List of the Wassenaar Agreement. As a result, export approvals would have to be obtained from the Russian Government and other relevant States and import licenses from the Australian Government before any of the above technology transfers can take place.

There may be instances where a launch operator may require re-export of the imported technology. For example, a launch operator in South Africa may have incorporated Russian technical data or launch vehicle specifications into launch control software that it has developed internally, in relation to which the domestic regulatory laws may require certification or review by an independent expert that is located in the United States. In this case:

1) the original technical data or specifications would have to be exported from Russia;

2) the technical data and specifications would have to be imported into South Africa;

3) the launch control software, as a controlled item, cannot be exported without a relevant export licence from the South African Government;

4) as the launch control software contains Russian controlled items, it may be necessary to obtain licences or permits for the re-export of those items from the Russian Government;

5) the launch control software would have to be temporarily imported into the United States where the certifying export consultant is located;

6) the return of the software to South Africa may attract export and import controls, though in some States the return of items to manufacturers after temporary import is exempt from export controls;

7) any modifications or even the report containing technical data produced by the American consultant would itself be a controlled item that would have to be exported from the United States to South Africa; and

8) if the contents of the report have to be disclosed to a Russian entity (as it concerns their launch vehicle), the report would have to be exported from South Africa and then imported into Russia, attracting any applicable export controls.

The issues would be further complicated if the launch control software itself was imported from a State other than Russia, as it would also attract the application of export controls of that State for the export and re-export of the software to South Africa and the United States.

It is clear that commercial launch operators and, perhaps more importantly, their specialist legal advisers, must have a good working knowledge of domestic and foreign export controls and their application in order to comply with all requirements.

Conclusions

Although generally high on the list of concerns in the commercial operation of a launch operator, the implications of the START framework and export controls do not appear to have been the focus of any major academic and legal analysis.

It is important in the interests of world peace and international security to maintain strict technology controls in relation to the flow of space launch and related technology. However, there is no reason why the Governments concerned should not recognise the economic importance and the global nature of the space industry and implement special streamlined and uniform rules of export controls. For example, a protocol to the Wassenaar Agreement may be developed to allow for a "Global Export Control Licence" which may be issued by a member State for the import-export of a specific list of items and technologies. Such a development can be subject to the existing transparency and accountability requirements of the Wassenaar Agreement and yet allows for a simplification of the regulatory burden of export controls as imposed on commercial launch operators.

Notes

This paper is written in the personal capacity of the authors and does not necessarily represent the views of any organisations with which they are associated.

* Member IISL and ILA.
Email: s.freeland@uws.edu.au.

† Member IISL, IBA, ILA and ANZSIL.
Email:ricky@myoffice.net.au

[1] Following the abandonment by the United States of the 1992 Antiballistic Missile Treaty in June 2002, the Russian Administration responded by declaring that it was no longer bound by the START II framework.

[2] "Retired" ICBMs, according to the Definitions Annex, are ICBMs of a type deployed when START entered into force but all of which were rendered non-deployed by virtue of the conversion or elimination of their launchers, other than test launchers and space launch facilities.

[3] The original START I treaty limited the number of mobile and silo launchers at space launch facilities to 10, which was subsequently raised by the Joint Compliance and Inspection Commission Agreement No. 45 of 17 July 2001 to the present limit of 12, of which the maximum number of mobile launchers is limited to 10.

[4] It is interesting to note that other major space nations are also implementing increasingly stringent regulations intended to restrict the export of missile and space-related technology. For example, China has recently introduced new regulations which it claims are stricter than the standards imposed under the Missile Technology Control Regime (MCTR).

[5] The member States to the Wassenaar Agreement are Argentina, Australia, Austria, Belgium, Bulgaria, Canada, Czech Republic, Denmark, Finland, France, Germany, Greece, Hungary, Ireland, Italy, Japan, Luxembourg, the Netherlands, New Zealand, Norway, Poland, Portugal, Romania, Russia, Slovakia, South Korea, Spain, Sweden, Switzerland, Turkey, Ukraine, the United Kingdom and the United States.

[6] Wassenaar Agreement, Art IV.

[7] *Ibid.*, Art II.

[8] *Ibid.*, Art II.

[9] The reference numbers referred to are those contained in the Australian Defence and Strategic Goods List, which correspond to the numbers used in the Dual-Use Goods and Technologies List under the Wassenaar Agreement.

[10] Wassenaar Agreement, Arts V and VI.

[11] The member States to the MTCR are Argentina, Australia, Austria, Belgium, Brazil, Canada, Czech Republic, Denmark, Finland, France, Germany, Greece, Hungary, Iceland, Ireland, Italy, Japan, Luxembourg, the Netherlands, New Zealand, Norway, Poland, Portugal, Russia, South Africa, Spain, Sweden, Switzerland, Turkey, Ukraine, the United Kingdom and the United States.

[12] MTCR Guidelines, Para 1.

[13] *Ibid.*, Para 3.

[14] *Ibid.*, Para 5.

[15] Part 2 of the Defence and Strategic Goods List contains nuclear and nuclear-related items.

[16] *Customs (Prohibited Exports) Regulations 1958* (Cth), Reg. 13E.

[17] *Law on Military-Technical Cooperation of the Russian Federation with Foreign States 1998*, Art 6.

[18] *Ibid.*, Art 1.

[19] *Ibid.*

[20] *Ibid.*, Arts 6 and 12.

[21] 22 CFR 120-130.

[22] International Traffic in Arms Regulations, s 122.1.

[23] *Ibid.*, s 123.1.

[24] *Ibid.*, s 123.4.

[25] *Ibid.*, s 125.2.

[26] *Ibid.*, s 126.1.

[27] The permanent import of defence items contained in the U.S. Munitions List are regulated by the Department of the Treasury under 27 CFR 47, 178 and 179.

LICENSING PROCEDURE ESTABLISHED IN THE MEXICAN LAW FOR THE OPERATION OF SATELLITE ORBITS ASSIGNED TO MEXICO AND FOR THE TRANSMISSION OF SIGNALS COMING FROM FOREIGN SATELLITES

Ramirez de Arellano, R.M.
Gurria y Ramirez de Arellano, S.C., Aniceto Ortega No. 1353, Col. Del Valle, Mexico City, Mexico
rramirez@gyra.com.mx

Arvide, Y.
Estaciones Estratosfericas de Mexico, S.A. de C.V., Aniceto Ortega No. 1353, Col. Del Valle, Mexico City, Mexico
yarvide@gyra.com.mx

Abstract- Federal Telecommunications Law in Mexico, in force since 1995, is the regulatory instrument which establishes the licensing procedures for satellite operations.

The importance of this law is the opening of the telecommunications competition in Mexico, which began with telephony in 1996, and in the satellite area, the first licenses for operating satellite orbits assigned to Mexico were granted in 1997 and for the transmission of signals coming from foreign satellites were granted for the first time just in 2001.

The purpose of this paper is to present the procedure established in the Mexican Law, to speak about these new licenses, the opportunity of investment that they represent in Mexico and the convenience or inconvenience of this procedure and the amendments that we are proposing to the Mexican Congress to include in the new Federal Telecommunications Law.

INTRODUCTION

The lack of a State policy in the telecommunications field in Mexico, has caused that its development has no objectives and that it does not correspond to the necessities of our country. The lack of such policy has been reflected in the deficient regulation that by now seems to be improvised in one field –the telecommunications one- which is the vertebral column of the development of any country. Via satellite communications has not been and is not an exception. The same as other activities, satellite communications was regulated based in two fundamental issues: I) as a strategy area reserved to the State, and therefore the services were provided by the Federal Government itself, and ii) as a main area in which the provision of services are subject to license and of course, with the participation of the private sector, of whose opening we will speak later on in this document.

II. REGULATORY BACKGROUND

The fundamental basis that regulates rights and obligations of the Mexican population and that establishes the departure point of the specific laws in Mexico, is the Federal Constitution of the Mexican Republic[1], issued on February 5, 1917, which included the part related properly to the constitutional rights of the Mexicans and a precept which is the basis of the provisions that today rule the areas reserved to the State and the foundations for the regulation in competency areas. The original text of the Federal Constitution established in article 28 that in Mexico, there would not exist monopolies, with the exception of telecommunications and to **telegraphy and radiotelegraphy.**

The Federal Constitution was amended on February 3, 1983, due to the fact that Mexico was about to launch its first satellite, Morelos I (1985). The amendment was made in the same article 28 itself, fourth paragraph and its text would include **via satellite communication** as strategic area, and therefore it was reserved for its provision to the State, without the participation of particulars.

In the justification of such amendment, which supported it, there was no explanation of why should it be considered as a strategic area.

Between the amendment to the Federal Constitution and the adoption of new laws in Mexico, in 1995, some commercial agreements became relevant. Mexico concluded some of them such as NAFTA.

On the other hand, there was a raise in the importance of the negotiations on the opening of the international trade services, initiated with the Tokyo Round in 1978 within the frame of the General Agreement of Trade and Tariffs[4] (GATT) and concluded within the Uruguay Round, when the final Record was executed in Marrakech on April 15, 1994. In said meeting GATT Secretariat was substituted by the World Trade Organization (WTO), which originated a new services trade system, in which the General Agreement of Services Trade, established relevant questions that subscribing countries are obliged to include in their own respective national regulations.

Mexico, the same as other countries amended its regulation in regards to opening to the competition the telecommunication services, within which we can find via satellite communication.

Based in those considerations, article 28 of the Mexican Federal Constitution, which we have mentioned, was amended once more in 1995, in order to establish via satellite communication as a priority area -not as a strategic area anymore-, opening to the private sector, the chance of investing in the satellite sector.

Simultaneously, the amendments to the Federal Constitution, the secondary laws in force, which regulated via satellite communication in terms and under the general rule established by the Supreme Mexican Law, the Federal Constitution, are:

- General Communication Means Law [2], and
- Federal Telecommunications Law[3].

The first one of them, General Communication Means Law, was published on February 19, 1940, and it is obvious that in such time it was very distant to speak about satellites, except for the Moon, which is the earth natural satellite, and inclusive telecommunications, which concept and actual definition, was not considered textually. Telephony and telegraphy were very basically regulated.

General Communications Means Law, established in article 11 –in accordance to the Federal Constitution- that:

"The provision of public telegraphy, radiotelegraphy and mail services was exclusively reserved to the federal Government and to the descentralized organizations established for those purposes".

Also were exclusively reserved to the Federal Government, the establishment of satellite systems, their operation and control, the provision of the public service of satellite signals transportation; as well as earth stations with international links for via satellite communication.

The Ministry of Communications and Transports, shall establish according to the Law and its regulations, the basis according to which the installation, operation and control of earth stations shall be carried out".

In relation to terrestrial segment –earth stations ES-, was managed, from my point of view, in a confiscatory way, this is, if a particular was interested in such service, and also he had the possibility of having the ES in his facilities, besides buying it and in order not to distortion such reserve in favor of the State, he was compelled to assign it to the Federal Government.

Such situation was amended, in a way, in the Telecommunications Regulation of 1990, in which there was a great chapter related to via satellite communications, in which only ES for international links should be assigned to the Federal Government.

It is important to remark that via satellite communication was operated by the Federal Government through the Decentralized Organization Telecomunicaciones de Mexico, until the semi-official corporation named Satelites Mexicanos, S.A. de C.V. (SATMEX), was incorporated on July 26, 1997, in which Mexican Government would temporarily participate.

III. CURRENT REGULATION

With the time, the reserve established in favor of the State, turned out to be a burden for the Federal Government itself, which did not have the budget necessary for providing it with the quality and efficiency required, therefore, ten years after it was established, and in accordance to the amendment of the Constitution of 1995 that we have referred to, that declared it as prioritary area, and based in the obligations obtained, basically in the WTO, competency was opened and of course, private national and foreign investment.

In the Federal Telecommunications Law, in force since June 8 1995, the following was established in satellite matter:

1. Are subject to license:

   1.1. Occupation of geo-stationary orbit positions and satellite orbits allocated to the Country, and exploitation of their respective frequency bands; and

   1.2. Exploitation of emission rights and reception of signals of frequency bands associated to foreign satellite systems that cover and might provide services in national territory.

2. General rules applicable to both type of licenses:

2.1. Licenses will only be granted to Mexican individuals or corporations;
2.2. Direct foreign investment might participate only for up to a 49%;
2.3. They will only be granted for a 20 year term, and could be prorogated for a similar term;
2.4. Rates will be freely fixed;
2.5. Services shall be provided with quality, competitivity, continuity and permanence;
2.6. Licensees shall refrain from applying crossed subsidies in services or in relation to its affiliates;
2.7. They should only provide licensed services.

III.1. Licenses for using orbital positions and satellite positions allocated to the Country, and exploitation of their respective frequency bands, with their respective frequency bands and rights of emission and reception of signals, are subject to the following requirements:

Additional to the general rules aforementioned in section 2, Federal Telecommunications Law establishes the following rules:

a. Federal Government might request payment for its granting;
b. Make available to the Federal Government, enough and adequate satellite capacity to the national security networks and to present social services, which will be granted free of charge;
c. They will be enforced to put in orbit a satellite, 5 (five) years after having obtained the license, the latest. In this case –in case of a variation of the provisions of Plenipotentiaries to be held in Marrakech from September 23 to October 18, 2002- as to the terms, in the respective license itself there will be established the maximum term for putting a satellite in orbit;
d. The control and operation centers of the satellites, shall be established in Mexican territory and must be operated by Mexicans;
e. The licensees might explode –provide services- in other countries based on the legislation in force in each country and in the Agreements subscribed by the Mexican Government;
f. Licensees shall respect the intellectual property rights and the signals they distribute through those satellites.

Under such regulation, the Federal Telecommunications Law and its Via Satellite Communications Regulation –published on August 1, 1997-, was carried out the privatization of the satellite corporation SATMEX, though a bidding procedure of the capital stock, including in the bidding bases that the patrimony of such semi-official company would be integrated, among others, with the licenses granted for occupying and exploding the geo-stationary orbital positions of 109.2°W; 113.0°W and 116.8°W, frequency bands C and Ku and the signals emission and reception rights.

The aforementioned procedure, originated privatization of via satellite communication in Mexico.

III.2. Licenses for exploding the emission and reception rights of signals of frequency bands associated to foreign satellite systems that cover and might provide services in the national territory.

As a part of the satellite opening, the Mexican Government granted on August 10, 2001, licenses to the following corporations: **Telesistema Mexicano, S.A. de C.V.** –which operates with PanAmSat satellites capacity-, **Controladora Satelital, S. de R. L. de C.V** –using PanAmSat International Sales, Inc. satellite capacity-, who is its shareholder at a 49%; **Sistemas Satelitales, S. de R. L. de C.V.** –using satellites of GE Americon-; and recently another licenses **Astrum Comunicaciones, S.A. de C.V** –which will operate with capacity of MSAT of Canada-

Notwithstanding that the Federal Telecommunications Law does not mention anything about the application of an specific procedure for granting such license, article 30 of such Law, establishes the following conditions for the provision us services in the Mexican territory to a foreign satellite operator:

1. Satellites should cover Mexican territory;
2. To have bilateral treaties in that subject with the country holding the signal origin;
3. That such treaties consider reciprocity for Mexican satellites;
4. The licenses shall only be granted to Mexican corporations and individuals.

Requirements and procedure for obtaining concessions are established in the Via Satellite Communication Regulations, in which we find:
i) Prove the relationship between a foreign satellite operator and the Mexican licensee; location of satellites in order to prove that they cover the Mexican territory; technical specifications of satellites; documents that prove that the Mexican licensee will hold "control" of the services provided in Mexico.

Different from the licensee of an orbital position, Federal Telecommunications Law does not establish the obligation of making a paying for the granting of such license, due to the fact that it is not subject to any bidding procedure.

An important question for granting such licenses is the existence of treaties executed with the origin signal country. Currently, Mexico has treaties with the following countries:

a. United States of America:

1. Treaty related to the transmission and reception of satellite signals for the provision of satellite services to USA users in Mexico (April 28, 1996), which is completed with the following Protocols:
    - For the provision of Via Satellite Direct to Home (April 7, 1997);
    - For the provision of Fixed Satellite Service (March 17, 1998);
    - For the provision of Mobile Satellite Service and Associated Connection Links (December 21, 1998);
2. Agreement for the use of satellites and earth stations for the provision of services included from and in the territories of USA and Mexico (December 21, 1998)

b. With Canada:

1. Treaty for the provision of satellite services (April 9, 1999) which is completed with the following Protocols:

- For the provision of Mobil Satellite Services and Associated Connection Links (January 16, 2001);
- For the provision of Fixed Satellite Service (January 16, 2001).

c. With Argentina:

1. Agreement related to the reciprocity in the use of Satellites and transmission and reception of signals from Satellites for the provision of Satellite Services to the Users of the United Mexican States and the Argentina Republic (July 7, 2000).

Based on the provision of the Federal Telecommunications Law, the Via Satellite Communications and in the referred treatises, as part of the satellite opening, the Mexican Government granted on August 10, 2001, licenses to the following corporations: **Telesistema Mexicano, S.A. de C.V.** –which operates with PanAmSat satellites capacity-, **Controladora Satelital, S. de R. L. de C.V** –using PanAmSat International Sales, Inc. satellite capacity-, who is its shareholder at a 49%; **Sistemas Satelitales, S. de R. L. de C.V.** –using satellites of GE Americon-; and recently another licenses **Astrum Comunicaciones, S.A. de C.V** –which will operate with capacity of MSAT of Canada-

Satellite opening in Mexico, could turned out to be easy, if we consider that the Federal Telecommunications Law and Via Satellite Communications Regulation establishes requirements, procedures and terms for its granting; nevertheless, even when nowadays licensees, in general, of satellite services are providing services, it is true that –the same as is has happened in other countries= the opening to competition caused that the existing satellite operator and one of its subsidiaries, promoted several judicial remedies, which have not been resolved yet.

Another aspect regulated by the Federal Telecommunications Law is the relative to the possibility of operating in the Mexican Territory, international satellites, established under multilateral international treatises of which it is member.

Before Federal Telecommunications Law entered in force in 1995, satellite services operated by INTELSAT and INMARSAT were held through the public organization of the Federal Government, Telecomunicaciones de Mexico (TELECOMM). Such situation was modified by the privatization of INTELSAT and INMARSAT, of which resulted in the incorporation of two private corporations which in order to continue providing services in Mexico must do it, either:

- Through a Mexican corporation that previously obtains a license from the Mexican Government. In case of INTELSAT, there is a Bilateral Treaty with USA, and not in the case of INMARSAT, who requests that in order to comply with the Mexican Law, to execute a treaty with England in order to keep providing services legally; or

- Through TELECOMM, whenever a direct allocation is expressively authorized for those purposes.

In that respect, the provision of such services has not been interrupted and keeps being administrated by TELECOMM, because the provision of services is of public interest.

In case of the **global positioning systems (GNSS),** they provide services in the national territory, and there is no existing license.

Also, it is true that such services are provided free of charge. If in the future, GNSS intended to exchange such position, it should be adjusted to the Mexican Law.

III. 3. Amendments to satellite legislation

On August 28, 2002, the Congress -Representatives- filed a proposal of a new Federal Telecommunications Law, which far from facilitating and giving legal certainty and promoting the satellite sector growth in Mexico, it will inhibit its growth and development and will raise the prices of those services.

This proposal:

1. Establishes new conditions to satellite operators, which use foreign satellite capacity, as there is an obligation to make a payment to the Federal Government –either with money or with satellite capacity- which is not provided in the current law;
2. It does not establish the requirement neither the procedure for obtaining the licenses for using satellite capacity of foreign operators;
3. In case of approval of the new Federal Telecommunications Law it will create for beginning trade barriers of satellite services in Mexico;
4. Is application will generate licensees with different obligations and rights.

It is not yet an applicable law, it is just a proposal which might be amended within the same legislative procedure, and with the comments made by the telecommunications industry.

IV. CONCLUSSIONS AND RECOMMENDATIONS

1. Privatization of satellite sector in Mexico, is the result of the barriers elimination to international trade of services, established upon competition and free concurrence;
2. Deregulation of such sector, which will begin with the amendments to the Federal Constitution in 1995, through which via satellite communication stopped being a strategy area reserved to the State, and therefore, the provision of satellite services was let to the private sector.
3. To the result of the multilateral commercial negotiations given within the WTO in the Agreements adopted in 1994 and 1997, for example the Basic Telecommunications Agreement.
4. In 2001, the Mexican Government granted some licenses to Mexican Companies to provide foreign satellite capacity services in Mexico, situation that the national operator, showed its inconformity through the legal ways, whose resolution is still pending.

5. Satellite opening in Mexico is a reality.
6. New regulation that in its case be approved as referred above, shall contribute to the development of satellite services- and in general to telecommunications- not to inhibit it; with no doubt it is an alternative for the Mexican Government to support in its infrastructure and capacity as an integration mean to the Mexicans.

BIBLIOGRAPHY

1. Constitución Política de los Estados Unidos Mexicanos, 1917 y sus reformas; (Mexican Constitution)
2. Ley de Vías Generales de Comunicación (Communications General Means Law)
3 Ley Federal de Telecomunicaciones (Federal Telecommunications Law);
4. General Agreements on Trade and Tariffs (GATTS) as adopted in within the framework of the WTO;
5 International Union Telecommunications Constitution, Geneva 1992 and its amendments adopted in Minneapolis, 1998.
6. North American Free Trade Agreement – NAFTA - 1994;
7 ITU Constitutional and Conventional Amendments, Alfonso A. Noll, presented in the Legal Framework for Commercial Satellite Telecommunications. Workshop on Telecommunications, Berlin, Germany, June 2000;
8. International Regulation of Radio Frequencies for Space Services.- Ram S. Jakhu and Virginia R. Serrano.- presented at the Legal Framework for Commercial Satellite Telecommunications. Workshop on Telecommunication, Berlin, Germany, June 2000;
9. Convention of International Mobile Satellite Organization and the Operating Agreement, 1979, as amended;
10 Agreement related to the International Organization of Satellite Telecommunications and the Operating Agreement, as amended, 1971.

Bilateral Agreements and its Protocols on Satellite Communications between Mexico and United States of America; Canada and Argentina

11.

IAC-02-IISL.4.11

THE BRAZILIAN SPACE LICENSING REGULATION

Altair Stemler da Veiga
W lteno Marques da Silva
Brazilian Space Agency
Bras lia — DF, Brazil
Stemler@aeb.gov.br
Walteno@aeb.gov.br

ABSTRACT

The prospects for space commercialization that have been showing up, specially in the case of the Alcantara Launch Center, direct the Brazilian legal system on a search for a statute law suitable for that aim.

In the context of the Brazilian legislative process, and due to a provision of the law which creates the Brazilian Space Agency (BSA), just this organization is in charge to establish rules and to issue licenses and authorizations regarding to space activities.

BSA has been working hard on that purpose, elaborating regulations that have been approved by its Superior Council. The rules on procedures and definitions required for application, assessment, issuing, controlling the indispensable license for launching space [2]activities on Brazilian territory have been established by BSA Resolution n. 51 of January 26th, 2001, as well as by BSA Edict n. 27 of June, 20th 2001.

According to this legislation, the adopted licensing procedure does not apply to space activities carried out by Brazilian governmental agencies.

It points out the intention of hastening the fulfillment of the necessary licenses and authorizations requirements related to the commercial uses of the Brazilian Launch Center (Alcantara and Barreira do Inferno) in order to attend potential partners interested on space launch business.

This paper aims to present the current stage of Brazilian Space Law, as well as its development and application. Special attention is give to the increasing demand for an even more dynamic space law making process in Brazil. The conclusion is that Brazil must create, as soon as possible, wide and efficient legal instruments.

1. INTRODUCTION

In order to implement its space policy, Brazil has been developing scientific and technological programs for research and development of space systems which, in addition to meeting its own needs, bring about collaborative ventures with other countries. In this context, the need for increased study and knowledge of space law becomes more evident, considering its singularity and the multiple and diverse aspects that so often characterize its application.

Following this line of thought, we must conclude that the joint efforts stemming from partnerships entered into with universities and other Brazilian institutions dedicated to the furtherance of space law studies take on a dominant and strategic role, for they are bound to generate an increased level of efficiency and efficacy in governmental programs. The latter encompass two Brazilian space launch centers, the Alc ntara Launch Center-CLA being particularly noteworthy because it possesses all the elements necessary to render the country internationally competitive in the commercial use of space services, due to its privileged geographic locale.

This situation highlights the need to put together a regulatory framework in the area of Brazilian space law, in order to discipline space activities in the national territory, the use of the available infrastructure, and the issuance, supervision and control of space launch licenses and authorizations, among a variety of other activities that may result therefrom.

This reality has certainly generated a great deal of international expectation over the matter of issuance of regulatory legislation regarding the services to be provided by the Brazilian State, through the use of the Alc ntara Launch Center-CLA, because that would provide a greater degree of certainty for those countries that have expressed an interest in carrying out launches from the national territory.

According to this perception, Brazilian competitiveness will hinge, to a large extent, on a most significant aspect, i. e., the enactment of legislative rules designed to bring about the degree of administrative and operational flexibility that is required for an effective handling of the demand for services, thereby ensuring that future negotiations on launches from that center will be as expedient as required.

My presentation is designed to give a description of the current state of Brazilian space law and the results already obtained, as well as the significance of the role that must be played by universities and similar institutions, not only in regard to the drafting of the much-awaited codification of Brazilian Space Law, but also - and perhaps more significantly - in connection with the study, development and application of that law.

2. THE BRAZILIAN LEGISLATIVE PROCESS

As set forth in Sec. 22 of the Brazilian Constitution, the Union has the power to legislate on matters of space law. Thus, the federal government is exclusively empowered to issue ordinary legislation on the matter. It should also be pointed out that, pursuant to national legislative procedures, all manner of bills introduced in the Senate or the Chamber of Deputies must first come under the scrutiny of the appropriate committees, that is, those having jurisdiction by reason of subject matter.

The requirement of examination by technical groups is in keeping with the universal principle of division of labor, and also fulfills the need of ensuring that the subject matter will be examined by legislators who are familiar with the respective field of knowledge. A favorable report by the committee constitutes a decisive step for the approval or rejection of a bill in either legislative house.

It should be stressed, moreover, that a report by the Committee on Constitution and Justice on a bill's compliance with basic legal, constitutional and parliamentary rules is a mandatory initial step with regard to practically the totality of bills introduced in any of the houses of the Brazilian Parliament.

The exclusive powers vested in the Union by the Constitution to regulate space law matters must conform however, to the principle that is at the essence of the democratic representative regime, to the effect that fundamental legal regulations must be enacted by the Legislative Branch, as the basic institution in a democratic representative regime. For this reason all bills of law dealing with essential reforms demanded by society at large must be submitted to It.

There is an awareness of the fact that such task is neither easy nor simple but, on the contrary, one that requires a great deal of time and must also comply with the requirement set forth in Decree n¡2,954 of January 29, 1999, whereby the enactment of politically or socially relevant regulatory statutes must be preceded by a process of ample public consultation.

3. THE ROLE OF THE BRAZILIAN SPACE AGENCY IN ESTABLISHING THE LEGAL FRAMEWORK

The BRAZILIAN SPACE AGENCY - AEB, a federal autarchic[1] [3]entity, under the Ministry of Science and Technology - MCT, was set-up by Law n¡8,854 of February 10, 1994, for the purpose of "furthering the development of space activities that are in the national interest" with, among others, the power to "establish rules and issue licenses and authorizations regarding space activities.

Decree n¡1,332 of December 8, 1994, in turn, gave approval to the Space Activities Development Policy - PNDAE and, in item II, n¡3 of its Appendix provided as follows:

"Space activities should be understood as consisting in the systematic effort to develop and operate space systems, and the necessary infrastructure, related therewith, for the purpose of enabling Man to increase his knowledge about the Universe and, in particular, of planet Earth and its atmosphere, as well as to explore, for utilitarian purposes, the availability of such systems."

This statutory citation makes it clear that the BRAZILIAN SPACE AGENCY is duly empowered **to establish rules and issue licenses and authorizations relative to space activities.**

It should also be mentioned that launch operations will have a major role in consolidating the efforts for the utilization of the Alc ntara Launch Center - CLA whose privileged geographic location may render Brazil internationally competitive in providing a wide range of services, especially for carrying out orbital launches.

In effect, there has been a great deal of speculation about the framework of the rules designed to discipline the services to be provided by the Brazilian State, particularly those pertaining to the launch center in question, given the need for legal safeguards that has been expressed by countries that have shown an interest in making launches from Brazil.

The BRAZILIAN SPACE AGENCY - AEB's decision to strive for the establishment of rules leading to future codification of Brazilian space law has met with a very positive reception, since there is a need for the country to develop its own set of legal rules, in harmony with the international accords signed by it, and designed to bring about the utilization of its space infrastructure.

AEB may be said to have initiated that process, through the issuance, by its Superior Council[2] and its president, of a set of regulations designed to achieve that purpose, through rules that establish procedures and define requirements to govern license application, evaluation, issuance, control, follow-up and oversight management, for the conduct of space launch activities in the Brazilian territory, as follows[3]:

- CHAPTER I - GENERAL PROVISIONS - (secs. 1 to 5): pertains to the definition of licenses and exempts therefrom those space activities that are carried out by governmental agencies or entities; allows the insertion of restrictive or conditional clauses; deals with the question of funding and criteria for the control, follow-up and inspection of licensee's activities, as well as the definition of damage, for civil liability purposes.
- CHAPTER II - DOCUMENTATION AND APPLICATION - (secs. 6 to 14): defines criteria for legal status documentation, technical qualification, economic-financial qualification and fiscal standing of interested legal entities, as well as the terms and conditions for document submission; makes it mandatory for the legal entity to be licensed in its country of origin, in order to engage in the activities it proposes to perform, and that it have a legal representative in Brazil, with express powers to receive summons and to be held administratively, as well as judicially, liable; requires that documents provided by foreign legal entities be submitted in the original language and the original text, by means of authentic copies, and that it be duly translated by a certified public translator; contemplates the possibility that AEB may require the submission to it of an instrument of commitment regarding technological safeguards, if this comes to be demanded by Brazilian government authorities; requires insurance coverage for possible third party damage, to the extent warranted in specific cases and in keeping with the degree of risk of the activities to be performed, such amounts to be set by AEB beforehand.
- CHAPTER III - PROCEDURES FOR APPLICATION - (secs. 5 to 19): defines, on a step-by-step basis, the procedures to be followed by legal entities for submission of their documentation and defines the jurisdiction of the Special Applications Commission.
- CHAPTER IV - ADMINISTRATIVE SANCTIONS - (secs. 20 and 21): defines administrative sanctions applicable to an infringer of the rules set forth in the Regulations and the criteria for their application.
- CHAPTER V - ADMINISTRATIVE APPEALS - (secs. 22 to 24): sets forth the procedure for filing appeals and their judgment.
- CHAPTER VI - FINAL PROVISIONS - (secs.25 to 27): deals with the publicity of administrative actions resulting from the application of the Regulations; contemplates the issuance of a normative act to deal with the matter of the charging of fees for the granting of licenses and with the question of supplementary instructions for the implementation of technical and administrative actions required to be carried out, in compliance with the licensing procedures.

At a later stage a set of rules was issued, to govern the procedure for authorizing a space launch operation in the Brazilian territory[4], likewise through the Superior Council and the President of AEB, according to the following outline:

Section 1, of 10.26.2001 and DIRECTIVE n¡5 of February 21, 2002 published in the DOU

Section 1, 02.25.2002.

- CHAPTER I - GENERAL PROVISIONS - (secs. 1 to 8): deals with the definition of space launch and excludes space activities carried out by governmental organs or entities; defines authorization and sets forth the general principles for its granting.

- CHAPTER II - PROCEDURE AND AUTHORIZATION - (secs. 9 to 11): defines the administrative proceeding to be followed by legal entities upon their obtaining an authorization.

- CHAPTER III - ADMINISTRATIVE PENALTIES - (secs. 12 and 13): defines administrative penalties applicable to an infringer of the rules set forth in the Regulations and the criteria for their application.

- CHAPTER IV - ADMINISTRATIVE APPEALS - (secs. 14 and 15): sets forth procedures for the filing and judging of appeals.

- CHAPTER V - FINAL PROVISIONS - (secs. 16 to 20): deals with the publicity of administrative acts arising out of the application of the Regulations; contemplates the issuance of a normative act regarding the charging of fees for the granting of an authorization; provides for the creation of a public register for the registry of space objects launched into outer space from the national territory, and defines the information that should be provided.

It should be stressed that, although these normative acts still fall short of meeting the expectations of international partners, their existence in the Brazilian space law is a sign of Brazil's resolve regarding the elaboration and systematization of a legal framework for space activities that are in the national interest.

VI - PARTICIPATION OF UNIVERSITIES AND SIMILAR ENTITIES IN THE STUDIES, DEVELOPMENT AND APPLICATION OF BRAZILIAN SPACE LAWS

There cannot be any doubt that the successful development of Brazilian space programs and the increase in the number of partnerships have unleashed a more effective phase in the race to marshal the human resources needed for attaining the national goals for this important market segment.

As a result, universities and similar institutions, which are fertile grounds
for specialized teams will certainly provide a decisive contribution to government sectors dealing with space law, as needed to face up to the challenge posed by this complex and relevant subject matter. One such example is in the work that has been performed by the Brazilian Aerospace Law Society - SBDA, whose pioneering efforts have provided incentive and spread the knowledge of space law.

A number of reasons come
together to recommend the involvement of the above-mentioned institutions in this relevant branch of the law, among them is the need to form groups made up of professors and jurists, all of them engaged in the study and application of space law, in a national as well as, in an international context. The growing attention to the matter is one of the upshots of Brazilian space activities carried out in the last years. This fact, together with the reality of the privileged location of the two launch sites existing in Brazil - one in Alc ntara, Maranh o and the other at Barreira do Inferno, in Natal, constitute vital signs of promising business prospects with regard to launch operations. This fact constitutes an added reason for accelerating the dissemination of knowledge and the training of professional cadres of specialists in this new branch of the law.

It is necessary, however, to advance a little more in this endeavor, and to that effect, the Brazilian Government ought to stop relegating to a secondary plane the need to introduce a course in space law as part of law course curriculum, even if it is on an optional basis. This would bring about increased awareness on the part of scholars and heighten their interest in this still novel branch of the law. Such action would be an unequivocal demonstration of the government's commitment and determination to promote the development of much needed human resources and the enhancement of their capability.

This represents yet another challenge that must be met by the Brazilian Government, as it cannot fail to keep abreast of technological progress and other advances, under penalty of compromising the goal of promoting the development of space activities of national interest, which encompass the study, development and application of their own legal system that is designed to meet such needs.

V - CONCLUSION

This presentation has sought to provide a picture of the present stage of development in the Brazilian legal system with regard to space activities that are in the national interest, and to highlight the innumerable reasons for an acceleration of the process of building the legal framework of Brazilian space law, in order to provide society with an effective regulatory instrument, one that fits in with the needs of the times.

The approach adopted was designed not only to report on what is being done in Brazil, in connection with its space legislation, but also to reach out to those responsible for the management of Brazilian institutions engaged in the study, discussion and application of the law, in the hope of increasing their awareness of this promising market. It is essential that they realize that the institutions in question must play an essential part as invaluable agents, and not merely as spectators, in the effort to achieve a better development and increased knowledge of space law, mindful of the fact that none of the branches of the law failed to go through a similar participatory process in their development.

Man will always be searching for knowledge and new experiences and, as such, has overcome the most diverse challenges, over the course of time. Once Brazilian universities are given new opportunities to gain a better knowledge of this matter, which is at present one of fundamental importance for the process of national and international development; this will bring about a new perspective for future professionals of this new legal field, one that is not so far behind, as well as the emergence of new academic works that will enlarge its universe and usher in new expectations and horizons.

In conclusion, it must be stated that, in the present stage of its space legislation, even if it may be still in an embryonic stage, Brazil is already able to meet the demands of the various areas that are encompassed by space activities, especially those having to do with the commercial development of the launch sector through the utilization of the Alcântara Launch Center structure.

References

[1] An autarchic entity is a governmental organization subject to Public Law, having its own assets and source of revenue and is established by law in order to carry out activities that are within the sphere of the public administration.

[3] RESOLUTION n¡51 of 01.26.2001 - published in the Official Gazette of the Union — DOU Section 1 of 06.21.2001

[4] RESOLUTION n¡55 of 10.24.2001 - published in the Official Gazette of the Union DOU — Section 1 of 10.26.2001

IAC-02-IISL.4.12

EVOLVING SPACE LAW AND WORLD POLITICAL HEGEMONIES

José Monserrat Filho
Brazilian Society of Aerospace Law, Rio de Janeiro
monserrat@alternex.com.br
Patrick A. Salin
CIASL, McGill University, and Orbicom, UQAM, Montreal
salin.patrick@UQAM.CA

"Without the ability to articulate political visions and critiques, international law becomes pragmatism all the way down, an all-encompassing internalization, symbol, and reaffirmation of power." Martti Koskenniemi (1)

Abstract

This paper examines some central aspects of the role exerted by world hegemony powers in the creation, development and orientation of Space Law since the beginning of the Space Age. It shows that from a very rich but also very lacunar experience of the initial bilateral hegemonic system we come to a unipolar one, which seems to be characterized by a disturbing paralysis of the international space law making process. As a conclusion it points out the importance of insisting on the preparation for a multipolar world, which surely will have an innovative impact, *inter alia*, in space politics.

Part I: The Age of Bipolarity

The Space Age – inaugurated by the Sputnik I launching in October 4th, 1957 – is only 45 years old but already knows two different superpower hegemony systems: a bipolar system hegemony systems: a bipolar system under the confronting leadership of the United States of America (USA) and the Union of Soviet Socialist Republics (USSR), as well as a unipolar one under the sole incomparable USA supremacy – "an imperial power the like of which has not been seen in the West since ancient Rome." (2)

These two systems have been characterized by very different impact on the space law making process. Almost all the *Corpus Iuris Spatialis* (3) was created during the process of development of the first system, which disappeared with the collapse of the USSR in 1991. Particularly in the 60s and 70s an intense activity took place in the treaty making process, producing remarkable outcomes at a speed seen as cosmic. And all this work was discussed and approved by just one legislative plenarium, the United Nations Committee on Peaceful Uses of Outer Space (Copuos) and its Legal and Scientific and Technical Subcommittees. This body has, in essence, been framed and regulated by the indispensable agreement between the USA and the USSR.

Triumphant in the Second World War, the two superpowers nevertheless were, from there on, separated by fierce political and strategic rivalry. They confronted each other in a Cold war which could at any moment become a hot one, including the use of weapons of mass destruction. Such weapons were initially transported by aircraft, as was the case in the American attack to Hiroshima and Nagasaki, in 1945. Later, however, they concluded that the better way to launch the atomic bomb was by intercontinental ballistic missiles, which modest forerunner was the Germany V-2. Then, the USA and the USSR propelled them headlong into a race, which aim was to create the first intercontinental ballistic missiles and to become the world's first space power.

"Space was a new frontier for the display of national prestige and power. The USA and the USSR demonstrated their leadership to other nations by waging propaganda war, exhibiting their technological and military superiority, and portraying the inherent greatness and excellence of their respective liberal democratic and communist regimes", as wrote Steven Lambrkis (4).

At that time there was also a great civil interest in space scientific research. The International Geophysical Year (July 1957 to December 1958) congregated scientific efforts of several nations – including from the USA and the USSR – to study the physical properties of Earth and the interaction between the Sun and our planet. It was a historic peaceful undertaking of worldwide magnitude, congregating the best scientific excellence then existing with very clearly peaceful purposes.

Although the Sputnik launching was part of this initiative, the beginning of the Space Age was due not to it but rather to strategic military mutual concerns and plans of the superpowers, vis-à-vis each other. Much more important than the inoffensive 184-pound ball Sputnik I – with diameter of 58 cm, as well as two radio transmitters of 1 W nourished by two chemical batteries – was the rocket (R-7, nicknamed Semyorka), which put into space the first artificial Earth satellite. Just as was the first Intercontinental Ballistic Missile (ICBM), duly tested and qualified. Besides, on November 8, 1957, the Soviet Government announced the testing of a new hydrogen bomb much more powerful.

Edward Teller, the so called "father of the hydrogen bomb" (5) narrated: "Sputnik caused fear. It was apparent that Russia, capable of throwing a satellite around the Earth, could also launch a device armed with an atomic or hydrogen bomb. Watching Sputnik flash overhead in the night, Americans realized as never before that our nation was in the range of Russian rockets – rockets that could carry the terrible destructiveness of nuclear weapons from launching pad to target, from continent to continent, from hemisphere to hemisphere in twenty minutes." (6)

Moscow commemorated the unexpected rocket superiority. Premier Nikita Khrushchev proclaimed: "The Soviet Union launched an intercontinental ballistic missile the testing of which yielded positive results. We can now send a missile to any point of the globe, carrying, if necessary, a hydrogen warhead. Our announcement to this effect was greeted by disbelief and regarded as an attempt by Soviet leaders to instill confidence in their own people and intimidate the Western governments. But then the Soviet Union, using the intercontinental ballistic missile, launched an artificial earth satellite, and when it started circling the globe and when everyone – unless blind - could see it by looking up to the sky, our opponents became silent." (7)

The USA was no longer an inviolable "sanctuary". It has lost its sacred invulnerability and absolute security, and now needed to urgently compensate this adverse situation. In 1958, after many failures, it finally succeeded in testing the prototype of the intermediate range ballistic missile (IRBM) Jupiter and of the intercontinental ballistic missile (ICBM) Atlas (8). Os its time the USSR seemed to be much better prepared to confront with American military bases around its territory, as well as to play a more active role in world politics, strengthening its superpower condition and its leadership upon an expressive group of countries, which in the first moment included China.

A new phase of confrontation then emerged. The new geopolitical landscape of Cold War defrosted the relationship between the two superpowers and led to an approximation, which was unthinkable before. Now, to negotiate was not only possible but necessary. Opportunities were opened, as well the demand for a quite considerable degree of cooperation between the USA and the USSR.

This was the environment in which the Space Age was inaugurated, and the basis of the Space Law was launched (meaning regulation of space activities).

Thus, Space Law was born from the Cold War, but from a stage of the Cold War which allows and requests some sort of mutual understanding, to the benefit of both sides of the potential conflict.

First big decision: the USA and the USSR agreed that all these newest space issues should be discussed and regulated under the auspices of the Organization of United Nations. For that end, a special body was created in 1959 – the COPUOS. At that time it permitted as open and transparent a treatment as possible of questions so closely linked to the arms race and to the tension between the superpowers.

Later, however, military problems between them with series space implications were solved separately, by bilateral agreements. This is how the 1963 Treaty Banning Nuclear Weapon Tests in the Atmosphere, in Outer Space and under Water – NTB Treaty (signed in Moscow by USSR, USA and United Kingdom and afterwards opened to adherence of other countries) and the 1972 Treaty Between the USA and the USSR on the Limitation of Anti-Ballistic Missile Systems – ABM Treaty (denounced by the USA last year), as well as the Convention on the 1977 Prohibition of Military or Any Other Hostile Use of Environmental Modification Techniques – Enmod Convention, were drafted.

The two superpowers came to the decision of transferring the space military issues from COPUOS to the United Nations Disarmament Commission and afterwards to the Conference of Disarmament. With this move COPUOS was deprived of the most crucial agenda of issues, on which depend all the peaceful uses of outer space, expressed in the very name of this organ.

Before the Sputnik I, the USA Government perceived a free and open international regime to be the most convenient for the outer space. Already then Washington made plans to use satellite to observe its enemies, starting with the USSR. President Dwight Eisenhower supported the freedom of space principle as the better way to defend the USA strategic interests. This position became even stronger after the Sputnik I. The importance of this project increased even more after the failure of the spy spacecraft U-2, which was overthrow by the USSR in 1960.

However, simultaneously with the Cold War, a large and diversified public opinion opposition movement was growing, due to the threats of a new worldwide conflict, particularly because of the probable use of nuclear weapons. Still earlier, in 1955, appeared the famous Russel-Einstein manifest against the nuclear war, defending an exclusively peaceful and humanistic posture in the matter of resolution of international controversies. (9) At the end of the 50s, and mainly in the 60s, the balance of political forces in the United Nations had dccply changed. From the ruins of the old colonial empires emerged dozens of new States. The "Third World", led above all by the Movement of Non-Aligned Countries, became an active player in the world political scene. It had no access to the strategic decision centers, but it assumes a claiming and demanding political capacity, while shaking entirely the work of the main international intergovernmental organizations. The United Nations General Assembly dynamics changed; it acquited more political weight; its agenda of debates paid much more attention to the interests and needs of developing countries.

The two superpowers had necessarily to take somehow into account this new force, mainly in the issues relating to international peace and security, as well as to space activities, given their obvious and increasing military relevance.

Thus, Space Law was born under concomitant war and peace pressures, although the first were stronger than the second. This became very clear in the first agreement of this area, the 1967 Space Treaty, which remains the central code of all space activities. In this treaty the idea of peace is mentioned only in the preamble, where "the common interest of all mankind in the progress of the exploration and use of outer space for peaceful purposes" is recognized. It is true that Article IV prohibits the installation in orbit around the Earth of any weapons of mass destruction (nuclear, chemical and biological). But it doesn't close the space to the transit of ballistic missiles carrying one of these weapons. Nuclear weapons are not currently prohibited, contrary to the chemical and biological ones. That is a legal breach where a devastating world war can pass.

Manfred Lachs has rightly assessed that the 1967 Space Treaty "was an important step on the road to the maintenance of peace, but it has not achieved the goal of outer space being reserved exclusively for peaceful purposes; no other agreement was possible". (10)

In fact, the bipolar hegemonic system, despite valuable partial concessions made to peace and development claims, did not prohibit the option of war.

However, it is not proper to underestimate the importance of the basic norms established by the two superpowers in their geo-strategic compromise relating to space activities:

non-appropriation, freedom of exploration and use of outer space and celestial bodies, starting from the Moon; and all the space actions always turned to the benefit and the interests of all countries, of all mankind – the principle well known as the clause of common benefit. (11) One can discuss whether these principles have been applied and accomplished in the better manner, for instance, in the current system of assignment and use of orbital positions and frequencies in the geo-stationary orbit. But nobody doubts that they are highly positive and must be preserved and strengthened in any case of future legislative reform.

In the other hand, one should not overestimate such principles. They can be easily changed and disfigured in practice. We are not yet protected from seeing the principle of non-appropriation simply transformed into an opposite custom. The free access to outer space continues to confront arbitrary and anti-competitive constraints. That is why it clearly deserves a specific and detailed international convention, designed to guarantee the maximum potential of all countries, and freed from unilateraly introduced discriminations and impediments. And what to say about the clause of common benefit, considering the current intense process of commercialization and privatization of space activities, in which powerful private interests compete with public interests and not seldom supplant them, in as much as these are not always duly safeguarded? How can such a fundamental clause be protected from the billionaire project directed to installing last generation weapons on Earth's orbit? Being generic and vague, this generous clause of unequivocal humanistic sense calls for a precise and detailed definition of its content and of its effective application.

Not by chance, Manfred Lachs, when evaluating the 25 years of the 1967 Space Treaty, strongly recommended that the process of Space Law development "cannot be arrested – it has to grow at ever great speed to follow life in order to resolve the many problems for the benefit and in the interests of all men". (12)

Part II: The Age of Unipolarity

The bipolar system did much for the Space Law, but left very serious lacunas. For instance, it did not demilitarized outer space as was done in Antarctica. According to Article 1st of the 1959 Antarctic Treaty, "Antarctica shall be used for peaceful purposes only. There shall be prohibited, inter alia, any measures of a military nature, such as the establishment of military bases and fortifications, the carrying out of military maneuvers, as well as the testing of any type of weapons". (13)

Even so, the EUA-USSR condominium did much more for the development of the space legal order than the current unipolar system, as we have been seeing since the beginning of the 90 and until now, as well as from forecasts for the next few years.

What seems to better characterize the unipolar system is its absolute impossibility to promote a great effort and to arrange a wide agreement in order to develop Space Law, responding to present and future demands. The present single superpower and some of its allies have been repeatedly manifested against any proposals to amend treaties that are in force. The increasing evidence of the need to fulfill the numerous lacunae does not matter. If it in the past this could be considered permissible, today it obstructs indispensable improvements and advances in the space legal order. Space activities, military as well as civil, are now in a very different stage from the one existing when the Space Law sources were elaborated. The lrgal framework in force is considerably bypassed by current social-political, as well as scientific-technological, changes in condition. Updating it becomes a clear and pressing need.

COPUOS has not succeeded in achieving the necessary agreement, nor even in starting a discussion on a need and a feasibility of an Universal Comprehensive Convention on the Space Law, as was fruitfully done in the 1982 Convention on the Law of the Sea (14); or on the necessity and feasibility of a convention on remote sensing of the Earth from outer space, starting from the principles on this matter approved by United Nations General Assembly in 1986. (15)

Such debates would certainly open way to new solutions to identifying coherent and cohesive formulae to consolidating the main principles and the most valuable achievements of Space Law registered in the documents already approved, as well as to fulfilling the existing lacunae and creating new norms in order to face many and important space problems not yet regulated.

The unipolar system has demonstrated to be incapable of admitting, and even less to living together with, an undertaking of such magnitude. It is like control of the legislative process would be lost, and one would be obliged to step down from dominant positions and to negotiate with less rich and powerful countries in conditions of legal equality. COPUOS seems to enjoy much less relevance than in other times, despite the fact that space activities today are effectively much more intense and relevant for all than in the past. The unipolarity, by its own nature, does not need necessarily to oppose the maintenance of this sort of forum. It is enough not to assign it a truly productive and creative role. At most, it will occasionally have the chance to ratify some project previously arranged in its essential topics in order to give it a wider supporting basis. In general, however, multilateral discussions and efforts for solutions are not seen as convenient and favorable to its interests. In its view, openness involves risks of unnecessary entanglements and annoyances. The one power hegemony reposes and keeps guard on its own force to reject any initiative it defines as affecting its interests and policies, disregarding the need to offer well proved and convincing arguments. That translates into the cold and reviewed right of veto into which the COPUOS rule of approval by consensus has not seldom been converted.

Unipolarity irresistibly tends to fail in paying "proper attention to the opinion of other" and in incorporating "a broad conception of justice" into its own national interest. These alerting words are from the Assistant Secretary of Defense in the Clinton Administration Joseph S. Nye Jr.. He also warns: "The danger posed by the outright champions of hegemony is that their foreign policy is all accelerator and no brakes." (16)

It absolutely doesn't help to deal with the increasing conflicts between national interest of the hegemonic power and interests of the international community, which has been minimized as "illusory" one. (17) The outcome is a series of difficulty to understand the global public goods, among them the international public order and the regime of exploration and use of outer space. (18) Hence another warming of Joseph S. Nye Jr.: “Too narrow an appeal to public good can become a self-serving ideology for the powerful.” (19) The consequences of it in the space practice is properly explained by H. Peter van Fenema: “To the extent that national security-based American policies maintain the gulf between U. S. space ‘haves’ and foreign ‘have nots’, and thus widen the technological and economic gap between the two groups, such policies have at the same time a peace, security and stability *threatening* effect. That effects not only the economic, political and security interest of the U. S. but also the corresponding interests of the world community at large.” Examining more specifically the unilateral obstructions in the launch technology transfer and industry, Fenema concludes that “laws, policies and practices, which virtually exclude cooperation” in such an essential sector of space activities, “violate the spirit” of the 1967 Space Treaty and of the 1996 Outer Space Benefits Declaration, which appeal to member States to engage to the maximum extent possible in international cooperation in the exploration and use of outer space. (20)

But the major threat of unipolarity is in its project, never so determined as now and to certain extend already in action, to militarize outer space entirely, including the use of nuclear weapons (21). The exploration and use of outer space for military purposes – *inter alia* observation, telecommunications, monitoring, reconnaissance, positioning and target precision – that intensively developed during the bipolar period, have been considered as “passives”, “auxiliaries”, “non-aggressive”. These kind of definitions, of course, are quite controvertial. In any case, all these military activities are no longer sufficient. The unipolar system, in its current shape, goes dangerously farther. It assumes the active military utilization of outer space. It considers indispensable the deployment of a missile defense system with space based weapons, as well as ground new arms capable to destroy space objects. It means the capacity to use the armed forces from the ground into space, from the space to the ground and in outer space itself. In order to justify this approach, an army of military legal experts has been mobilized in order to tailor an interpretation of the legal loopholes of the space law treaties and provide a legal basis for the military use of outer space (22). In this manner and for the first time in history, outer space is right now being transformed into a battlefield. This comes together with doctrines defending new concepts like “space power”, “space superiority” and “military space dominance”, as well as the “right” to deny access to space for countries that are one-sidedly labelled as “ennemies” (23). All these can open an entirely new phase in the Space Age, having plenty of arbitrariness and prepotence, and erasing the humanistic, constructive and freedom legacy of 1967 Space Treaty. Actually, the study of the actual legislative work that is under progress at the 107th US Congress shows it aims at granting this nation with a full fledged legal framework that ensures its political, technical, economic and financiel dominance in outer space over any potential contender (24).

Part III: Dominance or Multipolarity?

There are rational and feasible alternatives to this deleterious trend. We can take for granted a judicious premise: "As the century progresses, America will not be able to sustain the global preponderance that it enjoys today. A unipolar international system will over time give way to a world of multiple centers of power" (25). Then it is proper as well as prudent to insist right now on searching and preparing by all political, economic, legal and cultural means for a multipolar world that requires a renewed approach to collective international security (26). In this way, it urges to give genuine priority to the efforts to intensify – in much more deep and diversified manner – the international cooperation in the exploration and use of outer space, enhancing the benefits for all countries and stimulating the active participation of more and more countries. To this aim, it is highly necessary to improve the process of international governance of space activities. That includes to push and give prestige to the multilateralism anywhere, starting from multilateral bodies Copuos and International Telecommunication Union (ITU). It also embraces a renewed and creative political effort to remove obstruction to de free access to the agenda of Copuos, especially in the its Legal Subcommittee, permitting this way the present Space Law sources could be discussed and improved, if necessary, attending nowadays and future demands. In the same sense, it doesn't have to exclude the exam so many times postponed of the necessity of an international organization within the United Nations system particularly committed to enhance the space cooperation exclusively for peaceful purposes.

The better future of Space Age surely is a system truly global, multilateral and democratic. Just in this new phase, much more than in the previous ones, outer space "shall be free for exploration and use by all States without discrimination of any kind, on a basis of equality", and the common benefit clause – the global public interest – will have more favorable conditions to make concrete its huge potential and indeed become the cornerstone of Space Law.

References

1) KOSKENNIEMI, Martti, *The Gentle Civilizer of Nations – The Rise and Fall of International Law 1870-1960*, United Kingdom: Cambridge University Press, 2002, p. 516.

2) CHACE, James, *Imperial America and the Common Interest*, World Policy Journal, Volume XIX, N. 1, Winter 2002.

3) *Treaty on Principles Governing the Activities of States in the Exploration and Use of Outer Space, including the Moon and Other Celestial Bodies*, 1967; *Agreement on the Rescue of Astronauts, the Return of Astronauts and the Return of Objects Launched into Outer Space*, 1968; *Convention on International Liability for Damage Caused by Space Objects*, 1972; *Convention on Registration of Objects Launched into Outer Space*, 1975; *Agreement Governing the Activities of States on the Moon and other Celestial Bodies*, 1979 (See: UN Doc. A/AC.105/572/Rev.2). *Declaration of Legal Principles Governing the Activities of States in the Exploration and Use of Outer Space*, 1963; *Principles Governing the Use by States of Artificial Earth Satellites for International Direct Television Broadcasting*, 1982; *Principles Relating to Remote Sensing of the Earth from Outer Space*, 1986; *Principles Relevant*

to the use of Nuclear Power Sources in Outer Space, 1992; *Declaration on International Cooperation in the Exploration and Use of Outer Space for the Benefit and in the Interests of all States, Taking into Particular Account the Needs of Developing Countries*, 1996 (See: UN Doc. A/AC.105/572/Rev.2).

4) LAMBAKIS, Steven, *On the Edge of Earth – The Future of Space Power*, USA: The University Press of Kentucky, 2001, p. 211.

5) OHLWEITER, Otto Alcides, *A Energia Nuclear na Paz e na Guerra*, (Nuclear Energy in Peace and War) Rio de Janeiro: Editora Conquista, 1955, pp. 78-92 (in Portuguese).

6) CHACE, James, and CARR, Caleb, *America Invulnerable – The Quest for Absolute Secutiry from 1812 do Star Wars*, USA: Summit Books, NY, 1988, p. 306.

7) KHRUSHCHEV, N. S., *For Victory in the Peaceful Competition with Capitalism*, Moscow: Foreign Languages Publishing House, pp. 30-8. See also HUMBLE, Ronald D., The Soviet Space Programme, New York: Routledge, 1988, p. 5.

8) FONTAINE, André, *Histoire de la Guerre Froide (II) – De la guerre de Corée à la crise des alliances (1950-1967)*, Paris: Fayard, p. 316. O autor dedica um capítulo ao que ele chama de "Sa Majesté le Spoutnik".

9) *Einstein on Peace*, edited by OttoNathan and Heinz Norden, New York: Schocken Books, 1975.

10) LACHS, Manfred, *The Treaty on Principles of the Law of Outer Space, 1961-1992*, Netherlands International Law Review, XXXIX, 1992, p. 295.

11) RODOTA, Antonio, *Is there a specificity of outer space as an inalienable protected domain?*, Unesco Comest Sub-Commission on "The Ethics of Outer Space" Report, 2001, pp. 70-73.

12) LACHS, Manfred, idi ibid, p. 302

13) The Antarctic Treaty, signed in December 1st, 1959. See Basic Documents in International Law and World Order, selected and edited by Burns H. Weston, Richard A. Falk and Antony A. D'Amato, USA, St. Paul, Minn.: West Publishing Co., 1980, pp. 329-331.

14) KOLOSSOV, Iuri M., e TITUSHKIN, Vassili I, *Is it time to develop a Universal Comprehensive Convention on the Law of Outer Space?*, Revista Brasileira de Direito Aeroespacial (Brazilian Journal of Aerospace Law), October, Rio de Janeiro, 2002.

15) Brazilian proposal in Copuos Legal Subcommittee in 2002 session, supporting by many countries.

16) NYE JR., Joseph S., *Paradoxes of American Power – Why the World's only superpower can't go it alone*, New York: Oxford University Press, 2002, pp. 226-229.

17) LUDLOW, P, Wanted: A Global Partner, The Washington Quartely, Summer 2001, p. 167 (Quoted by NYE JR., id. ibid., p. 226)

18) KAUL, Inge, GRUNBERG, Isabelle, STERN, Marc A., *Global Public Goods – International Cooperation in the 21st Century*, New York: Oxford University Press, 1999.

19) NYE JR., Joseph S., id. ibid., p. 232.

20) FENEMA, H. Peter van, *The International Trade in Launch Services – The effects of U. S. laws, policies and practices on its development*, Doctor Dissertation approved in Meijers Institute of Legal Studies, Faculty of Law, Leiden University, The Netherlands, 1999, p. 380.

21) The nuclear issue in Outer Space is addressed from time to time. So far, the United States has no plans to arm anti-missile interceptors with nuclear explosives, according to the recent declaration of a defense official in Congress, but he acknowledged that some people are thinking about it. Please see on the web at: http://www.space.com/missionlaunches/missile_defense_020417.html

22) SALIN, P.A., *Space law, the National Missile Defense Initiative and the Common Concern for Global Security*, Proceedings of the 50th Anniversary

Conference, IASL, McGill University, Montreal, 20 April 2002.

23) MONSERRAT Filho, José, *Acts of Aggression in Outer Space*, Proceedings of Forty Fourth Colloquium on the Law of Outer Space, October 2001, Toulouse, France, AIAA, 2002, pp. 377-384; VLASIC, Ivan, *Space Law and the Military Applications of Space Technology*, in *Perspectives on International Law*, edited by Nandasiri Jasentuliyana/Foreword by Boutros Boutros-Ghali, United Kingdom: Kluwer Law International, 1995, pp. 385-410.

24) SALIN, P.A., *An Overview of US Commercial Space Legislation and Policies – Present and Future*, Air and Space Law Journal, Volume XXVII, No 3 (June 2002), pp. 209-236.

25) KUPCHAN, Charles A., ADLER, Emanuel, Coicaud, Jean-Marc, and Khong Foong Yen, *Power in Transition: The peaceful change of international order*, New York: United Nations University Press, 2001, pp. 1-2.

26) JIANMIN Wu, *Pour un nouveau concept de sécurité internationale*, Défense nationale, Janvier 2002, pp. 19-23. DUROURCQ Jean, *Pour de nouvelles combinaisons stratégiques*, same source, pp. 63-73.

IAC-02-IISL.4.13

U.S. EXPORT CONTROLS AND LITIGATION OF CONTRACTS: ANOTHER EXAMPLE OF THE LAW OF UNINTENDED CONSEQUENCES

F. Kenneth Schwetje, Esq.
Dennis J. Burnett, Esq.
Pierson & Burnett, L.L.P
517 South Washington Street, Alexandria, Virginia 22314
fkschwetje@comspacelaw.com djburnett@comspacelaw.com
http://www.comspacelaw.com

ABSTRACT

Lawyers engaged in aerospace matters, whether involved in high-tech complex transactions with multiple contractors and subcontractors, or involved in complex transnational litigation through national court systems or international arbitration tribunals, take for granted certain procedural rights and guarantees fundamental to due process and a fair and impartial adjudication of contracts. However, these rights and procedures cannot be taken for granted in transnational transactions because the restrictions and licensing requirements of the current export control regime of the United States can seriously impede if not frustrate normal trial and arbitration procedures. This paper reviews the conflict between the current export control regime of the United States and normal dispute resolution mechanisms and procedures. Particular attention is given to contract issues to be considered in contemplation of potential disputes in which "defense" technology transfer will be an issue. The authors also suggest some corrective measures to alleviate and minimize the conflicts between fundamental due process rights and the need to protect against unauthorized transfers of military technology.

INTRODUCTION.

The United States has the most sophisticated and complex export control system in the world. Initially designed to ensure U.S. neutrality, adapted for two world wars and then the Cold War, the system has evolved as an instrument of U.S. diplomacy--and a major problem for the aerospace industry. The implementation of the various laws and regulations governing the export and retransfer of space qualified items often result in consequences far beyond the original intent of the legislators, and on some occasions have a counter productive result.

U.S. commercial space industries are suffering as foreign satellite manufacturers and launch service providers actively seek alternatives to superior U.S. technology in an effort to avoid unpredictable delays, and sometimes denial of authorization to execute a carefully crafted business plan, due to the decisions made in the licensing process.

The U.S. State Department is not unaware, nor unfeeling, about the current situation. Within the Department of State, the Office of Defense Trade Controls works diligently to accommodate the policies of the US Government, as well as the needs of domestic and foreign industry. In cooperation with the U.S. Department of Defense, a series of initiatives have been developed to deal with the extreme cases.

EXPORT CONTROL REGIME

The *Arms Export Control Act, as amended*[i] *("AECA")* has been in place since 1968 and its predecessor legislation since the end of World War II. The AECA specifically authorizes the President of the United States to control the export and import of "defense articles and defense services" such as arms, ammunition and implements of war to protect U.S. national security and foreign policy. The Office of Defense Trade Controls ("ODTC"), in the Department of State administers the Act through implementing regulations called the International Traffic in Arms Regulations (the so called "ITAR").[ii] The ITAR contains a list of equipment considered to be arms, ammunition or implements of war. This list is called the "Munitions List" or "USML." Satellites (USML Category XV) and launch vehicles (USML Category IV) have been on the Munitions List for many years. In addition, "technical data" related to satellites and launch vehicles are also on the Munitions List.

In October 1996, the licensing responsibility for commercial communications satellites was transferred from the State Department to the U.S. Department of Commerce. The licensing requirements of the Department of Commerce were much less strict than those of the State Department. However, this transfer was to be short lived. Because of concerns in the U.S. Congress that the Commerce Department was not adequately scrutinizing satellite export licenses and because it was felt that the Department of Defense did not have an adequate role in the Department of Commerce licensing process, Congress required in *The Strom Thurmond National Defense Authorization Act of 1999*[iii] that the licensing responsibility for the communications satellites be transferred back to the State Department. In addition, special export controls were required for launch of U.S. satellites from or by countries other than NATO or major non-NATO allies of the U.S. The Act also required mandatory licensing for launch failure investigations.

This change was due in large part because in 1998, a bi-partisan investigative committee was formed in the U.S. House of Representatives, under the chairmanship of Congressman Christopher Cox (R-CA) to review the enforcement of the export control laws. The Cox Commission was formed as a result of allegations that the lax enforcement of the existing U.S. export laws had resulted in exports of critical technology without appropriate oversight and review. One of the concerns to be investigated was whether U.S. national security had been compromised by the participation of U.S. manufacturers and underwriters in the launch failure investigations for launch events involving China Great Wall Industries.

In general, the ITAR requires that no Munitions List items, including "technical data" can be exported from the United States without a prior license issued by ODTC. In addition, discussions or services involving "technical data," as defined by the ITAR, need a special prior authorization which can be granted only if the parties submit a Technical Assistance Agreement ("TAA") to ODTC for review and approval by various departments within the State Department, as well review by other U.S. government agencies such as the Department of Defense ("DOD"), NASA, and branches of the military (i.e. Navy, and Air Force).

The regulations expand the scope of the Munitions List in several respects:

- All satellites (except the International Space Station) are covered;

- All ground stations for tracking, telemetry and control ("TT&C") of satellites are covered;

- The definition of satellite components and parts has been expanded to include: satellite fuel, ground support equipment, test equipment, payload adaptor or interface hardware, replacement parts, and non-embedded solid propellant orbit transfer engines, and

- The definition of "technical data" under the ITAR has been expanded to include (for the first time): technical data provided to launch providers on form, fit, function, mass, electrical, mechanical, dynamic, environmental, telemetry safety, facility, launch pad access, and launch parameters, as well as interfaces for mating and parameters for launch.

The practical consequences of the expansion of the definition of technical data is that virtually any discussion between a U.S. services supplier and a non-U.S. services customer must be covered by an approved Technology Assistance Agreement.

Special requirements may be imposed by ODTC, such as a Technology Transfer Control Plan ("TTCP"). Furthermore, the parties to the license must arrange and pay for DOD monitoring of all discussions, as well as DOD's review of all documents to be exported.

While special requirements are not automatically imposed with regard to services provided by NATO countries or major U.S. allies, the new regulations specifically note that such requirements may be applied, when appropriate, in furtherance of the security or foreign policy of the United States.

US LITIGATION

Evidentiary and Procedural Rules

In the early days of the commercial space industry lawsuits between and among the participants were rare. Various reasons for this included the fact that NASA was often involved and required a "cross waiver of liability" form all involved; and that there was a certain club atmosphere within the industry which made it less likely that one company would make claims against another. This clubby atmosphere is changing as the commercial space segment matures and margins have decreased. Business practices typical in other sectors have become common, including the willingness to litigate.[iv]

In the past, litigants generally have been US persons within the meaning of the ITAR. Recently, the introduction of foreign plaintiffs and defendants into the US judicial system has created a problem unforeseen and unanticipated by the average litigator. The authors believe that export control issues in law suits involving controlled technology have been ignored due to a lack of awareness. Given sophisticated technical issues in a lawsuit involving space technology, it was inevitable that the issue would became part of the proceedings.

The application of the ITAR to arbitration and litigation present difficulties under the US system for civil (i.e., non-criminal) cases. At first impression, it appears that the export control regulations are inconsistent, if not in conflict with the Constitution of the United States, the Federal Rules of Civil Procedure, and the Federal Rules of Evidence. Foremost among these is the fact that no foreign person may have access to ITAR controlled technical data without the written permission of the ODTC. This includes witnesses, experts, and even the foreign clients of US law firms.

US pre-trial procedure, which is covered by the FRCP, allows the parties to gather a great deal of information in preparation for the actual trial. Many non-US attorneys are amazed at the depth and breadth of the "discovery" process. One of the features of discovery under the US system is that facts may be learned which are eventually inadmissible at trial. The discovery process certainly lengthens the judicial process, but most lawsuits are never tried because the parties are encouraged to settle when they are able to determine the relative merits of the case for all sides. Discovery also enables US lawyers to make motions before the Court prior to the trial date that are dispositive of part or all of the issues in the case. An example of this is a "Summary Judgment" in which the parties agree that no facts are in issue and the Court need only to determine the law to be applied. Another example is a Motion to Dismiss because, after conducting the discovery phase, the Court may determine that there is no case. Great latitude is required to make this system work as envisioned. When discovery begins US lawyers often do not know where discovery will lead them, what witnesses will eventually be needed for trial, and what information is material to the issues that will be tried.

In contrast, under the ITAR, a lengthy and detailed process must be completed before the exchange of US technical data is authorized. The necessary ITAR approvals have the potential for introducing delays in discovery. In addition to the impediment of not being able to discuss many aspects of the case with foreign witnesses and clients, the litigation attorneys cannot predict at the time a license is applied for at the US State Department precisely what the scope of the inquiry will be.

Constitutionally, the application of the export regulations raise many issues of fundamental fairness. The right to a trial by jury is granted by the VII Amendment to the Constitution of the United States in all common law cases in Federal courts.

The right includes the ancillary right to be present at all stages of such trial, except the deliberation of the jury.[v] However, a foreign party may be barred from testimony involving evidence of controlled data if his presence is not authorized. Likewise, a foreign expert witness may be prevented from listening to the testimony of a witness for purposes of evaluating the credibility of such, unless authorized to do so.

The litigation is conducted pursuant to the rules of the Federal Rules of Civil Procedure ("FRCP") and the Federal Rules of Evidence ("FRE"). The Federal Rules of Civil Procedure govern the procedure in the United States district courts in all suits of a civil nature. The rules are required to be construed and administered to secure the just, speedy and inexpensive determination of every action.[vi]

FRCP Rules 26 to 37 provide the legal machinery whereby the parties may learn for themselves the real points of controversy. Each party is required to disclose witness lists, document lists and expert reports[vii]. Any party has the right to examine any other party or any witness, either orally or upon written interrogatories.[viii] Any party may inspect relevant document and other tangible things in the possession of a party.[ix] The court also may compel parties to comply with the rules and impose sanctions for failure to comply.[x]

The Federal Rules of Evidence govern proceeding in the courts of the Untied States and were adopted by the United States Supreme Court [xi] Rule 615 of the FRE provides that witnesses cannot be excluded from hearing testimony in the case if they are either the representative of a party that is not a natural person or is a person whose presence is essential to the presentation of the party's case. Rule 705 provides that any expert providing testimony in the form of an opinion may be required to disclose the underlying facts or data on cross-examination.

Parties and Their Counsel

An initial problem in any litigation involving a foreign client is whether the US firm can disclose ITAR controlled data to its own client without the consent of the State Department. The troubling issue has been raised whether trial counsel are providing "defense services" to their clients by their representation, or are "exporting" technical data. Adding to the confusion is the fact that much of the information is a product of discovery, so the defendants need to be a party to any Technical Assistance Agreement; thereby allowing adverse parties to have some influence over the prosecution of the plaintiffs' case.

A seminal question is whether US law firms are "exporters" under the regulations since they would directly provide the technical data to the foreign witnesses and parties. The implication is that the law firms would then be subject to the rules and regulations administered by the ODTC for defense and aerospace contractors. This included reporting requirements, which may have been in conflict with the lawyer-client privileges; the possibility of periodic audits; and the requirement for registration with the Department of State.

Fashioning the appropriate licenses and technical assistance agreements is another difficult problem. Normally, all of the persons and organizations that will share the technical data are identified in the application to the ODTC. Since the process for approval can be lengthy and amendments take additional time, the best practice is to be as comprehensive in the initial application. For a trial attorney, this situation often reveals witnesses not immediately known to the adverse party; and may require an explanation of trial tactics far in advance of any requirements of the federal rules governing trials in US courts. Another awkward development results from the fact that all of the parties to the TAA must agree to the scope and application of the agreement submitted for approval. Litigants often have legitimate disagreement on these issues. There is always the potential that the negotiations over the TAA can be used to introduce more delay and uncertainty into the already complex litigation scenario.

As mentioned above, DoD has the right to review all documents for national security purposes and monitor discussions, which include testimony given during depositions, arbitration proceedings, or open sessions of a trial. The Defense Threat Security Agency (DTSA) has provided a monitor at hearings of arbitration tribunals and appears to be prepared to monitor any federal courtroom proceedings. This obviously presents an awkward and unusual situation for litigation attorneys and for the trial judge. While there is a procedure for government monitoring of classified testimony in federal trials, there is no statute that provides for the intervention of a DTSA official into the examination of witnesses or presentation of evidence. Unresolved issues include: (1) whether the DTSA monitor can "object" to evidence, (2) what are the consequences of notification to the Court that the evidence may be in violation of the ITAR, (3) is there any judicial review of the monitoring process, and (4) a host of other evidentiary and procedural issues.

Related to the participation of a DTSA monitor is the question of how the Court, the parties, ODTC or DTSA, guarantees that no spectator is an unauthorized recipient of the oral testimony. Under US law, most trials are open to the public and except for physical security measures no check is made of who may decide to participate as a spectator in a trial. Public trials are one of the recognized safeguards of fairness under American jurisprudence. Therefore, news reporters (who may then disseminate information further), industrial spies, and the curious are all given equal access to most proceedings. Judges and trial lawyers may therefore be surprised to learn that a U.S. trial is seen by some in the Deaprtment of defense as a potential "loophole" in the protection of national security screen for sensitive technical data.

<u>Foreign Litigation</u>

As difficult as the situation might be in the two actions described above, there is an extraterritorial aspect to the ITAR that foreign attorneys and their clients must be aware of. Arbitration often is governed by the Rules of the International Chamber of Commerce, or similar bodies. If a foreign arbitral body requires copies of testimony and exhibits, even if the arbitration is conducted in the United States and involves only U.S. parties, then the filing of the records would be considered an "export" under the generally accepted interpretation of the ITAR. The filing party or parties would need the permission of the ODTC. On a frequent basis, the ODTC will impose limitations on the handling of and access to such documents. Examples of these provisos include access being limited to the nationals of countries acceptable to the Department of State, special marking requirements, and periodic reports on the status of the file. This entire situation would also be subject to inspection by the US Department of Defense.

Even if the foreign litigation or arbitration is conducted outside the United States, solely among non-US parties and their domestic counsel, the extraterritorial aspects of the ITAR might come into play. This would be true if the information used in the proceeding included US origin data that was originally obtained by one of the parties under a US license. In order to share this information with the other parties, their counsel, and the courts the foreign party would need to request permission for re-export or retransfer from the ODTC. This could be refused or severely limited, which may violate the evidentiary or procedural rules of the nation in which the trial or arbitration is being held.

CONCLUSIONS

- The evidentiary and procedural rules for litigation and arbitration are not necessarily compatible with the export control regulations in litigation related to sophisticated technology, such as spacecraft.
- The export control laws and regulations of the United States do not contain exceptions for litigation; therefore, law firms, courts and witnesses are treated as if they are involved in the export of aerospace technical data that might present a threat to the national security of the United States.
- Lawyers and the US government should begin a dialogue with the Department of State, Department of Justice, Department of Defense to establish a means whereby the legitimate needs of national security can be met without imposing additional burdens to the trial teams and courts.
- These problems are not isolated to proceedings in the United States, or involving US parties. All attorneys in the aerospace industry must be aware of the provision of the ITAR to protect their clients from inadvertent disclosure during judicial proceedings that might result in sanction from the US government.

REFERENCES

[i] *22 USC 2778, et. seq.*

[ii] 22 CFR 120-130

[iii] *Public Law105-261*

[iv] This included litigation against the US Government space agency, NASA (*See Hughes Communications Galaxy v. The United States*) insurance litigation (*See Appalachian Insurance v. McDonnell Douglas)*; contract disputes over cross waivers *(See Martin Marietta v. INTELSAT and Certain Underwriters at Lloyds v. McDonnell Douglas Corp.)* and litigation resulting for faulty satellites (*See Lexington Insurance Co. v. McDonnell Douglas)* Cites upon request.

[v] Carlisle v. Nassau County, 408 N.Y.S. 2d 114, 64 A.D.2d 15 (1978).

[vi] FRCP, Rule 1

[vii] FRCP, Rule 26.

[viii] FRCP, Rules 27 to 33.

[ix] FRCP, Rules 34 and 35.

[x] FRCP, Rule 37.

xi Order of November 20, 1972 pursuant to authority provided by statute (Title 18 Sections 3402, 3771 and 3772 and Title 28, Sections 2072 and 2075).

LEARNING FROM THE X-PRIZE EXPERIENCE

C. HEATHER WALKER
WASHINGTON, D.C.
cheatherwalker@hotmail.com

Abstract

For several decades the space industry has dreamed of developing a reusable launch vehicle (RLV) to provide low cost access to space for human crews. Although governments traditionally sponsored these development initiatives, in 1995 a group of private investors decided to encourage development by private industry of a RLV by offering a monetary award. Aside from the obvious scientific and engineering challenges, these teams also face various non-technical challenges. Teams encountered their biggest initial non-technical challenge when seeking funding. Contest rules require competitors to secure non-governmental sponsors. To attract private investors and sponsors teams must convince them not only of the potential for success of their particular project but also that ultimately the vehicle will find a viable commercial market. Once able to develop prototypes for testing, teams must work with governmental regulatory agencies to obtain launch licenses for unproven vehicles that will ultimately carry crews. The new safety and liability issues raised by the presence of crews and the lack of governmental participation in the development raises a series of new challenges for licensing agencies. A quick review of the current experiences of participants and government officials involved reveals insights into the development of the commercial RLV industry.

Introduction

Since the inception of space programs governments and companies have envisioned the development of a completely reusable launch vehicle (RLV) that would enable frequent and reliable human space travel. Despite the recent high profile space adventures of a few private citizens, human space travel has not advanced significantly in the past few decades. Currently all human space flight occurs using the United States (US) Shuttle craft or Russian Soyez rockets; both vehicles entered into use several decades ago* and are only partially reusable. The extremely high cost per launch for these vehicles stagnated above the predicted price partly because both vehicles use expendable rockets that must be replaced or refitted prior to every launch. Also, due to the suppressed demand for launches at the current price, the economies of scale once anticipated for these space vehicles cannot be achieved.

To develop an economical alternative several countries actively support RLV development projects. For example in the US the National Aeronautical and Space Administration (NASA) participated in endeavors with private companies, military organizations and other countries to develop the numerically identified X-vehicles. The European Space Agency (ESA) began gathering support for its RLV program, Future Launch Technologies Programme (FLTP), during the 1990s, but, unfortunately, key players Britain and Germany declined to

* The US shuttle Columbia first launched on April 12, 1982, and the Russian Soyuz craft was first introduced in 1967.

join.[1] Germany declined to join because it supports a national program, as well as collaborating with NASA and the ESA on the X-38 vehicle that would serve as a crew return vehicle for the International Space Station. All of these programs experience waxing and waning support due bureaucratic and political reasons.

As government efforts to design a RLV flagged during the 1990's, a group of investors in St. Louis, Missouri originated the X-Prize. They modeled the X-Prize after the early aviation monetary awards sponsored by wealthy industrialists and companies to reward innovators who overcame specific problems or built aircraft that accomplished milestone missions.[†] The X-Prize, a monetary reward of $10 million dollars ($US), encourages private aeronautical development teams to design, build and successfully test reusable launch vehicles (RLVs) that can carry a crew into orbit and be reused. Under the conditions of the competition, the winning RLV program must fly two successful test flights, and the second launch of the vehicle must occur within fourteen days of the previous landing. The RLV will carry one person and a specified amount of ballast (demonstrating a capacity for a minimum of three adults) to an orbit of 100km (62 miles) before touching down safely. Additionally no more than 10% of the vehicles non-propellant mass may be replaced between flights. The award seeks to promote the development and flight of spaceships able to provide low-cost commercial transport of humans into space.

Currently, 20 teams have registered to compete for the X-Prize.[2] These teams are from various countries, including the US, Canada and Great Britain. The various X-Prize entrants operate at different stages of the development process. Several of the teams have prototypes for testing various aspects of the vehicle, while other still seek initial funding. The few already working with prototypes are beginning the process of getting appropriate government licenses and permits for test flights of an unproven space vehicle. Because these vehicles rely on unproven combinations of technology and launch methods the governmental agencies must adapt their current launch approval methods to accommodate new situations and concerns. The experiences of the teams in or nearing the test phase reveal interesting insights about the non-engineering issues and challenges that currently affect the development of commercial space flight vehicles.[‡] The issues discussed herein include challenges to securing financing during

---

[†] For example Charles Lindbergh won the $25,000 Orteig prize for his trans-Atlantic flight. Part of aviation's advancement and growth during its earliest years can be credited to the independent technological developments pushed by these awards.

[‡] Teams releasing current information about their projects originate in the US, Canada and Britain. While researching this paper attempts were made to contact these teams and several others. Teams from Canada and the US agreed to discuss their experiences; however, several requested that any information shared in the paper be kept anonymous. To respect their request no information is directly attributed to a specific team. Unfortunately, the British and Brazilian teams did not respond to inquiries for interviews nor do the governments make on-going licensing review information public, so the information and experience discussed focus on the experiences of Canadian and US teams. Several teams refuse to disclose any information including whether they are still actively involved in the RLV program. I would like to thank all the RLV development teams member who took time to talk with me and the government officials at Canada's LSO and the US's FAA who proved very helpful.

development, the licensing process and the current insurance situation. Finally, a few drawbacks and benefits of the X-Prize competition itself will be reviewed.

Financing for Development

Financing for infant industries often comes from the government, large financial investors or companies in related fields. The current X-Prize rules state that competitors are precluded from using a launch vehicle substantially developed under a government contract or grant.[3§] Entrants that receive direct funding, subsidies, grants of money, goods, or services from any government (or otherwise tax-supported entity) can be disqualified from the competition. Under this restriction participants in the contest must either make a strong case to the financing market for their vehicle to induce companies and investors to provide research and development financing or provide ample advertising opportunities.

Current Financing Status of Teams

The search for initial funding from private sources still dominates the project for many X-Prize registrants. Some teams seem to undergo funding drives in spurts to support particular portions of the development process, such as obtaining materials and skilled labor to build prototypes.[2] A few teams have begun promoting and even offering rides on their completed vehicle to attract funds.[2] Whether these financing difficulties reflect a dearth of financial sources or low confidence in the proposed plans that fail to secure steady backers remains to be seen. However, several teams have managed to overcome initial funding issues and appear to be able to proceed with development with adequate financial support.[2] Most of their acknowledged sponsorship comes from aerospace companies or other engineering or material suppliers. Undisclosed financing from investors may play a part in the private RLV industry, but until more information becomes publicly available this cannot be confirmed.

The Financial Case for Investing

An examination of the current demand for human space transportation and satellite launches reveals the challenges private RLV programs face in showing a future market for their product when soliciting investors. Historically, RLV developers envisioned enabling human space flight as the primary market for RLVs. However, the measurable market for crew transportation centers on measurements of the past and future needs of government space programs. Even if all government space programs began using a RLV for human space travel, these needs would not prove sufficient to justify private development. In the 1990's promoters of private RLV programs began promoting the use of RLV to launch non-geosynchronous orbit (NGSO) payloads with a specific focus on low-earth orbit (LEO) satellites. The satellite industry in the late 1990's anticipated a significant increase in the LEO launches needed per year. Unfortunately, recent developments in the satellite industry have adversely impacted the anticipated market for RLV services.[**] The limitations of these measurable markets force private RLV programs to rely on the development of a commercial space tourism industry.

Government-procured launches for human crews have high actual and opportunity cost because most government space agencies work within the constraints of a limited budget. Governments initially

[§] The current rules are considered tentative and will be confirmed once all funding of the $10 million dollar prize has been secured.

[**] Specifically the LEO launch market was adversely impacted by the demise and downsizing of several LEO satellite communications systems.

began developing RLVs anticipating that economies of scale and being able to amortize the cost over numerous yearly flights would reduce the cost of launches to a fraction of their current price making research in space more budgetable. Even though several governments directly finance development of their own RLV, investors and developers of private RLVs believe that governments could be induced to use a private RLV provider or purchase a privately designed RLV to meet crew launch needs if the RLV achieves the cost per flight goals.

In fact, the United States signaled it would be receptive to paying for a private vehicle when NASA terminated its X-33 and X-34 programs in the spring of 2001 due to the private contractors determined that the commercial launch market would not support their continued development investments.[4] At that time NASA announced a new program, the Strategic Launch Initiative (SLI), that shifted its involvement in the development work from active participant and partner in developing a RLV that meets NASA mission needs to sponsor through awarding contracts to private companies.[5] However, NASA envisions a limited role for the RLV. Using the RLV as a supplement to the Shuttle fleet to allow for increased flexibility in mission planning and provide an emergence space access vehicle. Even if other governments prove equally receptive, governmental budgets cannot immediately accommodate new expenses. Unless funds already budgeted for use on RLV development can be shifted to pay for immediate flights using a private RLV, this market will not develop until several years after the vehicle becomes commercially available. For example, Britain's current space objectives drove it to decline participating in the ESA's optional RLV program, so it has not allocated funds for crew launches in the near future. Therefore, unless governments change their current space flight plans to use the RLV as the primary space access vehicle and increase the anticipated number of space flights a year the government market demand for a private RLV service cannot support the cost of development.

While the satellite industry does not require a vehicle with the particular characteristics of a RLV, it would be interested in any proven, low cost access to launch services.[6] Launch companies currently use expendable launch vehicles (ELV) to satisfy the market needs for satellite launches. Developments over the past several decades increased the success rate of ELV launches while lowering the cost. To compete with ELV cost for satellite launches, RLV programs must focus on the niche launch market of NGSO payloads. Because of the high cost of using the powerful rockets often associated with ELVs to deliver light GEO payloads or short distance LEO payloads this market offers the greatest potential for RLVs to achieve an economic advantage.

The current market analysis does not look promising for RLV initiatives that plan to rely on the satellite market to recover development cost. A recent study by the Air Force's Developmental Planning Directorate at the Space and Missile Systems Center concluded that future RLVs would have to launch almost 40 payloads of 30,000 pounds (13,600 kilograms) each and upwards of 160 payloads of 10,000 pounds (4,536 kilograms) each per year to reach their "investment break-even" mark.[7] Clearly, this results in a capacity for which the satellite industry does not have demand. Additionally, the failure of several companies that were expected to increase the demand for LEO flights to launch communications satellites have further eroded this market.[8]

An untapped and unmeasurable market for RLV services exists in the budding tourist industry. Recent flights by private citizens at incredibly high cost rekindled the average armchair astronaut's dream of going into space. Unfortunately, this market cannot currently be quantifiably measured to ensure it will support investment in the design and development of a private RLV. RLV teams seeking to inspire investors draw on examples, such as the computer market. Several decades ago only governments and large corporations could afford computers, but technological innovations and innovative designs made computers available to the average consumer.

Fortunately, several investors appear willing to take a risk that the demand for RLV will develop. Several X-Prize teams obtained financial support from private investors or space industry corporations.[2] The exact amount of support from the various sponsors remains undisclosed, but at least three teams appear to have sufficient funds to allow them to develop prototypes for testing and have begun the preliminary licensing discussions for test launches.

Licensing Unmanned and Manned Test Flights

Teams from five different countries have registered for the X-Prize competition.[2] These X-Prize entrants who have advanced sufficiently to approach government agencies about licensing needs originate in the US, Canada and Britain. To date no one has plans for their vehicle to embark and return to different countries, therefore, each team deals with only one country during this process. Each team faces a slightly different regulatory process each with different advantages and disadvantages.

The licensing and permitting government agencies in each country primarily focus on protecting public safety during a launch. The current international liability regime places the burden for damages related to launch accidents on the launching state.[9] Therefore, government officials review the proposed launch and return flight plan to determine if applicants successfully minimize the probable losses to third parties from a launch accident and carry sufficient third-party liability insurance. Usually the launch vehicle providers and the launching facility sign cross-waivers, so the governments do not need to address the risk faced by the parties involved. RLV launch risks undergo additional scrutiny because the launch involves a landing and, ultimately, a crew.

Identifying Launch Risk

When considering a launch three readily identifiable risk to third parties must be evaluated.[6] First is the potential damage resulting from the vehicle impact during a crash. Depending on altitude achieved and the range of particle debris this could affect a relatively large area. Second, the risk of fire and explosion increases depending on the fuels used. Several proposed RLVs utilize explosive propellants and their payloads often would contain additional sources of explosive materials.[6] The amount of risk from these materials diminishes as the launch progresses and fuels are consumed. Finally, some materials and fuels used by RLVs and in payloads may be carcinogenic or toxic.[6] The resulting debris from a fire or crash would pose contamination risk to the impact area or non-consumed fuels could spread to contaminate areas not affected by the initial impact. Most licensing governments already posses a detailed methodology for evaluating these types of risks from previous experiences in licensing ELV launches.

Government officials anticipate additional concerns will need to be addressed when licensing a RLV launch. The unique considerations for a RLV launch center on the risk associated the landing and the presence of a crew. The risk calculation for a landing may account for the same factors but must be done separately, because velocities and the presence of explosive fuels or payloads would result in different calculated risk levels. The more problematic evaluation revolves around crew safety. Technically the crew does not qualify as a third party, however agency officials expressed that they would expect applicants to include information documenting the safety measures taken to provide for crew survivability if an accident were to occur.

United States: The teams operating in the United States obtain permits according to the rules established by the Federal Aviation Administration's (FAA) Associate Administrator for Commercial Space Transportation (AST).[10] All RLV launches need a mission specific license that evaluates safety risk based upon the design of the specific vehicle for identified launch and re-entry sites (including a possible alternative re-entry site).[††] AST issues a commercial space launch license when it determines that the proposed launch and reentry does not threaten public health and safety, the safety of property, national security or foreign policy interest.[11]

The licensing process involves a pre-application consultation, the formal application review and compliance monitoring. The pre-application review period does not have a time limit but exists to provide the applicant and the FAA a chance to ensure the application provides sufficient information for the FAA to complete its reviews and evaluations. Once the FAA accepts an application for review US statute mandates that the review be completed within 180 days. The complete application evaluation consists of a policy review, a safety review, a payload review, a determination of financial responsibility, and an environmental review.[11] Each stage in the review requires an independent approval before moving on to the next part of the application review. The rules and regulations give very specific instructions about the data needed in the application and the safety thresholds that must be met.[11] Most applicants appreciate the transparency of the review guidelines because it provides structure and allows them to anticipate potential problems in gaining final approval.

In the United States the licensing procedure places the burden on the applicant to demonstrate that the proposed flight missions meets all safety requirements.[11] Because of the judgment calls associated with providing this data for unproven vehicles, this part of the application process could easily be used to hinder a RLV developer's attempts to obtain a launch license for testing purposes. In the past such ventures often faced skepticism inside the government, as well as from private sources approached for funding and support. The natural progression of the private RLV industry was expected to follow that of the development and testing of a vehicle by or under the auspices of a government agency. A government developed vehicle seeking commercial launching authority would be able to demonstrate a proven success record and could provide information on the a variety of risk factors that now must be estimated by the applicant and agency. However, RLV developers dealing with the FAA indicate their expectations for private RLV development appears to be shifting.

In recent agency rule-makings the AST office worked with industry representatives to craft the launch application's requirements and develop

[††] The FAA does not release filed applications for public review, but does release environmental and final licensing information. To date no information indicates that any X-Prize competitors have filed a launch application. However, Kistler Aerospace Corporation apparently has an application pending to test a two-stage RLV at the Nevada Test Site. A final launch license has not yet been granted.

methods for calculating potential launch risk for RLVs.[‡‡] On September 19, 2000 the Federal Register published the final Commercial Space Transportation Reusable Launch Vehicle and Reentry Licensing Regulations.[12] Additionally, a recent Advisory Circular (Circular) provided information that will allow RLV launch applicants to submit an application for test launches that undergo a streamlined review process.[13] In the Circular the AST clarified that an operator does not need to have complete vehicle capabilities to be licensed as long as the vehicle meets the criteria of a RLV and the definition of a launch.[§§] The Circular stated that licenses are not given for test flights specifically, but could be obtained for a serious of mission flights where the vehicle operates at lower than maximum performance capabilities or flight for purposes other than design reference missions. The Circular then proceeded to explain a particular methodology for showing the vehicles fitness for flight and its satisfaction of safety requirements that would result in a streamlined application review. Any licenses issued under this review would have tailored and limited authority but would allow testing to proceed.[13] The major condition placed on applicants attempting to meet these streamlined requirements limited the testing range to remote or sparsely populated areas.

<u>Canada:</u> The teams operating in Canada work with the Launch Safety Office(LSO) at Transport Canada.[14] The LSO issues launch authorization when satisfied that adequate measures are in place to ensure the safety of the launch. The Canadian licensing process is not as meticulously outlined in regulations as the US procedures; however, it generally follows a similar pre-application review period before the filing of a final application. During the pre application review the LSO authorities ensure that the launch proposal has sufficiently considered all risk and implemented adequate safety precautions and procedures. During this period the LSO can provide additional information for the launch applicant to include or consider. The process truly resembles a partnership in creating a mission plan that meets the safety requirements than a judging of the information provided. While US companies openly expressed concerns about the potential arbitrariness of the informal pre-review process, no Canadian counterpart shared this concern. In fact the LSO authorities were commended on their willingness to work with teams and generally positive support for RLV endeavors.

The test licenses currently under discussion require a safety analysis substantially similar to a license for an ELV launch. How the LSO will address the additional safety concerns surrounding a crew in the RLV cannot be determined from this experience. Whether the final licenses needed for RLV test launches will contain restrictions or be granted quickly remains to be seen. However, given the overall positive experience RLV developers have enjoyed working with the LSO any extra scrutiny of safety related to the presence of a crew should not be a major stumbling block.

[‡‡] New laws directly addressing the development of a private RLV necessitated the rule-makings. During the rule-making process industry participants expressed concern with the inclusion of 14 CFR 431.11, which allows the FAA to place terms and conditions on a RLV mission license to ensure compliance with the safety rules. Developers objected on the grounds that this provision allowed for harassment and capriciousness in the licensing process.[12] To date this provision has not been a problem.

[§§] Generally, to be a RLV a vehicle or concept must have recoverable parts that are reused in later launches and must return to a reentry site on a planned trajectory.

Availability of Insurance

Licensing countries generally require private launch licensees to carry an amount of third-party insurance that will cover most of the estimated potential third party losses in case of an accident. In 2001 the typical amount of third-party liability insurance required fell in the $100 million-$300 million (US$) range.[15] The premium for typical third-party launch liability insurance was estimated to be in the range of $100,000 to $400,000 per launch.[15] Several events have occurred since this survey that dramatically increased the cost of insurance.

Within the past year insurance markets have experienced problems due to increased risk of exposure and economic problems. The aviation insurance market encountered more problems than most due to security issues and several pending large liability claims. However, Insurance policies for space launches represent a small fraction of the aviation insurance market. In fact a FAA study estimates that the amount of third-party liability insurance premiums collected for commercial space launches represent only about 0.1 percent of all aerospace insurance premiums.[15] Brokers for launch insurance generally use several underwriters to provide the overall policy coverage. The underwriters then tend to reinsure to insulate themselves from losses. This process spreads the risk. Prior to September 11, 2001, it was estimated that about $1 to $1.5 billion of capacity per launch is available for third-party liability insurance.[15] The capacity fluctuates with the general health of the aerospace insurance market. Because of the large losses experienced by the aerospace insurance market this capacity decreased to $500 million by February 2002.[15] An increase in premiums accompanied the contraction. By February 2002 premiums increased by 50 to 400 percent depending on the loss record of the insured and the risk aversion of the specific underwriters involved.[15] The launch liability niche may be partly insulated from some of the adverse impacts because exclusions for war risk or terrorism have appeared in the launch liability insurance certificates for years. Fortunately, government officials reported that no companies seeking launch authority have reported being unable to find and afford the required amount of insurance yet.

Benefits of the X-Prize Contest

With the availability of private and government financing for RLV projects the need for the X-Prize may be questioned. While, many people would be thrilled to win a ten million dollar prize, for most commercial space flight projects this award covers only a fraction of their budget to develop and get the RLV to market. So motivates teams to enter the X-Prize competition? The answer to this question is varied. Realistically most teams did not undertake this endeavors to win the monetary award. Most people become involved in these projects because they believe they can make money while developing an industry that excites the mind and spirit by pushing the limits of scientific and engineering accomplishment. Therefore it is fair to say the X-Prize more likely rewards innovation rather than encouraging it.

However, the prize provides benefits to participants despite not being the motivating factor behind the projects. First the X-Prize provides an immediately available source of positive publicity to the public and potential investors. Second, the contest defines a milestone based on the scientific accomplishment rather than financial returns to measure success. Finally, the X-Prize promises an infusion of cash when the development teams must shift focus from design the vehicle to development of a commercially viable company.

The X-Prize organization through its website and media activities provides a centralized source of information for the general public. By providing brief summaries and contact information on most registrants the X-Prize organization supplies the public with an easy way to identify groups developing commercial space flight technology and follow their progress. The contest gives the lengthy process of design and development an interesting hook to keep people's attention. But mostly importantly the publicity provides positive attention to help attract investors. Given the challenges of attracting financial support to develop a commercial vehicle for an unproven space travel market, the existence of the X-Prize enhances the argument that the space tourism industry will develop to support these endeavors. Many teams benefited from the added legitimacy provided by the contest when attracting sponsors. Further the constant publicity provides a channel through which the sponsor can be assured that they will receive a certain amount of advertising in return for sponsorship.

The X-Prize also provides a definition of success. As industries develop goals must constantly be moved to keep driving development. Because the focus remains on the next step, or next advance, people often feel that significant mid-project accomplishments fail to be rewarded. The X-Prize provides a point in the development of the commercial space flight industry when the attention of the public and the industry will be focused on appreciating and rewarding the accomplishments achieved thus far. The X-Prize also helps to counteract the tendency of commercial ventures to focus solely on fiscal accomplishments as the measure of success.

Finally the monetary reward does provide an incentive to meet the flight requirements outlined by the X-Prize rules. The monetary reward provides a guaranteed influx of capital at a pivotal business stage in the development of a commercially viable RLV company. Once the vehicle successfully completes test flights and then the group must begin to focus on making the transition from research project to launch market participant. To begin to market and produce more than just test prototypes, additional capital will needed. How successfully any team accomplishes this transition ultimately depends upon management skills, but the prize provides a stepping stone at a crucial time in the development of a viable company.

Drawbacks of the X-Prize Contest

For all the benefits of the X-Prize contest several drawbacks must be acknowledged due to the nature of competition and the structure of the rules. From the outside the most frustrating result of the prize has been the unwillingness of some participants to discuss their RLV projects. For the entrants the most frustrating limitation of the contest may prove to be the restriction against receiving government funds.

Competition can bring out the worst in people. Unfortunately, several of the teams contacted were hesitant to discuss anything related to the project. The competitive nature of the experience caused some teams to absolutely refuse to talk about their experiences, even once it was made clear to them that proprietary information was not sought. There may have been additional explanations for people's hesitancy to discuss their work and experiences, but everyone gave the competition as their reason for remaining silent. The inability to learn more from the experiences restricts the ability of financiers and government agencies to respond to the needs of the infant industry.

The X Prize organization states that the financing restrictions serve to exclude government-sponsored vehicles from the competition. However this blanket restriction may be remarkably short-sighted. The X-Prize organization does not explain how excluding teams that accept government funds promotes the development of a RLV for low-cost transport into space. For instance, some government programs, including the SLI, may allow any company to submit proposals and do not control or actively participate in the design stage. A RLV developed by a private company using these government funds would be available for private ventures. In promoting the development of a commercially available low-cost vehicle there may be no notable differences between government grants and corporate grants. NASA's SLI program began after many of the United States teams had registered for the contest. At least one registered X-Prize participant, Kelly Space & Technology may already be disqualified, as it received a SLI contract. Given the unpredictable future market for a RLV restricting access to funds appears unrealistic. RLV teams need to be able to accept funding from any source willing to support their work.

Many aspects of interpreting this rule could prove to be problematic. The rule claims it intends to exclude projects substantially developed under government sponsorship but fails to address the fact that government sponsorship could be funneled through a private company supporting the team. If the rule means to ban teams that access government technology or assistance then the rule should look at the assistance sponsoring corporations that work on space related projects with government agencies. Some of the participants enjoying the backing of large aerospace companies may have access to technology obtained through government projects that are not available to the general public. The rule also fails to consider that just because a government provides financing does not make the project a government-sponsored vehicle. The lack of control and direct participation in the project could mitigate any advantage from receiving government funds compared to receiving funds from any other source.

Additionally, the rule fails to tie its financial restriction to the ultimate goal of promoting a commercially available vehicle that allows for low cost space access. The large sponsoring companies might agree to support the development stages in return for sole access to any technology developed or place future sale restrictions on the vehicle.*** A restriction more consistent with the stated goal of the X-Prize might eliminate teams who accept finding from sources that try to control the development process, discriminate on factors other than feasibility of the proposal or place limitations on who may use the final product.

Conclusion

While the X-Prize may not be the driving factor behind the development of a RLV its has galvanized the community by focusing positive public and investor attention on this burgeoning industry. Even with positive community support the greatest challenge facing the participants, aside from any engineering and scientific problems, arises when seeking financial support. Making the case for a future market cannot rely solely on traditional market measures, so investors and sponsors must be induced to make a leap of faith or consider support merely a current advertising expense. Experience shows that while not all teams will successfully gain funding, there are sources of financing available. And once financed the current regulatory environment does not hinder launching an unproven vehicle.

*** These scenarios are all speculative. Because support agreements are not disclosed this type of information cannot be obtained at this time.

[1] ESA website at http://www.esa.int/export/esaLA/GGGMRJF3KCC_index_0.html and http://www.esa.int/export/esaLA/ESA95SG18ZC_index_0.html.

[2] The X-Prize website provides a list of teams accompanied by short descriptions of their proposals and links to entrants websites at http://www.xprize.com/teams/teams.html. Some of the more informative websites used to gather information on team activities include http://www.bristolspaceplanes.com/, http://www.canadianarrow.com/, http://www.kellyspace.com/, http://www.starchaser.co.uk/, http://www.davinciproject.com.

[3] X-Prize Competition Guidelines at http://www.xprize.com/teams/guidelines.html (last checked September 29, 2002).

[4] NASA News Release 01-31, March 1, 2001.

[5] *The Space Launch Initiative: Technology to pioneer the space frontier,* NASA Fact Sheet, FS-2002-04-87-MSFC, April 2002, http://www1.msfc.nasa.gov/NEWSROOM/background/facts/slifactstext.html last visited September 28, 2002)

[6] FAA and DOT *Liability Risk-Sharing Regime For U.S. Commercial Space Transportation: Study and Analysis*, Section 7.3.2 (April 2002).

[7] *Advanced Space Lift Architecture Study,* Directorate of Developmental Planning, *SMC/X*R, Space and Missile Systems Center, Los Angeles Air Force Base, Los Angeles, CA, April 2001.

[8] *The Space Launch Initiative: Technology to Pioneer the Space Frontie*r, NASA Fact Sheet, FS 2001-02-43-MSFC, January 2002, p. 3.

[9] United States Treaty, 1972, Convention on International Liability for Damage Caused by Space Objects, March 29 (24 U.S.T. 2389, T.I.A.S. 7762).

[10] 49 USC, Subtitle IX, Chapter 701 – Commercial Space Launch activities ; Commercial Space Transportation Competitiveness Act of 2000 (H.R. 2607/P.L. 106-405).

[11] 14 CFR §400-435.

[12] Fed. Reg., Vol. 65, No. 182, p. 56618-56667 (September 19, 2000).

[13] Advisory Circular, Licensing Test Flight Reusable Launch Vehicle Missions, AC 431.35-3, August, 2002.

[14] Transport Canada is responsible for rocket launch activities by virtue of the *Aeronautics Act*, which in Section 4. (1) and 4.9(w) authorizes the creation of the *Canadian Aviation Regulations*. LSO issues permits pursuant to the requirements of CAR 602.44.

[15] FAA and DOT *Liability Risk-Sharing Regime For U.S. Commercial Space Transportation: Study and Analysis*, Appendix D, D-2 (April 2002).

THE LUNAR BASE: LIABILITY IN PERSPECTIVE

Kenneth M. Weidaw III, Esq.
Kenneth M. Weidaw III & Associates
Pittsburgh, Pennsylvania U.S.A.
kweidaw@cobweb.net

ABSTRACT

Continuing exploration of the Moon will include the eventual construction of a lunar base for scientific research, solar power development and mining of surface and subsurface mineral resources. To embark on a major, long-term commercial enterprise, the private international consortium must first address its probably liability for acts of negligence committed by its employees against co-workers and others. Until appropriate commercial liability insurance is secured, the private consortium will be effectively unable to conduct business in this most challenging enterprise. This paper briefly discusses the most significant liability problems with which the consortium will have to deal as interpreted under the provisions of the Outer Space Treaty of 1967, the Moon Treaty, the Commercial Space Launch Activities, as amended, and the regluations promulgated by the U.S. Department of Transportation, enforced by the Federal Aviation Administration relating to the: (1) launch of space vehicles from the Earth destined for the Moon; (2) the robotic surface rover exploration of the lunar surface for sample return and lunar base site selection; (3) the initial human exploration of the lunar surface for lunar base site preparation and temporary occupancy; and (4) the construction of the first lunar base facility.

Finally, we explore the need for a new international treaty that clarifies the significant liability challenges faced by the future private international consortium when planning, organizing and financing the long duration program leading to lunar base development. A strong recommendation is made for limiting the liability of the private consortium to assure completion of the long-term development program. Absent clear, definitive guidance, scientific research and commercial development of lunar resources will prove exceedingly difficult and too costly.

INTRODUCTION

The private international consortium undertaking the long-term lunar base development project must fully examine and deal with both personal and property liability issues.

To address the significant, foreseeable liability issues, it is first necessary to outline a realistic prototype lunar base development project – describing its phases and what is to be accomplished during each phase. We will then separately examine each phase of the overall project addressing some of the significant liability issues that may affect the private consortium, its contractors, subcontractors, and others associated with the project.

In addressing these issues, we will assume that the launch location is within the jurisdiction of the United States of America; therefore, we will discuss the liability issues as they relate to extant international treaties, and statutes and regulations of the United States of America. The consortium would, however, fully examine the benefits and drawbacks of launching from another state offering comparable launch facilities and infrastructure to those found in the United States.

The phases of the lunar base development project described below are based on certain assumptions that we now have sufficient engineering skills and hardware available with which to undertake and complete the project. Given the many lessons learned from Project Apollo and numerous NASA projects and studies undertaken since 1968 on lunar base development, this is a project that can be accomplished.

THE PROTOTYPE LUNAR BASE DEVELOPMENT PROJECT

The phases of the lunar base development project are set forth below. After a brief outline of each of the four phases, we will examine each of them with respect to liability concerns to determine whether current laws, regulations and insurance industry practices now provide adequate protection. There are numerous management and engineering liability concerns not mentioned below in the four phases; they are intentionally omitted due to limitations on the size and scope of this paper. However, they must all be addressed and resolved by the consortium. Unanticipated liability concerns will arise throughout the project and will have to be resolved to insure completion of the lunar base.

PHASE I. DEVELOPMENT AND PLANNING THE MISSION

The goal of this phase is to accomplish the following objectives: formation of the private international consortium; planning the overall project; determining the launch site location; securing funding for the long-term project; determining the need for further mapping of the lunar surface to locate a base site; deciding whether to use robotic lunar rovers to explore a few potential base sites; determining liability exposure and then securing liability insurance coverage for Phases I, II and III and planning for insurance coverage for the missions to follow; determining the contractors and subcontractors that will provide the management, engineering and scientific services throughout the project; determining the hardware that will be required, such as, the rockets and launch systems and lunar base construction materials, construction machinery and equipment; training pilots, flight engineers and lunar base construction contractors; securing regulatory approvals to move forward with the mapping mission, the robotic, cargo and human missions to the Moon.

The only successful lunar transportation system to date was the Apollo system. It is no longer available. A new transportation system must be developed before the installation of a lunar base can occur. The concept selected for lunar base development will depend strongly on the size of the lunar base envisioned, on the length of the life cycle chosen, and on the mission profile selected.[1] Various lunar missions modes are available; for example, for cargo delivery

[1] PETER ECKART, ed., THE LUNAR BASE HANDBOOK 190 (1999)

missions, a direct one-way mission can be selected; or a one-way mission with lunar orbit staging.[2] The mission profiles will vary depending upon the launch vehicles used and the goal of each mission. For the purpose of examining the liability that a consortium might incur, a familiar crewed mission profile used in the Apollo program has been chosen. It involves: A launch from Earth into an Earth parking orbit; trans-lunar injection (TLI); establishment of a lunar parking orbit; Earth return vehicle remains in lunar orbit; landing vehicle desends to the lunar surface; landing vehicle ascends from the lunar surface; lunar orbit rendezvous (LOR) with the Earth return vehicle; trans-Earth injection (TEI); reentry of crew and cargo directly from a trans-Earth trajectory.[3]

PHASE II. LAUNCH MAPPING AND ROBOTIC MISSIONS

A lunar base site must be located during this phase. At least one mapping mission may be required to provide topographical and compositional data of the potential base site. One and possibly two robotic lunar rover missions, including a lunar sample mission, will provide considerable scientific data concerning the sites, such as the composition of the lunar soil for mining purposes and base construction. This phase does not include a human mission.

PHASE III. CARGO DELIVERY MISSIONS TO BASE SITE

With a base site located, construction materials and equipment must be safely delivered to the site. This phase does not involve a human mission.

2 *Id.* at 180-189

3 *Id.* at 182

PHASE IV. EARLY HUMAN MISSIONS TO BASE SITE

Construction engineers trained to work in the lunar environment must now be delivered to the base site to promptly assemble the first lunar base from the components using the machinery previously delivered to the site. The engineering specialists must assemble the primary base components – prepare living quarters, the water and oxygen generating facilities, communications facilities, activate the nuclear or solar power plant, prepare the protective shielding of all facilities, activate scientific equipment providing data needed at this early stage of base development and conduct necessary studies for future mining operations, undertake scientific studies and monitor scientific equipment for private industry and governments. During this phase, there is concern with problems that could develop involving the operation of a nuclear power plant providing electricity for the base, as well as protection and shielding for the base occupants from solar flares and meteoroids as well as damage to the equipment and scientific instruments. The missions anticipated during this phase are of a short-term nature. More than one human mission is anticipated to accomplish the base assembly work.

LIABILITY CONCERNS – PHASE I. DEVELOPMENT AND PLANNING THE MISSIONS

During this phase of development, liability concerns are determined by state and federal laws and regulations and certain international treaties entered into by the United States applicable to international business entities entering outer space.

The first concerns relate to the creation and financing of the private international consortium. The consortium will be composed of private companies and persons joining together for the common purpose of returning to the Moon motivated by commercial opportunities, particularly for the extraction of Helium-3 and other resources. Those forming the consortium must demonstrate to others that the opportunities for a return on investment are realistic, capable of being achieved. The consortium partners must be convinced that the legal regime under which they will operate – both on Earth, in orbit and on the lunar surface – will be beneficial to them. They will want to know the extent of their potential singular and collective liability throughout the duration of the long-term lunar base development project. Next, they will need to know whether there exists adequate insurance coverage to protect themselves and their companies in the likely event of death, injury and destruction or damage to property.

Some of the consortium partners will directly contribute hardware and engineering services to the project. As such, they will be governed by liability laws in force in their states. Consequently, the consortium will be compelled to consider potential liability in those states in which their consortium partners conduct business. Broad liability insurance coverage must be provided by a consortium of insurance companies. Given the high coverage limits and potential exposure of the partners, insurance companies must join together to provide coverage for death, injury, workers' compensation and damage to and destruction of property.

Phase I includes development of the business plan and securing regulatory approvals before going forward with the remainder of the ambitious project. Projects involving citizens of the United States or if the launch site is within its jurisdiction, the consortium will be required to work closely with the United States Department of Transportation ("DOT") and particularly with the Federal Aviation Administration (the "FAA"). Consortium partners not citizens of the United States may be supervised by their governments, perhaps under an intergovernmental agreement. International treaty law plays an important role in the affairs of the consortium.

The provisions of the Treaty on Principals Governing the Activities of States in the Exploration and Use of Outer Space, Including the Moon and Other Celestial Bodies, known as the Outer Space Treaty of 1967, become important in that they require specific actions by each State Party signing the treaty. Article VI requires that a State Party "shall require authorization and continuing supervision by the appropriate State Party to the Treaty." Therefore, the United States, in compliance with its international duties, must both authorize (by issuing and controlling launch licenses) and continually supervise the activities of the consortium (a "non-governmental entity"). Failure or negligence in complying with these duties subjects the United States to "international liability for damage to another State Party to the Treaty or to its natural or juridical persons by such object or its components on the Earth, in air space or in outer space…including the Moon…."[4] The Treaty goes on to state in Article VIII that the State Party retains jurisdiction and control over the "object and over any personnel thereof, while in outer space or on a celestial body." Given the foregoing mandates, the United States must exercise some control and oversight of the consortium from the outset of the project. Legislation to accomplish some of this task has been in force since the enactment of the former Commercial Space Launch Act of 1984.

[4] Outer Space Treaty, Article VII, 18 U.S.T. 2410, 610 U.N.T.S. 205, T.I.A.S. No. 6347 (entered into force October 10, 1967).

The consortium partners must be mindful of the requirements of 49 U.S.C. Subtitle IX, Chapter 701 – Commercial Space Launch Activities, formerly the Commercial Space Launch Act of 1984, as amended (the "CSLA") and the regulations promulgated by DOT.

REGULATORY COMPLIANCE ISSUES

Under the CSLA, the Secretary of Transportation is, among other things, to "oversee and coordinate the conduct of commercial launch and reentry operations, issue and transfer commercial launch licenses authorizing those operations, and protect the public health and safety, safety of property, and national security and foreign policy interests of the United States."[5] The Secretary is required to encourage, facilitate and promote commercial space launches and reentries by the private sector[6] as well as issue procedures for requesting launch and reentry licenses.[7]

The consortium will have to address numerous liability concerns of the FAA from the inception of its work. The jurisdiction of the FAA extends to "Earth orbit in outer space; or otherwise in outer space."[8] The author has been advised by a FAA legal representative that currently jurisdiction extends to Earth orbit only. Nevertheless, the consortium must be prepared to address safety and liability concerns of the FAA outside of Earth orbit due to the provision "…otherwise in outer space"[9] and the jurisdiction and control provisions in Article VIII of the Outer Space Treaty. It must be anticipated that the FAA will exert its jurisdiction past Earth orbit – indeed, onto the lunar surface - when it becomes expedient to do so. Continued FAA involvement and oversight may be a welcome development by the insurance carriers.

The Secretary is authorized to issue a launch license for launch and reentry[10] but may "…prevent the launch if the Secretary decides the launch would jeopardize the public health and safety, safety of property…."[11] To satisfy the regulations, the consortium must submit a completed application for launch license to the Secretary of Transportation. The FAA staff and other departments that have safety and political concerns (the most apparent being NASA, Department of State and Defense Department) must carefully examine it.[12] The Department of Transportation must carry out its duties consistent with international treaty obligations as well as take into account applicable foreign laws and regulations.[13] To ensure safety and reduce liability concerns, the FAA must assess the flight risk through orbital insertion as well as identify hazards.[14] The consortium must prepare an analysis that identifies "hazards and assesses risks to public health and safety…."[15] An accident plan will have to be prepared and submitted to the FAA.[16] Next, a payload review will be conducted by the FAA.[17] Since the FAA must comply with Article IV of the 1975 Convention on Registration of Objects Launched into Outer Space, the consortium

---

5 49 U.S.C. Section 70101(b)(3) and 14 CFR Parts 413 and 415
6 *Id.* at Section 70103 (b)
7 *Id.* at Section 70120
8 *Id.* at Section 70102(3)
9 *Id.* at Section 70102(3)(C)

10 *Id.* at Section 70104(a)(1), 14 CFR Parts 413 and 415
11 *Id.* at Section 70104(c)
12 *Id.* at Sections 70105(a) and 70109(b), 14 CFR 415.23 and 415.31
13 *Id.* at Section 70117(e)
14 14 CFR 415.35
15 *Id.* at 415.35
16 *Id.* at 415.41
17 *Id.* at 415.51

must provide the requested information.[18] Finally, the environmental impact associated with the proposed launches is also reviewed by the FAA.[19] The environmental impact of base construction and resource extraction may also be reviewed by the FAA although such a review process does not now exist.

During the early stages of launch vehicle construction, launch site selection and planning, United States Government employees or officers may act as observers (monitors) at the production facilities or at the assembly site a contractor of the consortium uses to produce or assemble the launch vehicles.[20] The observer will monitor the activity of the consortium or its contractors to the extent deemed necessary by the Secretary. The consortium will be required to cooperate with the observer.[21] Suspension or revocation of the launch license may occur if the consortium fails to "comply substantially" with the requirements of the launch license or the requirements of applicable law.[22] Public health and safety concerns are of primary importance – in addition to political concerns voiced by the international community and domestic government agencies.[23]

If a reusable launch vehicle is used, it must comply with additional regulations.[24] There exists a strong possibility that the consortium will use a non-reuseable reentry vehicle for the robotic (sample return) mission and may do so for the crewed missions. Therefore, close attention must be paid to the regulations governing the issuance of a license to reenter a reentry vehicle other than a reusable launch vehicle.[25] Special attention must be given to the FAA-conducted payload reentry determination.

Of great importance to the consortium is the setting of insurance coverage limits by the FAA. The Secretary of Transportation must determine the maximum probable loss to third parties and the United States Government associated with the consortium's lunar base development plans.[26] After the launch and reentry license is issued, the consortium must obtain liability insurance coverage or demonstrate financial responsibility in amounts to compensate for the "maximum probable loss" (defined as "the greatest dollar amount of loss for bodily injury or property damage that is reasonably expected to result from licensed launch activities.")[27] from claims by a third party for death, bodily injury or property damage or filed by the United States Government.[28] The coverage limits are set by the Secretary. The CSLA provides that for one launch, the consortium will not be required to obtain insurance of more than $500,000,000 for liability to third parties and no more than $100,000,000 for liability to the United States Government; and, if the world insurance market cannot support such limits, then the consortium must obtain the "maximum liability insurance coverage available on the world market at reasonable cost if the amount is less than $500,000,000."[29] The limits are subject, however, to adjustment on an annual basis.[30] If adequate coverage is unavailable on the world market, the consortium may request a waiver of the license terms or petition for rulemaking if market conditions make compliance impossible.[31]

---

18 *Id.* at 415.81
19 *Id.* at 415.101 and 103
20 49 U.S.C. at Section 70106
21 *Id.* at Section 70106(a)
22 *Id.* at Sections 70107(c) and 70108(a)
23 *Id.* at Section 70107(c)(2)
24 14 CFR Part 431
25 *Id.* at 435.1-435.43

26 49 U.S.C. Section 70112(c)
27 14 CFR 440.3(11)
28 49 U.S.C. Section 70112(a)(1)
29 49 U.S.C. Section 70112(a)(3), 14 CFR 440.9
30 49 U.S.C. Section (d)(2)
31 Department of Transportation: Responsibility Requirements for Licensed

Insurance coverage must remain in full force and effect for the period of time specified by the FAA.[32]

The contractors, subcontractors and customers of the consortium must also have insurance coverage.[33]

Finally, the FAA will require the consortium to "make a reciprocal waiver of claims with its contractors, subcontractors and customers… involved in launch services under which each party to the waiver agrees to be responsible for property damage or loss it sustains or for personal injury to, death of, or property damage or loss sustained by its own employees resulting from activity carried out by the licensee."[34] The intent of requiring reciprocal waivers is to limit the cost of managing launch risks by restricting litigation among launch participants and to protect the commercial launch industry from the risk of catastrophic losses from third party liability claims.[35]

Close adherence to the license requirements is demanded by the FAA. Civil and possible criminal penalties await those who violate the terms of the license and the regulations promulgated by the Secretary of Transportation.[36]

Insurance purchased by the consortium will have to provide broad coverage for the mapping and robotic rover missions from launch sites outside the United States. However, for crewed missions, they will launch from selected United States Government facilities that have the necessary launch infrastructure unless they prove to be unavailable or cost prohibitive.

Liability insurance coverage for contractor employees will be a paramount concern throughout the entire project starting with the construction and static testing of the launch vehicles and their innumerable components. Workers' compensation insurance will cover domestic work related bodily injury claims. With the construction of many components occurring outside the United States, appropriate insurance coverage for the foreign workers must be in place. Despite the reciprocal waivers, the consortium must be assured that the suppliers and aerospace workers are protected by their respective employers who may be consortium partners or investors.

Training must be provided for the crews and construction contractors that will travel to the Moon to assemble the first lunar base. Special insurance coverage must be provided for the crew members, contractors and their families for what will initially be deemed a hazardous undertaking. The FAA and other regulatory bodies will monitor all crew training that occurs at existing United States Government training facilities that are being leased by the consortium; it is expected that constructing new training facilities will be cost prohibitive.

The development of the first lunar base has been a matter of considerable discussion over the past 30 years with numerous suggestions for the design of the lunar base or outpost.[37]

Launch Activities; Final Rule, effective October 16, 1998, at http://ast.faa.gov/licensing/regulations/14cfr-440.html, page 51 of 80

32 14 CFR 440.11

33 49 U.S.C. Section 70112(4)(C)

34 49 U.S.C. Section 70112(b), 14 CFR 440.17

35 *Supra*, Responsibility Requirements for Licensed Launch Activities, 8 of 80 and 55 of 80

36 49 U.S.C. Section 70115

37 PETER ECKART, ed., THE LUNAR BASE HANDBOOK 203-422 (1999) and W.W. MENDELL, ed., LUNAR BASES AND SPACE

The first lunar outpost will be assembled with construction tools and equipment and component parts that have previously been placed at the base site by a lunar lander. Given the potential liability involved with malfunctioning base components, the so-called "construction shack"[38] or habitation module, power plant, communications facility and oxygen generating facility (the major base components) will come under intense scrutiny by the FAA and other domestic regulatory bodies and by those nations from which the consortium partners originate. Well-formulated backup plans must be in place in the event any of the base components are damaged on landing or later prove inoperable.

With property damage possible due to a faulty landing by the lunar lander and the harsh lunar environment, including the invasive lunar soil, property damage insurance coverage limits must be considerable. Given the possibility of damage to its precious base cargo, the consortium will have to devise a means by which to evaluate or monitor the physical condition of the cargo upon landing on the Moon. Careful monitoring is essential before launching a crew to the Moon.

Since no previous lunar missions have involved permanent habitation and construction activity on the Moon, the consortium should anticipate strong liability concerns by the insurance consortium. The first lunar base construction plans will include the layout of the habitation module that uses lunar regolith or lunar soil as shielding against meteorites, and radiation such as galactic and solar cosmic rays.[39]

ACTIVITIES OF THE 21st CENTURY 57-68, 363-373 (1985).

38 ECKART, *supra* at 277

39 *Id.* at 220, 253

During Phase I, the consortium partners will address numerous liability concerns not the least of which relates to the series of launch vehicles that will be used to accomplish the long-term mission goals. The mapping mission can be completed by utilizing existing launch systems. The robotic mission or missions will require new technology with more sophisticated orbital and lunar landing systems. The cargo delivery missions will demand heavy-lift launch vehicles and landers to deliver the necessary base components and equipment safely to the lunar surface. Finally, the early human or crewed missions will demand launch vehicles and systems not now available. A new lunar transportation system must be developed by the consortium before the installation of a lunar base.[40] However, some of the early missions can be undertaken with presently available launch vehicles, especially for the mapping and robotic missions. In the immediate future they may prove to be the easiest way to return to the Moon. However, commercial crewed missions to the Moon will require more sophisticated propulsion and cargo delivery systems than those now available; major changes are needed.

It has been suggested that an updated Saturn V heavy-lift booster (including use of the F-I rocket engines) could be used for early crewed missions since no better system has yet to be designed and built. "Updating the Saturn 5 with new materials for fuel tanks and advanced flight electronics technology would produce a launch vehicle that could put 150 – 200 tons into Earth orbit for perhaps less than a few hundred dollars per pound. Such a vehicle could put us back on the Moon with only two launches within five to seven years of the program's initiation."[41]

40 *Id.* at 190

41 PAUL D. SPUDIS, THE ONCE AND FUTURE MOON 242 (1996).

Despite the possibility of using an improved version of the Saturn V booster with updated technology to meet the crewed mission goals, considerable liability would remain necessitating the purchase of comprehensive liability insurance coverage. However, no coverage will be sufficient to protect the consortium partners against all the potential risks inherent in the lunar base development project.

Given the technological limitations still inhibiting lunar flights, it will be essential that a reliable, safe transportation system be devised, built, tested and utilized to assure the consortium partners and their investors that the commercial goals are being advanced and met. New or even updated launch systems entail major expense and substantial liability. Untried systems enhance the possibility of system failure with loss of equipment, cargo and crews. Only by means of thorough engineering, quality control and testing programs reminiscent of the Apollo program will reliable launch vehicles be available to crews.

The FAA must be satisfied that the launch vehicles are safe and reliable for the uses intended. Therefore, a primary goal during Phase I is for the consortium and its contractors to design and begin testing the new and updated launch vehicles, lunar landers, and base components needed for installation of the early lunar base.

The consortium planners will agree upon a lunar mission mode for each phase of the project. Each mission mode must be carefully devised to accomplish the mission's goal; various mission modes are familiar and will provide some degree of comfort.[42] Each mode is subject to scrutiny by the FAA and the insurance carriers' experts and may have to be revised to comply with their reasonable demands.

INTERNATIONAL TREATY COMPLIANCE ISSUES

Presently, no international treaty addresses all of the concerns of a private, commercial consortium intent on constructing a lunar base. The consortium is left to piece together a multitude of treaty provisions devised for an earlier time when commercial development activity on the Moon was not a reality. The primary international treaties that must be consulted when devising the lunar base development plan are: (1) the Outer Space Treaty of 1967; (2) the Moon Treaty of 1979; (3) the Convention On International Liability For Damage Caused By Space Objects of 1972; (4) the Convention On Registration of Objects Launched Into Outer Space of 1975; and (5) the Principles Relevant to The Use of Nuclear Power Sources In Outer Space.

In preparation for lunar base development, the consortium will scrutinize international treaty law that could expose it to legal liability for breach of treaty provisions. Special attention will be given to the terms of the Moon Treaty of 1979; it adheres to the property law doctrine of *res communis* – that outer space resources are the "common heritage of mankind" and may only be exploited through the auspices of an international authority acting on behalf of all nations.[43] The Moon Treaty represented a new generation of space legislation, creating legal concepts which extended beyond the 1967 Principles Treaty.[44] Eight nations have ratified the Treaty; consequently, the treaty provisions apply to those nations only. The consortium must determine whether it intends

---

42 ECKART, *supra* at 180-189

43 I. BROWNLEE, PRINCIPLES OF PUBLIC INTERNATIONAL LAW 222-32 (3rd ed. 1979)

44 NATHAN C. GOLDMAN, AMERICAN SPACE LAW: INTERNATIONAL AND DOMESTIC 90 (2nd ed. 1996)

to accept partners or investors from the eight nations bound by the treaty terms. If partners and investors are subject to the treaty provisions, they will be exposed to potential liability by their respective governments. To abate a possible international dispute, the consortium will want to consult with representatives of the eight nations to determine the extent they intend to enforce the treaty provisions against their citizens.

The United States does not support the *res communis* doctrine of property rights and was not a signatory to the Moon Treaty. The property rights doctrine supported by the United States and other developed nations is based upon the concept of Freedom of the High Seas/Outer Space – meaning that no state may claim or acquire exclusive sovereign rights to an area of pristine space; therefore, unless a state agrees to be bound in another manner, it may engage in or authorize the use and exploitation of space resources. The property rights concept of the United States must be the prevailing doctrine of the consortium; private commercial development on the lunar surface will not occur applying the *res communis* doctrine – even though the work performed on the Moon will ultimately be for the betterment of mankind. Nevertheless, the partners must conduct the lunar base activities giving reasonable regard for the rights of other nations and persons. To do otherwise would most certainly create a continuing source of liability for the consortium and its international investors.

In summary, the planning and regulatory compliance work completed during Phase I is critical to the overall health of the project. Dealing forthrightly with potential liability concerns will in some measure abate those concerns. The ability of the consortium partners to manage risk, however, will keep the project moving forward reducing the prospect of major time-consuming litigation or governmental intervention for safety reasons. Finally, the consortium legal advisors will seek the enactment of new legislation providing more protection from liability concerns than now exists in the United States; considerable attention must be given to this matter if the project is to avoid excessively expensive insurance coverage given the great number of risks inherent in the lunar base project.

LIABILITY CONCERNS - PHASE II. LAUNCH MAPPING AND ROBOTIC MISSIONS

The primary goals of Phase II are to (a) determine the final location of the lunar base site, and (b) if necessary, launch a lunar orbiter to complete topographic and compositional mapping to better examine the potential site and (c) after examining the data, launch a robotic lander mission to gather and examine or return resource samples from the vicinity of the site.

Let us first discuss the mapping mission that precedes the robotic lunar rover mission. More data about the lunar surface, especially a detailed site survey will be required to make sound scientific and operational judgments concerning lunar base siting.[45] Data, such as the regolith thickness, is required to determine whether or not proposed operations at a site are feasible.[46] The *in-situ* knowledge of the lunar surface and geology is restricted to the Apollo, Lunokhod, Luna and Surveyor landing sites and many questions remain to be answered.[47] It is also noted that "…a lunar base must be in a safe area for landing and launching spacecraft. Approaching

---

45 ECKART, *supra* at 212.
46 *Id.*
47 *Id.*

spacecraft must have acceptable clear area to land safely and the lunar base must not be located too close to steep slopes or near fresh craters where large rocks are common around the perimeter."[48]

MAPPING MISSION

Having established the mission plans, secured launch licenses for the early phases of the lunar base project, the consortium must make a final determination where the base site is to be located. Site characteristics are of great importance as previously noted. In Phase I, the consortium will have extensively discussed the matter and may have reached a tentative agreement on the base site. A determination would then be made whether existing topographical site data is available. If not, a mapping mission must be scheduled. Available topographical photographs of the lunar surface taken by spacecraft since the Lunar Orbiter series between August 1966 and August 1967 and the Clementine mission (taking topographical and compositional imagery) in February 20,1994 to May 3,1994 (taking 2.5 million pictures and making 330 orbits of the Moon)[49] would have been thoroughly examined to determine the need for further detailed photographs of potential base sites. However, it is believed that overall knowledge of the lunar surface is still patchy and incomplete – therefore, it is important to have detailed topographical and compositional maps of the sites, both with relatively high resolution imagery and remote sensing measurements to determine the chemical variability of lunar soil and by using an orbiting laser altimeter.[50] Given the additional cost and time expended in scheduling a mapping mission, the consortium will exert every possible effort to obtain and examine recent topographical photographs of the lunar surface especially those from the Clementine Mission. It may prove unnecessary to schedule a mapping mission provided that governmental agencies in the meantime map the potential lunar base sites under consideration. However, for the purposes of this paper, we will consider such a mission necessary.

The consortium will give careful consideration to selecting a polar site. "A major advantage of a polar site, from the stand-point of habitat design, is the almost constant thermal and illumination environment. Anywhere else on the Moon, the base design must cope with two-week day and night cycles."[51] And the possibility of water in the craters of the lunar south pole allowing the manufacture of hydrogen and oxygen for propulsion and life support must be considered when selecting a site. The Clementine Mission located a potential base site near the lunar south pole with a landing site in a nearby crater.[52] One possible disadvantage of a polar base site is that Earth-Moon communication will have to be by means of orbital or surface relays; and it is surmised that lunar surface resources are more suitably located near the equator and lunar limb (particularly a rare gas called Helium-3, to be used in future fusion reactors).[53] The prime motivation for the lunar base is resource extraction – therefore, it is believed that mature mare regolith offers the greatest flexibility, given present technology.[54] Given the foregoing, a follow-up lunar rover mission will prove helpful in determining the optimal location for mineral extraction.

---

48 *Id.*

49 SPUDIS, *supra* at 61, 185-186

50 ECKART, *supra* at 228, 230

51 *Id.* at 217

52 SPUDIS, *supra* at 187, 189

53 See: ECKART, Table 7.4, Summary of Some Advantages and Disadvantages of Potential Lunar Base Sites, *supra* at 220

54 *Id.* at 219

In an effort to conserve money, the consortium will learn from the experiences of the team that launched the Clementine Mission. Furthermore, it may be possible to secure funds from governmental agencies and private companies in need to high resolution lunar surface data. By using available technology and a familiar launch vehicle, costs can be contained and the liability reasonably predicted. Given the familiar technology to be used and the fact that the topographical and compositional data may be made generally available at a later time (although it would be deemed proprietary in nature), the FAA and other regulatory bodies should provide the necessary launch license. The insurance industry is familiar with liability concerns that pertain to the lunar mapping mission; therefore, insurance coverage for damage to and loss of property should be available.

With a successful mission, the consortium will have high resolution imagery and resource data pertaining to potential lunar base sites. Additional data obtained can be provided to those governmental bodies or private companies that contributed by paying a portion of the cost of the mission. After locating the lunar base site, the next resource discovery mission of the project will commence.

ROBOTIC LUNAR ROVER MISSION

We next proceed with the robotic lunar rover mission. The consortium will have already determined that such a mission is necessary. Alternatively, a decision could be made to proceed with the next phase of the project (Phase III) to reduce time delays and extra cost in developing a robotic lunar rover and lander if it is believed that sufficient resource data was acquired through the mapping mission. A robotic lander mission with lunar sample return may be planned for geological reconnaissance of the lunar surface in a selected area.[55] It is anticipate that the consortium will have earlier investigated whether a robotic lunar rover using an automation technique known as telerobotics (defined as the remote computer-assisted manipulation of equipment and materials) is available for use on the lunar surface. The consortium would seek a robot with telepresence features (allowing near simultaneous interaction with the field work being performed) so that it could be controlled by an operator from the Earth. It is reported that mobile lunar rovers are still in development but that their importance cannot be overestimated since they can, among other things, be used to traverse long distances on the Moon, performing chemical analyses and mapping the mineralogy of rock exposures.[56] To reduce potential liability resulting from human exposure to the extremes of space and conditions on the lunar surface, alternative means must be utilized to gather necessary resources data.

The increased technical complexity and cost of the robotic lunar rover mission will be justified only if the data obtained proves useful to the consortium. The likelihood of property damage or loss will be much greater since the lunar lander must perform as planned and deploy the robotic rover upon the lunar surface in the area to be mapped and examined. With no human involvement on this mission, except through robot telepresence, liability will be reduced. However, the insurance carriers will require that the mission be controlled by a fully trained and experienced team to increase the possibility of success. A successful mission will assure the consortium that the desired resources are readily available at the selected base site. Due to cost constraints and mission complexity, a sample return vehicle may be used but only if an *in-situ* examination of the

---

55 ECKART, *supra* at 232-235
56 *Id.* at 233

mineral resources cannot be successfully accomplished.

The ever-present concern about real property rights to a lunar base site and future mining activity in the vicinity will have been fully addressed for it may be a source of substantial liability for the consortium partners. Given the need to satisfy the concerns of the FAA and other governments overseeing the lunar base project[57], the insurance carriers will undoubtedly adopt a conservative stance with regard to international treaty compliance despite the property law doctrine of the United States, earlier set forth. For partners who come from nations that signed the Moon Treaty, they could be compelled (barring a waiver) by their governments to reveal what would otherwise be considered consortium proprietary information – such as "...the results of each mission, including scientific results" that would have to be furnished upon completion of the mission.[58] The consortium will be aware that under Article VI of the Moon Treaty, it does have "...the right to collect on and remove from the moon samples of its mineral and other substances." The consortium would have full control over the collected samples but could be compelled to share samples with other states and the international scientific community for scientific investigation. In the event the consortium wishes to use lunar resources to support its base project, for example, generating hydrogen and oxygen from lunar water and mineral resources, it is helpful to know that "State parties may in the course of scientific investigations also use mineral and other substances of the moon in quantities appropriate for the support of their mission."[59]
Given the international scope of the consortium partners and investors, the exchange of scientific information that will invariably result and the direct involvement of personnel from many nations who participate on the missions, there will be compliance with the spirit and, in most cases, the provisions of the Moon Treaty.[60]

The Moon Treaty provisions allow the installation of manned or unmanned "stations and installations anywhere on or below the surface of the moon."[61]

Questions concerning compliance with Article XI of the Moon Treaty will generate the most controversy. It provides generally that the natural resources of the Moon are the common heritage of mankind not subject to national appropriation by any claim of sovereignty, by means of occupation, or by any other means. To the consortium, a for-profit business entity, it is troubling that the Treaty, Article XI, 3., does not permit the natural resources in place to become the property of the consortium. The fact that no "international regime" has yet been established to "govern the exploitation of the natural resources of the moon as such exploitation is about to become feasible"[62] will give the consortium partners concern; such a regime may be established by those eight nations (and possibly others as well may accede to the Agreement at any time)[63] when it is determined that the consortium's lunar base site for resource exploitation is a reality. The uncertainty engendered by this possible political development must be addressed

57 See: Moon Treaty, Article XII, 1. regarding retention of jurisdiction and control over personnel, vehicles, equipment, facilities, stations and installations of State Parties
58 Moon Treaty, Article V, 1.

59 Moon Treaty, Article VI, 2.
60 Moon Treaty, Article VI, 3.
61 Moon Treaty, Article VIII, 2. (b), Article IX.
62 Moon Treaty, Article XI, 5. and Article XVIII.
63 Moon Treaty, Article XIX, 2.

during Phase I of the base project. In addressing this possible development, it will prove helpful for the consortium to seek written confirmation from each signatory nation and the United Nations that they will not later intercede when, on a limited scale, resource exploitation commences.

With a base site located, a site development plan ready, and a decision made to proceed with delivery of the construction materials and equipment, Phase III is ready to commence. In the meantime, crews will have already been trained to assemble the habitat from modular components and other critical life-support facilities with the specially designed equipment. Final plans will have been completed regarding the number of crew members and construction specialists required to complete assembly; the stay time at the lunar base to accomplish the preliminary habitat assembly work and geological site evaluation; and the number and frequency of resupply missions needed to complete base assembly and readiness for full-time occupancy. The phases of base growth for the purposes of mining operations will have been settled upon by the consortium during Phase I.[64]

Thorough crew training in leased government training facilities will have commenced many months prior; such training must meet with the approval of the FAA and, if successful, will reduce liability concerns. To further reduce liability concerns, the direct one-way mission mode[65] selected for the lunar lander missions will neither employ human crews nor involve assent or departure stages from the lunar surface because the component parts of the lander will be partially utilized in constructing the base facilities. With the basic plan decided, Phase III is ready to proceed.

LIABILITY CONCERNS – PHASE III. CARGO DELIVERY MISSIONS TO BASE SITE

The goal of the third phase is to safely deliver in one or more direct one-way missions the base components and support equipment to the base site. The contents of the cargo missions will have been earlier determined premised upon the base design selected by the consortium that best accommodates the mission goals. Since no human crews will be involved with the cargo missions, liability will be less of a concern. However, concerns will be expressed by the insurance carriers as to the reliability of the launch and propulsion systems used to soft-land the base components during one and possibly two or more landings on the Moon. Reliable launch systems and trained teams will abate some of the concerns. It will be useful to recall that there is a brief history of computer controlled lunar landers (such as Luna 16) successfully landing on the surface. However, there exists no prior experience with successfully landing heavy, bulky construction components and construction equipment.

Living and working on the lunar surface entails substantial risks. Therefore, every aspect of the design and fabrication of the lunar base will be carefully reviewed by both government engineers and insurance engineering experts. The base design will have been completed during Phase I to insure base component fabrication, testing and availability. A careful quality control program will again reduce chances of lunar site component failure and, thus, will assist in reducing the otherwise astronomical insurance premiums. At the outset, the lunar base will essentially be comprised of a power plant, a habitat, a laboratory, and construction

64 MENDELL, *supra* at 65, 70
65 ECKART, *supra* at 180; MENDELL, *supra* at 120

and transportation vehicles.[66] The site will have been developed taking into account the needs of the early crews and should minimize extra-vehicular activity, crew time requirements, transportation times, power transfer losses, and material handling requirements.[67]

The base components must be capable of fitting inside the cargo bay of the launch vehicles, not exceeding payload limits; and be able to survive loads during launch, flight and landing; numerous other design requirements and constraints must be fully considered.[68]

The anticipated nuclear power facility will be a ready source of liability concern both on Earth prior to and during launch (from the re-entry of radioactive space debris) as well as while being assembled on the Moon. Such a launch will be given extra scrutiny by the FAA and other involved governments that could be affected if the rocket must be destroyed prior to achieving Earth orbit. The insurance carriers may insist that the consortium comply with Principle 4 of the Principles Relevant To The Use of Nuclear Power Sources In Outer Space[69] requiring that a safety assessment be made by the launching state, or the United States, with results being made available to the public and the United Nations. From an insurance standpoint, it would prove less costly to employ the use of solar panels on the Moon to generate power; however, given the numerous heavy components that must be delivered, there will be insufficient space to accommodate the solar panels that would be needed to generate even a small portion of the power that would otherwise be generated by a compact nuclear reactor. That is not to say, however, that solar energy will not be utilized; indeed, it must be used to power certain station components outside of the base site area and act as a backup power source in the event of reactor repair, shutdown or failure.

The layout of the early base site has been a source of much interest by experts.[70] The manner in which the base is to be constructed will have a bearing on liability. Protection of the crew members is a paramount concern; therefore, the habitat, power source and oxygen generating facility will have to be promptly assembled, tested and made operational. While assembling the habitat, the crew will continue to return to the lander.

Safe delivery of the cargo will assure overall mission success. Close monitoring of every aspect of the missions will be required. An onboard monitoring system must be installed on the landers delivering the nuclear reactor to assure that the radiation level is acceptable and will not endanger the crew that later installs the reactor components nearby the base site.

The one-way mission mode selected would insure that the launch vehicles delivering the cargo spend more time getting to the Moon but will expend less propellant doing so. Speed is not a significant factor when delivering base components since no crew will be awaiting the arrival of the cargo. However, due to possible exposure damage to the components, it is important that the next phase of the project move forward promptly. It is time for the first crewed mission.

With successful completion of the cargo missions, Phase IV is ready to commence. The crews have been trained; the launch vehicles have been constructed, flight tested

66 ECKERT, *supra* at 245

67 *Id.*at 248

68 *Id.* at 258

69 See GOLDMAN, *supra* at 116

70 ECKART, *supra* at 241-262 and 747-772 – providing two significant examples of lunar base modeling and development

and are ready to take the crews back to the Moon.

LIABILITY CONCERNS – PHASE IV. EARLY HUMAN MISSIONS TO BASE SITE

The groundwork has been laid for humans to return to the Moon to establish a permanent settlement.

Concerns for the safety of the crews who will pilot the spacecraft and the construction engineers who will assemble the base facilities will be of paramount concern. In evaluating liability concerns, we must first consider the mission mode to be used for return to the lunar surface. The mode that will generate the least liability and is familiar from the Apollo program: Launch from Earth into Earth parking orbit; TLI (trans-lunar injection); establishment of a lunar parking orbit; Earth return vehicle remains in lunar orbit; landing vehicle descends to the lunar surface; upon completion of work on the lunar surface, landing vehicle ascends from the lunar surface; LOR (lunar orbit rendezvous) with the Earth return vehicle; TEI (trans-Earth injection); reentry of crew and cargo directly from a trans-Earth trajectory.[71] This mission mode would employ expendable stages and be suitable for crew exchange and resupply of a lunar base.[72] Although there are deficits inherent in using this mission mode, such as the need to establish a lunar parking orbit and for a vehicle to remain in lunar orbit until the landing vehicle returns as well as the increased developmental and hardware expenses, it may still prove to be the safest mode for the early crews. The consortium may wish to reconsider the mode involving Earth Orbit Rendezvous instead of Lunar Orbit Rendezvous[73] should it prove useful for the lunar missions. It is important that there be no accidents during the early missions for fear that it will dampen the enthusiasm of investors, consortium partners and governmental regulators. A major property loss or loss of life would undoubtedly trigger an investigation by the FAA and agencies of other involved nations. The insurance carriers providing coverage for the missions would also investigate to determine the extent of their liability and whether to revise or continue coverage for future missions. Given the foregoing, a familiar mission mode for the early crewed missions is of utmost importance.

Another equally important consideration involves the launch vehicles chosen to fly the crews to the lunar surface. At present, there is no launch vehicle available to complete the task. It was earlier suggested that the Project Apollo launch vehicles, configured as the Saturn V, could be constructed with new materials, electronics, computers and updated rocket motors. The early crewed missions could use similar vehicles to accomplish the base assembly although it would prove difficult to deliver the necessary crews given the size and weight limitations involved in using the former lunar lander (LEM). The consortium will undoubtedly give careful consideration to the choice of launch vehicle to be used to bring the crews to the lunar surface during Phase I; in so doing, it may elect to develop a new launch vehicle, lander and internal systems despite the substantial cost and time expenditure to test and qualify the new vehicles. With the need for at least four crew members to be available to assemble the base components, plus the added weight and subsistence requirements, it is almost certain that a new or substantially revised current or former (Saturn V) launch

---

71 ECKART, *supra* at 182

72 *Id.*

73 ROGER E. BILSTEIN, STAGES TO SATURN 60-67 (1996)

vehicle will have to be employed. If a new launch vehicle is to be developed, it involves added risk; consequently, enhanced liability is a factor to be considered by the insurance carriers and the consortium.

To complete base assembly it is believed that more than two missions will be required; crew members will be limited in the amount of time they can spend on the EVA's required to assemble the components. Safety and human needs considerations will compel the crews to periodically return to their lunar outpost or lander.[74] With limited space, oxygen and food in the lander, the first crews will be compelled to efficiently complete their assigned assembly work and then depart for Earth. The next crew will arrive shortly thereafter and continue the next phase of the assembly work continuing to make use of the lunar outpost or lander.

In Phase I, brief reference was made to the impact of the Outer Space Treaty and the Moon Treaty upon base development activity on the Moon as well as later mineral exploitation. Given the governmental "continuing supervision" requirements of Article VI of the Outer Space Treaty, the FAA or another agency will play a significant role in early base development. It has been the practice of the FAA to send a representative to oversee launches involving United States citizens or launches within its jurisdiction. With strict crew size requirements in place, it is doubtful that the FAA will be able to send along a representative; however, by overseeing the project as a whole and with post-mission reporting demands, the FAA will be advised of mission problems with which it must be involved. The insurance carriers will likewise be the recipients of ongoing and post-mission reports to better evaluate the need for oversight before future missions and for adjustments in the coverage limits.

Given the potential dangers of traveling to and from the Moon and working upon its surface, the consortium must provide appropriate insurance coverage for injury to or death of crew members and for their families. Retaining the loyalty of crews and their families will depend upon generous compensation and a comprehensive benefits package.

Liability problems may arise from hasty or improper selection of crew members who are unable to perform as required or who develop medical/psychological problems while in the line of duty. The consortium must determine early whether the workers' compensation laws are applicable to crew members or whether they are exempt given the nature of their duties and the place where those duties are performed. Although coverage for on-the-job injuries must be in place during the crews' training phase (in the state in which they are located), it is doubtful whether coverage is available or required while they are in orbit, in transit to the Moon or working on the lunar surface.

Additional liability concerns relate to operation of equipment and mobile devices (similar to the lunar rover vehicle) while performing work outside the lander or habitat. Careful attention must be given by the crews to provide adequate shielding of the habitat and other critical facilities from solar radiation. The early concern expressed in Phase I about the dangers to the crews and their equipment from meteoroids and radiation such as galactic and solar cosmic rays is now a reality. It is anticipated that the lunar regolith will be utilized as shielding in addition to other materials that can provide a high degree of protection. To accomplish the task of burying the habitation modules with

[74] *Id.* at 278-279

regolith and rocks, large amounts of lunar soil and rock must be excavated and moved to the base site.[75] To move the soil and rock, transportation vehicles must be sent to the Moon during Phase III and assembled by the first crew and will probably be terrestrial based equipment with track-type/dozer excavators.[76] In an effort at reducing the liability related with operating such large equipment on the lunar surface, the consortium must consider using robotic machines with various mechanical attachments to accomplish some of the heavy-lifting and moving tasks. Even with the reduced gravity on the Moon, heavy lifting and pushing will quickly tire the crews leading to shortened EVA's and possible injury.

One of the critical jobs for the first crew is to create a landing site to be used by future crews. It is anticipated that in the initial stages, a launch and landing facility will consist of not much more than a level area and, possibly, a navigational aid on the lunar surface.[77] The most important aspects of lunar launch/landing facility design include the effects of lunar lander engine exhaust blasting the lunar soil and chemical contamination from rocket plumes. This matter will affect virtually the entire lunar surface base layout.[78] It is expected that the early landing pads will be close to the habitat but in later, more developed bases, the landing pad will be considerably farther away accessible by motorized vehicle.

Next, we address the need for a nuclear power plant. "Due to the Moon experiencing long diurnal cycles, solar energy becomes an awkward energy source to rely on in a continuously inhabited and operated lunar settlement. This is mainly because massive energy storage devices would be needed for power in the night cycle. Nuclear energy offers a relatively compact power source that is not affected by the diurnal day/night cycle, and the technology should be available...."[79] Radioisotope generators have been used where long life, high reliability, solar independence, and operation in severe environments are critical.[80] The consortium will initially rely upon a compact nuclear reactor-based electric power plant for the early base. Given the work to be performed and the energy needs of the crews, they must be provided with a reliable source of electric energy. Despite the fact that liability concerns are raised by use of a nuclear power source, the alternatives (such as solar power or battery power) for providing the crews with sufficient power to complete their work and power their lander or outpost and other vehicles are inadequate. Since the nuclear power plant will have already been delivered to the base site in one of the cargo landers, there is minimal risk for the crew unless the reactor has sustained damage or becomes inoperable. In such event, given the critical need for power, the consortium will have devised backup plans for a redundant power plant that will have been delivered in another cargo lander.

Shielding the crews and their equipment against excessive radiation will be critically important. The shielding design approach consists of two steps: (1) predication of the astronaut risk and (2) evaluation of mission costs, before a mission is approved.[81] "No specific radiation exposure limits exist for crew members of exploratory-class space missions, including lunar base missions. However, radiation protection has to ensure that crew dose rates are kept as low as

75 *Id.* at 253
76 *Id.* at 254
77 ECKART, *supra* at 250
78 *Id.* at 250

79 MENDELL, *supra* at 91
80 *Id.* at 91
81 ECKART, *supra* at 526

reasonably achievable."[82] "Crew members on missions to the Moon will be unavoidably exposed to ionizing radiation … and there is the possibility for exposure radiation from *Solar Particle Events*."[83] Great care will have early been given by the consortium and their contractors to the shielding design process for the habitat and support facilities to insure that the selected materials will enhance the degree of protection. The manufacturer of the component parts of the habitat will be aware that "[A]s high-energy radiation traverses bulk matter, their radiation field changes composition through interactions with the materials in their path. As a result of these interactions, the internal radiation environment within the lunar habitat or a spacecraft can differ appreciably from the incident external environment."[84] In addition to sufficient shielding for the habitat and support facilities, it is suggested that crew members working on the lunar surface (during EVA) be provided with dedicated shelters so that they can rush to the shelter in case of a large solar particle event; the EVA suits now available do not provide sufficient shielding.[85] It will be important for the consortium to undertake studies of solar particle events in an effort to improve the rudimentary forecasting methods now used; the welfare of the crews may depend upon a timely warning of a solar particle event allowing the crews time to seek shelter. With the risk of radiation sickness and death a distinct possibility for all crew members, appropriate insurance coverage must be obtained by the consortium.

Protection for the crews can be enhanced by developing an EVA suit that provides better radiation shielding and by providing a readily accessible radiation shelter for the crews in the event of a large solar particle event or meteoroid impacts. "The actual risk of a meteoroid impact to an object on the lunar surface is difficult to estimate" and for a large but inert structure, like a regolith-shielded lunar base, the consequences of such an impact may be very small; but for a small but vital life support package, the consequences may be disastrous.[86] No means has yet been devised of protecting exposed crew members on EVA to the potential threat of meteoroids; a new space suit assembly and accompanying portable life support system will be required to provide some of the necessary protection. The welfare of the crews will depend upon a concerted research effort in finding new materials to improve shielding but give the crew member apparel flexibility to conduct EVA work.

Shielding the habitat and other vital facilities should prove easier. Use of regolith to shield the habitat has been a matter of scientific and engineering concern for some years and is considered useful but must be fully researched by the consortium and its contractors before designing the base.[87] Through careful research on the lunar surface the consortium's crews will be able to better devise ways in which to reduce their continuing exposure to radiation.

In addition to the hazards mentioned above, the consortium planners must consider other factors relating to the impact of the lunar environment while the crews are on EVA. These factors include: (1) the effects of working in microgravity conditions; (2) the abrasive effects of lunar dust on the space suits, rovers, tools and equipment; (3) lighting conditions that may inhibit EVA activity; (4) thermal and atmospheric conditions that require materials and equipment that can withstand the wide variations of temperature;

82 *Id.* at 514
83 *Id.* at 516
84 *Id.* at 518
85 *Id.* at 520
86 *Id.* at 536
87 *Id.* at 530-536

(5) lunar surface curvature that permits only line-of-sight communications without the aid of relay antennas or a communications satellite system.[88] By addressing each of the foregoing concerns, the consortium will reduce the hazards to its crews and, thus, reduce its liability exposure.

Plans to provide for crew member health care while on the lunar surface must also be implemented. Failing to provide for emergency medical problems will most assuredly be a source of liability for the consortium. Each of the crew members must receive sufficient health care training to provide for the basic medical needs of the others. When medical problems cannot be diagnosed by crew members, they must be provided with communications facilities to contact the assigned physicians on Earth who can diagnose the medical problem, monitor the crew member and advise what medical action must be taken. In certain critical situations where trained on-site medical attention (for complex surgical procedures) is unavailable, the crew member may die unless returned to Earth in a timely manner. Such an emergency return flight is unlikely with the lunar lander/return vehicle needed for the entire crew's return to Earth. Consequently, each crew member must be thoroughly examined on a routine basis, especially prior to each launch, to determine if they present a medical risk. Despite the most thorough examinations beforehand, medical emergencies on the lunar surface must be expected. Only by anticipating and providing for the medical needs of the crew will the consortium be able to reduce its continuing liability for injury and death.

Finally, we come to the lunar mining equipment that will be used initially to move the regolith and rock to shield the habitat and later be used to conduct mineral exploitation. One of the primary motivations for the consortium undertaking development of the lunar base is to make a profit from the lunar resources (such as Helium - 3) that will be used upon the Earth and to sustain (extracting oxygen and hydrogen from the lunar regolith) the lunar base. Substantial monetary losses will be sustained if the mining equipment is damaged or destroyed in the cargo landers. Given the unique, one-of-a-kind nature of the mining equipment, the insurance carriers involved will be required to pay out large sums of money to the consortium in the event of damage or total loss.

In order to conduct mining activity, special equipment will be required. "Designing lunar mining equipment will be an extremely challenging undertaking. Most mining and processing equipment and techniques used on Earth will not work on the Moon without significant modifications. Like all facilities and elements of a lunar base, mining and processing equipment must be designed to withstand the lunar vacuum, temperature extremes, low gravity, radiation, and the adherence of abrasive dust particles."[89] It is anticipated that early lunar surface mining/excavation activities will feature small, simple machines suitable for excavating lunar regolith.[90] But later mining activities will require dozers, scrapers, front-end loaders, hydraulic excavators and some form of truck or motorized vehicle to transport the lunar regolith. To continue its long-term mining plans, the consortium will have to provide the heavy mining equipment to enhance the efficiency of the extraction process. However, the liability associated with such activity is not considered within the scope of this paper.

Since mining and the extraction of minerals is the primary focus of the consortium in its

---

[88] *Id.* at 549-552

[89] *Id.* at 617

[90] *Id.*

efforts at generating revenue for its investors, and since standard Earth mining equipment cannot be used on the Moon, a major investment must be made by the consortium in developing specialized mining equipment. Appropriate insurance coverage must be made available to the consortium to protect its investment in the unique equipment. Thorough equipment design, testing, evaluation and the training of crews to operate it will assure investors and government regulators of the future success of the lunar base development project.

CONCLUSION

The purpose of this paper has been to discuss some of the sources of liability that a private, for-profit business entity will face when undertaking missions to the Moon to construct a lunar base for mineral exploitation.

Numerous liability issues must be addressed by the consortium planners in an effort to realize a successful project. Some of those issues have been briefly addressed in this paper. Apart from design, testing and evaluation of equipment, launch systems, launch vehicles and crew members, the consortium must address the critical need for both international and national legislation further limiting its liability; the current national (United States of America) legislation is inadequate to the task and still exposes the consortium to crippling monetary expenses in the event of major equipment losses or death. Furthermore, real property rights, especially relating to ownership of the permanent lunar base, the minerals and the mining rights upon and under the lunar surface must be dealt with promptly. The legislation must prove beneficial for commercial development activity upon the Moon before a private consortium undertakes financing a multi-billion dollar project that will involve thousands of worldwide citizens over a period of at least fifteen years.

The minerals and other resources obtained from the Moon will be of benefit to all the people of Earth. They will be used to fashion new materials for our use and provide relatively inexpensive, clean fusion energy to generate electric power on Earth. Given the long-term benefits to be derived from such a project, some of which we can only imagine now, it is well worth the investment by the consortium, its worldwide investors and contractors. Paving the way for a successful project will be those creating and enacting new laws and regulations controlling the project. Beneficial legislation and regulations will ensure a safe and profitable project for all involved and bring to people of all nations a wealth of new products and scientific discoveries while setting the groundwork for the future exploration of Mars and beyond.

IAC-02-IISL.4.18

Satellite technology as a source of integration. A comparative analysis: Europe / MERCOSUR.

Luis F. Castillo Argañarás, M.A

Universidad de Buenos Aires and Universidad Argentina de la Empresa.

Email: lfcastillo@uade.edu.ar

ABSTRACT[1]

The main purpose of this presentation is to show a comparative analysis between the development of European Integration for space activities and the first steps towards the same target on the part of MERCOSUR, in South America.

INTRODUCTION

The development satellite technology has produced several changes in the field of international law, creating the need to build a new framework for integration and cooperation.

The main purpose of this presentation therefore, as outlined in the abstract, is to show a comparative analysis between the development of European integration in the field of for space activities and the first steps towards a similar target taken by MERCOSUR.

We shall not be dealing with the powers conferred upon the European community in the field of research and development. We shall simply focus on the European Space Agency.

A review of the integration experience within MERCOSUR in the area of satellite technology, together wit a comparative analysis, will help to highlight the positive and negative side effects of its development up to our present time.

EUROPE AND THE EUROPEAN SPACE AGENCY

In the early 1960s, France, Germany, Italy , the Netherlands, the United Kingdom and Australia concentrated on the development of space launcher capacities leading to the creation of the "European Launcher Development Organization" (ELDO). The European Space Research Organization" (ESRO), which was created the same year as ELDO, in 1964.[i]

The European Space Agency was created after a diplomatic meeting that took place in Belgium in 1975. The ESA was set up after the European Space Research Organization (ESRO) and the European Launcher Development Organization (ELDO) with the some duties and rights.

The European Space Agency is a regional international intergovernmental organization with international legal personality[ii].

The members of this organization are: Austria, Belgium, Denmark, Finland, France, Germany, Ireland, Italy, Netherlands, Norway, Spain, Sweden, Switzerland, and the United Kingdom. On the basis of a special agreement, Canada cooperates with the said Organization.

The main target of this Organization is the encouragement of cooperation among its members and to provide and promote space research, space technology and its applications for peaceful purposes[iii]

ESA is a unique organization as it is the only international organization in the world dedicated to the research and development of space activities.[iv]

Briefly, its structure is as follows. The Agency is directed by a Council composed of the representatives of member States, and the chief officer, who is the Director-General [v]

The Organization has the following homebases: [vi]

1. Its headquarters are in Paris
2. The European Space Research and Technology Centre, in Noordwijk, the Netherlands. It is the principal technical office of this Agency, in which the majority of the team projects, space science department, and technological research and support engineers are located;
3. The European Space Operations Centre (Darmstadt- Germany), is in charge of satellite operations and its corresponding ground facilities and communications networks;
4. The European Space Research Institute (Frascati, Italy), whose main task is the exploitation of Earth observation data from space
5. The European Astronauts Centre (Porz – Wahn- Germany), which coordinates all European astronaut activities, including the training of the future European astronauts.

As stated earlier, we are not addressing the powers conferred upon the European community in the field of research and development

MERCOSUR

Since MERCOSUR was created in 1991, by the Treaty of Asunción. Its origin may be traced through bilateral agreements concluded between Argentina and Brazil

On 29th November, 1985 "Declaración de Iguazú" was signed, in which the Presidents of both countries declared their conviction that science and technology play an important role in the economic and social development.

The "Acta para la Integración Argentino-Brasileña" signed on 29th July 1986 established a Programme of Integration and Economic Cooperation between both countries

Two former Presidents of Argentina and Brazil (Menem and Sarney) signed the "Treaty of Integration, Cooperation and Development"[vii] on 29th November 1988. The main purpose was to consolidate the integration and economic cooperation among both with the purpose of establishing a joint economic space within their territories.

On 23rd August 1989 the "Argentine – Brazilian Joint Declaration concerning

Bilateral Cooperation in Peaceful Uses of Outer Space"[viii] was signed. On this occasion the intention was stated of increasing cooperation in the field of peaceful uses of outer space and working together in specific areas, to be later determinated.

This implementation of this agreement called for the creation of a "working group" under the responsibility of the Ministry of Foreign Affairs of both countries. This "working group" will be made up by the representatives of the entities involved in space activities.

On 26t March 1991 the Treaty of Asunción, which established the MERCOSUR, was signed by Argentina, Brazil , Uruguay and Paraguay.

On 9th April 1996 the Cooperation Framework Agreement on Peaceful Applications of Space Science and Technology[ix] was concluded between Argentina and Brazil. The National Commission for Space Activities (Argentina) and the Brazilian Space Agency (Brazil) were appointed to carry out the purposes of this agreement[x]

According to article 2, cooperation in this field included the following areas:

- Space sciences, apace technology, evaluation and monitoring the environment, natural resources by remote sensing and other space applications.
- Development of space missions for scientific and technological purposes, and space applications.
- Mechanisms of access and launch services
- Other fields to be agreed on by the Parties.

Both countries stated that they are exempt from taxes and import and export duties for goods, equipment and materials sent from one country to another. The idea is to enforce the cooperation programmes they subsequently may agree on (Article 5).

In this context the Parties decided to maintain "working group" system. To this end a Joint Working Group for the Peaceful Uses of Outer Space has been established between Argentina and Brazil.. The Brazilian side is composed of representatives of the Ministry of Foreign Affairs and the Brazilian Space Agency whilst the Argentine members are representatives of the Ministry of Foreign Relations and the National Commission for Space Activities. (Article.7).

The following treaties have been signed: so far

- A Cooperation Programme between National Commission of Space Activities (Argentina) and the Brazilian Space Agency regarding the SABIA3 Programme.
- A Cooperation Programme concerning sub-orbital launches.
- A Cooperation Programme relating to Ground Systems Infrastructure for Space Missions.

These Programmes were signed on 10th November 1998 in Buenos Aires.

The Argentine Space Programme 1997/2008 has stated that the National Commission for Space Activities should implement a long term Programme of remote sensing and global positioning. It should cooperate, to this end, with the other countries of MERCOSUR. The development of cooperation with Brazil concerning Earth observation and the monitoring of food and water resources, together with environmental issues (SABIA3)is considered a first priority goal[xi].

On 8th May 2001 an Agreement Capacity Building was signed between Argentina and Brazil in Río de Janeiro[xii]

The main targets of this agreement, pursuant to its Article 2, are:

- To facilitate the provision of capacity building activities in Argentina and Brazil between the Argentine and the Brazilian commercial satellites, to be coordinated in accordance with the Rules of the International Telecommunication Union .

- To establish conditions and technical standards for the supply of space capacities in fix-services by satellites.

On 14th August 2001, It was signed the Additional Protocol to the Cooperation Framework Agreement on Pacific Applications on Space Science and Technology[xiii] between Argentina and Brazil

This instrument states that the Parties have priority to provide systems, equipments or services if the other Party can obtain them from its own companies or agencies in order to carry out their duties.

CONCLUSION

As analyzed in the previous paragraphs, in Europe there is an Agency specialized on international cooperation within the countries of region. We have not considered the powers conferred upon the European community in the field of research and development but, instead, have especially focused on the European Space Agency example which provides the most appropriate ways and means that may be followed within the MERCOSUR system.

Integration in the field of space technology is non-existent in South America. There are, as previously indicated, some bilateral agreements between Argentina and Brazil which intend to develop international cooperation between the main parties of MERCOSUR.

Argentina and Brazil chose the mechanism of "working groups". This option means a sharp departure from the ESA pattern.

The above-named countries are the unquestionable leaders of the integration process in South America. They should involve Paraguay and Uruguay -both of them parties to the MERCOSUR system- to continue work towards the development of space science and satellite technology following the example provided by Europe regarding mechanisms adopted for the European Space Agency.

It is important to underline that, in spite of the political, economic and social crisis that Argentina and Brazil are going through at the moment, they should continue working together in order to develop satellite technology and space sciences for the benefit of developing countries.

---

[i] See Gasparini Alves, Pericles: "Access to outer space technologies: Implications for international Security". UNIDIR. Research Paper 15. United Nations. New York. 1992. Page 47

[ii] See Art. XV. ESA Convention.

[iii] See Art. II. ESA Convention.

[iv] Lafferranderie, Gabriel and Tuinder, Paul Henry: "The Role of ESA in the Evolution of Space Law" in Journal of Space Law. Volume 22, Numbers 1&2. 1994 Page 97

[v] United Nations. Office for Outer Space Affairs. "Space Activities of the United Nations and

International Organizations" United Nations. New York. 1999. Page 100

[vi] United Nations. Office for Outer Space Affairs. "Space Activities of the United Nations and International Organizations" United Nations. New York. 1999. Page 100

[vii] Tratado de Integración, Cooperación y Desarrollo.

[viii] Declaración Conjunta Argentino – Brasileña sobre Cooperación Bilateral en los Usos Pacíficos del Espacio Ultraterrestre

[ix] Acuerdo Marco de Cooperación en Aplicaciones Pacíficas de Ciencia y Tecnología Espaciales

[x] Article 1.

[xi] Argentine Space Programme1997/2008. Presidential Decree 1330/99. ADLA LIX-E. Page. 5363

[xii] Acuerdo Para la Provisión de Capacidad Espacial

[xiii] Protocolo Adicional al Acuerdo Marco de Cooperación en Aplicaciones Pacíficas de Ciencia y Tecnología Espaciales

IAC-02-IISL.4.19

SPACE DEBRIS MEASUREMENT, ANALYSIS AND STUDY A TOOL FOR GLOBAL COOPERATIONS

Bahrami, M.; Golrounia, A.; Moghani, T.; Shajiee, Sh.
Aerospace Research Institute
Tehran, I.R. IRAN
mbahrami@ari.ac.ir

ABSTRACT

Space activities and development have opened some new unprecedented frontiers for science and technology, and have created new hopes and goals for human society. At the same time like any other development in human history, there have been adverse effects on the environment. Of particular concern are the orbits around earth, which are polluted by space debris. Nonfunctional satellites, fragments due to satellite breakups, upper stages, etc. have created a kind of pollution that is highly dynamic.

More than 26000 objects have been officially cataloged in forty years of human space activities. One third of these are still in orbit. The cataloged objects are usually larger that 10cm in diameter in LEO and 1m in diameter in higher orbits. By January 1, 2000 about 8500 objects in orbit are cataloged, and approximately about 1000 objects exist which are not cataloged yet.

Measurement of debris is usually done either by radar or by optical instruments. About five countries are active in radar measurement and six countries in optical measurement. United states and Russia are also actively involved in cataloging.

In this paper after reviewing the current status of existing space debris, measurement, and cataloging activities, a suggestion is made for creating a global network for debris measurement, analysis, and study, for taking advantage of existing global possibilities and capabilities. This in turn will be useful in multinational activities involving space faring and user nations.

INTRODUCTION

Orbital debris includes any man-made object that was launched for a definite purpose, but it does not follow any practical and useful mission, any more. Nonfunctional spacecraft fragments due to satellite breakups, upper stages, and objects released in spacecraft operations are different kinds of orbital debris. They have created a kind of pollution that is highly dynamic, and are of considerable concern in space operations. Orbital debris has originated since the first satellite, Sputnik I, was launched in 1957. Fragmentation of space objects has the largest share in space debris population, Figure (1). It is interesting to note that only 6% of space objects in the earth orbits are functional spacecrafts. Non-functional spacecrafts have a considerable share of 22%, rockets upper stages have a share of 17% of orbital debris, while they are both potential sources for fragmentation debris.

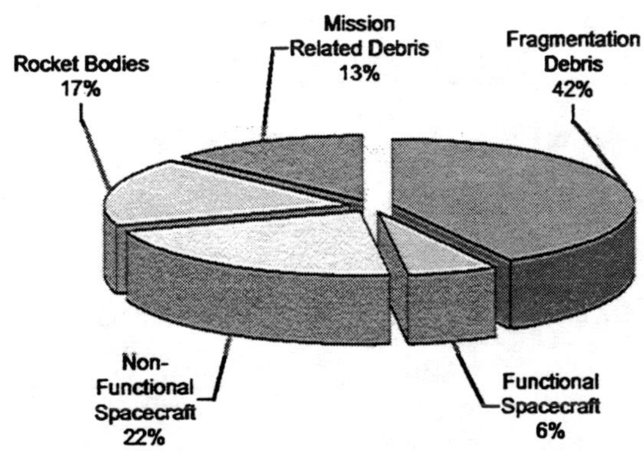

Figure 1. Space Objects in Earth Orbit Including Space Debris [1]

Due to the increased launching activities in commercial and non-commercial satellites business, over the past few years, the amount of space debris has been growing at an increasing rate. At the present, it is estimated to be about 8,600 objects with diameters of more than 10 centimeters, which are in known earth orbits. The figure depicts that 94% of man-made space objects are orbital debris.

Of particular concern are the orbits around earth, which are polluted by space debris. The orbital space around earth can be divided into three significant regions:

Low Earth Orbits (LEO)
Semi Synchronous Orbits
Geo-synchronous Earth Orbits (GEO)

LEO region has a height between 200 and 2000 km. The risk of collision in LEO is much higher than in GEO, because of the higher relative velocities and the much smaller regional volume. In LEO the average relative velocity between any two orbiting objects is about 10 km/s. At this speed a 1 kg orbiting object has the kinetic energy equivalent to a 10-ton object at speed 360 km/hr. The 1-kg orbiting object can destroy a typical LEO satellite of mass 500-1000 kg [1].

Semi-synchronous orbits from 10,000 to 20,000km high are important for navigation.
GPS satellites use these orbits.

GEO is about 36000 km high. Due to lack of atmosphere drag, the orbital lifetime is much longer in GEO than LEO; thus, a GEO satellite is likely to orbit the earth for many years.
So, special considerations are needed in these regions. Figure(2) shows the distribution of debris in different orbital distance. Note that higher density can be observed in three aforementioned regions.

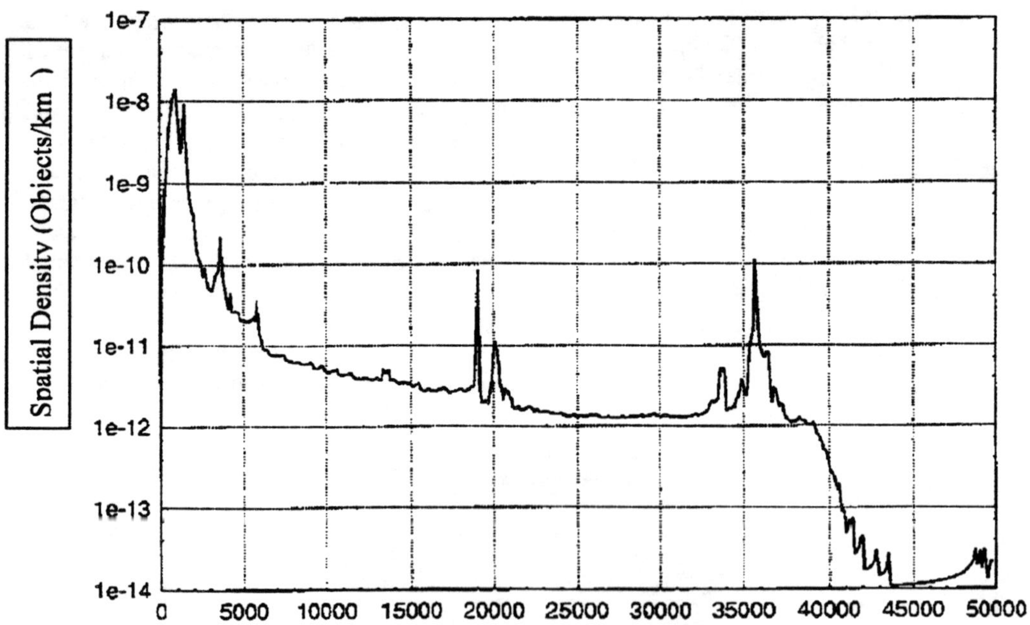

Figure 2. Spatial density of the 1994 U.S. Space Command Satellite Catalog[2].

The growth of cataloged objects in orbit at the end of each year is presented in Figure(3) with the break down of object type. The figure shows monthly number of objects in earth orbit by object type.

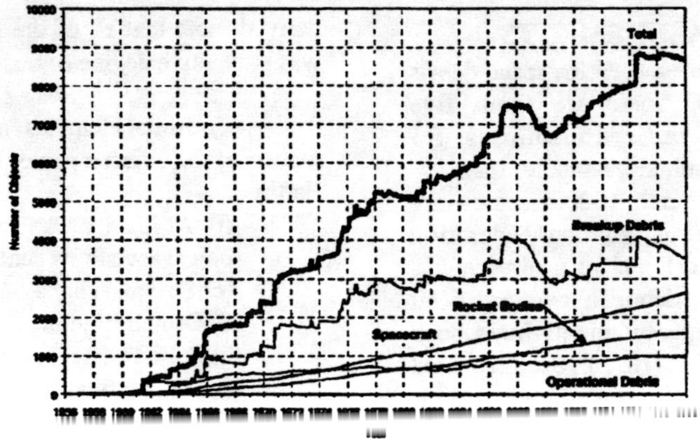

Figure 3. Growth of cataloged debris population[3]

ORBITAL DEBRIS MEASUREMENTS

Orbital debris can be detected by both ground-based and space-based measurements. The main advantage of space-based sensors is that they can be much closer to orbital debris than ground based sensors. It provides data on debris that are very difficult to detect from Earth. On the other hand, it is much more expensive to detect space debris from space. Generally orbital debris measurements fall into three categories:

- Radar measurements
- Optical measurements
- Research on retrieved surfaces

The capabilities of sensors are function of altitude. Figure (4) shows the US Space Command sensor altitude limitation. It can be observed that the operation system capability to detect objects depends strongly on the altitude.

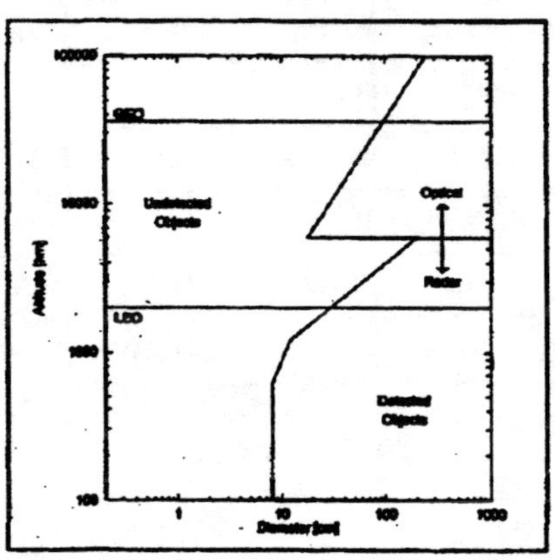

Figure 4. US Space Command sensor altitude limitation on debris measurement [4]

RADAR MEASUREMENTS

Radars generally have been used for space debris measurement in LEO. There are about five countries that have radar capabilities for observation of debris with sizes smaller than 10-30 cm in diameter beneath 1000km, they are Germany, Japan, Ukraine, Russian Federation and United States. Typically, radar measurements have been used for space debris in low Earth orbit (LEO), while optical measurements have been used for high Earth orbit (HEO). Ground-based radars are well suited to observe space objects because of their all-weather and day and night performance. The radar power budget and operating wavelength are limiting factors for detection of small objects at long ranges.

From radar measurements principally, the following space object characteristics can be derived; note that all of the following parameters will have some degree of uncertainty[]:

(a) Orbital elements, describing the motion of the object's center of mass around Earth;

(b) Attitude, describing the motion of the object around its center of mass;

(c) Size and shape of the object;

(d) Orbital lifetime;

(e) Ballistic coefficient, specifying the rate at which the orbital semi-major axis decays;

(f) Object mass;

(g) Material properties.

The existing and planned radar capabilities for observation of debris for sizes smaller than 10-30cm in diameter are given in Table(1).

Table(1) Radar facilities for debris observation [5]

Country	Organization	Facility	Type	Primary operation mode	Configuration	Field of View	Wave-length (m)	Sensitivity diameter (m)	Status
Germany	FGAN	TIRA	Dish	Mixed	Monostatic	0.5	0.23	0.02 at 1,000 km	Operational
Germany	MPIfR	Effelsberg	Dish	Stare	Bistatic with TIRA	0.16	0.23	0.009 at 1,000 km	Experimental
Japan	Kyoto University	MU Radar	Phased Array	Stare	Monostatic	3.7	6.4	0.02 at 500 km	Operational
Japan	ISAS	Uchinoura	Dish	Mixed	Bistatic	0.4	0.13	0.02 at 500 km	Experimental
Japan	ISAS	Usuda	Dish	Mixed	Bistatic	0.13	0.13	0.02 at 500 km	Experimental
Ukraine/Russian Federation	—	Evpatoria	Dish	Stare	Bistatic	0.1	0.056	0.003 at 1,000 km	Development
United States	NASA/NSF	Arecibo	Dish	Stare	Bistatic	0	0.13	0.004 at 575 km	One-time experiment
United States	NASA/DOD	Haystack	Dish	Stare	Monostatic	0.1	0.03	0.006 at 1,000 km	Operational
United States	NASA/DOD	HAX	Dish	Stare	Monostatic	0.1	0.2	0.05 at 1,000 km	Operational
United States	NASA	Goldstone	Dish	Stare	Bistatic	0	0.035	0.02 at 500 km	Operational
United States	DoD	TRADEX	Dish	Mixed	Monostatic	0.61/0.30	0.23/0.10	0.03 at 500 km	Operational

NASA's main source of data for debris in the size range of 1-30cm is the Haystack radar[6]. The Haystack radar, operated by MIT Lincoln Laboratory, has been collecting orbital-debris data for NASA since 1990 under an agreement with the U.S. Air Force. Haystack statistically samples the debris population by "staring" at selected pointing angles and detecting debris, which flies through its field of view. The data are used to characterize the debris population by size, altitude, and inclination. From these measurements, scientists have concluded that there are over 100,000 debris fragments in orbit with sizes down to 1cm.

Japan has decided to strengthen the monitoring setup necessary to forecast potential collisions[7]. According to a plan by the Science and Technology Agency, a dome-shaped radar facility and a large optical telescope with an aperture of 1 meter and a range three times that of an ordinary telescope will be constructed in Okayama Prefecture, which is considered the best site in Japan for monitoring space at a total cost of 2 billion yen. This radar facility, that is scheduled to go into operation in 2004, will be able to track objects 1 meter in diameter at an altitude of about 600 kilometers.

OPTICAL MEASUREMENTS

Debris can be also detected by optical measurements. Optical measurements have been used for higher orbits. A telescope can detect debris when the object is sunlit, while the sky, background is dark. There are about six countries that have optical capabilities for optical observation of debris namely France, Japan, Russian Federation, Switzerland, United Kingdom and Northern Island and United States.

Debris larger than 1m in diameter can be detected in GEO by ground based telescopes. The existing and planned optical capabilities for optical observation of debris are summarized in Table(2).

Table (2) Optical facilities for debris observation [8]

Country	Organization	Telescope Aperture (m)	Field of View (deg)	Detection Type	Limiting Magnitude	Status
France	ESA	1	1	CCD	19	In development
France	French National Centre for Scientific Research	0.9	0.5	CCD	19	In development
Japan	JSF[a]/NAL[b]/NASDA	1.0	3.0	CCD	19.5	In development
Japan	JSF[a]/NAL[b]/NASDA	0.5	2.0	CCD	18.5	In development
Japan	Sundai	0.75	0.04	CCD	17	Operational
Japan	CRL	1.5	0.28	CCD	18.7	Operational
Russian Federation	RAS[c]	1	0.2	CCD	19	Operational
Russian Federation	RAS[c]	0.6	0.2	CCD	18	Operational
Russian Federation	RSA[d]	0.6	0.2	TV	19	Operational
Switzerland	University of Berne	1	0.5	CCD	19.5	Operational
United Kingdom of Great Britain and Northern Ireland	Royal Greenwich Observatory/MOD	0.4	0.6	CCD	18	Two telescopes operational, United Kingdom and overseas
United States	NASA	0.3	1.5	CCD	17.1	Operational
United States	NASA	3	0.3	CCD	21.5	Operational

[a] Japan Space Forum.
[b] National Aerospace Laboratory of Japan.
[c] Russian Academy of Sciences.
[d] Russian Space Agency.

NASA is using two optical telescopes for measuring orbital debris: A 3 m diameter liquid mirror telescope, which is referred to as the LMT; and a charged coupled device equipped with 0.3m Schmidt camera, which is commonly referred to as the CCD Debris Telescope or CDT[9].

The LMT consists of a 3 m diameter parabolic dish that holds four gallons of liquid mercury. The dish is spun up to a rate of 10 revolutions per minute. Centrifugal force and gravity cause the mercury to spread out in a thin layer over the dish creating a reflective parabolic surface that is as good as many polished glass mirrors.

RESEARCH ON RETRIEVED SURFACES

Remote sampling of debris from orbit provides data on debris that are very difficult to detect from Earth. Space based sensors contain both radar and optical measurements. The main advantage of space-based sensors is that they can be much closer to orbital debris than ground based sensors.

Debris measurements can be also followed by research on retrieved surfaces and impact detectors. The Long-Duration Exposure Facility (LDEF) is an example covered by more than 30,000 craters visible to the naked eye; 5000 of which had a diameter larger than 0.5 mm. The largest crater, 5mm in diameter, was probably caused by particle of 1mm[].

Table 3. Examples of retrieved spacecraft and surfaces [10]

Name	Orbit	Duration In Orbit	Stabilization	Exposed Area
Salyut 4 and 6	350 km 51.6 degrees	1974-1979	Various	~7 m^2 of sensors and cassettes
STS-7 Window NASA	295-320 km 28.5 degrees	June 1983	Various	~2.5 m^2
Solar Maximum Solar Maximum	500-570 km 28.5 degrees	February 1980-April 1984	Sun-pointing	2.3 m^2
STS-52 (Canada/NASA)	350 km 28.4 degrees	October 1992	Various	1 m^2
LDEF (NASA)	340-470 km 28.5 degrees	April 1984-January 1990	Gravity-gradient	151 m^2
EURECA (ESA)	520 km 28.5 degrees	July 1992-June 1993	Sun-pointing	35 m^2 of spacecraft plus 96 m^2 of solar arrays
HST Solar Array (NASA/ESA)	610 km 28.5 degrees	May 1990-December 1993	Sun-pointing	62 m^2
Mir/EUROMIR 95 (RSA/ESA)	390 km 51.6 degrees	October 1995-February 1996	Gravity-gradient	20 x 30 cm (cassette)
Mir	390 km 51.6 degrees	1986-1998	Various	~15 m^2 of cassettes and other elements
Mir (Canada/Ukraine)	390 km 51.6 degrees	November 1997-February 1999	Various	1 m^2
SFU (Japan)	480 km 28.5 degrees	March 1995-January 1996	Sun-pointing (except 1 month IR telescope operation)	50 m^2
Space Shuttle Orbiter (NASA)	300-600 km 28.5-51.6 degrees	1992-present	Various	100 m^2

GLOBAL COOPERATION BY MEAN OF DEBRIS STUDIES

Even though space activities are mainly developed in few countries, but almost all nations are using the space technologies and products. In this regards all users are in some degrees involved in generation of debris. In another view debris, in its own right creates danger and cost that is reflected on consumer price directly or indirectly. Thus, we can expect research centers and academia to have interest in debris related research all over the world.

From the forgoing discussion on debris measurements, it is observed that even though the space based study of debris might give better measurements, but still the main activity is performed on earth. For selecting a proper site some general parameters can be considered:

1. Geographical Latitude
2. Clear and dark sky
3. Low smog and dust
4. Water vapor density
5. Aerosols Density

The current sites are mainly located in northern America and Western Europe and Russia, however, many location in other countries are suitable for establishment of observation facilities, while, the educated manpower is also available in some of these countries to take part in debris measurement and study.

Here, taking into consideration the reasoning presented here, we propose a new international cooperation scheme in development and decimations of space science and technology

- Setting up observation centers in suitable sites other than traditional places like Europe.

  The cost of establishing of the site is bored mainly by the Space Fairing Nations (SFN)
- The operating cost of the center is bored by the host country (HC).
- The manpower is provided by both countries as necessary, with emphasis on

providing mainly consultation and technical leader ship from SFC.

- The measurement and analyzed information is released to interested parties, with priority given to participating countries.

There are advantages to this cooperation:

- Those who use space technology will provide budget for space research.
- Knowledge of space science and technology is decimated in practical and efficient manner.
- Involving all space technology users in space research, knowing that they are directly or indirectly benefited from it.
- Measurements that are more versatile are provided.
- Manpower is used where it exits and is not involved in space research at this time.

This cooperation paves the way to open the door for space research in many countries that are interested and have interested educated personnel. These countries also provide some financial resources that is otherwise not available to space research communities.

REFERENCES

[1] Position Paper on Orbital Debris, updated 2000, International Academy of Astronautics, 2000, p3

[2] Ibid, p7

[3] Orbital Debris: A Technical Assessment. Committee on Space Debris Aeronautics and space Engineering Board Committee Commission on Engineering and Technical Systems National Research Council, USA, 1995, P66.

[4] Position Paper on Orbital Debris, Updated 2000, International Academy of Astronautics, 2000, pp11.

[5] Ibid, p29.

[6] Technical Report on Space Debris, Text of the report adopted by the Scientific and Technical Subcommittee of the United Nations Committee on the Peaceful Uses of Outer Space, USA, 1999, p6.

[7] Radar Measurements, available: "http://www.orbitaldebris.jsc.nasa.gov/measure/radar.html"

[8] COSMIC LITTER: Japan Moves to Counter Space Debris, available:

"http://jin.jcic.or.jp/trends98/honbun/ntj980630.html"

[9] Technical Report on Space Debris, Text of the report adopted by the Scientific and Technical Subcommittee of the United Nations Committee on the Peaceful Uses of Outer Space, USA, 1999, p8.

[10] Optical Measurements, available: "http://sn-callisto.jsc.nasa.gov/"

[11] Ibid, p9.

WORLD SPACE CONGRESS: "LEGAL AND POLICY FACTORS"

Thierry THORIN

CNES (Centre National d'Etudes Spatiales)
18 avenue Edouard Belin - 31401 TOULOUSE CEDEX 4 - FRANCE
Tel: (33) 05 61 28 32 50, Fax: (33) 05 61 27 31 67
E-mail: thierry.thorin@cnes.fr

To start with, I would like to explain why some years ago I became interested in the topic addressed today. The reason is that at the time I conducted a study on the impact of 'defective products related to space activities' for insurance purposes. You may be legitimate in objecting that the link with an attempt to set a boundary between both spaces is somewhat tenuous but I shall try to demonstrate that the opposite is true. As part of said study, I had tried to inventory not only the products but also the objects that contribute to the implementation of space activities. In doing so, I had underlined how difficult it was to determine the precise moment when a given object acquires or, on the contrary, loses its "space" nature. Nevertheless, as my research was progressing, I realized that it was not easy to dissociate the products that I wanted to analyze from the physical framework in which they were implemented. Through a misleading short cut I was tempted to affirm first of all that the defective products I was concerned with and related space activities occured exclusively in space. However, this was not as straightforward as it could appear, as the example of such activities known as pre-launching showed it. First and foremost, it was necessary to define the concept of "space". In retaining only the restrictive meaning of this term by reasoning a contrario i.e. all that is not located on the ground is in space, we can see that all activities for the last thirty years, generated first by mere machines of elementary design then by man himself and now by his varied robots and instruments, cover many locations and positions. The extent of such diversity is due both to technological development and the objectives to be reached.

This said, we could assert that the concept of space over the years has shifted from our terrestrial suburbs towards the boundaries of our galaxy due in particular to deep-space probes. As for the question regarding the activities we are concerned with, we cannot dodge the fundamental issue of space delimitation. However, it can arguably be said that, from a statutory standpoint, no accurate and universally accepted définition has been adopted yet, although this topic has been a concern of the international "space" community for a few decades already, encompassing so-called "space" powers as well as international bodies. As a matter of fact, beyond the unilateral stance or claims of a given state more particularly involved, it is obvious that the international community has abstained from legislating on the matter, except through sparse ad hoc or even symbolic provisions.

Most certainly this deliberate legal vagueness reflects the assertion of nations stepping up their demands in addition to discrepancies or even antagonism between states fueled by hypothetical profits, as was the case during attempts to delimit the ocean space.

In addition to the purely binary apprehension of space i.e. all that is not located on the ground is in space, another approach has to be considered whose scope keeps on developing as far as space activities are concerned. In this approach, space is no longer considered only in its metaphysical and geophysical aspects. More prosaically, space is seen as a virgin experimentation ground similar to a new boundary and mankind, after pursuing scientific goals in a disinterested manner, has quickly realized the profit to be made from a commercial exploitation of space.

Thus, space activities shall encompass a dual aspect involving transport, routing and design operations on the one hand, to put things simply while accurately reflecting reality, as well as research and development, pre-industrialization and even marketing on the other hand.

SPACE ACTIVITIES – SPACE

As these two concepts overlap, we are lead to ask a fundamental question: what does the concept of space –within which space activities are supposed to take place, thus so called simply because these activities physically occur in space– cover?

If space is endless, does it have at least a beginning? By opposition, one can affirm that although Earth is located itself in space, it represents, when legally apprehending this concept, the item zero from which indeed space starts insofar as our current knowledge allows us to spatially position the immediate satellites of the Earth like the Moon and also a great number of planets and celestial bodies.

Actually, to give a legal or even physical definition of space would be difficult since on the international level, the so-called space powers themselves have not imposed a common meaning to date. According to certain authors who were precursors in this field such as professor Bin Cheng, three different schools of thought have formed, namely the spatialist, the functionalist and the negativist ones. First, let us examine the "Spatialist" approach which could also be described as pragmatic. In the Spatialist approach, it is basically logical that national airspace is clearly and legally delimited. Regarding delimitation, it goes without saying that one should understand height or more correctly altitude.

Consequently, and logically, the end of airspace would mark the beginning of outer space.

The second school of thought known as the "Functionalist" questions the legitimate existence and even the capacity to implement such a delimitation of space. According to the functionalist approach in the delimitation of airspace from outer space, only the character of the (space) activity performed, coupled with the related objects, should make it possible to put them under regulation or conversely, to let them evolve in a realm of lawlessness.

Lastly, a third and last alternative that could be described as negativist considers the principle of the right to know as legitimate. For its supporters, only a minority would be likely to assert the right to know where space is and this based only on the need to know. Consequently, according to defenders of this theory, raising the issue of locating outer space, let alone discussing it, is useless. At the end of the day, we should agree this is a somewhat obscurantist vision of our environment and, beyond that, of the place of the human being in the universe.

Questionable as they may appear, these last two theories find substantiation in the fact that to delimit precisely airspace as opposed to outer space seems extremely difficult not to say impossible even when considering only the geophysical aspect of the problem. Moreover, even if that proved to be possible, after all the distance from the Earth to the Moon has been precisely calculated, this virtual boundary would remain abstract for most people, and that is all it would be.

Although this analysis is far from being totally illogical, it plays down the case of a famous precedent, the maritime field.

Indeed, how to be unaware of the efforts made since centuries by countries with a maritime frontage to attempt to set a spatial

boundary between territorial sea and high seas and to reign there?
When searching for international texts of a statutory nature or other, it becomes quickly obvious that few reference texts exist to define outer space. As Mr. G. LAFFERANDERIE stresses it, it is not necessary to search for an additional definition in the Astronauts Rescue Convention of 1968 or in the Convention on the Moon and other celestial bodies of 1979. Nonetheless, one might attempts to refer to the Treaty on principles governing the activities of states in the exploration and use of outer space, including the moon and other celestial bodies of 1967. First of all, it is to be noted that both the title and the recitals of this text underline the innovative nature of this concept since they feature both the terms "entry" and "exploration", the latter being mentioned six times in a row.
Although the situation has considerably evolved since 1967, we find ourselves in an almost virgin field, especially legally speaking. The prime objective of the Treaty being so clearly enunciated, one could expect that its authors would be somewhat more explicit regarding its object of application. The Treaty fails however to define outer space, since from the title to article XIII (the last four articles being dedicated to the implementation of the treaty), only "outer space, including the moon and other celestial bodies " is mentioned. No definition, even a contrario, is given to tell us what the outer space covers. Nonetheless, we should not be too critical. Indeed, even if the authors did not wish to codify this point, they have, voluntarily or not, provided us with the beginning of an answer through article VII in mentioning the liability of the states "on the Earth, in air space or in outer space". One can therefore conclude, keeping a simplistic terminology, that the lower boundary of outer space is located at the upper limit of air space and that its upper boundary remains indefinite to date. This interpretation is reinforced by the use of the exclusive prefix "extra" which leads us to assume that all that is not covered by air space is taken into account by the broad sense definition of outer space. We are forced to admit however that the phrase "outer space" has a meaning unanimously acknowledged without any other form of definition. For example, a convention on international liability for damage caused by space objects in 1972 mentions the outer space without going into further details.

Although international conventions have almost unanimously retained the term of outer space, they do not give any precise definition, as we have just seen it. Thus, able as we may be to scientifically position our planet and most of the celestial bodies, if not in our universe at least within our galaxy, we are however unable to delimit outer space. In fact, in observing international practice, one would be tempted to affirm that despite everything, a consensus based on logic exists to recognize and define outer space. The result is that all artificial satellites orbiting or having orbited around the Earth are located in outer space. This analysis could be also extended to natural satellites and go also beyond the concept of strict gravitation, irrespective of the planet concerned, Earth, Moon or other. For example, comets and meteorites or deep-space probes do not relate to a phenomenon of gravitation or orbit but fall within a course from a given point to another, both being located in outer space. However, this is not exactly the case for space probes insofar as their starting point is Earth therefore out of the outer space, which can have an impact regarding involvement in the scope of responsibility.

According to professor Bin Cheng still, the establishment of a rule of public international law setting the beginning of

outer space at the lowest perigee or altitude of an artificial satellite of the Earth initially stems from the absence of any claim from a state denouncing violation of the sovereignty of its national space because of satellites placed in terrestrial orbit. Secondly, there is the explicit acknowledgment by certain states of the fact that artificial satellites of the Earth orbit *de facto* in outer space. Generally speaking, this boundary could be set at an altitude of approximately a hundred kilometers subject to the application by certain states of a policy similar to that adopted regarding delimitation of territorial waters, namely a claim aimed at modifying the boundary separating the national airspace from the outer space by extending it or restricting it.
Historically speaking, the dissension between the spatialist and the functionalist approach, the very people who aimed at defining outer space, appeared even before the beginning of the space era. The views expressed on the issue at the time emanated from multiple and varied interlocutors and horizons, be it authors specialized in space law (a topic hardly tackled by international law), politicians, learned societies, or even governments or specialized agencies and other bodies from the United Nations. Within the latter, the supporters of a functionalist approach, initially backed by the great space powers which had no interest in setting boundaries likely to limit their freedom in space (for civil or military purposes), asserted the preponderance of their doctrine. To this end, they used the conclusions of the report from the ad hoc Committee on the Peaceful Uses of Outer Space. According to this report, the definition of outer space was not a priority issue, as we shall see it later on.

In 1966, the spatialist school of thought also expressed their views by means of resolution 2222 (XXI) adopted by the General Assembly, which invited the space committee to study the question. This resolution resulted from the approach chosen by some countries including Mexico, with a view to define outer space as part of the Outer Space Treaty to come. The chance or the handicap of the spatialist school in this debate laid in the existence of major and persistent dissensions within their community regarding universal acceptance of outer space. In this polemic, the most elementary debate consisted in delimiting air space as opposed to outer space. Another spatialist approach yet insisted on the introduction of triple zones or even multiple zones. In this respect, the diversity of methods and criteria used to set the higher or lower limits depending on whether airspace or outer space is considered reflects the variety of participants in this topic. Those methods and criteria included gravitational effect, effective control of a space object, lowest theoretical or actual perigee point regarding orbiting satellites, air resistance effect, farthest atmosphere layer, maximum capacity of an air flight or more arbitrarily a point representing the thousandth of the distance measured on a meridian line from the equator to the pole i.e. 100 kilometers or eventually the hundredth of the Earth radius i.e. 64 kilometers as the Canadian government suggested.

In fact, the United Nations Legal Sub-Committee in charge of outer space answered the General Assembly's interrogations by soliciting the scientific and technical sub-committee. At the time, in 1967, this sub-committee concluded that it was impossible to retain technical or scientific criteria making it possible to lead to a precise and unanimously acknowledged definition of outer space. Consequently, it was agreed that the Legal Sub-Committee had to come to a definitive conclusion on the topic. However, over the years, the functionalist supporters were gradually supplanted by the spatialist school even though they had widened their spectrum of outer space by including not only the nature of activities performed but also the missions carried out by "space vehicles". Italy in particular shared the spatialist approach. As early as 1958, the Italian representative at the United Nations committee demanded that a country national sovereignty apply at the outer space boundaryline, which according to this representative was set at approximately a hundred kilometers starting from the Earth surface. Thereafter, an increasing number of countries abandoned the functionalist theory in favor of the spatialist approach. For instance Belgium which, following the Italian example, suggested a delimitation based on the 100-kilometer limit. The Soviet Union, the other space power, also aligned with the spatialist doctrine by declaring in 1979:

1) Outer space is at a distance of 110 kilometers above the sea level.

2) The boundary of the airspace and outer space shall have to be the subject of agreements between the states and shall in consequence give rise to a treaty in which the outer space shall appear at an altitude which shall not exceed 110 kilometers above sea level.

3) The space objects concerned with the sovereignty of a state shall have the right to fly over the territory of other states at an altitude lower than 110 kilometers only for the purpose of reaching the necessary orbit or to return to Earth on the territory of the state of launching.

This last detail is very important because it confirms the fact that any object leaving the terrestrial ground shall have to cross the airspace of several states, made necessary by orbit positioning, before reaching this kind of " No man's land " which is the outer space and conversely on the return trip. However, in this last case, only the American shuttle is to date concerned, recoverable launch vehicles still being in the state of prototypes. The question has then arisen of whether air law must apply in such cases or on the contrary must one resort to the rules of the international space law insofar as a space type vehicle is involved. One of the explanations put forward on the change to the Soviet Union policy, consisted of the claim on behalf of the equatorial states in favor of the positioning of the geostationary orbit at a 36,000 kilometers altitude and this at the time of the declaration in Bogota of December 3, 1979. As for the United States, followed by the Federal Republic of Germany and the United Kingdom, they continued to support the uselessness of a delimitation to airspace and outer space for the following reasons:

- The incapacity of most states to manage such a concept
- The insufficiency of a scientific, legal, technical analysis and suitable policy
- Lastly, the obstacles that the introduction of such a boundary could represent if one considers future ambitions with regards to commercial use and exploration of outer space.

The controversy between the two schools of thought continued beyond the reasoning and the analyses of the respective supporters of each school. However, it is essential to reconsider the spatialist and functionalist approaches within the framework of the bases of the international law if one wants to succeed in better understanding them. It should first of all be recalled that contrary to a generally spread belief, there is no independent legal system on "space laws" treating outer space amongst other matters. In this case, space law is more like a compilation of national and international legal provisions treating outer space as well as artificial objects whether or not human activities take place there. One can thus say that there are international rules of space law and the rules of space law depending on the different national legal systems. The debate must however be primarily focused on international law insofar as the various national legal provisions should in this field only clarify international rules and not replace them. As regards international law and more precisely international space law, two jurisdictional sources can be identified. The first jurisdictional source stems from international law in its broadest sense, the second results from treaties, to which one could give a quasi contractual character insofar as only the signatories are named. It is indeed unanimously accepted that, even if there are many signatories to a treaty, it cannot be a creator of rights with regard to third parties without their prior assent, principle reaffirmed by article 24 of the convention of Vienna in 1969 on the right of treaties. It is thus fundamental, being international law, to dissociate the universal rules of international law applicable to all, from those which only the adherent states of a treaty belong. This distinction is all the more significant in space law as legal provisions on the matter are relatively very few whereas multiple international treaties concluded on the initiative the United Nations govern them in this field. Besides, it is not superfluous to point out that the charter of the United Nations itself does not form part as such of the international rules of law, that the United Nations, if I am not mistaken, do not have any legislative authority and that finally the resolutions of the General Assembly, as far as I know, are not binding to members except on budgetary matters.

I believe that we all agree to consider that the territorial delimitation of the competence of a state represents one of the basic functions of international law. Thus, the development of the national organization of the states during recent centuries and in parallel the development of international law have confirmed the principle of the exclusive competence of the sovereign state over its own territory. Territorial sovereignty always belongs to a single state excluding any other. On the contrary, the fact that state prerogatives can be exerted by other states on a determined area concerns the legal situation prevailing in certain places of the globe such as the high seas, which cannot constitute the territory of a state.

Generally, territorial sovereignty is based on natural and uncontested boundarys or reciprocal engagements between neighboring states such as conventions on territorial divisions or acts of reconnaissance of states based on given boundarys. This concept of territorial sovereignty makes it possible to divide between the nations the air space in which the activities of the citizens of this state are carried out. According to International law, the world including outer space is thus divided into three categories, namely: the "national territory", "territorium extra-commercium" and "territorium nullius".

- "national territory" is that on which a state exerts its national sovereignty without any interventions by any other state.
- "territorium extra-commercium" is defined on the contrary as that not being able to constitute the territory of a state, such as for example, the high seas.
- "territorium nullius" does not yet represent the territory of a state. In fact, they are territories which do not yet depend on the sovereignty of a subject of international law no matter, but which may nevertheless be acquired by a state according to the international legal provisions applicable to this type of procedure. Moreover, the treaty of 1979 on the Moon introduced a new and fourth category of territory under the name of "territorium commune humanitatis". This territory, like territorium extra-commercium, cannot be the subject of appropriation by a state but the two concepts defer for other reasons. Thus being "territorium extra-commercium" and in normal circumstances of peace as long as a state respects the sovereignty of other states regarding their aircraft, ships and other objects, international law confers on the said state a particularly

wide freedom of use of the territory concerned. It can indeed take over the resources, carry out military type tests and even what seems to be the latest trend, make use of it as immense discharge for its industrial waste.
Concerning this last point, if the open sea has for a long time and still continues to occupy the front of the scene, the fate reserved for outer space becomes increasingly crucial with in particular the problem of the space debris. In this matter, the International Instrument adopted by the International Law Association (ILA) conference in Buenos Aires in 1994 defined space debris as "man-made objects in outer space".

On the other hand, the emergent concept of "territorium commune humanitatis" considers that sharing of the resource of these territories and, generally, the problem of their appropriation, come under the responsibility of the international community (or more restrictively to the signatories to a given treaty as in the case of the treaty on the moon). However, certainly not in any case to individual states and even less their nationals. The objective of this classification is to determine above all, through international law, what states can or cannot do and this whether on their own territory or on the territories enumerated above. Consequently, the functionalist classification of the state activities between those which are legal and those which are not can only be consecutive and not precede classification spatialist. In fact, in international law, there are very few state activities that are of totally legal or totally illegal nature.
For example, the question of whether a state has the right to hail a ship to control its electronic monitoring means shall not depend on the nature of the act on boarding itself but above all on the place where the act of spying and the act of boarding occurred; being in the territorial waters of the state concerned, in those of a non-member state, in open sea or in one of the territories listed above. A second element in answer to this question shall consist in identifying the links existing between the spy vessel and the boarding state. Is it the act of a ship under the flag of its original country, or a ship of a non-member nationality or without any nationality?

NATURE, EXTENT AND LIMIT OF THE JURISDICTION OF A STATE

As regards international law, three types of jurisdiction are conferred to states
a) Territorial jurisdiction that the state is entitled to exert on its own territory.
b) Quasi territorial jurisdiction exerted on the ships, aircraft, spacecraft in the broadest sense and generally any means of transport whose vocation is to travel through territories other than its own territory and which belong to a given state due to their membership, nationality or registration.
c) Personal jurisdiction that a state can take over on nationals, whether they are natural persons or corporate entities except for material objects indicated in the preceding subparagraph. Each type of jurisdiction is subdivided in two subcategories:
- capacity of a state to enact laws applicable to its territory and its nationals and also capacity to interpret these same laws if need be,
- capacity of a state to apply these laws.

At this stage in our study, it is now time to examine in detail the functionalist approach on the delimitation of outer space vs. the Spatialist approach.
If, as we saw previously, the Spatialist school can not manage to harmonize their approach for the delimitation of airspace as well as for outer space, nor the functionalist approach proposes a standardized vision. They only converge on the point that the delimitation as meant by the spatialist school

is not useful and this even less nowadays. For the functionalist school, spatialist delimitation is not essential because only reference to the nature of the activities and objects involved make it possible to find an answer for present. For the functionalist school, it does not matter where an event takes place to determine its legality or its illegality, what is crucial is the nature of this event. However this approach goes against the international law as shown in the example of the ship boarded, referred to above. As defined by international law, monitoring the defense of a foreign state constitutes an act which is neither legal nor illegal and the functionalist analysis of this act does not make it possible to qualify it. Only the localization of the act makes it possible to determine its legality. Insofar as it is performed from the territory of the observing state or even at high seas, but not on the territory of the state observed, it is at first sight a perfectly legal act. On the other hand, assuming that this act is located above the territory of a sovereign state, this state has full rights to declare this act illegal in accordance with its own national law. This is the well-known case of the U2 American spy planes, one of which was shot down in 1960 above the territory of the Soviet Union: the United States acknowledged the legality of this act without hesitating. On the other hand, if this act of spying occurs outside the jurisdiction of the state observed, it does not violate international law and consequently any hostile attempt from spied state would be against this right. This is what happened in the same situation as in the preceding example but two months later in July 1960 above the high seas.

What is true for ships and aircraft also applies more and more to satellites. The monitoring activity of a state by means of spy satellites shall or shall not constitute an international statutory offence according to whether the activity carried out is or is not above the territory of the state in question. In this line of thought, it is difficult to solve the problem of the limit between airspace and outer space by supporting the fact that satellite monitoring is against international law irrespectively of the place where this activity is carried out, as defended by the functionalist theory. This line of thought is backed up by the fact that current technologies give the possibility to a satellite of a state A to observe a state B while remaining above the territory of state A. Another line of thought has been put forward according to which the absence of total consent as to the precise delimitation of territorial waters is not likely to generate a particular prejudice, which itself is questionable, and that the same should apply to outer space. This line of thought is true except that the limit of territorial waters claimed by any state is always known even if there is no international agreement. The same does not apply to outer space, perhaps because for a number of states the determination of its limits is not of a character as economically crucial as for territorial waters. In this respect, the functionalist school should contemplate the hypothetical situation according to which a state would not claim any limitation for its territorial waters and only retain the criterion of act contrary to its safety in its "near waters". Without reaching such a level of indetermination, the case of Pueblo, the American spy ship, which hit the news back in 1968 is revealing. At the time, the problem was not to know if the activity in question, spying, was or was not against the law but rather to know where the limit of sovereignty of the spied state was — North Korea in this case: 3 miles, 12 miles, and where the ship was when it was spying and when it was boarded.

While spatialist and functionalist schools were still confronting each other, an agreement on where air space ends and outer space begins had yet to be reached. The said

Professor Bin Cheng thought in 1965 that states were sufficiently advanced in this field to make it possible to define a new rule according to which airspace would be that reserved to conventional aircraft and outer space that devoted to satellites. Consequently this implied an upper boundary or a lower limit of approximately 50 miles i.e. 80 kilometers with a 25-mile tolerance in either direction. For the professor, the question lay in the interpretation by the states of a pre-existing rule of international law, i.e. the emergence of a new customary rule. His theory of a 50-mile limit was based on implicit recognition by the states discussing the matter at the United Nations that, when orbiting, satellites never penetrate in the airspace except when stationing or returning to earth and consequently, the question of satellites within airspace is irrelevant. This opinion was the basis for the draft resolution introduced at the Helsinki conference of the International Law Association (ILA) in 1966. In this resolution, the ILA legitimized the principle of the lowest perigee point. According to the same professor, this draft resolution was no more than an acknowledgment of an established fact and a consensus between states that all satellites to date orbited in outer space. Conversely, states could consider that their air sovereignty did not reach beyond the lowest perigee of an orbiting satellite. Hence the conclusion that the position adopted by states during the conference did not prejudge on any account their attitude towards future generations of satellites.

In addition, this draft resolution was far from establishing a precise and final boundary and did not even set the top limit of air sovereignty; it simply claimed that the top limit was not located beyond the point indicated in the project. Consequently, it could be located below the lowest point of perigee but never above. In conclusion, the professor mentioned three different layers hence three different legal statutes superimposed above the earth surface. Airspace is the first layer and undeniably depends on a state national sovereignty. Outer space is the second layer, starting above the lowest point of perigee, and incontestably independent of any state. Lastly, sandwiched in-between these two strata lies a relatively undetermined area above airspace and below outer space, undetermined due to satellite technical capabilities. However, original as it may be, this "three zone" approach does not reflect the stance of most states in favor of the more conventional coexistence of two spaces. For all that, the relevance of the lowest perigee rule has often been questioned, considering the factor of inaccuracy implied by this rule. At the most, it can be said that this rule reflects a latent finding at a given moment. As we have just seen, the definition and delimitation of outer space is far from being the subject of an international consensus. Quite the opposite in fact since this question seems to have been and remain a favorite showcase for the display of national peculiarities and specificities. This is perhaps the distinctive sign of great international law issues: in dealing with unexplored areas, devoid of any preexisting legal framework, such issues raise the most antagonistic claims under cover of protecting national interests. This said, and though unexplored, this question has been examined within the most prestigious existing international authority, i.e. the United Nations and ensuingly through its various committees. Given the rapid technological breakthroughs in the space field, this question was bound to trigger off attempts at codification if only to answer money-driven concerns — hidden though undoubtedly actual — of the main players on the international space stage.

Though not an immediate issue and still one unresolved, the topic discussed here has been thought about deeply and reflected upon giving rise to numerous suggestions over the last decades. France was the first country to put forward a proposition at a General Assembly of the United Nations in 1966. However, for lack of interest or conflicting opinions from certain participants, the work undertaken within the Legal Sub-Committee following the French initiative has been really slow, how else to explain that still no regulation on the matter has been laid down?

For the first time in 1967 during its sixth Session, the Legal Sub-Committee started to debate over matters relating to the "definition and delimitation" of outer space. These were the concerns of a number of delegations whose admitted objective was to found a legal regime applicable to space activities that were still in their infancy at the time. Opposite what was then best described as a legal void, it was only natural to take as a starting point the intangible principles of international law including the supremacy of sovereignty and national independence, equal rights, and noninterference in current home affairs. As commendable as they may be, we shall see that unfortunately these noble intentions were to conflict with the expression of national interests, as already mentioned. Nevertheless, at this very early stage of progress, two schools of thought emerged. The first school of thought favored a direct and pragmatic approach based on a distinction between two natural environments. In my opinion, the second school of thought was more subtle and augured of the difficulties to come. Its theory was based on the location or environment in which spacecraft would fly and where related activities would take place. It is easy to imagine how difficult it can be to define and delimit outer space based on this approach. In opposition to this, supporters of a direct approach — including France and Italy in line with their stance — presented a precise and concrete proposition based on an altitude determined from the earth surface and setting a boundary between the two spaces. Bearing in mind these positions, the Legal Sub-Committee thereafter consulted the Scientific Sub-Committee with the aim of getting a broader perspective on the question. Out of prudence or for lack of relevant information on the subject – we were then in the 1960's –, the Scientific Sub-Committee declared itself unqualified thus giving the go-ahead to lawyers who, although qualified, would have appreciated a scientific and technical opinion. Thereafter and as I mentioned previously, the question remained pending between 1970 and 1976. No doubt it was not considered a priority in comparison with what was at stake at a world level. Only in 1971 did France and Argentina request the reopening of the debate on the occasion of the tenth Session of the Sub-Committee. The delegates were certainly aware of the difficulties raised by such a large field of investigations related to the problem as presented initially, and so they scaled down their approach by dividing the question into two distinct interrogations. The elected terminology was from now on: "Questions relating to the definition AND/OR the delimitation of outer space and space activities". Only in 1975 did Italy suggest setting a precise limit of the two spaces according to a "vertical boundary" located at approximately 90 kilometers above the surface of the Earth. We had to wait until 1978 during the seventeenth Session for two issues to be raised which are essential in my eyes, i.e. the need to define "space objects" on the one hand and "space activities" on the other hand. Bearing in mind that at the time, artificial satellites had been orbiting for nearly twenty years, it was high time to define these terms. But this said, there is the risk of overlooking that any yearning for codification, however positive and constructive it may be, is likely to trigger an opposite reaction stating that such codification could infringe a pseudo freedom found in the absence of law. This explains that some delegations inferred that there was no need to legislate with regard to the smooth operation of space activities over the last twenty years. The same delegations added that any attempt at codification was in itself a potential hindrance to the development of space activities. They also evoked the difficulties related to the incapacity of most states to observe and control a conventional limit.

However, more and more delegations had a different view, being aware that the development of space activities and also of the states operating in space would ineluctably generate problems of liability in the short or medium term, which the existing bases of air law could not resolve. Some states had even anticipated the problem of dual localization according to which a space vehicle, acting first as a launch vehicle and then a shuttle, would be led to operate under both the legal provisions of air law and space law. In spite of that, the supporters of a space approach were still opposed to the supporters of a functional theory. The former wanted to apply a legal regime suitable according to the criterion of altitude, while the latter preferred as a preliminary to define objects and activities.

In 1983, on the occasion of the twenty-second Session of the Sub-Committee, the USSR, one of the two main players in worldwide space policy, proposed a boundary at an altitude of 110 km which had to be confirmed by a mandatory instrument of international law. This proposition incorporated a key provision in that it recognized the right to peacefully overfly states' territories at a lower altitude for orbit insertion and Earth return.

In the same year, the General Assembly drew again the attention of the Legal Sub-Committee to this topic that was still pending but also wanted for the first time to start thinking about drafting general principles relating to the use of geostationary orbit. The USSR, in line with its propositions drafted in 1983, again expressed its will to reach an agreement by introducing a draft text laying the basis for a future treaty, which unfortunately did not meet with approval by the delegations. Failing to reach an agreement in 1987, i.e. nearly twenty years after this question was first brought to light, some delegations went as far as expressing their wish to see this question banned from the Sub-committee's agenda. Despite these reactions, the Russian Federation presented an innovative approach in 1992 by listing a certain number of questions referring to the legal regime of space objects. Again this attempt met a refusal in 1996 after the delegations had deemed it useless to revive such a debate. Nevertheless, during the thirty-seventh meeting held in 1998, a trend emerged aiming at dividing into two the problems relating to space objects. This new approach could seem relatively logical in that it established a distinction between two periods, from 2000 to 2005 and from 2005 to 2010. These two phases were supposed to be representative of the increase in space activities. During the first period, it was planned that the design and the relatively limited use of space objects and related legal questions would be based on a legal status quo between the existing air law and space law provisions. Subsequently, during the second period supposed to be that of increased space activities, the experience gained was to lead to the development of a genuine legal corpus including both air law and space law concepts and legal provisions. This proposition came to naught. In 1999, the thirty-eighth session of the Legal Sub-Committee saw the emergence of a consensual approach in that it based its legitimacy on the reference to the 1967 Treaty on the Principles governing the activities of states in the exploration and use of outer space, including the moon and other celestial bodies. According to the delegation that initiated this proposition, it was necessary to follow a reasoning by analogy with existing and effective texts. This methodology was logical and eliminated at the same time any divergence inherent to the unilateral character of any given proposition. Such reasoning consisted in stating that any legal principle, part of a possible legal regime which would be applicable in the future, was to comply with the principles and rules stated in the Outer Space Treaty which constituted the general framework of all activities carried out in space.

However and since then, one can but notice that despite the reappointment of the working group entrusted with examining the item on the agenda concerning "the questions relating to the definition and the delimitation of outer space... ", no consensus has yet emerged among the delegations. Some delegations remain convinced that legislation is necessary with regard to the increasing risks of damage related to the possible collisions between airspace objects and aircraft. Other delegations persist in their position according to which the absence of codification had in no way hampered the development of the space-related activities.

NEED FOR COMBINING SPACE LAW WITH ENVIRONMENTAL LAW AND GLOBAL FEDERALISM

Professor S. Bhatt
Formerly Professor of Space Law, and
Honorary Professor of International Law
School of International Studies
Jawaharlal Nehru University, New Delhi – 110067
Commentator to UNISPACE III Conference, Vienna, July 1999

Abstract

This paper concerns the need to combine the principles of international space law with the principles of modern environmental law and ideas of global federalism. The requirement of a world order of 21st century is based on considering this planet being one large ecological unit. The stability of world order is dependent upon the stability of the global environments. As a result, space law is increasingly concerned with environmental law and federal management of this planet.

MODERN SPACE LAW

The broad contours of space law are provided in the excellent Space Treaty of 1967. These legal principles have shaped not only the order in outer space, but also the global order on this planet. A few predominant principles of space law need to be mentioned here. The freedom of exploration, scientific investigation, information contained in the Space Treaty changed the world order from a close, sovereignty-oriented international system to an open and collaborative system based on international cooperation.[1] Even in national defence matters and in matters related to threats from terrorism from external sources space law and space satellites provide active information at the global level to prevent such threats to world order and federal and national security. International cooperation in space exploration is another important principle of space law for which the United Nations has held important conferences like the UNISPACE III 1999 in Vienna. These conferences of states have helped the global community shape cooperation between states and share the benefits of space exploration. Global communication through space exploration has helped all states and people to live in great ease and interact with convenience. It has helped the whole global management of day to day life through phones, e-mails etc. The last important use of space law has been in the remote sensing of global resources and monitoring of global environments in general. Space law and exploration has a great role to play in the protection of global environments by monitoring eco-systems, disaster management and promoting international cooperation in the conservation movement and protection of global environments.

Indeed at the global level, there is need to install joint outer space/environment management boards to help provide information on the state of global environments. This can include information on training of terrorists and their camps and other sources of threats to peace and world order. The destruction to global environments by terrorism, by laying of mines, by destroying forests has assumed alarming proportions. The unfortunate terrorist attacks of September 11, 2001 in New York could have been prevented if we had a global disaster management monitoring system which could have given advance warning of terrorist training camps in Afghanistan and elsewhere. Monitoring and responding to global terrorism has become an important function of space law.

GLOBAL ENVIRONMENTAL LAW: ITS MAJOR CONCERNS

Modern environmental law has major concerns with the protection of global environments and with sustainable development. The Stockholm Declaration of 1972 is a world charter for environmental law. It says in the preamble that there is "the need for a common outlook and for common principles to inspire and guide the peoples of the world in the preservation and enhancement of the human environment." It calls for more prudent care for environmental consequences, acceptance of responsibility by all citizens, communities and institutions as also by individuals for the care of environments. It calls for conservation of earth's resources, control of rising global populations, sound environmental policies that enhance development potential, especially among the developing countries. Above all, the Declaration like the Space Treaty recommends international cooperation in the protection of environments. Indeed the World Charter for Nature 1982 also gives a new direction to environmental law to seek harmony with nature. It sets forth a few general principles of environmental law which inter alia states that nature shall be respected, genetic viability shall not be compromised, conservation of all resources shall be promoted, various eco-systems and organisms shall be protected, and nature shall be secured against degradation by warfare or other hostile activities (to this we may add global terrorism activities). Then there are vast areas of concern for modern environmental law that relate to forest fires, disaster like earthquakes, floods in major river systems, desert formation, scarcity of water resources etc. It is in this field of monitoring of environments and the preservation of eco-systems that space law must be tailored for the decades ahead. We have by and large solved the problems of space law for direct broadcasting, for remote sensing of global resources, for economic exploitation and the issues related to intellectual property rights. Laws are in the making on above issues. Nevertheless space law must be addressed to help solve problems of monitoring of, and degradation to, global environments, and global security of peoples of the world secured from unwanted acts of terrorism. In general, space law should promote sustainable development of environments. The global order is taking note of the stability of climates and other ecological issues. We have to respect nature and renew our lost resources of wild life and some beautiful eco-systems.

GLOBAL FEDERALISM

Federalism has emerged at the global level in recent decade or so in response to globalisation of world economy and cultural interaction. In simple terms federalism is a concept of governance taking into view the needs of local habitat within the overall needs of the region or a state. Thus, federalism ensures diversity of economy or cultures within the overall ambit of national or global economy. Federalism like the notion of sovereign provides for national polity but within the unified world order made possible by globalisation. The environment management has close nexus with federalism. An eco-system approach to resource management is an ecological manner of use of global resources. Federalism as a means of governance goes well with the eco-system management. Therefore space law should promote a life-style of people of the world based on federalism and ecological balance of eco-systems. Whereas space law has provided the unity of mankind for various resources like communications etc., it should help evolve a stable world order based on federal system and in conformity with the environmental needs. Thus, local safety and security of life of people anywhere in the world should be protected by monitoring of disasters and information systems regarding environments and security matters. The United Nations Charter is based on unity and diversity of global life. Modern space law and environmental law also help realise goals of UN Charter for security and economic well-being of people of the world. We have, therefore, the space exploration and its impact on world society. We have the global environmental revolution when life-style on this planet is changed to adjust to the common needs of the people. And, thirdly, we have the emerging federal view of management of states and geographical areas so as to ensure the stability of the biosphere, harmony with nature and cultural harmony world over. Federalism teaches us unity in diversity of global life. It is in conformity with the creation of nature based on diversity with an overall unity of the global ecological system.

I have attempted to describe the above world order in some of my recent and previous publications.[2]

Summary

It is time to look upon space law with a new perspective so that it can combine with the needs of environmental law and the federal management of global life. Space law can promote unity in diversity of global life. It can help ecological stability by meeting the needs of environments. It can ensure working of global federalism and the elimination of all forms of terrorism by efficient monitoring and response. Space law can help achieve a stable and creative environmental order. It should be in harmony with the needs of federalism. Because an efficient federal means of governance can promote cultural diversity within the unified economic and social order in the world.

Footnotes:

1. See S. Bhatt, Legal Controls of Outer Space: Law, Freedom and Responsibility with a foreward by Prof. Quincy Wright, S. Chand and Company Ltd., New Delhi, 1973, pp. 372. See also, V.S. Mani, S. Bhatt, B. Reddy, Eds., Recent Trends in Space Law and Policy, Lancers Books, New Delhi, 1997, pp. 683.

2. See S. Bhatt and B.D. Nag Chaudhuri, The Global Environment Movement: A New Hope for Mankind, Sterling Publications, New Delhi, 1987; S. Bhatt, "The Role of Environmental Law for the World Order of 21st Century", International Conference on International Law in the New Millennium: Problems and Challenges Ahead, 4-7 October, 2001, organised by Indian Society of International Law, New Delhi, vol. III, pp. 31-39; S. Bhatt and Akhtar Majid, Eds., Environmental Management And Federalism: The Indian Experience, Uppal Publishing House, New Delhi, 2002, pp. 256.

ADDENDA

INTERNATIONAL INSTITUTE OF SPACE LAW
of the
INTERNATIONAL ASTRONAUTICAL FEDERATION

Standing Committee on the Status of International Agreements Relating to Activities in Outer Space

Chairman:
Andrei D. Terekhov
Senior Legal Officer
Office of Legal Affairs
United Nations

ANNUAL REPORT – 2002

Background

At the meeting of the IISL Board of Directors held at Brighton, United Kingdom, in October 1987, the Board decided to create a standing committee of the Institute to prepare and submit at each annual Colloquium a report on the status of agreements relating to activities in outer space.

Institute members who can contribute substantively to the work of the committee are invited to serve on it. Membership is open to any interested IISL member. The committee members help collect, review and verify data concerning selected space agreements. Agreements of general global applicability or regional applicability are selected for reporting. Bilateral agreements are not included in the report. In general, the agreements included in the present report, and their status, are believed to be valid as of 1 January 2002.

Coded entries are used in the table as follows:

R = ratification, accession or succession
S = signature only
D = declaration of acceptance of rights and obligations

When no entry is made in a column opposite a state's name, that state has not signed that agreement, or is not a party to it, or that state has withdrawn from the agreement. Changes from last year are highlighted by "**".

At the meeting of the IISL Board of Directors held at Paris, France, in April 1998, the Board decided that the report should also contain basic data concerning Declarations of Principles Relating to Activities in Outer Space adopted by the General Assembly of the United Nations.

COMMITTEE MEMBERSHIP

Prof. Dr. K.-H. Böckstiegel
Institut für Luft- und Weltraumrecht
University of Cologne
Albertus-Magnus-Platz 5000
Cologne, 41 GERMANY

Prof. Carl Q. Christol
1041 Anoka Place
Pacific Palisades, CA 90272
USA

Prof. Dr. Aldo Armando Cocca
Lavalle 1527, piso 10
1048 Buenos Aires
ARGENTINA

Prof. Dr. Isabella Diederiks-Verschoor
President Emeritus, IISL
Leestraat 43, 3743 EH Baarn
NETHERLANDS

Dr. Stephen E. Doyle
3431 Bridget Brae
Shingle Springs
CA 95682
USA

Dr. Eilene Galloway
4612 29th Place, NW
Washington, D.C. 20008
USA

Prof. Dr. Vladimir Kopal
IAF General Counsel
Vidlicová 2200
16000 Prague 6 - Dejvice
CZECH REPUBLIC

Prof. Francis Lyall
Department of Public Law
University of Aberdeen
Aberdeen, AB92UB
SCOTLAND

Mr. G. Lafferranderie
Legal Adviser, ESA
8-10, rue Mario Nikis
Paris 75738 FRANCE

Mrs. Tanja L. Masson-Zwaan
38 rue des Carmélites
81000 Albi
FRANCE

Dr. HE Qizhi
Legal Advisor
Department of Treaty & Law
Ministry of Foreign Affairs
Beijing CHINA

Mr. David Sagar
Flat 4, 51 Cadogan Gardens
London SW3 2 TH
UNITED KINGDOM

Dr. A. D. Terekhov (Chairman)
Office of Legal Affairs
Room 3430G, UN Secretariat
New York, NY 10017 USA

Mr. Leo A. Webb
5597 Seminary Road, No. 2305
Falls Church, VA 22041
USA

AGREEMENTS INCLUDED

1. **1963 NTBT** - **Treaty Banning Nuclear Weapon Tests in the Atmosphere, in Outer Space and Under Water; done at Moscow on 5 August 1963; entered into force on 10 October 1963. (14 UST 1313; TIAS 5433; 480 UNTS 43)**
http://www.tufts.edu/departments/fletcher/multi/texts/BH454.txt

2. **1967 OST** - **Treaty on Principles Governing the Activities of States in the Exploration and Use of Outer Space, including the Moon and Other Celestial Bodies; done at Washington, London and Moscow on 27 January 1967; entered into force on 10 October 1967. (18 UST 2410; TIAS 6347; 610 UNTS 205)**
http://www.oosa.unvienna.org/SpaceLaw/outerspt.htm

3. **1968 ARRA** - **Agreement on the Rescue of Astronauts, the Return of Astronauts and the Return of Objects Launched into Outer Space; done at Washington, London and Moscow on 22 April 1968; entered into force on 3 December 1968. (19 UST 7570; TIAS 6599; 672 UNTS 119)**
http://www.oosa.unvienna.org/SpaceLaw/rescue.htm

4. **1972 LIAB** - **Convention on International Liability for Damage Caused by Space Objects; done at Washington, London and Moscow on 29 March 1972; entered into force on 1 September 1972. (24 UST 2389; TIAS 7762; 961 UNTS 187)**
http://www.tufts.edu/departments/fletcher/multi/texts/BH595.txt

5. **1975 REG** - **Convention on Registration of Objects Launched into Outer Space; done at New York on 14 January 1975; entered into force on 15 September 1976. (28 UST 695; TIAS 8480; 1023 UNTS 15)**
http://www.oosa.unvienna.org/SORegister/regist.htm

6. **1979 MOON** - **Agreement Governing the Activities of States on the Moon and Other Celestial Bodies; done at New York on 18 December 1979; entered into force on 11 July 1984. (18 ILM 1434; UN doc. A/RES/34/68 of 14 December 1979, Annex)**
http://www.oosa.unvienna.org/SpaceLaw/moon.htm

7. **1971 INTL** - **Agreement Relating to the International Telecommunications Satellite Organization (INTELSAT) with annexes, and Operating Agreement Relating to the International Telecommunications Satellite Organization with annex; done at Washington on 20 August 1971; entered into force on 12 February 1973. (23 UST 3813, 4091; TIAS 7532)**
http://www.tufts.edu/departments/fletcher/multi/texts/BH585.txt

8. **1976 INMR** - **Convention on the International Maritime Satellite Organization (INMARSAT) with annex, and the Operating Agreement on the International Maritime Satellite Organization with annex; done at London on 3 September 1976; entered into force on 16 July 1979. (31 UST 1, 135; TIAS 9605)**
http://www.tufts.edu/departments/fletcher/multi/texts/BH688.txt

9. **1971 INTR** - **Agreement on the Establishment of the "Intersputnik" International System and Organization of Space Communications; done at Moscow on 15 November 1971; entered into force on 12 July 1972. (862 UNTS 3)**
http://www.intersputnik.com/doc2.shtml

10. **1976 INTC** - **Agreement on Cooperation in the Exploration and Use of Outer Space for Peaceful Purposes (INTERCOSMOS); done at Moscow on 13 July 1976; entered into force on 25 March 1977. (16 ILM 1)**
http://www.nasda.go.jp/lib/space-law/chapter_2/2-2-2-7_e.html [Note: *The document served from this website omits the words "and Use" in the title and is incorrectly dated "1973" instead of "1976".*]

11. **1976 ARBS** - **The Agreement of the Arab Corporation for Space Communications (ARABSAT); done at Cairo on Wednesday, 14 Rabi Al Akhar 1396 H., corresponding to April 14, 1976; entered into force on July 16, 1976. (Space Law and Related Documents, U.S. Senate, 101st Congress, 2nd Session, 395 (1990))**
http://www.nasda.go.jp/lib/space-law/chapter_2/2-2-2-15/index_e.html

12. **1975 ESA** - **Convention for the Establishment of a European Space Agency (ESA) with annexes; done at Paris on 30 May 1975; entered into force on 30 October 1980. (14 ILM 864)**
http://www.esa.int/convention/

13. **1982 EUTL** - **Convention Establishing the European Telecommunications Satellite Organization (EUTELSAT); done at Paris on 15 July 1982; entered into force on 1 September 1985. (XI Annals of Air and Space Law 416 (1986); UK Misc. No.4, Cmnd. 9154 (1984))**
http://www.nasda.go.jp/lib/space-law/chapter_3/3-2-2-2/index_e.html

14. **1983 EUMT** - **Convention for the Establishment of a European Organization for the Exploitation of Meteorological Satellites (EUMETSAT); done at Geneva on 24 May 1983; entered into force on 19 June 1986. (Federal Republic of Germany Bundesgesetzblatt, Jahrgang 1987, Teil 11, p. 256 (1987). This Convention has been published in the national bulletins of the ratifying States)**
http://www.nasda.go.jp/lib/space-law/chapter_3/3-2-2-6/index_e.html

15. **1974 BRUS** - **Convention Relating to the Distribution of Programme-carrying Signals Transmitted by Satellite; done at Brussels on 21 May 1974; entered into force on 25 August 1979. (1144 UNTS 3)**
http://www.nasda.go.jp/lib/space-law/chapter_2/2-2-2-11_e.html

The texts of all the above agreements, except 1974 BRUS, 1982 EUTL and 1983 EUMT, were published in Space Law and Related Documents, U.S. Senate, 101st Congress, 2nd Session, June 1990.

Treaty Status Table as of January 1, 2002

TREATY — STATE	(1) 1963 NTBT	(2) 1967 OST	(3) 1968 ARRA	(4) 1972 LIAB	(5) 1975 REG	(6) 1979 MOON	(7) 1971 INTL	(8) 1976 INMR	(9) 1971 INTR	(10) 1976 INTC	(11) 1976 ARBS	(12) 1975 ESA	(13) 1982 EUTL	(14) 1983 EUMT	(15) 1974 BRUS
Afghanistan	R	R					R		R						
Albania													R		
Algeria	S	R		S			R	R			R				
Andorra													R		
Angola							R								
Antigua and Barbuda	R	R	R	R	R										
Argentina	R	R	R	R	R		R	R							S
Armenia	R						R						R		R
Australia	R	R	R	R	R	R	R	R							R
Austria	R	R	R	R	R	R	R					R	R	R	R
Azerbaijan							R						R		
Bahamas	R	R	R				R	R							
Bahrain							R	R			R				
Bangladesh	R	R					R	R							
Barbados		R	R				R								
Belarus	R	R	R	R	R			R	R				R		
Belgium	R	R	R	R	R		R	R				R	R	R	S
Benin	R	R		R			R								
Bhutan	R						R								
Bolivia	R	S	S				R								
Bosnia and Herzegovina	R		R	R			R	R					R		R
Botswana	R	S	R	R			R								
Brazil	R	R	R	R			R	R							S
Brunei Darussalam							R	R							
Bulgaria	R	R	R	R	R		R	R	R	R			R		
Burkina Faso	S	R					R								
Burundi	S	S		S	S		S								
Cambodia				S											
Cameroon	S	S	R				R	R							
Canada	R	R	R	R	R		R	R				(1)			
Cape Verde	R						R								
Central African Republic	R	S		S			R								
Chad	R						R								
Chile	R	R	R	R	R	R	R	R							
China		R	R	R	R		R	R							
Colombia	R	S	S	S			R	R							
Comoros							R								
Congo			S				R								
Costa Rica	R		S	S			R	R							R
Cote d'Ivoire	R						R								S
Croatia	R						R	R					R		R
Cuba		R	R	R	R		*R*	R	R	R					
Cyprus	R	R	R	R	R		R	R					R		S

Note: (1) Canada has a Cooperation Agreement with ESA, but is not a Member.

Treaty Status Table as of January 1, 2002

TREATY — STATE	(1) 1963 NTBT	(2) 1967 OST	(3) 1968 ARRA	(4) 1972 LIAB	(5) 1975 REG	(6) 1979 MOON	(7) 1971 INTL	(8) 1976 INMR	(9) 1971 INTR	(10) 1976 INTC	(11) 1976 ARBS	(12) 1975 ESA	(13) 1982 EUTL	(14) 1983 EUMT	(15) 1974 BRUS
Czech Republic	R	R	R	R	R		R	R	R	R			R		
Dem. People's Rep. of Korea							R		R						
Dem. Rep. of the Congo (formerly - Zaire)	R	S	S	S			R								
Denmark	R	R	R	R	R		R	R				R	R	R	
Djibouti											R				
Dominican Republic	R	R	S	R			R								
Ecuador	R	R	R	R			R								
Egypt	R	R	R	S			R	R			R				
El Salvador	R	R	R	S			R								
Equatorial Guinea	R	R					R								
Estonia													R		
Ethiopia	S	S					R								
Fiji	R	R	R	R			R								
Finland	R	R	R	R			R	R				R	R	R	
France		R	R	R	R	S	R	R				R	R	R	S
Gabon	R		R	R			R	R							
Gambia	R	S	R	S			*R*								
Georgia							*R*		R				R		
Germany	R	R	R	R	R		R	R	R			R	R	R	R
Ghana	R	S	S	S			R	R							
Greece	R	R	R	R			R	R					R	R	R
Guatemala	R			S		S	R								
Guinea							R								
Guinea-Bissau	R	R	R				*R*								
Guyana		S	R												
Haiti	S	S	S	S			R								
Holy See		S					R						R		
Honduras	R	S		S			R								
Hungary	R	R	R	R	R		R	R	R	R			R		
Iceland	R	R	R	S			R	R					R		
India	R	R	R	R	R	S	R	R	R						
Indonesia	R	S	R	R	R		R	R							
Iran (Islamic Republic of)	R	S	R	R	S		R	R							
Iraq	R	R	R	R			R	R			R				
Ireland	R	R	R	R			R					R	R	R	
Israel	R	R	R	R			R	R							S
Italy	R	R	R	R			R	R				R	R	R	R
Jamaica	R	R	S				R								R
Japan	R	R	R	R	R		R	R							
Jordan	R	S	S	S			R				R				
Kazakhstan		R	R	R	R	R	R		R				R		
Kenya	R	R		R			R	R							R
Kuwait	R	R	R	R			R	R			R				
Kyrgyzstan							R		R						
Lao People's Dem. Republic	R	R	R	R					R						

Treaty Status Table as of January 1, 2002

TREATY — STATE	(1) 1963 NTBT	(2) 1967 OST	(3) 1968 ARRA	(4) 1972 LIAB	(5) 1975 REG	(6) 1979 MOON	(7) 1971 INTL	(8) 1976 INMR	(9) 1971 INTR	(10) 1976 INTC	(11) 1976 ARBS	(12) 1975 ESA	(13) 1982 EUTL	(14) 1983 EUMT	(15) 1974 BRUS
Latvia								R					R		
Lebanon	R	R	R	S			R	R			R				S
Lesotho		S	S												
Liberia	R							R							
Libyan Arab Jamahiriya	R	R					R	R			R				
Liechtenstein				R	R		R						R		
Lithuania													R		
Luxembourg	R	S	S	R			R						R		
Madagascar	R	R	R				R								
Malawi	R						R								
Malaysia	R	S	S				R	R							
Maldives			R												
Mali	S	R		R			R								
Malta	R		S	R			R	R					R		
Marshall Islands								R							
Mauritania	R						R				R				
Mauritius	R	R	R				R	R							
Mexico	R	R	R	R	R	R	R	R							R
Micronesia (Fed. States of)							R								
Monaco			S				R	R					R		
Mongolia	R	R	R	R	R		R		R	R					
Morocco	R	R	R	R		R	R	R			R				R
Mozambique							R	R							
Myanmar	R	R	S												
Nepal	R	R	R	S			R								
Netherlands	R	R	R	R	R	R	R	R				R	R	R	
New Zealand	R	R	R	R			R	R							
Nicaragua	R	S	S	S	S		R		R						R
Niger	R	R	R	R	R		R								
Nigeria	R	R	R				R	R							
Norway	R	R	R	R	R		R	R				R	R	R	
Oman				S			R	R			R				
Pakistan	R	R	R	R	R	R	R	R							
Panama	R	S		R			R	R							R
Papua New Guinea	R	R	R	R			R								
Paraguay	S						R								
Peru	R	R	R	S	R	S	R	R							R
Philippines	R	S	S	S		R	R	R							
Poland	R	R	R	R	R		R	R	R	R			R		
Portugal	S	*R*	R				R	R				R	R	R	R
Qatar				R			R	R			R				
Republic of Korea	R	R	R	R	R		R	R							
Republic of Moldova													R		
Romania	R	R	R	R		S	R	R	R	R			R		
Russian Federation	R	R	R	R	R		R	R	R	R			R		R

Treaty Status Table as of January 1, 2002

TREATY — STATE	(1) 1963 NTBT	(2) 1967 OST	(3) 1968 ARRA	(4) 1972 LIAB	(5) 1975 REG	(6) 1979 MOON	(7) 1971 INTL	(8) 1976 INMR	(9) 1971 INTR	(10) 1976 INTC	(11) 1976 ARBS	(12) 1975 ESA	(13) 1982 EUTL	(14) 1983 EUMT	(15) 1974 BRUS
Rwanda	R	S	S	S			R								R
Samoa	R														
San Marino	R	R	R										R		
Saudi Arabia		R		R			R	R			R				
Senegal	R		S	R			R	R							S
Seychelles	R	R	R	R	R										
Sierra Leone	R	R	S	S											
Singapore	R	R	R	R	S		R	R							
Slovakia	R	R	R	R	R			R		R			R		
Slovenia	R		R	R									R		R
Somalia	S	S	S				R				R				
South Africa	R	R	R	S			R	R							
Spain	R	R	R	R	R		R	R				R	R	R	S
Sri Lanka	R	R		R			R	R							
St. Vincent and Grenadines		R	R	R	R										
Sudan	R						R				R				
Suriname	R														
Swaziland	R		R				R								
Sweden	R	R	R	R	R		R	R				R	R	R	
Switzerland	R	R	R	R	R		R	R				R	R	R	R
Syrian Arab Republic	R	R	R	R			R		R		R				
Tajikistan							R		R						
Tanzania							R	R							
Thailand	R	R	R				R								
The former Yugoslav Republic of Macedonia													R		R
Togo	R	R		R			R								
Tonga	R	R	R												
Trinidad and Tobago	R	S		R			R								R
Tunisia	R	R	R	R			R	R			R				
Turkey	R	R	S				R	R					R	R	
Turkmenistan									R						
Uganda	R	R					R								
Ukraine	R	R	R	R	R			R	R				R		
United Arab Emirates		*R*		*R*	R		R	R			R				
United Kingdom	R	R	R	R	R		R	R				R	R	R	
United Rep. of Tanzania	R			S			R								
United States of America	R	R	R	R	R		R	R							R
Uruguay	R	R	R	R	R	R	R								
Uzbekistan							R								
Venezuela	R	R	S	R			R								
Viet Nam		R					R	R	R	R					
Yemen	R	R	R				R		R		R				
Yugoslavia	R	S	R	R	R		R	R					R		R
Zambia	R	R	R	R			R								
Zimbabwe							R								

Treaty Status Table as of January 1, 2002

~ Totals for 178 States ~

TREATY — STATE	(1) 1963 NTBT	(2) 1967 OST	(3) 1968 ARRA	(4) 1972 LIAB	(5) 1975 REG	(6) 1979 MOON	(7) 1971 INTL	(8) 1976 INMR	(9) 1971 INTR	(10) 1976 INTC	(11) 1976 ARBS	(12) 1975 ESA	(13) 1982 EUTL	(14) 1983 EUMT	(15) 1974 BRUS
"Old" Ratifications	124	95	88	80	44	10	144	86	24	10	20	15	49	17	25
"New" Ratifications		2		1			4								
Total Ratifications	**124**	**97**	**88**	**81**	**44**	**10**	**148**	**86**	**24**	**10**	**20**	**15**	**49**	**17**	**25**
"Old" Signatures	10	27	24	26	4	5	1								10
"New" Signatures															
Total Signatures	**10**	**27**	**24**	**26**	**4**	**5**	**1**								**10**

~ Changes in status since the 2001 Report ~

Agreements for which status has changed:		(2) 1967 OST		(4) 1972 LIAB			(7) 1971 INTL								
Cuba		R	R	R	R		*R*	R	R	R					
Gambia	R	S	R	S			*R*								
Georgia							*R*		R				R		
Guinea-Bissau	R	R	R				*R*								
Portugal	S	*R*	R				R	R				R	R	R	R
United Arab Emirates		*R*		*R*	R		R	R			R				

Treaty Status Table as of January 1, 2002, for certain IGOs

TREATY *(See Note below.)* ---- ORGANIZATION	(3) 1968 ARRA	(4) 1972 LIAB	(5) 1975 REG	(6) 1979 MOON
European Space Agency (ESA)	D	D	D	
European Org. for the Exploitation of Meteorological Satellites (EUMETSAT)			D	
European Telecommunications Satellite Org. (EUTELSAT)		D		
Totals for 3 Organizations:	1	2	2	

Note: The Committee believes that only four of the agreements covered in the report (1968 ARRA, 1972 LIAB, 1975 REG and 1979 MOON) provide for a declaration of acceptance of rights and obligations ("D") by IGOs.

Declarations of Principles Relating to Activities in Outer Space adopted by the General Assembly of the United Nations

1. Declaration of Legal Principles Governing the Activities of States in the Exploration and Use of Outer Space (General Assembly resolution 1962 (XVIII)). Adopted without vote on 13 December 1963.
http://www.oosa.unvienna.org/SpaceLaw/gares/html/gares_18_1962.html

2. Principles Governing the Use by States of Artificial Earth Satellites for International Direct Television Broadcasting (General Assembly resolution 37/92). http://www.un.org/documents/ga/res/37/a37r092.htm Adopted by 107 votes to 13, with 13 abstentions, on 10 December 1982 as follows (voting results are reproduced from UN document A/37/PV.100 of 17 December 1982):

> **In favour: Afghanistan, Algeria, Argentina, Bahrain, Bangladesh, Barbados, Benin, Bhutan, Bolivia, Botswana, Brazil, Bulgaria, Burma, Botswana, Burundi, Byelorussian Soviet Socialist Republic, Central African Republic, Chad, Chili, China, Colombia, Comoros, Congo, Cuba, Cyprus, Czechoslovakia, Democratic Kampuchea, Democratic Yemen, Djibouti, Dominican Republic, Ecuador, Egypt, El Salvador, Ethiopia, Fiji, Gabon, Gambia, German Democratic Republic, Ghana, Guyana, Haiti, Honduras, Hungary, India, Indonesia, Iran (Islamic Republic of), Iraq, Jamaica, Jordan, Kenya, Kuwait, Lao People's Democratic Republic, Liberia, Libyan Arab Jamahiriya, Madagascar, Malaysia, Maldives, Mali, Malta, Mauritania, Mauritius, Mexico, Mongolia, Mozambique, Nepal, Nicaragua, Niger, Nigeria, Oman, Pakistan, Panama, Papua New Guinea, Peru, Philippines, Poland, Qatar, Romania, Rwanda, Sao Tome and Principe, Saudi Arabia, Senegal, Sierra Leone, Singapore, Solomon Islands, Somalia, Sri Lanka, Sudan, Suriname, Syrian Arab Republic, Thailand, Togo, Trinidad and Tobago, Tunisia, Turkey, Uganda, Ukrainian Soviet Socialist Republic, Union of Soviet Socialist Republics, United Arab Emirates, United Republic of Cameroon, United Republic of Tanzania, Upper Volta, Uruguay, Venezuela, Viet Nam, Yemen, Yugoslavia, Zaire, Zambia.**
>
> **Against: Belgium, Denmark, Germany, Federal Republic of, Iceland, Israel, Italy, Japan, Luxembourg, Netherlands, Norway, Spain, United Kingdom of Great Britain and Northern Ireland, United States of America.**
>
> **Abstaining: Australia, Austria, Canada, Finland, France, Greece, Ireland, Lebanon, Malawi, Morocco, New Zealand, Portugal, Sweden.**

3. Principles Relating to Remote Sensing of the Earth from Outer Space (General Assembly resolution 41/65). Adopted without vote on 3 December 1986. http://www.un.org/documents/ga/res/41/a41r065.htm
[Note: *The document served from this website omits the word "Outer" in the title.*]

4. Principles Relevant to the Use of Nuclear Power Sources in Outer Space (General Assembly resolution 47/68). Adopted without vote on 14 December 1992. http://www.un.org/documents/ga/res/47/a47r068.htm

5. Declaration on International Cooperation in the Exploration and Use of Outer Space for the Benefit and in the Interests of All States, Taking into Particular Account the Needs of Developing Countries (General Assembly resolution 51/122). Adopted without vote on 13 December 1996.
http://www.un.org/documents/ga/res/51/a51r122.htm

Note: A copy of this report can be downloaded from the Institute's web site– http://www.iafastro-iisl.com/main%20pages/committee_8.htm

IAA-IAC/IISL/COSPAR Joint Session:
Planetary Protection Issues in Space Exploration, Legal Aspects

PROTECTION OF THE LIFELESS ENVIRONMENT IN THE SOLAR SYSTEM

I. Almár
Konkoly Observatory, H-1525, Budapest, POB 67, Hungary

ABSTRACT

The main concern of planetary protection policy is how to protect the (hypothetical) extraterrestrial life against contamination and back-contamination. There is almost no interest in the preservation of the existing lifeless surfaces of extraterrestrial bodies, although some planetary transformation plans (in order to exploit hypothetical resources) were made public a long time ago. It should be remembered that planetary environments are practically unchanged since ages and damage caused by any human intervention would be irreversible. Our intention is not to prevent any commercial utilization of Solar System resources, but to make space exploration and exploitation of resources a controlled and well-planned endeavor. The three main issues connected with the protection of the lifeless space environment are the following:

1/ The scientific aspect: a limited, well-defined initiative to select by scientific investigation areas and objects of highest priority on different celestial bodies.

2/ The legal aspect: to start the drafting of a declaration of principles supporting the protection of selected areas and objects on celestial bodies with solid surface. It might evolve into an international legal instrument or treaty in order to limit the "free-for-all" intervention and use of Solar System resources.

3/ The societal aspect: to initiate a large-scale discussion on the possible "ethical values" of the lifeless environment.

INTRODUCTION

In a previous paper (Almár 2000) we emphasized the need for an environment protection policy within the Solar System for the sake of future generations. The task of planetary scientists would be to survey and evaluate all known planetary environments with regards to their scientific value. Based on such a survey a list of scientifically important planetary environments can be drawn up by an international panel. The result would be a limited list of sites and objects open to scientific investigation but closed to exploitation of natural resources. These international scientific preserves or "wilderness areas" should be legally protected within the frame of an international environment-protection treaty.

In the present paper our intention is to further elaborate this suggestion and separate its scientific, legal and societal aspects. Our intention is not to prevent any commercial or other utilization of Solar System resources, but to make space exploration and exploitation of resources a controlled and well-planned endeavor taking into account the interest of environmental protection for the sake of future generations.

What happened since 2000 in this respect? Some papers have been published in order to draw the attention of the space community to the issue (Williamson 2000, Spall 2002, Almár and Williamson 2002). The landing of the *NEAR-Shoemaker* space probe on asteroid Eros on 12 February 2001 and its functioning until 28 February on the surface demonstrated clearly the technical capacity of some nations to search and to exploit asteroidal resources. *Deep Impact,* a NASA Discovery Programme mission to fly by a comet and blow a large crater into it for analysis of its composition, was approved on 25 May 2001. The space probe is scheduled to be launched to Comet Tempel-1 in January 2004 and impact the comet on 4 July 2005. The crater will be produced by releasing a 350 kg projectile that will hit the comet at a speed over 35,000 km/hr. The resulting crater is expected to be about 100 m in diameter and 30 m deep. The experiment will demonstrate the capability of NASA to cause significant changes on the surface of a pristine celestial body in the Solar System. Environmental or ethical issues were not raised at all in this case. With the permission of NASA, NOAA and the State Department *TransOrbital* intends to launch its lunar probe *Trailblazer* in June 2003. This will be the first step by a private company in Solar System exploration – again without any international agreement on its rights and responsabilities.

Another event which should be mentioned in this respect is the visit of the first *space tourist*, Denis Tito on the International Space Station in April 2001. His spaceflight was neither legally nor politically well prepared in advance. The confusion – on the part of NASA in particular – was a consequence of the official skepticism that such an event may occur in the near future. Tito's flight proved that – in cases when a new kind of activity starts - an international agreement is absolutely needed well in advance in order to reduce the risks and misunderstanding.

Space tourism within near-Earth space is not an issue for planetary protection, but space tourism on the Moon or later on Mars would be a real danger for the conservation of these important planetary surfaces – as Mr. Nicholas Spall correctly points out. Space tourism will be without doubt an important industry in the 21st century and we ought to be prepared. With reference to the flight of the second space tourist, Mark Shuttleworth in 2002, we can conclude that regular space tourism started earlier than expected, and there is a chance that tourists will appear on the Moon also earlier than we are prepared with regulations. It is an international problem, closely related to the "protection of the planetary environment" issue, which is not properly discussed and regulated yet.

It is evident that there is almost no interest in the preservation of the existing *lifeless* surfaces of extraterrestrial bodies, the main concern of planetary protection policy is at the present time how to protect the (very hypothetical) extraterrestrial *life* against contamination.

THE SCIENTIFIC ASPECT

Classification of Planetary Bodies

In addition to the "classification of the problem" raised in our previous paper, one further important point is the age of the solid planetary surfaces. Io has the youngest surface in the Solar System, also Europa, Earth, and several cometary nuclei show relatively fast changes on their surface. Although in certain cases the interaction from humanity may be important for the future of the celestial body (e.g. the nucleus of a comet as the target of an impacting rocket may fall into pieces), nevertheless on fast changing surfaces there is generally less danger that human interaction would destroy something which otherwise would stay unaltered for billions of years.

On the other side very old, non-variable surfaces (Moon, Mercury, several satellites and asteroids) are absolutely vulnerable and their scientific value would be irrevocably damaged if a large-scale intervention occurs.

Mr. Mark *Lupisella* in his review of my previous COSPAR paper (Almár 2000) made several suggestions how my classification scheme should be improved. His remarks are worth further consideration and complement our previous classification scheme (Lupisella 2002). He emphasizes that when creating ecosystems (named *ecopoeisis)* the activity need not be constrained as to the type of ecosystem I was dealing with in the paper, but it could be done also to assist existing extraterrestrial biota. It may imply the creation of a planet-wide ecosystem, but also a regional or local one. Accordingly he is suggesting the following additional classification of this kind of activity:

Ecopoeisis – Creating Ecosystems

Terraforming – creating an earth-like ecosystem
Anthroterraforming – creating an ecosystem for humans
Non-anthroterraforming – creating an ecosystem for terrestrial life (e.g. microbes)
Planetary ecopoeisis – creating any kind of global ecosystem
Assistive (or indigenous) ecopoeisis – creating an ecosystem to assist
Indigenous biota, perhaps limited to locations or regions
Planetary assistive ecopoesis – planet-wide ecosystem development/creation to
assist indigenous biota on a global scale

According to his opinion there is a need to distinguish between colonization and terraforming: colonization can occur with or without terraforming and the environmental consequences could be quite different.

Different Kinds of Protection

He suggested also a classification, which can be applied to planetary surfaces:

Complete protection, which might imply remote sensing only,

Robotic exploration only, which might imply in-situ robotic exploration (perhaps with only a certain number of missions, and maybe sub-categories distinguishing between biological and non-biological experiments)

Controlled human exploration implying high levels of control over disturbance activities and contamination

Uncontrolled human exploration perhaps suggesting little or no control of activities and contamination required.

The first *objective* of the scientific part of such a project would certainly be to start a limited, well defined and organized initiative to select the highest scientific priority areas and objects on different kinds of planetary bodies (Moon, Mars, Mercury, satellites of outer planets, asteroids, comets, KBOs including Pluto), and then to give the position, the description (with a scientific definition) and the kind of protection it needs to each of the regions and objects in question.

Diagram of planetary surfaces as well as possible and permissible astronautical interventions on them

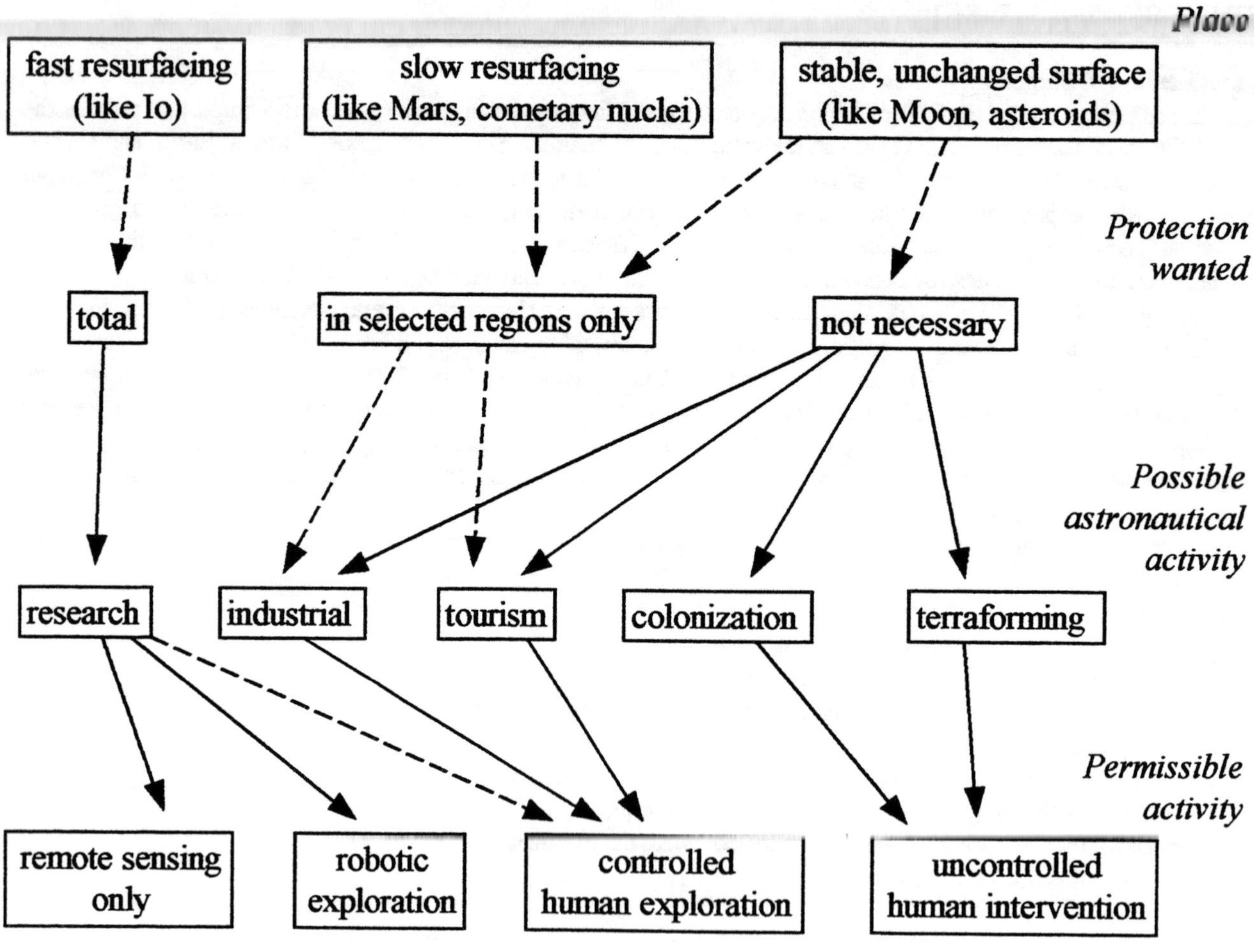

Fig.1 The diagram tries to summarize the different aspects of the planetary protection problem, without unnecessary details. It does not attempt to give definite answers. (Dotted lines mean uncertain connections.)

THE LEGAL ASPECT

It is not the task of the present paper to give a standpoint in the debate on the legal position of different celestial bodies or to elaborate on the legal side of the protection of the planetary environment. There is, however, one point, which is worth mentioning.

According to N. Spall (2002): *"Non of the UN Outer Space Treaties provide any legislation or protection policies to address this future problem."*

This is definitely true if only UN Treaties signed and ratified by the majority of nations are taken into consideration. But there is an *Agreement Governing the Activities of States on the Moon and Other Celestial Bodies (MA79)* adopted by the UN General Assembly on 5 December 1979, which entered into force on 11 July 1984 (United Nations Treaties 1996). Only 9 governments, excluding most of the leading space powers have ratified it. It contains, however, several important paragraphs from our point of view, which are definitely suitable to lay the foundation of another international agreement on the preservation of planetary surfaces.

According its *Article 1* 1. The provisions of this Agreement relating to the moon shall also apply to other celestial bodies within the solar system, other than the earth...

Article 4 1. The exploration and use of the moon shall be the province of all mankind and shall be carried out for the benefit and in the interest of all countries ... Due regard shall be paid to the interest of present and future generations...

Article 7 1. In exploring and using the moon, State Parties shall take measures to prevent the disruption of the existing balance of its environment, whether by introducing adverse changes in that environment, by its harmful contamination through the introduction of extra-environmental matter or otherwise.

3. States Parties shall report to other States Parties and to the Secretary-General concerning areas of the moon having special scientific interest in order that, without prejudice to the rights of other States Parties, consideration may be given to the designation of such areas as international scientific preserves for which special protective arrangements are to be agreed upon in consultation with the competent bodies of the United Nations

Article 11 1. The moon and its natural resources are the common heritage of mankind, which finds its expression in the provisions of this Agreement...

3. Neither the surface nor the subsurface of the moon, nor any part thereof or natural resources in place, shall become property of any State, international, intergovernmental or non-governmental organization, national organization or non-governmental entity or of any natural person.

Although the *Moon Agreement* has been the subject of several serious critical remarks (see Reijnen, 1993, Williamson, 1997), we repeat that it has entered into force in 1984 and so is the last of the "space agreements". This Moon Agreement may be the fundament to start the drafting of a declaration of principles supporting the protection of selected areas and objects on celestial bodies with solid surfaces. It might evolve into a special international legal instrument or treaty in order to limit the "free-for-all" kind intervention and use of Solar System resources.

As mentioned in our previous paper (Almár, 2000) although the "Vienna Declaration" of UNISPACE III does not mention explicitly the planetary protection problem, its *Technical Forum on Space Activities in the Twenty-first Century* recommends the following: *"Defining roles for the protection and preservation of the planetary and space environment and establishing a framework for implementation."* (Par.9 point h). It corresponds exactly to the intention of the present paper; therefore our suggestions are following up directly the recommendation of this UN Forum.

THE SOCIETAL ASPECT

The most important societal or philosophical question connected with the protection of the non-living planetary environment is probably asked by Callicott (and quoted by M. Lupisella, 2000): *"In addition to human beings, does nature (or some of nature's parts) have intrinsic value?* That is the critical theoretical question in environmental ethics." Robert Hynes, Chris McKay and Don MacNiven conclude that existing ethical theories exclude the extraterrestrial environment because they are geocentric and cannot be applied to extraterrestrial environments, hence leaving a vacuum for *a cosmocentric ethic.*

Is there any way to assess and measure such values objectively? Several authors argue that if the Universe creates objects of formed integrity (e.g. objects worthy of a proper name) they might have intrinsic value, which should be respected. According to Rolston "If a thing has formed integrity, or is worthy of a proper name, it should be respected." This is practically linked closely to the value measurement problem. IAU has given names to different parts of known surfaces of planetary bodies, but neither the hierarchy nor the exact boundaries of these features are defined exactly. Whether a feature has an official name or not is almost accidental, depending on the resolution of space probe images being at our disposal. There is plenty of work to be done before all celestial bodies in the Solar System will be mapped homogeneously.

We suggest initiating a profound professional discussion on the possible "ethical values" of the lifeless environment.

CONCLUSIONS

There is a general consensus that no NASA policy or international protocol exists for the proper handling of planetary bodies and their environment.

According to the general opinion, activities in space such as colonization will be unavoidable since it is consistent with the dominant practice of our civilization. Historically human exploration has seldom been concerned about its effect on the original biological or geological environment, even aboriginal population. Is this kind of attitude unavoidable? There is, however, another tendency: the formation of strong environmentalist and animal rights movements in the 20th century. It would be highly desirable to extend similar attitudes to *extraterrestrial environments* as well; we need to be proactive in this respect.

We emphasize again that only the dedicated effort of an international group or task force of experts can draft the necessary recommendations, serving as a basis of the legal discussion. (Sterns and Tennen, 1990) The societal or ethical background should be worked out as well. The whole effort should be initiated and coordinated by international space organizations (like COSPAR, IAF, IAA, IISL or UN COPUOS). This will definitely be an important task in the present decade in order to prevent confusion and irreparable damage in the future, when planetary surfaces will become places, where a large-scale astronautical activity might occur at any time.

REFERENCES

Almár, I., What could COSPAR do for the protection of the planetary and space environment? 33rd COSPAR Congress, Warsaw, accepted for *Adv. Space Res.* 2000.

Almár, I. and Williamson M., Protection of the planetary environment, *Spaceflight* (Correspondence) **44**, 260, 2002.

Lupisella, M., Humans and Martians, *Earth Space Review,* **9**, 50-60, 2000.

Lupisella, M., private communication (2002)

Reijnen, B., Interpretation of the space treaty texts, IAA.5.2-93-726 (44th IAF Congress, Graz) 1993.

Spall, N., Conservation of the planets – the case for regulation, *Spaceflight* (Into Space) **44**, 176, 2002.

Sterns, P. and Tennen, L., Preserving pristine environments: the planetary protection policy, in: *Space Safety and Rescue 1988-89,* ed. G.W. Heath, pp. 399-420, AAS, San Diego, 1990.

United Nations Treaties and Principles on Outer Space, United Nations, New York, 1996.

Williamson, M., Protection of the space environment under the Outer Space Treaty, IISL-97-IISL.4.02 (48th IAF Congress, Turin) 1997.

Williamson, M., Planetary spacecraft debris – the case for protecting the space environment, *Acta Astronautica,* **47**, 719-729, 2000.

E-mail address of I. Almár: almar@konkoly.hu

Planetary Protection - Some Legal Questions

E. Fasan

Honorary Director, International Institute of Space Law,
Raimundweg 2, A 2620 Neunkirchen, Austria

ABSTRACT

When we legally investigate the topic of planetary protection, we have to realize that there are primarily two very distinct parts of our juridical work: We have to study *lex lata*, the existing applicable law, especially space law, and also *lex ferenda*, what should be the law. With this in mind, we have to deliberate the legal meaning of the notions "planetary", and "protection".

About "planetary": Our own Earth is our most important planet. At present only here do exist human beings, who are *sensu strictu* the only legal subjects. We make the law, we have to apply it, and we are to be protected as well as bound by it. But what is further meant by "planetary"? Is it planets in an astronomical sense only, the nine planets which revolve around our fixed star, namely the sun, or is it also satellites, moving around most of these planets, as our own Moon circles Earth. "The Moon and other Celestial Bodies (C.B)" are subject to space law, especially to international treaties, agreements, resolutions of the UN etc. I propose that they and not only the planets in an strictly astronomical sense are to be protected. But I do not think that the said notion also comprises asteroids, comets, meteorites etc. although they too belong to our solar system. Our investigation comes to the result that such bodies have a different (lesser) legal quality.

Also we have to ask protection from what? I suggest the following:

Natural bodies: Meteorites, NEO asteroids, comets that could hit Earth or C.B.

Artificial objects: Space debris threatening especially Earth and near Earth orbits.

Terrestrial life: No infection of other celestial bodies.

Alien life forms which could bring about harmful contamination of Earth and the life, above all human life, etc. Here, astrobiological questions have to be discussed.

Special realms on C.B. which should be protected from electronic "noise" such as craters SAHA or Deadalus on the Moon, also taking into account the Common Heritage principle.

Then we have to examine: protection where, of whom and of what:

On Earth: Humans, and nature, namely other life forms, air, water and soil, but also all man made things.

On Other celestial bodies: Crew of manned space missions, stations on C.B., possible alien life forms, or remnants of such, water, other environment on C.B.- even if completely barren ? Protection of C.B. from becoming " an area of international conflict."

Finally we have to discuss overriding interests, such as deflection of asteroids which threaten to hit Earth, then the legally permitted "use" of C.B., also mining versus protection, then, too high costs of absolutely sterile spacecraft etc.

With this we have *de lege ferenda* to create an order of values of protection, whereby the protection of the higher category has priority over the lesser ones.

THE NEED FOR LEGAL REGULATIONS.

We speak about planetary protection, we want planetary protection, and we - not the lawyers but the scientists and technicians - even invent and/or adapt devices for such protection. Several papers today deal with this, on a very learned level. So why does planetary protection create legal problems?

Legal entities, legal subjects, be it individuals, juridical persons, and thus even States, are bound by a framework of laws. In the still valid definition of Kant (1) "Law is the total of conditions, by means of which the discretion of the one with the discretion of the other can be reconciled under a general rule of freedom".

Law is the rule of social conduct. It establishes the obligation to act or not to act in a certain way, and enables every legal subject to expect from all others that they do the same. Thus, it gives legal security, and prevents the otherwise unavoidable collision of interests. Without law, such collisions would be solved by brute force only. Law that is in force, presently existing law, is called *lex lata* (2).

Such rules of conduct may be -on a national basis - created, but also altered or abolished, by a relevant body (king, government or parliament etc.) or they can be concluded between legal subjects themselves; that is what we call treaties or agreements. On an international basis such treaties and agreements can be concluded by sovereign states. Then, they constitute (among others) the international law. When a sovereign nation concludes and ratifies a treaty, then it has the obligation to adhere to it (*pacta sunt servanda*), and to adapt its national laws in a way compatible with those treaty regulations (obligations and rights) (3).

For our investigation, the main legal framework of international law is the Law of Outer Space(4). Therefore, we at first will have to examine which codified space legal rules do exist, applicable to planetary protection. But after that, we will have to deliberate which changes or additions of or to space law seem necessary in order to better serve the desired protection. This will be deliberations of *lex ferenda* (5).

Legal rules show a tendency to demonstrate sometimes a kind of "hierarchy" This is not a modern idea. However, it was the Vienna school of Law with Kelsen (6) and Merkl (7) who systemized this notion in the framework of the so called "Pure Theory of Law" (8). In short, they taught that all national legal systems are based upon a constitution. Even in countries where such a constitution formally does not exist there are basic legal rules, which the so called "simple" or general laws may not violate. A Congress, a Parliament "shall make no law" contradicting the basic constitutional norms. And decisions, court sentences, administrative decrees may - following this system - not contradict those general laws. Usually a Constitutional or Supreme Court can be appealed to if this order of norms is violated. In a rude scheme, the hierarchy of norms shows the following picture:

Constitution
»
General (simple) Law
»
Decisions

In international law, too, there is a kind of hierarchy: Treaty Law usually derogates Customary Law, and General Principles of International Law recognized by civilized nations are applicable on a subsidiary basis only(9). Our above scheme would look as follows:

Treaty Law
»
Customary Law
»
General Principles

As we have seen, International Legal Treaties and Agreements have therefore the highest order in our hierarchy of norms. And there are such norms - *leges latae* -which already regulate several topics of planetary protection. But if we study these existing rules and examine the work of many distinguished authors we must come to the conclusion that the most important task is yet to be undertaken, and a clear system of law and procedure is still lacking.

Existing International Space Law (10) is codified mainly in the so called Space Treaties and Agreements. In addition, there are "Legal Principles" of space law which have been adopted by the United Nations General Assembly, not having the force of treaties.

The main document of space law, often called *"Magna Charta of Space"*, is the "Treaty on Principles Governing the Activities of States in the Exploration and Use of Outer Space, including the Moon and Other Celestial Bodies" of Jan 27., 1967 (OST). It has been signed and ratified by 98 Nations, and (merely) signed by 26 more. (11)

In chronological order there follows the Agreement on the Rescue of Astronauts and the Return of Objects Launched into Outer Space (Rescue Agreement), of April 22nd, 1968, the Convention on International Liability for Damage, Caused by Space Objects (Liability Convention) of March 29th, 1972, the Convention on Registration of Objects Launched into Outer Space (Registration Convention) of January 14th, 1975, and finally the Agreement Governing the Activities of States on the Moon and other Celestial Bodies (Moon Agreement) of December 18th, 1979 (12).

There was, and still is, a decreasing number of States having signed and ratified these Treaties and Agreements. So the last one, the "Moon Agreement merely received 10 ratifications and 6 more signatures. We shall not explore the reasons for this today, but examine now the space legal norms, applicable to our problem.

EXISTING SPACE LAW ON PLANETARY PROTECTION:

The OST states in Art. I the freedom for Exploration and Use of Outer Space, including the Moon and Other Celestial Bodies, and (Art. IV) the exclusive use for peaceful purposes, and prohibits in Art. II national appropriation. In Art V. it requests immediate information . . ."of any phenomena . . . which could constitute a danger to the life or health of astronauts."

Still more important to our topic is Art. IX., which requests to conduct national space activities in a way ". . . as to avoid their (*of space and C.B.*) harmful contamination and also adverse changes in the environment of the Earth resulting from the introduction of extraterrestrial matter. . . ."

Whereas the Rescue Agreement shows no norms specifically applicable to our problem, the Liability Convention states in its Art. II the absolute liability of the launching State for damage, caused by its space objects on Earth. Art. III requests that State (States) be liable for damages caused elsewhere only in case of fault.

We will not examine the Registration Convention in detail for our work (13) but the Moon Agreement goes far more into details: In Art. 3 it prohibits the placement of nuclear weapons or other weapons of mass destruction, and the conduction of military manoeuvres on C.B.

Of other multinational treaties the most important is the "Treaty Banning Nuclear Weapon Tests in the Atmosphere, in Outer Space and Underwater, of Aug.5., 1962 (the Moscow Test Ban Treaty) between (originally) USA, GB and the USSR with the intention, as expressed in the preambula, to end the contamination of humankinds environment by radioactive matter.

Each Party "undertakes to prohibit, to prevent, and not to carry out any nuclear weapon test explosion, or any other nuclear explosion, at any place under its jurisdiction or control . . . including Outer Space." This treaty received in the meantime all in all 104 ratifications, and 7 more signatures (14).

The "Principles" on outer space matters, adopted by the General Assembly of the UN can be used as demonstration of that organizations and its members intention to protect environment, even if those Principles deal mainly with other space topics.

In short: P. 15 of the "Principles Governing the Use of States of Artificial Satellites for International Direct Television Broadcasting" (15) refers to the "unavoidable overspill of radiation of satellite signal", about which reference is made to the International Telecommunication Union (ITU).

Principle X of the "Principles Relating to Remote Sensing of the Earth from Outer Space" (16) reads as follows:

" Remote Sensing shall promote the protection of the Earth's natural environment. To this end, States participating in remote sensing activities that have identified information in their possession that is capable of averting any phenomenon harmful to the Earth's natural environment shall disclose such information to the States concerned."

The Principles Relevant to the Use of Nuclear Power Sources in Outer Space (17) request in 3., I, (a) ".States launching space objects with nuclear power sources on board shall endeavour to protect individuals, populations and the biosphere against radiological hazards . . . and not cause a significant contamination of outer space".

Principle 7. 2. requests launching States to ". . . provide promptly the necessary assistance to eliminate actual and possible harmful effects . . ."

This, then is our starting platform (*lex lata*) of International Law and Regulations about Planetary Protection. They are, as indicated, not sufficient. But before requesting new regulations of our problem (*leges ferendae*), we have to quote some works and opinions of the last years, even decades.

AN OVERVIEW OF THE LEGAL HISTORY OF PLANETARY PROTECTION ISSUES

The following short and not complete overview of conferences and papers about our topic demonstrates that the main concern of authors was the important problem of space debris. This is correct and understandable because space debris endangers not only future space flights but the terrestrial environment as well (debris, especially larger exemplars crashing unto the Earth's surface). Also, the possible influence of military operations on the environment as a whole - terrestrial and extraterrestrial - was investigated. But also other important questions of planetary protection, such as militarisation and terrorism from and into outer space, cross contamination, radio activity, were dealt with as well as procedural problems, and possible solutions. This is shown by the following examples.

Olmstead (18) quoted the legal principle "*sic utere tuo ut alienum non laedes*" - One must use ones own rights so as not to do injury to another. He referred to the Corfu Channel Case (1949) I.C.J. Rep.4, that States are obliged "not to allow knowingly their territory to be used for acts contrary to the rights of other States". And he refers to the well known Trail Smelter Arbitration (between USA and Canada) - Decision of Mar.11., 1941, U.N.Rep., Int'l arbitration Awards 1905, (1945), citing the passage that "under the principles of international law as well as the Law of the United States, no State has the right to use or permit the use of its territory in such a manner as to cause injury by fumes in or to the territory of another or the property of persons therein..." *Olmstead* states quite correctly, that..."effective action to maintain the global environment requires co-operative international community action" (19).

G.S.Robinson in his 1976 paper "Earth exposure to Martian Matter: Back contamination procedures and international Quarantine Regulations" (20) points out that the US Public Health Service Act gave "...authority to the Surgeon General to promulgate and enforce regulations for prevention of the introduction and spread of communicable diseases into and throughout the United States." And he requested and proposed a "Convention on the International Prevention of harmful contamination of Earth by extraterrestrial matter".

In his "Free Enterprise and the proposed Moon Treaty" (21) *A. Dula* discussed among others the principle of "Common Heritage of Mankind", as used p.e. in the Moon Treaty. He pointed out that for the developing countries this means "common ownership of the resources and majority control over their disposition". This might be " a dangerous and unnecessary abandonment of the basic legal rights free enterprise will need...." The question, whether the common heritage principle would also include the obligation of planetary (lunar) protection, was not discussed, and was not the theme of that paper.

In 1984, at the 27th Colloquium of Outer Space, questions of "Military uses of Outer Space" were discussed (22) by P. M. Sterns and L. I. Tennen. N. Jasentuliyana spoke on "Debate Concerning Arms Control in Outer Space in the Context of the Conference on Disarmament," (23), and legal problems arising from the adaptation of Asteroids into Space Stations were investigated by E. Fasan,(24). At the same Colloquium there took place a Scientific - Legal Round Table under the chairmanship of V. Kopal "Present and expected Uses of Outer Space and Problems of protecting the Space Environment" with papers of L. Perek, E. A. Roth, C.Q.Christol, G. Gßl, N. Jasentuliyana, and P. M. Sterns & L. I. Tennen.

In 1988 ESA published a report of its Space Debris Working Group (25) which under Chapter 9 discussed legal aspects, and especially the applicable provisions of the Space Treaties and Agreements. And it came to the conclusion that "the necessary legal instruments should be negotiated at an early date, following Art. IX. of the OST".

In 1989 the International Institute of Space Law (IISL) dealt in its second session with: "Legal Aspects of Protection of Outer Space Environment". Chairman was M.Menter.

H.A.Baker (26) spoke on the "Current Space Debris Policy and its Implications." He quoted the revised US National Space Policy of 1988, that "all space sectors will strive to minimize the creation of space debris...", and he dealt extensively with the "Declaration of the United Nations Conference on the Human Environment of 1970", and the Vienna Convention for the protection of the ozone layer, of 1985.

K.H.Bockstiegel examined "Procedures to clarify the Law regarding the Environmental Aspects of Activities in Outer Space" (27). He reported on the 1988 Cologne Colloquium, and requested above all the clarification of several terms in space law texts. He requested an interdisciplinary approach, and especially mandatory exchange of information, mandatory consultations and cooperation.

A.A.Cocca saw "Environment as a Common Heritage of Mankind" (28). He reported of the first environmental law, namely the 1306 a.D.(!) Royal Proclamation of King Edward I. of England, prohibiting "open Furnace". He called "space armamentism the worst pollution" and reported on the Ottawa Meeting 1989 which had found that the atmosphere is a "resource of vital interest to mankind".

I.H. Ph.Diederiks Verschoor spoke on the "...increasing Problems of Space Debris and their Legal Solutions" (29). She requested a clarification of the term space object as used in the Space Law Texts and quoted several proposals to prevent damage caused by debris.

E.Fasan, your present author, started with the "*neminem laedere* " principle of Art 51 of the UN Charter, and gave tables of "Types and Causes of Emissions", "Space Legal Sources about Damage" etc. He expressed his doubts regarding the Convention on the prohibition of military and other hostile use of environmental modification techniques (30). This Convention, he pointed out, in its Art. III(1) states that its provisions "shall not hinder the use of environmental modification for peaceful purposes".

J.F.Galloway (31) spoke on "Mission to the Atmosphere" and taught about the various Conventions to protect the Atmosphere, as Montreal (1987), Sofia (1988), Bangalore (1987), adopting the 1985 Vienna Convention, and stated that the "winding down of the cold war necessitates a new definition of national security".

S.Gorove (32) gave an overview on "Space Debris in International Legal Perspective". He demonstrated the importance of clarifying whether "space debris" could be subsumed under the term "Space Object". He criticized the "non committal attitude of the major space powers" towards our problem.

E.Konstantinov (33) requested in his paper "The Outer Space Environment and its Legal Protection" to "find out the correct ratio between the interests of the States deriving direct benefit from ecologically adverse space activity, and in the interests of all States of the preservation of the ecological equilibrium"

V.Kopal (34) gave his paper the clear title " The Need for International Law Protection of Outer Space Environment against Pollution of any kind, particularly against Space Debris." He said:" It seems that preventive measures are technically feasible while future remedies such as cleaning of Outer Space are beyond the possibilities of present science and technology". He reported that COSPAR and IAF had in 1982 explained "that no concrete evidence had been found that rocket effluences may be deleterious to our environment". And he found that the present international law principles to protect the human environment and also space law are far from being satisfactory for that requested protection.

N.S.Natov spoke on "Some Ecological Problems in the Area of the Exploration and Use of Outer Space" (35) and posed five questions still to be answered to solve our related problems.

C.C.Okolie discussed "International Law Principles for the Protection of Outer Space Environment" (36). He taught about the US National Environmental Protection Agency, and the necessity to "maintain the natural balance between Humans and the Environment".

B.Reijnen reported on " Pollution of Outer Space and International Law" (37). She clearly pointed out the responsibility of States for space activities and with this also for pollution, caused by that. Regarding the Terrestrial atmosphere, she quoted the 1979 Convention on Long-Range Transboundary Air Pollution; regarding the ozone layer and radio-active pollution, she quoted the 1987 Conventions following the Chernobyl accident, and she then examined the relevant contents of the Space Treaties and Agreements. Her conclusion was the responsibility of States, according to the (imperfect) *legas latae*.

H.Safavi read about "Legal Aspect of Outer Space Environment (38), and was of the opinion that the terms "benefit" and interests of all countries" would comprise environmental protection.

G.Catalano Sgrosso (39) in her paper "Protection of Outer Space Environment; The present International Law Rules and Suggestion for New Legal Measures and Instruments" defined the terms "pollution", "debris", and spoke about the often debated term of "space object". She concluded: "A Convention dealing with pollution of Outer Space environment should specify duties and to keep their observances under control . . ."

R.Stamps had the Title: " Space Debris, an International Agreement is needed" (40). He spoke on tort liability, the destruction and removal of space debris, and especially stressed the importance of Art. IX of the OST for our problem.

P.M.Sterns and L.I.Tennen (41) put before the audience the question: "Recent Developments in the Planetary Protection Policy: Is the Outer Space Environment at Risk?" They reported about the COSPAR Planetary quarantine Requirements of 1964 and called them correctly a "significant deviation in the approach to preservation of pristine celestial environments", "because PQR allowed a limited microbial burden to be present at launch." They then reported, quoting a paper by J. Rummel on the US-American SBB, about the acceptance of those American standards by COSPAR in 1984. They found the situation still suffering "from a fundamental inconsistency and concluded that "the planetary protection policy must apply to every target body in which there is any possibility for the existence of life, its remnants and precursors...."

K.Tatsuzawa (42) spoke on "The Protection of Space Environment: The Problem of Space Wreckage". That term seemed to the author preferable to Space Debris, discussing papers of *Diederiks Verschoor, Kolosov, Reijnen, Gorove*, and others. In conclusion, an international agreement was requested.

S.M.Williams (43) discussed "Environmental risks arising from space activities, some legal issues". She discussed Art. IX of the OST, the 1985 Vienna Convention and requested also a convention, which would have to define the terms "pollution" and "debris".

W.B.Wirin spoke under the short and clear title "Space Debris 1989" (44). He taught on the U.S. Space Debris Report of Feb., 1989, and President Reagan's Space Policy Directive, released in 1988. *Wirin* quoted shocking numbers of debris in LEOs, mid earth orbit and GEO, and the dangers obviously connected with this. He called for an international agreement after serious studies but warned: "One of the (U.S.) goals will be to ensure that the commercial space industry is not significantly disadvantaged by regulatory steps that are not followed by the competitors of the United States".

E.G.Zhukova-Vasilevskaja in the last - but not least paper of this session - "Progressive Development of Space Law and Protection of Environment" (45) discussed the provisions of the OST, and of the Liability Convention. She warned from damage "from military activities in space". This should be referred to as "international crime". She concluded that international legal rules should be elaborated, which should be a task of UNCOPUOS.

In 1992, ten years ago, at the World Space Congress in Washington D.C. the Colloquium on the Law of Outer Space dealt in its session X.3. with "Managing environmental Issues including space debris" (46). Here, C.Q.Christol started his paper on "The Stratosphere Ozone Problem and Space Activity" with the following remarkable statement: " Humans have demonstrated a remarkable capacity to threaten Mother Earths natural environment". J.Galloway spoke on "The implementation of environmental treaties", and discussed the Montreal Protocol and its London Amendment. Further papers were by S.Courteix, E.Fasan, I.Kuskuvelis, M.Na Idu, L.Perek, and M.Rothblatt.

In 1993, there took place "The First European Space Debris Conference" in Darmstadt, Germany. A detailed overview in given by W.Flury, the Conference Organiser (47). The purpose was "to present the results from research on space debris . . . and to discuss international implications and policy issues". J.P.Loftus Jr. gave an overview on current mitigation practises, and asked for international agreements. W.Flury and D. McKnight discussed the Space Debris position Paper of the International Academy of Astronautics (IAA). The authors recommended furthermore several debris control measures, mainly to facilitate prevention measures. G.C.M.Reijnen, first legal author of the conference, explained in detail the importance of Art.IV., par.2. of the Registration Convention. She also thought that a new custom of consultation between the space powers seems to be emerging. M.Benko, K.U.Schrogl, and G.Gruber requested that space debris legal problems ought to be solved within the United Nations, and called especially for immediate work at UNCOPUOS.

H.A.Baker offered "recommendations for consideration when developing space debris policy" He found that international space law, and international environmental law were to be applied.

In 1996 on occasion of the 35th Session of the Legal Subcommittee (LSC) of UNCOPUOS in Vienna, Austria, there took place the annual Symposium, organised by IISL under its president, N. Jasentuliyana, and ECSL under its president G.Lafferranderie. The topic was Protection of the Space Environment (48.) Here, in his paper "Space Debris: Discussion in the Scientific and Technical Subcommittee in Feb., 1996." L.Perek quoted the proposed definition of space debris as "...inactive man-made objects, such as spent upper stages, spent satellites, fragments or parts generated during launch or mission operations, or fragments from explosions and other break-ups."

Lafferranderie discussed the Status and Organisation of the Inter-Agency Space Debris Co-ordination Committee, and requested examination of future legal regulations by UNCOPUOS.

F.B.Cheuvront reported on the industry viewpoint on space debris with special regards to the mitigation efforts of the "IRIDIUM Project".

V.Kopal spoke about the "Current Regulatory System about Space Debris", especially pointing out the provisions of the Space Treaties and Agreements, which he correctly deemed as being "too general . . . and far from being satisfactory."

For an overview of this symposium see "Protection of the Space Environment" by your present author who had served as coordinator (49).

In their paper "Preliminary Jurisprudential Observations Concerning Property Rights on the Moon and other Celestial Bodies in the Commercial Space Age" (50) P.Sterns, H. Stine and L. Tennen stressed Art V, and X of the OST, and stated: "Activities in space shall be conducted to prevent harmful contamination of outer space and celestial bodies, and also prevent adverse changes to the environment of the Earth through the introduction of extraterrestrial matter . . ."(51).

At the 40st Colloquium on the Law of Outer Space (52) P.Sterns and L.Tennen discussed "Exobiology and the Outer Space Treaty: From Planetary Protection to the Search for Extraterrestrial Life." They warned for the possible unforeseen and catastrophic consequences, "Cross-contamination" might bring about, discussed the 1964 COSPAR PQR requirements, the NASA Pub. No. SP-530, Exobiological Strategy for Mars Exploration, and in conclusion requested the legal protection of natural celestial environments to be supported by effective policies and procedures of the international scientific community. "Thus, the law of outer space should contain clear and express requirements to disclose and provide detailed information concerning the nature scope, extent and location of the contamination and the risk of harm . . . and the obligation to disclose the discovery of organic life, found on the Moon or elsewhere."

During the same Colloquium (53) A.Debus, J.Runavot, G.Rogovsky, V.Bogomolov, N.Khamidullina, and V.Trofimov discussed the "Mars 96 Planetary Protection Program and Implementations for Mars Environment Preservation". They spoke extensively about the COSPAR recommendations, both old and new, and implementations, decontamination methods, documentation, and studies.

There followed the paper "Dangers from Asteroids and Comets" by E. Brooks (54). The author gave an astronomical - scientific background and said that "there are an estimated .5 million to 1,5 million asteroids larger than 50 meters, whose orbits cross the orbit of Earth. He discussed the 1981 University of Arizona "Spacewatch", and especially the new (1995) "Near Earth Asteroid Tracking System (NEAT) of Air Force, NASA, and JPL. And as important conclusion, Brooks stated: "Present technology exists or can be adapted to deflect or destroy an offending body. This includes rockets, launch vehicles, tracking and homing,, and finally the energy delivery to the offending body." With sharp observational clarity he pointed out that several legal instruments, namely the Moscow Test Ban Treaty, the OST, the Environmental Modification Treaty of 1978, and the Moon Treaty seemed to restrict the proposed measures to deflect an asteroid or comet. And he asked for "human ingenuity" to solve the (seemingly contradictous) topics of avoiding danger and using and exploiting asteroids.

Furthermore, I would like to quote M.Williamson's "Protection of the Space Environment under the Outer Space Treaty" (55). He pointed out the danger to the lunar environment by space debris, discusses the Space Treaties, and found them insufficient for the said protection. A suitable choice - plunder or protection - is requested.

The late J. Heidmann had always been a stout defender of keeping some sites of the Earth-averted side of the Moon clean, and reserved for scientific purposes, especially for SETI. This should be SAHA, "a little crater near *Mare Smithii*". In "What Legal Questions are raised by the Establishment of a dedicated Lunar Far Side Specific Crater for High Sensitivity Radioastronomy?"(56) he gave astronomical details, and requested to discuss and solve the relevant legal problems.

In January, 1997, there took place in Alpbach, Austria, a Seminar "Space Futures and Human Security"(57). The Second Session (chair S. Doyle) dealt with "Space and Environmental Security". Papers were presented among others by R. Winter, "Environmental Monitoring from Space", and V. M. Canuto, "Space Activities and Environmental Security".

Also in 1997 G.Lafferranderie with Co-Author D.Crowther published the "Outlook on Space Law over the Next 30 Years (58). Chapter 9 deals with the "Environment of Earth and Space". In this book J.M.deFaraminan Gilbert discussed space debris, and requested legal solutions with "recommended minimum standards." C.Catalano Sgrosso followed suit with "Prevention and Management of Natural Disasters". She gave an extensive bibliography on the policy of preventing natural disasters, and the methods available. She showed, that the "Rio Declaration of 1992, UN Doc. A/Conf.151/5" goes farther as the former "Soft Law Contents". And she concluded: "The United Nations must absolutely guarantee the leadership of the international system for the prevention and management of calamities . . ."

In 1998, S.Doyle published a paper "Using extraterrestrial resources under the Moon Agreement of 1979" (59). Approaching our problem (correctly) from the other side, he pointed out the legality of not only exploitation but also use of Outer Space and the C.B. Not without reason he called the Moon Agreement imperfect etc. But the necessity of planetary protection versus exploitation of C.B. was not his topic.

F.Lyall in his paper "On The Moon" (60) was not quite as critical about the Moon Agreement. But he also made clear that the "Common Heritage" concept is one of the reasons why the said agreement is not widely accepted". In detail, Lyall requested that "certain areas of the moon should be set aside for scientific study..", and proposes especially the area of the (far side) crater SAHA.

N.Jasentuliyana wrote in the same issue of J.Space L. (61) on "Space Debris and International Law". The author discussed not only the Space Treaties and Agreements, but in detail and extensively the work within UNCOPUOS, especially its scientific and technical Subcommittee, including problems of nuclear power sources. He reported that some studies "suggest that, in the crowded orbital regimes of LEO, the number of collision partners will reach the critical level required to sustain collisional cascading within the next 10 to 15 years." He taught then about national and multinational space debris mitigation measures. He did not think that one treaty or convention would be the solution but - as he had advocated earlier (62) - that expert technical groups should develop recommended standards.

The UNISPACE III Conference in Vienna, 1999 (63) in its Workshop on Space Law had a special session "Maintaining the Space Environment" under the chairmanship of ambassador Qizhi *He*. One heard the discussion paper by *L.Perek*, one of the best authors on the topic of Space Debris. Perek made special reference to the Technical Report on Space Debris of the UNCOPUOS Scientific and Technical Subcommittee, A/AC.105/720. He pointed out that "Every year about 500 pieces of trackable debris and a very large number of debris too small to be detected, decay in the atmosphere". The total mass of all artificial objects in earth orbit is between 2000 and 3000 tons ." And he requested to maintain the space environment in a state suitable for future Space Activities.

In 2001, A.A.Cocca, M.M.E.de Cocca, P.M.Sterns and L.I.Tennen published a paper "Autonomous Settlements and Environmental Protection in the Law of Outer Space" (64). Although this paper mainly deals with "habitats in outer space and on C.B.", it very extensively investigates the questions of environmental protection, resulting from establishing such habitats. They find clearly, quoting Williamson, that "...it is inevitable that the exploration of celestial bodies will cause some impact on the natural environment". They continue that ". . . environment is a concept inseparable from life. . . ." And they request, quoting a 1993 paper of Sterns and Tennen the establishment of an "International Agreement of Recognition and Capacity" which would include relevant protective measures.

The International Academy of Astronautics (IAA) has dealt with problems of space debris since more than ten years. Its first Position Paper on Orbital Debris was issued in 1993, and an updated and extended "Edition 2001" was published in Sept., 2001 (65). This excellent report gives an overview on the present status and the future development, and deals then with debris control options, i.e. prevention and removal. One of these options is "reorbiting of geostationary satellites into a disposal orbit, at least 300 km above GEO". The booklet contains an extensive bibliography, deals with the early report of AIAA of 1981, and gives in Appendix E a very good political/legal historical overview. Here, the work of UNCOPUOS and its Scientific and technical Subcommittee and of COSPAR is quoted. The most important chapter for our legal problems and procedure is "Approaches to Implementation". After "technical discussions within - among others - COSPAR, IAA, IAF, IISL" there should be discussions at the UNCOPUOS, leading ultimately to a "Code of Conduct", international standards, or space law ." This, of course, is a very sensible proposal, which is recommended by your author also for all the problems of planetary protection of which space debris issues are only one (but most important) chapter.

The United Nations Office for Outer Space Affairs annually prepares a "Highlights in Space" volume in cooperation with IAF, COSPAR, and IISL. The 2001 edition carries a Chapter XV, "PLANETARY PROTECTION". The presentation defines planetary protection as "the activity that seeks to prevent the biological cross contamination of solar system bodies, especially those that may (or do) harbour living entities." And it comes to the solution, "...that the contamination of other solar system bodies by Earth organisms is possible, and that the potential for life elsewhere in this solar system exists". It requests prudence, "both to protect Earth and to shield those other bodies from Earth contamination." Legally, the paper referred especially to Art IX of the OST, as quoted above. Under Chapter XI. it dealt under the title "Potentially Environmentally Detrimental Activities in Space", especially with the problems of space debris as one of the most important topics.

Furthermore, I want to quote the UNGA Resolution of 21 Jan., 2002, which in its part E. deals with "Ensuring the safety of space activities to human health, property and the environment"(66). It points out the importance of the Liability Convention, but especially the relevant national laws of space faring nations. Australia, the Russian Federation, South Africa, Ukraine, UK., USA., Guiana, and Art.10 of the International Space Station Agreement are quoted.

Finally, we have seriously to consider the Report "COSPAR/IAU Workshop on Planetary Protection", Williamsburg, Virginia, 2-4 April 2002 (67). It proposes "five categories for target body/mission type combinations and their respective suggested ranges of requirements . . . ." It goes deep into the matter and details, especially regarding Missions to Mars and Europa. It contains the draft to be presented to the Council and Bureau.

THE MEANING OF THE TERMS "PLANETARY" AND "PROTECTION".

Before trying to come to a conclusion, we will now have to examine the exact meaning of the two main terms of our topic, namely "planetary", and "protection".

The notion of "planetary" seems to be an astronomical one. The definition seems (but only seems) to be clear: A planet is a celestial body which revolves around a fixed star; in our case, that star would be the sun. Our own Earth is one of those (nine) planets. But all studies demonstrated very quickly, that "planetary protection" would not only apply to such planets but to natural satellites, to moons, of such planets as well, especially to our own Moon.

Our Earth itself is our most important planet. At present only here do exist human beings, who are *sensu strictu* the only legal subjects. We make the law, we have to apply it, and we are to be protected as well as bound by it. Thus Earth is the planet to be protected above everything else. But then, we have to discuss what is further meant by "Planetary". "The Moon and other Celestial Bodies" are, as indicated above, subject to Space Law, especially to International Treaties, Agreements, Resolutions of the UN etc. They, and not only the planets in an strictly astronomical sense are to be protected. We can not - contrary to existing Space Law norms as quoted above - protect Pluto but neglect to protect Luna. In this sense, S. Gorove (68) equalled the Moon with "other planets of the solar system". On the other hand, I do not think that our notion 1"Planetary" also comprises small asteroids, comets, meteorites etc. although they too belong to our solar system. Some such objects might cross Earths orbit at quite close distances. A typical example is Asteroid 253 Mathilde. It was one of the first C.B. which approached Earth 1997 in a way which caused the NASA program of near Earth asteroid rendezvous (NEAR) to study and photograph it (69). And in the same time issue AIAA invited for April, 1998 to the "Leonid Meteorids Storm and Satellite Threat Conference". Such bodies, most of them without detectable orbits, may constitute high danger to Earth and its inhabitants, including Astronauts. Protection from them is requested, not protection of them. They must have a different legal quality. Maybe, they, or some of them, are also to be protected themselves. An example might be an asteroid which might be mined for valuable materials.

But such protection need not be on the same level as that of the C.B themselves. And the question of living entities - be it on Earth or on other C.B.- is of foremost importance (70).

Lachs had raised the question of minimum size of a natural object in space in order to be deemed a C.B. The definition of the latter should be "land areas in space" (71).

A solution might be, and this I propose , the definition of "Planetary Body" as it was defined by the then Working Group Three of the IISL: "Celestial Bodies in (legal) sense are natural objects in Outer Space, including their eventual gaseous coronas, which can not artificially be moved from their natural orbits" (72).

"Protection" (the latin root of this notion is *tectum* - the roof, and *tegere*, to cover) means averting, fending off, shielding from injury or destruction, and other harmful influences - be it by voluntary acts or from natural occurrences (73).

A protecting measure is one which prohibits or at least decreases such harmful influences. The prohibition would be factual (physical - technical). It will have to be based on legal rules, in order to avoid misunderstandings, duplications or even disputes(74).

With this we have to ask Protection from what? From:

Natural bodies: Meteorites, NEO asteroids, comets which could hit Earth or C.B.

Artificial Objects: Space debris threatening especially Earth and near Earth orbits.

Militarisation of outer space and its effects, terrorism from Outer Space.

Radiation, especially from nuclear sources.

Terrestrial Life - no infection of other celestial bodies.

Alien life forms which could bring about "harmful contamination" of Earth and life, above all human life. Here, astrobiological questions have to be discussed.

Special realms on C.B. should be protected from electronic "noise" such as craters SAHA or Deadalus on the Moon, also taking into account the "Common Heritage" Principle.

Then we have to examine: Protection where, of whom and of what:

On Earth: Human life above all, but of course our whole nature, including other life forms (animals and plants), and soil, air, water etc. etc. And all man made things, all artificial objects, immovable or movable as well.

On Other celestial bodies: Crews of manned Space Missions, Stations on C.B., possible alien life forms, or remnants of such, water, other environment on C.B.- whereby it seems questionable whether areas should be included, even if they are completely barren. And protection of C.B. is necessary from becoming "an area of international conflict".

Finally we have to discuss overriding interests, such as deflection of asteroids which threaten to hit Earth, then the legally permitted "use" of C.B., especially mining versus protection, and the possibly too high costs of absolutely sterile Spacecraft etc.

May I add that it would be illogical to protect natural resources on the Moon more strictly than those on Earth. The Moon should remain free, free of appropriation. But its natural resources should serve all mankind. And he who can bring them here, should be rewarded in the sense of a clear space legal regulation.

CONCLUSION: LEX FERENDA.

To find solutions, we at first have to ask: How shall we proceed, and what is our aim?

As we have seen, there are several categories of dangers to planetary environments. To evaluate these categories, and to find practical solutions, we need the expertise of scientists and technicians on the highest level, and we need a forum for these knowledgeable people. But we need an international legal forum as well, on the same supreme level. These fora should be on the broadest international basis and acceptance, and experienced in matters of Outer Space. I strongly propose - in accordance with many authors, as quoted above - that to be the Committee on the Peaceful Uses of Outer Space of the United Nations (UNCOPUOS).

UNCOPUOS was established by UNGA Resolution 1472 (XIV) of Dec. 12., 1959. It has two Sub-Committees, namely the Scientific - Technical, and the Legal ones. It was the most important body, in whose realms the formulations of the Space Treaties, and the "Principles" were worked out (75). It would be insensible, not to rely on the expertise of these bodies, of their excellent procedural knowledge, and the outstanding cooperation of Nations there.

At the Scientific and Technical Subcommittee, possible protective measures could be elaborated against the various dangers to our planetary environment, as elaborated above in <u>Protection from what</u>.

After that, we will have to forge a legal framework for those technical solutions. States might be interested to have the discussion on a basis as broad as possible in an reliable institution, knowledgeable in the formulation of Space Law principles. This once more would be UNCOUPOS, and its Legal Subcommittee.

Thus, States might want to decide on this, and to propose and pass an UNGA Resolution, requesting UNCOPUOS and its two Subcommittees, to work on suitable texts. Those texts could then be the basis of a new set of "Principles", to be voted upon by UNGA itself. Whether then a new Agreement should follow, or whether these new "Principles" themselves would be found to be sufficient, would be a question to be solved, once the said Resolution is passed.

About the content of these Principles, I believe, and I propose, to create an order of values of protection as follows, <u>whereby the protection of the higher category has priority over the lesser ones</u>:

Therefore we have to protect:

1) Human life, be it on Earth or beyond it,
2) Other terrestrial life, i.e., animate nature,
3) Inanimate terrestrial environment, i.e. inanimate nature,
4) Possible alien life forms or their remnants on the Moon or other C.B.,
5) The natural environment of the Moon and other C.B.,
6) In some cases even asteroids, comets etc.

And with this, I submit that the work could start immediately.

Notes and References.

(1) Metaphysics of Morals, Berlin 1912, VII, 31.
(2) Roman law concept: existing valid law.
(3) Treaties must be adhered to, contractual obligations must be kept.
(4) Although Space Law - especially in its beginnings - was International Law, there have been developed more and more national Laws and regulations, applicable to Outer Space.
(5) Roman law concept (see (2): Law to be created.
(6) Reine Rechtslehre, 1934, 1960, General Theory of State and Law, 1945.
(7) Prolegomena einer Theorie des rechtlichen Stufenbaus, Gesellschaft, Staat und Recht, 1931, 252ff.
(8) Legal System, based on human logic.
(9) See Art. 38 of the Statutes of the International Court of Justice, also *Tunkin* Remarks on the juridical nature of customary norms in international law, Calif. Law Rev. 49, 419ff (1961).
(10) See *Kopal* about the "layers of regulations of space activities" in "Existing United Nations Treaties and Agreements", UNISPACE III, Proceedings of the workshop on Space Law in the twenty first century, UN Doc. A/CONF.187/7.
(11) See "United Nations Treaties and Principles on Outer Space", annually published by the UN Office for Outer Space Affairs, Vienna, Austria. It annually contains a list of all relevant documents with indication which States have signed and/or ratified the relevant Treaties and Agreements, prepared by *A. Terekhov*.
(12) Texts in (11).
(13) But see *Reijnen* in (47).
(14) Text in (11).
(15) Dec.10., 1982, No. 37/92.
(16) Dec.3.,1986. No. 41/65.
(17) Dec.14., 1992, No. 47/68.
(18) Prospects for Regulation of Environmental conservation under International Law, Centenary Celebration of the International Law Association, Kluver 1973, 245ff.
(19) ibidem, 248.
(20) 18 Proc. Colloq. L. Outer Space, 1976, 134ff
(21) Houston Journal of International Law, Vol.2., 1979, No.1.
(22) 27.Proc. Colloq. L. Outer Space, 1984, 134ff.
(23) ibidem 326ff.
(24) ibidem 243ff.
(25) esa SP-1109, Technical Coordinator *W.Flury*.
(26) 32. Porc. Colloq. L. Outer Space, 1989, 59ff.
(27) ibidem65ff.
(28) ibidem 71ff.
(29) ibidem 77ff.
(30) of May. 18., 1977 UNGA Res. 31/72.
(31) ibidem 89ff.
(32) ibidem 97ff.
(33) ibidem 100ff.
(34) ibidem 107ff.
(35) ibidem 118 ff.
(36) ibidem 123ff.
(37) ibidem 130ff.

(38) ibidem 138ff.
(39) ibidem 146ff.
(40) ibidem 152ff.
(41) ibidem 163ff.
(42) ibidem 173ff.
(43) ibidem 177ff.
(44) ibidem 184ff.
(45) ibidem 197ff.
(46) I would like to refer to the Book of Abstracts - AIAA, NASA, and NAS - which contains also the scientific - technical papers.
(47) J.Space L. 1993, No 1., 46ff.
(48) 39. Proc. Colloq L. Outer Space, 298ff.
(49) J.Space L., 1996, No. 1., 48ff .
(50) 39 Proc. Colloq. L Outer Space, Beijing, 1996, p.50ff.
(51) ibidem p. 52.
(52) 40.Proc. Colloq. L. Outer Space,Turin, 1997.
(53) ibidem 220ff.
(54) ibidem 238ff.
(55) ibidem 296ff.
(56) ibidem 302ff.
(57) Proceedings edited by *N. Jasentuliyana* and *K. Karnik* United Nations Office for Outer Space Affairs, Vienna, 1997.
(58) Kluwer, The Hague.
(59) J.Space L. 1998, 111ff.
(60) J.Space L. 1998, 129.
(61) ibidem, p.139ff.
(62) 27 Proc. Colloq. L. Outer Space , 395, 1985.
(63) Proceedings of the Workshop on Space Law in the Twenty First Century, UN Doc. A/CONF.184/7.
(64) IAF Paper No. IISL-01-IISL.4.07.
(65) Published by IAA under its Director of Publication *J.M.Contant*.
(66) A/AC.105/768
(67) The Report was prepared by the COSPAR Planetary Protection Panel under the chairmanship of *John D. Rummel*.
(68) Space Law, its challenges and prospects, Sijthoff, Leiden, 1977, 174.
(69) Aerospace America, Dec. 1997, 63 and 70.
(70) The question of extraterrestrial intelligence is not discussed in this paper.
(71) The Law of Outer Space, Sijthoff, Leiden, 46.
(72) *Cocca*, in 7 Proc. Colloq. L. Outer Space 16, 1962. But we will have to be careful there, in order not to exclude the Mars moons Phobos and Deimos from such protection.
(73) Websters New Collegiate Dictionary, 926.
(74) *Fasan*, How to legally protect Outer Space Environment", 32 Proc. Colloq. 1989, 81ff.
(75) See UN Doc. A/AC.105/193 New York, 1973, "Space Activities and Resources", especially p. 2ff.

PROTECTION OF THE SPACE ENVIRONMENT: THE FIRST SMALL STEPS

Mark Williamson

Space Technology Consultant, The Glebe House, Kirkby Thore, Cumbria, CA10 1UR, UK

ABSTRACT

The development of the space environment - for industry, commerce and tourism - is a natural extension of our current business and domestic agenda. Unfortunately, this brings with it the ability to pollute, degrade and even destroy aspects of the space environment. This paper briefly reviews the evidence of mankind's pollution of the space environment in the first 45 years of the Space Age, and extrapolates the potential for further degradation into its second half-century. It also makes recommendations concerning the first steps towards a solution to the problem, including the formation of an international consultative body and consideration of a 'set of guidelines' or 'code of practice' as a precursor to more formal policies or legislation.

INTRODUCTION

It has often been said that mankind's desire for exploration is one of the aspects that set us apart from the other creatures with which we share the Earth. A natural extension of this is the desire to explore the space environment - a philosophy expressed concisely in the well-worn phrase 'space...the final frontier'. From this point of view, it is important for the long-term psychological well-being of the human race that we maintain the ability explore space.

Moreover, as the development of industry, commerce and tourism here on Earth has shown, our desire and ability to explore leads inexorably to a desire to develop and exploit. This strongly suggests, therefore, that exploration of the space environment will lead to its development and exploitation, and there is evidence that this is the case. Indeed, it has been suggested that, particularly as it becomes increasingly accessible, the space environment will become a natural extension of our current business and domestic environment (Williamson, 2001).

As previous papers - most notably those presented at an IAA/IISL Scientific-Legal Round Table in 1999 (see references) - have shown, this ability to explore and develop brings with it an ability to pollute, degrade and even destroy aspects of the space environment. This is, arguably, a natural extension of an ability we have developed and practised here on Earth.

It is these abilities, and their long-term effects, that compel us to consider protection of the space environment in much the same way as terrestrial environmental degradation has compelled others to call for its protection.

The task is a difficult one in either realm - terrestrial or extraterrestrial - because those who seek to develop and exploit the environment in question are usually those with the most to lose, particularly if protection means denial of their business income.

This is, by its nature, an emotive subject, which many will tend to shun because of its difficulty and potential to set different parts of the space community against each other. This would obviously be counterproductive. The only solution is to take an entirely pragmatic stance. As on Earth, the solution for protection of the space environment lies in convincing the 'polluters' and 'degraders' that it is in their long-term business interests to protect the environment they are developing and exploiting.

No-one is suggesting that protection of the space environment is easy, but then neither is space exploration - and mankind has managed to do that quite successfully. This paper attempts to make the first small steps towards a goal that would, arguably, constitute another "giant leap for mankind": the preservation of the space environment for future generations of space explorers and developers.

EVIDENCE

The evidence of mankind's pollution or degradation of the space environment, which includes the surfaces of the planetary bodies, has been presented in some detail in previous papers (Almar; Johnson; Williamson, 1999), and is summarised here. Although pollution and degradation are emotive and pejorative terms, and definitions of the terms may differ between observers, this discussion is not intended as an exercise in laying blame; it is simply an attempt to highlight a few historical facts.

For most observers, degradation of the space environment begins and ends with space debris, or man-made orbital debris - the inactive remnants or products of space hardware which remain in Earth orbit. This includes defunct satellites, launch vehicle upper stages, hardware jettisoned from manned and unmanned spacecraft, and even the combustion products of solid rocket motors in the form of tiny metallic particles.

The larger objects are tracked on a continual basis and the evolution of their orbital paths is well understood, but many other smaller objects remain undetectable. For example, objects in low Earth orbit (LEO) at least 10cm in diameter can, in principle, be tracked on a routine basis by the US Space Surveillance Network (SSN); indeed, about 10,000 objects are tracked, some 8,600 of which are officially catalogued. Objects greater than 1m in diameter can be detected in geostationary orbit (GEO), but the ability to detect them depends on many factors, including shape, material composition and the eccentricity of their orbit. About 2000 objects in GEO, including active and inactive satellites, are currently tracked by the SSN.

According to NASA estimates, the population of particles between 1cm and 10cm in diameter is greater than 100,000, while the number of particles smaller than 1cm probably exceeds tens of millions. Individual objects as small as 3mm can be detected by ground-based radars, providing a basis for a statistical estimate of their numbers, while assessments of the debris population smaller than 1mm can be made by examining impact features on the surfaces of returned spacecraft (albeit limited to spacecraft operating at altitudes below 600km).

Most orbital debris resides within 2000km of the Earth's surface, although the amount of debris varies significantly with altitude and is concentrated at around 800km, 1000km and 1500km. A good deal of theoretical work has been done concerning predictions of how these debris populations may evolve, largely based on the premise that a single collision can produce a cascade effect, producing more and more debris. Some have concluded that certain low Earth orbits may become unusable by the middle of the century (Eichler and Rex, 1989; United Nations, 1999). Interestingly, the first validated collision between two catalogued objects occurred in July 1996 when the French microsatellite Cerise was hit by part of an Ariane rocket.

Although there was originally a good deal of resistance towards warnings of the dangers of orbital debris, it is now widely accepted as a cause for concern. As a result, in order to reduce the probability of collision and the resulting accumulation of debris, geostationary satellites are now removed to a 'graveyard orbit' at the end of their operational lives and satellites in LEO are generally de-orbited to burn up in the Earth's atmosphere. Likewise, cleaner separation and deployment devices which do not produce debris have been developed, and propellant tanks are now 'passivated' by venting residual propellant to avoid subsequent explosions.

These procedures and technologies have not been developed to protect the space environment for its own sake; they are pragmatic and self serving measures which help to protect the orbital environment for future use, either for scientific or financial gain. Again, no judgement is intended; it is simply a fact.

Unfortunately, the same pragmatism has so far not been extended beyond Earth orbit, and there are no similar debris mitigation measures for spacecraft which orbit or land on other planetary bodies (including of course our own Moon).

In the early years of the Space Age, a large number of spacecraft and rocket stages were intentionally crashed onto the lunar surface, littering the surface with debris (Williamson, 1999). It began with the Soviet Lunas and American Rangers of the 1950s and 1960s, and continued into the early 1970s with the impact of Lunar Orbiters, Apollo lunar module ascent stages and Saturn V third stages. Interestingly, however, the potential danger posed by inactive orbiting spacecraft was realised in the case of the Lunar Orbiters, which were deorbited specifically to avoid 'potential interference' with the later (manned) Apollos.

While the catalogue of a few dozen impacts may be viewed as insignificant on a planetary scale, in the absence of a policy against impacts it has continued to the present day. The most recent example was the impact of

Lunar Prospector onto the Moon's south pole in 1999, designed as an attempt to produce a plume of water molecules from suspected polar ice deposits.

The only reason there have not been more intentional impacts is that no lunar missions were conducted between Luna 24's landing in August 1976 and the launch of Japan's Hiten/Hagoromo spacecraft in January 1990; and there were only two other missions in the 1990s (Clementine in 1994 and Lunar Prospector in 1998/99).

Likewise, the only reason the other bodies of the solar system are not littered with debris from manned and unmanned spacecraft is the dearth of missions. With the single exception of targeting the Galileo orbiter into Jupiter's atmosphere to avoid a possible contaminating impact with Europa, there is little indication that these bodies are afforded any protection against contamination when it comes to their scientific exploration. What hope then when they become the target of commercial exploitation?

EXTRAPOLATION

It is difficult to extrapolate the potential for further degradation of planetary orbits and surfaces into the second half-century of the Space Age (2007-2056), because no-one knows with any certainty what missions will be launched in that period. However, it is possible to predict the *likely* consequences of *currently expected* progress in space exploration and development.

For the most popular Earth orbits, the case has already been made and broadly agreed upon for debris mitigation measures. As a result, we expect to continue using low, medium and high altitude orbits for at least the next half-century without experiencing significant problems. However, this will depend on the continuation and improvement of those mitigation measures, since a single cascade event could make a given orbit unusable (perhaps for thousands of years).

Moreover, current mitigation measures for the higher orbits (e.g. graveyard boosts for geostationary satellites) simply delay the eventual solution. At the current launch rate of 20-25 geostationary satellites per year, between 1000 and 1250 spacecraft would be added to the GEO population over a 50-year period. Even assuming longer operational lifetimes for the newer satellites, this means that some 10-20 defunct satellites will be added to the graveyard each year (i.e. 500-1000 in 50 years).

The fact that these satellites are, almost by definition, abandoned and uncontrolled means that one day a collision will occur in a graveyard orbit, producing debris in orbits that will intersect the geostationary ring and threaten operational satellites. The probability of such a collision can only increase until the graveyard population is reduced.

At present, the technology to remove defunct satellites from high altitude orbits does not exist; nor are there any funded programmes to develop this technology. A significant part of any policy advocating protection of the space environment would, by necessity, include consideration of this matter.

At one point in the 1990s, it appeared that a similar if not greater potential for collision would be provided by the number of multi-satellite constellations planned for launch into low and medium Earth orbits (LEO and MEO). As it turned out, only two significant constellations - Iridium and Globalstar - were deployed, and they were commercial failures. However, a number of companies still have plans to deploy other constellations when market conditions allow, so the potential threat to LEO and MEO remains.

Current commercial applications apart, it is important - as with all aspects of space development - to realise that the situation does not remain static for long. Simply because most of our spacecraft are confined to Earth orbit today does not mean that this will always be the case. There are already plans to place a network of what, in Earth orbit, would be termed communications satellites in orbit around Mars. In the first instance, they would be used to transfer data from science stations on the surface, or flying in the Martian atmosphere, back to Earth; later they could serve as relay stations supporting a manned mission. There is no reason why areostationary orbit - the Mars equivalent of GEO - should not become an important resource in the future, eventually requiring the same protection as GEO.

Perhaps before that, similar orbits around the Moon may be developed for communications, lunar imaging and manned applications as they are today around the Earth. The example of the Lunar Orbiters quoted above shows that a precedent for protection has already been set.

At the beginning of the 21st century, we are still - by analogy - in the pre-commercial airline days of the 1920s; once the promised innovation of space tourism arrives, a Pandora's box of problems, issues and challenges will open, most of them concerned with the safety of fare-paying tourists. If measures are not in place by then to protect the usability of certain orbits, mitigate the production of debris, and maintain communications services to space stations, lunar shuttles and surface bases, there is little hope that space tourism will succeed.

PROTECTION FOR THE ENVIRONMENT'S SAKE

Protecting the space environment to maintain its qualities for commercial exploitation is surely the first line of attack in any pragmatic protection programme, since it addresses the primary concern of the commercial developer: continuity of income. However, it is also worth considering protection for its own sake. Too often, we hear of irreversible environmental degradation here on Earth. As we expand our influence into the solar system, we have the potential to carry our penchant for environmental degradation with us, as shown by historical evidence. The question must be one of balance: how much degradation is allowable in the name of progress?

While few space professionals would advocate a slash and burn philosophy in our exploration and development of the solar system, many would choose to turn a blind eye to the occasional pollution or degradation event in favour of budgets, project timelines or personal advancement. This is human nature; and it illustrates why protection of the space environment requires a human dimension.

This human dimension is effectively summarised in the term 'space ethics', a subject worthy of consideration in its own right (Pompidou, 2000), and covered in a parallel session of the 2002 World Space Congress (IAA.8.1 Ethical Issues Arising in Space Activities). Ethics can be defined as "the philosophical study of the moral value of human conduct, and of the rules or principles that ought to govern it". More practically, it represents "an approved code of behaviour" adopted, for example, by a group or profession. If a set of ethics is to be developed for space, it is important that what we refer to as the 'space community', or 'space profession', is intimately involved. Indeed, if it is not, the profession risks having the job done for it, for example by politicians and members of the general public, who for their own reasons may wish to place restrictions on space development, or ban it altogether. The terrestrial nuclear power industry, for example, has already suffered this fate, while widespread ignorance of 'nuclear matters' has led to a moratorium on the use of radioisotope thermoelectric generators (RTGs) in spacecraft.

Practical questions include the extent to which development of the lunar surface should be allowed. For example, strip mining the surface for helium 3 or other elements and materials would, by definition, disfigure the surface. Should we only sanction mines that are small enough to remain invisible from Earth and, if so, do we mean invisible to the naked eye or through a telescope? Or should we confine such development to the back side of the Moon? In which case, should the development remain invisible from naked eye observers in a lunar orbiting hotel, or not? Alternatively, should any scale of mining be allowed as long as the surface is returned to its former visual appearance after a given period?

Similar questions may be posed for other planetary bodies, and it is worth repeating the concern of astronomer Ivan Almar who has pointed out that a typical open cast mine on the Martian moon Phobos, which is smaller than a city the size of London, could destroy its unique groove system forever (Almar, 1999). These and many other specific questions are worth asking. However, it is not for individuals to decide on the answers - especially individuals with a financial interest in the outcome. This much we may learn from terrestrial experience. So, who will decide, on what information will they base their decisions, and how will those decisions be enforced?

RECOMMENDATIONS

The above discussion indicates that much, but certainly not all, of this subject is theoretical and dependent on actual progress in space exploration and development. However, it also argues that there is no time like the present to begin serious and organised consideration of the subject of protection of the space environment.

In a sense, the first small steps have already been taken. Individual space professionals have published articles and papers drawing attention to some of the issues, and the 1999 IAA/IISL Scientific-Legal Round Table made a more formal attempt to present the issues to the international space community.

While these attempts are laudable, they represented only a fraction of the effort required, firstly, to convince the space community of the need to consider protection and, secondly, to formulate a policy.

PROMULGATING IDEAS

The next small step in the process is, in fact, more of a continuing background task: that of spreading the word. Those with an interest in protection of the space environment, or those with particular expertise to share, should continue talking to their peers in industry, space agencies, etc, and promulgating the issues at conferences and in publications.

If the aims of the 'protection lobby' are to be realised, the discussion of the subject will require a good deal more collective knowledge, understanding and maturity than has been evident in similar discussions regarding the

Earth's environment. At present, that knowledge resides largely within a small subset of the professional space community. Thus there is a need for promulgation, both within and beyond that community. This will be no easy task, because there are many who will see this as another layer of bureaucracy and yet another restriction on progress.

The analogy with the terrestrial environmental movement has already been drawn; one could also compare the space protection lobby with the Luddite machine-breakers of the early 19th century. This would, however, be controversial and counterproductive, since the space protection lobby is not against the industrial development of space; it simply wishes to ensure that development takes place in a sustainable and environmentally-friendly manner.

By definition, most people with an interest in protection of the space environment are those with some knowledge of space science, technology, and so on; and most of them have a vested interest in the continuation of space exploration and development. One of the many challenges in communicating information and views on space protection to a wider audience will be that of demonstrating that the lobbyists are not latter-day Luddites.

FORMULATING POLICY

Small steps aside, significant progress in any subject is made by giant leaps, and the giant leap in protection of the space environment would be the formulation and agreement of a policy.

The first step towards that goal is the formation of an international consultative body to consider the relevant issues and raise awareness of the subject among the growing body of space professionals and practitioners. The question is, of course, under whose auspices should this body be inaugurated? Obviously, given the increasingly international nature of space exploration and development, it is important for the body to be as international as possible, ideally including representatives from all major spacefaring nations.

Given the forum in which this paper is presented, a first suggestion might be the formation of a working group under the joint auspices of the International Academy of Astronautics (IAA) and the Committee on Space Research (COSPAR). An alternative might be organised under the UN, possibly affiliated with the United Nations Committee for the Peaceful Uses of Outer Space (UNCOPUOS), which has already taken an interest in space debris. A third option might be a form of space agency/space industry forum. The pros and cons of these and other options may have to be discussed at some length before a decision is made.

Even this is only a start, however. One needs only to look at the body of space law - and the disappointing fact that certain major spacefaring nations have not ratified the Moon Treaty ("Agreement Governing the Activities of States on the Moon and Other Celestial Bodies", adopted by the United Nations General Assembly on 5 December 1979) - to realise that well-meaning work on behalf of the international space community is not always appreciated. Another example is the International Telecommunications Union (ITU), which aims to coordinate the use of the radio frequency spectrum and geostationary orbital positions, among other things, to avoid harmful interference. Although, in most cases, this works well - since an interferer will generally also suffer interference - the ITU can only make recommendations; it has no legal powers of enforcement.

Any future 'International Space Protection Union' may have to function under the same restrictions. The key to success will be to get as many parties with vested interests 'on side' as soon as possible. Thus, to represent the science community, one might seek to gain backing from major space agencies, such as NASA, ESA and the future combined Japanese space agency. To represent industry, one might seek the support of national space industry associations or, better still, the leading prime contractors themselves. However, to make the organisation as democratic as possible and to allow a broad-based 'ownership' of the ideas, issues and eventual policies, one would have to accept representations from a much wider field.

This is important because we appear to be on the cusp of a true commercialisation of space: witness in-space burials, tourists on the International Space Station and plans to send teleoperated 'theme-park' rovers to the Moon. There is no point in formulating policies to which only the industrial prime contractors will adhere; there has to be a way to include the smaller operators.

Of course, this raises the issues of legislation, policing, conviction and punishment. If an operator or developer ignores the policies and breaks the rules, will there be a mechanism to cope with this? Unfortunately, experience regarding the Moon Treaty and the ITU suggests not.

Despite this, it is too early in the process to declare defeat. Despite the limitations of current space law and policies - and however little they have been tested in the hostile environment of space commerce - space exploration and development has continued unabated for the past 45 years and shows little sign of ceasing.

So, assuming the formation of an international consultative body goes to plan, what should it do? The first small steps should surely include the following:

- formation and enactment of a policy to maintain and expand the constituency of the body, specifically regarding its international nature
- formation and enactment of a policy to obtain funding and other support from key space-related organisations
- formation and enactment of a policy to ensure the promulgation of ideas among the space community and the media
- consideration of a 'set of guidelines' or 'code of practice' as a precursor to more formal policies or legislation.

Although the last point is the *raison d'être* for the body, the preceding points are also important. Their importance can be illustrated by considering the ramifications of omitting them:

- if the body is not international in nature it will be considered by those outside as partisan, and however well-meant its eventual policies they will be ignored.
- if the body cannot secure at least some regular funding, it will be unable to operate a secretariat or provide expenses to those members unable fund their activities in support of the body.
- if the body does not appoint an experienced promulgator - a press and public relations officer, for example - the ideas and issues considered by the body will remain 'in-house', much as they are today.

NEXT SMALL STEPS

Detailed suggestions concerning the content and coverage of the guidelines or code of practice will undoubtedly be made in due course, as one of the next small steps towards the goal of protecting the space environment. In formulating these guidelines, it will be important to recognise the need to strike a balance between unbridled exploration and development, and a stifling regime of rules and regulations. It is not in the nature of mankind to open a new frontier and then close it again without fully exploring its potential. Specifically, it is not in mankind's best interests to place a moratorium on space exploration and development.

The challenge for 21st century space practitioners will be to find a way to explore, develop and exploit the unique properties of the space environment - including the surfaces and orbital spaces of the planetary bodies - without degrading or destroying the environment which holds so much promise for the future of mankind.

CONCLUSION

As the space frontier becomes accessible to a wider variety of individuals, corporations and other bodies, the requirement for protection of the space environment grows. If the space environment is to remain available for the study of and use by successive generations of explorers and developers, we must make the first steps towards protection now. In another twenty years or so - when the second generation of lunar explorers is making footprints on the surface - it may be too late.

REFERENCES

Almar, I., Protection of the planetary environment - the point of view of an astronomer, IAA-99-IAA.7.1.02 *

Eichler, P. and Rex, D., Chain reaction of debris generation by collisions in space - a final threat to spaceflight?, IAA-89-628 (40th IAF Congress, Beijing), 1989

Fogg, M., The ethical dimensions of space settlement, IAA-99-IAA.7.1.07 *

Johnson, N., Man-made debris in and from lunar orbit, IAA-99-IAA.7.1.03 *

Lyall, F., Protection of the space environment and law, IAA-99-IAA.7.1.05 *

Pompidou, A., The ethics of space policy, COMEST/UNESCO, June 2000

Sterns, P., The scientific/legal implications of planetary protection and exobiology, IAA-99-IAA.7.1.06 *

United Nations, Technical Report on Space Debris, A/AC.105/720, 1999

Williamson, M., Planetary spacecraft debris - the case for protecting the space environment, IAA-99-IAA.7.1.01 * [also published in *Acta Astronautica*, **47**, Nos. 2-9, 719-729, 2000]

Williamson, M., Exploration and protection - a delicate balance, IAA-01-IAA.13.1.03 (52nd IAF Congress, Toulouse), 2001

* (IAA/IISL Scientific-Legal Round Table on Protection of the Space Environment, 50th IAF Congress Amsterdam), 1999

E-mail address of M. Williamson: markwilliamson1@compuserve.com

PLANETARY PROTECTION: LESSONS LEARNED

L. Perek

Astronomical Institute, Academy of Sciences, Boční II 1401, 141 31 Praha 4, Czech Republic

ABSTRACT

Planetary protection is a very wide subject because of the variety of physical conditions on individual planets and their moons. At present, we have good photographs or imagery, as well as other evidence, from most planets and from a selection of their moons. The most important factor is the presence or absence of any form of life. Material samples are available from the Moon and possibly, in the form of a few meteorites, from Mars. The danger of contamination has been recognized in the past and it became clear that some measures would have to be taken. The adoption of measures will have to be universal in missions to planets and their moons because for an undesirable contamination to occur, one failed measure of protection may be enough. The question is, if we can learn from experience gained in the last forty years in adopting laws, rules or unbinding recommendations for space activities. Several examples will be discussed, such as the amount of knowledge at a time when international treaties on space law were adopted, the consequences of the failed discussion at the United Nations on the definition of outer space, or of the break-up of Cosmos 954. Special attention will be devoted to the ongoing discussion of space debris in the UN Committee on the Peaceful Uses of Outer Space and its relevance for planetary protection, to the general compliance with the Registration Convention and to the experience gained with the recommendation to re-orbit geostationary satellites.

POLITICAL WILL

Political will to establish rules for space activities was very strong in the first years after the launch of the first satellite. The UN General Assembly decided to establish an ad hoc Committee on the Peaceful Uses of Outer Space already in 1958[1]. The committee was directed to consider (a) the activities and resources of the UN system of organizations relating to the peaceful uses of outer space, (b) international cooperation and programs, (c) organizational arrangements to facilitate international cooperation, and (d) legal problems that might arise. That decision shows that the international community realized from the beginning that space activities have a global character requiring international cooperation and that legal problems are likely to arise and will have to be considered and ultimately solved. The COPUOS was converted into a standing committee in 1959[2].

In the course of the following years, a number of international organizations, intergovernmental as well as non-governmental, have been granted observer status, among them COSPAR, IAF, IAA, the European Space Agency, the International Astronomical Union, the International Law Association and several others. The Committee and its two Subcommittees, Scientific and Technical, and Legal, work on the principle of consensus.

Already in 1963, the committee adopted a Declaration of Legal Principles Governing the Activities of States[3] in the Exploration and Use of Outer Space. Among the principles are:

- Freedom of exploration and use by States,
- Non-appropriation of outer space by any country,
- Liability for damage caused by space objects,
- Safety and rescue of astronauts,
- Notification of registration of space objects.

It has to be realized that in the years 1958-1963, between the start and completion of the work, there were in space only a few scientific satellites, there was no experience with space applications and no experience with the reaction of non- space-faring countries to space activities. Yet the political will was so strong that a list of important principles of very high moral value was set up and adopted. In the following years, five international treaties were elaborated[4], transforming the principles into legally binding language. Never again was such a miracle performed.

During the 1960's, the Committee discussed also the question of adopting a definition or delimitation of outer space. In that instance, no strong political will appeared and the discussion were concluded in the Scientific and Technical Subcommittee in 1967[5] by stating that it was not possible at that time to identify scientific and technical criteria which would permit a precise and lasting definition of outer space. Such an argument is not logical because it is not the task of scientific and technical consideration to derive a "precise" limit between airspace and outer space. Scientific considerations can lead only to suggesting a certain range in altitudes where a legal limit would not be in conflict with scientific or technical facts. The "precise" value is needed only in application of legal rules. The Scientific and Technical Subcommittee just had no political will to adopt a fixed value of the limit.

Political will, in particular in a committee working on the principle of consensus, is of prime importance for reaching any result, be it the adoption of basic principles for space activities, be it the question of the delimitation of outer space, or be it the question of adopting rules for planetary protection.

FACTS

The latin saying, *Ex facto sequitur lex,* suggests that some facts require regulation by law. The saying does not elaborate on the nature and amount of facts needed before a regulation is desirable. That decision is left to lawmakers.

When the Principles Governing Space Activities were adopted in 1963, the need for more detailed knowledge was overrun by the political will to regulate the newly emerged field of activities by principles of a high moral value.

This has not always been the case. The question of space debris came to the attention of the scientific and technical community in late 1970's. The UN Secretariat prepared a number of studies[6] for the UN COPUOS between 1979 and 1987 on various aspects of space debris. It was only in 1988-1990 when official studies were prepared, first by the ESA Space Debris Working Group[7], later by the US Interagency Group[8] and by the US Congress[9]. The International Academy of Astronautics prepared a Position Paper on Orbital Debris[10]. The ESA organized three international conferences on Space Debris in 1993, 1997, and 2001[11]. The proceedings of 700, 800, and 900 pages respectively, reflected the wealth of information presented by participants. A special periodical devoted to Space Debris started to appear in 1999. An Interagency Space Debris Coordinating Committee has been created by space-faring countries for the purpose of studying space debris. Yet, it took the years 1990 to 1994 to adopt an item on space debris to the agenda of the Scientific and Technical Subcommittee. A Technical Report[12] reflecting all the available knowledge on space debris was elaborated and adopted by the Subcommittee in 1999.

Compared to the knowledge of space activities available in 1959, which was deemed sufficient to start elaborating the main principles governing space activities, our present knowledge of space debris is orders of magnitude more extensive and detailed. But no consensus has been reached in 2002 in the Scientific and Technical Subcommittee[13] to start legal considerations on space debris.

It will be a long way between the start of legal considerations and the adoption of a decision on what to do on international level about space debris. Whether the fragile environment of the geostationary orbit, or possibly of other orbits, will absorb all the space debris produced and to be produced, is a question without an answer at present.

In the case of planetary protection, an important point will be to agree on specific facts needed to start meaningful discussions on general rules.

WIDE VIEW

On 24 January 1978, Cosmos 954 disintegrated over northwestern Canada and several radioactive fragments. The debris was located, collected and investigated. The specific aspect of radioactivity attracted more attention that the fact of danger posed by debris in general. The COPUOS and its Subcommittees started to discuss an item entitled "Nuclear Power Sources" and countries were exhorted to pay attention to collisions with radioactive fragments. From hindsight, it would have been logical to consider the topic of space debris in general, because some harmful effects can come from space debris, whether they are radioactive or not. Finally, in 1992, a set of Principles on Nuclear Power Sources[14] was adopted, while the topic of space debris appeared on the agenda of the Scientific and Technical Subcommittee as late as 1994.

Evidently, questions of environmental protection should be seen in a sufficiently wide context. This finding may be of consequence for future discussions of environmental protection of celestial bodies.

VOLUNTARY REGULATION

Voluntary regulation is, of course, preferable because it is inexpensive and can be changed flexibly in accordance with the facts and techniques of the day. As a necessary and sufficient condition of success, all participants have to implement what they have agreed on. They will do it either if the universal implementation of the regulation is in their interest, or if they wish to maintain their image as fair players.

An example of the first case is the voluntary use — by all operators of satellites – of communication frequencies and nominal orbital positions assigned by the International Telecommunication Union. It is in the interest of operators to avoid harmful interference in satellite communications by adhering to the results of the ITU coordinating process.

An example of the second case is the careful registering of objects launched into outer space in compliance with the Registration Convention by the two space superpowers and some other States.

On the other hand, there are several examples of failures of operators to comply with recommendations of a non-binding nature:

- In May 2002, it was found in the On-line Index of Objects Launched into Outer Space[15], that 30% of objects launched in the year 2000 have not been registered with the UN, in spite of Article XX of the Convention to register "as soon as feasible".
- The recommendation by the ITU of 1993, to re-orbit satellites approaching the end of their active lives into disposal orbits at least 300 km beyond the nominal geostationary orbit, has been complied with by only 2 out of 14 satellites, which approached the end of their active lives in 2001. In the four years, 1996-2000, the same picture emerged. Thus in the five last years, a total of 50 satellites was left in or near the nominal geostationary orbit, posing a risk of collision with one or other of the active satellites.

It seems that the international community would act in a foolish way if it always relied on voluntary compliance with non-binding regulation. In Planetary Protection, the situation will have to be considered carefully. If the club of Planetary Visitors has very few members, all of them fair players and reliable partners in international cooperation, voluntary arrangements will have a chance. If the club is opened widely, there will be no substitute for an efficient policeman in the background, ready to write stiff penalties to trespassers.

REFERENCES

[1] United Nations, General Assembly Resolution 1348(XIII) , New York, 13 December 1958.

[2] United Nations, General Assembly Resolution 1472(XIV), New York, 12 December 1959.

[3] United Nations, General Assembly Resolution 1962 (XVIII), New York, 13 December 1963.

[4] **Outer Space Treaty**, United Nations, General Assembly Resolution 2222 (XXI), New York, 19 December 1966, in force on 10 October 1967, 98 ratifications, 26 signatures;
Rescue Agreement, United Nations, General Assembly Resolution 2345 (XXII), New York, 19 December 1967, in force on 3 December 1968, 89 ratifications, 25 signatures;
Liability Convention, United Nations, Gneral Assembly Resolution 2777 (XXVI), New York, 29 November 1971, in force 1 September 1972, 84 ratifications, 25 signatures;
Registration Convention, United Nations, General Assembly Resolution 3235 (XXIX), New York, 12 November 1974, in force 15 September 1976, 43 ratifications, 3 signatures;
Moon Treaty, United Nations, General Assembly Resolution 34/68, New York, 5 December 1979, in force 11 July 1984, 9 ratifications, 5 signatures.

[5] United Nations, Report of the Scientific and Technical Subcommittee, A/AC.105/39, Fifth session, New York, 6 September 1967.

[6] For the list of studies see L. Perek, Space Debris at the United Nations, accepted by the periodical Space Debris.

[7] European space agency, Space Debris, A Report from the ESA Space Debris Working Group, ESA SP-1109, Paris, November 1988.

[8] Report on Orbital Debris by Interagency Group (Space) for National Security Council, Washington, D.C., February 1989.

[9] Congress of the United States, Office of Technology Assessment: Orbiting Debris, A Space Environmental Problem, Background Paper, OTA-BP-ISC-72, Washington D.C., September 1990

[10] International Academy of Astronautics: Position Paper on Orbital Debris, compiled by an ad hoc expert group, Paris 1995; Updated edition published in 2001.

[11] European Space Agency: Proc. of the First European Conf. on Space Debris, ESOC Darmstadt, Germany, ESA SD-01, Paris, July 1993, Edited by W. Flury;
European Space Agency, Proc. of the Second European Conf. on Space Debris, ESOC Darmstadt, Germany, ESA SP-393 (SD-02), ESA Publications Division, ESTEC Noordwijk, The Netherlands, May 1997, Edited by B. Kaldeich-Schürmann and B. Harris;
European Space Agency, Proc. of the Third European Conf. on Space Debris, ESOC Darmstadt, Germany, ESA SP-473, ESA Publication Division, ESTEC, Noordwijk, The Netherlands, October 2001. Edited by H. Sawaya-Lacoste.

[12] United Nations: Technical Report on Space Debris (Rex Report), A/AC.105/720, New York, 1999, UN publication sales No. E.99.I.17.

[13] United Nations: Report of the Scientific and Technical Subcommittee, 39th session, A/AC.105/786, paragraphs 120-126, Vienna, 15 March 2002.

[14] United Nations: Principles Relevant to the Use of Nuclear Power Sources in Outer Space, General Assembly Resolution 47/68, New York, 14 December 1992.

[15] The index lists all functional objects launched into outer space. It contains data from governmental announcements made in compliance with the Registration Convention. Where such data are missing, other sources are quoted. Prepared by the UN Office of Outer Space Affairs, at the website registry.oosa.unvienna.org/oosa/index/index.stm.

E-mail address of L. Perek perek@ig.cas.cz

EVOLUTION OF THE PLANETARY PROTECTION POLICY: CONFLICT OF SCIENCE AND JURISPRUDENCE?

L.I. Tennen

Law Offices of Sterns and Tennen, 849 North Third Avenue, Phoenix, Arizona 85003 U.S.A.

ABSTRACT

The policy of protecting pristine celestial environments is accepted with virtual unanimity, and has been incorporated into positive international law. Originally phrased by the scientific community in terms of planetary quarantine requirements, the implementation of the strictures of planetary protection have been drastically relaxed over the years for most bodies within the solar system, which now are deemed to be of little or no biological or chemical interest in regard to the search for the origins of life. However, the jurisprudential considerations which underlie the planetary protection policy do not necessarily recognize the same scientific distinctions and assumptions which have provided the rationalization for the reduced application of active planetary protection mechanisms. This paper examines the potential for conflict between the scientific and jurisprudential considerations of planetary protection.

INTRODUCTION

The necessity of protecting natural celestial environments was among the earliest policies articulated at the dawn of the space age. There are three basic interests which are sought to be safeguarded by the planetary protection policy: first, the prevention of contamination of pristine celestial environments by terrestrial sources; second, the prevention of the contamination of the Earth by the return of extraterrestrial materials; and third, the prevention of interference with the activities of states in the peaceful exploration and use of outer space. Comprised of both scientific as well as legal considerations, the subject of planetary protection has received attention from several international fora, most notably the United Nations, COSPAR, and the International Institute of Space Law of the International Astronautical Federation.

The planetary protection policy has not been static, but has been re-examined over the years, with revisions made by the scientific and the legal communities. These revisions, however, were not made in conjunction with each other, nor were they necessarily consistent. The divergences in the scientific and the legal perspectives of planetary protection become apparent by an examination of the development of the separate components of the policy.

ORIGINS OF THE PLANETARY PROTECTION POLICY

The subject of protecting natural celestial environments was considered in 1956 at the Congress of the International Astronautical Federation in Rome, under the foresight of Andrew Haley. The development of the planetary protection policies followed parallel courses. One the one side were the activities of the international scientific community, while on the other side were the diplomatic and legal actions. In 1957, the U.S. National Academy of Sciences requested the International Council of Scientific Unions (ICSU) to assist in the development of means to prevent contaminating celestial environments.[1] In response and reaction to the launch of Sputnik, the United Nations General Assembly created the *Ad Hoc* Committee on the Peaceful Uses of Outer Space (COPUOS), and directed that it identify legal problems associated with the advent of mankind's exploration of space.[2]

SCIENTIFIC DEVELOPMENT OF THE PLANETARY PROTECTION POLICY

The ICSU acted on the request of the National Academy of Sciences, and formed the *Ad Hoc* Committee on Contamination by Extraterrestrial Exploration (CETEX).[3] CETEX considered celestial bodies to be scientific preserves, and stated four primary objectives: freedom of exploration of celestial bodies, subject to limitations such as planetary quarantine requirements; disclosure to COSPAR of information concerning activities and experiments; the conducting of experiments only which are likely to yield useful scientific data; and nuclear explosions should not occur near the surface of celestial bodies. In the case of the Moon, CETEX also recommended that no soft landings requiring the use of large quantities of gas should take place pending further investigations.[4]

In 1961, pursuant to an ICSU request to assume the duties of studying the potential for contamination by extraterrestrial exploration, COSPAR formed the Consultive Group on Potentially Harmful Effects of Space Experiments.[5] In 1964, the COSPAR Consultive Group published recommended planetary quarantine requirements in the form of a COSPAR resolution.[6] Pursuant to the resolution, decontamination techniques were to be employed to reduce the probability of contamination of a celestial environment by a single viable terrestrial organism aboard any spacecraft intended for planetary landing or atmospheric penetration to less than 1×10^{-4}. The probability limit established by COSPAR for an accidental planetary impact by an unsterilized fly-by or orbiting spacecraft was to be 3×10^{-5} or less.

The probability of contamination was to be determined by a mathematical formula, which multiplied the initial microbial burden, after decontamination, of an interplanetary probe at launch, by factors relating to the probability of survival of the rigors of launch, transit, entry, release and growth in the target alien environment. These planetary quarantine requirements were to apply for the initial period of planetary exploration of ten years.[7] Nations were allocated specific fractions of the overall probability limits which were apportioned by the recipient state among the missions planned to be conducted under its jurisdiction.[8]

The planetary quarantine requirements were re-examined periodically, and revisions made thereto, often at the initiative of NASA.[9] In 1969, COSPAR revised the planetary quarantine requirements, and stated:

> as the basic objective for planetary quarantine of Mars and other planets deemed important for the investigation of extraterrestrial life, or precursors or remnants thereof, a probability of no more than 1×10^{-3} that a planet will be contaminated during the period of biological exploration . . . ending in 1988.[10]

This decision by COSPAR made two significant alterations to the planetary quarantine requirements: first, it reduced the probability of contamination limit by a full order of magnitude; second, it limited the application of the quarantine requirements to "**Mars and other planets deemed important**" in the search for extraterrestrial life.

In 1978, the Space Studies Board (SSB) of the National Research Council re-evaluated the application of the formula for determining the probability of contamination. The SSB concluded that for many planetary bodies of the solar system, the probability of growth of a terrestrial organism in their hostile extraterrestrial environments was sufficiently low so as to negate the necessity of engaging in any active decontamination techniques.[11] As a matter of policy, the assignment of negligible values to the probability of growth factors began to transform planetary protection from the planetary quarantine requirements, whereby the application of active bioload reduction techniques would no longer be the norm but would be the exception.[12]

In 1984, the transformation from planetary quarantine requirements was completed, when the applicable guidelines were relaxed to provide that planetary protection constraints may be imposed, depending upon the nature of the mission and the target body or bodies to be explored. These guidelines completely eliminated the overall probability of contamination restrictions. For missions to target bodies which were deemed not to be of biological interest in the search for life, including the Moon, the policy did not require any planetary protection techniques to be utilized, nor was any specific documentation required. The classification of missions to other target bodies was to be determined on a case by case basis for planetary protection purposes.[13]

The planetary protection policy was revisited again and revised in 1994, particularly in relation to exploratory missions to Mars. Specifically, the 1994 revisions to the policy tied the utilization of decontamination and cleanliness controls to whether the mission objectives included life-detection experiments. That is, craft landing on Mars which carried life detection instruments were subject to Viking level sterilization. However, landing craft without such life detection instruments were subject to substantially less stringent decontamination techniques.[14]

Pending before COSPAR is a proposed update and consolidation of the planetary protection policy. Pursuant to this proposal, planetary missions will be classified into one of five categories, depending upon the pre-determined "planetary protection status" of the target body, and the mission plan. The categories range from targets which are "not of direct interest for understanding the process of biological or chemical evolution," to missions which involve the return of extraterrestrial samples to Earth.[15] An intermediate category has been introduced for planetary bodies which, while of interest concerning biological or chemical evolution, can be considered to present "only a remote chance that contamination by spacecraft could jeopardize future exploration."[16]

Stringent bioload reduction requirements are imposed only for a limited range of missions, to a small number of target bodies, notably Mars and Europa. Viking level sterilization is mandated only for landing craft which are intended to conduct life detection experiments. Other landing crafts and fly-by missions are subject to lesser strictures, with a notable exception: a new category, that of "special region," has been established, where it is believed that H_2O, in the form of surface or subsurface ice, may be present. For these "special regions," landing craft must achieve Viking level sterility, even where the craft is not intended to conduct life detection experiments.[17]

JURISPRUDENTIAL DEVELOPMENT OF THE PLANETARY PROTECTION POLICY

The General Assembly directed the *Ad Hoc* COPUOS to identify the legal issues presented by the movement of mankind into space. In July, 1959, the *Ad Hoc* COPUOS reported:

> Scientific studies indicate that certain activities related to lunar and planetary impacts might result in biological, chemical, and radiation contamination jeopardizing subsequent physical and chemical studies and endangering possible living organisms. Release of chemical markers, radio-activity resulting from nuclear explosions, generation of gases in connexion (sic) with 'soft' landings and the spreading of terrestrial micro-organisms carried within space vehicles represent possible sources of contamination to the moon and planets. The re-entry of space vehicles which have effected landings on the moon and planets might contaminate the earth on their return. It will probably be desirable to continue such studies of this problem as are already under way, for example, in COSPAR, with a view to arriving at appropriate agreements to minimize the adverse effects of possible biological, radiological, and chemical contamination.[18]

In March of 1962, Chairman Khrushchev wrote an eloquent letter to President Kennedy about, what he termed, "heavenly matters." Included in the points he urged to be considered was: "It should, perhaps, be specified that any experiments in outer space which may hinder the exploration of space by other countries should be the subject of preliminary discussion and of an agreement concluded on a proper international basis."[19] In this letter, the issue of contamination of a celestial environment was inexorably linked to the potential for such contamination to interfere with the rights of states to conduct activities in space. The focus of concern was not on the negative impact contamination may have on the celestial body, but rather with how the contamination may impact on the activities of other states.

Khrushchev's letter was only one of several significant events which occurred in 1962 that would have important implications for planetary protection. COPUOS, which by then was a permanent Committee reporting to the General Assembly,[20] agreed to establish two sub-committees: a legal sub-committee, and a scientific and technical sub-committee.[21] COPUOS also agreed to dispense with voting and conduct its activities on the basis of consensus.[22] Finally, the Soviet Union submitted for consideration a draft document entitled "Declaration of the Basic Principles governing the Activities of States pertaining to the Exploration and Use of Outer Space."[23]

The proposal of the Soviet Union incorporated the linkage established by Khrushchev between contamination of a celestial environment and interference with the activities of other states. The U.S.S.R. Draft Declaration provided:

> 6. Co-operation and mutual assistance in the conquest of outer space shall be a duty incumbent on all States; the implementation of any measures that might in any way hinder the exploration or use of outer space for peaceful purposes by other countries shall be permitted only after prior discussion of and agreement upon such measures between the countries concerned.[24]

The primary thrust of this proposal was to give states a veto over the activities of other states by withholding agreement. The interest in maintaining the integrity of pristine celestial environments was implied only obliquely in the Soviet draft. During the course of the discussions of the COPUOS Legal Sub-Committee, some representatives noted this deficiency, and it was suggested that "prevention of contamination of or from outer space and celestial bodies" be given further examination.[25] Such further examination was conducted the following year by both the COPUOS Scientific and Technical Sub-Committee, as well as by the Legal Sub-Committee.

The Legal Sub-Committee reached consensus on the Soviet draft Declaration of Principles in 1963. The Declaration set forth several fundamental principles to govern the movement of mankind into space, including the non-appropriation doctrine, and that outer space is to be utilized exclusively for peaceful purposes.[26] Significantly, among the initial principles adopted by the global community was:

> 6. In the exploration and use of outer space, States shall be guided by the principle of co-operation and mutual assistance and shall conduct all their activities in outer space with due regard for the corresponding interests of other States. If a State has reason to believe that an outer space activity or experiment planned by it or its nationals would cause potentially harmful interference with activities of other States in the peaceful exploration and use of outer space, it shall undertake appropriate international consultations before proceeding with any such activity or experiment. A State which has reason to believe that an outer space activity or experiment planned by another State would cause potentially harmful interference with activities in the peaceful exploration and use of outer space may request consultation concerning the activity or experiment.

Paragraph 6 of the Declaration incorporated the consultation concept embodied in the U.S.S.R. draft proposal, and maintained the nexus between the contamination of a celestial environment and interference with the activities of other states. It was noted by COPUOS that this provision took into account the conclusion of the Scientific and Technical Sub-Committee that the problem of preventing potentially harmful interference with the peaceful uses of outer space required urgent attention.[27] The Canadian delegation commented that states were not specifically asked in the Declaration to partake in consultations if an experiment would harm the natural environment of the Earth. However, they were confident that any state contemplating such an experiment "would spontaneously undertake consultation."[28]

On November 22, 1963, COPUOS unanimously agreed to submit the Declaration of Principles to the General Assembly, which adopted the instrument as Resolution 1962 in December, 1963.[29]

The Scientific and Technical Sub-Committee took keen interest in the COSPAR planetary quarantine requirements recommended by the Consultive Group on Potentially Harmful Effects of Space Experiments in 1964. The matter was considered sufficiently significant that COPUOS reprinted in its official report the full COSPAR resolution of May, 1964.[30] The Chairman of COPUOS remarked, in his opening statement, "For the first time since the United Nations has been dealing with outer-space matters, reference has been made in the Scientific Sub-Committee's report to a COSPAR resolution of 20 May 1964, affirming that the search for extra-terrestrial life is an important objective of outer space research."[31]

The Scientific and Technical Sub-Committee recommended a form of resolution to be adopted by COSPAR as follows:

> Urges that all Member States proposing to carry out experiments in space should give full consideration to the problem of possible interference with other peaceful uses of outer space, as well as of possible harmful changes in the natural environment caused by space activities and, where Member States consider it appropriate, should seek a scientific analysis of the qualitative and quantitative aspects of those experiments from the COSPAR Consultative Group on Potentially Harmful Effects of Space Experiments, and should give due consideration to the results of this analysis; this does not preclude other recourse to international consultations as provided for in General Assembly resolution 1962 (XVIII).[32]

The Report of COPUOS additionally noted the Report of the Executive Council of the COSPAR Consultative Group, which stated: "The Group recommends early action to *declare Mars a biological preserve* to ensure that in the exploration of this planet, *considerations of biological research receive priority* over others (emphasis added)."[33] Finally, COPUOS recognized the Report of the Panel on Standards for Space Probe Sterilization, which stated:

> (3) A study of the prebiological chemistry of a planet which proves to be sterile would nevertheless be of major biological significance.[34]
>
> * * *
>
> The standards of space vehicle sterilization are, we believe, unrelated to the probability of indigenous life on a planet in question; except in the limiting case that indigenous life and the proliferation of terrestrial contaminants can both be firmly excluded. While there is a sizeable probability that the surface temperatures of Venus are too high for either indigenous or exogenous organisms, this conclusion is based on indirect lines of argument. Also, we cannot entirely exclude the possibility of biological contamination of the clouds of Venus. Until unambiguous astronomical information is available, we recommend that Martian standards of sterility control should also apply to Venus. In the case of the Moon, the surface conditions are rigorous enough to reliably exclude biological contamination of the surface. We cannot exclude the possibility that conditions several tens of metres below the lunar surface will permit microbial replication. Such depths, however, are unlikely to be reached unintentionally during lunar landings. Accordingly, we recommend such less rigorous sterilization techniques as biocleanroom assembly and terminal gaseous sterilization of all spacecraft intended for lunar landings; but rigorous sterilization of drills designed for lunar subsurface boring. Our information about the conditions on other planets is insufficient to form a basis for definitive recommendations at this time."[35]

The parallel courses in the development of the planetary protection policy converged in COPUOS. From the perspective of jurisprudence, the Legal Sub-Committee had drafted the Declaration of Principles which was approved by the General Assembly. On the scientific side, the Scientific and Technical Sub-Committee recognized, endorsed and encouraged the dissemination of and adherence to the stringent planetary quarantine requirements adopted by COSPAR.

The COSPAR planetary quarantine requirements were a function of scientific self-regulation, but did not carry the force of law. Similarly, the Declaration of Principles, as a resolution of the General Assembly, did not constitute positive international law. It was recognized that a more formal treaty document would serve the interests of mankind in the exploration and use of outer space. On May 7, 1966, President Johnson issued a statement in which he proposed a draft treaty specifically applicable to activities in outer space. Among the points to be included in the consideration of such a treaty was to "avoid harmful contamination" of celestial environments.[36]

The following month, the U.S. submitted a Draft Treaty Governing the Exploration of the Moon and Other Celestial Bodies to COPUOS.[37] Article 10 of the draft treaty provided that "States shall pursue studies of, and, as appropriate, take steps to avoid harmful contamination of celestial bodies and adverse changes in the environment of the Earth resulting from the return of extraterrestrial matter."[38] The U.S. draft expanded the concern regarding contamination to both forward and back contamination, and expressed the rights of all states to freedom for scientific exploration. However, unlike the Declaration of Principles, the U.S. draft did not provide for consultations for activities which may cause interference with the activities of other states.

The Soviet Delegation, in June, 1966, made its own proposal concerning a Draft Treaty of Principles Governing the Activities of States in the Exploration and Use of Outer Space, The Moon and Other Celestial Bodies. In article VIII of the U.S.S.R. proposal, the provisions of paragraph 6 of the Declaration of Principles were restated, with the addition of the following new sentence, which was inserted after the original first sentence: "States Parties to the Treaty shall conduct research on celestial bodies in such a manner as to avoid harmful contamination."[39] The U.S. and the U.S.S.R. draft treaties went beyond the provisions of paragraph 6 of the Declaration of Principles by referring to the concept of "avoiding harmful contamination."[40]

The U.S. and Soviet draft proposals were referred to the Legal Sub-Committee, which met in two sessions in the summer and fall of 1966.[41] During the first session, discussions were conducted through a Working Group, and consensus was reached on nine articles of a proposed treaty.[42] These nine articles, in general, incorporated and carried forward the provisions of the Declaration of Principles, including the policy of protecting natural celestial environments.

The expression of the planetary protection policy was not met with serious opposition in the Legal Sub-Committee, and therefore did not provoke extended debate. The primary issues that emerged during the discussions related to the voluntary versus compulsory nature of disclosures to be made regarding activities conducted, and the role, if any, of the Secretary General of the United Nations.[43] Within the Legal Sub-Committee and the Working Group, only the Japanese delegation raised objections, based on its belief that neither proposed draft was sufficient to protect natural celestial environments, and noted: "Great care must therefore be taken to preserve their resources and their natural milieu."[44]

The Japanese delegation was not convinced that the text, as adopted by the Working Group, was adequate to require states to exercise maximum care for the preservation and conservation of the natural resources and environment of celestial bodies. Japan was unsuccessful in offering an amendment to that effect. The Japanese delegation suspected that the amendment was rejected due to fears that it might unduly restrict future activities on celestial bodies. In the view of Japan's delegation, such fears were groundless, but in a spirit of co-operation did not press the amendment, thereby allowing consensus to be achieved.[45]

The language that emerged as article IX of the Outer Space Treaty[46] is as follows:

> In the exploration and use of outer space, including the moon and other celestial bodies, States Parties to the Treaty shall be guided by the principle of co-operation and mutual assistance and shall conduct all their activities in outer space, including the moon and other celestial bodies, with due regard to the corresponding interests of all other States Parties to the Treaty. States Parties to the Treaty shall pursue studies of outer space, including the moon and other celestial bodies, and conduct exploration of them so as to avoid their harmful contamination and also adverse changes in the environment of the Earth resulting from the introduction of extraterrestrial matter and, where necessary, shall adopt appropriate measures for this purpose. If a State Party to the Treaty has reason to believe that an activity or experiment planned by it or its nationals in outer space, including the moon and other celestial bodies, would cause potentially harmful interference with activities of other States Parties in the peaceful exploration and use of outer space, including the moon and other celestial bodies, it shall undertake appropriate international consultations before proceeding with any such activity or experiment. A State Party to the Treaty which has reason to believe that an activity or experiment planned by another State Party in outer space, including the moon and other celestial bodies, would cause potentially harmful interference with activities in the peaceful exploration and use of outer space, including the moon and other celestial bodies, may request consultation concerning the activity or experiment.

The Working Group blended the U.S. and Soviet drafts, and the provision as adopted was similar to paragraph 6 of the Declaration of Principles. The modifications to the text of paragraph 6 of the Declaration incorporated the terminology proposed by the Soviets to protect against forward and back contamination. In addition, minor grammatical adjustments were made, and the phrase "including the moon and other celestial bodies" was added to the reference to outer space. The final modification from the Declaration restricted the applicability of the paragraph to "states parties," that is, all other states party to the treaty, rather than "other states" as referenced in the Declaration.

On July 3, 1970, Argentina proposed a "draft agreement on the principles governing activities in the use of the natural resources of the moon and other celestial bodies."[47] This proposed agreement focused on the sharing of benefits from the use of extraterrestrial resources, and did not mention either contamination of celestial environments nor the potential for interference with the activities of "other states" or "states party."[48] The following year, on June 4, 1971, the U.S.S.R. proposed a "Draft Treaty Concerning the Moon" to the General Assembly,[49] which referred the document to the COPUOS Legal Sub-Committee.[50] The Soviet Draft provided, in article VI:

> 1. States parties shall explore and use the Moon by reasonable means avoiding the disruption of the existing balance of the lunar environment.

2. States Parties shall explore and use the Moon in such a way as to prevent adverse changes in the lunar environment and its contamination through the introduction of extralunar matter. Where necessary, consultations shall be held between the States Parties concerned.

In 1972, the Legal Sub-Committee reported that agreement had been reached on 21 substantive articles, including much of article VI. A lack of consensus still remained, however, concerning a number of issues, including whether the treaty was to be restricted to the Moon or whether it was to include other celestial bodies within its scope.[51] The approved text of draft article VI, with areas of dispute in brackets, was as follows:

1. In exploring and using the Moon [and circumlunar space] [and other celestial bodies] States parties shall take measures to prevent the disruption of the existing balance of [its] [their] environment[s] whether by introducing adverse changes in such environment[s] [its] [their] harmful contamination through the introduction of extra-environmental mater or otherwise. States parties shall also take measures to prevent harmfully affecting the environment of the earth through the introduction of extra-terrestrial matter or otherwise.

2. [States parties planning missions to the Moon [and other celestial bodies] shall notify the Secretary-General of measures being adopted to minimize the disruption of the existing balance of the environment[s] of [those bodies]. Such reports shall include the trajectories to be flown the distance of closest approach, and specific measures taken to control micro-organisms on and in the spacecraft.]

3. [States parties shall notify the Secretary-General of plans to place radio-active material on or in orbit or other trajectory around the Moon [or other celestial bodies] and shall give similar notification with regard to the conditions and effects of such placement when it occurs.]

4. States parties shall report to other States parties and to the Secretary-General concerning areas of the Moon [and other celestial bodies] having special scientific interest in order that consideration may be given to their designation as international scientific preserves for which special protective arrangements are to be agreed, without prejudice to the rights of other States parties to this Treaty.[52]

The draft text required the disclosure of detailed information, including the specific measures taken to control the number of micro-organisms on and in a spacecraft. Consensus was reached by the Legal Sub-Committee on the text of a revised draft article VI in 1973. This revised text modified the reporting requirements, and combined paragraph 3 with the balance of the previous paragraph 2. The revised text provided:

1. In exploring and using the Moon, States parties shall take measures to prevent the disruption of the existing balance of its environment whether by introducing adverse changes in such environment, its harmful contamination through the introduction of extra-environmental matter or otherwise. States parties shall also take measures to prevent harmfully affecting the environment of the Earth through the introduction of extra-terrestrial matter or otherwise.

2. States parties shall inform the Secretary-General of the measures being adopted by them in accordance with paragraph 1 of this article and shall also notify him of all placements by them of radio-active materials on the Moon and of the purposes of such placements. (Points of time of information and notification to the Secretary-General to be resolved.)

. . .

4. States parties shall report to other States parties and to the Secretary-General concerning areas of the Moon having special scientific interest in order that, without prejudice to the rights of other States parties, consideration may be given to the designation of such areas as international scientific preserves for which special protective arrangements are to be agreed in consultation with the competent organs of the United Nations.[53]

The Moon Agreement incorporated this revised text, with minor modifications, as article 7.[54] The General Assembly, without a vote, approved and opened the Moon Agreement for signature in December, 1979.[55] In addition, the General Assembly specifically took note of the Report of COPUOS, which clearly expressed that the intention of this article was not to prohibit exploitation of natural resources, but rather to protect the existing balance of the natural celestial environments.[56]

The Moon Agreement entered into force in 1984,[57] but it has been ratified by only a handful of states.[58] Nevertheless, the Moon Agreement does establish a legal regime applicable to the states which have ratified or signed the instrument.[59] The provisions of the Moon Agreement also may be applicable to all states which participate in a cooperative mission with one or more states which have signed the document. In such circumstances, states will have an affirmative duty to take steps to prevent the disruption of the existing balance of the environment, and to inform the Secretary General of the measures so adopted.

CONFLICTS BETWEEN SCIENTIFIC AND LEGAL APPROACHES TO PLANETARY PROTECTION

The planetary protection policy as set forth in the law of outer space has been consistent in both its philosophy and its expression. While modifications have been made in terminology from the Declaration of Principles, to the Outer Space Treaty, to the Moon Agreement, those changes have expanded the scope of the policy to encompass the three main considerations of preventing forward contamination, back contamination, and interference with the activities of states. The *corpus juris spatialis* has refrained from grafting exclusions, exemptions and exceptions to the policy. The same cannot be said of the scientific approach to planetary protection. What began as a presumption by CETEX that celestial environments are scientific preserves, has evolved into a selective policy applicable only to a limited subset of missions only to a limited subset of target bodies.

The origins of the planetary protection policy were based on the recognition that pristine celestial environments presented a unique opportunity for scientific study and exploration which must be protected. The criterion was expressed that definitive recommendations should not be made in the absence of unambiguous astronomical information. However, alterations began to be introduced to the planetary protection policy based on indirect lines of reasoning, much of which concerned a re-evaluation of the factor of the probability of growth of a terrestrial organism in an alien environment.

These alterations consistently have eroded the requirement to employ active decontamination techniques, even for Mars. The result of this process is that the original planetary quarantine requirement, *i.e.*, that the probability of contamination by a single viable organism be less than 1×10^{-4}, has been eliminated in favor of a standard which can allow for a pre-launch contamination level of 300 spores per square meter for landing craft for Mars.[60] The situation is even more unsettling in relation to fly-by crafts. The probability limit of less than 3×10^{-5} has been abandoned, and crafts have been sent to Mars which were subject to relatively minimal decontamination techniques.

The intention to conduct life detection experiments should not be the determining factor in whether to apply strict bioload reduction requirements to an interplanetary spacecraft, nor should the presence of a craft in a "special region." There have been significant failures of both landing and fly-by craft sent to Mars in the recent past. These missions have not just ended in failure, but the space objects were lost after reaching the red planet. These lost craft could have impacted the surface at unknown locations, including within "special regions." Thus, probes sent to Mars, even if not intended to land in a special region, or to land at all, have carried a substantial risk of contaminating undetermined areas of the planet.

The reductions in the applicability of strict decontamination techniques often have been effected based on little or no relevant data from *in situ* experimentation for the search for life. Moreover, the definition of "life" is constantly expanding, and the experimentation which has been conducted frequently enhances the arguments in favor of strengthening rather than lessening the planetary protection policy.[61]

There are two distinct developments which converge in astrobiology, and which support a robust planetary protection policy: first, the discovery of H_2O on a variety of celestial bodies, which hitherto were unimaginable as sources of water, including the Moon, asteroids, and Mars; and second, the study of extremophiles. The confirmed discovery of water on many celestial bodies is a crucial development for the search for life on alien worlds.[62] The study of extremophiles has expanded the realm of what is considered possible for life to exist, even to thrive, in formerly unthinkably hostile environments. Clearly, the possibility must be acknowledged that life, as we are capable of detecting it, or perhaps as we are as yet unable to comprehend or even recognize, may exist or have existed in celestial environments. The indications are that we should find life on Mars, as all of the essential building blocks are present. If we do not discover life, or the remnants or precursors thereof, it would underscore the uniqueness of Earth.[63] We are still in the early stages of planetary exploration and discovery, and definitive astronomical information must await future experimentation.

Two revisions which have been made to the planetary protection policy merit special mention, as they represent a positive approach: first, the creation of the category of target bodies which are of interest for biological or chemical evolution, but which are considered to present only a remote chance that contamination could jeopardize future exploration; second, the establishment of "special regions" where it is believed H_2O may be present. The first of these revisions carries the implicit recognition that target bodies may be of interest in the search for life, even if it is believed that target body is barren. Nevertheless, as recent discoveries have demonstrated, virtually all celestial bodies should be considered of potential interest for biological or chemical evolution. The "special region" designation, on the other hand, while significant, also may be too restrictive, especially if the refining element is the possible existence of water. Given the extensive evidence of liquid water on the surface of Mars in the past, can the presence of subsurface water, past or present, be definitively ruled out in the absence of experimentation, even in areas regions outside of the "special regions?"

CONCLUSION

The law of outer space requires states to avoid harmful contamination of celestial environments. The *corpus juris spatialis* does not distinguish between celestial bodies based on whether or not they are "deemed important for [the] investigation of extraterrestrial life,"[64] nor whether or not they are deemed of interest for biological or chemical evolution.[65] The modifications of the planetary protection policy based on such distinctions unfortunately have failed to adequately protect Mars from possible contamination. As such, the policy may be deficient *vis-a-vis* international treaty commitments. Moreover the evolution of the planetary protection policy has lost sight of one of the basic propositions on which the policy was founded: a sterile celestial environment would be of major biological significance.[66] Finally, an important distinction must be noted in the perspective of the two major disciplines engaged in the search for life on celestial bodies: astrobiologists and SETI. The planetary protection policy has been driven by astrobiology, and the universe of celestial bodies which are subject to rigorous planetary protection techniques consistently has been reduced, based on the indirect deduction that life is incapable of growth in such alien environments. The SETI community, on the other hand, has been actively searching the skies for new planetary systems, with the implicit assumption that not just life, but intelligent life, may be present on any worlds which may be discovered. It is respectfully submitted that reductions to the planetary protection policy are premature in the absence of extensive study and experimentation.

1. *See* C.R. PHILLIPS, THE PLANETARY QUARANTINE PROGRAM: ORIGINS AND ACHIEVEMENTS 3 (1975), NASA Pub. No. SP-4902, U.S. GPO Stock No. 3300-00578; Stabekis, *History and Processing of Changes*, in REPORT, COSPAR/IAU WORKSHOP ON PLANETARY PROTECTION, Appendix C (2002).
2. G.A. Res. 1348 (December 13, 1958).
3. Phillips, *supra* note 1, at 3; H.S. LAY & H.J. TAUBENFELD, THE LAW RELATING TO THE ACTIVITIES OF MAN IN SPACE, AN AMERICAN BAR FOUNDATION REPORT 189, n. 7 (1970).
4. Lay & Taubenfeld, *supra* note 3, at 189, n. 37; C.Q. CHRISTOL, THE MODERN INTERNATIONAL LAW OF OUTER SPACE 132 (1982); *see also* CETEX, *Contamination by Extraterrestrial Exploration*, 183 NATURE 925-28 (1959); CETEX, *Development of International Efforts to Avoid Contamination by Extraterrestrial Exploration*, 128 SCIENCE NEWS 887-89 (1958); Atwood, *Basis for the Sterility Requirement*, in SPACECRAFT STERILIZATION TECHNOLOGY 3 (L. Hall ed. 1966), NASA Pub. No. SP-108.
5. W.C. JENKS, SPACE LAW 34 (1965).
6. COSPAR Res. 26, 20 COSPAR INFO. BULL. at Annex 4 (1964); see text & notes 30-35, *infra*.
7. Report, Committee on the Peaceful Uses of Outer Space, at 13, U.N. Doc. A/5785 (November 13, 1964). *See* Committee on Planetary Biology and Chemical Evolution, Space Science Board, RECOMMENDATIONS ON QUARANTINE POLICY FOR MARS, JUPITER, SATURN, URANUS, NEPTUNE AND TITAN 27 (1978).
8. Sterns & Tennen, *Protection of Celestial Environments Through Planetary Quarantine Requirements*, in PROCEEDINGS OF THE 23RD COLLOQUIUM ON THE LAW OF OUTER SPACE 107 (1981).
9. *See, e.g., Outbound Spacecraft Basic Policy Relating to Lunar and Planetary Quarantine Control*, NASA Policy Directive 8020.7 (1967); *Outbound Planetary Biological and Organic Contamination Control*, NASA Policy Directive 8020.10A (1972); *Quarantine Provisions for Unmanned Extraterrestrial Missions*, NASA Hand Book 8020.12A (1976); *Biological Contamination Control for Outbound and Inbound Planetary Spacecraft*, NASA Management Instruction 8020.7A (1988).
10. COSPAR Decision No. 16, 50 COSPAR INFO. BULL. 15-16 (July, 1969), *quoted by* Stabekis, *supra* note 1.
11. Space Science Board, Recommendations, *supra* note 7, at 27-28 (Appendix C).
12. *Id.* Nevertheless, the SSB continued to recommend that crafts intended for such celestial bodies employ clean room techniques. It justified such recommendation not on planetary protection considerations, but on the basis that the use of clean rooms would reduce the possibility of growth of organisms which might compromise the functioning of the spacecraft or its payload. *Id.* at 15-16.
13. COSPAR Internal Decision 7/84, *quoted by* Stabekis, *supra* note 1, Appendix C, at C-6.
14. *See* AN EXOBIOLOGICAL STRATEGY FOR MARS EXPLORATION 49 (1995), NASA Pub. No. SP-530; *see also* DeVincenzi, *Planetary Protection Issues and the Future Exploration of Mars*, in 12 ADV. S. RES., No. 4, 121 (1992); D.L. DEVINCENZI, H.P. KLEIN & J.R. BAGBY, JR., PLANETARY PROTECTION ISSUES AND FUTURE MARS MISSIONS, NASA Conf. Pub. 10086 (1991).
15. *See generally* COSPAR/IAU Report, *supra* note 1.
16. *Id.* at chap. 1.
17. *Id.*
18. Report, *Ad Hoc* Committee on the Peaceful Uses of Outer Space, U.N. Doc. A/4141 (July 14, 1959).
19. Letter dated March 21, 1962, transmitting letter of March 20, 1962, from Chairman Khrushchev to President Kennedy, at 5, U.N. Doc. A/AC.105/2 (March 21, 1962).
20. G.A. Res. 1472 (December 12, 1959).
21. Report, Committee on the Peaceful Uses of Outer Space, at 4, U.N. Doc. A/5181 (September 27, 1962).

22. *Id.* at 3-4.
23. *Id.* at 5, *text reprinted in* U.N. Doc. A/AC.105/C.2/L/1.
24. Report, Legal Sub-Committee, Committee on the Peaceful Uses of Outer Space, U.N. Doc. A/AC.105/6 (July 9, 1962).
25. *Id.* at 8, ¶ 14.
26. *See* G.A. Res. 1721 (December 20, 1961).
27. Report, 1962 Legal Sub-Committee, COPUOS, *supra* note 24, at Annex, p.3.
28. *Id.* at 10.
29. Additional Report, Committee on the Peaceful Uses of Outer Space, at 2, U.N. Doc. A/5549/Add.1 (November 27, 1963).
30. 1964 Report of COPUOS, *supra* note 7, at 17.
31. *Id.* Annex I, at 6.
32. *Id.* at 17-18, ¶ 3.
33. *Id.* Annex III, at 3.
34. *Id.* Annex III, Appendix 4, at 11.
35. *Id.* at 13-14.
36. Christol, *supra* note 4, at 134, n. 16; *Agreement Governing the Activities of States on the Moon and Other Celestial Bodies*, Senate, Comm. On Commerce, Science and Transportation, 96th Cong., 2nd Sess., 5-6 (Comm. Print 1980).
37. U.N. Doc. A/AC.105/32 (June 17, 1966).
38. *Id.* at 6.
39. Report, Legal Sub-Committee, Committee on the Peaceful Uses of Outer Space, Annex I, at 11, U.N. Doc. A/AC.105/35 (September 16, 1966); *see also* Report, Committee on the Peaceful Uses of Outer Space, U.N. Doc. A/6431 (September 22, 1966) (U.S. and U.S.S.R. drafts).
40. Christol, *supra* note 4, at 135.
41. 1966 Report of COPUOS, *supra* note 39, at 1, ¶ 1.
42. *Id.* at ¶ 3.
43. *See generally* Legal Sub-Committee, Committee on the Peaceful Uses of Outer Space, Summary Record of the 68th Meeting, 26 July 1966, Geneva, at 3-11, U.N. Doc. A/AC.105/C.2/SR.68 (October 21, 1966) (statements of U.S.S.R., U.S., Japan, and Canada); Legal Sub-Committee, Committee on the Peaceful Uses of Outer Space, Summary Record of the 71st Meeting, 4 August 1966, Geneva, U.N. Doc. A/AC.105/C.2/SR.71 and Add.1, at 13-14 (October 21, 1966) (statements of Japan, Australia, and Bulgaria).
44. Legal Sub-Committee, COPUOS, Summary Record of the 68th Meeting, *supra* note 43, at 6.
45. Legal Sub-Committee, COPUOS, Summary Record of the 71st Meeting, *supra* note 43, at 13-14.
46. Treaty on Principles Governing the Activities of States in the Exploration and Use of Outer Space, Including the Moon and Other Celestial Bodies, *opened for signature* January 27, 1967, 18 U.S.T. 2410, T.I.A.S. No. 6347, 610 U.N.T.S. 205, *text reproduced in* UNITED NATIONS TREATIES AND PRINCIPLES ON OUTER SPACE 3 (2000) [hereinafter referred to as the "Outer Space Treaty"].
47. Report, Legal Sub-Committee, Committee on the Peaceful Uses of Outer Space, Annex I, at 6-7, U.N. Doc. A/AC.105/101 (May 11, 1972).
48. Committee On Commerce, Science and Transportation, *supra* note 36, at 7.
49. U.N. Doc. A/8391 and Corr. 1, annex (1971); *see also* U.N. Doc. A/AC.1/L.568 (November 5, 1971).
50. G.A. Res. 279 (XXVI) (November 29, 1971).
51. Report, Committee on the Peaceful Uses of Outer Space, GAOR 27th Session (Supp. 20), Part II, Report, Legal Sub-Committee, at 3, ¶ 12, U.N. Doc. A/8720 (1972).
52. Report, Committee on the Peaceful Uses of Outer Space, 28th Session (Supp. 20), at 28, U.N. Doc. A/9020 (1973).
53. *Id.* at 34-35.
54. The modifications were, in paragraph 1, the terms "that" was substituted for "such" and "avoid" for "prevent"; in paragraph 2, notification was to be made to the maximum extent feasible in advance; and paragraph 4 was renumbered to paragraph 3.
55. G.A. Res. 34/68, U.N. Doc. A/RES/34/68 (December 14, 1979).
56. *See* Committee on Science, Technology & Commerce, *supra* note 36, at 44.
57. Agreement Governing the Activities of States on the Moon and Other Celestial Bodies, *entered into force* July 11, 1984, 1363 U.N.T.S. 3, *text reproduced in* UNITED NATIONS TREATIES AND PRINCIPLES ON OUTER SPACE 27 (2000), *and* 18 I.L.M. 1434 (1979) [hereinafter referred to as the "Moon Agreement"].
58. As of January 1, 2001, the Moon Agreement has been ratified by Australia, Austria, Chile, Kazakhstan, Mexico, Morocco, the Netherlands, Pakistan, the Philippines, and Uruguay. In addition, the Moon Agreement has been signed by France, Guatemala, India, Peru, and Romania. See Terekov, *Annual Report 2001: Status of International Agreements Relation* (sic) *to Activities in Outer Space*, in PROCEEDINGS OF THE 44TH COLLOQUIUM ON THE LAW OF OUTER SPACE 389, 393-401 (2002).
59. Vienna Convention on the Law of Treaties, art. 18, *text reproduced in* 8 I.L.M. 679 (1969).

60. Debus, Runavot, Rogovsky, Bogomolov, Khamidullina & Trofimov, *Mars 96 Planetary Protection Program and Implementation for Mars Environment Preservation*, in PROCEEDINGS OF THE 40TH COLLOQUIUM ON THE LAW OF OUTER SPACE 220 (1998).
61. *See, e.g.*, "Hydrogen-Fed Bacteria May Exist Beyond Earth," NASA Press Release 02-37AR (April 3, 2002); "NASA Scientists Create Amino Acids in Deep-Space-Like Environment," NASA Press Release 02-33AR (March 27, 2002).
62. "Jupiter's Moon UA Scientist Finds Water and Life Sustaining Nutrients on Europa," University of Arizona, *Report on Research* 5 (2002); "Odyssey Finds Water Ice in Abundance Under Mars' Surface," 2001 Mars Odyssey Press Release (May 28, 2002).
63. 1964 Report of COPUOS, *supra* note 7, Annex III, at 3.
64. COSPAR Decision 16, *supra* note 10.
65. COSPAR/IAU Report, *supra* note 1.
66. 1964 Report of COPUOS, *supra* note 7, Annex III, appendix 4, at 11.

This paper is dedicated in memory of my grandmother, Mary Liberbaum.

ENVIRONMENTAL IMPACT ASSESSMENT AND SPACE ACTIVITIES

L.E. Viikari

University of Lapland, Faculty of Law, PB 122, 96101 Rovaniemi, Finland

ABSTRACT

Environmental Impact Assessment (EIA), the prior assessment of the possible effects of a proposed activity on the environment, is a common tool for environmental protection and management on Earth today. It was the first major step in the development of impact assessment procedures, which are probably the most obvious examples of an approach that integrates economic, social and environmental considerations. Environmental impact assessment is not a well-established tool in the international law of outer space, however. Despite the peculiarities in assessing the potential impacts of space activities, the premise of this paper is that also this field of human endeavor would benefit greatly from the adoption of EIA procedures and, moreover, such an approach is even becoming vital for the safe and rational conduct of these activities. This is particularly true inasmuch as any adverse environmental impacts of space activities are highly difficult to mitigate once they have materialized.

BRIEF INTRODUCTION TO ENVIRONMENTAL IMPACT ASSESSMENT

History of EIA

The earliest mandatory EIA procedures were introduced back in 1969 through the US National Environmental Policy Act (NEPA; 42 U.S.C. § 4321-47). Since then, the terrain has broadened dramatically. The idea of EIA as part of national policy has been adopted in the international arena, too, and there have been significant increases in both the type of activities to which assessments are applied and the scope of the activities, which nowadays extends far beyond the purely environmental (Cordonier Segger et.al., 2002, pp. 58-59). For instance, assessing social and health impacts is now a standard component of EIAs (Cordonier Segger et.al., 2002, p.61). Consequently, environmental impact assessment has often allowed the selection of an alternative which is environmentally, economically and socially superior to the original choice (Harrop and Nixon, 1999, p. 9).

The increasing recognition of environmental impact assessment, and its potential value as an instrument to promote sustainable development in particular, was also reflected in the 1992 Rio Declaration, Principle 17 of which provides: " Environmental impact assessment, as a national instrument, shall be undertaken for proposed activities that are likely to have a significant adverse impact on the environment and are subject to a decision of a competent national authority " (Rio Declaration on Environment and Development, Report of the United Nations Conference on Environment and Development, UN Doc. A/CONF.151/6/Rev.1, 31 I.L.M. 874 (1992)). Principle 15, promoting the more general precautionary approach (of which the impact assessment procedures are a vital part) states: "In order to protect the environment, the precautionary approach should be widely applied by States according to their capabilities. Where there are threats of serious or irreversible damage, lack of full scientific certainty shall not be used as a reason for postponing cost-effective measures to prevent environmental degradation".

Obligations under international environmental law that required EIAs were first introduced in the context of the potential transboundary impacts of particular projects (in the historic US-Canada Trail Smelter Arbitration 1938/1941, for instance, the tribunal held that a state may be held internationally liable for causing transboundary harm. See, e.g., Cordonier Segger et.al., 2002, p. 60). With growing recognition of international interdependence, international obligations to conduct EIAs have arisen also in relation to activities that are proposed to take place in areas beyond the limits of national jurisdiction: such obligations can be found, for instance, in the 1991 Protocol to the Antarctic Treaty on Environmental Protection (Art. 8) (30 I.L.M. 1455 (1991)), and in the 1982 United Nations Convention on the Law of the Sea (Art. 206) (21 I.L.M. 1245 (1982)). It may well be argued that there even exists an obligation under customary international law to conduct an EIA in such circumstances (for instance, in the 1997 Gabcikovo-Nagymaros case, the International Court of Justice found a duty to conduct EIAs before proceeding with serious transboundary projects under customary international law as well as treaty and customary obligations to consult and cooperate in implementation of projects which might affect other states′ interests. See, e.g., Cordonier Segger et.al., 2002, p.60).

Currently, there are regulations for project-level EIA in over 100 countries, but with considerable variations in the types of projects assessed, details of the procedures, and the numbers of assessments carried out (Cordonier Segger et.al., 2002, p. 59). In addition to countries and states, international organizations may have their own environmental assessment procedures - amounting to over 200 EIA systems altogether (Koivurova, 2002, p.131). There are also international agreements on EIA which establish their own EIA systems (e.g., the 1991 Espoo Convention on Environmental Impact Assessment in a Transboundary Context; 30 I.L.M. 800 (1991)).

Procedure and Aims of the EIA

EIA is primarily meant to provide the decision-makers with information that is as comprehensive as possible about the different environmental effects the proposed activity would entail, including alternative courses of action and the zero-alternative (i.e., the no-action alternative). Additionally, plans for mitigation in respect of each alternative are to be outlined.

Typically, an EIA includes a preliminary information-gathering phase and a report, followed by a possible decision to proceed with the project in question. There may also be additional measures, such as full investigations and studies, public meetings and consultations. The assessments take account of, among other things, environmental impacts on ecosystems, diminution of aesthetic and scientific values, long-term or cumulative effects, as well as transboundary implications. They also consider issues such as pollution control, environmental protection measures, reporting, post-project analysis, and rehabilitation. Uncertainties in the assessment process must also be expressly presented. Another common requirement is that the results of the impact assessment should be presented in a way that makes them comprehensible to the general public. (On the EIA procedure, see, e.g., Koivurova, 2002, pp. 131-134.)

Although the central aspect of an EIA is to provide decision-makers with scientific information, the process has other important implications, too. One of the most relevant of these is the involvement of those potentially affected by the proposed activity: most EIA systems require in some way the participation of the public alongside the relevant governmental authorities and other stakeholders. Such public involvement has various aims and goals: it may serve as testimony to good governance in general, or, in more practical terms, be considered improved planning due to the concrete contribution of the public to the decision-making process. Clearly, it is also a tool for reducing conflict and developing wider support for the eventual decisions. In any case, it enables the public to gain information about planned activities and influence these developments in some way.(On the aims of EIA, see, e.g., Morgan 1998, pp. 12-21.)

ENVIRONMENTAL IMPACT ASSESSMENT AND SPACE LAW

Space Treaties

Despite its success in many other fields, environmental impact assessment is not a well-established tool in the international law of outer space. The UN space treaties were drafted at a time when such considerations were definitely not among the highest-ranking items on national agendas in any field of endeavor. Therefore, these instruments lack provisions regarding impact assessment, and the rest of the environmental content found in them is rather modest, too. The nearest equivalent to any impact assessment is contained in Article IX of the Outer Space Treaty, which requires prior consultations in the case of a planned space activity or experiment that might cause "potentially harmful interference" with the space activities of other States Parties.

Domestic Space Laws

The national legislation of some spacefaring countries provides at least for the supply of some kind of information assessing the possible environmental consequences of proposed space activities. In the USA, for instance, regarding the 1969 NEPA, the court decided in Environmental Defense Fund v. Massey (986 F. 2d 528 (1993)) that this Act also applies to Antarctica. By analogy, it should be applicable to space activities as well. In addition to these general obligations, there is a requirement of "formal assessment" on NASA programs of "[orbital] debris generation potential and debris mitigation options" (NASA Policy for Limiting Orbital Debris

Generation, Art. 1.b).

Also, the Russian Statute on Licencing Space Operations requires that in order to obtain a license for space operation in the Russian Federation, the applicant has to supply, among other things, "documents confirming the safety of space operations (including ecological, fire and explosion safety) and the reliability of space equipment'"(Art.5.h). However, such provisions are obviously not enough for ensuring effective regulation of the issue, whereby the possibility of international environmental impact assessment for space activities deserves further examination.

PROSPECTS FOR ENVIRONMENTAL IMPACT ASSESSMENT OF SPACE ACTIVITIES

Problematic Aspects

The space environment is a unique arena in many ways. An obvious problem for any impact assessment is the deficiency in knowledge about processes taking place in outer space. Space activities involve not only natural processes but also complex technological phenomena. These factors together contribute to the fact that the inclusiveness of information most often leaves a great deal to be desired and the outcome of proposed space activities cannot be assessed in detail.

The quality of the impact information is, however, of paramount importance to the effectiveness of the entire EIA system. Scientists are usually expected to produce information that is as unambiguous as possible for the use of decision-makers, but the above limitations considerably increase uncertainty about the conclusions in this case. This means that a substantial gray area exists between scientific resolution and political choice, which enables non-scientific factors to become significant components of debates regarding space missions. Additionally, since much of the subject matter is poorly understood and the tools available are often inappropriate for the task of assessment, the assessment of impacts on space is rather expensive to implement and likely to be comparatively time-consuming. Indeed, lack of time and resources is in practice likely to pose a serious constraint on the development of responsible conduct in space.

However, outer space is a global common, and any adverse environmental effects of space utilization are likely to be severe, irreversible and wide in scope. At the same time, the tragedy of the commons problem (i.e. free-riders) renders many nationally adopted strategies for combating adverse environmental consequences ineffective. Additionally, some of the environmental principles applied on Earth have not been too warmly welcomed among the spacefaring nations and other entities involved. For instance, it is still an issue under debate whether space has any intrinsic value or is merely a resource for human utilization. Understandably, as there is presently no permanent human settlement in space, the environs thereby remain a somewhat remote issue in the everyday life of the vast majority of humankind.

Furthermore, the space industry is a highly commercialized and militarized area of international activity, and spacefaring nations and other entities are seldom very keen on distributing detailed information about their planned activities. The relevance of the precautionary principle and sustainable development, for instance, might seem to rest on a bit shakier ground when applied in outer space. Also, the fact that any activity taking place in outer space may be regarded as ultra-hazardous, although during normal operation the environmental harms usually are minor, renders for instance the due diligence principle, and the transboundary impact assessment duty it entails, somewhat less applicable as well.

Benefits of Space EIAs

Nevertheless, sustainable development and the precautionary principle are important issues for all space activities, and such goals would obviously necessitate better environmental protection, and, thereby, the application of impact assessment procedures. The large scale of potential impacts of space activities would require an equally wide scope of assessment. Also, health and social impacts should be studied in space EIAs as far as possible, since space activities are likely to involve at least indirect social effects, too (the 1991 Espoo Convention, for instance, refers to "any effect. . . on the environment including human health and safety. . . landscape and historical monuments " and includes even "effects on cultural heritage or socio-economic conditions", in addition to effects on more "natural" parts (such as flora and fauna) of the environment; Art. 1.vii). The uncertainty created by the lack of time and resources for impact assessment can partly be amended by ongoing monitoring programs, and, in any case, the potential damage resulting from space activities is of such magnitude that we can hardly afford to omit a thorough assessment of the environmental and other impacts, regardless of the costs.

In the long run, the use of EIA may even reduce direct long-term project costs as well as the time taken to reach a decision by identifying and quantifying not only the beneficial effects but also the possible environmental consequences that might require expensive pollution abatement technology, compensation payments or other costs, and so on (Harrop and Nixon, 1999, p.9). Additionally, democracy would seem to require the possibility of enhanced public participation, or at least more open distribution of information about human enterprises in space. A more communicative approach is becoming increasingly vital for mission planners and policy-makers as well, because the present development of a myriad of groups with specialized interests in space, combined with laws facilitating access to the courts, considerably heightens the probability that a mission or program will attract opposition, even legal challenge (Sterns and Tennen, 1995, pp. 268-269). Effective use of EIA can thereby help to avoid significant administrative delays and increased costs (Sterns and Tennen, 1995, p. 280). Effective EIA is of course also likely to benefit the environment itself - not least in the outer space environment, where many of the environmental amenities can be considered to have more or less unique value.

STRATEGIC ENVIRONMENTAL ASSESSMENT

Environmental Impact Assessment, modified to address the particular features of space activities, would indeed seem to be a tool worth considering for the spatial sphere, too. The (formal) aims of EIA are, however, often already contained in some broader policy statements (Morgan, 1998, p. 12). Space activities are a good example of a field regulated for the most part on the policy level. Therefore, Strategic Environmental Assessment (SEA), as the next "level" of impact assessment procedures, would seem to be a good option for supplementing individual EIAs of space missions. As distinct from project EIA, SEA means carrying out EIAs of plans themselves, thereby directly addressing the environmental implications of proposed strategies and policies. Strategic-level assessments extend the scope of assessment to cover earlier stages in planning cycles (policies, plans and programs), offering a way of dealing with cumulative impacts and making possible the examination of alternatives which project level assessments cannot deal with efficiently (Harrop and Nixon, 1999, p.7). This also often results in reducing the time and costs involved in the lower, project-level assessments (Cordonier Segger et.al., 2002, p.62).

The multiple causes of the deterioration of the space environment also seem to necessitate more proactive, integrated approaches than those found in conventional EIAs, which only represent a limited response to problems. Additionally, there are major non-project-level factors behind individual space missions that determine the course of space activities - starting from the basic principle of international space law, namely, the freedom-of-use rule established by Article I of the Outer Space Treaty of 1968. On the political scene, government macro-economic and security policies often address space issues (either directly or indirectly) with only modest consideration of the full scale of their impacts. Similarly, the international tendency to privatize space activities is only likely to diminish recognition of environmental and social impacts. On balance, the cumulative assessment enabled by SEAs would seem very appropriate. But, at the same time, the fundamental freedom-of-use principle and the right of every state to retain jurisdiction and control over its space missions (Outer Space Treaty, Art. VIII) also need to be respected. The more significant the potential international impacts of space projects, the more easily the balance should, however, be tipped away from state discretion.

Formerly, the governmental authorities tended to regard SEA with suspicion because of the involvement of public interest groups in policy-making that the SEA entails (Morgan 1998, 36). However, the SEA is currently a highly topical issue in the international arena, particularly because of the ongoing discussions within the United Nations Economic Commision for Europe about adopting a Protocol on Strategic Environmental Assessment to amend the Espoo Convention, and of the recent EU Directive (2001/42/EC) on the assessment of the effects of certain plans and programmes on the environment. These instruments could also serve as feasible models for SEA in the outer space environment.

SUSTAINABILITY IMPACT ASSESSMENT

Finally, the most recent "innovation" in the integrated impact assessment field is the introduction of so-called Sustainability Impact Assessments (SIAs). They take into consideration environmental, social and economic factors and apply to policies, plans and programs as well as projects, seeking strategies which will result in long term sustainability. SIAs are increasingly concerned with processes, i.e., with the soundness of institutional planning and management, including mechanisms for the meaningful involvement of the appropriate stakeholders. Access to information and public participation are considered essential, and efforts are made to involve public interest groups in all aspects of the SIA system. Currently, there are still few existing concrete international legal obligations referring to SIAs. (Cordonier Segger et.al.,2002, pp.64-65).

As regards space activities, conducting SIAs would be a substantial improvement and could, for instance, better integrate both the increasingly important private sector proponents as well as the numerous public interest groups into the assessment procedures. However, for the moment, adopting even somewhat effective environmental impact assessment and strategic environmental assessment procedures seems like a demanding enough task. Yet, one might hope that sustainability impact assessment systems will become a reality in the future of space activities, too.

REFERENCES

Cordonier Segger, M.-C., A. Khalfan, and S.A. Nakhjavani, *Weaving the Rules for Our Common Future: principles, practice and prospects for international sustainable development law*, Centre for International Sustainable Development Law, Quebec, Canada, 2002.

Harrop, D.O., and J.A. Nixon, *Environmental Assessment in Practice,* Routledge, London and New York, 1999.

Koivurova, T., *Environmental Impact Assessment in the Arctic: a study of international legal norms,* Ashgate, Burlington, VT, USA, 2002.

Morgan, R.K., *Environmental Impact Assessment: a methodological perspective,* Kluwer Academic Publishers, Dordrecht, Boston and London, 1998.

Sterns, P.M., and L.I. Tennen, Space and the environment: public perceptions and policy considerations, *Proceedings of the 37th Colloquium on the Law of Outer Space,* October 9-14, 1994 (Jerusalem, Israel), pp. 268-280, American Institute of Aeronautics and Astronautics, Washington D.C., USA, 1995.

E-mail address of L.E. Viikari lotta.viikari@urova.fi

IISL Program at UN COPUOS Legal Subcommittee: Prospects for Space Traffic Management

IISL-ECSL Program at UN COPUOS
Legal Subcommittee
2002 Session

On April 2. 2002, a Symposium „PROSPECTS FOR SPACE TRAFFIC MANAGEMENT" was held shortly after the opening of the 40th Session of the Legal Subcommittee of the UN Committee on the Peaceful Uses of Outer Space in Vienna. The Symposium was organised by the International Institute of Space Law (IISL) and the European Center for Space Law (ECSL).

On request of the President of the IISL, *Dr. Nandasiri Jasentuliyana,* the session was coordinated by *Dr. Ernst Fasan,* Honorary Director of IISL. Mr. Philippe Lacoste, Associate Legal Affairs Officer with the UN Office for Outer Space Affairs, served as Rapporteur.

Fasan was able to welcome the President of the Legal Subcommittee, *Prof. Vladimir Kopal;* the President of ECSL, *Dr. Gabriel Lafferranderie;* and many of the distinguished delegates and guests. He transmitted the greetings and best wishes of *Dr. Nandasiri Jasentuliyana,* President of IISL, and introduced the speakers in the order of the agenda as follows:

The Discussion paper will be presented by *Dr. Kai-Uwe Schrogl*, Head, Corporate Development and external relations of German Aerospace Center, DLR.
Then the Discutants start with *Space Traffic Management* by *Dr. Armel Kerrest de Rozavel*, Professor at the Université de Bretagne Occidentale, Faculté.
Next speaker is Professor *Jose Monserrat Filho*, Brazil, member of the board of directors of the IISL, presenting *Space Traffic Management: Comparative Legal Aspects.*
There follows Professor *Dr. Lubos Perek*, also director of the IISL Academy of Sciences of the Czech Republic, and member of the Czech Delegation, to this distinguished subcommittee, taking *A look back to early concepts for space traffic.*
Next speaker will be Professor *Patrick Salin*, Centre of Air and Space Law, McGill University, on *Existing Elements of Traffic Management in the Field of Telecommunication.*
And then follows the concluding paper By *Dr. William Ailor*,Director, Center for orbital and reentry Debris Studies on the Aerospace Cooperation on the *Role of Aerospace Objects in the future.*

After presentation of these papers by the speakers, there followed an extensive questions and answers period. In conclusion, the Chairman of the Legal Subcommittee, *Prof. Vladimir Kopal,* expressed his appreciation for the speakers and discutants, and to the International Institute of Space Law (IISL), and the European Center for Space Law (ECSL) for organising the event. On behalf of the Subcommittee, he expressed the wish that a similar Symposium on Space Law would again be organised for the 42nd Session of the Subcommittee in 2003.

A little reception closed the event.

Dr. Ernst Fasan, Hon. Director, IISL.

Space Traffic Management : Comparative Legal Aspects

Armel Kerrest
Professeur des Universités
Institut de Droit des Espaces Internationaux et des Télécommunications
Université de Bretagne Occidentale

Sooner or latter, it will be necessary to manage space traffic. For the time being the same problem already poses in relation with other human activities, i.e. in the high sea and in the air. It is of great interest to consider how this issue is handled in those spaces.

First of all let us consider the problems:

States can exercise territorial jurisdiction on their territory and personal jurisdiction on their nationals. Territorial jurisdiction is unique on a territory; as far as traffic regulation is concerned, it prevails over personal jurisdiction of other States. When we travel back to the centre of Vienna in our cars, Austrian jurisdiction applies as territorial jurisdiction, it overcomes personal jurisdiction, the rule applicable in our national original countries.

This solution is of course very efficient. There is only one territorial State but there is many States of nationality. Driving to Vienna we will apply Austrian law whatever our nationality may be. What a mess if we apply our national regulations. Only one applies: the Austrian.

If we want to go a little further, when we consider traffic regulation, we have three various legal issues:

- We need rules
- These rules must be applied, a control of their application must be done.
- If the rules append to be violated a sanction is needed.

If I go on with the example of Vienna traffic management, these three activities are efficiently conducted by Austrian legislative, administrative and judicial powers. Doing so Austria respects international and European law, but as far as we are concerned, we have to respect Austrian laws and regulations, we are under the control of Austrian police and may be prosecuted before the Austrian judge.

In international spaces the situation is quite different. The corner stone of the system misses: no State can exercise its sovereignty, there is no territorial State, no State able to exercise its territorial jurisdiction. Only personal jurisdiction applies. When there is only one territorial jurisdiction on a national territory, there is many personal jurisdictions applying on an international space if nationals or many States are using this space. When traffic management is concerned the problem is obvious. Who is going to make the rules, who is going to control their implementation, who is going to punish violations ?

As a matter of principle, if no special international regime is created, only personal jurisdiction applies. The State of nationality, registration, flag is the only competent State to set the rules, control and punish.

This situation has at least two very detrimental consequences: the plurality of applicable rules in a unique international territory, the possibility for some to change registration flag or even nationality in order to change and choose the law, control and sanction applicable to their activity. It is the well known problem of flag of convenience which poses for instance in high sea.

There is fortunately some solutions as far as the issue of regulation is concerned three of them may be highlighted: The creation of rules by an international body, the setting of an international convention, the entrustment of one State to set up regulations.

As far as the issues and control and repression are concerned, these competences may be recognised to

- the State having personal jurisdiction (State of registration or flag) (it is the common rule) or
- A State specially invested for instance a State involved for some other reasons -like practical ones- like costal State or port State.
- An international body

How does it work in the high sea and in air above the high sea ?

They are spaces out of the territorial jurisdiction of any State, for that respect they are the same as outer-space.

I Traffic management in the High Sea.

As a mater of principle navigation is free in the high sea, only the State of the flag has jurisdiction over its ships. Since some decades, following major oil splits, costal States have tried to extend their control over ships endangering their coasts.

According to the Law of the sea convention, they can regulate the passage in their territorial water:

Article 21

1. The coastal State may adopt laws and regulations, in conformity with the provisions of this Convention and other rules of international law, relating to innocent passage through the territorial sea, in respect of all or any of the following:

a) the safety of navigation and the regulation of maritime traffic;

...

This article is precised by article 22 which deals with sea lanes and traffic separation schemes in the territorial sea.

Article 22

Sea lanes and traffic separation schemes in the territorial sea

1. The coastal State may, where necessary having regard to the safety of navigation, require foreign ships exercising the right of innocent passage through its territorial

sea to use such sea lanes and traffic separation schemes as it may designate or prescribe for the regulation of the passage of ships.

2. In particular, tankers, nuclear-powered ships and ships carrying nuclear or other inherently dangerous or noxious substances or materials may be required to confine their passage to such sea lanes.

3. In the designation of sea lanes and the prescription of traffic separation schemes under this article, the coastal State shall take into account:

(a) the recommendations of the competent international organization;

(b) any channels customarily used for international navigation;

(c) the special characteristics of particular ships and channels; and (d) the density of traffic.

4. The coastal State shall clearly indicate such sea lanes and traffic separation schemes on charts to which due publicity shall be given." [1]

In some cases coastal States wanted to move away from their shore the navigation of some ships carrying dangerous goods. The passage was to be made in the high sea. The legal basis for such a decision is far less obvious. The costal State has no power to regulate the passage of foreign ships in the high sea.

A solution was founded thanks to an International Organisation: the International Maritime Organisation. (IMO). It was necessary to use the Safety of Life at Sea Convention, called "SOLAS convention" at its regulation V point 8. and the "Convention on the International Regulations for Preventing Collisions at Sea" 1972 "COLREG convention", in its article 10 which provides for traffic separation schemes adopted by the International Maritime Organisation.

When a costal State wants to set a traffic separation scheme it makes a proposal to IMO's Sub-Committee on Safety of Navigation which will discuss the issue and put it forward to the Maritime Safety Committee (MSC) IMO's senior technical body. If accepted as a recommendation, the traffic separation scheme may be put in place by the costal State[2]

This recommendation is not compulsory, even if every ship master knows it is in his interest to follow these rules. Thus the coastal State has no real possibility to control the implementation of this "rule" and even less the right to punish wrongdoing.

Nevertheless, most of the time, these rules are accepted and implemented by the ships, because, at the end of the voyage the ship must enter a port. Then, as a territorial State, the State of the port may control and even refuse the entrance of any ship.

II Traffic management in the Air above the High Sea.

As a matter of principle, according to the law of the sea convention in its article 87:

"... Freedom of the high seas ... comprises, inter alia, ...

(a) freedom of navigation;

(b) freedom of overflight;"

Flight is free over the high sea, only the State of flag or registration has jurisdiction over its ships and aircrafts.

Fortunately, as far as commercial air navigation is concerned, the

[1] United Nations Law of the Sea Convention, Montego Bay 1982 part II : territorial sea and contiguous zone, article 21.

[2] See IMO Resolution A.572(14) *"General Provisions on Ship's Routeing"*.

practical situation is quite different. Thanks to an other International Organisation, the International Civil Aviation Organisation -ICAO- rules are applicable.

Specifications proposed to be given the status of "Standards or Recommended Practices" are, after consultation with all Contracting States and interested international organisations, finalised by the Air Navigation Commission and submitted to the ICAO Council where they require a two-third majority for adoption.

Following their adoption and provided a majority of Contracting Parties do not disapprove them, they become applicable at dates set by the Council.

As far as air navigation is concerned, these Standards and Recommended Practices are considered binding for their application on air over the high sea.

During the flight over the high sea, commercial aircrafts are controlled by a State in charge of a route. In practice, there is very few breaches of the rules as, whatever their State of registration may be, companies know that States in charge of the traffic control may blacklist them and forbid them to land on their territory.

Conclusions :

Some principles are common to sea and air traffic regulation. A distinction may be done between creation of the rule, control of its implementation and prosecution of offenders. For the creation of the rule, an elaboration within an international organisation seems rather efficient. In the case of sea traffic separation schemes, the action of the costal State is essential.

For the control of implementation of the rule, The control by the State of registration or flag is the principle but is not really efficient. The real control is made in both cases by a State whose territory will be used by the aircraft or ship at the end of its voyage (costal State, State of the port or of the airport. This point out the importance of territorial jurisdiction in that respect.

As far as prosecution of offenders is concerned, the State of flag or registration is the only competent State. In practice, at least for air regulation, because of their considerable commercial impact, measures by the territorial States are sufficient threat.

How Sea and Air traffic regulation may give us indications for Space traffic regulation ?

On the first point, the same solution may be used: an international organisation may be responsible for making the rules.

For control in air and sea, the control by States of the flag or registration proved not to be efficient enough. Other States must intervene through their territorial jurisdiction.

For Space activities, the situation is quite different, there is no territorial jurisdiction of a State which may be used. No costal State, no State of the port or of the airport.

An original solution must be proposed.

IISL/ECSL Symposium Prospects for Space Traffic Management
UNCOPUOS Legal Subcommittee
Vienna, 2 April 2002

Space Traffic Management: Comparative Institutional Aspects

José Monserrat Filho *

"Tout en étant parfaitement au courant des faits de l'histoire, il doit s'appliquer à étudier les prolongements futurs de l'évolution actuelle et le faire avec une probité résolue, temperée par une appréciation exacte des problèmes pratiques que posent les réalités de la vie." Manfred Lachs (1)

1. Introduction

To know exactly where each spacecraft is, in the air or in the outer space, where it comes from and where it is going to, what it is doing and how it is working in a given moment. Aiming to assure safety of space activities by preventing collisions and harmful interference, as well to protect the outer space and Earth environment. (2)

This is briefly what we are dealing with when the point is space traffic management

To have all these data in a real time we need by no means:

- A new kind of international co-operation as deep and confident as we do not have yet;
- A complex and competent international system (network) with highly qualified international teams and last generation hardware to fulfil all involved tasks;
- A global space traffic management institutionally established.

Without a permanent, efficient and self-sufficient institutional framework, a true global space traffic management seems to be impracticable.

Human being has been able to create very sophisticated systems of maritime, railway, railroad, and air traffic management. However, until now, in 44 years of Space Age, he was unable to work out a space traffic management system.

Is it really needed? Yes, it is, today more than yesterday and even more tomorrow than today.

"How much space traffic is necessary before you institute some space traffic control?" - William O. Glascoe III asked in 1999. He answered that "traffic arises from a lot of vehicles vying for the same space at the same time whether or not they are destined for the same place."

In fact, the geostationary orbit already faces a traffic jam in many passages. Conflicts caused by crowding of space vehicles can reach critical mass. At the same time, the question of space debris is becoming challenging. As yet there is no international solution - neither in perspective - for the problem of increasing amount of space debris the heavy used orbits are going to be more and more polluted.

Hence the reasonable Glascoe recommendation: "We need a Space Traffic Control System under development now than later." (3) It is a prudent and wise approach. It makes possible to anticipate knowledge and solutions for future inevitable problems, as well as to prepare expertise, to create hardware for such a crucial task and to gather experience in the field.

The foundation of the Space Traffic Management System could be laid down at the same time with the construction of the Global Air Traffic Management System, thought the later is far more urgent, of course. Operationally, the two systems are very different, but technically, politically and legally all works relating to the Global Air Traffic System will be quite beneficial for the Space Traffic System.

There seem to have no insurmountable technical obstacles to start shaping a Space Traffic Management System. The main barriers for this program are undoubtedly economic and political.

"It would be necessary to put some order in this" ("Il faudrait y metre un peu d'ordre"), Roger-Maurice Bonnet, Scientific Director of the French Space Agency (Cnes), said, speaking specifically about the European Earth Observation Strategy. (4) Yet this commentary is as well as suitable to the question of space traffic today. It is evident that here also there is no appropriated international order.

Demands for a global Space Traffic Management are already wide and multiples. A symptomatic indication is the proposal recently presented by José Achance, Earth Observation Director of the European Space Agency (ESA). According to him, "the demographic, industrial and economic development of mankind demand that we organize in planetary scale an integrated administration of the terrestrial and maritime environment, as well as of the natural resources". It would be a Global Monitoring for Environment and Security (GMES). In José Achance view, this administration passes necessarily thought the understanding and the surveillance of the nature' complex processes, to which the space tools are absolutely indispensable. (5)

It is obvious that such a planetary integrated administration will be much more secure and efficient if it could count on a global space traffic management that could contribute to assure safe and orderly functioning of all space tools linked to the system.

An huge difficult for working out of an entire space traffic management system would surely be the deployment of weapons in outer space and consequently its transformation into battlefield. (6) The new, space armed race it would engender, as well as the clear predominance of military doctrines defending a national control of and superiority in outer space will undermine the cooperative and trustful foundation indispensable for the space traffic management.

2. Institutional aspects

As Glascoe pointed out, "the existing body of International Space Law does not consider an authority controlling 'space traffic' anywhere in its text. This void must be filled before progressing." Once again it is the sound preventing approach.

What kind of institutional structure could be better to develop and to set up a space traffic management in the foreseeable future?

It is not easy to answer this question today. However, we already have some practical and historic references to think about it and to envisage some ways to arrive there.

The International Telecommunication Union (ITU), to certain extend, manages the traffic of geostationary satellites, practically since the beginning of the use of this relevant orbit in the sixties. Under the ITU supervision the satellite operators coordinate their demanded orbital positions and radio frequencies. The ITU also controls the assignments of communication radio frequencies in space and of service areas on the ground.

Although the ITU work is extremely important, it is limited to the telecommunications programs and not to all aspects of them. In fact, it doesn't encompass many tasks required for a space traffic management: satellite collision preventing service, re-orbiting and re-entering regime for non-functional space objects and general outer space debris regime (7), among others. It means:

1) We have no a international system, based in a complete and precise directory with information about all objects launched into outer space, capable to track them and to alert their close encounters, as well as to provide them the optimal guidance option;

2) We have the 1993 ITU recommendation to re-orbit geo-stationary satellites, but it is not yet a legal obligation. Far beyond this we need to conceive an international regime for operations of re-orbiting or re-entering into the atmosphere of any kind of spacecraft.

3) It is also necessary to conceive an international regime for all issues rosed by space debris, starting from its legal definition, as well as the removal of space debris and the minimization of the arising of new ones. Of course, it includes the development of industrial standards and their implementation by all States and private enterprises.

"Who is going to coordinate all this activities in a place that doesn't fall under any nation's jurisdiction or doesn't have an internationally recognized boundary?" - Glascoe asks.

Some of these tasks have being accomplished, at least partially, by States individually. For instance the US Space Command for many decades tracks debris objects larger than 10cm in low orbits and larger ones at higher orbits - 1m at geostationary orbit.

The deeply unequal current world geopolitical situation strongly favors national unilateral solutions, as they seem better to safeguard the national economic and strategic interests of the most powerful countries.

That is why the first institutional question we need to answer is whether a national structure of one or some great powers is sufficient and legitimate to meet with all space traffic management requirements.

A restricted national solution to this essential issue hardly will be acceptable by the international community as a whole, unless another embracing and cooperative way will be absolutely impossible, which certainly is not the case. Emblematic in this sense is the recent

European Union decision to implement the Galileo satellite navigation system, rejecting the GPS worldwide monopoly position. (8)

To manager the space traffic it seems necessary, at last, three international bodies, working in close relationship:

1) Data Base body with real time information about the situation of all spacecrafts;

2) Regulation body in charge of the creation of operational rules, a kind of standards and recommended practices;

3) Permanent coordination body in charge of monitoring and evaluating the accomplishment and the efficiency of the adopted rules.

These bodies should be essentially technical and autonomous. They could be composed by and render account to the United Nations Committee for the Peaceful Uses of Outer Space (Copuos). They could be created gradually, trying to overcome step by step all kind of resistance existing today.

Above all, the most important action is to start such a process. The first step certainly must be a Copuos decision to produce in its Legal and Scientific and Technical Subcommittees a wide and deep discussion on the necessity and the possibility of the creation of a Space Traffic Management System. In this sense, it probably would be quite reasonable to establish a special working group to study this issue. In short, we should include this item in Copuos agenda. It would be wiser to do this now as we all are aware that it will have to be done one day in not so remote future.

3. Comparative Institutional Aspects

We already have accumulated different international institutional experiences, particularly in the United Nations system, which can be useful to develop our project. (9)

It seems that the most valuable of them is the institutional model established by the 1944 Chicago Convention, the Charter of the International Civil Aviation Organization (ICAO). (10)

As Dr. N. Jasentuliyana has stressed properly, "the regulatory structure of the [Chicago] Convention's Annexes, in particular, has brought international uniformity, to a great extent, to international civil aviation, and has led to the greater safety, regularity and efficiency of air transport". (11) Safety, regularity and efficiency also will be the permanent purposes of the Space Traffic Management.

Special significance for us has the ICAO structure and law-making process. This system is responsible for adopting and amending international standards and recommended practices and procedures. It has been working successfully all along more than half a century.

There are many reasons for the success of the ICAO system. One of them has being the ability to delimitate the matters falling under its competence and the matters belonging to the domestic jurisdiction of each State. It surely will be one of the most arduous issues to cope with in shaping the Space Traffic Management system.

This extremely hard point led us to the very sensitive political area. The ICAO has been succeeded in separating the technical and political aspects of International civil aviation, as Dr. N. Jasentuliyana pointed out. Yet this task will be much more challenging in space activities due to its incomparable huge strategic and political problems. Nevertheless, we will probably have no another choice than to leap over this wall if we really want to achieve a worldwide safe, regular and efficient Space Traffic Management.

It means that firstly we are "condemned" to construct a consensual political will strong enough to face such a complex and historical undertaking.

A timely motivation for doing this great effort are the recent warning words from the Finnish Professor Martti Koskenniemi: "Without the ability to articulate political visions and critiques, international law becomes pragmatism all the way down, an all-encompassing internalization, symbol, and reaffirmation of power". (12)

4. Conclusions

It is necessary to place the question on Space Traffic Management in the Copuos agenda as soon as possible.

To approve this almost impossible decision in our time, it is necessary to make a political miracle, which is as well as indispensable to solve many others even more pressing world problems.

Let's make a miracle.

* Professor of Space Law, Vice-President of the Brazilian Society of Aerospace Law (SBDA) and Member of the Board of the International Institute of Space Law (IISL). E-mail: <monserrat@alternex.com.br>

Notes and references

1) Lachs, Manfred, Le Monde de la Pensée en Droit International - Theories et pratique, France, Paris: Economica, 1989, p. 228.
2) Perek, Lubos, Traffic Rules for Outer Space, Proceedings of the 25th Colloquium on the Law of Outer Space, AIAA, 1983, pp. 37-42.
3) Glascoe III, William O., Controlling the Spaceways, Space Policy Digest, October 12, 1999.
4) Liberation, March 2, 2002.
5) Liberation, March 2, 2002.
6) Krepon, Michael, Lost in Space - The Misguided drove Toward Antisatellite Weapons, Foreign Affairs, May/June 2001, pp. 2-8.
7) Perek, Lubos, Traffic in Outer Space, paper of January 19, 1999.
8) Black, Ian, EU and America Clash on navigation system, The Guardian, March 9, 2002; Mckie, Robin, Euro satellite to be _£2bn eye in the sky for blind, Observer, March 17, 2002.
9) Trindade, Antônio Augusto Cançado, Direito das Organizações Internacionais, Belo Horizonte, MG, Brazil: Del Rey 2002.
10) Convention on International Civil Aviation, December 7, 1944, 15 UNTS 295; ICAO Doc 7300/6.
11) Jasentuliyana, Nandasiri, Lessons for Space Law Through The Experience of Air Law; Recent and Future Developments in Space Law: Preparing for the 21st Century; in International Space Law and the United Nations, The Netherlands: Kluwer Law International, 1999, pp. 372-373. See also from the same author Celebrating Fifty Years of the Chigaco Convention Twenty-Five Years after the Moon Landing: Lessons for Space Law, Annals of Air and Space Law, Vol. XIX-II, 1994; and Future Perspectives of Space Law, in Perspectives of Air Law, Space Law, and International Business Law for the Next Century, Edited by Karl-Heinz Böckstiegel, Proceedings of an International Colloquium, Cologne, June 7-9, 1995, Carl Heymanns Verlag KG, Germany, 1996.
(12) Koskenniemi, Martti, The Gentle Civilizer of Nations - The Rise and Fall of International Law 1870-1960, United Kingdom: Cambridge University Press, 2001, p. 516.

IISL / ECSL Symposium
Prospects for Space Traffic Management
UNCOPUOS Legal Subcommittee
Vienna, 2 April 2002

Discussion Paper: Prospects for Space Traffic Management

By: Kai-Uwe Schrogl
German Aerospace Center, DLR

Space Traffic Management

... so far an academic venture ...

- early, but still excellent, ideas by Lubos Perek in 1982
- AIAA / CEAS / IAA / UNOOSA Workshops 1999 and 2001
- IAA study group 2001-2003

... but soon a „real“ issue

- today approximately 600 active satellites
- approximately 9000 debris larger than 10 cm
- rising number of spacefaring nations
- rising number of launch ventures and facilities
- rising number of non-governmental actors
- new technologies, in particular aerospace objects in the future

What does Space Traffic Management have to achieve?

- Safe access to outer space
- Safe operations in outer space, in particular collision avoidance
- Prevention of pollution of outer space, safeguarding the (limited) natural resources (the orbits)
- To combine existing rules developed in various bodies (UNCOPUOS, ITU) and regimes (international and national space law, air law, telecommunication law)

Elements of Space Traffic Management to be considered regarding the three phases of space activities

- Launch phase
  - expendable and re-usable launch systems, aerospace objects, commercial and private ventures, debris mitigation

- In-orbit phase
  - use of orbits, monoeuverability of spacecraft, collision warning and avoidance, use of disposal orbits, specific use of outer space (e.g. advertising, funerals)

- Re-entry phase
  - re-usable launchers and aerospace objects, intentional deorbiting, unintentional deorbiting

Elements for a regulatory framework for the three phases

- Information needs (information / observation / notification)
- Regulatory needs on the international and national level
- Organizational and institutional aspects

A long-term perspective 2010-2020:

- Shared knowledge about the status of space activities at any given time (shared observation capabilities and capacities)
- Comprehensive set of binding rules for all three phases negotiated internationally and implemented through national legislation for governmental as well as non-governmental activities
- Organizational structures comparable to air traffic management as in existence today

Early Concepts for Space Traffic

Luboš Perek
Astronomical Institute
Academy of Sciences, Prague, Czech Republic

1. Sources

Some aspects of space traffic have been dealt with in several papers in the past and some space traffic rules have been enacted without calling them traffic rules. Systematic treatments of the question are, however, rare. In the 1980's, two papers dealing with general problems of traffic in outer space were presented at the Colloquia of the IISL[1],[2]. Both papers pointed out that traffic problems had been known for a long time on the land, on the sea and in the air. Both papers also stressed that space environment differs substantially from the three environments around us and that traffic rules for outer space will have to reflect this fact. Both papers also referred to the Registration Convention and its possible modification. None of the two papers anticipated that in the year 2002 Traffic Rules for Outer Space would still be a matter for an undetermined future and not a matter, which already proved its value and usefulness.

The first paper discussed:

- Traffic Rules on the Road, on the Sea, in the Air,
- Travel in Outer Space,
- Principles of Outer Space Traffic Rules, such as
  - Coordination of Communications,
  - Traffic Separation,
  - Removal of Inactive Satellites,
  - Disposal Orbits,
  - Reducing the Amount of Debris,
  - Identification of Space Objects, and
  - Minimizing Environmental Pollution.

[1] L. Perek: Traffic Rules for Outer Space, Proceedings of the 25th Coll. on the Law of Outer Space, AIAA p. 37, 1983.

[2] P.Q. Collins, T.W. Williams: Towards Traffic Systems for Near-Earth Space, Proc. of the 29th Coll. on the Law of Outer Space, AIAA p.161, 1987.

The second paper dealt with:

- Spacecraft Orbits,
- Traffic Separation into Zones,
- The Geostationary Orbit,
- Satellite Power Station Scenario, and
- Space Tourism Scenario.

The American Institute of Aeronautics and Astronautics (AIAA) initiated in the 1990's a series of Workshops on international space cooperation. The Fifth Workshop[3] of that series, held in Bermuda, 12-15 April 1999, established a Working Group on The Growing Number of Satellites in Orbit: Facing the Issues. It dealt with:

- Orbital Resource Management,
- Collision Avoidance,
- Orbital Debris, and
- Regulatory Framework.

The Sixth Workshop[4], held in Seville, Spain, 11-15 March 2001, had a Working Group on Space Traffic Management. The discussions were directed in

- Legal and Regulatory Environment,
- Developing Rules of the Road for Space,
- Enabling Collision Warning,
- Using Disposal Orbits,
- Actively Managing Launch and Reentry,
- Reducing the Creation of Orbital Debris, and
- Protecting the Geostationary Orbit.

Let us summarize the contents of those four sources from today's point of view.

2. Traffic Rules in the Three Environments

Traffic rules play an important role in three environments: on the road, on the sea and in the air. Although the conditions are quite specific for each of the environments, there are some general features. The main aim is to maintain safety of traffic by:

- **Establishing rules for avoidance of collisions**. Knowledge of traffic rules enables drivers, helmsmen or pilots to anticipate the actions of their counterparts and to choose the optimal action. Many rules exist in the rules of the road, such as rules on right of way, priority at crossings, etc. Marine traffic is regulated by special International Regulations for Preventing Collisions at Sea. For the prevention of collisions in the air sophisticated practices and technical elements have been introduced.

---

[3] Report of an AIAA, UN/OOSA, CEAS, CASI Workshop, April 1999, International Space Cooperation: Solving Global Problems, AIAA, 1999.

[4] Report of an AIAA, UN/OOSA, CEAS, IAA Workshop, March 2001, International Space Cooperation: Addressing Challenges of the New Millenium, AIAA, 2001.

• **Separating traffic in opposite directions**. This principle is very efficient because it diminished relative velocities of vehicles. It is being used on highways, in channels near ports, and in the air space.

• **Establishing specific rules on inactive vehicles**. Such rules deal with parking places, with signals to be exhibited by automobiles and ships. For inactive balloons specific rules have been established.

• **Requiring proper identification of vehicles**. Vehicles in all three environments have to exhibit names, license plates, or other designations.

• **Requiring high quality of technical equipment and qualification of personnel**. Technical elements for safety are numerous, certificates of safety of vehicles and competence of drivers or pilots are obligatory. Safety in traffic, though very expensive, is generally recognized as preferable to the risk and cost of accidents.

• **Establishing rules on protection of environment**. Rules and obligatory equipment restricting the pollution of the environment apply in all three environments.

Some of these principles can be applied also to space traffic, if the very specific conditions of outer space are respected. Manned spacecraft are rather the exception than a rule. The vast majority of objects in space are inactive and have no means of maneuvering, objects "at rest" are moving under natural forces at high velocities, and no scavenging service is operating, to name just some examples.

3. Space Traffic Rules in Force

Surprisingly, some space traffic rules are in force and, what more, are followed by all space users. The International Telecommunication Union has been applying traffic rules to geostationary satellites for a long time, almost since the beginning of the use of that orbital belt. An assignment of a nominal position in the GEO (Geostationary Orbit) is, in fact, equivalent to traffic separation of one satellite orbit against another. Close encounters among active satellites can happen only in cases when the same nominal position has been assigned to more than one satellite or when satellites are being transferred to another nominal position. The present practice is to leave the coordination of relative positions to operators of satellites concerned. Difficult moments may arise also during the insertion of a satellite into, or removal from, the geostationary orbital belt.

Satellites in the GEO keep their nominal orbital positions – within permitted tolerances – by periodical application of corrective impulses, i.e., during their active lives only. Objects left in orbit after the termination of their activities pose a hazard of a destructive collision.

The ITU takes care also of assignments of communication radio frequencies in space and of service areas on the ground. All operators comply with the coordination rules.

4. Traffic Separation

Traffic separation could apply, in a form different from that used in GEO, to Low Earth Orbits, in particular to communication satellite systems. Each of the systems consists of a number of satellites located in a fixed configuration in an orbital shell, defined by its altitude above the ground. Reserving a shell for each satellite system would separate orbits of one system from orbits of all other systems, excluding thus collisions under normal operating conditions. Passage through a shell for satellites launched into higher shells or for de-orbiting maneuvers would have to be coordinated.

5. Avoidance Maneuvers

Avoidance maneuvers have been used in particular in the GEO. Whenever the computed distance between an active and an inactive satellite became smaller than a predetermined limit, the active satellite used its station keeping capability to perform a maneuver to get out of the way of the inactive object. In order not to spend valuable fuel on unnecessary maneuvers, the orbits have to be calculated with high precision. The current databases and catalogues are incomplete and inaccurate. Therefore it was felt (see footnote 3,4) that:

Finding -- A mechanism is needed to warn satellite operators of close encounters and to provide guidance as to optimum actions. The service provider, be it government or commercial entity, should be reviewed by an international body that includes representatives of both government and industry.

6. Disposal Orbits

De-orbiting of satellites from the GEO to the ground or to the dense layers of the atmosphere would be too costly because large amount of fuel would be necessary for the maneuvers. Less fuel is needed to raise the perigee of the orbit in such a way that the new orbit, called disposal orbit, does not interfere with active satellites located in the vicinity of the nominal GEO. The first to recognize and use the advantage of disposal orbits was INTELSAT. In May 1977, the perigees of three INTELSAT satellites were raised by 400 km, or more, beyond the nominal GEO. In the following years, other operators used the same procedure. Finally, in 1993, the ITU adopted a recommendation to re-orbit satellites approaching the end of their active lifetimes into disposal orbits. The necessary distance, following from the ITU definition of the GEO, is at least 300 km above the nominal orbit. A more refined formula for determining the minimum distance for the disposal orbits was developed by the IADC in 1995. The formula respected the degree of compactness of satellites and the resulting distance is between 245 km for very compact satellites to 435 km for loosely built objects.

The recommendation is being followed by some operators but not by all. Possibly the technical difficulties connected with the complex maneuver of re-orbiting has not been mastered, or commercial operators are reluctant to stop a profitable operation and to use the remaining fuel for re-orbiting. The situation is not likely to change if the respective recommendations are not made into binding provisions through incorporation into the ITU Radio Regulations[5].

Finding – Since the recommendation to re-orbit geostationary satellites into disposal orbits is not followed in all cases, it should be changed into a binding provision through incorporation into the ITU Radio Regulations.

The principle of disposal orbits could be used at other altitudes for the 12 hours orbits of the navigation satellite systems. It could be useful even for lower orbits as long as they are less costly than de-orbiting.

7. Space Debris in Orbit

The total mass of objects in space up to about 2000 km altitude is between 2000 and 3000 tons. About one quarter of that amount is in active spacecraft, three quarters in space debris. If all the inactive objects are left in orbit, they will eventually be fragmented by collisions into smaller debris. In particular large objects may generate very large number of small, but still deadly, fragments. The collision probability may consequently increase dramatically in the future. It is rather probable that the amount of mass of objects in space will have to be reduced, in order to keep near-Earth space fit for future space activities. Even if available technology and financial means do not allow any significant cleaning of near-Earth space at present, there are theoretical studies of methods to de-orbit inactive objects. There is a good chance that such efforts will be successful and that adequate ways and means will appear in the future.

The Outer Space Treaty, in its Article VIII, is quite clear on the provision that launching state retains the jurisdiction and control over a space object while it is in outer space. The ownership of objects is not affected by their presence in space. In this sense also the agreements on anti-satellite activities support the rights of the owner. Unless specific provisions are introduced for space debris, space law will pose an important obstacle to de-orbiting of space debris.

Source 3 addressed the problem of on-orbit debris and proposed 1) moving large debris, such as satellites at the end of operational lifetime, out of the way of active satellite orbits; and 2) by the active removal of visible but untracked smaller debris.

Finding -- In a long perspective, also the active removal of large bodies has to be considered. Legal obstacles in the form of protection of all space objects, including space debris, by the Outer Space Treaty should be reconsidered.

8. Restricting New Space Debris

All the sources recommend that it is necessary to restrict the formation of space debris in the near term on a worldwide basis, because the hazards could

[5] See footnote 4, p.12.

escalate significantly within 10 years. Of particular importance are standards adopted by national and international space agencies, recommendations of the IAA Position Paper, and standards developed by the IADC. The standards deal with control of debris released during launch and operation, with the prevention of explosions, with re-orbiting into disposal orbits and de-orbiting from space. Let us quote, in a succinct form, from the recommendations in sources 3 and 4:

Recommendation – The Working Group participants strongly support work being done by the UN, the IADC, the IAA, and others to develop guidelines designed to minimize the creation of new debris objects. However, the acceptance of these guidelines is not yet universal. Industry standards, based on these guidelines should be developed for consideration by the International Organization for Standardization.

9. Status of Space Objects: Valuable Asset or Space Debris

An important lesson can be learned from the early, as well as from the not quite so early, discussions of space traffic rules. It concerns the frequent use of the term "active space object". The term is very important because any rules will be different for active spacecraft from those applying to inactive objects. In other words, the status of a space object is the most important characteristic to be considered in the discussion of traffic rules or management of space.

The number of trackable active space objects is relatively small. There are only some 600 to 700 active objects compared to the total number of all trackable objects, which exceeds 9000. Active objects, however, are very valuable assets. The cost of manufacturing, launching and operation is high. The investment yields considerable profit, if the satellite provides continuous services. Inactive objects, i.e. space debris, on the other hand, have no value and pose a hazard to active objects.

With regard to their importance, it is rather curious that there is no officially recognized list of active space objects. There are good estimates of the total number, there are unofficial and unpublished lists, but when it comes to enumerating all such objects, authoritative sources are silent.

The adjective "active" could be understood as referring to receiving or emitting radio signals. But spare communication satellites, which will be put into service at a later time, do not receive or emit radio signals for extended periods of time. Or scientific satellites, such as those used in investigating the field of gravity, may not send any messages, their only function being to reveal their position by reflecting light.

A launching state may keep being interested in the fate of a space object even after it has become non-functional. That may happen when the object contains industrial or military classified information. The term "active" could be understood to cover also the keeping of classified information.

Finding -- The opposite to space debris are not only objects, which are active in the narrow sense of the word, but all spacecraft which are considered valuable assets by their launching states or operators.

In fact, the change of an "active space object" into space debris occurs only by decision of the owner and that is the launching state. There are examples: The Mir station or the Compton Gamma Ray Observatory were functional objects as long as the respective launching countries considered them functional and useful. It was only after a decision of the launching state that the object became officially non-functional[6].

Information on the status of a space object is quite important for scientists and technicians investigating all aspects of space debris. It is vitally important for objects, which are more or less intact and of a large size, because these can be confused easily with active objects.

Two scenarios have to be considered. If launching states provide information on which of their space objects are active spacecraft, then all other objects could be considered space debris. The second scenario may be more probable. If launching states do not provide information on all of their active satellites, perhaps they might be willing to provide information on which space objects terminated their activities and are not considered valuable asset anymore.

There is, fortunately, a mechanism for authoritative announcements on the status of objects in space, which could be useful in either of the two scenarios. The Registration Convention contains a provision for announcements by launching states not only on the launching but also on other important phases in the life of space objects. Practically all launching states -- and some launching organizations -- keep announcing the launching of space objects. Some launching states have even made use of the opportunity in a wider sense and announced the termination of activities of their satellites[7]. That practice should become universal. With the appearance of the Online Index of Objects Launched into Outer Space[8], the relevant information could be easily and widely accessed.

Finding – Existing space law does not use the term *space debris* and does not differentiate between valuable spacecraft and worthless space debris. The value and status of a space object can be important in determining how the object is to be treated. Launching states should keep announcing changes in the status of their objects.

Objects, which cannot be confused with active spacecraft, may not require individual announcements. Their status as space debris may be recognized by their small size, or, by agreement, by their characteristics as rocket bodies, stages, component parts, or fragments.

---

[6] L. Perek, Definition of Space Debris, Paper IISL-01-IISL.4.01, presented at the Int. astron. congress, Toulouse, 2001.

[7] E.g., Sweden announced the termination of activities of three of its satellites in UN documents ST/SG.SER.E/318, 335, and 364.

[8] Online Index of Objects Launched into Outer Space is an index of governmental announcements made by launching states to the UN Secretary General in compliance with the Registration Convention. It was prepared by the Office of Outer Space Affairs at the website registry.oosa.unvienna.org/oosa/index/index.stm .

10. Conclusion

Setting up traffic rules for outer space is a very complex problem. Conditions in outer space differ radically from traffic conditions in the three environments, we are familiar with: the road, the sea and the air. Yet, some of the general principles encountered in traffic around us might find their way into space, such as traffic separation, collision avoidance or protection of environment.

A very special problem concerns the status of a space object. As long as the spacecraft is active, it is a valuable asset providing important services. Once the object terminates its activities, it becomes a burdensome piece of debris posing a potential hazard to active spacecraft. The status of a space object depends on the decision or intention of its owner, that is its launching state. Without learning about that decision or intention, other users of outer space, in particular those who intend to devise traffic rules, are left in the dark about the true nature of some vehicles participating in the traffic.

2002 IISL/ECSL SYMPOSIUM

Prospects for Space Traffic Management
On Occasion of the 41st Session of the Legal Subcommittee of the United Nations Committee on the Peaceful Uses of Outer Space
2 April 2002, Vienna (Austria)

EXISTING ELEMENTS OF TRAFFIC MANAGEMENT IN THE FIELD OF TELECOMMUNICATIONS

Dr. Patrick A. Salin[1]
CIASL, McGill University
Orbicom (Uqam), Montreal, Canada
salin.patrick@uqam.ca

Abstract:

The use of the frequency spectrum by satellite services has exploded within the last ten years, forcing the ITU to adapt itself to a rapidly evolving environment. Space traffic management is primarily concerned by radio frequency utilization rules that aim at allowing sound communications between satellite operators. Technology innovation for both geostationary and low earth orbits satellite systems is strong and leads towards a profound renovating process of ITU radio regulations. While still being framed by rules that have mostly been crafted before the progressive world radio conferences of the second half of the 1990s, an evolutionary process seems to be initiated to accommodate new services within the fragile outer space environment in order to allow for their being used for the benefit of all.

Introduction

Telecommunications traffic rules as they exist now with reference to the geostationary orbit (GSO) and to the low earth orbits (LEOs) are different because of the fact that the GSO provided satellite system operators with the physical advantage to place a satellite in an apparent stationary position in relation to the Earth. As a consequence, being more easily operational than the other orbits, they have been utilized almost since the beginning of the commercial space adventure for telecommunications and television services, while LEOs have only been utilized since the mid-1980s for commercial remote sensing services and since the mid-1990s for mobile satellite services. Both sets of rules are in the process of being revised for different reasons in order to continue offering a rational and efficient utilization of the frequency spectrum. GSO telecommunication rules are threatened by the clogging of satellites on a limited number of available orbit slots, while rules for the low earth orbits are not elaborate enough to accommodate the heavy

[1] DCL (McGill), MBA (New York), DEA (Paris). Author of: *Satellite Communications Regulations in the Early 21st Century - Changes for a New Era*. Utrecht Studies in Air and Space Law (Volume 19). Kluwer Law International - Martinus Nijhoff Publishers, Den Haag (The Netherlands). 592 pages. October 2000. ISBN 90-411-1238-3.

utilization of LEO systems in a close future. We will therefore successively address (i) traffic rules for the GSO, (ii) traffic rules for the LEOs and, (iii) the present evolutionary for both sets of rules.

I – Telecommunication traffic rules for the geostationary orbit

Telecommunications rules are set by the ITU and have been in use as to satellite operations for the last three decades. Two situations should be considered, the one of the allocation of frequencies before the project is under elaboration, and the situation when the satellite(s) is (are) in orbit. To sum up the whole procedure in one sentence, we can say that existing telecommunications traffic rules are centred around the use of a limited dual resource: the radio frequency-orbital slot (RF-OS) resource. The specific identification of orbital slots on the GSO makes the RF-OS a very unique resource in the sense that for one orbital position, there are several radio frequencies that can be used, but since there is only one available orbital position, there is a bottleneck effect on that orbital position, which resembles to an inverted triangle resting on one of its head (the orbital position) while the available frequencies lie on top of it. Hence the need to coordinate the use of those frequencies because they correspond to different services that can be used by different satellite operators, while there is only one orbital position available.

For the sake of the reader, let us first recall the role of the ITU and, second, its legal consequences offering suggestions for possible changes in the future.

1.1. The role of ITU as a coordinator

Contrary to a largely spread opinion, ITU is the oldest specialized agency of the United Nations and acts not as a regulator but as a coordinator. The whole ITU coordination procedure is a consequence of Article 44 of its Constitution that requires a use of radio-frequency spectrum and orbit that is *rational*, *efficient* and *economical*, together with *equitable access*, while Member States retain jurisdiction on the objects they launch into Outer Space. ITU principles incorporate two basic principles, which rule the use of radio communications in Outer Space by Member States, which have ratified the various space treaties and conventions:

(i) Direct and absolute state responsibility backs any activity that one of its registered nationals may conduct in outer space (Liability Convention, Art. VI).

(ii) The Member State itself must fill-in a registration procedure in order to place a satellite on the geostationary orbit (Registration Convention, Art. II).

ITU's role is directly played towards Member States or international institutions whose members are also members of ITU, and not towards corporate operators. Member States must follow several steps, knowing that, it is the "*first come, first served*" rule which applies in the distribution of slots on the geostationary orbit. And since it is a limited resource and there is no priority privilege granted to anyone, this rule becomes a *de facto* rule, which gives an advantage to those nations that have the capacity to place a satellite on orbit or to have it being placed by somebody else. Advance notification and registration by the Radio Regulations Board is requested in order to identify possible incompatibilities. The Board then examines (i) the conformity of the demand with the ITU Convention, (ii) the conformity with the Table of frequency allocation, (iii) the conformity with the procedure of pre-notification, and (iv) the probability of harmful interference. When the national administration has accepted the notified orbital position and frequency, it is recorded in the Master Register. It should be noted here that an assignment which would not conform to the Convention could still be used and be recorded in the Master Registry, provided that it does not provide interference.[2] There is a possibility of legal loophole here, since the responsibility of the operating plan of the system lies with the operator of such system and, in last resort, with the state of registration.

Three main different tasks are shared by three different actors: the Radio Regulations Board (RRB) controls the "*allocation*" procedure, ITU conferences control the "*allotment*" procedure, while national administrations control the "*assignment*" procedure.[3] It follows that the RRB implements the frequency assignments that have been decided by the Member States after specific frequencies have been allotted by ITU conferences.

The purpose of these procedures is to let the RRB organize an orderly recording of frequencies which have been allotted to specific uses by international conferences. States themselves, whether or not they are members of ITU and are within the orbital position they have been allotted, assign specific frequencies to those of their national operators which have presented a request, the technical characteristics of which correspond to the general allotment parameters which have been identified for all states.

In case interference should occur during time, in the use of radio communications, interfering stations must, upon receipt of advice, immediately eliminate the harmful interference. Every user has a right of international protection against harmful interference when using the GSO, provided (i) it has an assigned orbital position and (ii) this position has an allocated radio frequency.

A national administration may suspend the use of any of its recorded frequencies or orbital positions during 18 months, provided it informs the RRB. If the suspension was to last for a longer period, say more than six months, the assignment would no longer be protected and could be reassigned to some other operator. The Board may also cancel or

---

[2] For satellite radio-broadcasts, it is an "*a priori*" procedure which is used, which implies a fairly rigid plan and freezes the orbital slot and the technical characteristics once they are identified.

[3] Excerpts from: *ITU Radio Regulations*, volume 1, chapter 1, section II: Specific terms related to frequency management:

2.1: *ALLOCATION* (of a frequency band): Entry in the Table of Frequency Allocations of a given frequency band for the purpose of its use by one or more terrestrial or space radiocommunication services or the radio astronomy service under specified conditions ...

2.2: *ALLOTMENT* (of a radio frequency or radio frequency channel): Entry of a designated frequency channel in an agreed plan, adopted by a component conference, for use by one or more administrations for a terrestrial or space radiocommunication service in one or more identified countries or geographical areas and under specified conditions.

2.3: *ASSIGNMENT* (of a radio frequency or radio frequency channel): Authorisation given by an administration for a radio station to use a radio frequency or radio frequency channel under specified conditions.

modify a recorded assignment, if the use of the frequency or of the position was not in conformity with the Convention and after having consulted with the national administration, since the use of frequencies on the GSO is derived from a right of access (even perpetually) and not from ownership. One country may allow another country to use its allotted positions provided that an agreement with respect to Convention obligations is signed by the receiving nation. The registered nation may replace a dead satellite and may have more allotted slots than it has satellites.

These rules conceal an important flaw: they are *de facto* directed towards the use of the geostationary orbit, i.e. the only orbit where one can precisely assign orbital positions. Consequently, with regard to low Earth orbits satellite systems, the international community, i.e. the ITU, only has the harmless interference rule at its disposal in order to discipline the arrival of the LEO constellations of satellites and impose a code of satellite circulation.

1.2. Legal consequences of the use of the frequency spectrum by outer space systems

On the GSO, ITU rules are fairly well established and have only been slightly altered by recent conferences.[4]

1.2.1. A right to "use" and not to "own"

This is a direct consequence of space law principles: the recording of an assigned orbital position does not confer national property rights, whether those rights have been granted on a "first-come, first-served" basis, or on an "a priori" plan.

1.2.2. A right to use perpetually

The general rule is that the notifying country is allowed continuous use without a time limitation. However, in the "a priori" plan, the procedure is designed to meet the requirements of the concerned country for specified periods of time.

1.2.3. A right to barter a GSO slot

This right does not officially exist, since the right to use a particular orbital position/radio frequency is non transferable. This right is the *de facto* consequence of the established "a priori" procedure which opens the way for adjacent countries to exchange allotments in situations when the proposed modification or inclusion of a new frequency assignment could affect the nearby allotments.

1.2.4. A right to replace a dead satellite

The protection of assigned frequencies against harmful interference requires that any change be notified with regard to an assignment which has been recorded in the Master Registry. What is at stake here in terms of identification is the name of the space object and the effective use of the frequency. In practical terms, nothing prevents a nation from

[4] For a more in depth study, please see Ram Jakhu, *International Regulations of Satellite Communications*, pages 78-101, in: Legal Aspects of Space Commercialization, Edited by K. Tatsuzawa, CSP Japan, 1992. Professor Francis Lyall of the University of Aberdeen is also a regular commentator on ITU issues.

simply replacing an expired satellite with an identical one which carries the same technical characteristics. This leads to consider that the "temporary" use of frequencies translates itself into a *de facto* permanent or even quasi-appropriation of the orbital/frequency position.

1.2.5. A right to more recorded assignments than satellites

The reasons why such situation may occur for a nation, could come from the need to hoard positions for future use or to make the best use of available satellites in providing service wherever and whenever needed. This led to the "paper satellite" controversy that was raised in the early 1990s and showed the limit of the regulatory procedure.

II – Traffic rules for non-GSO orbits

For non-GSO orbits there is a regulatory vacuum if we want to be exhaustive in the expectation of a complete set of rules as those which do exist for the GSO. Actually, the vacuum is not total since space systems are constrained by the interference-free obligation which emanates from Article IX of the 1967 OST.[5] When we say "obligation", this is not true since consultation should occur in relation with the activity causing the interference. Beyond what we would qualify as being a quasi-obligation, the assignment of positions is totally free. Moreover, the recording of orbital parameters required by Article IV of the 1976 Registration Convention may reveal itself to be incomplete or may lack precision in case of large size satellite constellations.[6] When we think of large projects that were much heralded not long ago, we easily can imagine the complexity of management and maintenance difficulties such fleets will create and how easily it can turn into a technical (and legal) nightmare for both the owner and other satellite system operators.

III – Traffic rules for LEO systems

When considering the making of ITU Radio Regulations, it appears that the mindset of the redactors did not anticipate the fantastic development of satellite communications. Even with "standard" GSO-dedicated World Radio Conferences, it is only recently that the international community became conscious of the soon-to-come *de facto* extremely massive utilization of near-Earth outer space, i.e. the LEO area in the close vicinity of the Earth.

Apart from standard regulations concerning the use of radio frequencies and until WRC-

---

[5] Article IX of the 1967 Outer Space Treaty (extract) : « ... A State Party to the Treaty which has reason to believe that an activity or experiment planned by another State Party in outer space ... would cause potentially harmful interference with activities in the peaceful exploration and use of outer space ... may request consultation concerning the activity or experiment ».

[6] Article IV of the 1976 Registration Convention (extract) : « 1. Each State of registry shall furnish to the Secretary-General of the United Nations, as soon as practicable, the following information concerning each space object carried on its registry : .(a) Name of launching State or States ; (b) An appropriate designator of the space object or its registration number ; (c) Date and territory or location of launch ; (d) Basic orbital parameters, including : (i) Nodal period, (ii) Inclination, (iii) Apogee, and (iv) Perigee ; (e) General function of the space object ...

3. Each State of registry shall notify the Secretary-General of the United Nations, to the greatest extent feasible and as soon as practicable, of space objects concerning which it has previously transmitted information, and which have been but no longer are in earth orbit ».

95, there were no specific ITU regulations for the use of non-GSO orbit locations. Even now, the use of non-GSO orbits is not really addressed, since ITU only focuses on the use of specific radio frequencies which will be used by these systems. So far, multi-million $ non-GSO satellite systems are concerned by ITU regulations only to the extent that they use radio frequencies, just like any individual or isolated amateur radio.

In the end, the only constraint that does exist emanates from the ITU Radio Regulations as it is illustrated by the diagram of the exploded view of the location of several satellites on closely located orbital spots, which appears on the following page. But this is only of concern to geostationary satellites. No such constraints exist for LEO satellites, for the simple reason they are in motion relative to one another, while GSO satellites are fixed relative to one another. At that stage, engineers have to tell us what is feasible and what is not in terms of assigning specific LEO locations (meaning "orbit plans" within which the satellites are moving) and their available spectrum frequencies for which only the non-interference rule exist, in association with the implied non-physical assault (collision) rule that always exist in a legal environment, because of the legal pursuits that it would trigger.

FIGURE 9
Exploded view of geostationary satellite orbit

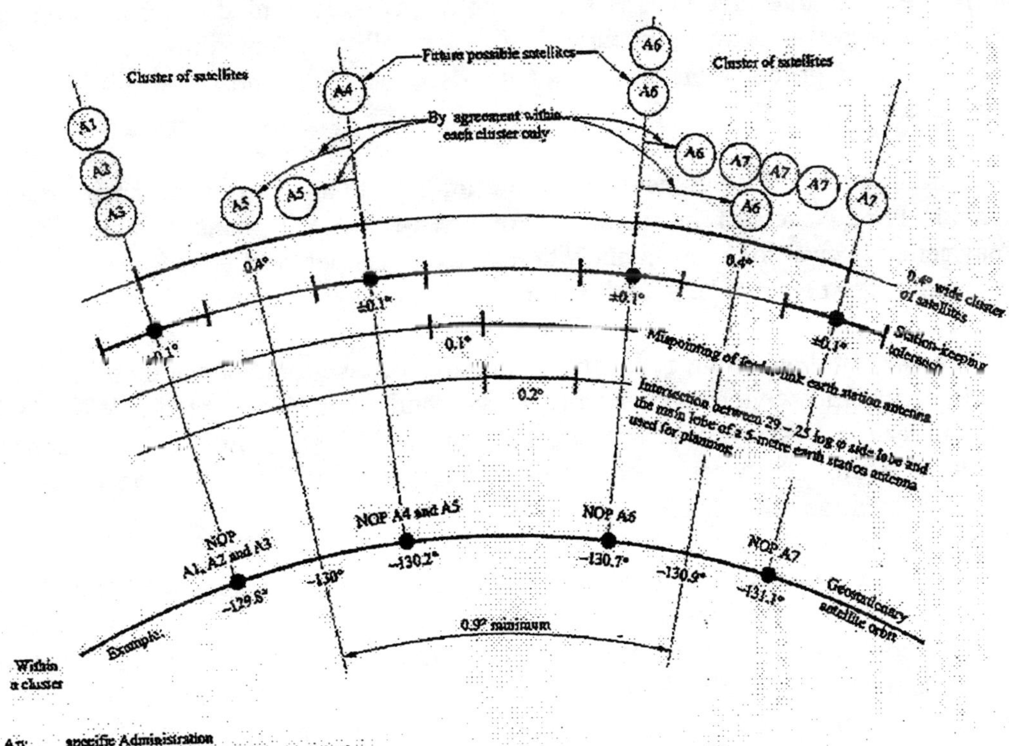

IV – The evolution of the present system for both the GSO and the LEOs

Evolution is now engineered into the ITU regulatory process that will impact on both GSO and LEO system operators in their handling of the radio frequency spectrum. It is of concern to GSO systems because of the limited accommodation capacity of the GSO, and to LEO systems because of the non-regulated dimension of these orbits apart from the non-interference obligation and the general care duty that emanates from international obligations, mostly from the Outer Space treaty.

Different resolutions have been adopted by previous World Radiocommunication Conferences (WRC), timidly starting with WARC-95 until the last WRC-2000 held in Istanbul. They illustrate technical solutions that are ventured in order to face potential difficulties in the utilization of radio frequencies by an increasing number of space stations and platforms of all types on both types of orbits.

First, we may consider that increased harmful effects could be created as a consequence of the backlog in satellite filings at the ITU. This may simply result from the acceleration of the filing procedure by the ITU, considering that current efforts to solve this backlog issue may be shortened for the sake of being pragmatic (i.e. leaving the registering State assuming the consequences of licensing a "careless" satellite project that would be authorized without due supervision). Oddly enough, we may think that this backlog has a positive side-effect in slowing the access of new satellite systems into Outer Space by means of lack of proper registration. But this is done under the responsibility of the registering state.

Second, additional spectrum seems to be the immediate and only solution in order to accommodate new users of the spectrum. For a non-engineer it seems as simple as that, we may certainly envision constraints with regards to this perspective, because the use of spectrum may not be extendable to the infinite.

Third, the view of developing countries should also be taken into consideration. The re-planning of specific services (BSS) in Regions 1 and 3 has been agreed at WRC-2000, which will lead to a review of power limits during WRC-2003. This is concurrent to the principle of equity of access to spectrum that may border the expansion of satellite systems by developed countries.

Fourth, WRC-2000 tried to balance the sharing of constraints between GSO and non-GSO systems. We have here a wealth of new services such as high speed Internet, corporate intra/extranets, e-commerce, videoconferencing and other interactive services that are planned to be offered by means of satellites. Such constraints also aim at protecting terrestrial uses that operate in the same frequency bands.

Fifth, newly engineered projects, such as High Density Systems, have been allocated specific frequencies and protected by power limits from other systems. We are here at the vanguard of these new services that may benefit very much to developing countries. Other services that we already know, such as High Altitude Platform Stations, Earth

Exploration Services and Radioastronomy Service, have also benefited from new allocations of spectrum.

Sixth, allocations have also been made to the promising and front-guard radionavigation systems in order to allow for the expansion of the existing services like the GPS and GLONASS, while allowing for the coming of Galileo that has just been officially approved by European authorities.

Quite obviously, mentioning these new approaches is not enough, engineers have to tell us about their technical feasibility and how far they allow for their compatibility with other services and systems.

Conclusion

Space Telecommunications are the ultimate frontier of standard telecommunications that we all know on earth, which are so important to socio-economic development. The most recent UN Report on Human Development has stressed the positive impact of high technology exports for developing countries in their development. So far, it appears that the evolution of the rational and efficient use of the frequency spectrum inevitably leads to the additional allocation of new frequency bands for new types of services and networks. Economic interests are huge, they are worth billions of dollars for those who engineer those systems, as well as for those who operate them, and also to those who benefit from them as users. This translates into offering and having access to new services that did not exist before or to services that did exist before but at a higher price. WRC-2003 will be a new milestone in this evolution towards a increased use of the frequency spectrum by satellite systems for the betterment of mankind.

However, before ending this brief presentation, we must bring a slightly minoring tone to our reasonable optimism. A very strong commercialization trend has been developed since the mid-1990s, whereby space powers are increasingly considering that national security considerations coupled with self-imposed budget constraints justify the dual use of commercial satellites for both private and public strategic purposes. In parallel, commercial satellites serving sole private business purposes that represent financial assets in large amounts are increasingly considered to be exposed to all sorts of malfunctions, if not to straightforward intentional destruction by adverse interests. This raises the topic of space warfare that will increase in importance in the coming years. Radiocommunications are extremely vulnerable to warfare, whether traditional or high technology, for the simple reason that telecommunications have historically always been a strategic instrument, and it will remain so in the future.

The vulnerability of Outer Space as an environment has been recognized since the beginning of the space adventure and this recognition should, and must, allow for a different approach of space matters so that they are not dragged into earthly-considerations. Some space analysts and practitioners already say that Outer Space is a mere extension of the air space that States control with their sovereign rights when their strategic needs are threatened, very similar to the right of "hot pursuit" in standard public international law. In our opinion, this is the ground on which the debate will inevitably relocate in the next years. This will prevail on the standard discussions on the sharing of frequency spectrum by various services, especially because huge financial interests are at stake. More than the sharing of radio frequencies, the debate will concentrate on the sharing or lack of sharing of benefits to be returned from an extensive utilization of the frequency spectrum, yet, a natural resource that belongs to all.

Space Traffic Control: Data Access Defines the Future

William Ailor, Ph.D.
The Aerospace Corporation
2350 East El Segundo Blvd
El Segundo, CA 90245
william.h.ailor@aero.org

Abstract

The evolution of space traffic control services will be strongly affected by how issues related to data access and protection are resolved. Several governments and many private companies own portions of the data required for these services, but the best quality services require that data from all sources be merged. One possible solution is the formation of an international nonprofit or equivalent organization, with responsibilities, data access, and services defined by agreement of space faring nations.

Introduction

Given the increasing number of operating satellites and associated debris, it is inevitable that collisions in space will seriously damage or destroy operating vehicles. It is also likely that a collision involving a critical asset will lead to the institution of a "space traffic control" system designed to help operating satellites avoid collisions. The question is: how might such a system evolve?

Background

Over the last 40 years, mankind has launched over 20,000 metric tons[1] of material into orbit around our planet Earth. While much of this has come back to Earth, some of this material is still in orbit and will remain there for a few years to millions of years.

We're adding new satellites and creating new debris at a rapid rate. Some estimates put the total number of operating satellites at over 2000 by the year 2020—an increase of nearly 300% from the approximately 700 satellites operating today.

Typically, operating satellites release debris as they are launched and placed into their operating orbits. This debris ranges from spent stages to hardware required for deployment, to lens covers and the like. In addition, satellites and stages that are currently in orbit can create debris by accidentally exploding or colliding with other objects.

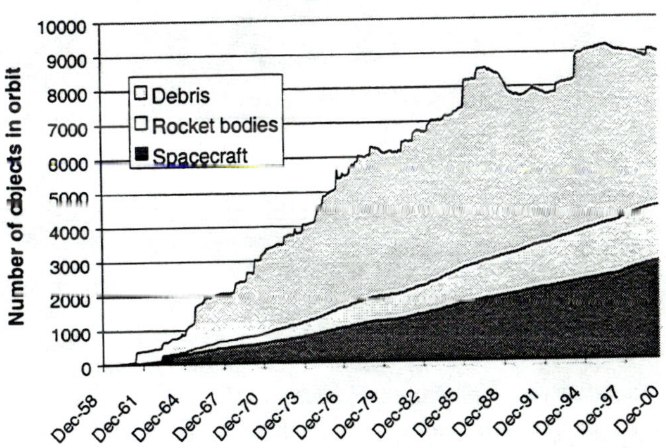

The number of spacecraft and rocket bodies is increasing steadily while debris mitigation efforts and increased cleansing of debris in low orbit due to solar storm-induced atmospheric density increases are decreasing the population of debris.

As a result, the population of non-operating hardware and debris can also be expected to increase from the approximately 9,000 currently tracked (generally, tracked objects are larger than a 10-30 cm in low earth orbit and a meter and larger at geosychronous equatorial orbit (GEO) altitude[2]).

Fortunately, some objects in low earth orbit will slowly be removed from orbit by atmospheric drag.

In addition, there are efforts among space-faring nations to develop regulations to reduce the quantity of debris. Current drafts call for satellite operators to move their vehicles to disposal orbits (or remove them from orbit altogether) and to vent propellant tanks and discharge batteries at end of life to prevent later explosions. The emerging regulations will also require that debris created during deployment and operations be minimized.

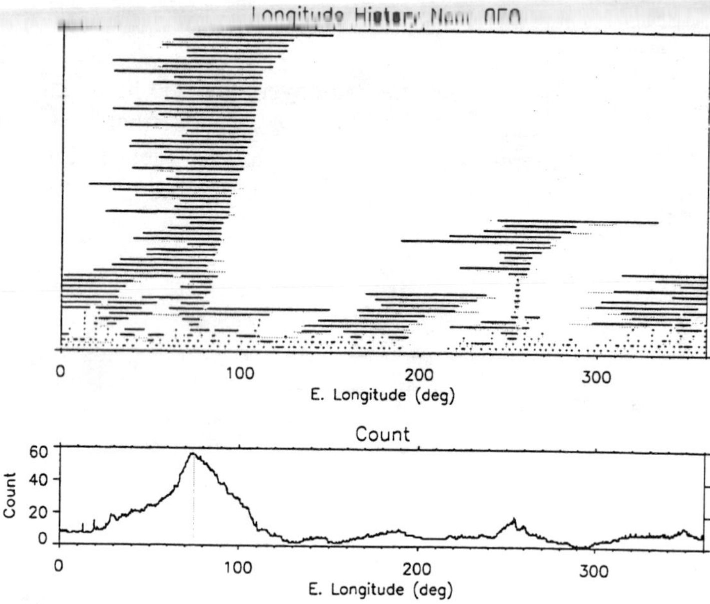

These figures show the number of satellites sharing the same region of space. The bottom figure shows the number of GEO satellites as a function of longitude; the upper figure shows the range of longitudes over which each satellite operates. Operational satellites tend to have much smaller longitude variations (near the bottom of the upper plot).

There are also efforts to track and catalog more of the debris in orbit (at orbital velocities, even a centimeter-sized fragment represents a serious threat to the International Space Station and operating satellites). The United States Space Command (USSPACECOM) maintains the 9000-object Resident Space Object (RSO) catalog that includes information on each object's orbit so that its position may be predicted at times in the future. Other countries maintain similar catalogs. It is estimated that adding information on smaller objects would increase the number of objects in the RSO catalog to over 100,000.

Information in the RSO catalog has been used for several years to provide information on objects passing close to the Space Shuttle, the former Mir Space Station, and now the International Space Station. Analysts have used this information to move these satellites—the Shuttle has been moved eight times to date, the Space Station three times, and the Mir cosmonauts moved to their escape pod at least once because of concern with passing objects.

Many satellite operators believe that the chance of collision is so small that they need not worry about collision avoidance. For example, the probability of collision at GEO for a single active satellite is approximately one in 3000 over a 10-year mission; however, the collective probability of a collision involving an active GEO satellite over the next 10 years is approximately one in 10. Other operators realize that their satellites are frequently approached by debris as well as by satellites operated by others and are interested in knowing if and when a threat exists.

As with the manned vehicles, some operators have chosen to move their satellites to decrease the possibility of a collision. In some cases, however, such moves have been ill advised based on the relatively poor quality of the tracking data used for the predictions.

Given this background, the 1999 AIAA workshop on International Space Cooperation: Solving Global Problems has called for the creation of an "internationally recognized entity" to provide collision avoidance and other services.[3] This group also noted that available "catalogs [of tracked objects] must be greatly improved" to enable effective collision avoidance.[4] Reference 5 raises a number of questions and issues about this service, and Ref. 6 proposes an organizational structure.

Ellipsoids are used to represent position uncertainties of two converging objects. The size of the ellipsoids, sometimes exceeding several kilometers in length, reflects the uncertainty in the position of each object. Collision avoidance analysis produces a probability that the two objects within the ellipsoids will actually collide.

Accurate, meaningful predictions of satellite close approaches require that:

- Tracking data be generated in a manner that is suitable for this application; that is, the catalog of orbiting objects must be maintained with observations of a quality and frequency that permits collision risk reduction using a reasonable number of avoidance maneuvers for each satellite.[7]
- Data used for predicting future collisions must incorporate operator data, including operator estimates of orbital ephemeris and information on upcoming station keeping or other planned maneuvers. Without knowledge of where a satellite is going, collision avoidance predictions are impossible.

Operator data and predictions are also critical for satellites that use low thrust motors to move to operational orbits or for orbit transfer maneuvers. It may be difficult or impossible to develop reliable predictions of future locations of such satellites without such input.

Data May Define Directions

One of the areas that must receive substantial focus, and will ultimately play an important role in the architecture of these types of services, is the catalog itself. The data collection, maintenance, and use of this information database, and the controls established to limit its use and availability, will have important implications for the quality of service available to worldwide operators.

Some examples of how this data may be used illustrate this point:

- Governments can use information on satellite orbits to assess whether operators are abiding by end-of-life disposal rules, to determine if operators are violating guidelines about release of debris during deployment and operations, to assure compliance with regulations in other areas, or to see what other governments are doing in space.
- Companies can use information to establish the health of a competitor's constellation or to gain insight into a competitor's technological status or business plan for communications or other services
- Lawyers and insurance companies can use this information to assign blame and collect damages in the event of an on-orbit collision with another company's satellite or launch vehicle or debris
- Investors can gain insight on the health of a company by looking at the company's constellation of satellites and determining whether satellites are maintaining their station correctly, if the constellation is fully populated and has on-orbit spares, etc.
- Service providers can offer radio frequency interference and other

services to help operators avoid problems and minimize liabilities.

Of course, the data required for all of these activities can come from many sources. Operators in each of the space faring nations maintain perhaps the best and most up-to-date information on their own vehicles.

Private companies like Intelsat and Iridium maintain data on their satellites and constellations. Governments and amateurs track satellites and maintain catalogs. Information on many tracked objects is available for free on the World Wide Web.

There are some indications that private companies may be moving to establish tracking stations to catalog data on orbiting objects. This independent tracking data could be provided to operators for a fee.

Evolutionary Paths

Given the fact that collision avoidance services require the best information on all objects, and given the fact that the best information is not available from a single source, how might collision avoidance services evolve?

The highest priority service to be provided would be close approach warnings and collision avoidance. Services could evolve to include launch collision avoidance, collision avoidance for maneuvering and deorbiting spacecraft, and potentially radio frequency interference, laser impingement avoidance, and other services dependent on the RSO database. It is possible that overall "situational awareness" services, providing operators information on space weather conditions local to their spacecraft, would also emerge as part of this evolution.

The evolutionary pathways for the service provider depend on how access-to-data issues are resolved. For example, one can envision the following options:

1. **Data could be made available for free for anyone to use.** Potentially sensitive information would be available to everyone. Commercial companies would most likely develop and market services based on this data, would contract with satellite operators and receive maneuver plans for those under contract, and each would provide services affecting only a portion of the operating satellites. A drawback is that no entity would have full information on all objects, potentially increasing the chance of a satellite managed by one company being unaware of potentially hazardous situations caused by maneuvers of a satellite managed by another. In addition, companies or nations who wished to protect data would most likely elect not to participate in this approach, further limiting the quality of the services possible.

2. **One or more commercial companies could be authorized to bid for the right to provide services using government-supplied data.** By this approach, a commercial company or companies would charge for services and would interact with the government for additional data required for close approach and other assessments.

Under this scenario, the company would have access to proprietary information that could, by merger or acquisition, find its way to a competitor. Also, if the company selected was a subsidiary of or had financial or other ties to a satellite manufacturer or operator, it could be viewed as having a conflict of interest in certain close approach situations, possibly raising questions about its recommendations.

Again, based on concern about these factors, some commercial companies would elect to use in-house capabilities, or none at all, rather than participate.

Finally, there will be issues to be resolved regarding the government, in effect, subsidizing a for-profit company both by providing data and by providing support to requests for additional data from government owned and operated sensors.

3. **One government and government agency could take responsibility for the data and services.** There are complicating factors to this option, as well. For example, would the government agree to make services available even in a time of war? Would that government agree to pay for services to everyone, or if not, how would fees be set? Would other governments and companies agree to give data despite concerns that the data might conceivably be used to put the data provider in a less favorable position? Would the government guarantee financial support required to assure good-quality service? Could the government agency guarantee to protect an operator's proprietary data from release to other companies or other government agencies to the satisfaction of commercial operators?

4. **A private, nonprofit organization could be chartered in the United States to utilize government-supplied RSO catalog data, incorporate customer-supplied satellite orbit information and maneuver plans, and provide basic collision avoidance services to all.**

   The organization must be considered a "trusted agent" by both government and operators. For example, the government would establish rules for how government-supplied information would be handled and released, and satellite operators would use legal agreements to establish similar restrictions for their data. As a nonprofit, the organization would be free of potential conflicts-of-interests noted earlier.

   This entity would offer services for a nominal fee—critical to assuring the satellite operators that the services they need would be available, and allowing each operator to control and customize the services provided.

   Another factor to be considered is the cost for services. Given the "public benefit" nature of this work and the desire to encourage satellite operators to participate, the government might decide to subsidize the service, or even provide a basic level of service for free. The fee might apply only to services above the basic level. The government could work closely with the nonprofit entity to structure a fee schedule to accomplish this goal.

   An advantage of this approach, and to some degree that of Options 1 and 2, is the potential for assuring that the services remain state-of-the-art. As a private company, the nonprofit can remain flexible and can grow quickly to meet operator requirements (sometimes a challenge for a government agency). In addition, as a nonprofit, any "profits" from providing these services can be rolled back into research and new tools and capabilities.

   Problems to be worked with this concept include refining the nature of the organization, developing a working relationship with government agencies responsible for tracking and other data, establishing an agreed-on set of services and fee structure, assuring that export licensing issues are expedited, and assuring the permanence of the organization so that it will remain a trusted agent over the long term.

   This latter point means that operators must be assured that the entity will not be taken over or go out of business, potentially putting their data and services at risk. Similarly, government must be confident in the special access relationship critical to the work.

5. **Nations could jointly establish an international nonprofit, or equivalent, entity to maintain the data and provide services.**

   In this case, international agreements would define the operational, funding, fee structure, data access, and data protection issues. For example, the agreement would establish the ground rules under which data would be released to governments (as noted earlier, governments may wish to use catalog data to assure that operators are abiding by regulations or for other purposes).

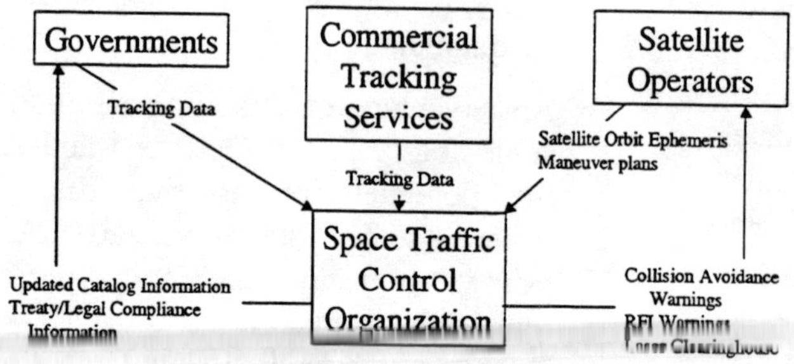

The conceptual international space traffic control organization[6] *would receive data from several sources and provide processed results and data to commercial satellite operators and government organizations.*

The organization would be funded by governments and potentially by fees charged to satellite operators (a portion of a government's contribution could be in the form of tracking data or other "in kind" support). It would receive tracking data from government, private sources, and satellite operators, would develop an integrated database, and would use this database to provide agreed-upon services.

It is likely that governments will withhold from this organization information on some sensitive satellites, so that the database will never actually be "complete." Thus, the entity would probably provide a set of agreed-on data to governments for their use in protecting sensitive assets and regulatory enforcement. The use of an incomplete database could hamper the overall development and acceptance of this approach.

While the organization itself would provide technical services, its operations, services, and output would be governed by international agreements. This fact may mean that it may be challenging for the organization to be innovative and provide state-of-the-art services to the satellite operations community.

Another challenging area will be data protection: operators and governments must be confident that their data will be secure and protected in accordance with prior agreements. The organization would need to be established with this as a paramount concern and requirement.

Near Term Possibilities

The obvious challenge in agreeing on and negotiating the framework for an international entity, assuring its funding, providing tracking data from multiple nations and operators, etc., as suggested in Option 5, suggests a phased approach for space traffic control should the international approach be the desired end point.

For example, at present the nonprofit organization suggested in Option 4 might be the most palatable approach. It maintains the "government function" nature of this work, allowing the government to be closely involved with the evolution and structure while a more mature understanding of data protection issues develops. It also assures all satellite operators that the services provided are the most complete and accurate possible at the earliest date.

As services under an Option 4 approach evolve, the organization could be transitioned to another form. For example, if negotiations on the international entity have progressed to the point of agreement, the existing organization could be the basis and model for the new international service provider. Properly established, the government would have maximum flexibility in long-term options by this approach.

In the Meantime...

There are increasing calls for debris avoidance and collision avoidance services. At present, such services are provided by USSPACECOM for manned vehicles, with The Aerospace Corporation and the European Space Agency offering prototype services and MIT/Lincoln Laboratory conducting cooperative research with several GEO operators.

Over the next several years, research and prototype services in areas related to collision avoidance will continue to develop requirements for these services. Progress toward and demand for generally available services would be dramatically increased should there be a high-profile collision in orbit.

---

[1] Johnson NL, "Monitoring and Controlling Space Debris," Scientific American, August 1998, p. 62-67.

[2] Spencer DB, "Orbital Debris and the Environmental Restoration of Space: A Report to the Congressional Defense Committees," AFRL-VS-PS-TR-1998-1024, Air Force Research Laboratory, February 1998.

[3] "International Space Cooperation: Solving Global Problems," AIAA, Report of an AIAA, UN/OOSA, CEAS, CASI Workshop, April 1999.

[4] "International Space Cooperation: Addressing Challenges of the New Millennium," AIAA, Report of an AIAA, UN/OOSA, CEAS, CASI Workshop, March 2001.

[5] Ailor WH, "Controlling Space Traffic," Aerospace America, November 1999, p. 34-38.

[6] Ailor WH, "Space Traffic Control: A View of the Future," to be published in Space Policy.

[7] Jenkin AB, "Effect of Orbit Data Quality on the Operational Cost of Collision Risk Management," Paper No. AIAA 2002-1810, SatMax 2002, Arlington, Virginia, April 22, 2002.

11th Manfred Lachs Space Law Moot Court Competition 2002

The Case Concerning International Liability Utopia v. Friendlistan

PART A: INTRODUCTION

The 11th Manfred Lachs Space Law Moot Court Competition was held during the Houston Colloquium. Semi-finals were held on Tuesday 15 October, and the Finals were held on Thursday 17 October. Three Judges of the ICJ judged the Finals: H.E. Judge Koroma, H.E. Judge Buergenthal and H.E. Judge Elaraby. The Institute is very grateful that they accepted to travel to Houston, thus enabling us to continue our unique tradition of having World Court Judges for the Finals.

In the European Round, 7 teams participated, in the USA 5, and in the Asia-Pacific region there were 11 teams. The winners of the preliminary rounds were, respectively, the University of Warwick, UK, Georgetown University Law Center, Washington DC, USA, and the University of New South Wales, Sydney, Australia. Australia, the team with the highest score for written briefs, moved directly to the Finals, whereas the USA and UK first met in the Semi Final. The USA won this, then met Australia in the Final, was victorious there as well, and brought home the Manfred Lachs Trophy. The Sterns and Tennen Award for Best Oralist was won by Victoria Williams of the US team, and the Eilene M. Galloway Award for Best Brief was won by the Australian team. All students received certificates.

With the invaluable help of Ms Daria Lopez-Alegria of SpaceBridges, a Houston-based consultant, we had managed to secure the support of a large number of law firms, space corporations, universities, government agencies, international organizations and individual IISL Members, to whom IISL is most grateful. Their names are mentioned in an annex.

The Colombe d'Or, an elegant restaurant in Houston was the location for the IISL Dinner that followed the Finals. The University of Houston had provided the location for the finals, and had also hosted a special luncheon for the ICJ Judges, the IISL Board and Faculty officials.

For the first time, a Brochure had been prepared for the World Finals, which, apart from general information about the IISL and the Competition, gave all relevant information regarding the moot court, such as a summary of the case, the full programme, the names of all sponsors, all Judges and juries for written briefs in the semi-final and final, all universities that participated in each regional round, the names of members of the three finalist teams, and a list of all prizes and awards, including a photo of the Manfred Lachs Trophy. Another major innovation for this year is that we will have video coverage of the finals, recorded by a professional company, as well as digital photographs. All these will be used for promotion of the moot court in various regions.

Summary information:

RESULTS OF THE WORLD FINALS:

- Winner: Georgetown University Law Center, Washington DC USA (Victoria Williams, Kelly Gable, Petra Vorwig)

- Runner up: University of New South Wales, Sydney Australia (Victoria-Anne Davidson, Caroline Ang, Johanna O'Rourke)

- 2nd runner up: University of Warwick School of Law, UK (Sethu Nandakumar, Sagee Sasikumar)

- Eilene M. Galloway Award for Best Written Brief: University of New South Wales, Sydney Australia

- Sterns and Tennen Award for Best Oralist: Victoria Williams, Georgetown University Law Center

PARTICIPANTS IN THE REGIONAL ROUNDS

USA:
Georgetown University, Washington DC
University of North Carolina, North Carolina
Hamline University, Minnesota
University of Mississippi, Mississippi
Golden Gate University, San Francisco
University of St. Thomas, Miami
Valparaiso University, Indiana

Europe:
Universita' degli studi di Padova, Italy
Université de Paris I, France
Université de Paris Sud, France
University of Granada, Spain
University of Lüneburg, Germany
University of Warwick, UK

Asia Pacific:
Bond University, Australia
Chulalongkorn University, Thailand
Jawaharlal Nehru University, India
Monash University, Australia
National University of Singapore, Singapore
Sophia University, Japan
University of Canterbury, New Zealand
University of New South Wales, Sydney, Australia
University of Queensland, Australia
University of Technology Sydney, Australia
University of Tokyo, Japan

CONTACT FOR REGIONAL ROUNDS:
USA:
Milton (Skip) Smith, SSMITH@sah.com
Europe:
Alberto Marchini, Alberto.Marchini@esa.int
Asia Pacific:
Ricky J. Lee, ricky@myoffice.net.au

AUTHORS OF THE PROBLEM:
Ram Jakhu
William Wirin
John Gantt

JUDGES FOR WRITTEN BRIEFS:
Joann Clayton-Townsend, USA
Peter van Fenema, The Netherlands
Armel Kerrest de Rozavel, France
Martha Mejia-Kaiser, Mexico
Leighton Morris, Australia
Sylvia Ospina, USA/Colombia

JUDGES FOR SEMI FINALS:
Ernst Fasan, Austria
Joanne Gabrynowicz, USA
Sylvia Ospina, USA/Colombia

JUDGES FOR FINALS:
H.E. Judge Abdul Koroma, ICJ
H.E. Judge Thomas Buergenthal, ICJ
H.E. Judge Nabil Elaraby, ICJ

PART B: THE PROBLEM

Spaceliner Inc., a private company incorporated in the State of Utopia, operates from its home port in Utopia which it owns as well as from air/spaceports which it serves in other places mentioned herein, a fleet of three similar transportation vehicles for both passengers and cargo from its equatorial port to the International Space Station (ISS), the Moon and several points on the surface of the Earth. In order to capture a highly profitable market, Spaceliner Inc. uses exclusively one of these vehicles for the carriage of high paying business passengers between different cities on the Earth as Spaceliner can reach its destination on the other side of the globe within an hour by passing through both air space and outer space. Its flight path takes it through the airspace of all of the states named herein. There exists an open sky policy with respect to all reusable vehicles that can be operated in airspace and outer space. Under Utopia law no flight plan is required and Utopia as a matter of practice does not notify the United Nations of each flight.

Utopia is located on the equator and does not have a strong financial position. The World Bank financed the operations of Spaceliner Inc. up to 65 percent with a view to encourage private enterprises in this developing country and on the condition that at least 25 percent of the remaining financing should come from foreign private investors. Only 10 percent of the shares of Spaceliner Inc. are owned by the private sector in Utopia. Being a member of the World Trade Organization, Utopia is committed to total privatization and deregulatory industrial policies in all economic activities and the Spaceliner Inc.

venture is not an exception. Thus, as a matter of practice, Utopia adopts a somewhat hand-off regulatory policy towards Spaceliner Inc. Utopia does not carry insurance, nor does it require Spaceliner Inc. to carry insurance or obtain an airworthiness certificate for its fleet of Spaceliner transporters. Utopia Law requires Spaceliner Inc. to include in its transportation contracts with all passengers and cargo shippers a provision limiting its liability in accordance with the 1929 Warsaw Convention (i.e. the Convention for the Unification of Certain Rules Relating to International Carriage by Air, Warsaw, October 12, 1929). In addition, passengers are able to purchase higher coverage limits in the private insurance market should they so desire. Utopia and a few of its equatorial neighbors provide limited navigational services. It routinely relies upon the Global Positioning Satellite (GPS) system, operated by the State of Friendlistan, which is the only such system available for use by aircraft, ships and other various vehicles worldwide. However, the system was encrypted on 1st July 2030 due to anonymous threats of terrorism directed toward Friendlistan. On the same day, Friendlistan issued a worldwide notification that GPS signals would not be available for the near future.

On 2nd June 2030, Utopia signed a five-year agreement worth US$200 million with the State of Equatorian to image remotely certain areas of Friendlistan. In this agreement, Spaceliner Inc. was named the prime contactor for actually performing such imagery activities when a Spaceliner passes over Friendlistan territory, though with some technical help from the Equatorian remote-sensing experts. Equatorian is friendly towards, but is in economic and industrial competition with, Friendlistan. Friendlistan, a rich and strong space-faring nation, objected to such imaging because the areas to be imaged were possibly highly profitable mining areas and Utopia refused to provide copies of the imagery to Friendlistan and its companies. Friendlistan sent Utopia a formal diplomatic note objecting to the capture of the imagery unless copies were made available to Friendlistan. The Utopian Embassy in Friendlistan replied to this note stressing that international law allows its citizens to carry out all remote sensing activities, Spaceliner Inc. would continue such activities, and would not make the copies of the captured imagery available to Friendlistan and its companies, since under the June 2nd agreement the State of Equatorian is exclusively entitled to all proprietary rights in all forms of the collected remote sensing data.

On 4th July 2030, a Spaceliner vehicle commenced its journey from Utopia and after a short stopover in Equatorian picking up an Equatorian passenger, it continued flying with 40 passengers and a crew of 5 with the ISS as immediate destination and Equatorian as the return destination. Nine of the passengers were officials from various nations on an inspection mission of the ISS, one was an Equatorian remote sensing expert and the remaining 30 from various nations were tourists who were to spend twenty four hours on the ISS before returning to Earth. The flight path of the Spaceliner took it over Friendlistan at an altitude of 110 kilometers (approximately 70 miles). While the Spaceliner was at this altitude over Friendlistan territory, a Friendlistan Air Force station lit a laser beam illuminating the Spaceliner in an attempt to frustrate the capturing of imagery. As a result of this illumination, several computers and other electronic equipment on board the Spaceliner malfunctioned. Such malfunctions caused the Spaceliner to be unstable but it continued its flight towards the ISS.

Learning about the instability of the Spaceliner, the Commander of the ISS refused to allow it to dock with the ISS even though the Captain of the Spaceliner had declared an emergency. Having no other choice, the Spaceliner began its journey back to Earth. Being unstable and uncontrollable, the right wing of Spaceliner hit Milsat, a private remote sensing satellite belonging to Davidson Corporation, which was carrying out reconnaissance activities under a multi-million dollar commercial contract with several like-minded States, including Friendlistan. Davidson Corporation is a multinational corporation having its headquarter in Equatorian but 70% of its shares are owned by the citizens of Friendlistan. Within a few minutes of the accident, Milsat developed a serious malfunction and all communications with the ground stations stopped. It was later discovered that in the accident with Spaceliner, the antennae and solar arrays of Milsat were damaged. Consequently, Milsat had to be declared totally dead. The destruction of Milsat forced Davidson Corporation to declare bankruptcy, as it was unable to pay its creditors due to the lack of sufficient and timely cash flow.

The Spaceliner continued its return to home base in Utopia. However, On its way back, it collided with the Stationary High Altitude Relay Platform (SHARP) belonging to Airspacecom, a company incorporated in the Peoples Republic of Hitono, a colony of Friendlistan. This unmanned lightweight platform, circling at an altitude of 20 kilometers, was a fuel-less platform powered by microwave energy transmitted from a ground station on Earth. At the time of collision, SHARP was relaying television signals from the final match of World Soccer Competition to a major broadcasting system for global coverage. SHARP was operating with the use of radio frequency band of 47.2 - 47.5 GHz, which had been allocated by ITU World Radiocommunication Conference in 1997 to the Fixed Service for High-Altitude Radio-Relay Platform Stations. SHARP was destroyed and after floating for some time in the air, its debris smashed to the ground in the territory of Hitono creating a large (200 m diameter) crater on a wheat field.

Thereafter, while attempting to return to its home base in Utopia and being even closer to the Earth, the Spaceliner crossed through international air traffic lanes inadvertently due to its inability to navigate and control its descent. As it crossed, there was a near miss with a Friendlistan aircraft, but the resulting air turbulence caused the Captain of the Spaceliner to lose total control and ditch within the territorial waters of Utopia. Although all of the crew and passengers were alive at the time of crash landing it took two days for the Utopian rescue teams to reach the Spaceliner. By that time the Spaceliner had sunk in 600 m of water and everyone had drowned. Friendlistan had refused repeated requests by Utopia for assistance in finding the location of the crash and rescuing the crew and passengers. Friendlistan's refusal was based on its belief that Utopia and Spaceliner, Inc. were operating illegally.

After several unsuccessful attempts to resolve the dispute between the Government of Utopia and the Government of Friendlistan, on 20th September 2031, Utopia commenced this action against Friendlistan before the International Court of Justice.

In particular, the Applicant, Utopia, requests the Court to adjudge and declare:

1. that Friendlistan has violated international law and consistent state practice by objecting to Utopia and Spaceliner Inc's. carrying out of remote sensing activities over the territory of Friendlistan and thereafter illuminating the Spaceliner by laser beam which resulted in the on-board malfunctions of several computers and other electronic equipment;
2. that Friendlistan has violated international law by not providing the requested timely assistance to Utopia and Spaceliner crew and passengers; and
3. that Friendlistan is responsible and liable under international law to adequately compensate Utopia for the loss of the Spaceliner vehicle, its equipment, its crew and passengers, and
4. that Utopia is not responsible or liable under international law for the destruction of Milsat and SHARP and thus for any payment of compensation for the loss suffered by the Friendlistan shareholders of Milsat or the operators of SHARP.

The Respondent, Friendlistan, asks the Court to adjudge and declare:

1. that Friendlistan was not required by any rule of international law or consistent state practice to allow Utopia's Spaceliner to carry out remote sensing of Friendlistan's territory contrary to Friendlistan's vital interests;
2. that Friendlistan is entitled under international law to take unilaterally

all precautionary measures to protect its vital interests, and thus the foregoing claims of Utopia in this regard must be rejected;
3. that Utopia and Spaceliner, Inc. were operating illegally and thus Friendlistan had no obligation under international law to assist Utopia and the Spaceliner astronauts following the accident and emergency landing, and
4. that Utopia is responsible and liable under international law for the destruction of Milsat and SHARP and thus must adequately compensate for the loss suffered by the Friendlistan shareholders of Milsat and by the operators of SHARP.

Both States have accepted the jurisdiction of the International Court of Justice without any reservation; there are no issues of exhaustion of local remedies or of the jurisdiction of the Court. All relevant international law and consistent state practice are as they existed on 1 July 2001, and have not during the interim thirty years changed or been revised to take into account the developments and evolution in the use of re-usable space vehicles.

Both the Applicant and Respondent are members of the United Nations, the International Telecommunication Union, the Convention on Damage Caused by Foreign Aircraft to Third Parties on the Surface of the Earth of 1958, and the International Civil Aviation Organization (i.e., the Chicago Convention of 1944). They are also parties to the 1967 Treaty on Principles Governing the Activities of States in the Exploration and Use of Outer Space, including the Moon and other Celestial Bodies, the 1968 Agreement on the Rescue of Astronauts, the Return of Astronauts and the Return of Objects Launched into Outer Space, the 1972 Convention on International Liability for Damage caused by Space Objects, and the 1975 Convention on Registration of Objects Launched into Outer Space.

On 2nd February 2010, Utopia ratified the 1979 Agreement Governing the Activities of States on the Moon and other Celestial Bodies. Both States had participated in the discussions on and adoption of the UN Principles Relating to Remote Sensing of the Earth from Outer Space, that were adopted without vote on 3 December 1986. The State of Utopia is a party to the Convention for the Unification of Certain Rules Relating to International Carriage by Air, Warsaw, October 12, 1929, but Friendlistan withdrew from this Convention effective 4th July 2020.

PART C: WINNING BRIEFS

A. WRITTEN BRIEF FOR UTOPIA

AGENTS:

Victoria Williams, Kelly Gable, Petra Vorwig, Georgetown University Law Center, Washington DC, USA

ARGUMENT

I. INTRODUCTION

The events of July 4, 2030 resulted in a terrible, yet avoidable, tragedy. As activity in outer space increases, so does the need for application of international law to preserve peace and security in the outer space arena. Utopia respectfully submits to this Court a petition requesting allocation of international liability and reparation for the great losses suffered.

II. FRIENDLISTAN VIOLATED INTERNATIONAL LAW AND PRACTICE WHEN IT INTERFERED WITH UTOPIA'S RIGHT TO USE OUTER SPACE BY FIRING THE LASER THAT SEVERELY DAMAGED THE SPACELINER.

Friendlistan breached its obligations under international law when it obstructed by force the remote sensing activities conducted by Utopia and Spaceliner Inc. Under international law, Utopia has a right to conduct remote sensing activities in outer space without interference. While Friendlistan attempts to justify its actions, its claims cannot stand under the applicable law. International law and practice make clear that Friendlistan, not Utopia, acted illegally.

A. Friendlistan Violated International Law When It Interfered with Utopia's Right to Use Outer Space by Firing a Laser at the Spaceliner to Prevent it from Gathering Data.

Outer space is free for use and exploration to all States.[1] Peripheral data gathering[2] from outer space, such as the remote sensing conducted by the Spaceliner, whether of data in outer space or of the Earth, is permissible under international law. Any interference with this right by another state constitutes a violation of international law.[3]

1. *Friendlistan Violated the Principle of Equality Under Article I of the 1967 Outer Space Treaty.*

Friendlistan's refusal to allow Utopia to conduct remote sensing activities violated the fundamental principle of the most important legal instrument governing the activities of States in space, the Outer Space Treaty. Article I sets forth the principle of equality, declaring outer space "free for exploration and use by all States without discrimination of any kind."[4] The treaty also declares outer space free for scientific investigation, to be facilitated and encouraged by all States.[5] Contrary to the demands of Article I, Friendlistan not only refused to acknowledge Utopia's right to use outer space, but also went so far as to deny Utopia access to the resources of outer space by beaming a laser at the Spaceliner.[6] Friendlistan's actions are even more indefensible in light of the legislative history of Article I, whose principle of equality was established primarily to protect the interests of developing countries, such as Utopia, which feared being squeezed out of access to space by space powers like Friendlistan.[7] The actions taken by Friendlistan legitimate the developing countries' concerns. Using its significant scientific and military resources, Friendlistan denied Utopia its right to use outer space in direct contravention of the guarantee of equality extended to all States in Article I of the Outer Space Treaty.

2. *Friendlistan Violated the Principle of Non-Appropriation of Space in Article II of the Outer Space Treaty and Acted Contrary to State Practice.*

Friendlistan also breached a binding obligation under Article II, which clearly prohibits any claims of sovereignty in outer space, by use, occupation, or any other means.[8] Friendlistan violated this provision by treating the outer space above its territory, where the Spaceliner was flying at the time it was struck by the Friendlistan laser, as its sovereign territory. By firing a laser at the Spaceliner, Friendlistan effectively treated the vehicle as a threat within its sovereign air space, while in actuality the Spaceliner, flying at an altitude of 110 kilometers, was in outer space.[9]

While the delineation between air space and outer space has not been codified, the practice of states in the use of satellites has led to the formation of a customary rule of international law that the region at and above the line determined by the lowest perigee[10] of satellites so far placed in orbit constitutes outer space. Customary law is formed when states agree to accept a constant and uniform practice as binding law.[11] By not protesting that any of the satellites thus far put into orbit

[1] Treaty on Principles Governing the Activities of States in the Exploration and Use of Outer Space, including the Moon and Other Celestial Bodies, art. I, Jan. 27, 1967, 18 U.S.T. 2410, T.I.A.S. No. 6347, 610 U.N.T.S. 205. [hereinafter "Outer Space Treaty"]

[2] Peripheral data gathering is performed from outside a state's sovereign territory, as opposed to penetrative data gathering, which is conducted from within another State's territory. BIN CHENG, STUDIES IN INTERNATIONAL SPACE LAW 578 (1997).

[3] *Id.* at 578.

[4] Outer Space Treaty, *supra* note 1, art. 1.

[5] *Id.*

[6] Compromis, ¶ 4.

[7] NANDASIRI JASENTULIYANA, INTERNATIONAL SPACE LAW AND THE UNITED NATIONS 175 (1999).

[8] Outer Space Treaty, *supra* note 1, art. 2.

[9] Compromis, ¶ 4.

[10] The lowest perigee refers to the lowest point above the surface of the Earth that is passed by a satellite on its elliptic orbit around the Earth. ROBERT GOEDHART, THE NEVER ENDING DISPUTE: DELIMITATION OF AIR SPACE AND OUTER SPACE 47 (1996).

[11] *See Case Concerning Right of Passage Over Indian Territory* (Port. v. Ind.), 1960 I.C.J. 6; *North Sea Continental Shelf Cases* (F.R.G. v. Den.; F.R.G. v. Neth.), 1969 I.C.J. 3.

have entered sovereign airspace, states have expressly or tacitly agreed that the lowest perigee of satellites constitutes the baseline demarcation of outer space. The lowest perigee thus far achieved is 96 kilometers,[12] though most satellites have perigees at or above 110 kilometers. Therefore, "one is arguably in outer space when one reaches 96 kilometres above the earth, clearly so at 110 kilometres, and definitely so at 130 kilometres."[13] Several states have even urged that the boundary be set at 100 kilometers.[14] Thus, at 110 kilometers, where the Spaceliner was attempting to gather data when hit by the laser, even a conservative estimate would place the Spaceliner in outer space, outside the jurisdiction of any assertion of sovereignty.

Even if the Court is not inclined to determine a spatial boundary, a functional approach confirms the Spaceliner's position in outer space.[15] When struck by the Friendlistan laser, the Spaceliner was performing an outer space activity en route to an outer space destination. The applicable legal regime is therefore the law of outer space, which prohibits Friendlistan from making any territorial claims.

Nor can Friendlistan make any claim of sovereignty to the data gathered from its territory by the Spaceliner. Such an extension of the concept of sovereignty does not exist in international treaty or customary law, and would directly conflict with the principle of freedom of exploration and use of outer space resources set forth in Article I of the Outer Space Treaty.[16]

3. *Friendlistan Violated the Principle of Peaceful Use of Outer Space in Article IV of the Outer Space Treaty.*

Friendlistan also violated Article IV of the treaty, which establishes that outer space is to be used for peaceful purposes only.[17] When Friendlistan directed its Air Force to fire the laser at the Spaceliner, Friendlistan breached its duty to act peacefully in outer space by ordering aggressive military action in an arena where the use of such a weapon is expressly prohibited.[18] Friendlistan's act of aggression is all the more deplorable considering it was directed without cause at a civilian commercial entity.

Friendlistan may attempt to justify its military action as a self-defense measure, but this argument is invalid under the circumstances. Under the United Nations Charter, a self-defense measure must be both necessary and proportional and may only be executed against an *armed attack*.[19] The laser was not necessary because military threats were not involved, and even Friendlistan's economic concerns were purely speculative.[20] Furthermore, the laser was not proportional, as evidenced by the tragedy that occurred. Having suffered no damage and with no evidence of any legitimate threat, Friendlistan directed its military to employ a weapon against an unarmed civilian party, destroying the Spaceliner and killing the forty-five civilians it carried on board.

4. *Friendlistan Violated the Principle of International Cooperation By Refusing to*

---

[12] The United Kingdom's Skynet-IIA achieved a perigee of 96 kilometers in 1974. CHENG, *supra* note 2, at 498.

[13] CHENG, *supra* note 2, at 498.

[14] Russia and the former Soviet Union have long advocated a 100 km limit, and this boundary has also been implicitly recognized by others such as the United States and South Africa. *See* Frans G. von der Dunk, *The Delimitation of Outer Space Revisited: The Role of National Space Laws in the Delimitation Issue*, Proceedings of the 41st Colloquium on the Law of Outer Space 254, 256 (Sept. 28-Oct. 2, 1998) (1999).

[15] The spatial approach focuses on where the vehicle was located, and requires drawing some distinction between air space and outer space in order to determine the applicable legal rules. The functional approach determines the applicable legal regime by focusing on the capabilities and activities of the vehicle. *See* CARL CHRISTOL, *Legal Aspects of Aerospace Planes*, *in* THE HIGHWAYS OF AIR & OUTER SPACE OVER ASIA (Chia-Jui Cheng ed., 1992).

[16] Jefferson Weaver, *Lessons in Multilateral Negotiations: Creating a Remote Sensing Regime*, 7 TEMP. INT'L & COMP. L.J. 29, 53 (1993).

[17] Outer Space Treaty, *supra* note 1, art. IV.

[18] Friendlistan also violated the provision in art. IV of the Outer Space Treaty outlawing the use of weapons of mass destruction in outer space. While weapons of mass destruction have traditionally been interpreted as nuclear, biological, or chemical, a laser could arguably be used in such a way to achieve the same effect, especially in an area of heightened risk such as outer space.

[19] U.N. CHARTER, art. 51. (emphasis added)

[20] Compromis, ¶ 3.

Respect the Needs of Utopia as a Developing Country.

By disregarding the special concerns of Utopia as a developing State, Friendlistan also violated international law by acting contrary to the principle of international cooperation, mentioned no less than six times in the Outer Space Treaty.[21] The principle of international cooperation is complemented in Article IX, which requires "due regard" for the interests of other States.[22] Developed countries' obligations to cooperate internationally and to encourage space science development in developing countries is clarified in the United Nations Declaration on International Cooperation in the Exploration and Use of Outer Space for the Benefit and in the Interest of all States, Taking into Particular Account the Needs of Developing Countries.[23] Friendlistan failed to cooperate and take into account Utopia's needs as a developing country by preventing a Utopian company from maximizing its revenues, and by disregarding Utopia's contractual obligations to Equatorian. Given the extraordinarily high investment required for entry into the remote sensing market,[24] a breach of the contract by Utopia would result in dire consequences. Not only would Utopia have sustained major losses, but it also would have gained a dishonorable business reputation, thereby jeopardizing all future commercial remote sensing opportunities. Friendlistan ignored these considerations in violation of its duty to cooperate internationally.

B. Utopia's Remote Sensing Activities Did Not Violate International Law or Practice.

Remote sensing is the collection of data from outer space that can be processed into imagery of the Earth. Remote sensing has many applications, including weather forecasting, environmental monitoring, and military reconnaissance.[25] While there are no treaties on remote sensing, there is general agreement that the Outer Space Treaty permits remote sensing by virtue of Article I, which declares outer space free for exploration and use by all states.[26]

Friendlistan may argue that Utopia's remote sensing activities were illegal, relying primarily on the Principles Relating to Remote Sensing of the Earth from Outer Space,[27] which mention respect for the sovereignty of the sensed state[28] and access to the processed data for the sensed state.[29] Even if these Principles represented binding law, which they do not, the actions of Utopia and Spaceliner Inc. were consistent with both international law and practice.

Furthermore, Friendlistan should be estopped from claiming Utopia's remote sensing activities were unlawful, as Friendlistan itself conducts remote sensing. Friendlistan performs remote sensing for reconnaissance purposes and does not automatically provide the states it senses with the data gathered.[30] Friendlistan cannot protest against the very same activities it conducts.[31]

1. *The Principles on Remote Sensing Impose No Binding Obligations on Utopia as They Are Neither Treaty Nor Customary Law.*

Any claim by Friendlistan that Utopia acted contrary to the Principles on Remote Sensing is irrelevant to determining whether Utopia's remote sensing was legal because the Principles are not binding. The Principles on Remote Sensing emerged as a General Assembly resolution rather than a legally binding treaty, or even a more formal

---

[21] Outer Space Treaty, *supra* note 1, preamble and articles I, III, IX, X, XI.

[22] *Id.* art. IX.

[23] United Nations Declaration on International Cooperation in the Exploration and Use of Outer Space for the Benefit and in the Interest of all States, Taking into Particular Account the Needs of Developing Countries, G.A. Res. 51/122, U.N. Doc. A/AC.105/572/Rev. 1 (1996).

[24] Youssef Sneifer, *The Implications of National Security Safeguards on the Commercialization of Remote Sensing Imagery*, 19 SEATTLE UNIV. L.R. 539, 568 (1996).

[25] CHENG, *supra* note 2, at 578.

[26] JASENTULIYANA, *supra* note 7, at 317.

[27] G.A. Res. 41/65, 42 U.N. GAOR, 28th Sess, 95th plen. Mtg., U.N. Doc. A/RES/41/65 (1987). [hereinafter "Principles on Remote Sensing" or "Principles"]

[28] *Id.* principle IV.

[29] *Id.* principle XII.

[30] Compromis, ¶ 5.

[31] *See Case Concerning the Land and Maritime Boundary Between Cameroon and Nigeria* (Cameroon v. Nig.), 1998 I.C.J. 275, 303 (Preliminary Objections) (Order of June 11).

"declaration of principles."[32] Under the Charter of the United Nations, the General Assembly may make only *recommendations*.[33] As such, the Principles created no new legal rights or obligations; instead, they merely "underscore the legitimacy of the customary rules of international law which do little more than support the right of states to engage in remote sensing activities."[34]

The Principles on Remote Sensing also lack binding force as customary international law because they lack the elements necessary to constitute custom. A customary rule of law comprises two elements: state practice, the material element, and *opinio juris*, the subjective element.[35] There is little evidence of any state practice based on the Principles, and no indication that States have accepted the Principles as binding law. To give one example, the domestic remote sensing legislation of the United States, a major space power, contains several provisions that are not consistent with the Principles on Remote Sensing.[36] In addition, customary international law must follow from state practice that is "both extensive and virtually uniform" within the period of time required for the evolution of a custom into law.[37] The lack of such uniformity with respect to remote sensing is evidenced by the arduous nature of the negotiations of the Principles on Remote Sensing. Consensus came only after many years of battling between developed and developing states and resulted in little more than a tenuous compromise of their views. Therefore, the Principles have no significant legal effect on remote sensing activities – not only because they are non-binding, but also because they are the product of nearly twenty years of intense debate among countries with radically different viewpoints, which indicates their inability to form a basis for custom.[38]

2. *Even If the Principles on Remote Sensing Were Binding, Utopia and Spaceliner Inc. Did Not Violate Them.*

Friendlistan is likely to point to Principles IV and VII as establishing obligations that Utopia breached, but the remote sensing activities conducted by Spaceliner Inc. violated neither provision. Principle IV declares that remote sensing activities "shall be conducted on the basis of respect for the principle of full and permanent sovereignty of all States and people over their own wealth and natural resources ... Such activities shall not be conducted in a manner detrimental to the legitimate rights and interests of the sensed State."[39] Given the vague wording of the Principle IV, it is unclear what the nature of the obligation is, if there is any obligation at all. There is certainly no duty to obtain the prior consent of the sensed country, as Friendlistan would argue, nor is there any duty to attempt prior consultation, as both of these proposals were specifically rejected during the negotiation of the Principles.[40] With respect to Principle IV, "stripped of all the verbiage about respect for this and respect for that, the bottom line is that data gathering from outer space directed at any object anywhere on earth is permissible."[41] Furthermore, the remote sensing was not "detrimental" to the "legitimate rights and interests" of Friendlistan. Friendlistan had no evidence of any potential adverse effects resulting from the remote sensing; in fact, the activities were being conducted to protect the environment.[42]

Friendlistan may attempt to rely on Principle XII to claim it had a right to the remote sensing data gathered over its territory,

---

[32] JASENTULIYANA, *supra* note 7, at 314.

[33] U.N. CHARTER, *supra* note 19, art. 11.

[34] WEAVER, *supra* note 6, at 59.

[35] *See North Sea Continental Shelf Cases*, (F.R.G. v. Den.; F.R.G. v. Neth.), 1969 I.C.J. 3; *Case Concerning Military and Paramilitary Activities in Nicaragua* (Nicar. v. U.S.), 1986 I.C.J. 14.

[36] The U.S. Land Remote Sensing Commercialization Act, 15 U.S.C. § 4201 (1998), contains different categorizations of data than those in the Principles, and obligates the State to provide copies of "unenhanced data" only. *See* Cynthia Hayward, *Remote Sensing: Terrestrial Laws for Celestial Activities*, 8 B.U. INT'L L.J. 157, 177 (1990).

[37] *North Sea Continental Shelf Cases*, (F.R.G. v. Den.; F.R.G. v. Neth.), 1969 I.C.J. 3, at para. 74.

[38] Susan Jackson, *Cultural Lag and the International Law of Remote Sensing*, 23 BROOK. J. INT'L L. 853, 871 (1998).

[39] Principles on Remote Sensing, *supra* note 27, principle IV.

[40] The requirements of prior consent and consultation were put forth in the Argentina/Brazil draft and rejected. CHENG, *supra* note 2, at 66-67.

[41] *Id.* at 67.

[42] Clarifications to Compromis, Set 4, #5.

and to argue that Utopia breached an obligation by making it available only to Equatorian. This argument fails for two reasons. First, the Principles do not address commercial remote sensing, and thus do not prohibit exclusive commercial contracts such as the one held between Utopia and Equatorian. The practice of many states, including Canada and the United States, demonstrates the legality of such exclusive contracts under international law.[43] Therefore, Utopia was under no obligation to breach its contract with Equatorian in order to make the data available to Friendlistan.

Second, by the terms of Principle XII, Utopia had no duty to make the data available at the time it was requested. Principle XII entitles the sensed state to access "as soon as the primary data[44] and the processed data[45] concerning the territory under its jurisdiction are *produced*."[46] While Utopia had primary data, it did not have processed data, which would be available only after Equatorian completed the processing of the data.[47] At the time Friendlistan requested the data, Utopia was not obligated to honor the request because the data was not yet processed. In fact, the request should have been put to Equatorian, the country responsible for processing the data, but Friendlistan addressed its demand to Utopia only.[48] Because Utopia was not obligated to provide Friendlistan with raw data, its actions did not violate the Principles on Remote Sensing.

C. Spaceliner Inc. Was a Legal Operation Under International Law.

Utopia satisfied its duties under international law even though it did not require Spaceliner Inc. to file flight plans and did not notify the United Nations of each flight. Similarly, Utopia's "hands-off" regulatory policy was not unlawful. While detailed industry regulation may be required of aircraft under the Chicago Convention,[49] the Spaceliners are specialized dual-use vehicles, not airplanes. The Spaceliners' outer space capabilities and services subject them to the legal regime of outer space,[50] which does not require insurance, airworthiness certificates, or report modifications for registered space objects.[51]

While Friendlistan argues that Utopia failed its obligations under the Registration Convention, Utopia did fulfill its obligations in good faith as required by the Vienna Convention on the Law of Treaties. The Vienna Convention states: "A treaty shall be interpreted in good faith in accordance with the ordinary meaning to be given to the terms of the treaty in their context and in light of its

---

43 Canada's RADARSAT has exclusive dissemination rights over the remote sensing data it collects. Martha Mejia-Kaiser, *An International Remote Sensing Cartel?*, Proceedings of the 36th Colloquium on the Law of Outer Space 322, 325 (Oct. 16-22, 1993). The United States Department of Defense has an exclusive contract with Space Imaging, Inc. for all its imagery of Afghanistan. *See* James Risen, *Afghanistan Maps for Pilots Were Delayed by Foul-Ups*, N.Y. TIMES, May 11, 2002, at A12.

44 Primary data is defined as "raw data." Principles on Remote Sensing, *supra* note 27, principle I.

45 Processed data is the product of processing the raw data in order to make it usable. *Id.*

46 Principles on Remote Sensing, *supra* note 27, principle XII. (emphasis added)

47 *See* Clarifications to Compromis, Set 5, #5. The processing of remote sensing data, which requires specialized computer application and interpretation by experts, was beyond the capabilities of Utopia as a developing country. Charles Davies, Susan Hoban, and Braden Penhoet, *Moving Pictures: How Satellites, the Internet, and International Environmental Law Can Help Promote Sustainable Development*, 28 STETSON L. REV. 1091, 1114 (1999).

48 Clarifications to Compromis, Set 1, #1.

49 Convention on International Civil Aviation (Chicago), 61 Stat. 1180 T.I.A.S. No. 1591, 15 U.N.T.S. 295 (Dec. 7, 1944).

50 The U.S. Shuttle, an early dual-use vehicle and predecessor to the Spaceliner, was determined by the United States to be a "space object," and was subject to regulation by the National Aeronautics and Space Administration, rather than the Federal Aviation Authority. *See* Claudio Zanghi, *Aerospace Object*, *in* OUTLOOK ON SPACE LAW OVER THE NEXT 30 YEARS (Gabriel Lafferrandere ed. 1997).

51 *See* Convention on Registration of Objects Launched into Outer Space, 28 U.S.T.695, T.I.A.S. 8480, 1023 U.N.T.S. 15, art. IV (2): Each State of registry *may*, from time to time, provide the Secretary-General of the United Nations with additional information concerning a space object carried on its registry. [hereinafter, "Registration Convention"] (emphasis added)

object or purpose."[52] Therefore, while the treaty language of the Registration Convention calls for registration, the object and purpose of the treaty can be upheld without actual registration.

The *travaux préparatoires* of the Registration Convention explain that the essential function of registration is twofold. First, registration discourages the furtive placement of weapons of mass destruction in outer space. Second, registration serves the important purpose of identifying a space object that has caused damage.[53] These concerns were not implicated, however, with respect to the Spaceliner's operations. As a purely commercial enterprise, the Spaceliner was never involved in the transport of weapons, and because its operations were publicly based in Utopia, registration was not necessary to trace the Spaceliner in the event of an accident. Thus, the nature of the Spaceliner's operations rendered the registration requirement moot. Even though Utopia may not have fully complied with the Registration Convention, it fulfilled its obligations under the treaty by acting consistently with the Convention's object and purpose.

Furthermore, state practice does not indicate that Utopia acted contrary to any established international custom. Several parties to the Registration Convention, including China, France, Germany, Great Britain, Italy, Canada, Japan and the United States, routinely fail to register their space objects.[54] Evidence of a lack of *opinio juris* among states indicates that the Registration Convention, unlike the Outer Space Treaty, does not have the force of customary international law. Spaceliner Inc. acted legally, operating consistently with the object and purpose of the Registration Convention as well as general state practice.

III. FRIENDLISTAN VIOLATED INTERNATIONAL LAW BY REFUSING TO ASSIST UTOPIA'S RESCUE ATTEMPT OF THE SPACELINER CREW AND PASSENGERS.

After disabling the Spaceliner with the laser, Friendlistan again violated international law by breaching its duty to assist in the recovery of the vehicle after it crashed. Friendlistan defied its obligations under international law, resulting in the loss of the vehicle and the lives of those on board.

A. Friendlistan Breached Its Duty Under International Law to Render Humanitarian Assistance.

The duty to provide humanitarian assistance in an international emergency is imposed by international treaties, state practice, and general principles of law. Friendlistan's refusal to provide even slight assistance is condemned by each of these sources of international law.

1. *Friendlistan Violated International Treaty Law of Outer Space by Refusing to Assist the Rescue Effort.*

States' recognition of the importance of international cooperation and assistance in outer space activities and recovery efforts is evidenced by the rescue provisions in both the Outer Space Treaty and the Agreement on the Rescue of Astronauts, the Return of Astronauts and the Return of Space Objects Launched into Outer Space.[55]

(i) Friendlistan Breached Its Obligations Under Article V of the Outer Space Treaty.

Article V of the Outer Space Treaty imposes a duty to regard astronauts as "envoys of mankind," and to render to them "all possible assistance in the event of accident, distress, or emergency landing on the territory of another State Party or on the high seas." While "astronaut" has never been specifically

---

[52] Vienna Convention on the Law of Treaties between States and International Organizations or between International Organizations, art. XXXI, opened for signature May 23, 1969, 115 U.N.T.S. 331, UN Doc. A/CONF.39/27. [hereinafter Vienna Convention]

[53] I.H. Ph. Diederiks-Verschoor, AN INTRODUCTION TO SPACE LAW 47 (2d rev. ed., 1999).

[54] Christopher Noble Reuters, *U.S., China, G7 Countries Flout Satellite Registry*, (Aug. 16, 2001), *available at* http://www.space.com/news/satellite_orbits_010816.html.

[55] Agreement on the Rescue of Astronauts, the Return of Astronauts and the Return of Space Objects Launched into Outer Space, Apr. 12, 1968, 19 U.S.T. 7570, T.I.A.S. 6599, 672 U.N.T.S. 119. [hereinafter "Rescue Agreement" or "Agreement"]

defined in international law, the term has been understood to include "any person who ventures into outer space or who travels on board a spacecraft."[56] Under this definition, all of the people on board the Spaceliner were astronauts and deserved the immediate attention of State parties in a position to render assistance. Even if "astronaut" were interpreted more narrowly, so as to encompass only those individuals traveling in outer space in an official capacity, Friendlistan's duty to assist would still be implicated, as nine of the Spaceliner passengers were officials on an inspection mission of the International Space Station.[57] At the least, those nine officials were astronauts, and Friendlistan violated the Outer Space Treaty by refusing to come to their aid, even to locate the crash site, when they crashed in the territory of another State, Utopia.[58]

(ii) Friendlistan Breached Its Obligations Under the Rescue Agreement.

The duty to assist imposed by the Outer Space Treaty is bolstered by the Rescue Agreement, which extends assistance to "personnel of a spacecraft," indicating a desire among States to extend benefits to all persons on board.[59] Under the Rescue Agreement, if the personnel of a spacecraft land "in territory under the jurisdiction of a Contracting Party," that party shall "immediately take all possible steps to rescue them and render them all necessary assistance."[60] By refusing to respond to Utopia's call for help, Friendlistan failed to fulfill its obligations under the Agreement with requisite good faith.[61]

Friendlistan attempts to justify its blatant disregard of its commitment to international cooperation and respect for human life by denying any obligation to help because the Spaceliner crashed into Utopian waters, but Friendlistan's reliance on formal distinctions does not disguise the illegality of its conduct. Even if Friendlistan were not obligated to render assistance under Article 2, it would be obligated under Article 3, which extends the duty to rescue to "the high seas or in any other place not under the jurisdiction of any State" and obligates all Contracting Parties "in a position" to render assistance to do so.[62] The Spaceliner was effectively in an area "not under the jurisdiction of any state" within the meaning of Article 3, because Utopia did not have the resources to reach it. Friendlistan, by contrast, with its significant resources, was "in a position" to render assistance and violated the Agreement by failing to do so.

It is important to note that there are no limitations or restrictions on the obligations of States to rescue and return under the Rescue Agreement.[63] In fact, during negotiations of the Rescue Agreement, a proposal that States should be obligated only to assist to the extent they deemed practicable was not included in the final agreement.[64] This signals the broad reach of the Agreement, obligating its Contracting Parties to provide assistance *whenever possible*. The specific mandates of the Outer Space Treaty and the Rescue Agreement indicate that the drafters intended to establish a general atmosphere of cooperation among states.

2. *Friendlistan Violated Customary Law by Refusing to Assist the Rescue Effort.*

The Rescue Agreement may also be seen as customary law because it is humanitarian by nature and forms part of international custom, even if there is little or no state practice.[65] There is strong evidence that states are dedicated to providing assistance in the event of an emergency related to space activities without hesitation or qualification. The speed with which the Agreement was passed – less than six weeks – is one reflection of the commitment by all States to international cooperation in rescue efforts.[66] During negotiations of the Agreement, a number of states, including France and India, indicated their willingness to give every assistance to astronauts in distress, for humanitarian

[56] CHENG, *supra* note 2, at 457.
[57] Compromis, ¶ 4.
[58] Compromis, ¶ 7.
[59] Rescue Agreement, *supra* note 55, art. 1; CHENG, *supra* note 2, at 277.
[60] Rescue Agreement, *supra* note 55, art 2.
[61] States are obligated to fulfill in good faith their treaty obligations. U.N. CHARTER, *supra* note 19, art. 2.

[62] Rescue Agreement, *supra* note 55, art. 3.
[63] JASENTULIYANA, *supra* note 7, at 189.
[64] *Id.* at 277.
[65] *Id.* at 195 (Comment by Maureen Williams).
[66] CHENG, *supra* note 2, at 265.

reasons.[67] Both the *Asylum Case*[68] and the *Right of Passage Case*[69] indicate that *opinio juris* may be established by a small number of States, or even between two States. In addition, given States' wide acceptance of the Outer Space Treaty as binding customary law, even non-parties to the treaty probably have a duty to provide general assistance to a rescue effort.[70]

States also recognize a similar duty to assist in international maritime law.[71] The United States Coast Guard, for example, follows as a guiding principle that its "vessels and aircraft have a duty to provide assistance to other vessels, aircraft or persons in distress, without regard to location, nationality or circumstances."[72]

The breadth of this recognized commitment forms the basis for a duty to render assistance as a matter of customary international law. By failing to render any assistance, even to locate the crash, Friendlistan acted contrary to the practice of States under customary international law.

3. *Friendlistan Violated General Principles of International Law By Refusing to Assist the Rescue Effort.*

This Court may also consider "general principles of law recognized by civilized nations" to determine Friendlistan's violation of international law in refusing to aid the Spaceliner.[73] Chief among the principles disregarded by Friendlistan but recognized by civilized nations is the notion of respect for human life. General principles may be divided into categories, one of them involving the concept of "natural justice."[74] Natural justice manifests itself in international law in two respects: first, as a minimum standard of decency and respect for human life, and second, as related to the concept of equity.[75]

The requirement of respect for human life appears in the United Nations Charter and has been elaborated in several international human rights instruments.[76] As such, it may be considered an obligation *erga omnes*, one of a class of obligations owed to the international community as a whole, whose breach "shocks the conscience of mankind."[77] In the *Corfu Channel Case*, this Court recognized "elementary considerations of humanity" as a general and well-recognized principle "even more exacting in peace than in war."[78] Respect for human rights was again emphasized in the *Case Concerning Military and Paramilitary Activities in and Against Nicaragua*, where the Court also invoked the duty of states not to encourage disrespect for humanitarian law.[79] Friendlistan not only encouraged disrespect for humanitarian law; it actively flouted the law by dismissing the value of the lives of the forty-five people it refused to assist.

The natural justice inherent in equity balancing is also relevant to this case. This Court may also render its decision based on equity, *ex aequo et bono*, according to what is right and good.[80] Notwithstanding Friendlistan's legal duties, its blatant disregard for the lives lost aboard the Spaceliner was deplorable and must be deemed a violation of

---

[67] *Id.* at 276.

[68] *Asylum Case*, (Col. v. Peru), 1950 I.C.J. 266.

[69] *Case Concerning Right of Passage Over Indian Territory* (Port. v. Ind.), 1960 I.C.J. 6.

[70] Vienna Convention, *supra* note 52, art. 38. Under Article 38 of the Vienna Convention, a treaty is binding on non-parties if it becomes customary international law.

[71] *See, e.g.*, International Convention on Maritime Search and Rescue, Apr. 27, 1979; International Convention for the Safety of Life at Sea, Nov. 1, 1974, *available at* http://www.imo.org.

[72] U.S. Coast Guard Search and Rescue Manual, *available at* http://www.uscg.mil/.

[73] Statute of the International Court of Justice, June 26, 1945, 59 Stat 1055, T.S. No. 993, 3 Bevans 1179, art. 38.

[74] OSCAR SHACHTER, INTERNATIONAL LAW IN THEORY AND PRACTICE 54-55 (1991).

[75] *Id.*

[76] *See, e.g.*, U.N. CHARTER, *supra* note 19, art. 55; Universal Declaration of Human Rights, Dec. 10, 1948, U.N.G.A. Res. 217; American Convention on Human Rights, Nov. 22, 1969, 9 I.L.M. 673 (1970).

[77] James R. Crawford, *The Earl A. Snyder Lecture in International Law: Responsibility to the International Community as a Whole*, 8 IND. J. GLOBAL LEGAL STUD. 303, 314 (2001).

[78] *Corfu Channel Case*, (U.K. v. Alb.), 1949 I.C.J. 4, 22.

[79] *See Case Concerning Military and Paramilitary Activities in Nicaragua* (Nicar. v. U.S.), 1986 I.C.J. 14.

[80] Statute of the International Court of Justice, *supra* note 73, art. 38.

international law. Furthermore, even assuming *arguendo* that Utopia and Spaceliner Inc. were acting illegally, Friendlistan acted in bad faith by refusing to aid the passengers, who were not responsible for any breach of law. Unless Friendlistan's conduct is condemned, it may be repeated, resulting in another avoidable tragedy.

B. Even if There Was No Duty to Render Assistance, Friendlistan's Refusal to Aid Would Still Be Unlawful as an Illegal Countermeasure.

Friendlistan refused to aid the Spaceliner rescue effort because it believed that Utopia and Spaceliner Inc. were operating illegally.[81] By denying aid in response to the perceived illegal acts of Utopia, Friendlistan's refusal effectively constituted a countermeasure.[82] Friendlistan's countermeasure was unlawful under the circumstances of this case.

1. *Utopia and Spaceliner Inc. Were Not Operating Illegally.*

A State may only take countermeasures if it is injured by another State's violation of an international obligation.[83] Friendlistan suffered no injury, and neither Utopia nor Spaceliner Inc. violated international law. Utopia has a right under the Outer Space Treaty to use outer space and send vehicles there, and it acted in compliance with the law applicable to the operations of Spaceliner Inc. Because Utopia was not operating illegally, Friendlistan's countermeasure of refusing to aid the rescue was unjustified and unlawful.

2. *Even if Utopia and Spaceliner Inc. Were Operating Illegally, Friendlistan's Refusal to Assist the Rescue Was an Unlawful Countermeasure.*

Friendlistan's countermeasure would be unlawful even if Utopia and Spaceliner Inc. were operating illegally. A lawful countermeasure must be proportional to the original alleged breach, because the proper aim of a countermeasure is "to restore equality between the Parties and to encourage them to continue negotiations to reach an acceptable solution."[84] Friendlistan's refusal to assist the rescue of the Spaceliner did not restore equality nor foster negotiation; the denial of assistance was a grossly disproportionate response to any breach committed by Utopia. Friendlistan suffered no harm, while Utopia lost the Spaceliner and all forty-five of its passengers. International law does not legitimate any countermeasures that violate fundamental rules of human rights.[85] Friendlistan's refusal to aid the rescue blatantly disregarded the human rights of the people who lost their lives in the Spaceliner tragedy. Friendlistan cannot justify its refusal to provide assistance as a countermeasure.

IV. FRIENDLISTAN IS RESPONSIBLE AND LIABLE UNDER INTERNATIONAL LAW FOR THE LOSS OF PROPERTY AND LIFE RESULTING FROM THE SPACELINER DISASTER.

The Outer Space Treaty distinguishes responsibility and liability in Articles VI and VII. A State incurs responsibility when it breaches an international obligation; if the breach causes injury to another State, the breaching State incurs liability and an obligation to provide reparation for the damage it caused.[86] Friendlistan is both responsible and liable for the loss of the Spaceliner and its passengers. Friendlistan breached international law by firing the laser at the Spaceliner and then refusing to aid the rescue effort, causing the loss of the Spaceliner and the deaths of the people on board.

---

[81] Compromis, ¶ 7.

[82] Friendlistan's countermeasure could be viewed as either reprisal or retorsion. Reprisal refers to countermeasures that would be unlawful if not for the prior illegal act of the State against which it was taken. Retorsion refers to countermeasures against an offending State that are generally permissible in international law. LOUIS HENKIN ET AL, INTERNATIONAL LAW: CASES & MATERIALS, (3d ed. 1993) 570.

[83] *See Case Concerning Air Services Agreement Between France and the United States*, (Fr. v. U.S.), 18 U.N.R.I.A.A. 417 (1978).

[84] *Id.* at para. 90.

[85] *See* Draft Articles on State Responsibility, II Yb. I.L.C. (1974), art. 14 (1) (b) (i): "An injured State shall not resort, by way of countermeasure, to any conduct which is not in conformity with the rules of international law on the protection of fundamental human rights."

[86] *See id.*

A Friendlistan Is Responsible Under International Law for the Spaceliner Tragedy.

Article VI of the Outer Space Treaty requires States to bear "international responsibility for national activities in outer space ... whether such activities are carried on by governmental agencies or by non-governmental entities, and for assuring that national activities are carried out in conformity with the provisions set forth in the present Treaty."[87] Certainly Friendlistan must bear responsibility for the violations of law it committed directly: its military discharged the laser at the Spaceliner, and its government made the decision to deny assistance to the rescue effort.[88] Friendlistan must answer for the consequences of its illegal actions.

B. Friendlistan Is Liable Under International Law for the Spaceliner Tragedy and Must Compensate Utopia for the Loss of the Spaceliner and Its Passengers.

Friendlistan's liability follows from its responsibility for the Spaceliner tragedy. Friendlistan's breaches of international law caused tremendous loss of life and property and it is now obligated to compensate Utopia.

1. *Friendlistan Is Liable for the Loss of Property and Life Under the Outer Space Treaty.*

Under the Outer Space Treaty, Article VII, a State that "launches or procures the launching of an object into outer space" is liable for damage to another State party caused by the object on the Earth, in air, or in outer space.[89] The laser was an object launched into outer space,[90] where it caused severe damage to the Spaceliner. As a result of that damage, the Spaceliner crashed, causing the complete loss of the vehicle and the deaths of the people it carried on board. Under the Outer Space Treaty, Friendlistan is liable to compensate the losses stemming from its illegal use of force in outer space.

2. *Friendlistan Is Liable for the Loss of Property and Life Under the Convention on International Liability for Damage Caused by Space Objects.*[91]

Friendlistan is also liable under the Liability Convention, which divides fault into two categories: absolute liability and fault-based liability. Absolute liability applies when damage has been caused on the surface of the Earth or to an aircraft in flight.[92] Fault must be shown for liability to apply to damage caused "elsewhere than on the surface of the Earth."[93]

Under Article II, Friendlistan is *absolutely* liable for the damage caused to the Spaceliner as an aircraft in flight. While the Spaceliner was in outer space when fired upon by Friendlistan, it is a specialized dual-use vehicle and may be considered simultaneously as a spacecraft and an aircraft. Indeed, Utopia treats the Spaceliner as an aircraft in certain contexts, requiring Spaceliner Inc. to limit its liability under the Warsaw Convention, an instrument of international aviation law providing for air carrier liability to passengers and for cargo.[94] Because Friendlistan damaged the Spaceliner while it was in flight, Friendlistan is absolutely liable to pay for the damage it caused. Alternatively, under Article III, Friendlistan is liable because it was at fault. Friendlistan breached international law when it fired the laser at the Spaceliner with the intent to cause damage, and when it refused to minimize the damage it had caused by denying any aid to the Spaceliner rescue.

Friendlistan is not eligible for exoneration under the Liability Convention. Under Article VI (I), exoneration from absolute liability is granted only when the damage has resulted either wholly or partially from gross negligence or from an act or omission done with intent to cause damage on

---

87 Outer Space Treaty, *supra* note 1, art. VI.

88 Compromis, ¶ 4, 7.

89 Outer Space Treaty, *supra* note 1, art. VII.

90 The laser may be construed as a "space object." "Space object" has not been precisely defined under the outer space treaties, but it has been interpreted to include "anything that human beings launch or attempt to launch into space." CHENG, *supra* note 2, at 599. The photons in the laser beam constitute matter, making it possible to consider the laser an "object."

91 Convention on International Liability for Damage Caused by Space Objects, Oct. 9, 1973, T.I.A.S. No. 7762, 961 U.N.T.S. 2389. [hereinafter "Liability Convention"]

92 Liability Convention, *supra* note 91, art. II.

93 *Id.* art. III.

94 Compromis, ¶ 2.

the part of the claimant state.[95] Neither of these conditions is present here. Utopia did not act in a grossly negligent manner or with any intent to cause damage; on the contrary, Utopia merely attempted to carry out a commercial activity that it had a legal right to perform. In addition, Article VI (2) revokes any exoneration where damage has resulted from activities not in conformity with international law.[96] Friendlistan's use of force in outer space and subsequent refusal to aid the victims of its aggression were in direct contravention of international law. As a result of its illegal actions, Friendlistan may not be exonerated from liability.

3. *Friendlistan Is Liable for the Loss of Property and Life Under General International Law.*

Under general international law, a State is at fault for damages caused to another state if it has failed to carry out an international obligation.[97] In the *Chorzow Factory Case*, this Court outlined three elements necessary to prove fault under international law: (1) a legal obligation imputable to a state; (2) a breach of the obligation by that state; and (3) a discernible link between the illicit act and the harm suffered.[98] Each of these elements applies to Friendlistan, making it liable for the damages it caused.

First, Friendlistan clearly had a legal obligation under international law not to use force against the Spaceliner. In the *Corfu Channel Case*, this Court emphasized "every State's obligation not to allow knowingly its territory to be used for acts contrary to the rights of other States."[99] Similarly, the tribunal in the *Trail Smelter Arbitration* held that "a State owes at all times a duty to protect other States against injurious acts by individuals from within its jurisdiction."[100] If a State must prevent its territory and its citizens from committing harm, surely it must refrain from causing injury itself. In addition to the obligation not to use force, Friendlistan had a legal obligation to offer assistance to the Spaceliner rescue effort, especially given that its own act of aggression caused the Spaceliner's crash.

With respect to the second element outlined in *Chorzow Factory*, Friendlistan breached both obligations under international law by firing the laser at the Spaceliner and by refusing to aid the rescue of the vehicle after it crashed.

Finally, there is a direct link between Friendlistan's breaches of international law and the damages suffered by Utopia and the Spaceliner. Not only did Friendlistan disable the Spaceliner with the laser, but it also denied the Spaceliner GPS guidance, and then allowed a Friendlistan aircraft to fly into the path of the Spaceliner, which had been forced to fly blind. This last near collision is what finally sent the Spaceliner down.[101] Finally, Friendlistan magnified the damage it caused by refusing to aid the rescue of the craft or even to pinpoint its location.[102] Friendlistan's actions led directly to the destruction of the Spaceliner and the deaths of the people on board. It is liable for these losses and must provide reparation. Under the *Chorzow Factory Case*, "reparation must, as far as possible, wipe out all the consequences of the illegal act."[103] While it is impossible to recover the forty-five lives lost, Friendlistan must compensate the loss of the Spaceliner and its passengers to the fullest extent possible.

V. UTOPIA IS NOT RESPONSIBLE OR LIABLE UNDER INTERNATIONAL LAW FOR THE DESTRUCTION OF MILSAT OR SHARP.

The destruction of Milsat and SHARP adds to the tragedy of the Spaceliner disaster, but did not result from any breach of international law

---

95 Liability Convention, *supra* note 91, art. VI (1).
96 *Id.* art. VI (2).
97 *See Case Concerning Military and Paramilitary Activities In and Against Nicaragua* (Nicar. v. U.S.), 1986 I.C.J. 14; *Barcelona Traction, Light & Power* (Belg. v. Spain), 1970 I.C.J. 3; *Corfu Channel Case* (U.K. v. Alb), 1949 I.C.J. 4.
98 *Chorzow Factory Case* (Germany v. Pol), 1928 P.I.C.J. 47.
99 *Corfu Channel Case* (U.K. v. Alb), 1949 I.C.J. 4, 23.
100 *Trail Smelter Arbitration* (U.S. v. Can.), 3 R.I.A.A. 1905, 1911 (1941).
101 Compromis, ¶ 2, 7.
102 Compromis, ¶ 7.
103 *Chorzow Factory Case*, 1928 P.I.C.J. (ser. A) No. 17 at 47.

by Utopia. On the contrary, Friendlistan caused the objects' destruction by disabling the Spaceliner with the laser. Severely damaged by the laser, the Spaceliner was unable to navigate its descent, and struck Milsat and SHARP through no fault of its own.

A. Utopia Is Not Responsible Under International Law for the Destruction of Milsat or SHARP.

While Article VI of the Outer Space Treaty declares that States "shall bear international responsibility for national activities in outer space,"[104] Utopia cannot be held responsible for the destruction of Milsat or SHARP because the cause of the damage did not follow from any breach of international law by Utopia. Neither Milsat nor SHARP would have been destroyed had Friendlistan not illegally fired upon the Spaceliner. After being crippled by the laser fired by Friendlistan, the Spaceliner lost control and could not avoid striking either Milsat or SHARP.[105]

Even if Utopia were found to be responsible for the damage to Milsat or SHARP, its responsibility would be absolved under the doctrine of *force majeur*. In the *Rainbow Warrior Case*, the arbitral tribunal found that a State may invoke *force majeur* to justify "involuntary, or at least unintentional conduct" due to an irresistible force or an unforeseen external event."[106] Utopia's conduct was both involuntary and unintentional; indeed, the Spaceliner would have steered away from Milsat and SHARP if it could have in order to avoid causing further harm to itself. The shooting of the laser by Friendlistan was an unforeseen external event that deprived the Spaceliner of any ability to control its path. Utopia is not responsible for the damages it caused due to *force majeur*.

B. Utopia Is Not Liable Under the Liability Convention for the Destruction of Milsat Because Friendlistan Lacks Standing to Bring Its Claim and Cannot Recover Remote Damages.

Friendlistan's claims for Milsat and SHARP cannot be brought under the Liability Convention. Friendlistan lacks standing and asks for irrecoverable damages, attempting to apply the Liability Convention beyond its proper scope.

Friendlistan lacks standing to claim damages on behalf of the shareholders of Davidson Corporation, the owner of Milsat. In the *Case Concerning Barcelona Traction, Light and Power Company*, this Court rejected Belgium's standing to bring a claim on behalf of its nationals who were shareholders in a Canadian corporation: "whenever a shareholder's interests are harmed by an act done to the company, it is to the latter that he must look to institute appropriate action."[107] Similarly, Friendlistan cannot claim on behalf of its nationals because they were shareholders in an Equatorian corporation.[108] The Friendlistan shareholders can look only to Equatorian to obtain relief.

Even if Friendlistan had standing to bring the claim, Utopia cannot be held liable to the shareholders of the Davidson Corporation because the damages claimed are remote and indirect. The bankruptcy of the Davidson Corporation may be linked to Milsat's destruction, but only remotely, and any damage suffered by the shareholders is indirect. Remote and indirect damages are not recoverable under the Liability Convention, nor are they recoverable under international law generally.[109] This rule is embodied in the Liability Convention, which expressly limits recovery to direct losses such as "loss of life, personal injury or other impairment of health; or loss of or damage to property of States or of person, natural or juridical, or property of international intergovernmental

---

[104] Outer Space Treaty, *supra* note 1, art. VI.

[105] Compromis, ¶ 5, 6.

[106] *Rainbow Warrior Case*, (N.Z. v. Fr.), 82 I.L.R. 499 (1990), at para. 77.

[107] *Case Concerning Barcelona Traction, Light and Power Co., Ltd.* (Belg. v. Spain), 1970 I.C.J. 3, para. 44.

[108] Clarifications to Compromis, Set 1, #4.

[109] *See The Naulilaa Claims*, (Port. v. Germany), 2 R.I.A.A. 1013 (1928), where the arbitral tribunal found that the damages caused to Portuguese colonial territory were too remote to be attributable to Germany's activities. *See also* Stephen Gorove, *Some Comments on the Convention on International Liability for Damage Caused by Space Objects*, PROCEEDINGS OF THE SIXTEENTH COLLOQUIUM ON THE LAW OF OUTER SPACE (1973).

organizations."[110] The losses claimed by the Davidson Corporation shareholders simply do not fall within the definition of compensable damages under the Liability Convention and cannot be recovered.

C. Even of the Liability Convention Does Apply, Utopia Is Not Liable for the Destruction of Milsat or SHARP.

Utopia would not be absolutely liable nor liable for proof of fault under the Liability Convention. No fault can be attributed to Utopia for fault-based liability, and Utopia is exonerated from any absolute liability because of the illegal acts of Friendlistan.

1. *Utopia Is Not Liable Under the Liability Convention Because It Was Not at Fault.*

Both Milsat and SHARP were damaged "elsewhere than on the surface of the earth," which invokes Article III and requires a showing of fault.[111] The circumstances make clear, however, that Utopia was not at fault. Friendlistan, not Utopia, was at fault for disabling the Spaceliner. Friendlistan's illegal use of force severely damaged the Spaceliner, depriving it of control over its flight path. Friendlistan further disabled the Spaceliner by denying it navigational services, rendering it unable to avoid striking Milsat or SHARP. While SHARP was positioned only 20 kilometers above the Earth, the Liability Convention defines damage as including all personal and property damage caused by a space object. Therefore, Friendlistan's actions absolve Utopia of liability for SHARP in the same way they do for Milsat. Utopia is not at fault for the destruction of Milsat or SHARP and cannot be held liable under the Liability Convention.

2. *Utopia Is Exonerated from Absolute Liability Under the Liability Convention.*

While Utopia may be absolutely liable for the damage caused by SHARP's fall to the surface of the Earth,[112] Utopia is exonerated from liability under the Liability Convention. Under Article VI (1), Friendlistan cannot demand reparation for damage that it caused by its own gross negligence and deliberately injurious acts.[113] First, Friendlistan's use of a laser in outer space was grossly negligent, given the heightened risk associated with space activity, and even amounted to a violation of international law. Second, Friendlistan fired the laser beam with intent to cause the Spaceliner damage; indeed, Friendlistan's aim was to disable the vehicle's remote sensing capabilities.[114] Even if Friendlistan did not intend to damage the Spaceliner to the extent that it did, Friendlistan was still grossly negligent in failing to consider the risks involved. Because Friendlistan's act was both grossly negligent and injurious, Utopia is exonerated from any liability.

D. Utopia Is Not Liable Under General International Law for the Damage to Milsat or SHARP.

A state cannot be held liable for damages unless there is a direct causal link between its actions and the damage caused.[115] Utopia is not liable, first, because it has breached no international obligation, and second, because there is no direct casual link between Utopia's conduct and the damages caused. Under established tort standards, the breach must be the proximate cause of the damages.[116] Proximate causes requires avoidability and foreseeability of risk, neither of which applies to Utopia in this case.[117] The Spaceliner could

[110] Liability Convention, *supra* note 91, art. I (a).

[111] Liability Convention, *supra* note 91, art. III.

[112112] Liability Convention, *supra* note 91, art. II. If the Court finds that art. II liability applies to all damage suffered in air space, then Utopia would also be absolutely liable for the damage caused to SHARP upon impact with the Spaceliner. Utopia is absolved of this liability, however, under art. VI (1).

[113] Liability Convention, art. VI (1).

[114] Compromis, ¶ 4.

[115] *Chorzow Factory Case*, 1928 P.I.C.J. 47.

[116] While the concept of proximate cause has not been widely applied in the international realm, the principles of international tort law are informed by domestic laws, particularly of the Anglo-American tradition, which rely upon proximate causation. *See* Jay Ginsburg, *The High Frontier: Tort Claims and Liability for Damages Caused by Man-Made Space Objects*, 12 SUFFOLK TRANSNAT'L L.J. 515 (1989).

[117] Liability only applies when the risk involved is both real and not farfetched, and when avoidance of the risk could have been easily achieved. *See*

not avoid the damage caused to Milsat and SHARP because its navigational capabilities had been destroyed by the Friendlistan laser.[118] Furthermore, the Spaceliner could not have foreseen the damage to Milsat or SHARP because it could not possibly have anticipated the series of unfortunate events that prevented it from completing its journey safely, including being hit and disabled by the Friendlistan laser and being refused landing at the ISS. Each of these events broke any chain of causality that could be traced to Utopia. Under general international law, as under the Liability Convention, Utopia cannot be held liable for damages.

VI. CONCLUSION

Friendlistan's actions are completely unjustifiable whether Utopia acted legally or illegally. The loss of the Spaceliner, its equipment, and the lives of the forty-five people on board directly resulted from Friendlistan's violations of international law. The Court has found monetary damages to be an appropriate remedy where there has been a breach of international law.[119] Accordingly, Utopia asks the Court to require Friendlistan to compensate Utopia for the costs of the Spaceliner and its equipment and for the great loss of life suffered. Friendlistan must make reparations to the fullest extent possible.

SUBMISSIONS

For the foregoing reasons, the Government of Utopia, Applicant, respectfully requests the Court to adjudge and declare that:

1. Friendlistan violated international law and practice by interfering with the remote sensing activities conducted by Utopia and Spaceliner Inc. and discharging the laser which crippled the Spaceliner vehicle;
2. Friendlistan violated international law by refusing assistance to Utopia in the rescue of the Spaceliner crew and passengers;
3. Friendlistan is responsible and liable under international law to adequately compensate Utopia for the property and lives lost by the destruction of the Spaceliner;
4. Utopia is not responsible or liable under international law for the destruction of Milsat or SHARP and thus owes no compensation to the Friendlistan shareholders or operators

---

Overseas Tankship (U.K.) Ltd. V, Miller Steamship Co. Pty. Ltd., (1966) 1 All E.R. 709.

[118] Clarifications to Compromis, Set 4, #1.

[119] *Corfu Channel Case*, (U.K. v. Alb.), 1949 I.C.J. 4, 23.

INTERNATIONAL INSTITUTE OF SPACE LAW
OF THE INTERNATIONAL ASTRONAUTICAL FEDERATION

INSTITUT INTERNATIONAL DE DROIT SPATIAL
DE LA FEDERATION ASTRONAUTIQUE INTERNATIONALE

3-5, RUE MARIO NIKIS
75015 PARIS - FRANCE

Tél. 33-1-45.67.42.60
Telefax 33-1-42.73.21.20

STATUTES

ARTICLE I

The name of the Institute shall be the International Institute of Space Law of the International Astronautical Federation.

ARTICLE II

The purposes and objectives of the Institute shall include:

(a) The providing of advice to the President of the International Astronautical Federation when requested;
(b) Cooperation with appropriate international organizations and national institutions in the field of space law;
(c) The holding of meetings, colloquia and competitions on juridical and social science aspects of space activities, thereby providing forums for individuals from different legal systems and regions of the world to engage in the free expression and exchange of ideas relevant to space law and policy;
(d) The preparation or commissioning of studies and reports;
(e) The publication of books, proceedings, reports and other papers;
(f) The granting and presentation of awards and certificates;
(g) The conduct of such other activities as may be considered desirable in fostering the development of space law and studies of legal and social science aspects of the exploration and use of outer space.

ARTICLE III

Section 1

Individuals distinguished by their contributions to or of proven interest in the field of space law or other social science aspects related to space activities, may be elected as members of the Institute by the Board of Directors upon an application recommended in each case by a Director, or by three members of the Institute.

Section 2

Corporate bodies and other institutions actively engaged or otherwise interested in the field of space law or other social science aspects related to space activities, may be elected by the Board of Directors as institutional members of the Institute upon an application recommended in each case by a Director, or by three members of the Institute. Corporate bodies and other institutions that are members of the International Astronautical Federation (IAF) may be elected as institutional members of the Institute so long as no prejudice to the IAF is thereby incurred.

Section 3

Election to membership of the Institute shall be by a majority vote of the Board of Directors in attendance at a regular or special meeting of the Board, or by a majority of affirmative answers of the members of the Board if the vote is held by mail.

ARTICLE IV

Section 1

All members of the Institute shall pay annual membership dues in accordance with the Bye-laws. These dues are expressed in terms of units.

Section 2

The Board of Directors shall establish the value of the unit in which membership dues are expressed. Alterations in the value of the unit shall take effect for each member or institutional member at the end of the period for which the relevant membership dues have been paid.

Section 3

Members of the Institute who are in default of their membership fee shall lose the right to vote in an annual or other meeting. Members of the Institute may be removed from the membership of the Institute by decision of the Board of Directors, if they are in arrears of membership dues for more than two years.

Section 4

On cause shown, the Board of Directors may reduce or remit the membership fee for a particular member.

Section 5

The Board of Directors may remove from membership of the Institute any member whom they judge to have violated the principles of the Statutes. Such decisions shall be taken by a two thirds vote of members of the Board present at the meeting at which the decision is taken.

ARTICLE V

Section 1

An annual meeting of the Institute shall be held each year, and special meetings may also be held, at such times and places as the Board of Directors may determine.

Section 2

The Board of Directors shall submit to each annual meeting a report on the activities of the Institute. The report shall outline the events and accomplishments of the preceding year and put forward the policy and projects of the Institute for the future.

Section 3

The annual meeting shall elect from among the members of the Institute, by a majority vote of the members present, officers and members of the Board of Directors, with due regard to the provisions of Article VI, Sections 2 and 3.

ARTICLE VI

Section 1

The governing body of the Institute is the Board of Directors. The officers of the Institute are the President, the two Vice-Presidents, the Secretary and the Treasurer. The President, Presidents Emeriti, two Vice-Presidents, and twelve other members shall be the voting members of the Board. Any Honorary Directors of the Institute and the Presidents of the International Astronautical Federation and of the International Academy of Astronautics ex officio shall be non-voting members of the Board of Directors.

Section 2

The Institute will seek that the membership of the Board of Directors shall reflect and represent the different regions of the world and different legal systems, due regard being paid especially to those countries in which significant space programmes or considerable efforts to develop space law have been made.

Section 3

The officers and members of the Board of Directors shall be elected for a period of three years, and may be re-elected. Members of the Nomination Committee acting in accordance with the Bye-laws, and members of the Institute when electing officers and other members of the Board, shall take account of the desirability of ensuring both a continuity and an adequate rotation of membership within the Board.

Section 4

In the case of a vacancy occurring in the Board between two annual meetings, the Board of Directors may appoint an acting Director to fill the vacancy until the expiry of the relevant term, subject to the approval of the appointment by the next annual meeting.

Section 5

An outgoing President, who has served in that capacity over several years and has contributed substantially to the development and the activities of the Institute, may be elected for life as a President Emeritus.

Section 6

Persons who have made outstanding contributions to international cooperation in the peaceful uses of outer space, or to the development of space law, as well as officers of the Institute and members of the Board of Directors who have served for several succeeding terms and have contributed substantially to the work of the Institute, may be elected as Honorary Directors. They may attend meetings of the Board of Directors in a consultative capacity, but without a right to vote.

ARTICLE VII

Section 1

The President of the Institute shall guide and supervise the activities of the Institute pursuant to its Statutes and in accordance with its Bye-laws. The President shall represent the Institute in its external relations, including those with the International Astronautical Federation.

Section 2

The Board of Directors shall:

(a) Carry out the purposes and objectives of the Institute as set forth in Article II of these Statutes;
(b) Implement the resolutions and directives adopted at the annual meetings of the Institute;
(c) Create standing committees with appropriate terms of reference and powers for their functions;
(d) Create ad hoc committees and working groups for specific purposes and functions;
(e) Appoint members of the Institute to fill vacancies occurring in the membership of the Board of Directors in accordance with Art. VI (4) of these Statutes;
(f) Supervise the correspondence of the Institute and provide for the safekeeping of the archives thereof;
(g) Establish a secretariat as appropriate, designate its duties and supervise all its activities;
(h) Arrange for meetings and colloquia;
(i) Arrange for the publication of books, proceedings, reports and other papers;
(j) Make recommendations concerning the awarding of medals, certificates and prizes;
(k) Approve budgets and supervise accounts;
(l) Accept donations and legacies, and funds from private sources, and contributions from national and international organizations, governments and agencies;
(m) Approve the annual reports of the President and the Treasurer to be presented at the annual meetings of the Institute, and the annual report of the President to be presented at the plenary meeting of the General Assembly of the Federation.

Section 3

At least eight of the voting members of the Board of Directors present at its meeting, including the President or Acting President shall constitute a quorum. Where in exceptional cases a matter has to be decided by mail, the same number of answers shall be required for a valid decision of the Board if a vote is held by mail.

Section 4

Decisions of the Board of Directors shall be taken, so far as possible, by consensus. Where a decision is taken by vote, Directors may cast their votes by mail or other written means as to any action proposed to be taken by the Board. Except where these Statutes and relative Bye-laws provide otherwise, decisions by vote of the Board shall be valid when taken by a majority of members present, or indicating their view in writing. In the case of a tie, the President shall have a casting as well as a deliberative vote.

Section 5

The ordinary affairs of the Board of Directors and of the Institute shall be conducted in accordance with the Bye-laws of the Institute. These Bye-laws shall be adopted by the Institute at an annual or special meeting by a majority vote of its members present upon a recommendation of the Board of Directors.

Section 6

The membership of standing committees, of ad hoc committees and of working groups, shall be determined by the President in consultation with the Board of Directors.

Section 7

The President, in consultation with the Board shall, by the end of April of each year, appoint the Chairman and members of the Nomination Committee responsible for nominating candidates for election as officers or other Board members whose terms of office are to begin after each annual meeting. The Committee shall be composed of not less than three, but not more than five members. The Report of the Nomination Committee shall be submitted to the President not later than one month before the annual meeting.

ARTICLE VIII

Section 1

These Statutes and Bye-laws shall be adopted at a meeting of the Board of Directors by a two-thirds majority vote of all members of the Board, subject to confirmation of this adoption at the next annual meeting of the Institute by a simple majority of members of the Institute present at that meeting.

Section 2

These Statutes and relative Bye-laws may be amended at any meeting of the Board of Directors by a two-thirds majority vote of all members of the Board, subject to confirmation of the amendment at the next annual meeting of the Institute by a simple majority of members of the Institute present at that meeting. All members of the Institute shall be informed of the intention to present such an amendment for confirmation at least six weeks prior to the next annual meeting.

Section 3

The Institute shall not enact Statutes or Bye-laws or amendments to either which are inconsistent with the provisions of the Constitution of the International Astronautical Federation, or its resolutions pertaining to the Institute.

BYE-LAWS

1. The President of the Institute shall preside at meetings of the Institute and of the Board of Directors. If unable to do so, the President may appoint one of the Vice-Presidents, and, if either of them is unable to do so, another member of the Board, to preside at a particular meeting. If the President is unable so to appoint or has not done so in time, a Vice-President, or if necessary another member of the Board, appointed by a majority of the members of the Board present, shall so preside and have the powers of the President for the purpose.

2. The Board of Directors shall endeavour to take decisions by consensus, but, if necessary, voting in the Board of Directors shall be by a show of hands, the President or Secretary informing the meeting of the views of those not present who have notified their view in writing on a matter. Such written views shall, wherever possible, be treated as votes on the matter under discussion.

3. The Board of Directors shall cause minutes to be kept of its meetings and of all actions taken by the Board. Such minutes shall be deposited with the Secretariat of the International Astronautical Federation and any member of the Institute in good standing may inspect them at any reasonable time.

4. A Nomination Committee, itself appointed by the President in consultation with the Board, shall make recommendations to the annual meeting as to elections to the offices of the Institute and membership of the Board of Directors. A person may be elected to the Board of Directors even though his or her name is not included in the list of recommendations made by the Nomination Committee. The Board and members attending shall be informed of the recommendations of the Nomination Committee which shall be made available at the latest by forty-eight hours prior to the annual meeting. In making its recommendations the Nomination Committee shall have regard to the distinction of the contribution made to space law by potential

nominees, as well as to the provisions of Article VI Sections 2 and 3 of the Statutes of the Institute.

5. The responsibilities of the Secretary of the Institute include:

(a) Maintaining the list of members of the Institute;
(b) Maintaining all necessary records, including financial records;
(c) Making arrangements for meetings of the Board;
(d) Taking the minutes of the meetings of the Board, and the annual and other meetings of the Institute;
(e) Depositing copies of the minutes of the Board with the International Astronautical Federation, and with the approval of the Board, making suitable arrangements for, the custody of the records of the Institute;
(f) In consultation with the Board and with the Secretariat of the International Astronautical Federation, making arrangements for the annual and other meetings of the Institute;
(g) Coordinating the Institute's involvement in the preparation of and making arrangements for any moot court or other competition involving or run by the Institute;
(h) Conducting the routine correspondence of the Institute;
(i) Communicating with members of the Institute, including preparing and seeing to the circulation of the Newsletter.

6. The responsibilities of the Treasurer of the Institute include:

(a) Ingathering membership dues and receiving donations and other monies received for or arising from the work of the Institute;
(b) Operating appropriate bank accounts on behalf of the Institute;
(c) Preparing appropriate budgets for approval by the Board;
(d) Paying bills incurred by the Institute or its officers in the carrying out of the purposes of the Institute from monies held by the Institute.

6. The President of the Institute shall refer an application for membership of the Institute to a membership committee, which he shall appoint, and the Board shall be informed of the report of that committee before it decides on the election of the applicant.

7. The Secretary of the Institute shall be informed in writing of any proposals for the amendment of the Statutes or Bye-laws of the Institute, other than those made by the Board, at least twelve weeks prior to the annual meeting, and any such proposal must be supported in writing by at least twenty individual fully paid-up members of the Institute.

8. The annual membership dues payable by an individual member of the Institute shall be one unit of contribution dues. Honorary Directors, if not otherwise members of the Institute, are exempt from the requirement to pay annual membership dues. Corporate or institutional members of the Institute shall pay three or more units of contribution dues of membership dues a year, the level of contribution being selected by the Institutional member in agreement with the Board of Directors.

9. A corporate or institutional member paying three contribution units per year has the right to nominate up to three representatives to vote in the annual meeting. Each additional contribution unit allows the institutional member to nominate one additional such representative.

10. A member of the Institute remains in good standing in the Institute provided that membership dues are not in arrear, and that a current mailing address has been received by the Secretary.

AUTHOR INDEX